The Great American Documents

VOLUME II: 1831–1900

UNCLE SAM

PRESENTS

The Great American Documents

VOLUME II: 1831–1900

Ruth Ashby

ILLUSTRATED BY
Ernie Colón

EDITORIAL CONSULTANT
Russell Motter

A NOVEL GRAPHIC FROM HILL AND WANG
A DIVISION OF FARRAR, STRAUS AND GIROUX
NEW YORK

Hill and Wang
A division of Farrar, Straus and Giroux
120 Broadway, New York 10271

This is a Z File, Inc. Book
Text copyright © 2019 by Ruth Ashby
Artwork copyright © 2019 by Ernie Colón
All rights reserved
Printed in the United States of America
Published simultaneously in hardcover and paperback
First edition, 2019

Library of Congress Control Number: 2013956401
Hardcover ISBN: 978-0-8090-9459-2
Paperback ISBN: 978-0-374-53737-1

Our books may be purchased in bulk for promotional, educational, or business use. Please contact your local bookseller or the Macmillan Corporate and Premium Sales Department at 1-800-221-7945, extension 5442, or by e-mail at MacmillanSpecialMarkets@macmillan.com.

Editor: Howard Zimmerman
Editorial Consultant: Russell Motter
Designer: Richard Amari
Project Manager: Steven A. Roman

www.fsgbooks.com
www.twitter.com/fsgbooks
www.facebook.com/fsgbooks

1 3 5 7 9 10 8 6 4 2

Editor's Note: Dialogue attributed to major historical figures appearing in this volume is taken or condensed from actual statements made by the respective individuals or is paraphrased based on relevant accounts and interviews.

Front cover image of "The Gettysburg Address delivered by Abraham Lincoln Nov. 19 1863 at the dedication services on the battle field" courtesy of the Library of Congress (reproduction #LC-USZC4-12220). Originally published in 1909 by M.T. Sheahan (Boston, Mass.).

To our wonderful grandsons: Calder, Lachlan, and Eirnin

CONTENTS

Manifest Destiny 1	Lincoln's Second Inaugural Address 88
The Declaration of Sentiments 19	The Thirteenth Amendment 93
The Compromise of 1850 30	The Fourteenth Amendment 97
Uncle Tom's Cabin 39	The Fifteenth Amendment 104
The Kansas-Nebraska Act 45	*Plessy v. Ferguson* 111
Dred Scott v. Sandford 51	The Chinese Exclusion Act 118
The "House Divided" Speech 57	The Dawes Severalty Act 126
The Emancipation Proclamation 65	White Man's Burden 138
The Gettysburg Address 75	The Mother of Exiles 150

A NOTE ABOUT THE NARRATOR 155

SUGGESTED READING 157

SUGGESTED WEBSITES AND MULTIMEDIA 157

ACKNOWLEDGMENTS 159

Manifest Destiny

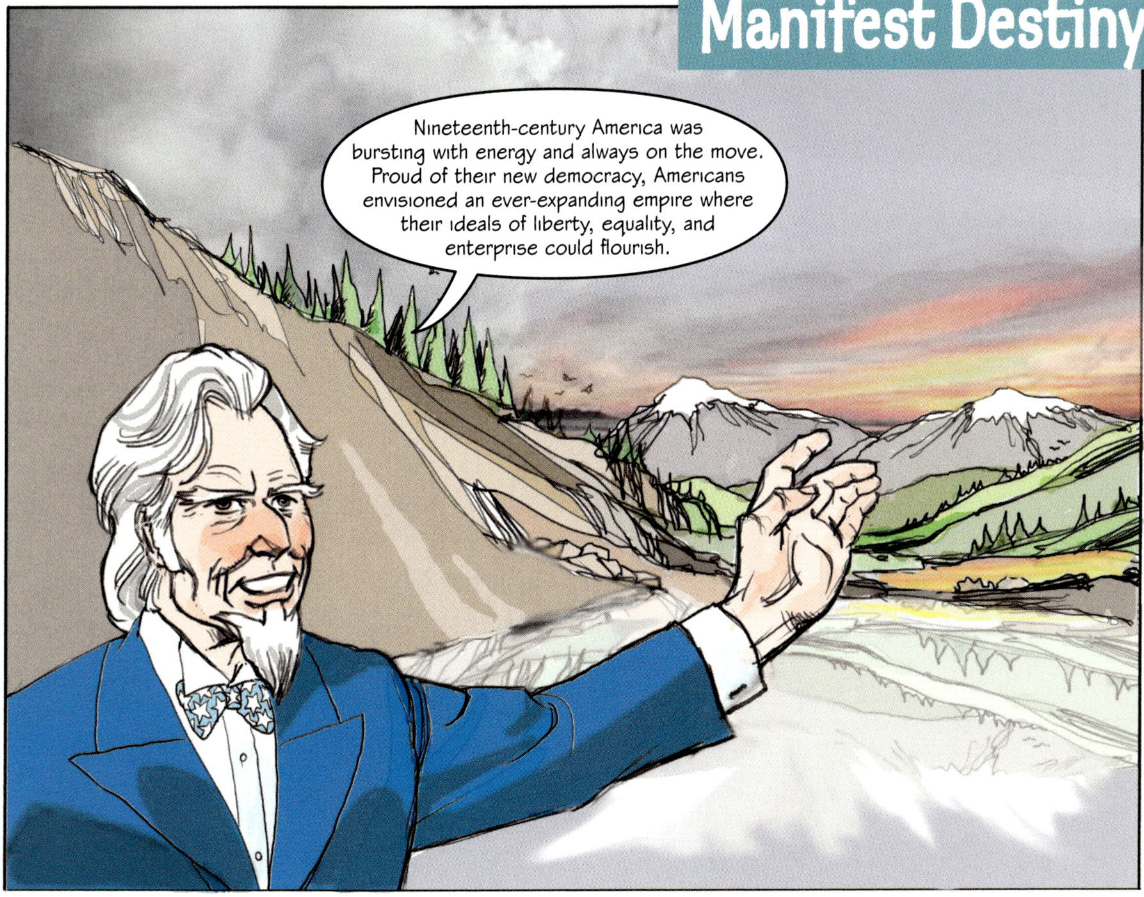
Nineteenth-century America was bursting with energy and always on the move. Proud of their new democracy, Americans envisioned an ever-expanding empire where their ideals of liberty, equality, and enterprise could flourish.

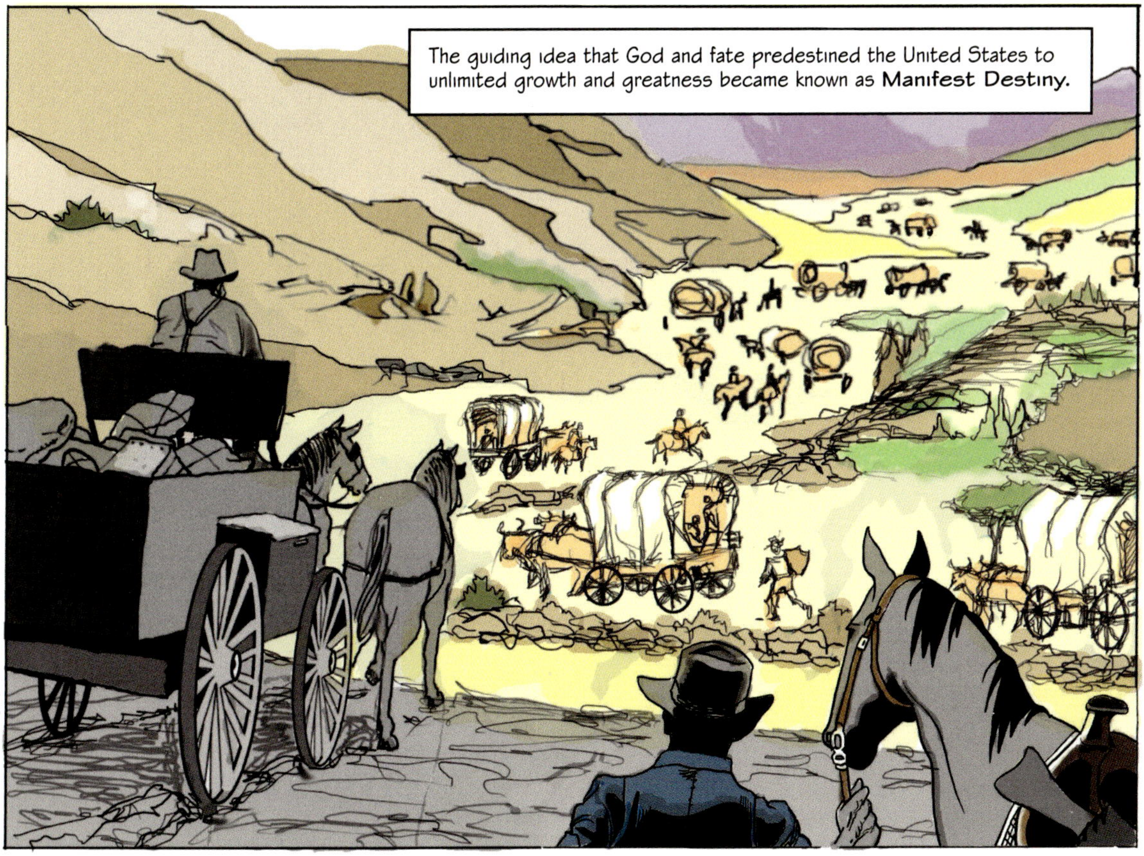
The guiding idea that God and fate predestined the United States to unlimited growth and greatness became known as **Manifest Destiny.**

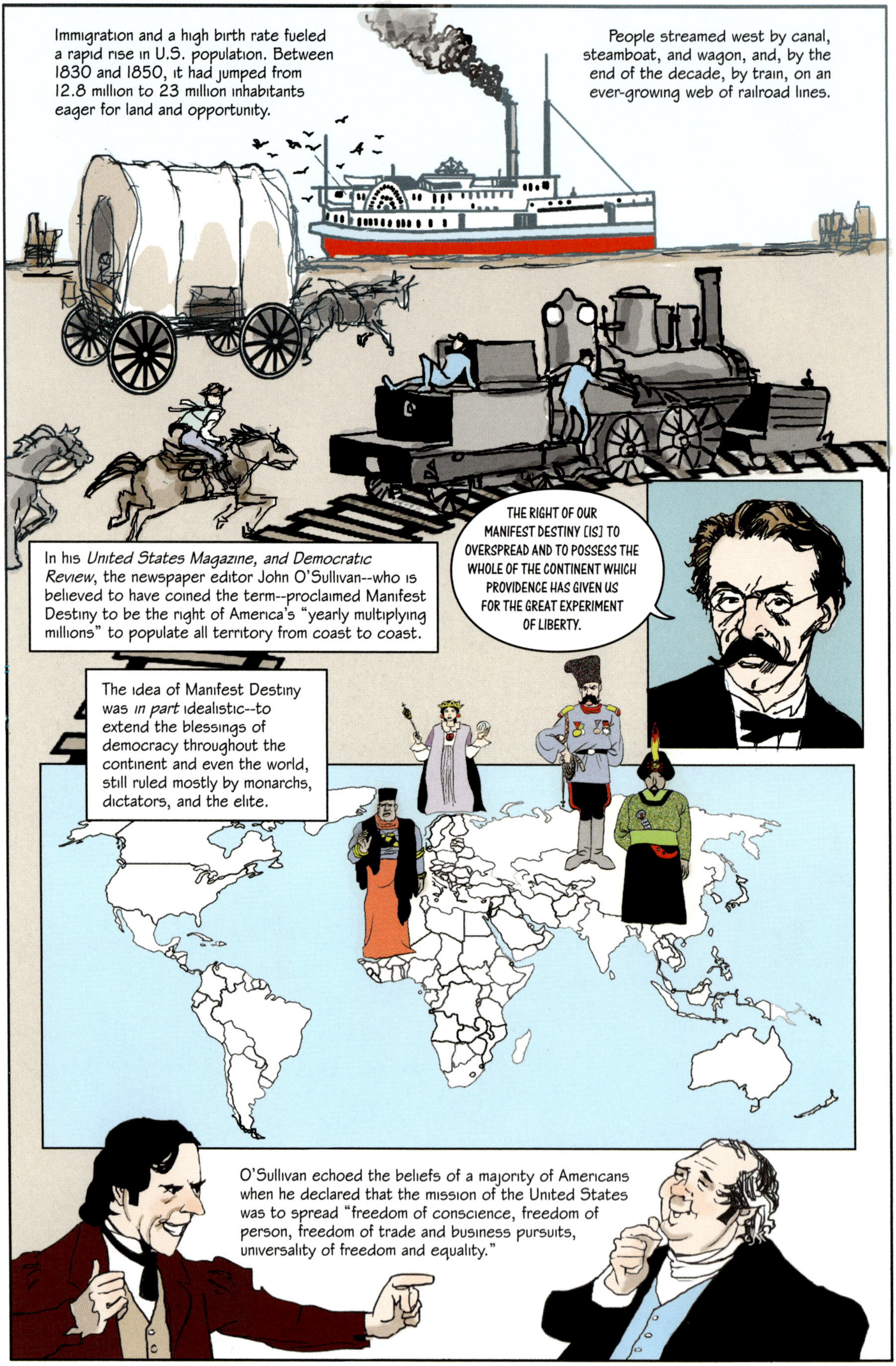
Immigration and a high birth rate fueled a rapid rise in U.S. population. Between 1830 and 1850, it had jumped from 12.8 million to 23 million inhabitants eager for land and opportunity.
People streamed west by canal, steamboat, and wagon, and, by the end of the decade, by train, on an ever-growing web of railroad lines.
In his *United States Magazine, and Democratic Review*, the newspaper editor John O'Sullivan--who is believed to have coined the term--proclaimed Manifest Destiny to be the right of America's "yearly multiplying millions" to populate all territory from coast to coast.
THE RIGHT OF OUR MANIFEST DESTINY [IS] TO OVERSPREAD AND TO POSSESS THE WHOLE OF THE CONTINENT WHICH PROVIDENCE HAS GIVEN US FOR THE GREAT EXPERIMENT OF LIBERTY.
The idea of Manifest Destiny was *in part* idealistic--to extend the blessings of democracy throughout the continent and even the world, still ruled mostly by monarchs, dictators, and the elite.
O'Sullivan echoed the beliefs of a majority of Americans when he declared that the mission of the United States was to spread "freedom of conscience, freedom of person, freedom of trade and business pursuits, universality of freedom and equality."

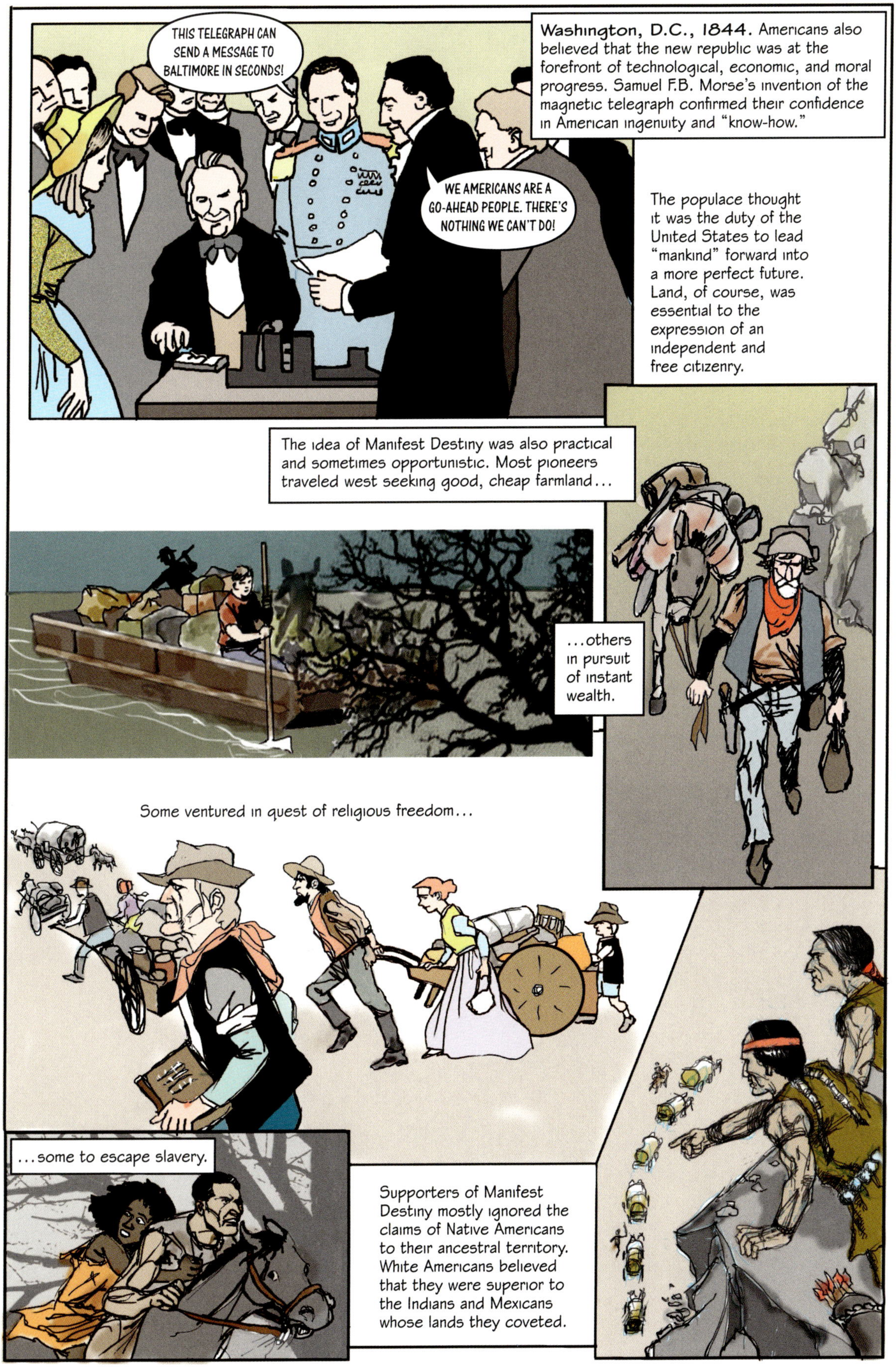
Washington, D.C., 1844. Americans also believed that the new republic was at the forefront of technological, economic, and moral progress. Samuel F.B. Morse's invention of the magnetic telegraph confirmed their confidence in American ingenuity and "know-how."
THIS TELEGRAPH CAN SEND A MESSAGE TO BALTIMORE IN SECONDS!
WE AMERICANS ARE A GO-AHEAD PEOPLE. THERE'S NOTHING WE CAN'T DO!
The populace thought it was the duty of the United States to lead "mankind" forward into a more perfect future. Land, of course, was essential to the expression of an independent and free citizenry.
The idea of Manifest Destiny was also practical and sometimes opportunistic. Most pioneers traveled west seeking good, cheap farmland...
...others in pursuit of instant wealth.
Some ventured in quest of religious freedom...
...some to escape slavery.
Supporters of Manifest Destiny mostly ignored the claims of Native Americans to their ancestral territory. White Americans believed that they were superior to the Indians and Mexicans whose lands they coveted.

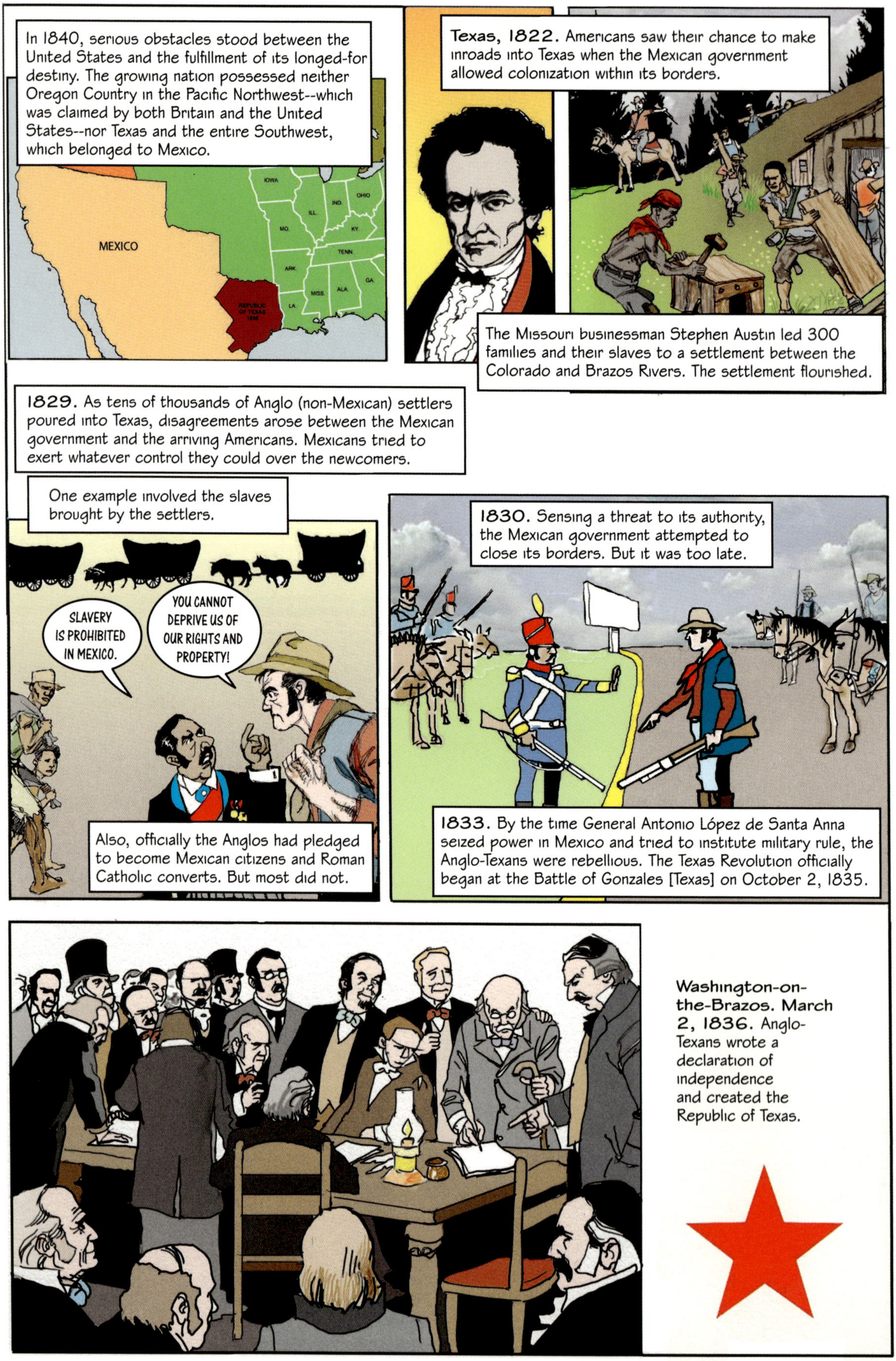
In 1840, serious obstacles stood between the United States and the fulfillment of its longed-for destiny. The growing nation possessed neither Oregon Country in the Pacific Northwest--which was claimed by both Britain and the United States--nor Texas and the entire Southwest, which belonged to Mexico.
MEXICO
IOWA
ILL.
IND.
OHIO
MO.
KY.
TENN.
ARK.
MISS.
ALA.
GA.
LA.
REPUBLIC OF TEXAS 1836
Texas, 1822. Americans saw their chance to make inroads into Texas when the Mexican government allowed colonization within its borders.
The Missouri businessman Stephen Austin led 300 families and their slaves to a settlement between the Colorado and Brazos Rivers. The settlement flourished.
1829. As tens of thousands of Anglo (non-Mexican) settlers poured into Texas, disagreements arose between the Mexican government and the arriving Americans. Mexicans tried to exert whatever control they could over the newcomers.
One example involved the slaves brought by the settlers.
SLAVERY IS PROHIBITED IN MEXICO.
YOU CANNOT DEPRIVE US OF OUR RIGHTS AND PROPERTY!
Also, officially the Anglos had pledged to become Mexican citizens and Roman Catholic converts. But most did not.
1830. Sensing a threat to its authority, the Mexican government attempted to close its borders. But it was too late.
1833. By the time General Antonio López de Santa Anna seized power in Mexico and tried to institute military rule, the Anglo-Texans were rebellious. The Texas Revolution officially began at the Battle of Gonzales [Texas] on October 2, 1835.
Washington-on-the-Brazos. March 2, 1836. Anglo-Texans wrote a declaration of independence and created the Republic of Texas.

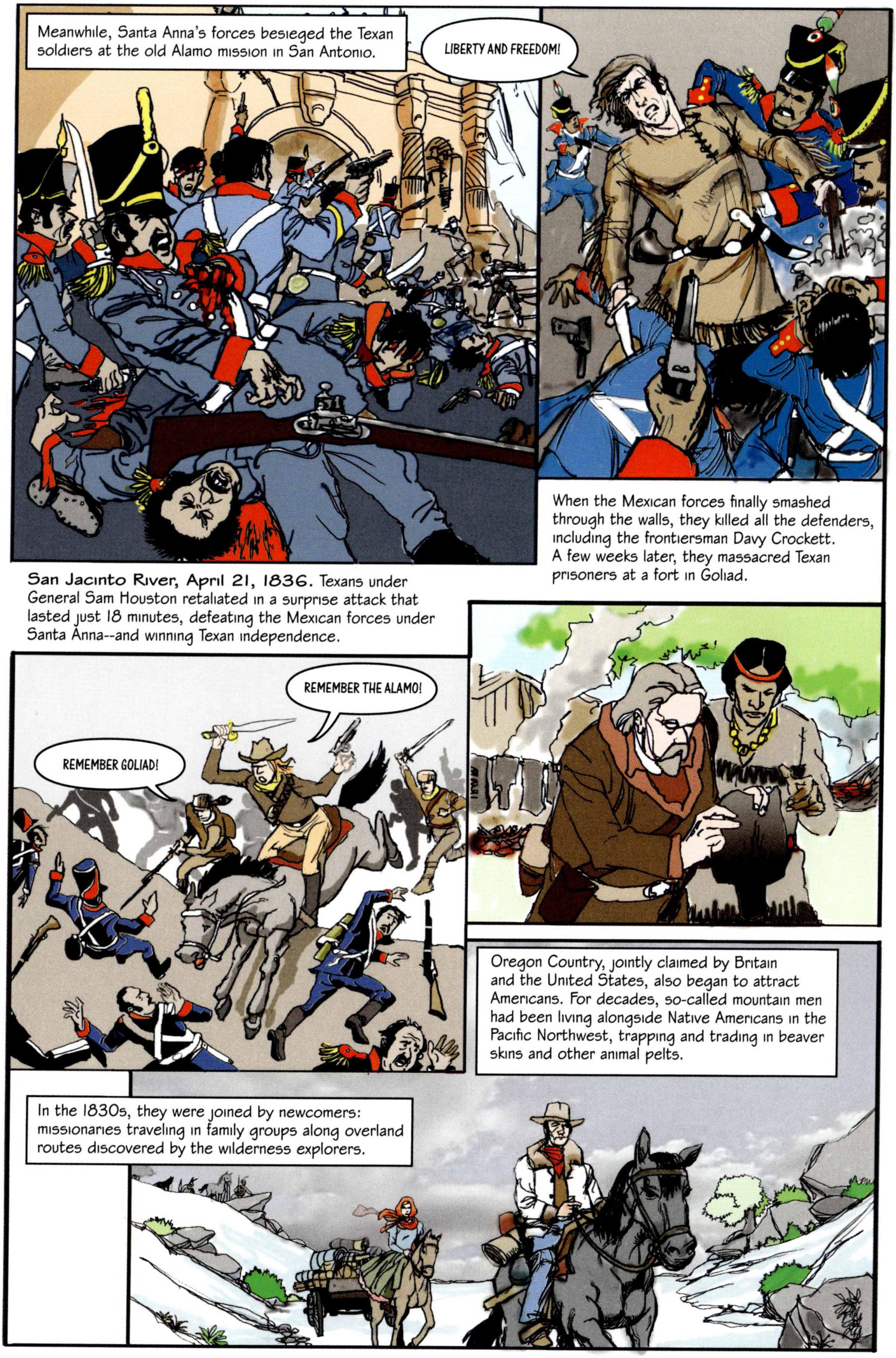

Meanwhile, Santa Anna's forces besieged the Texan soldiers at the old Alamo mission in San Antonio.
LIBERTY AND FREEDOM!
When the Mexican forces finally smashed through the walls, they killed all the defenders, including the frontiersman Davy Crockett. A few weeks later, they massacred Texan prisoners at a fort in Goliad.
San Jacinto River, April 21, 1836. Texans under General Sam Houston retaliated in a surprise attack that lasted just 18 minutes, defeating the Mexican forces under Santa Anna--and winning Texan independence.
REMEMBER THE ALAMO!
REMEMBER GOLIAD!
Oregon Country, jointly claimed by Britain and the United States, also began to attract Americans. For decades, so-called mountain men had been living alongside Native Americans in the Pacific Northwest, trapping and trading in beaver skins and other animal pelts.
In the 1830s, they were joined by newcomers: missionaries traveling in family groups along overland routes discovered by the wilderness explorers.

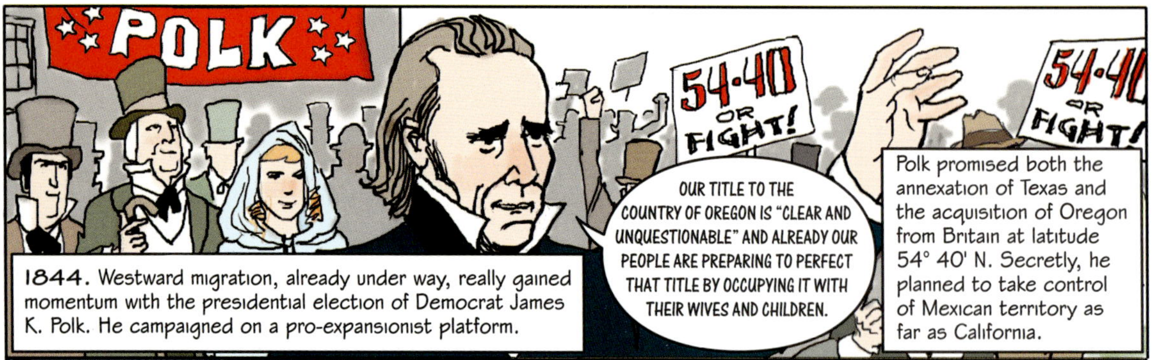
POLK
54-40 OR FIGHT!
54-40 OR FIGHT!
1844. Westward migration, already under way, really gained momentum with the presidential election of Democrat James K. Polk. He campaigned on a pro-expansionist platform.
OUR TITLE TO THE COUNTRY OF OREGON IS "CLEAR AND UNQUESTIONABLE" AND ALREADY OUR PEOPLE ARE PREPARING TO PERFECT THAT TITLE BY OCCUPYING IT WITH THEIR WIVES AND CHILDREN.
Polk promised both the annexation of Texas and the acquisition of Oregon from Britain at latitude 54° 40' N. Secretly, he planned to take control of Mexican territory as far as California.

In response to public opinion, outgoing president John Tyler persuaded Congress to annex Texas in 1845. Northerners who supported the acquisition of what would doubtless become a slave state, saw Oregon as a counterbalance.

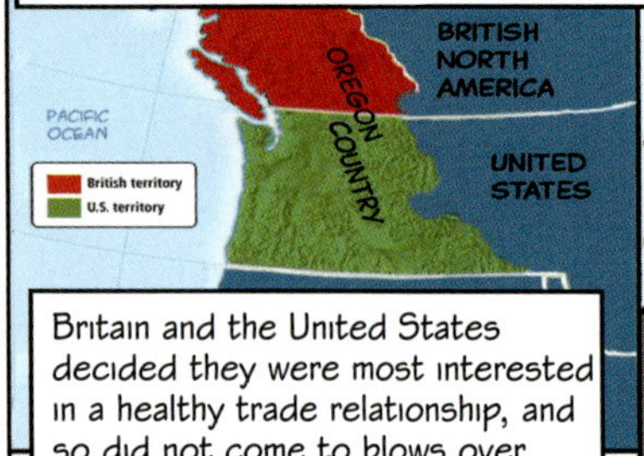
BRITISH NORTH AMERICA
OREGON COUNTRY
PACIFIC OCEAN
UNITED STATES
British territory
U.S. territory

Britain and the United States decided they were most interested in a healthy trade relationship, and so did not come to blows over latitude 54° 40' N. Instead, they divided the Oregon Country right down the middle.

The United States was in the grip of a major economic depression that caused people to lose their jobs and their farms. But in the West, they could start over again.

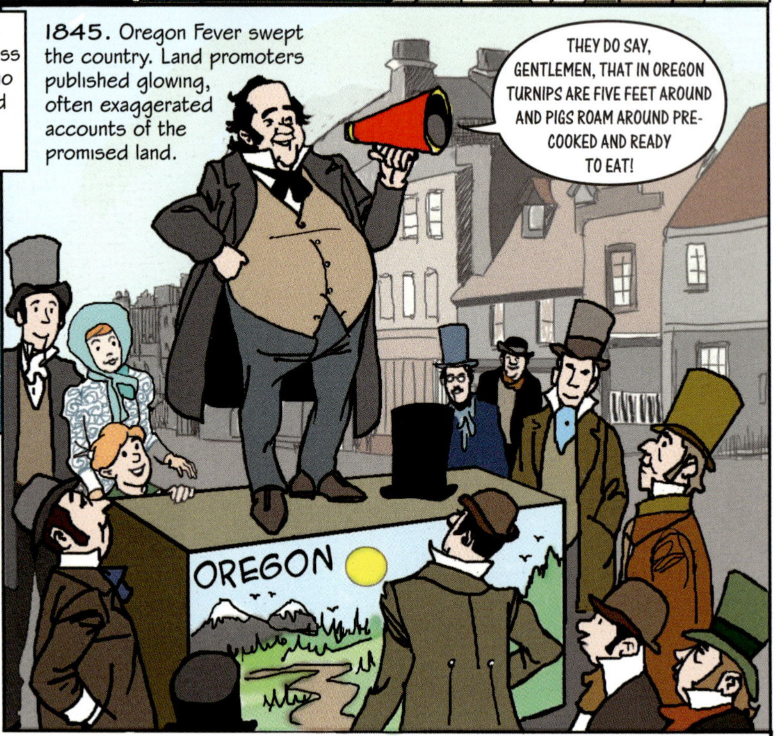
1845. Oregon Fever swept the country. Land promoters published glowing, often exaggerated accounts of the promised land.
THEY DO SAY, GENTLEMEN, THAT IN OREGON TURNIPS ARE FIVE FEET AROUND AND PIGS ROAM AROUND PRE-COOKED AND READY TO EAT!
OREGON

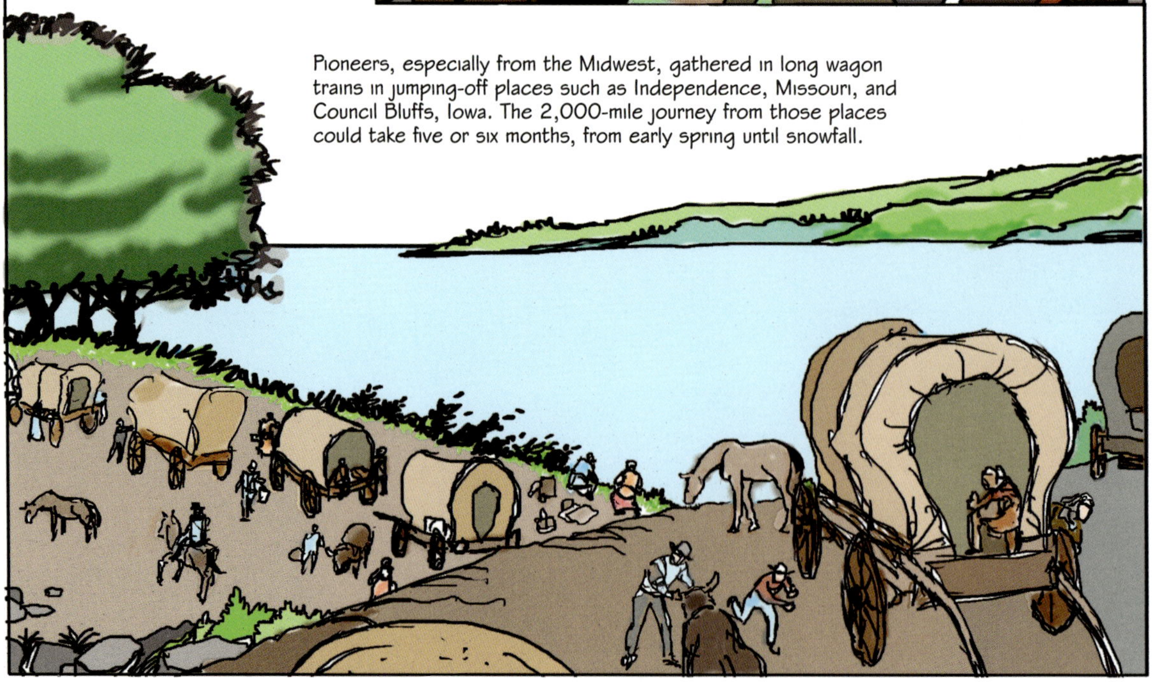
Pioneers, especially from the Midwest, gathered in long wagon trains in jumping-off places such as Independence, Missouri, and Council Bluffs, Iowa. The 2,000-mile journey from those places could take five or six months, from early spring until snowfall.

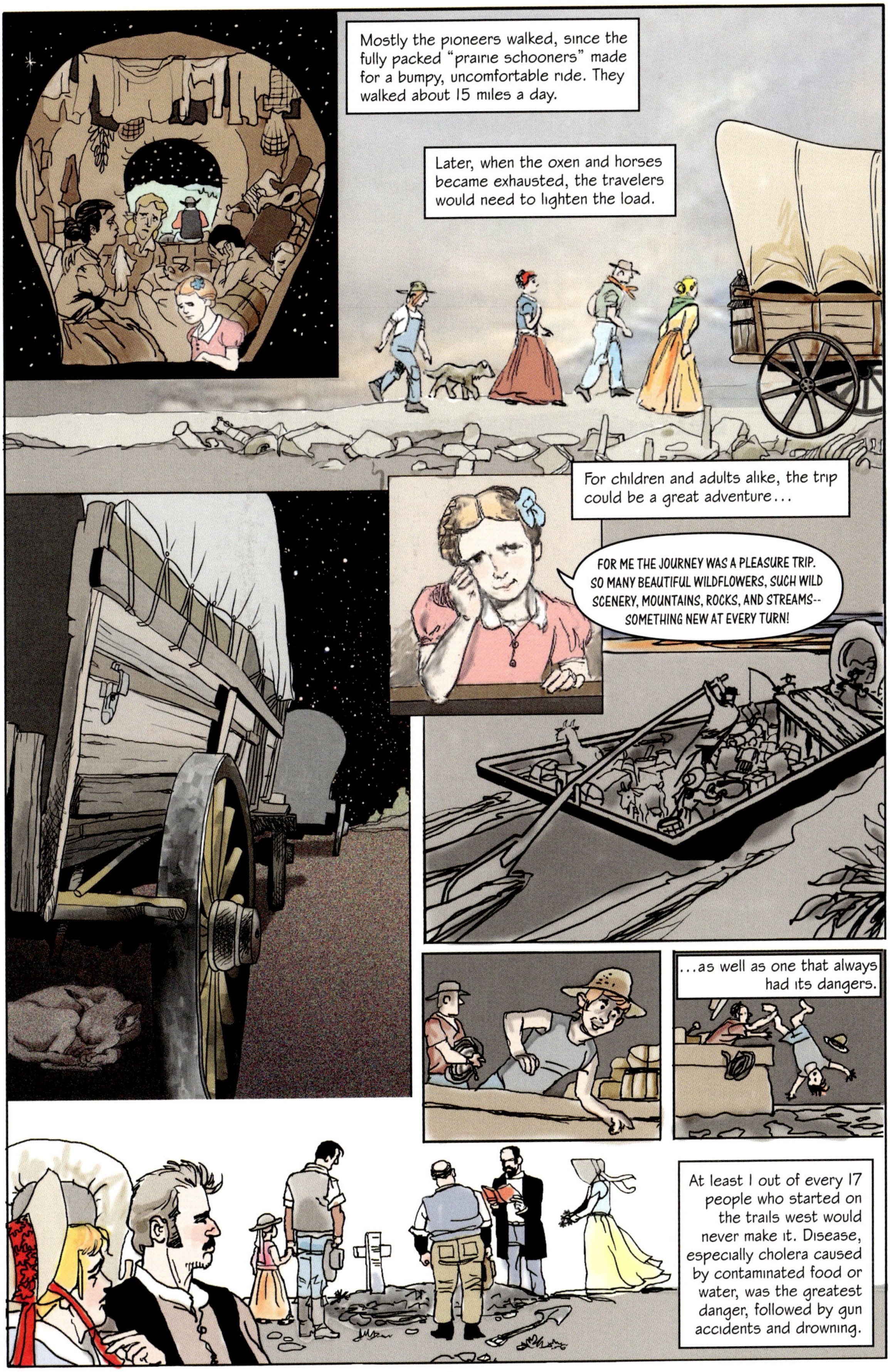

Mostly the pioneers walked, since the fully packed "prairie schooners" made for a bumpy, uncomfortable ride. They walked about 15 miles a day.
Later, when the oxen and horses became exhausted, the travelers would need to lighten the load.
For children and adults alike, the trip could be a great adventure...
FOR ME THE JOURNEY WAS A PLEASURE TRIP. SO MANY BEAUTIFUL WILDFLOWERS, SUCH WILD SCENERY, MOUNTAINS, ROCKS, AND STREAMS-- SOMETHING NEW AT EVERY TURN!
...as well as one that always had its dangers.
At least 1 out of every 17 people who started on the trails west would never make it. Disease, especially cholera caused by contaminated food or water, was the greatest danger, followed by gun accidents and drowning.

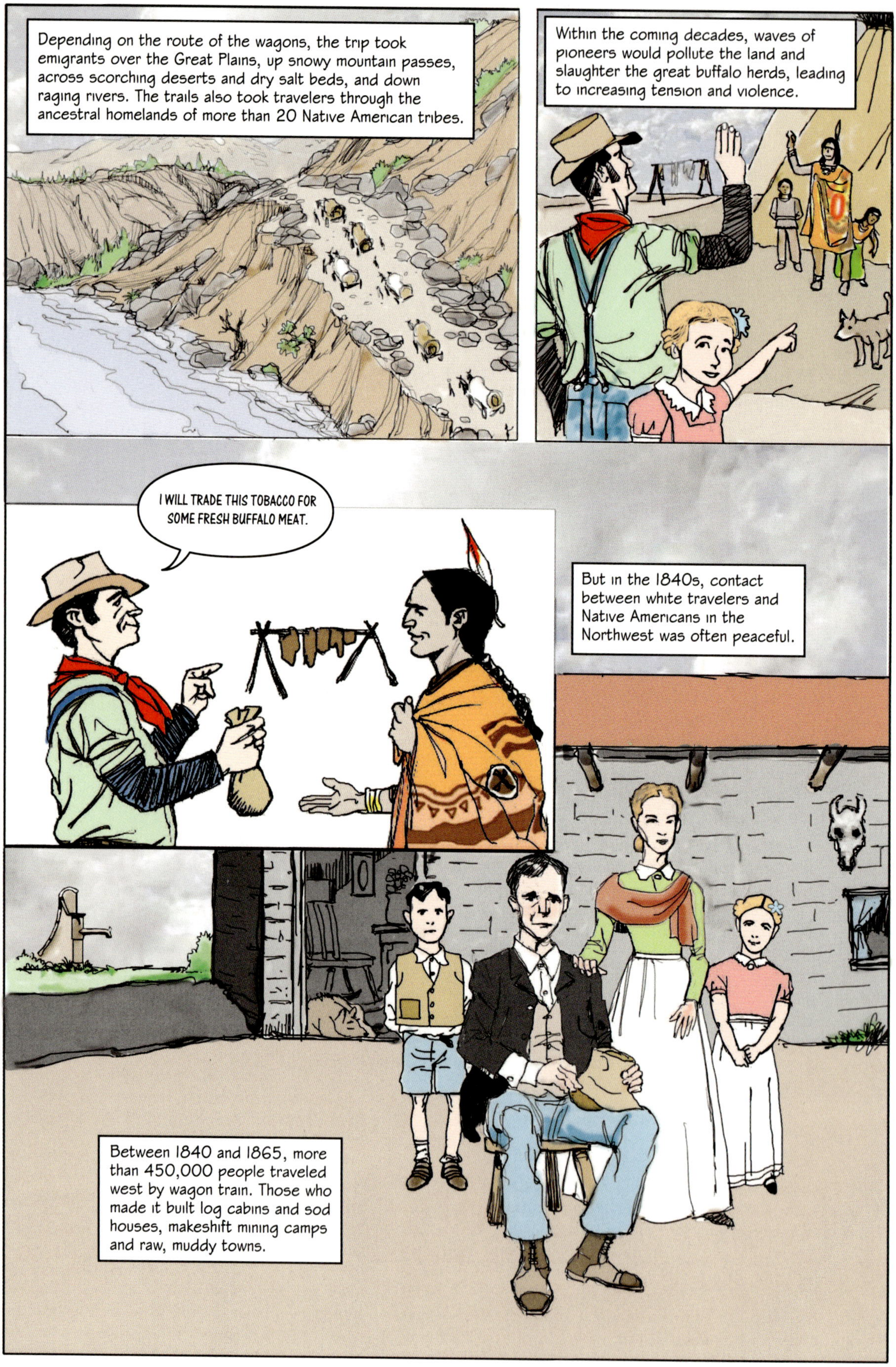
Depending on the route of the wagons, the trip took emigrants over the Great Plains, up snowy mountain passes, across scorching deserts and dry salt beds, and down raging rivers. The trails also took travelers through the ancestral homelands of more than 20 Native American tribes.
Within the coming decades, waves of pioneers would pollute the land and slaughter the great buffalo herds, leading to increasing tension and violence.
I WILL TRADE THIS TOBACCO FOR SOME FRESH BUFFALO MEAT.
But in the 1840s, contact between white travelers and Native Americans in the Northwest was often peaceful.
Between 1840 and 1865, more than 450,000 people traveled west by wagon train. Those who made it built log cabins and sod houses, makeshift mining camps and raw, muddy towns.

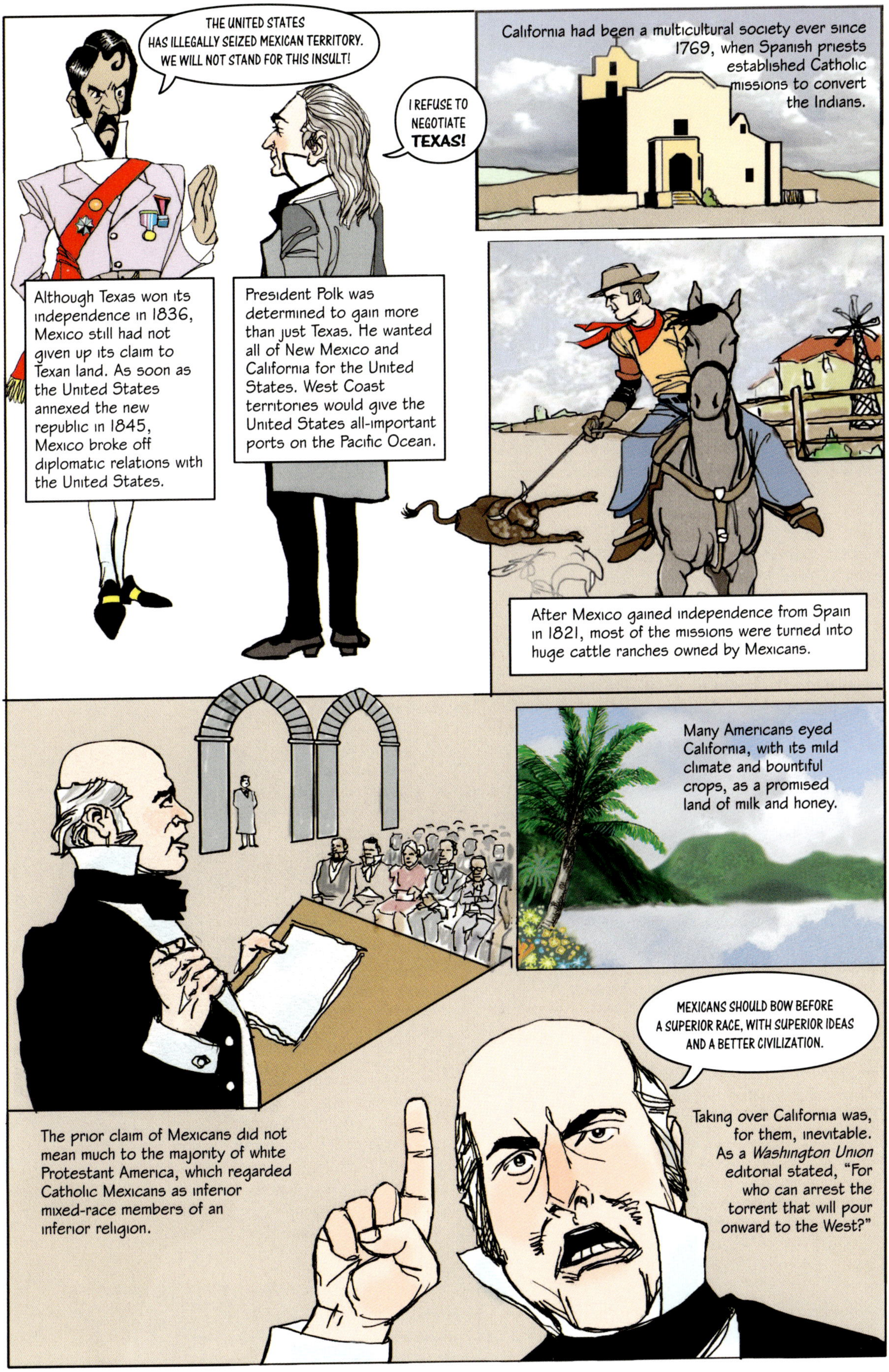
THE UNITED STATES HAS ILLEGALLY SEIZED MEXICAN TERRITORY. WE WILL NOT STAND FOR THIS INSULT!
I REFUSE TO NEGOTIATE TEXAS!
Although Texas won its independence in 1836, Mexico still had not given up its claim to Texan land. As soon as the United States annexed the new republic in 1845, Mexico broke off diplomatic relations with the United States.
President Polk was determined to gain more than just Texas. He wanted all of New Mexico and California for the United States. West Coast territories would give the United States all-important ports on the Pacific Ocean.
California had been a multicultural society ever since 1769, when Spanish priests established Catholic missions to convert the Indians.
After Mexico gained independence from Spain in 1821, most of the missions were turned into huge cattle ranches owned by Mexicans.
Many Americans eyed California, with its mild climate and bountiful crops, as a promised land of milk and honey.
MEXICANS SHOULD BOW BEFORE A SUPERIOR RACE, WITH SUPERIOR IDEAS AND A BETTER CIVILIZATION.
The prior claim of Mexicans did not mean much to the majority of white Protestant America, which regarded Catholic Mexicans as inferior mixed-race members of an inferior religion.
Taking over California was, for them, inevitable. As a *Washington Union* editorial stated, "For who can arrest the torrent that will pour onward to the West?"

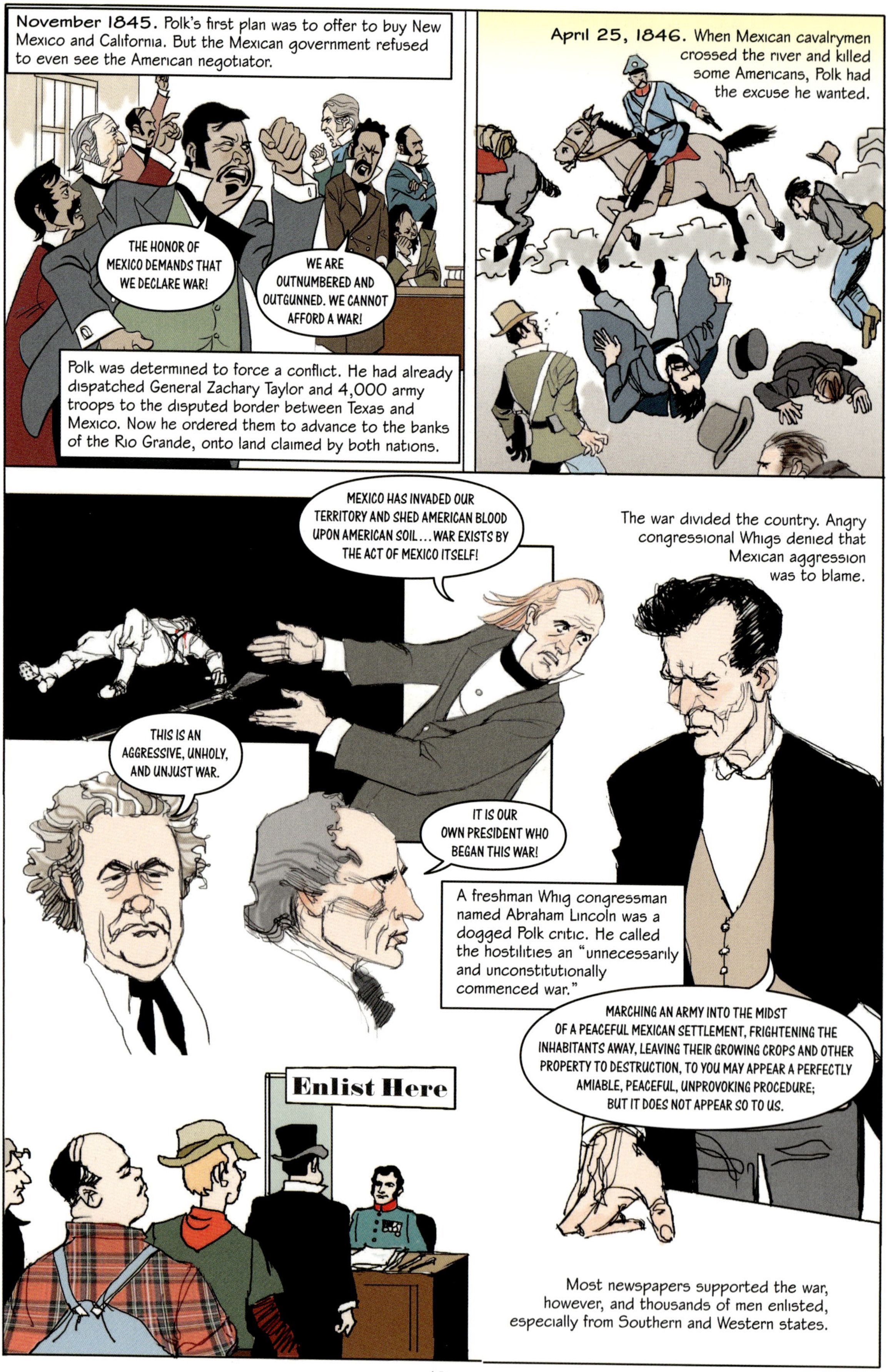
November 1845. Polk's first plan was to offer to buy New Mexico and California. But the Mexican government refused to even see the American negotiator.
THE HONOR OF MEXICO DEMANDS THAT WE DECLARE WAR!
WE ARE OUTNUMBERED AND OUTGUNNED. WE CANNOT AFFORD A WAR!
Polk was determined to force a conflict. He had already dispatched General Zachary Taylor and 4,000 army troops to the disputed border between Texas and Mexico. Now he ordered them to advance to the banks of the Rio Grande, onto land claimed by both nations.
April 25, 1846. When Mexican cavalrymen crossed the river and killed some Americans, Polk had the excuse he wanted.
MEXICO HAS INVADED OUR TERRITORY AND SHED AMERICAN BLOOD UPON AMERICAN SOIL... WAR EXISTS BY THE ACT OF MEXICO ITSELF!
The war divided the country. Angry congressional Whigs denied that Mexican aggression was to blame.
THIS IS AN AGGRESSIVE, UNHOLY, AND UNJUST WAR.
IT IS OUR OWN PRESIDENT WHO BEGAN THIS WAR!
A freshman Whig congressman named Abraham Lincoln was a dogged Polk critic. He called the hostilities an "unnecessarily and unconstitutionally commenced war."
MARCHING AN ARMY INTO THE MIDST OF A PEACEFUL MEXICAN SETTLEMENT, FRIGHTENING THE INHABITANTS AWAY, LEAVING THEIR GROWING CROPS AND OTHER PROPERTY TO DESTRUCTION, TO YOU MAY APPEAR A PERFECTLY AMIABLE, PEACEFUL, UNPROVOKING PROCEDURE; BUT IT DOES NOT APPEAR SO TO US.
Enlist Here
Most newspapers supported the war, however, and thousands of men enlisted, especially from Southern and Western states.

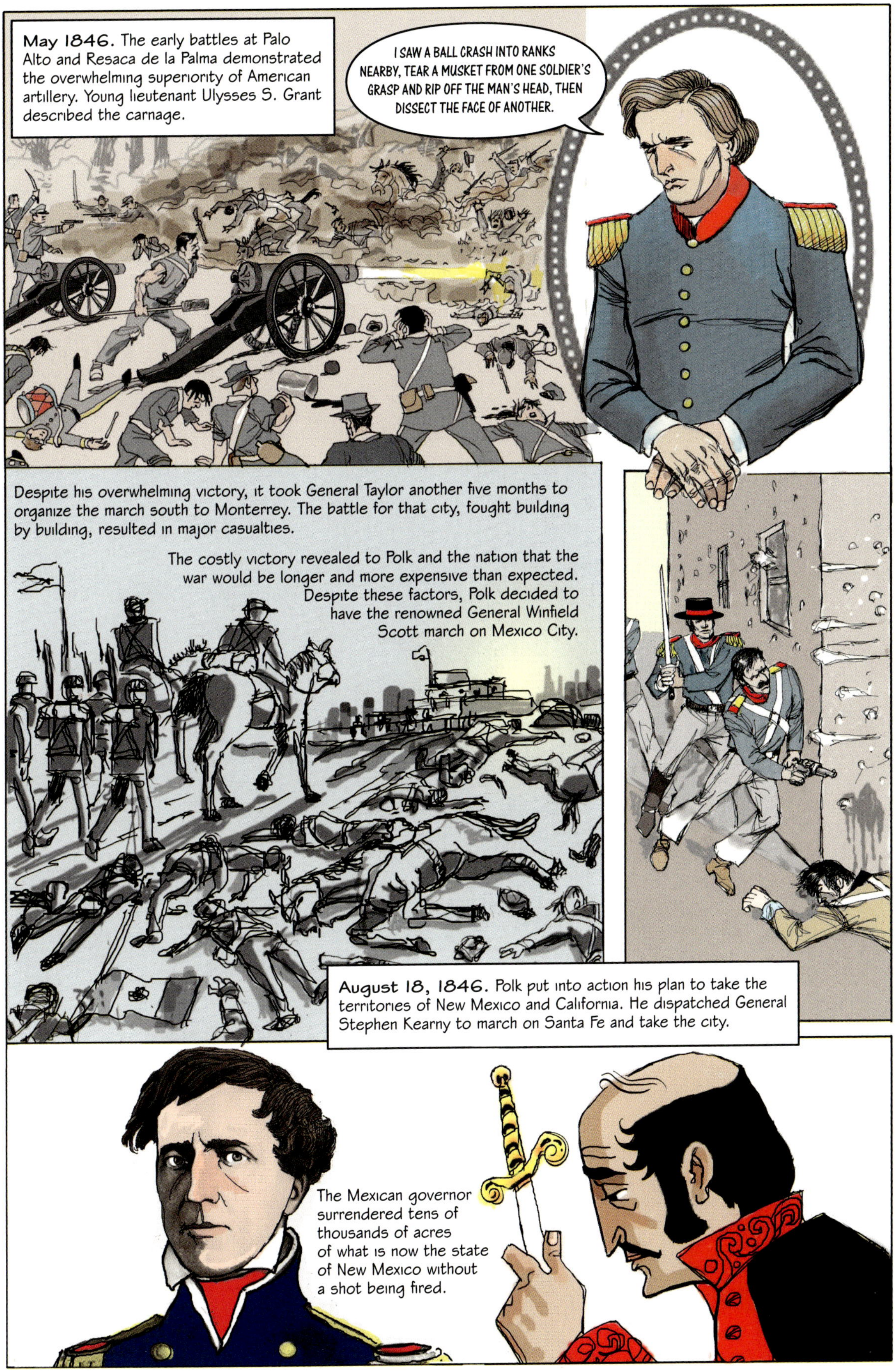
May 1846. The early battles at Palo Alto and Resaca de la Palma demonstrated the overwhelming superiority of American artillery. Young lieutenant Ulysses S. Grant described the carnage.
I SAW A BALL CRASH INTO RANKS NEARBY, TEAR A MUSKET FROM ONE SOLDIER'S GRASP AND RIP OFF THE MAN'S HEAD, THEN DISSECT THE FACE OF ANOTHER.
Despite his overwhelming victory, it took General Taylor another five months to organize the march south to Monterrey. The battle for that city, fought building by building, resulted in major casualties.
The costly victory revealed to Polk and the nation that the war would be longer and more expensive than expected. Despite these factors, Polk decided to have the renowned General Winfield Scott march on Mexico City.
August 18, 1846. Polk put into action his plan to take the territories of New Mexico and California. He dispatched General Stephen Kearny to march on Santa Fe and take the city.
The Mexican governor surrendered tens of thousands of acres of what is now the state of New Mexico without a shot being fired.

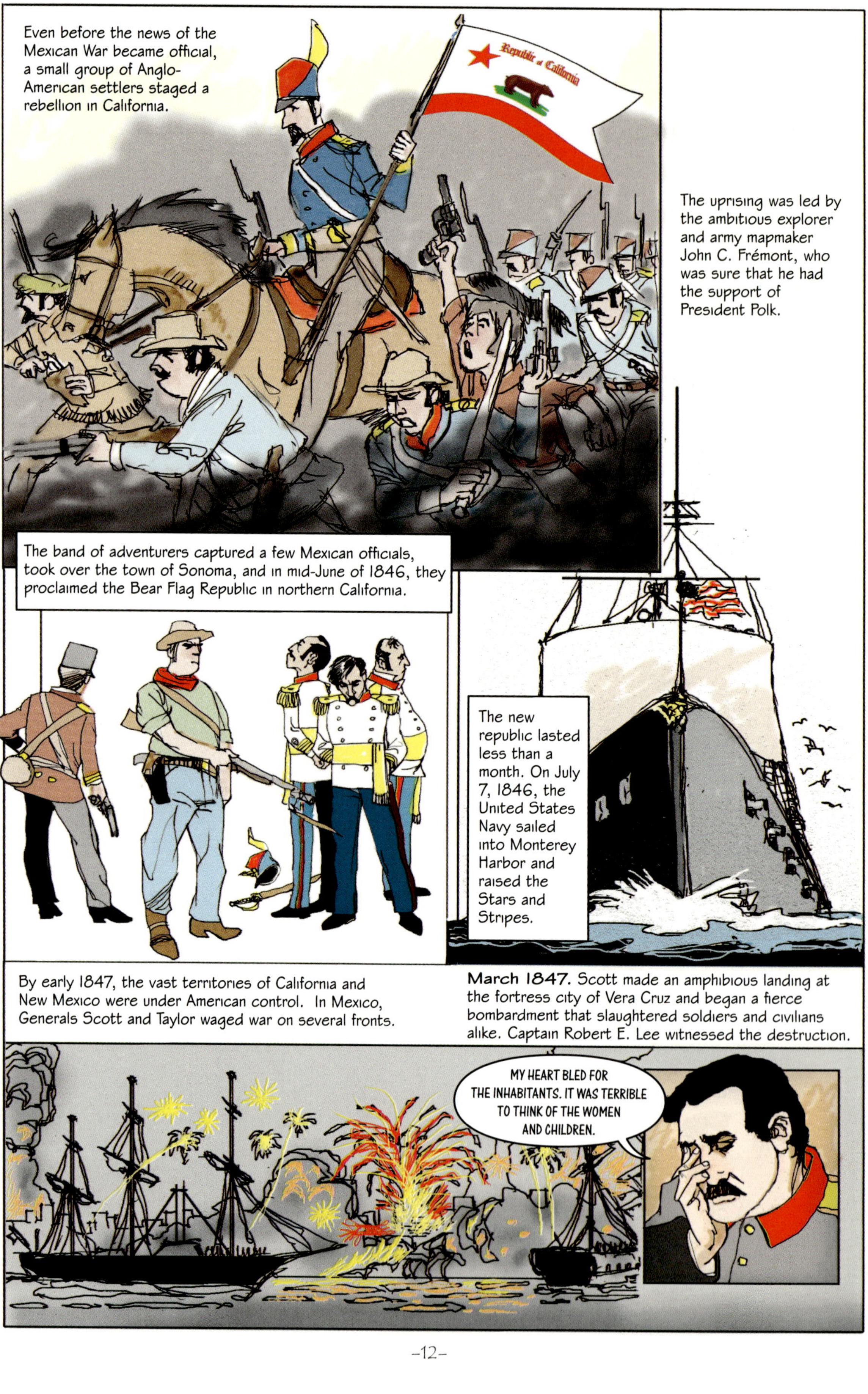
Even before the news of the Mexican War became official, a small group of Anglo-American settlers staged a rebellion in California.
Republic of California
The uprising was led by the ambitious explorer and army mapmaker John C. Frémont, who was sure that he had the support of President Polk.
The band of adventurers captured a few Mexican officials, took over the town of Sonoma, and in mid-June of 1846, they proclaimed the Bear Flag Republic in northern California.
The new republic lasted less than a month. On July 7, 1846, the United States Navy sailed into Monterey Harbor and raised the Stars and Stripes.
By early 1847, the vast territories of California and New Mexico were under American control. In Mexico, Generals Scott and Taylor waged war on several fronts.
March 1847. Scott made an amphibious landing at the fortress city of Vera Cruz and began a fierce bombardment that slaughtered soldiers and civilians alike. Captain Robert E. Lee witnessed the destruction.
MY HEART BLED FOR THE INHABITANTS. IT WAS TERRIBLE TO THINK OF THE WOMEN AND CHILDREN.

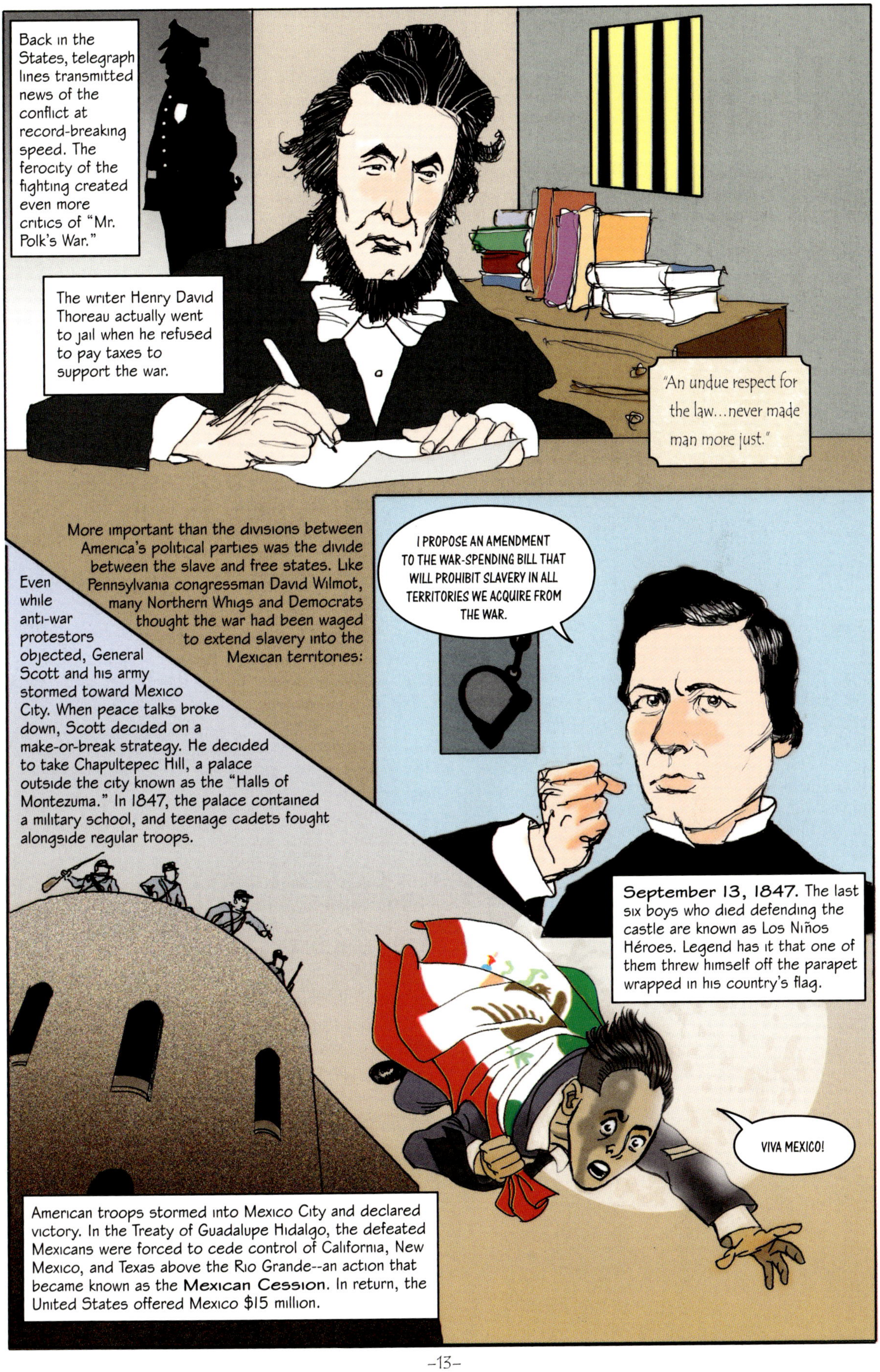
Back in the States, telegraph lines transmitted news of the conflict at record-breaking speed. The ferocity of the fighting created even more critics of "Mr. Polk's War."
The writer Henry David Thoreau actually went to jail when he refused to pay taxes to support the war.
"An undue respect for the law…never made man more just."
More important than the divisions between America's political parties was the divide between the slave and free states. Like Pennsylvania congressman David Wilmot, many Northern Whigs and Democrats thought the war had been waged to extend slavery into the Mexican territories:
I PROPOSE AN AMENDMENT TO THE WAR-SPENDING BILL THAT WILL PROHIBIT SLAVERY IN ALL TERRITORIES WE ACQUIRE FROM THE WAR.
Even while anti-war protestors objected, General Scott and his army stormed toward Mexico City. When peace talks broke down, Scott decided on a make-or-break strategy. He decided to take Chapultepec Hill, a palace outside the city known as the "Halls of Montezuma." In 1847, the palace contained a military school, and teenage cadets fought alongside regular troops.
September 13, 1847. The last six boys who died defending the castle are known as Los Niños Héroes. Legend has it that one of them threw himself off the parapet wrapped in his country's flag.
VIVA MEXICO!
American troops stormed into Mexico City and declared victory. In the Treaty of Guadalupe Hidalgo, the defeated Mexicans were forced to cede control of California, New Mexico, and Texas above the Rio Grande--an action that became known as the Mexican Cession. In return, the United States offered Mexico $15 million.

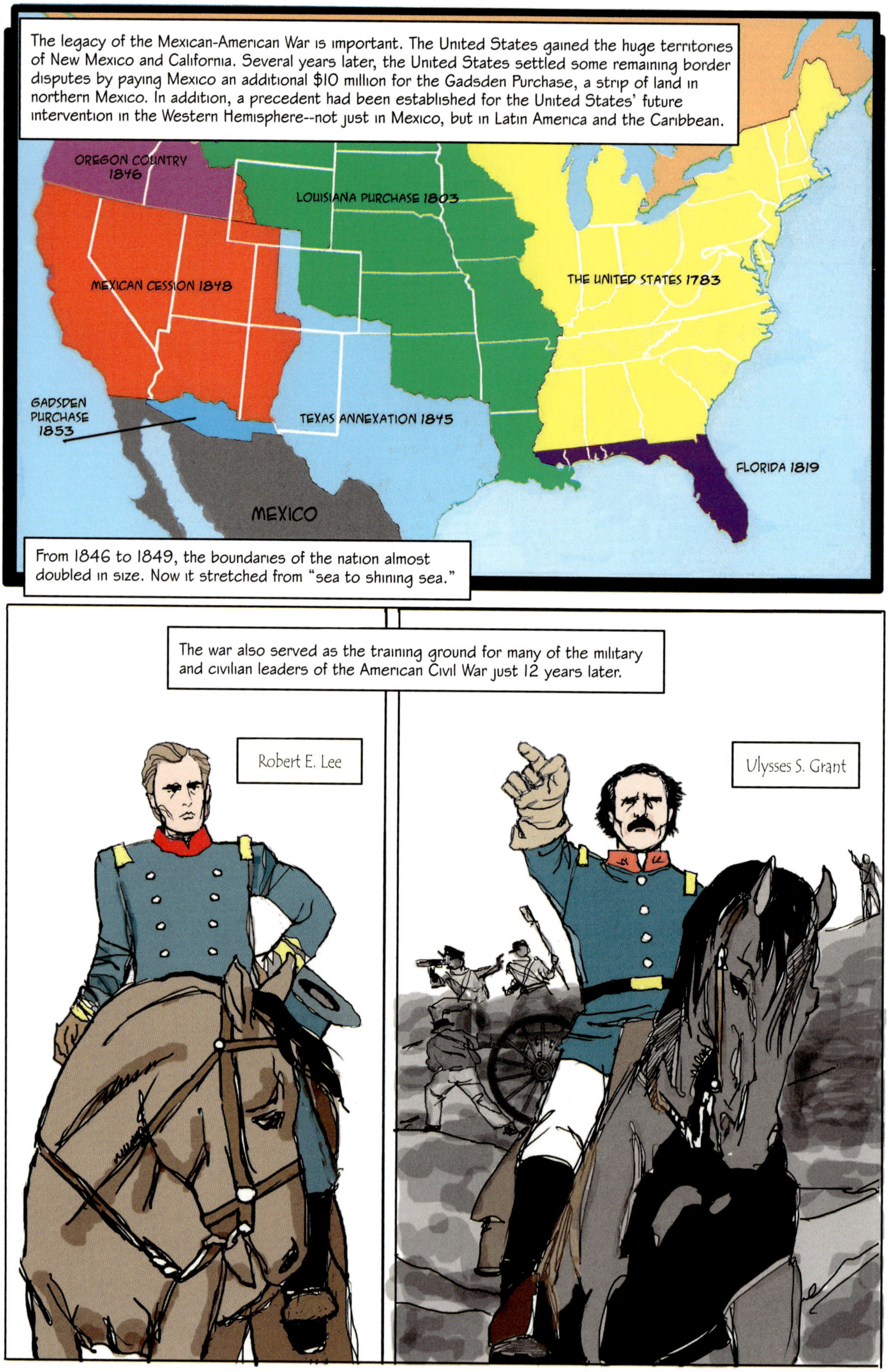
The legacy of the Mexican-American War is important. The United States gained the huge territories of New Mexico and California. Several years later, the United States settled some remaining border disputes by paying Mexico an additional $10 million for the Gadsden Purchase, a strip of land in northern Mexico. In addition, a precedent had been established for the United States' future intervention in the Western Hemisphere--not just in Mexico, but in Latin America and the Caribbean.
OREGON COUNTRY 1846
LOUISIANA PURCHASE 1803
MEXICAN CESSION 1848
THE UNITED STATES 1783
GADSDEN PURCHASE 1853
TEXAS ANNEXATION 1845
FLORIDA 1819
MEXICO
From 1846 to 1849, the boundaries of the nation almost doubled in size. Now it stretched from "sea to shining sea."
The war also served as the training ground for many of the military and civilian leaders of the American Civil War just 12 years later.
Robert E. Lee
Ulysses S. Grant

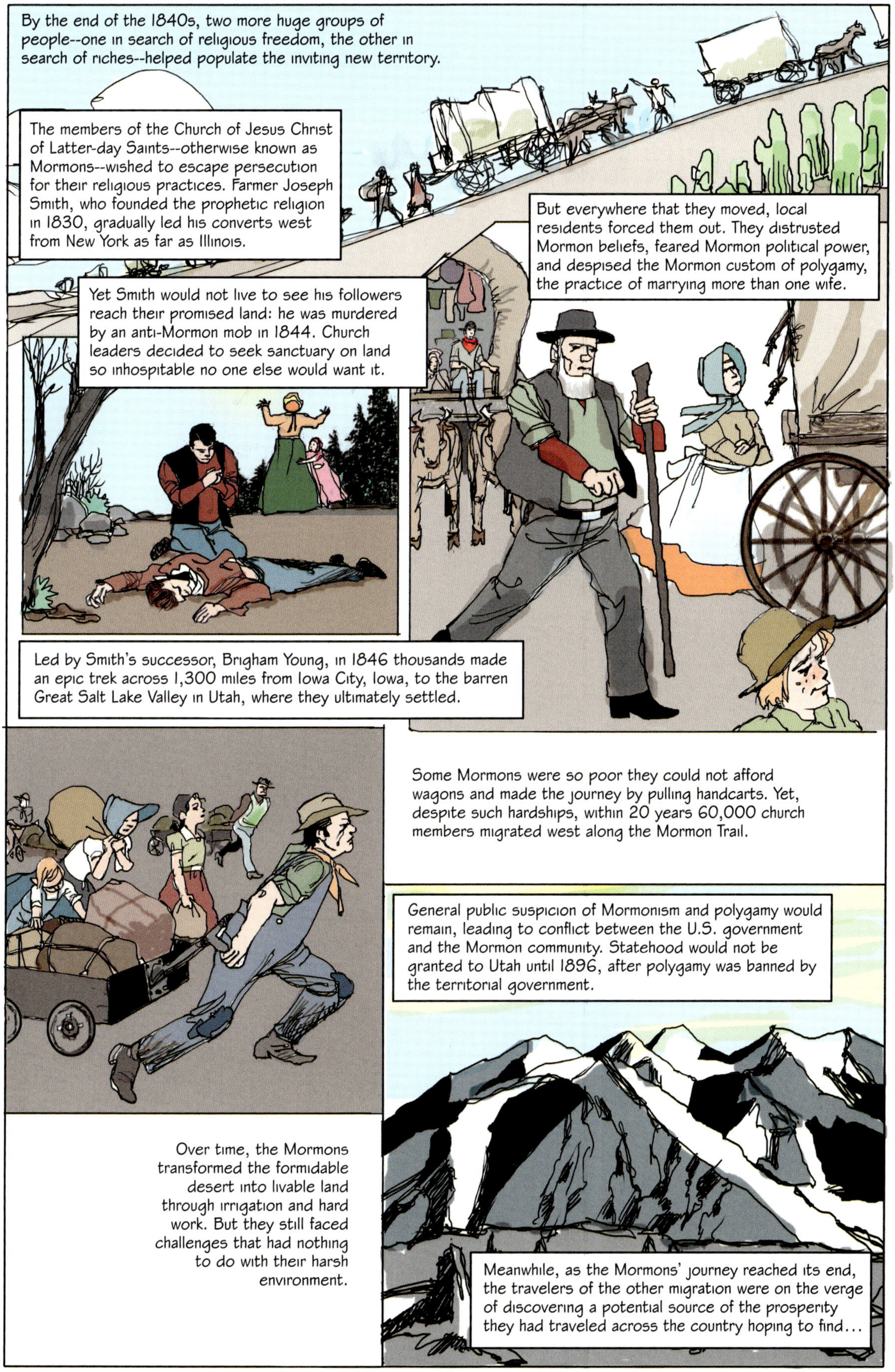
By the end of the 1840s, two more huge groups of people--one in search of religious freedom, the other in search of riches--helped populate the inviting new territory.
The members of the Church of Jesus Christ of Latter-day Saints--otherwise known as Mormons--wished to escape persecution for their religious practices. Farmer Joseph Smith, who founded the prophetic religion in 1830, gradually led his converts west from New York as far as Illinois.
But everywhere that they moved, local residents forced them out. They distrusted Mormon beliefs, feared Mormon political power, and despised the Mormon custom of polygamy, the practice of marrying more than one wife.
Yet Smith would not live to see his followers reach their promised land: he was murdered by an anti-Mormon mob in 1844. Church leaders decided to seek sanctuary on land so inhospitable no one else would want it.
Led by Smith's successor, Brigham Young, in 1846 thousands made an epic trek across 1,300 miles from Iowa City, Iowa, to the barren Great Salt Lake Valley in Utah, where they ultimately settled.
Some Mormons were so poor they could not afford wagons and made the journey by pulling handcarts. Yet, despite such hardships, within 20 years 60,000 church members migrated west along the Mormon Trail.
General public suspicion of Mormonism and polygamy would remain, leading to conflict between the U.S. government and the Mormon community. Statehood would not be granted to Utah until 1896, after polygamy was banned by the territorial government.
Over time, the Mormons transformed the formidable desert into livable land through irrigation and hard work. But they still faced challenges that had nothing to do with their harsh environment.
Meanwhile, as the Mormons' journey reached its end, the travelers of the other migration were on the verge of discovering a potential source of the prosperity they had traveled across the country hoping to find...

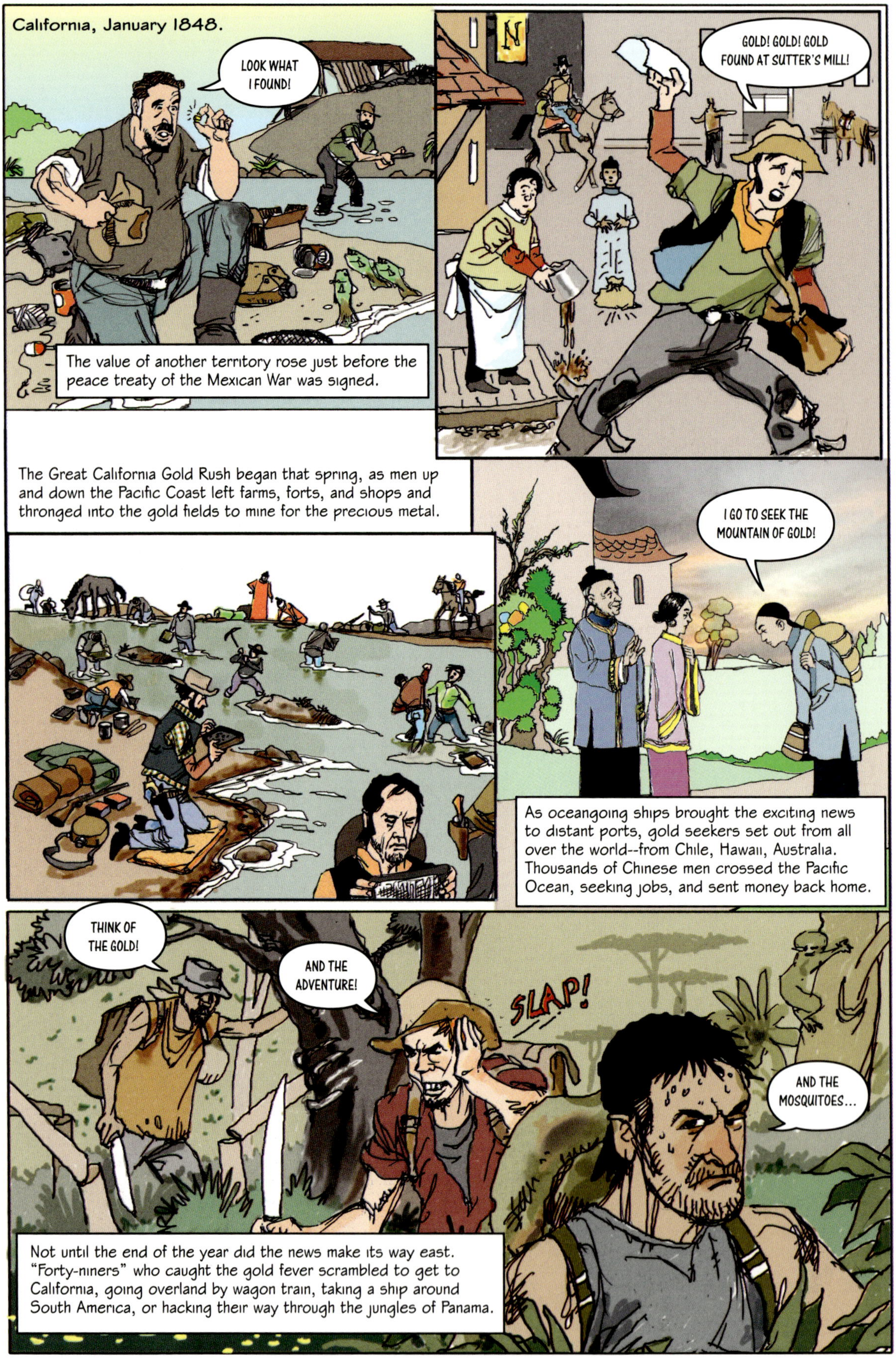
California, January 1848.
LOOK WHAT I FOUND!
The value of another territory rose just before the peace treaty of the Mexican War was signed.
GOLD! GOLD! GOLD FOUND AT SUTTER'S MILL!
The Great California Gold Rush began that spring, as men up and down the Pacific Coast left farms, forts, and shops and thronged into the gold fields to mine for the precious metal.
I GO TO SEEK THE MOUNTAIN OF GOLD!
As oceangoing ships brought the exciting news to distant ports, gold seekers set out from all over the world--from Chile, Hawaii, Australia. Thousands of Chinese men crossed the Pacific Ocean, seeking jobs, and sent money back home.
THINK OF THE GOLD!
AND THE ADVENTURE!
SLAP!
AND THE MOSQUITOES...
Not until the end of the year did the news make its way east. "Forty-niners" who caught the gold fever scrambled to get to California, going overland by wagon train, taking a ship around South America, or hacking their way through the jungles of Panama.

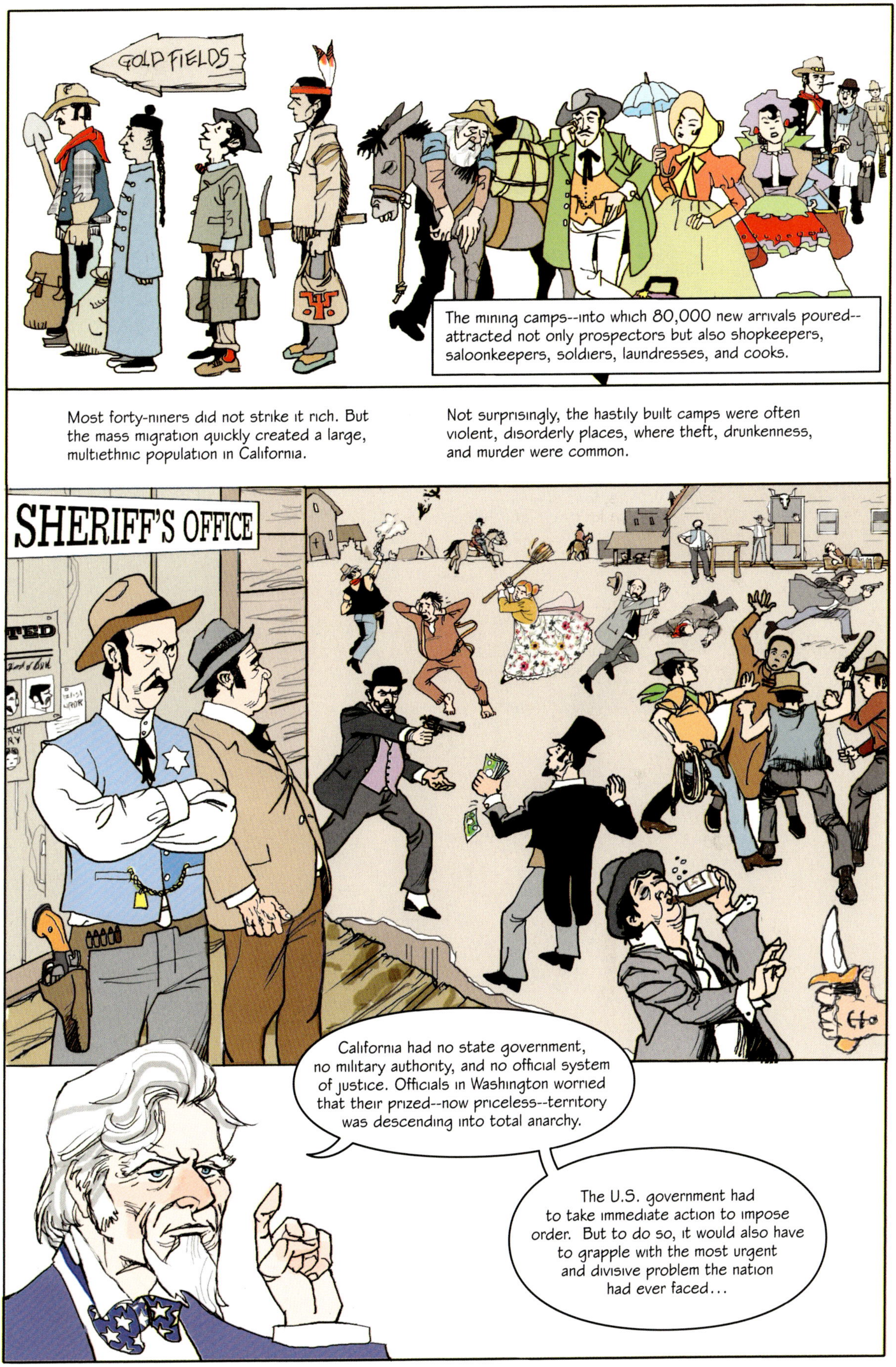
GOLD FIELDS
The mining camps--into which 80,000 new arrivals poured--attracted not only prospectors but also shopkeepers, saloonkeepers, soldiers, laundresses, and cooks.
Most forty-niners did not strike it rich. But the mass migration quickly created a large, multiethnic population in California.
Not surprisingly, the hastily built camps were often violent, disorderly places, where theft, drunkenness, and murder were common.
SHERIFF'S OFFICE
California had no state government, no military authority, and no official system of justice. Officials in Washington worried that their prized--now priceless--territory was descending into total anarchy.
The U.S. government had to take immediate action to impose order. But to do so, it would also have to grapple with the most urgent and divisive problem the nation had ever faced...

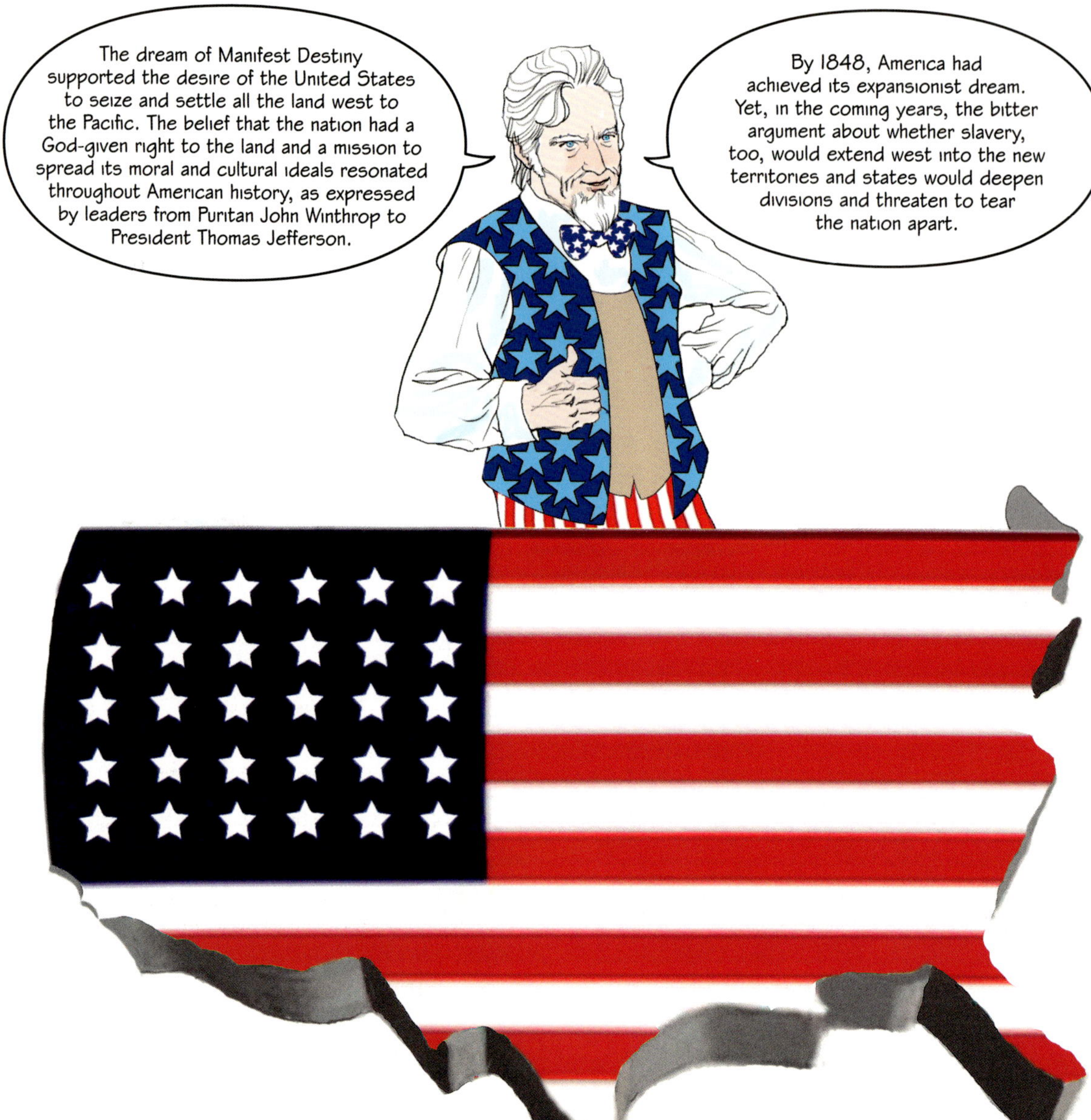
The dream of Manifest Destiny supported the desire of the United States to seize and settle all the land west to the Pacific. The belief that the nation had a God-given right to the land and a mission to spread its moral and cultural ideals resonated throughout American history, as expressed by leaders from Puritan John Winthrop to President Thomas Jefferson.
By 1848, America had achieved its expansionist dream. Yet, in the coming years, the bitter argument about whether slavery, too, would extend west into the new territories and states would deepen divisions and threaten to tear the nation apart.

EXCERPT FROM JOHN O'SULLIVAN'S
UNITED STATES MAGAZINE, AND DEMOCRATIC REVIEW

"The far-reaching, the boundless future will be the era of American greatness…Yes, we are the nation of progress, of individual freedom, of universal enfranchisement…We must onward to the fulfilment of our mission—to the entire development of the principle of our organization—freedom of conscience, freedom of person, freedom of trade and business pursuits, universality of freedom and equality. This is our high destiny, and in nature's eternal, inevitable decree of cause and effect we must accomplish it. All this will be our future history, to establish on earth the moral dignity and salvation of man—the immutable truth and beneficence of God. For this blessed mission to the nations of the world, which are shut out from the life-giving light of truth, has America been chosen; and her high example shall smite unto death the tyranny of kings, hierarchs, and oligarchs, and carry the glad tidings of peace and good will where myriads now endure an existence scarcely more enviable than that of beasts of the field. Who, then, can doubt that our country is destined to be the great nation of futurity?"

The Declaration of Sentiments

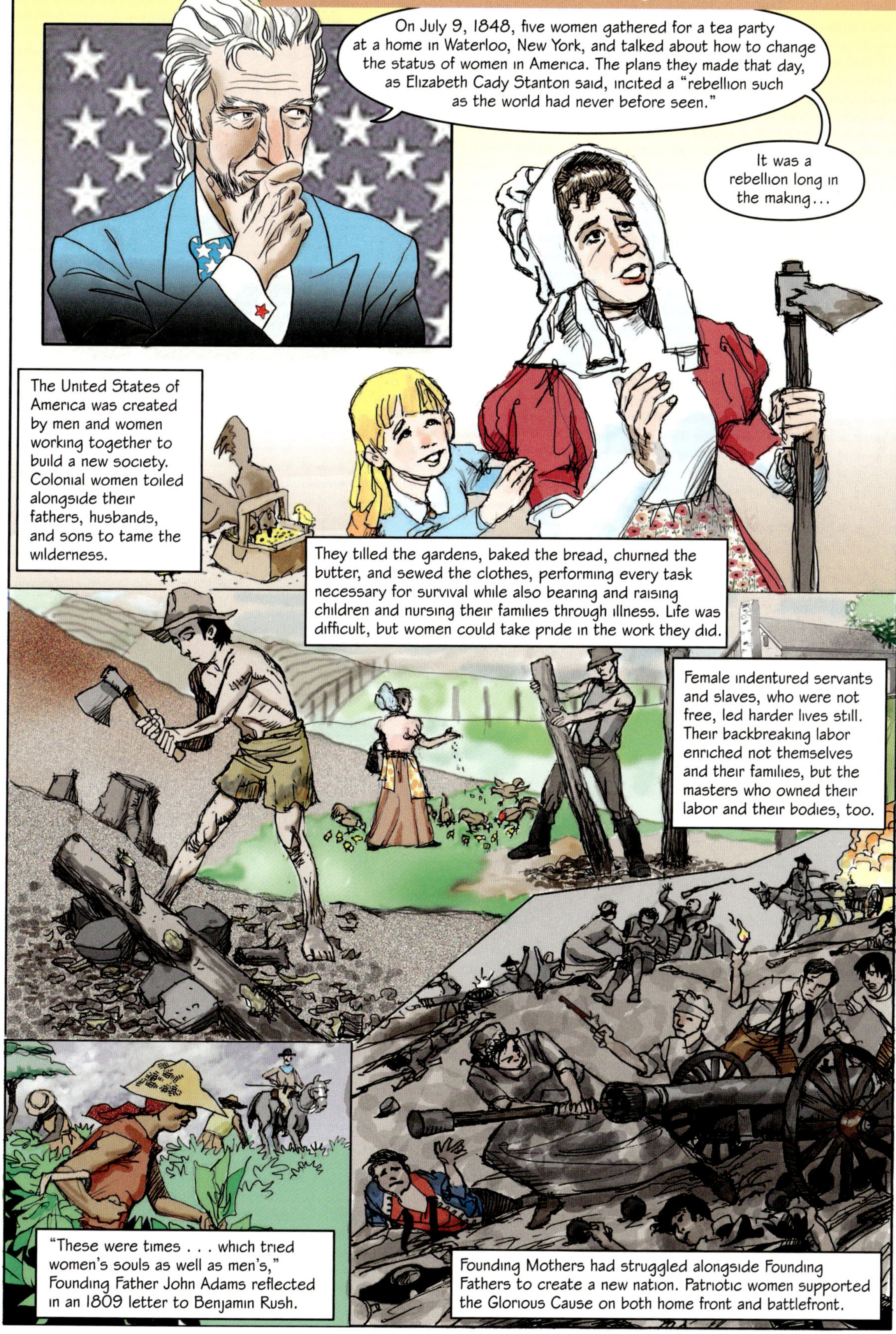
On July 9, 1848, five women gathered for a tea party at a home in Waterloo, New York, and talked about how to change the status of women in America. The plans they made that day, as Elizabeth Cady Stanton said, incited a "rebellion such as the world had never before seen."
It was a rebellion long in the making...
The United States of America was created by men and women working together to build a new society. Colonial women toiled alongside their fathers, husbands, and sons to tame the wilderness.
They tilled the gardens, baked the bread, churned the butter, and sewed the clothes, performing every task necessary for survival while also bearing and raising children and nursing their families through illness. Life was difficult, but women could take pride in the work they did.
Female indentured servants and slaves, who were not free, led harder lives still. Their backbreaking labor enriched not themselves and their families, but the masters who owned their labor and their bodies, too.
"These were times . . . which tried women's souls as well as men's," Founding Father John Adams reflected in an 1809 letter to Benjamin Rush.
Founding Mothers had struggled alongside Founding Fathers to create a new nation. Patriotic women supported the Glorious Cause on both home front and battlefront.

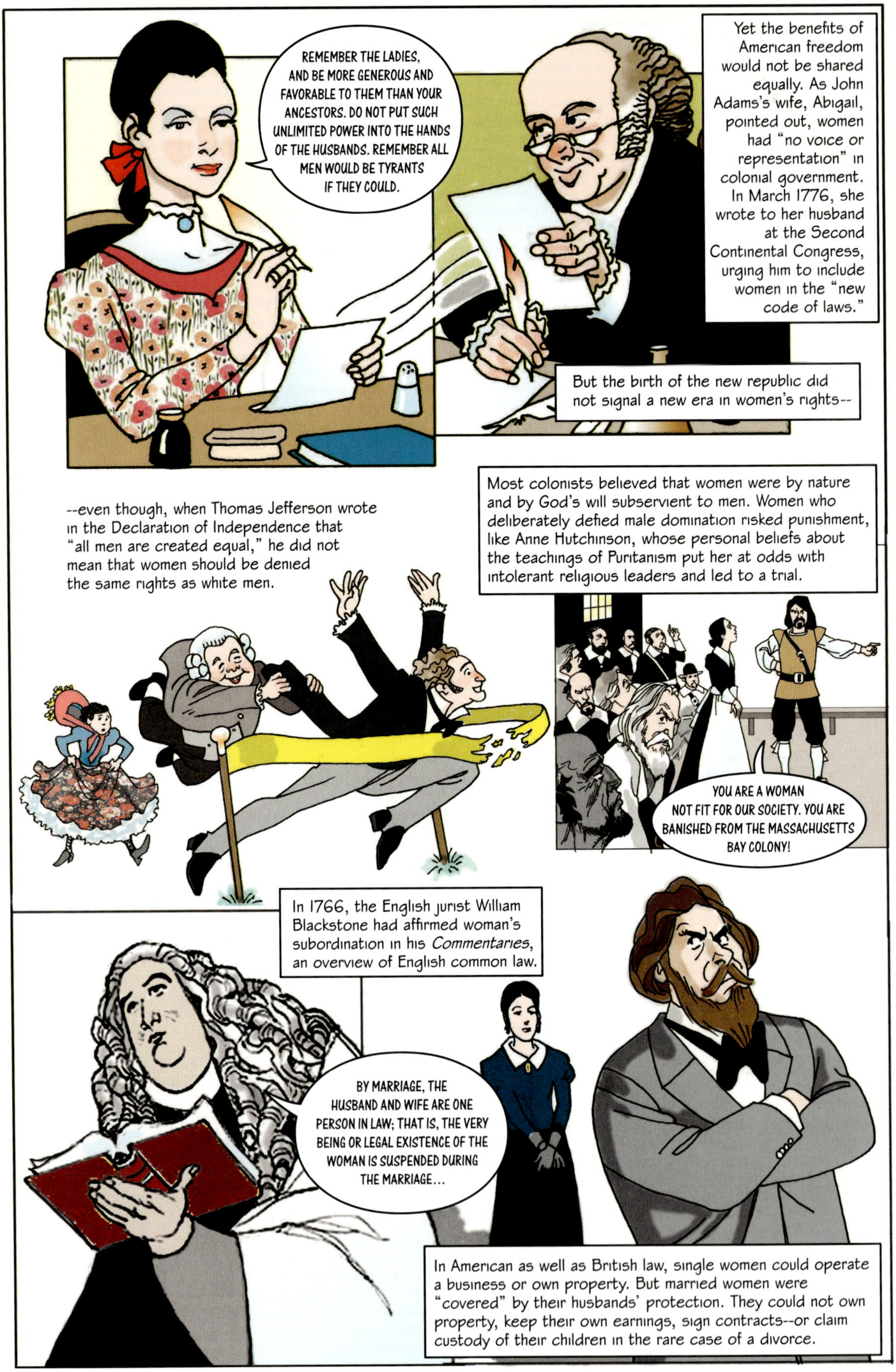
REMEMBER THE LADIES, AND BE MORE GENEROUS AND FAVORABLE TO THEM THAN YOUR ANCESTORS. DO NOT PUT SUCH UNLIMITED POWER INTO THE HANDS OF THE HUSBANDS. REMEMBER ALL MEN WOULD BE TYRANTS IF THEY COULD.
Yet the benefits of American freedom would not be shared equally. As John Adams's wife, Abigail, pointed out, women had "no voice or representation" in colonial government. In March 1776, she wrote to her husband at the Second Continental Congress, urging him to include women in the "new code of laws."
But the birth of the new republic did not signal a new era in women's rights--
--even though, when Thomas Jefferson wrote in the Declaration of Independence that "all men are created equal," he did not mean that women should be denied the same rights as white men.
Most colonists believed that women were by nature and by God's will subservient to men. Women who deliberately defied male domination risked punishment, like Anne Hutchinson, whose personal beliefs about the teachings of Puritanism put her at odds with intolerant religious leaders and led to a trial.
YOU ARE A WOMAN NOT FIT FOR OUR SOCIETY. YOU ARE BANISHED FROM THE MASSACHUSETTS BAY COLONY!
In 1766, the English jurist William Blackstone had affirmed woman's subordination in his *Commentaries*, an overview of English common law.
BY MARRIAGE, THE HUSBAND AND WIFE ARE ONE PERSON IN LAW; THAT IS, THE VERY BEING OR LEGAL EXISTENCE OF THE WOMAN IS SUSPENDED DURING THE MARRIAGE...
In American as well as British law, single women could operate a business or own property. But married women were "covered" by their husbands' protection. They could not own property, keep their own earnings, sign contracts--or claim custody of their children in the rare case of a divorce.

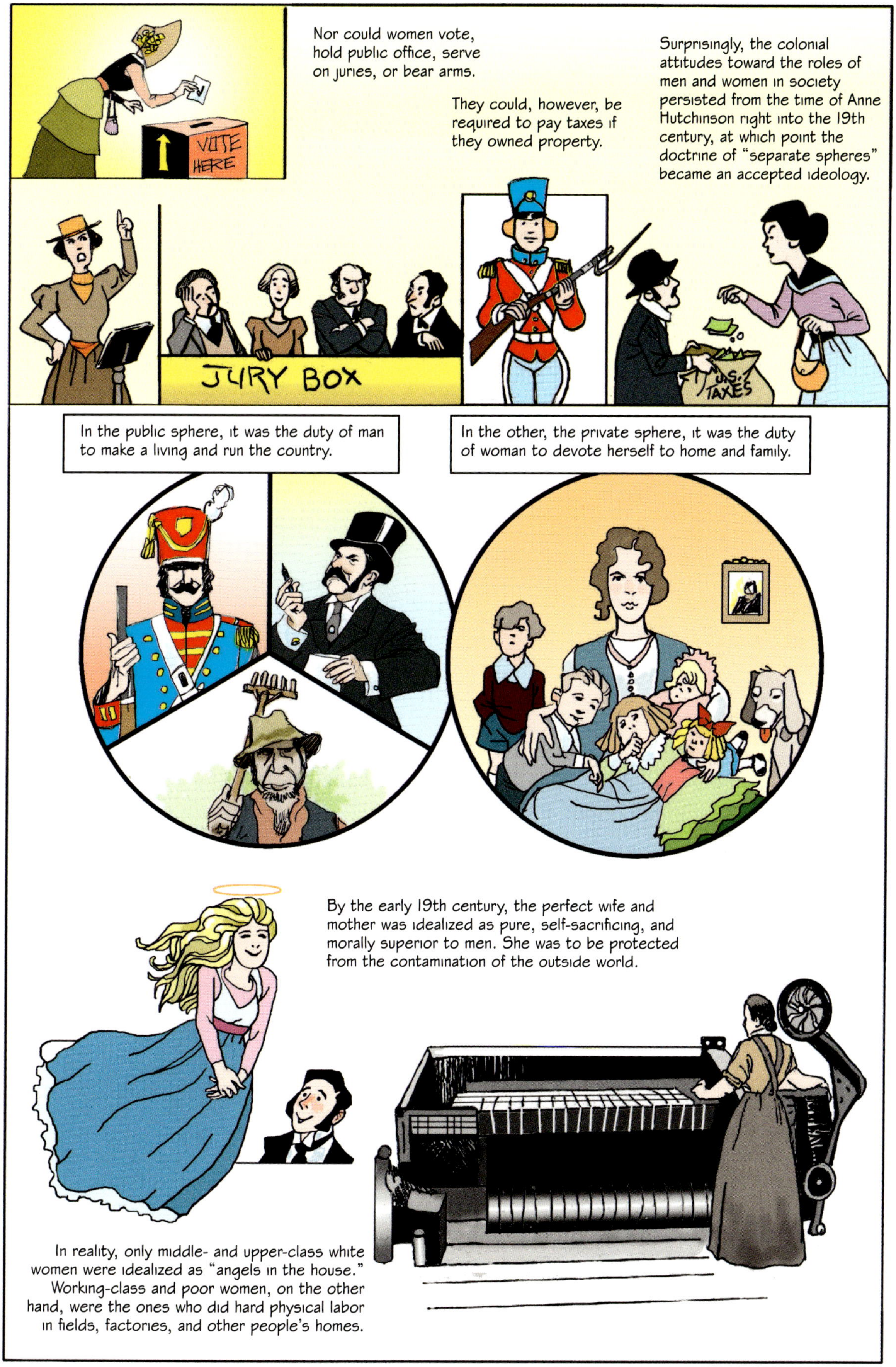
Nor could women vote, hold public office, serve on juries, or bear arms.
VOTE HERE
They could, however, be required to pay taxes if they owned property.
Surprisingly, the colonial attitudes toward the roles of men and women in society persisted from the time of Anne Hutchinson right into the 19th century, at which point the doctrine of "separate spheres" became an accepted ideology.
JURY BOX
U.S. TAXES
In the public sphere, it was the duty of man to make a living and run the country.
In the other, the private sphere, it was the duty of woman to devote herself to home and family.
By the early 19th century, the perfect wife and mother was idealized as pure, self-sacrificing, and morally superior to men. She was to be protected from the contamination of the outside world.
In reality, only middle- and upper-class white women were idealized as "angels in the house." Working-class and poor women, on the other hand, were the ones who did hard physical labor in fields, factories, and other people's homes.

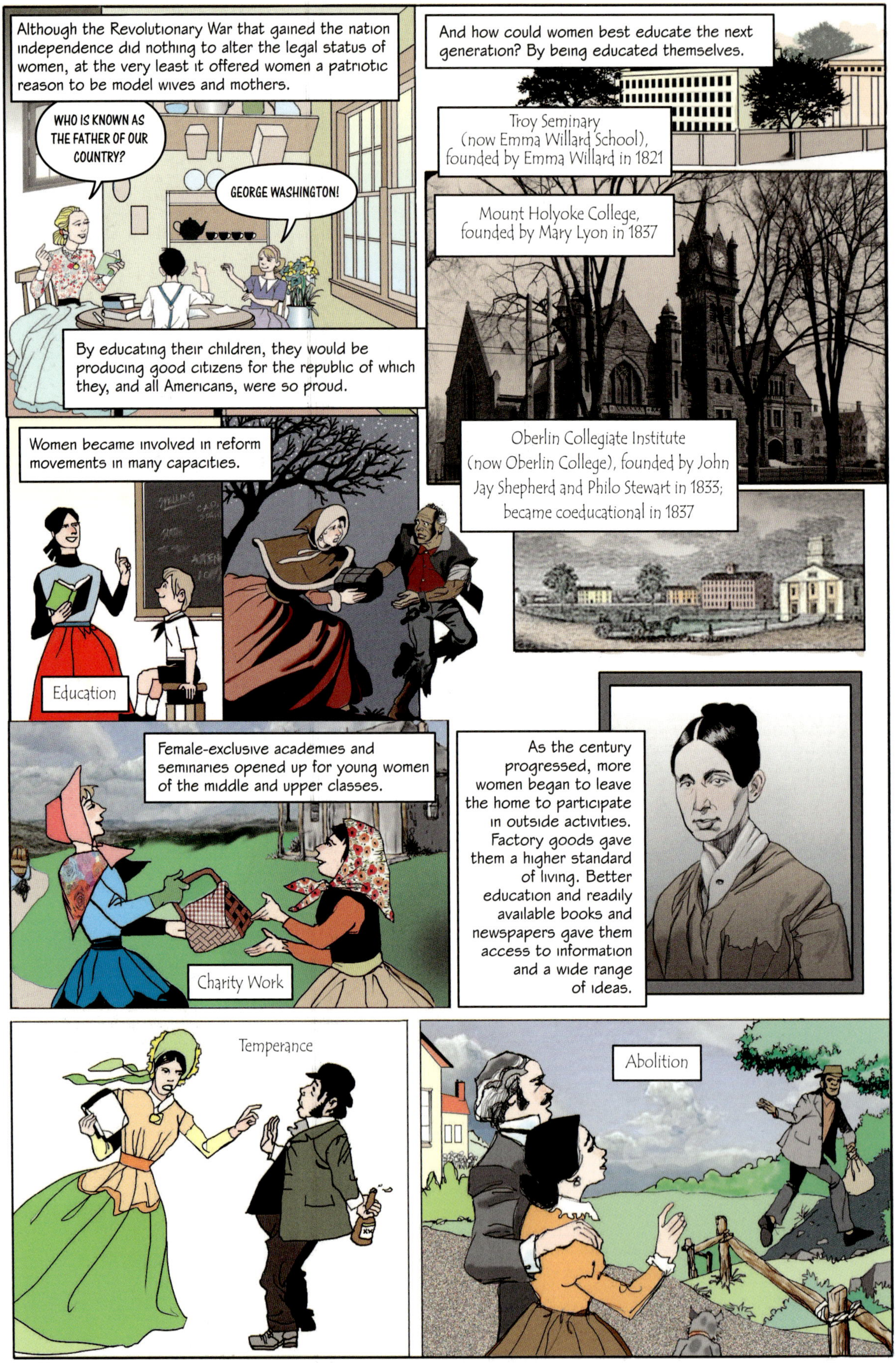
Although the Revolutionary War that gained the nation independence did nothing to alter the legal status of women, at the very least it offered women a patriotic reason to be model wives and mothers.
WHO IS KNOWN AS THE FATHER OF OUR COUNTRY?
GEORGE WASHINGTON!
By educating their children, they would be producing good citizens for the republic of which they, and all Americans, were so proud.
And how could women best educate the next generation? By being educated themselves.
Troy Seminary (now Emma Willard School), founded by Emma Willard in 1821
Mount Holyoke College, founded by Mary Lyon in 1837
Oberlin Collegiate Institute (now Oberlin College), founded by John Jay Shepherd and Philo Stewart in 1833; became coeducational in 1837
Women became involved in reform movements in many capacities.
Education
Female-exclusive academies and seminaries opened up for young women of the middle and upper classes.
Charity Work
As the century progressed, more women began to leave the home to participate in outside activities. Factory goods gave them a higher standard of living. Better education and readily available books and newspapers gave them access to information and a wide range of ideas.
Temperance
Abolition

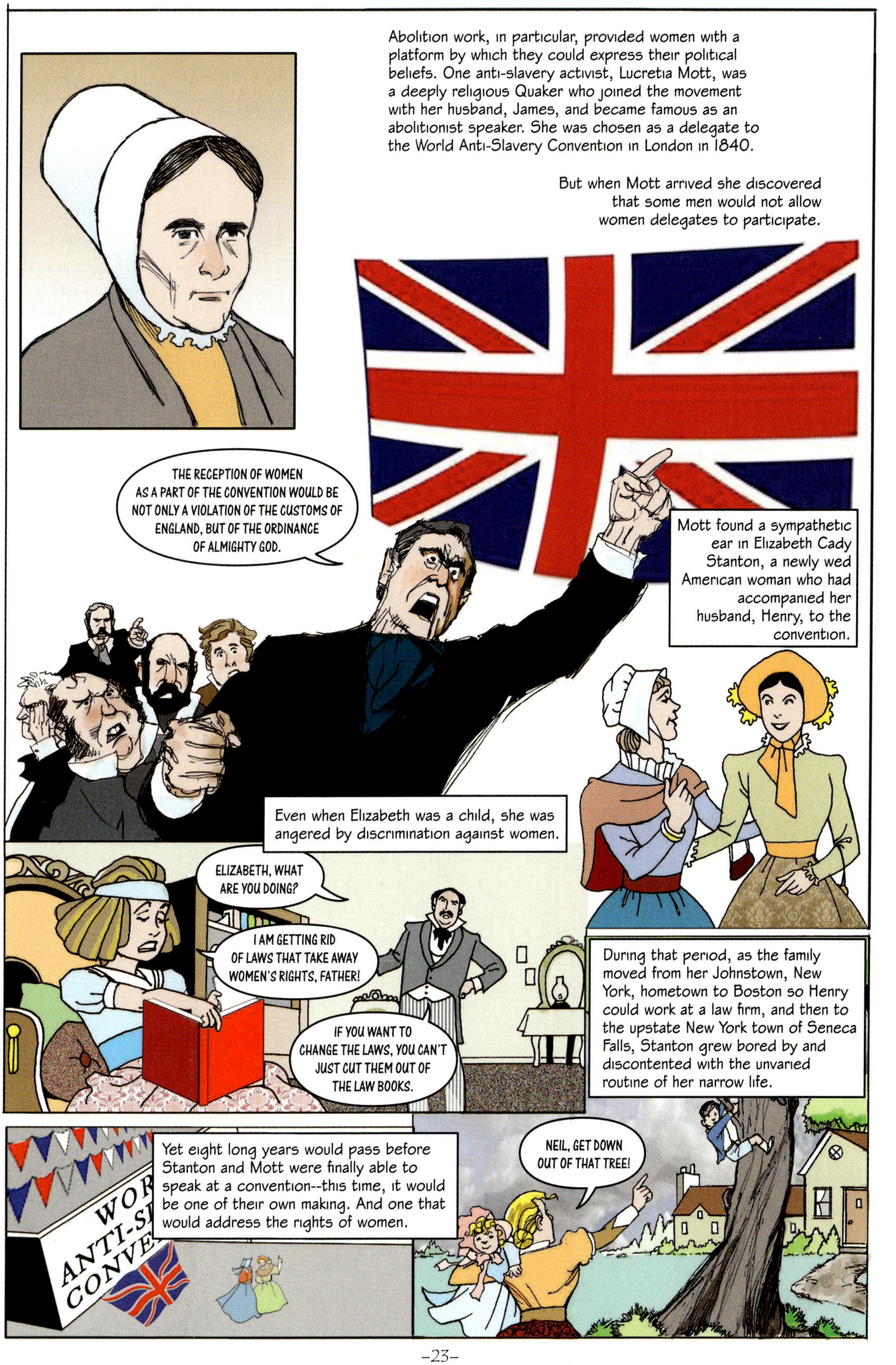
Abolition work, in particular, provided women with a platform by which they could express their political beliefs. One anti-slavery activist, Lucretia Mott, was a deeply religious Quaker who joined the movement with her husband, James, and became famous as an abolitionist speaker. She was chosen as a delegate to the World Anti-Slavery Convention in London in 1840.
But when Mott arrived she discovered that some men would not allow women delegates to participate.
THE RECEPTION OF WOMEN AS A PART OF THE CONVENTION WOULD BE NOT ONLY A VIOLATION OF THE CUSTOMS OF ENGLAND, BUT OF THE ORDINANCE OF ALMIGHTY GOD.
Mott found a sympathetic ear in Elizabeth Cady Stanton, a newly wed American woman who had accompanied her husband, Henry, to the convention.
Even when Elizabeth was a child, she was angered by discrimination against women.
ELIZABETH, WHAT ARE YOU DOING?
I AM GETTING RID OF LAWS THAT TAKE AWAY WOMEN'S RIGHTS, FATHER!
IF YOU WANT TO CHANGE THE LAWS, YOU CAN'T JUST CUT THEM OUT OF THE LAW BOOKS.
During that period, as the family moved from her Johnstown, New York, hometown to Boston so Henry could work at a law firm, and then to the upstate New York town of Seneca Falls, Stanton grew bored by and discontented with the unvaried routine of her narrow life.
Yet eight long years would pass before Stanton and Mott were finally able to speak at a convention--this time, it would be one of their own making. And one that would address the rights of women.
NEIL, GET DOWN OUT OF THAT TREE!

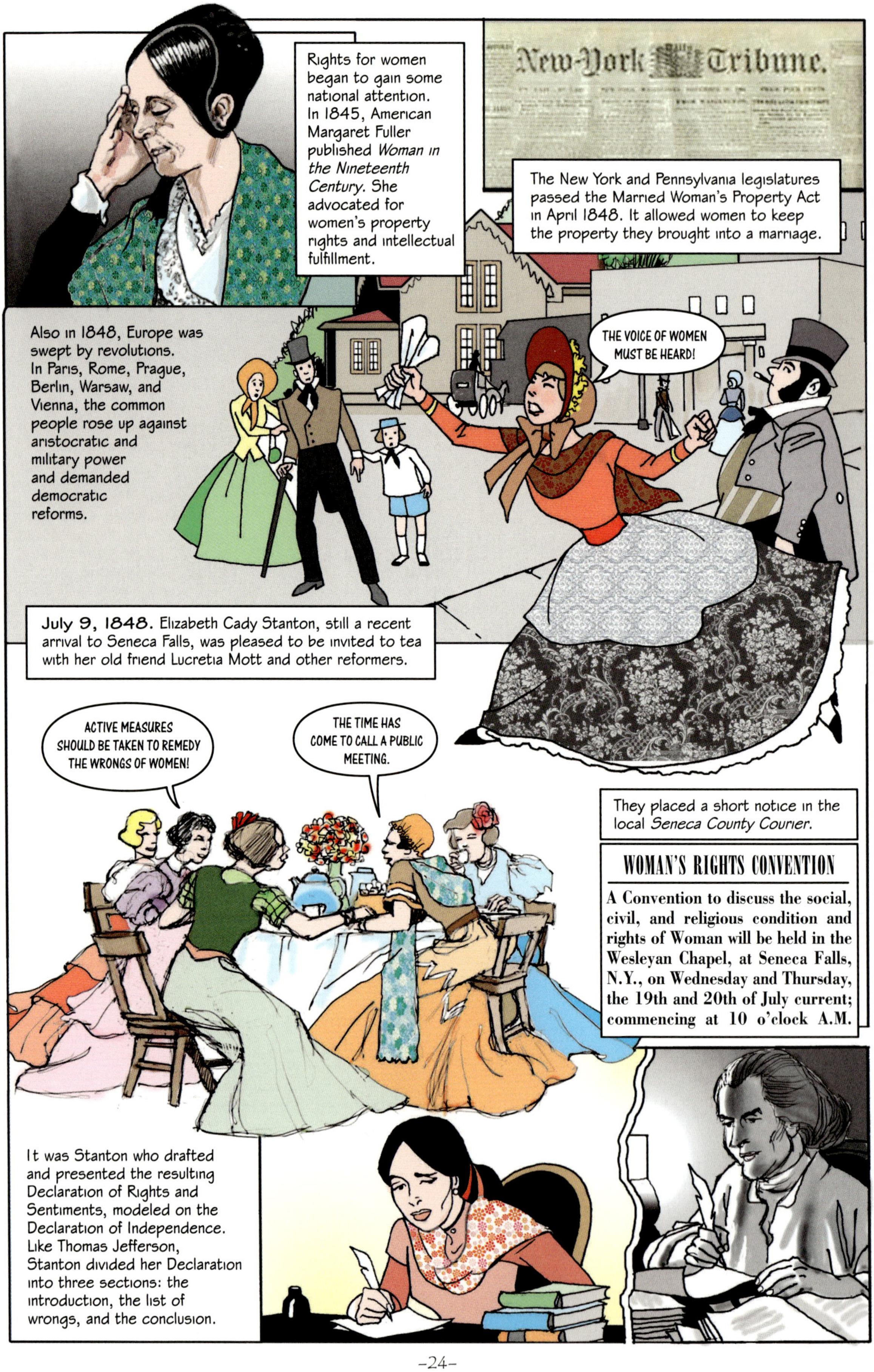
Rights for women began to gain some national attention. In 1845, American Margaret Fuller published *Woman in the Nineteenth Century*. She advocated for women's property rights and intellectual fulfillment.
New-York Tribune.
The New York and Pennsylvania legislatures passed the Married Woman's Property Act in April 1848. It allowed women to keep the property they brought into a marriage.
Also in 1848, Europe was swept by revolutions. In Paris, Rome, Prague, Berlin, Warsaw, and Vienna, the common people rose up against aristocratic and military power and demanded democratic reforms.
THE VOICE OF WOMEN MUST BE HEARD!
July 9, 1848. Elizabeth Cady Stanton, still a recent arrival to Seneca Falls, was pleased to be invited to tea with her old friend Lucretia Mott and other reformers.
ACTIVE MEASURES SHOULD BE TAKEN TO REMEDY THE WRONGS OF WOMEN!
THE TIME HAS COME TO CALL A PUBLIC MEETING.
They placed a short notice in the local *Seneca County Courier*.
WOMAN'S RIGHTS CONVENTION
A Convention to discuss the social, civil, and religious condition and rights of Woman will be held in the Wesleyan Chapel, at Seneca Falls, N.Y., on Wednesday and Thursday, the 19th and 20th of July current; commencing at 10 o'clock A.M.
It was Stanton who drafted and presented the resulting Declaration of Rights and Sentiments, modeled on the Declaration of Independence. Like Thomas Jefferson, Stanton divided her Declaration into three sections: the introduction, the list of wrongs, and the conclusion.

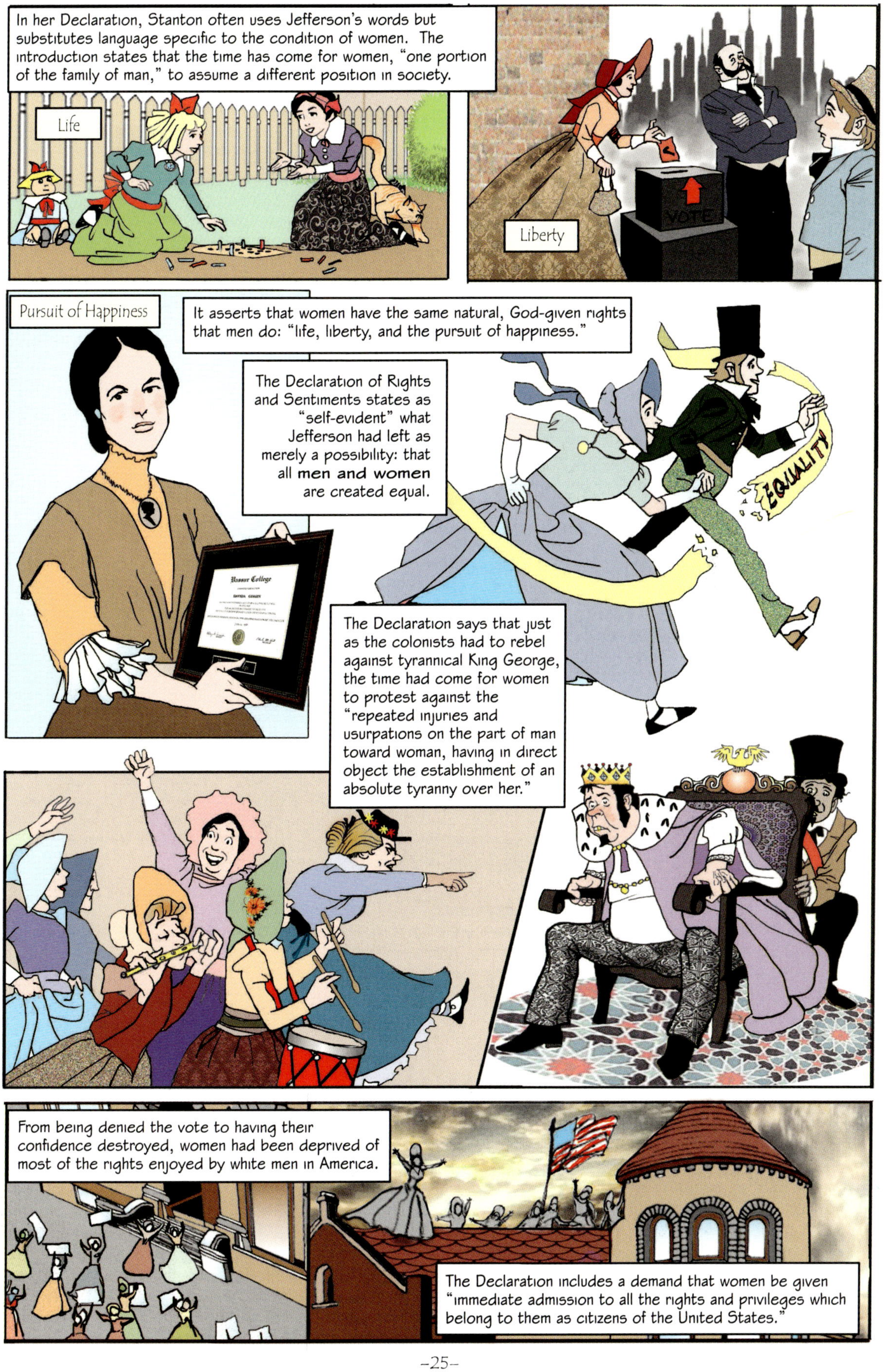
In her Declaration, Stanton often uses Jefferson's words but substitutes language specific to the condition of women. The introduction states that the time has come for women, "one portion of the family of man," to assume a different position in society.
Life
VOTE
Liberty
Pursuit of Happiness
It asserts that women have the same natural, God-given rights that men do: "life, liberty, and the pursuit of happiness."
The Declaration of Rights and Sentiments states as "self-evident" what Jefferson had left as merely a possibility: that all **men and women** are created equal.
EQUALITY
The Declaration says that just as the colonists had to rebel against tyrannical King George, the time had come for women to protest against the "repeated injuries and usurpations on the part of man toward woman, having in direct object the establishment of an absolute tyranny over her."
From being denied the vote to having their confidence destroyed, women had been deprived of most of the rights enjoyed by white men in America.
The Declaration includes a demand that women be given "immediate admission to all the rights and privileges which belong to them as citizens of the United States."

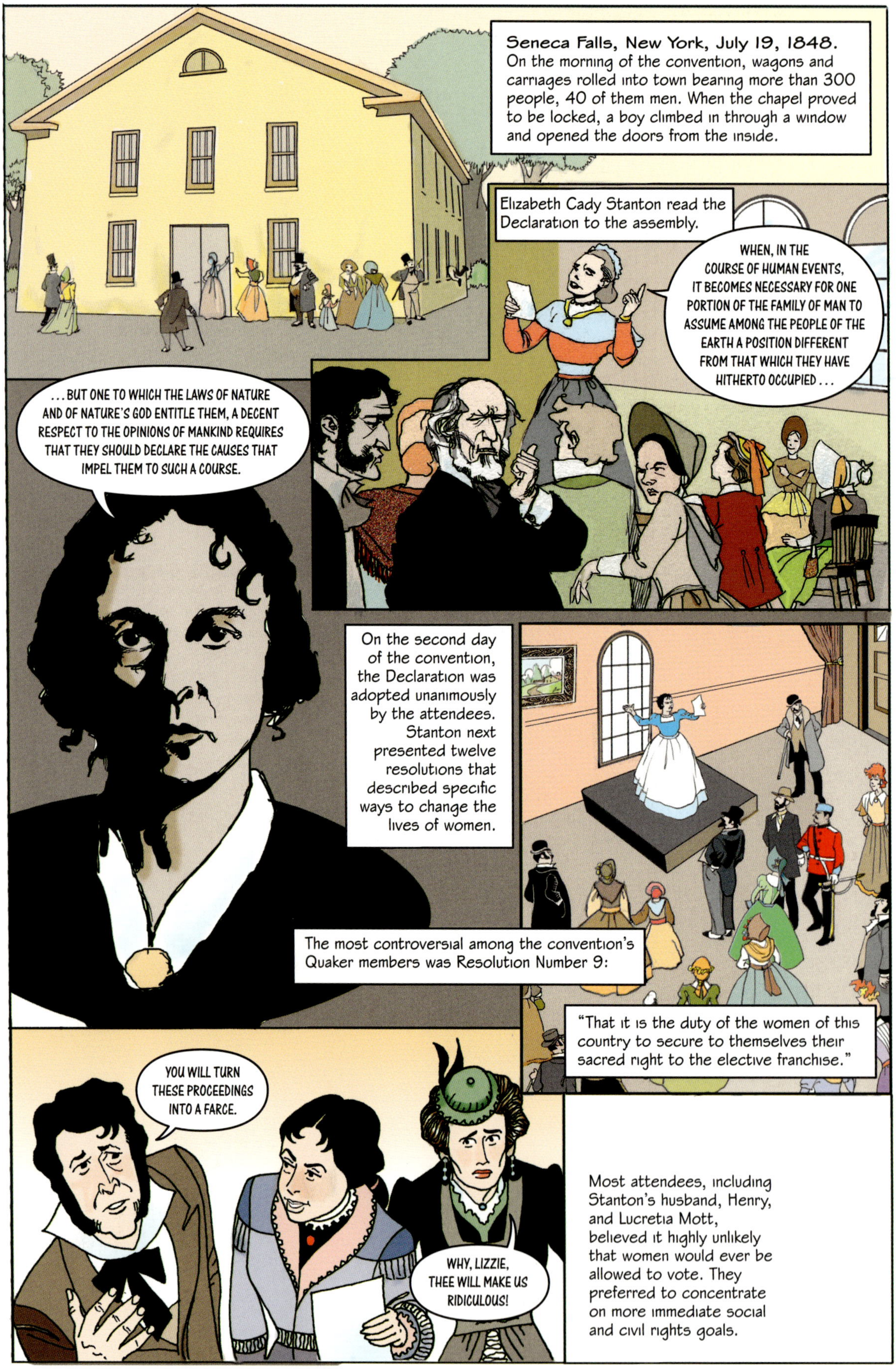
Seneca Falls, New York, July 19, 1848.
On the morning of the convention, wagons and carriages rolled into town bearing more than 300 people, 40 of them men. When the chapel proved to be locked, a boy climbed in through a window and opened the doors from the inside.
Elizabeth Cady Stanton read the Declaration to the assembly.
WHEN, IN THE COURSE OF HUMAN EVENTS, IT BECOMES NECESSARY FOR ONE PORTION OF THE FAMILY OF MAN TO ASSUME AMONG THE PEOPLE OF THE EARTH A POSITION DIFFERENT FROM THAT WHICH THEY HAVE HITHERTO OCCUPIED . . .
. . . BUT ONE TO WHICH THE LAWS OF NATURE AND OF NATURE'S GOD ENTITLE THEM, A DECENT RESPECT TO THE OPINIONS OF MANKIND REQUIRES THAT THEY SHOULD DECLARE THE CAUSES THAT IMPEL THEM TO SUCH A COURSE.
On the second day of the convention, the Declaration was adopted unanimously by the attendees. Stanton next presented twelve resolutions that described specific ways to change the lives of women.
The most controversial among the convention's Quaker members was Resolution Number 9:
"That it is the duty of the women of this country to secure to themselves their sacred right to the elective franchise."
YOU WILL TURN THESE PROCEEDINGS INTO A FARCE.
WHY, LIZZIE, THEE WILL MAKE US RIDICULOUS!
Most attendees, including Stanton's husband, Henry, and Lucretia Mott, believed it highly unlikely that women would ever be allowed to vote. They preferred to concentrate on more immediate social and civil rights goals.

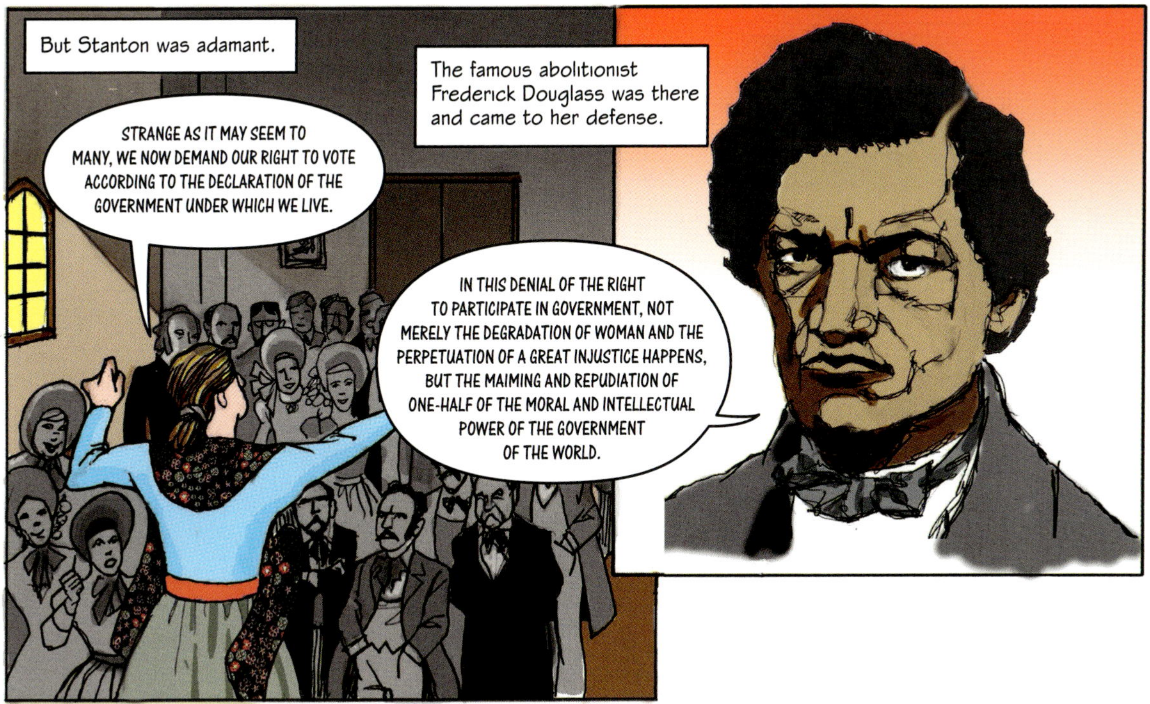
But Stanton was adamant.
STRANGE AS IT MAY SEEM TO MANY, WE NOW DEMAND OUR RIGHT TO VOTE ACCORDING TO THE DECLARATION OF THE GOVERNMENT UNDER WHICH WE LIVE.
The famous abolitionist Frederick Douglass was there and came to her defense.
IN THIS DENIAL OF THE RIGHT TO PARTICIPATE IN GOVERNMENT, NOT MERELY THE DEGRADATION OF WOMAN AND THE PERPETUATION OF A GREAT INJUSTICE HAPPENS, BUT THE MAIMING AND REPUDIATION OF ONE-HALF OF THE MORAL AND INTELLECTUAL POWER OF THE GOVERNMENT OF THE WORLD.

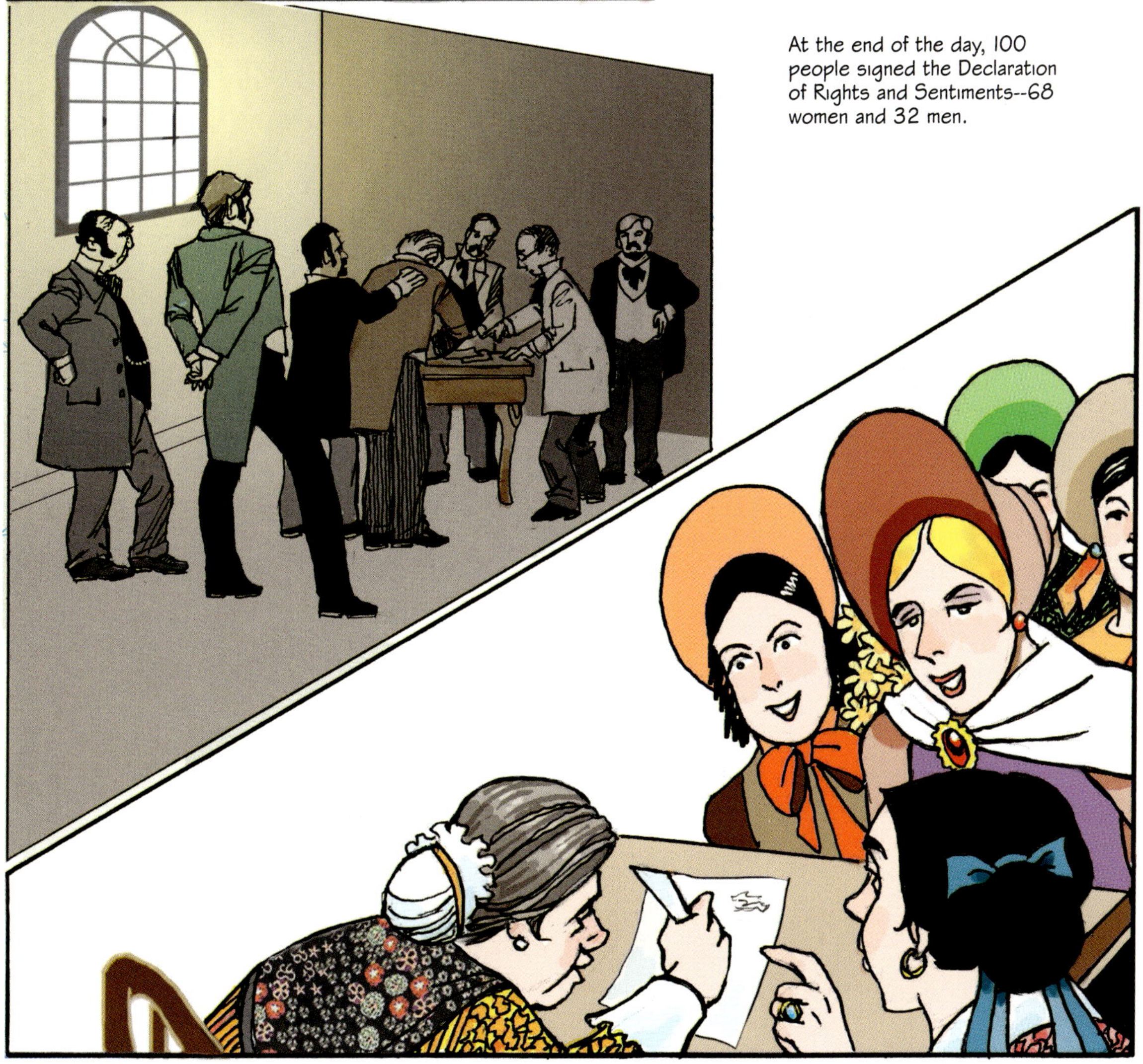

At the end of the day, 100 people signed the Declaration of Rights and Sentiments--68 women and 32 men.

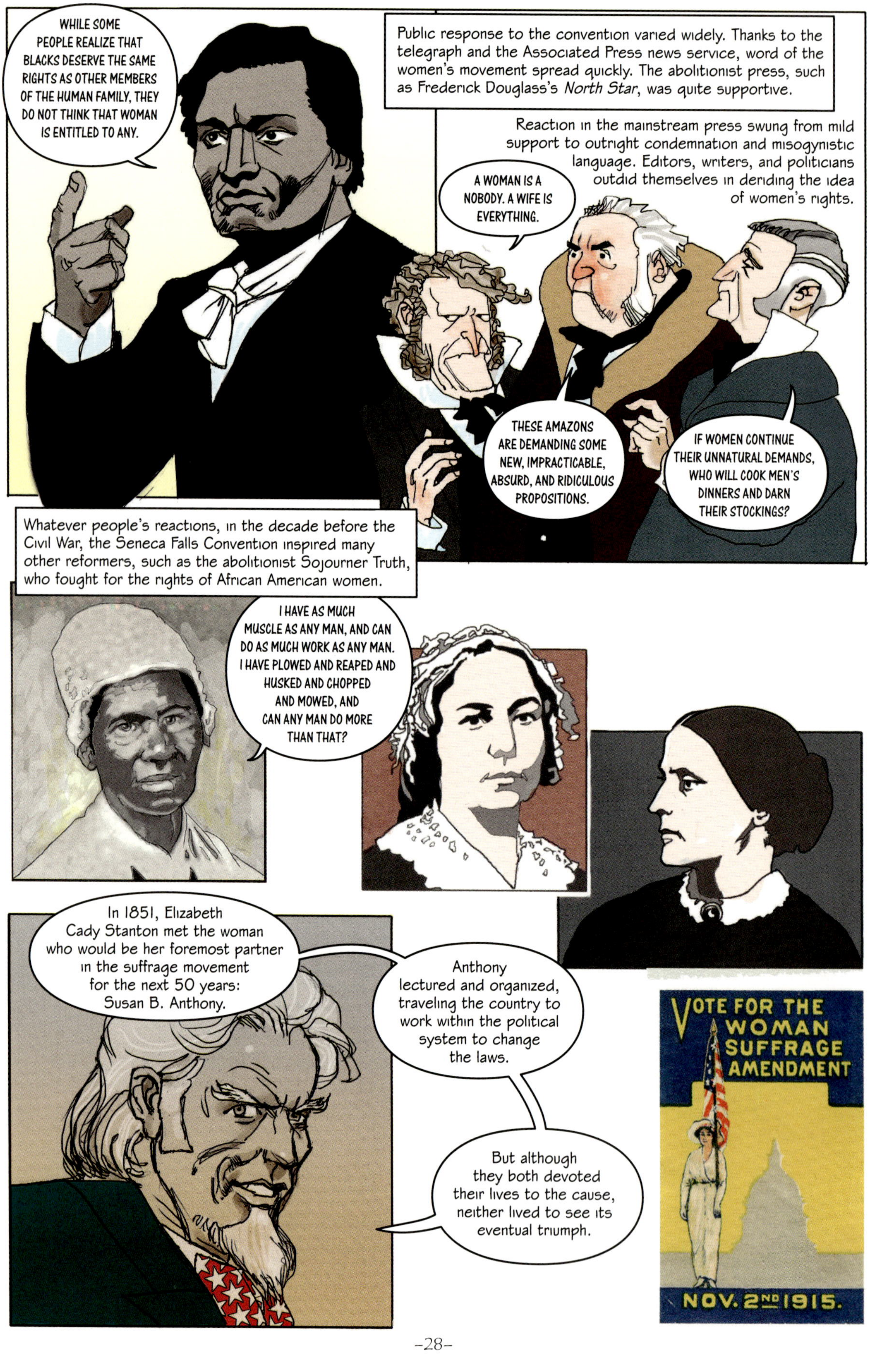
WHILE SOME PEOPLE REALIZE THAT BLACKS DESERVE THE SAME RIGHTS AS OTHER MEMBERS OF THE HUMAN FAMILY, THEY DO NOT THINK THAT WOMAN IS ENTITLED TO ANY.
Public response to the convention varied widely. Thanks to the telegraph and the Associated Press news service, word of the women's movement spread quickly. The abolitionist press, such as Frederick Douglass's *North Star*, was quite supportive.
Reaction in the mainstream press swung from mild support to outright condemnation and misogynistic language. Editors, writers, and politicians outdid themselves in deriding the idea of women's rights.
A WOMAN IS A NOBODY. A WIFE IS EVERYTHING.
THESE AMAZONS ARE DEMANDING SOME NEW, IMPRACTICABLE, ABSURD, AND RIDICULOUS PROPOSITIONS.
IF WOMEN CONTINUE THEIR UNNATURAL DEMANDS, WHO WILL COOK MEN'S DINNERS AND DARN THEIR STOCKINGS?
Whatever people's reactions, in the decade before the Civil War, the Seneca Falls Convention inspired many other reformers, such as the abolitionist Sojourner Truth, who fought for the rights of African American women.
I HAVE AS MUCH MUSCLE AS ANY MAN, AND CAN DO AS MUCH WORK AS ANY MAN. I HAVE PLOWED AND REAPED AND HUSKED AND CHOPPED AND MOWED, AND CAN ANY MAN DO MORE THAN THAT?
In 1851, Elizabeth Cady Stanton met the woman who would be her foremost partner in the suffrage movement for the next 50 years: Susan B. Anthony.
Anthony lectured and organized, traveling the country to work within the political system to change the laws.
But although they both devoted their lives to the cause, neither lived to see its eventual triumph.
VOTE FOR THE WOMAN SUFFRAGE AMENDMENT
NOV. 2ND 1915.

It would take more than 70 years for the dream of women's suffrage to be realized. By the time the Nineteenth Amendment to the Constitution granting women the right to vote, finally became law in 1920, only one signer of the Declaration of Rights and Sentiments was still alive.

EXCERPTS FROM THE DECLARATION OF RIGHTS AND SENTIMENTS

"When, in the course of human events, it becomes necessary for one portion of the family of man to assume among the people of the earth a position different from that which they have hitherto occupied, but one to which the laws of nature and of nature's God entitle them, a decent respect to the opinions of mankind requires that they should declare the causes that impel them to such a course.

"We hold these truths to be self-evident: that all men and women are created equal; that they are endowed by their Creator with certain inalienable rights; that among these are life, liberty, and the pursuit of happiness; that to secure these rights governments are instituted, deriving their just powers from the consent of the governed…

"The history of mankind is a history of repeated injuries and usurpations on the part of man toward woman, having in direct object the establishment of an absolute tyranny over her. To prove this, let facts be submitted to a candid world.

"He has never permitted her to exercise her inalienable right to the elective franchise.

"He has compelled her to submit to law, in the formation of which she had no voice…

"He has made her, if married, in the eye of the law, civilly dead.

"He has taken from her all right in property, even to the wages she earns…"

The Compromise of 1850

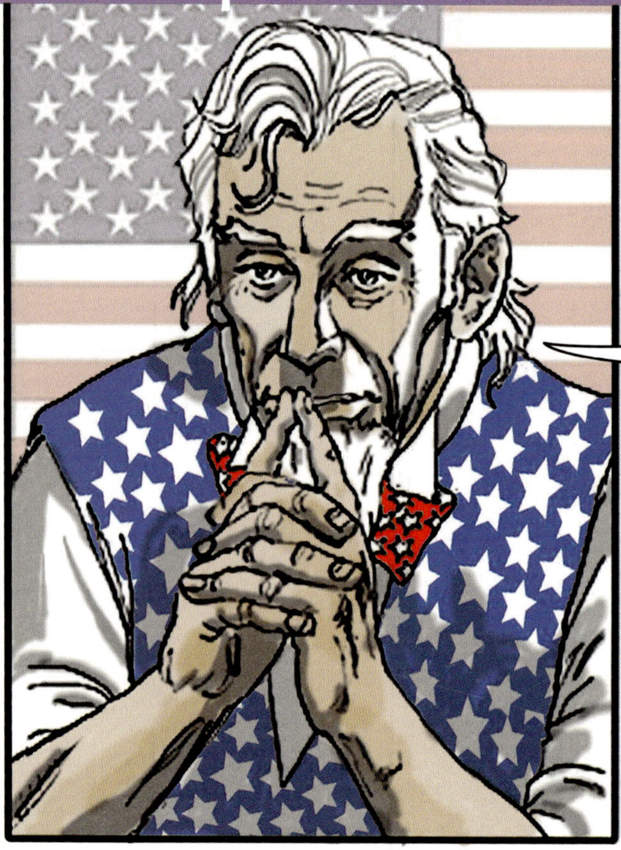

Westward expansion brought not only additional land and opportunity to the United States, but also a new set of problems. The most urgent--and dangerous--dilemma had to do with the expansion of slavery. Would the new territories include slaveholding states? Or would all these states be free? If they were free, would the South secede from the Union? How would the North respond?
The answers to these questions would determine the future of the country.

THE UNITED STATES IN 1850

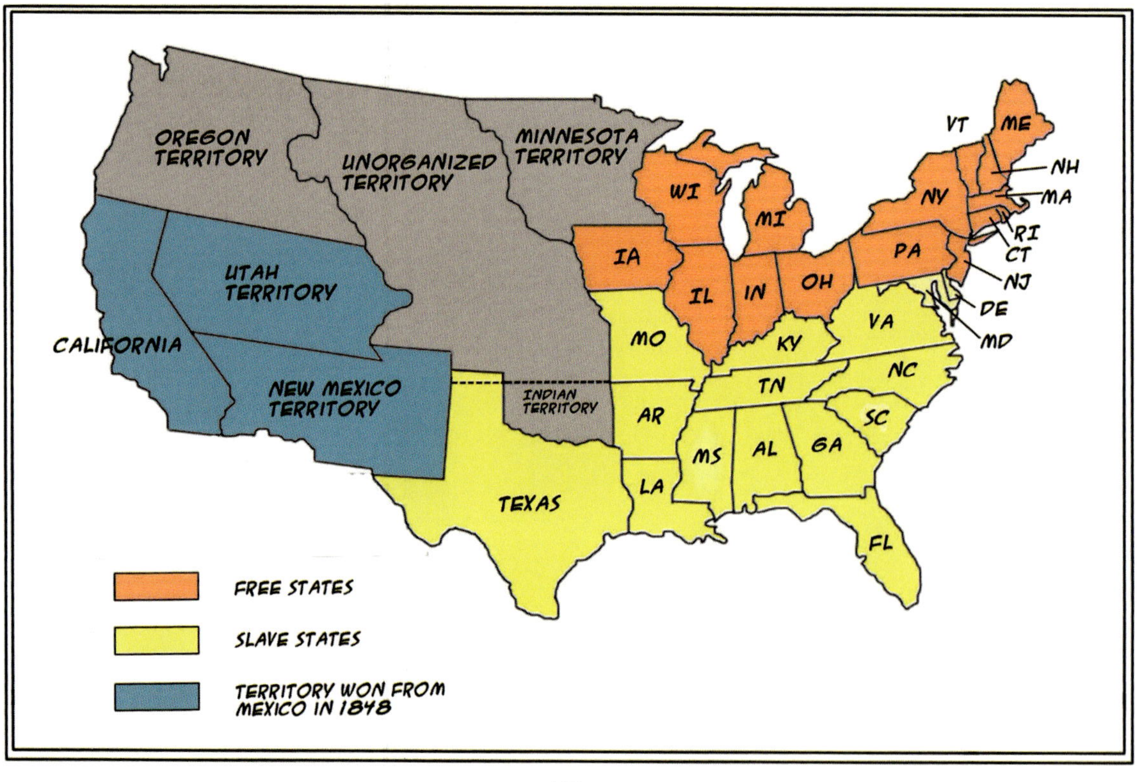

OREGON TERRITORY
UNORGANIZED TERRITORY
MINNESOTA TERRITORY
UTAH TERRITORY
CALIFORNIA
NEW MEXICO TERRITORY
INDIAN TERRITORY
TEXAS
WI
MI
IA
IL
IN
OH
PA
NY
VT
ME
NH
MA
RI
CT
NJ
DE
MD
VA
MO
KY
NC
TN
AR
SC
MS
AL
GA
LA
FL
FREE STATES
SLAVE STATES
TERRITORY WON FROM MEXICO IN 1848

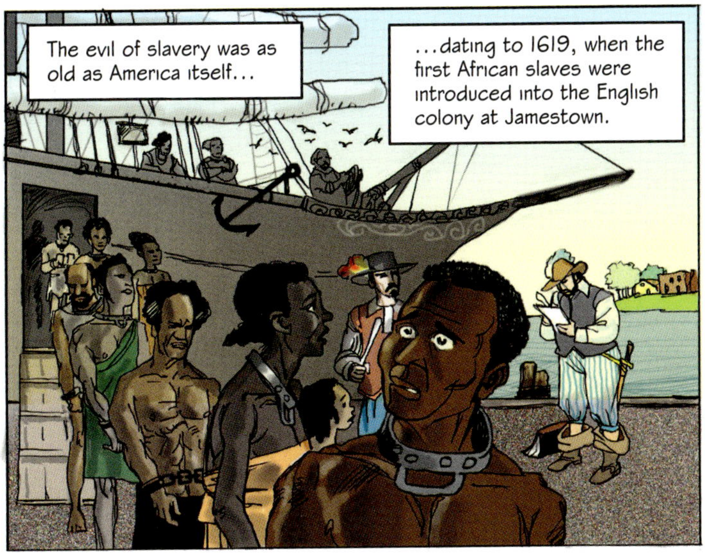
The evil of slavery was as old as America itself...
...dating to 1619, when the first African slaves were introduced into the English colony at Jamestown.

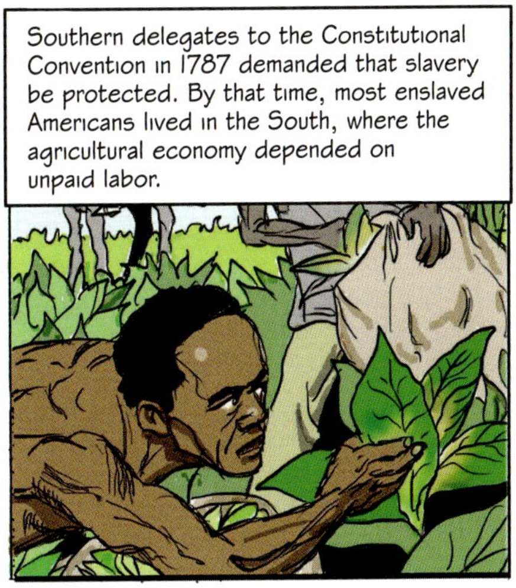
Southern delegates to the Constitutional Convention in 1787 demanded that slavery be protected. By that time, most enslaved Americans lived in the South, where the agricultural economy depended on unpaid labor.

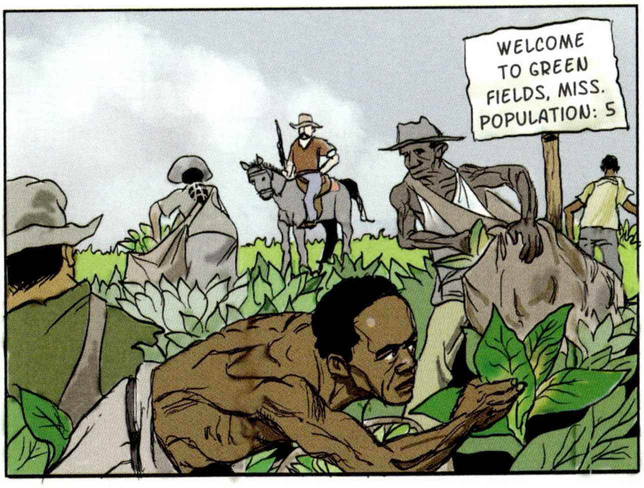
WELCOME
TO GREEN
FIELDS, MISS.
POPULATION: 5

The Southern states also wanted enslaved people--who made up about 40 percent of their total population and were not allowed to vote--to count for purposes of congressional representation. In a compromise with the North, it was agreed that each slave would be counted as three-fifths of a person.

This would guarantee close to a 30 percent increase for the South in both the number of Congressional seats they had and in electoral votes.

Political compromises aside, it was profitability that the South was more interested in, as the invention of the cotton gin in 1793 made growing cotton a much more lucrative industry--one that benefited from slavery.

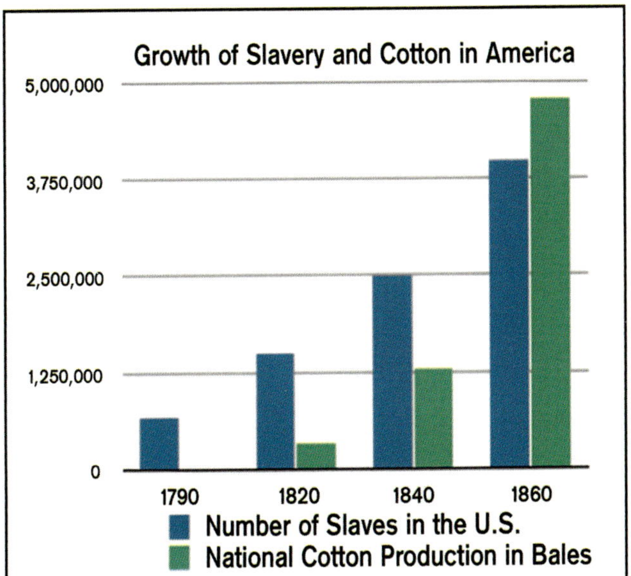
Growth of Slavery and Cotton in America
5,000,000
3,750,000
2,500,000
1,250,000
0
1790
1820
1840
1860
Number of Slaves in the U.S.
National Cotton Production in Bales

Between 1800 and 1860, the number of enslaved people in the United States ballooned from 900,000 to nearly 4 million...

...while cotton became the single most profitable industry, accounting for nearly 60 percent of American exports.

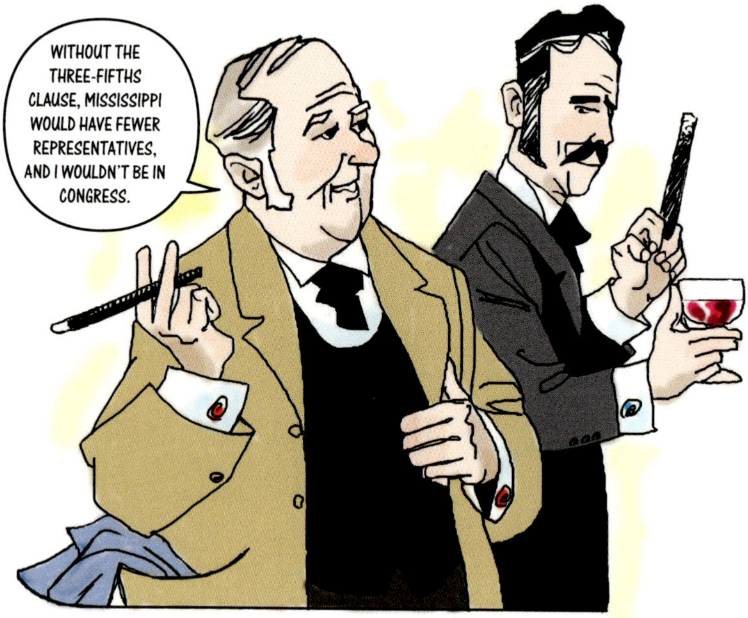
WITHOUT THE THREE-FIFTHS CLAUSE, MISSISSIPPI WOULD HAVE FEWER REPRESENTATIVES, AND I WOULDN'T BE IN CONGRESS.

In Congress, the three-fifths rule continued to grant slaveholding states a disproportionate influence in the House of Representatives, even though the population of the North was much larger than that of the South. For instance, in 1850, the slave population gave the Southern states 21 additional congressmen.

In the Senate, however, there was an evenly matched balance at 30 representatives, consisting of two senators each from the 15 free states and two each from the 15 slave states.

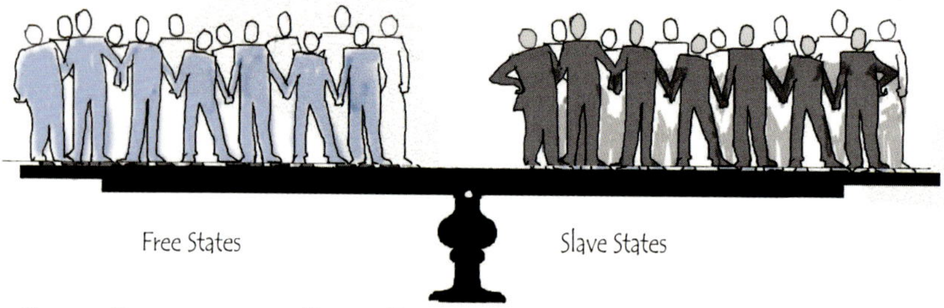
Free States
Slave States

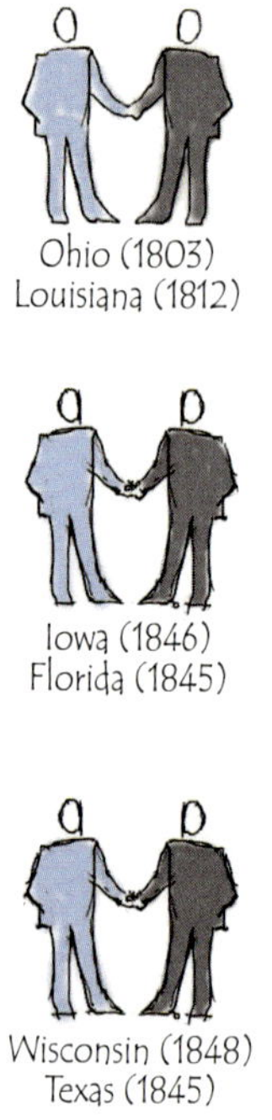
Ohio (1803)
Louisiana (1812)
Iowa (1846)
Florida (1845)
Wisconsin (1848)
Texas (1845)

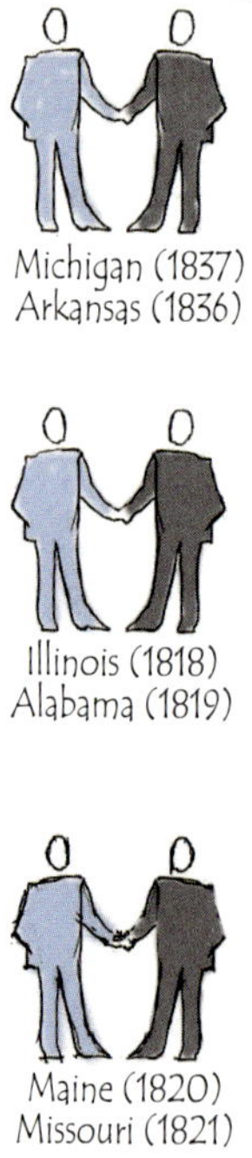
Michigan (1837)
Arkansas (1836)
Illinois (1818)
Alabama (1819)
Maine (1820)
Missouri (1821)

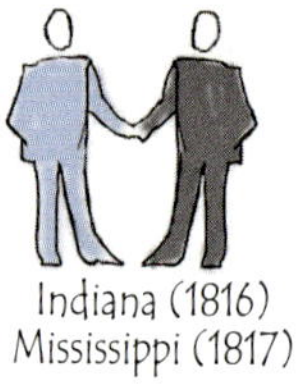
Indiana (1816)
Mississippi (1817)

Maintaining that balance in the Senate was important to both South and North. Since the beginning of the 19th century, states had essentially entered the Union *in pairs*, averting a political conflict.

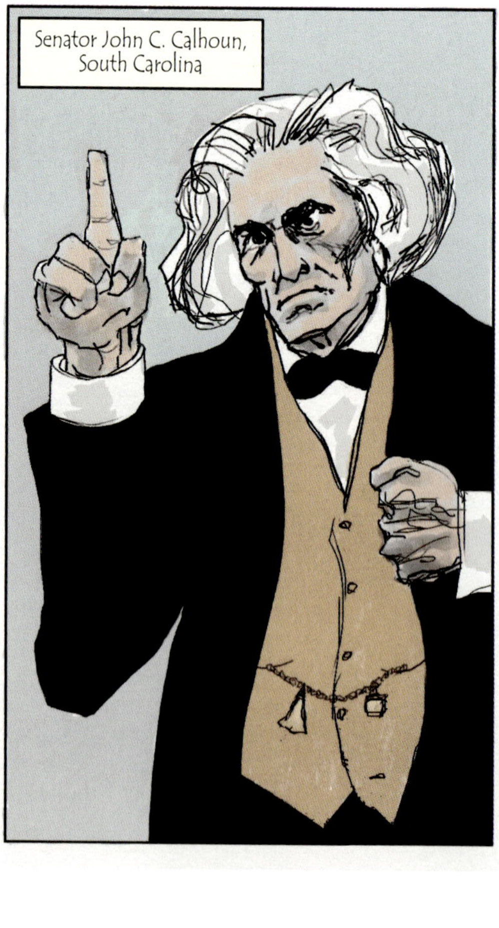
Senator John C. Calhoun, South Carolina

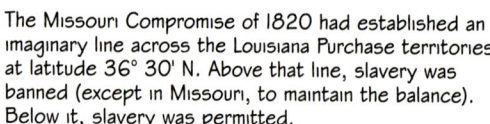

The Missouri Compromise of 1820 had established an imaginary line across the Louisiana Purchase territories at latitude 36° 30' N. Above that line, slavery was banned (except in Missouri, to maintain the balance). Below it, slavery was permitted.

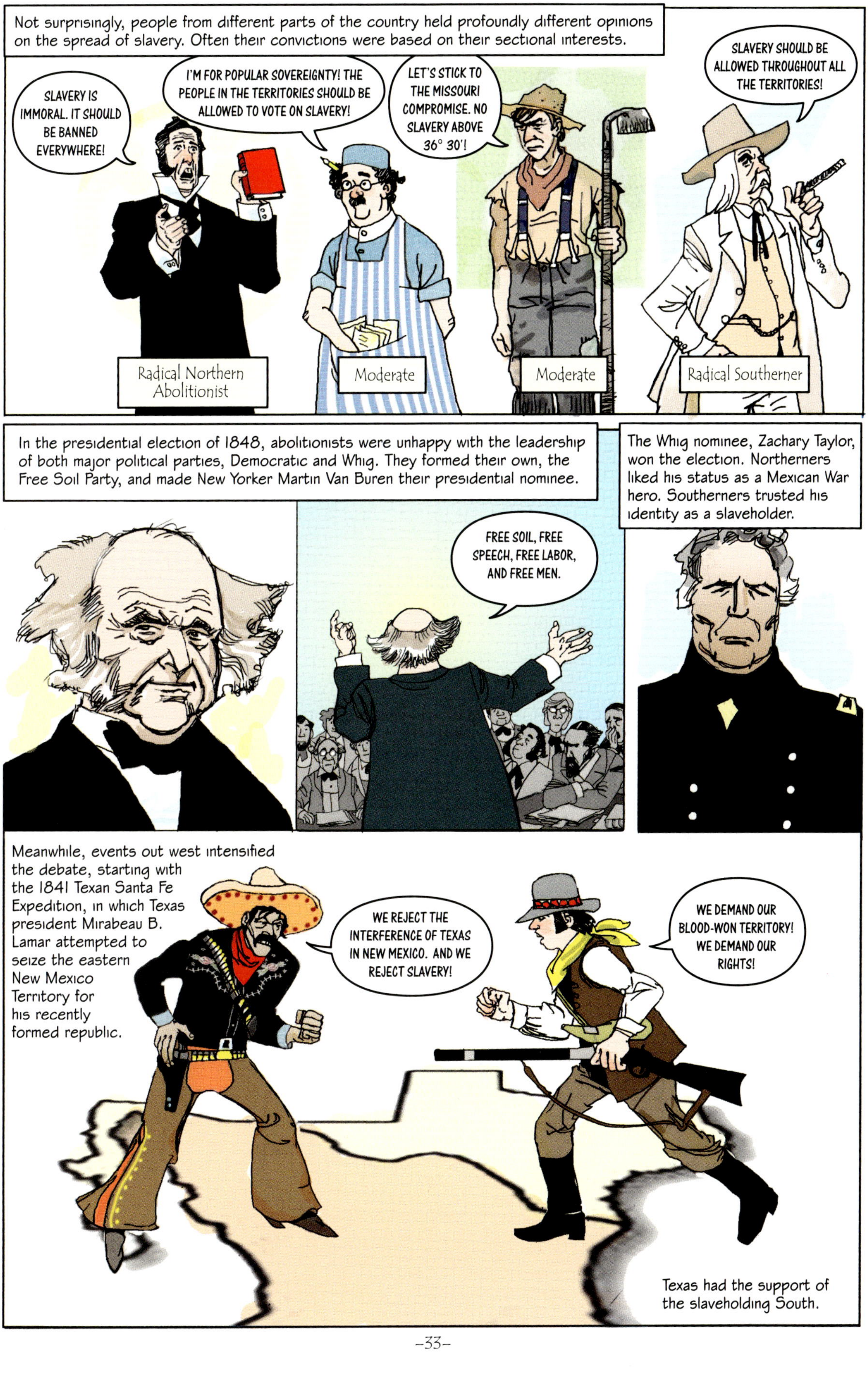
Not surprisingly, people from different parts of the country held profoundly different opinions on the spread of slavery. Often their convictions were based on their sectional interests.
SLAVERY IS IMMORAL. IT SHOULD BE BANNED EVERYWHERE!
Radical Northern Abolitionist
I'M FOR POPULAR SOVEREIGNTY! THE PEOPLE IN THE TERRITORIES SHOULD BE ALLOWED TO VOTE ON SLAVERY!
Moderate
LET'S STICK TO THE MISSOURI COMPROMISE. NO SLAVERY ABOVE 36° 30'!
Moderate
SLAVERY SHOULD BE ALLOWED THROUGHOUT ALL THE TERRITORIES!
Radical Southerner
In the presidential election of 1848, abolitionists were unhappy with the leadership of both major political parties, Democratic and Whig. They formed their own, the Free Soil Party, and made New Yorker Martin Van Buren their presidential nominee.
FREE SOIL, FREE SPEECH, FREE LABOR, AND FREE MEN.
The Whig nominee, Zachary Taylor, won the election. Northerners liked his status as a Mexican War hero. Southerners trusted his identity as a slaveholder.
Meanwhile, events out west intensified the debate, starting with the 1841 Texan Santa Fe Expedition, in which Texas president Mirabeau B. Lamar attempted to seize the eastern New Mexico Territory for his recently formed republic.
WE REJECT THE INTERFERENCE OF TEXAS IN NEW MEXICO. AND WE REJECT SLAVERY!
WE DEMAND OUR BLOOD-WON TERRITORY! WE DEMAND OUR RIGHTS!
Texas had the support of the slaveholding South.

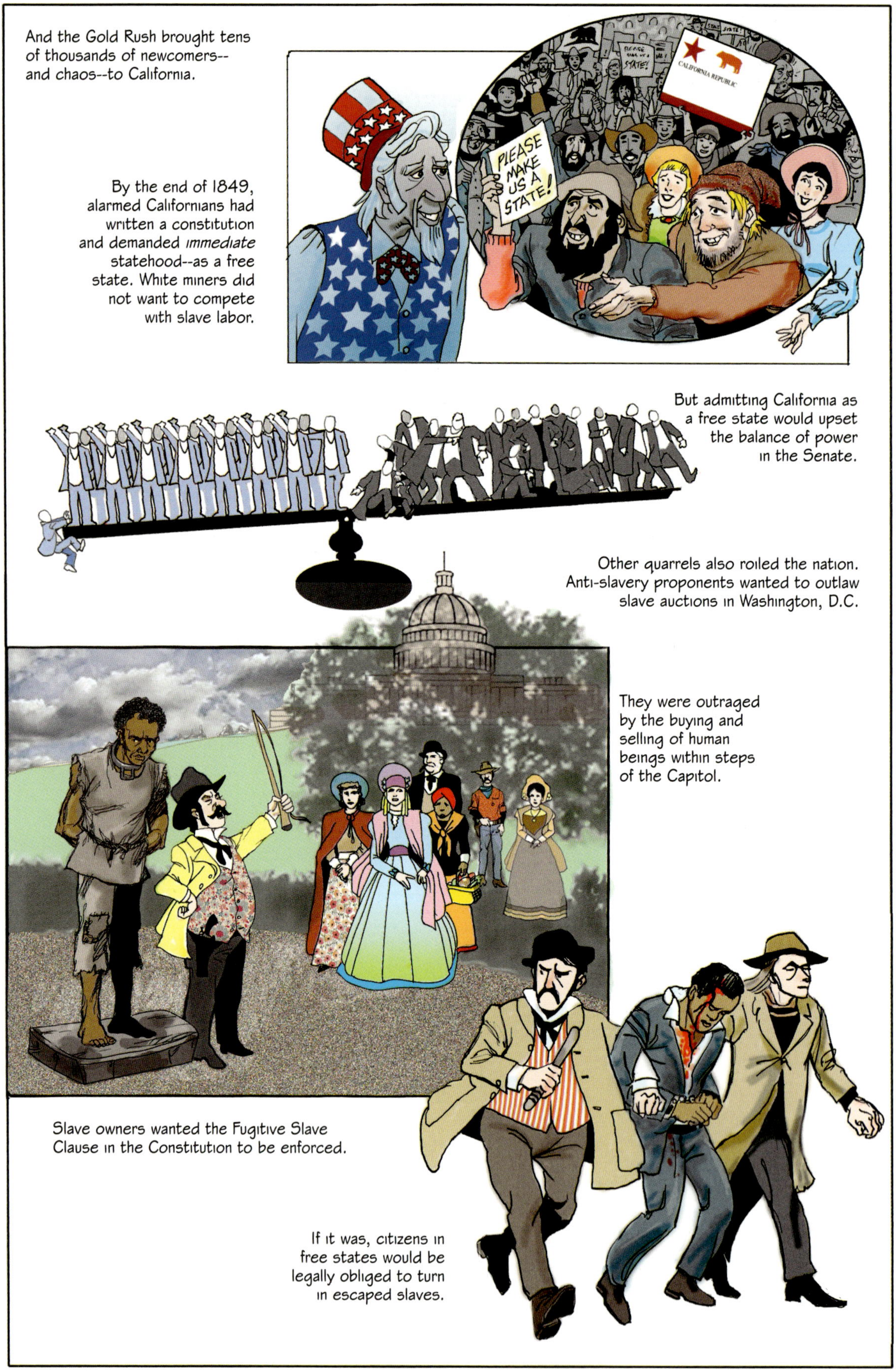
And the Gold Rush brought tens of thousands of newcomers--and chaos--to California.
By the end of 1849, alarmed Californians had written a constitution and demanded *immediate* statehood--as a free state. White miners did not want to compete with slave labor.
CALIFORNIA REPUBLIC
PLEASE MAKE US A STATE!
But admitting California as a free state would upset the balance of power in the Senate.
Other quarrels also roiled the nation. Anti-slavery proponents wanted to outlaw slave auctions in Washington, D.C.
They were outraged by the buying and selling of human beings within steps of the Capitol.
Slave owners wanted the Fugitive Slave Clause in the Constitution to be enforced.
If it was, citizens in free states would be legally obliged to turn in escaped slaves.

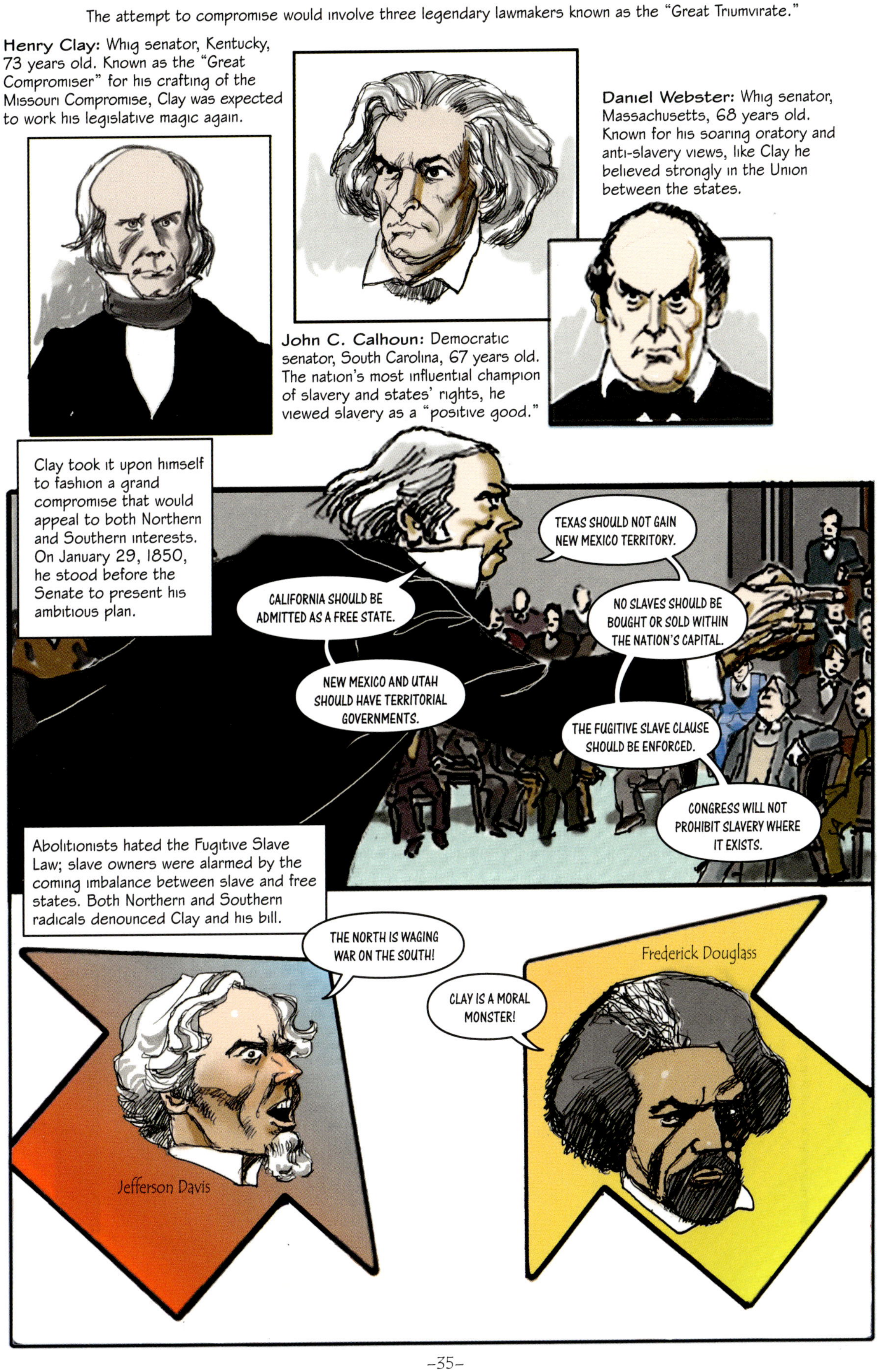
The attempt to compromise would involve three legendary lawmakers known as the "Great Triumvirate."
Henry Clay: Whig senator, Kentucky, 73 years old. Known as the "Great Compromiser" for his crafting of the Missouri Compromise, Clay was expected to work his legislative magic again.
John C. Calhoun: Democratic senator, South Carolina, 67 years old. The nation's most influential champion of slavery and states' rights, he viewed slavery as a "positive good."
Daniel Webster: Whig senator, Massachusetts, 68 years old. Known for his soaring oratory and anti-slavery views, like Clay he believed strongly in the Union between the states.
Clay took it upon himself to fashion a grand compromise that would appeal to both Northern and Southern interests. On January 29, 1850, he stood before the Senate to present his ambitious plan.
CALIFORNIA SHOULD BE ADMITTED AS A FREE STATE.
NEW MEXICO AND UTAH SHOULD HAVE TERRITORIAL GOVERNMENTS.
TEXAS SHOULD NOT GAIN NEW MEXICO TERRITORY.
NO SLAVES SHOULD BE BOUGHT OR SOLD WITHIN THE NATION'S CAPITAL.
THE FUGITIVE SLAVE CLAUSE SHOULD BE ENFORCED.
CONGRESS WILL NOT PROHIBIT SLAVERY WHERE IT EXISTS.
Abolitionists hated the Fugitive Slave Law; slave owners were alarmed by the coming imbalance between slave and free states. Both Northern and Southern radicals denounced Clay and his bill.
THE NORTH IS WAGING WAR ON THE SOUTH!
Jefferson Davis
Frederick Douglass
CLAY IS A MORAL MONSTER!

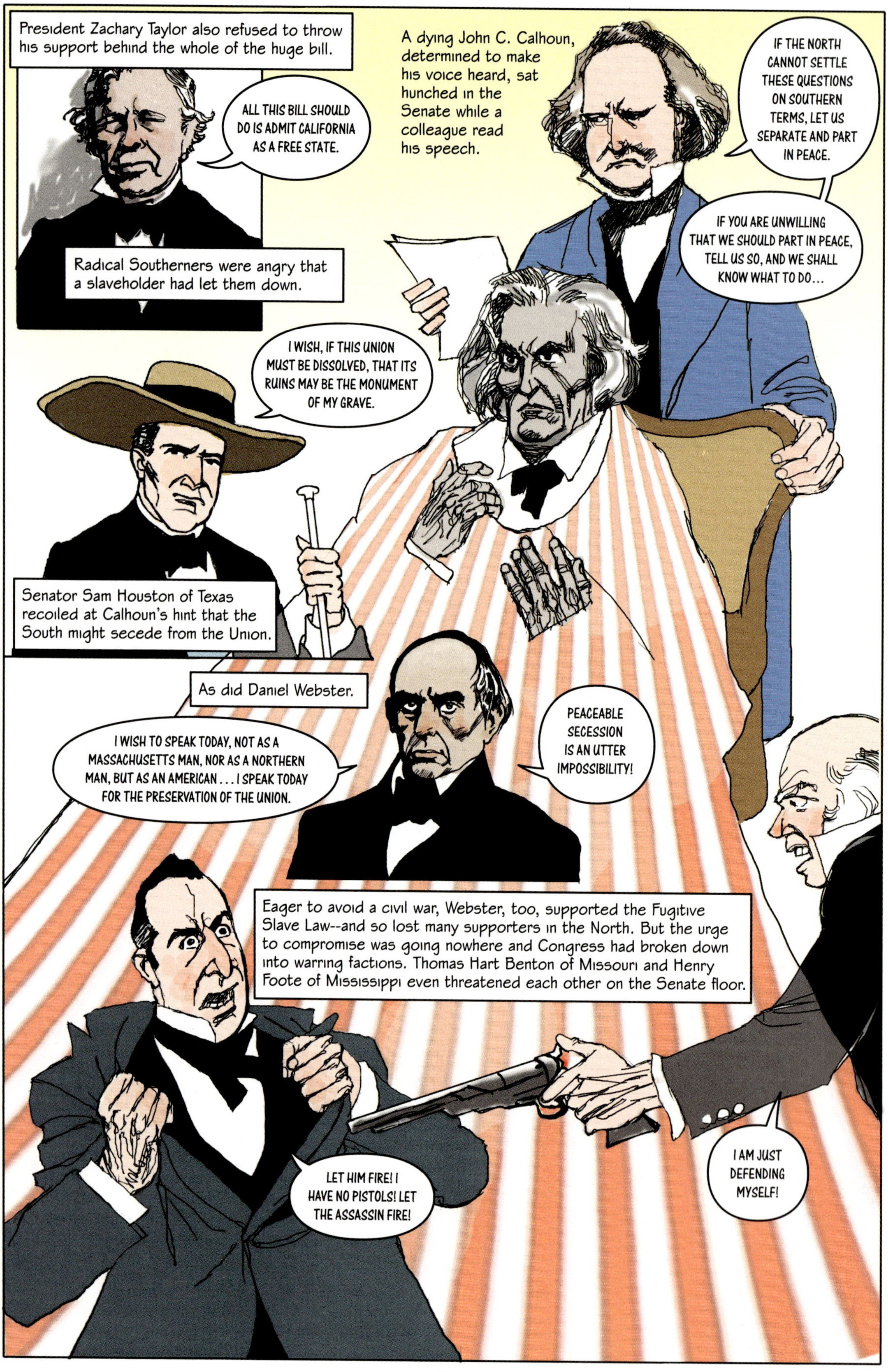
President Zachary Taylor also refused to throw his support behind the whole of the huge bill.
ALL THIS BILL SHOULD DO IS ADMIT CALIFORNIA AS A FREE STATE.
Radical Southerners were angry that a slaveholder had let them down.
A dying John C. Calhoun, determined to make his voice heard, sat hunched in the Senate while a colleague read his speech.
IF THE NORTH CANNOT SETTLE THESE QUESTIONS ON SOUTHERN TERMS, LET US SEPARATE AND PART IN PEACE.
IF YOU ARE UNWILLING THAT WE SHOULD PART IN PEACE, TELL US SO, AND WE SHALL KNOW WHAT TO DO...
I WISH, IF THIS UNION MUST BE DISSOLVED, THAT ITS RUINS MAY BE THE MONUMENT OF MY GRAVE.
Senator Sam Houston of Texas recoiled at Calhoun's hint that the South might secede from the Union.
As did Daniel Webster.
I WISH TO SPEAK TODAY, NOT AS A MASSACHUSETTS MAN, NOR AS A NORTHERN MAN, BUT AS AN AMERICAN . . . I SPEAK TODAY FOR THE PRESERVATION OF THE UNION.
PEACEABLE SECESSION IS AN UTTER IMPOSSIBILITY!
Eager to avoid a civil war, Webster, too, supported the Fugitive Slave Law--and so lost many supporters in the North. But the urge to compromise was going nowhere and Congress had broken down into warring factions. Thomas Hart Benton of Missouri and Henry Foote of Mississippi even threatened each other on the Senate floor.
LET HIM FIRE! I HAVE NO PISTOLS! LET THE ASSASSIN FIRE!
I AM JUST DEFENDING MYSELF!

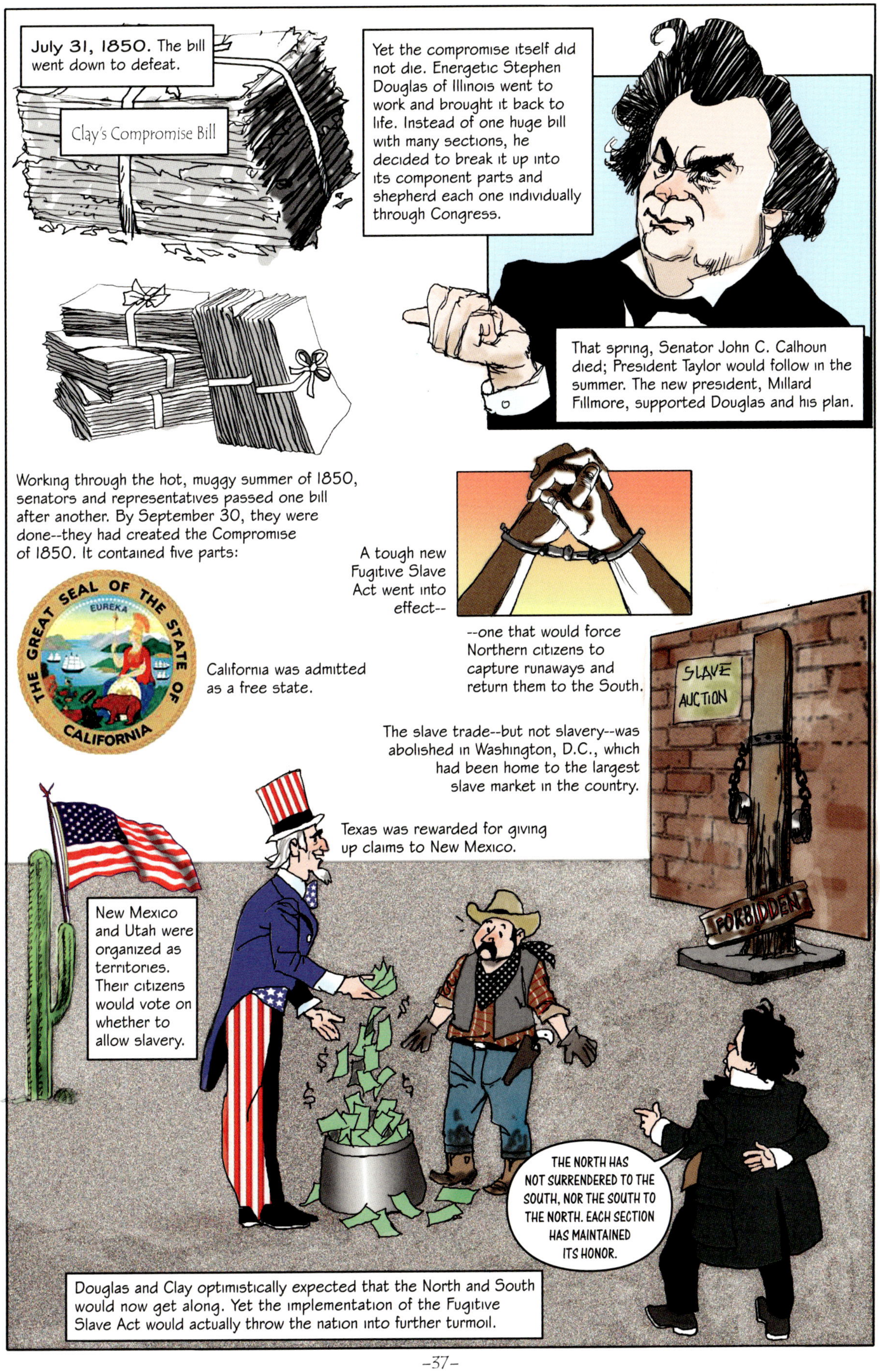
July 31, 1850. The bill went down to defeat.
Clay's Compromise Bill
Yet the compromise itself did not die. Energetic Stephen Douglas of Illinois went to work and brought it back to life. Instead of one huge bill with many sections, he decided to break it up into its component parts and shepherd each one individually through Congress.
That spring, Senator John C. Calhoun died; President Taylor would follow in the summer. The new president, Millard Fillmore, supported Douglas and his plan.
Working through the hot, muggy summer of 1850, senators and representatives passed one bill after another. By September 30, they were done--they had created the Compromise of 1850. It contained five parts:
A tough new Fugitive Slave Act went into effect--
--one that would force Northern citizens to capture runaways and return them to the South.
THE GREAT SEAL OF THE STATE OF CALIFORNIA
EUREKA
California was admitted as a free state.
SLAVE AUCTION
The slave trade--but not slavery--was abolished in Washington, D.C., which had been home to the largest slave market in the country.
FORBIDDEN
Texas was rewarded for giving up claims to New Mexico.
New Mexico and Utah were organized as territories. Their citizens would vote on whether to allow slavery.
THE NORTH HAS NOT SURRENDERED TO THE SOUTH, NOR THE SOUTH TO THE NORTH. EACH SECTION HAS MAINTAINED ITS HONOR.
Douglas and Clay optimistically expected that the North and South would now get along. Yet the implementation of the Fugitive Slave Act would actually throw the nation into further turmoil.

> The Compromise of 1850 established important guidelines for the future of Western territories and states. The men who labored for nearly a year to hammer out a bill knew that the consequences of not reaching some sort of a compromise between slave and non-slave states would be disastrous for the Union.

> Their achievement delayed serious clashes for ten years. However, the Fugitive Slave Law offended individual consciences, outraged communities, and led to further strife.

EXCERPTS FROM THE DEBATE OVER THE COMPROMISE OF 1850

Daniel Webster:

"I speak today for the preservation of the Union. Hear me for my cause. I speak today out of an anxious heart, for the restoration to the country of that harmony that makes the blessings of this Union so rich and so dear to us all…

"I hear with pain, and anguish, and distress, the word secession. Secession! Peaceable secession! Sir, your eyes and mine are never destined to see that miracle. The dismemberment of this vast country without convulsion. Who is so foolish as to expect to see such a thing. There can be no such thing as peaceable secession. Sir, I see it plainly as I can see the sun in heaven—see that disruption must produce such a war as I will not describe."

William Seward:

"I am opposed to any such compromise in any and all forms in which it has been proposed, because I think all legislative compromises radically wrong and essentially vicious…

"There is a higher law than the Constitution which regulates our authority over the domain, and devotes it to some noble purpose. The territory is no inconsiderable part of the common heritage of mankind, bestowed upon them by the Creator of the universe… And now the simple, bold and even awful question which presents itself to us, is this: Shall we, who are founding institutions, social and political, for countless millions—shall we, who know by experience the wise and the just, and are free to choose them, and to reject the erroneous and unjust—shall we establish human bondage, or permit it by our sufferance, to be established?"

John C. Calhoun:

"I have, Senators, believed from the first that the agitation of the subject of slavery would, if not prevented . . . end in disunion . . . The agitation has been permitted to proceed, with almost no attempt to resist it, until it has reached a period when it can no longer be disguised or denied that the Union is in danger . . . I refer to the relation between the two races in the Southern section, which constitutes a vital portion of her social organization. Every portion of the North entertains views and feelings more or less hostile to it. Those most oppressed and hostile regard it as a sin, and consider themselves under the most sacred obligation to use every effort to destroy it . . . The Southern section regards the relation as one which cannot be destroyed without subjecting the two races to the greatest calamity, and the section to poverty, desolation, and wretchedness; accordingly, they feel bound by every consideration of interest and safety to defend it. . . ."

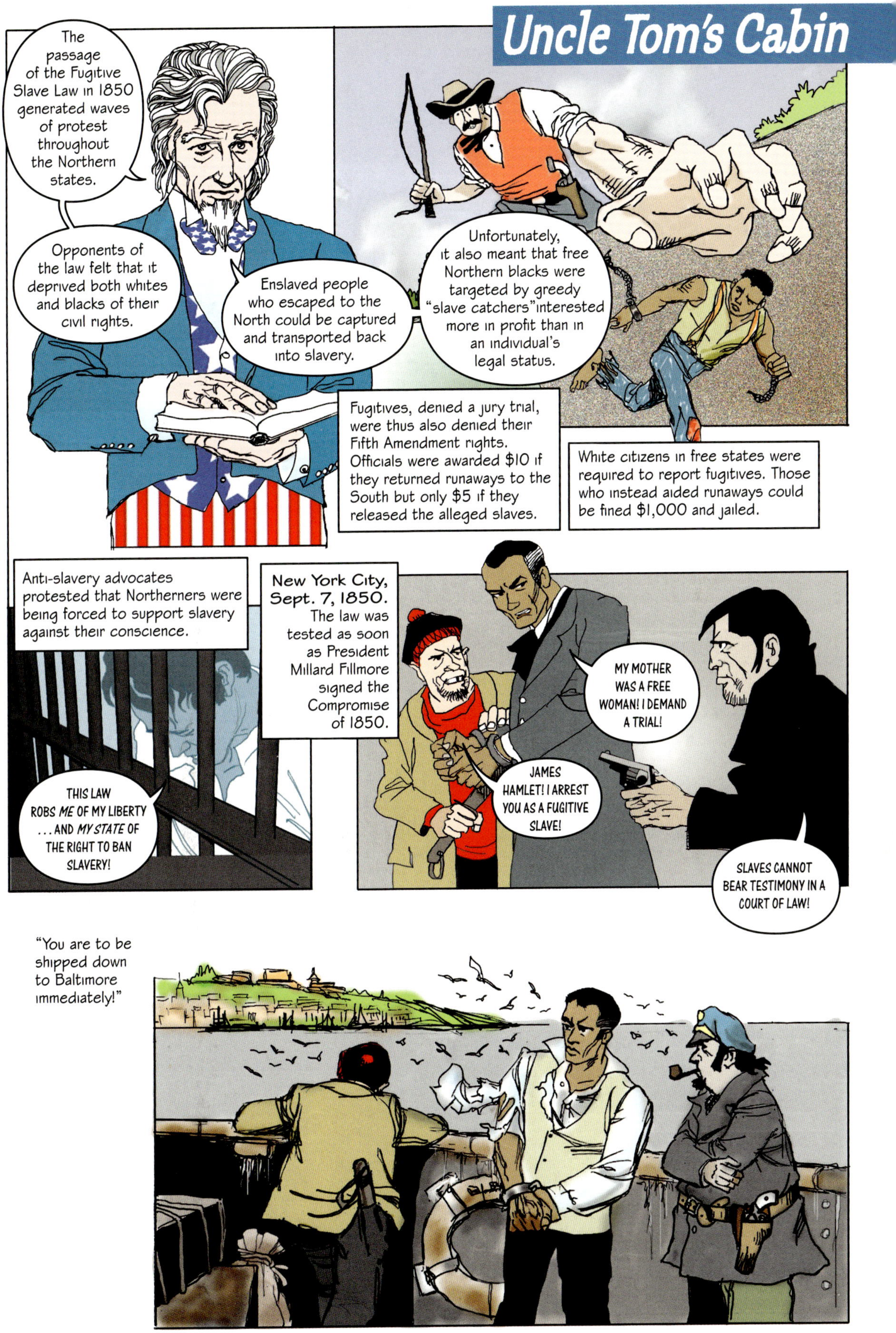
The passage of the Fugitive Slave Law in 1850 generated waves of protest throughout the Northern states.
Opponents of the law felt that it deprived both whites and blacks of their civil rights.
Enslaved people who escaped to the North could be captured and transported back into slavery.
Unfortunately, it also meant that free Northern blacks were targeted by greedy "slave catchers" interested more in profit than in an individual's legal status.
Fugitives, denied a jury trial, were thus also denied their Fifth Amendment rights. Officials were awarded $10 if they returned runaways to the South but only $5 if they released the alleged slaves.
White citizens in free states were required to report fugitives. Those who instead aided runaways could be fined $1,000 and jailed.
Anti-slavery advocates protested that Northerners were being forced to support slavery against their conscience.
THIS LAW ROBS *ME* OF MY LIBERTY . . . AND *MY STATE* OF THE RIGHT TO BAN SLAVERY!
New York City, Sept. 7, 1850. The law was tested as soon as President Millard Fillmore signed the Compromise of 1850.
MY MOTHER WAS A FREE WOMAN! I DEMAND A TRIAL!
JAMES HAMLET! I ARREST YOU AS A FUGITIVE SLAVE!
SLAVES CANNOT BEAR TESTIMONY IN A COURT OF LAW!
"You are to be shipped down to Baltimore immediately!"

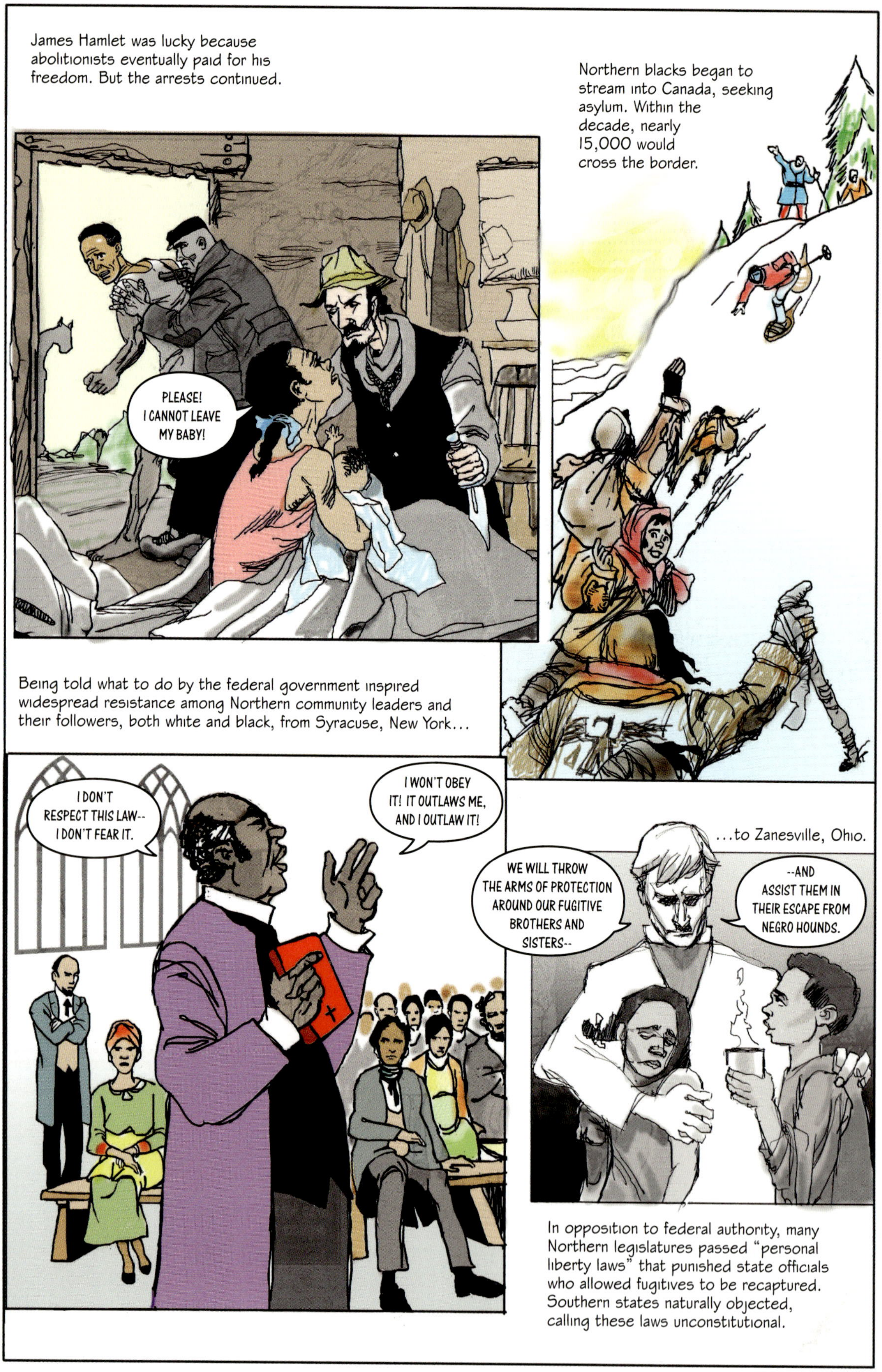
James Hamlet was lucky because abolitionists eventually paid for his freedom. But the arrests continued.
PLEASE! I CANNOT LEAVE MY BABY!
Northern blacks began to stream into Canada, seeking asylum. Within the decade, nearly 15,000 would cross the border.
Being told what to do by the federal government inspired widespread resistance among Northern community leaders and their followers, both white and black, from Syracuse, New York...
I DON'T RESPECT THIS LAW-- I DON'T FEAR IT.
I WON'T OBEY IT! IT OUTLAWS ME, AND I OUTLAW IT!
...to Zanesville, Ohio.
WE WILL THROW THE ARMS OF PROTECTION AROUND OUR FUGITIVE BROTHERS AND SISTERS--
--AND ASSIST THEM IN THEIR ESCAPE FROM NEGRO HOUNDS.
In opposition to federal authority, many Northern legislatures passed "personal liberty laws" that punished state officials who allowed fugitives to be recaptured. Southern states naturally objected, calling these laws unconstitutional.

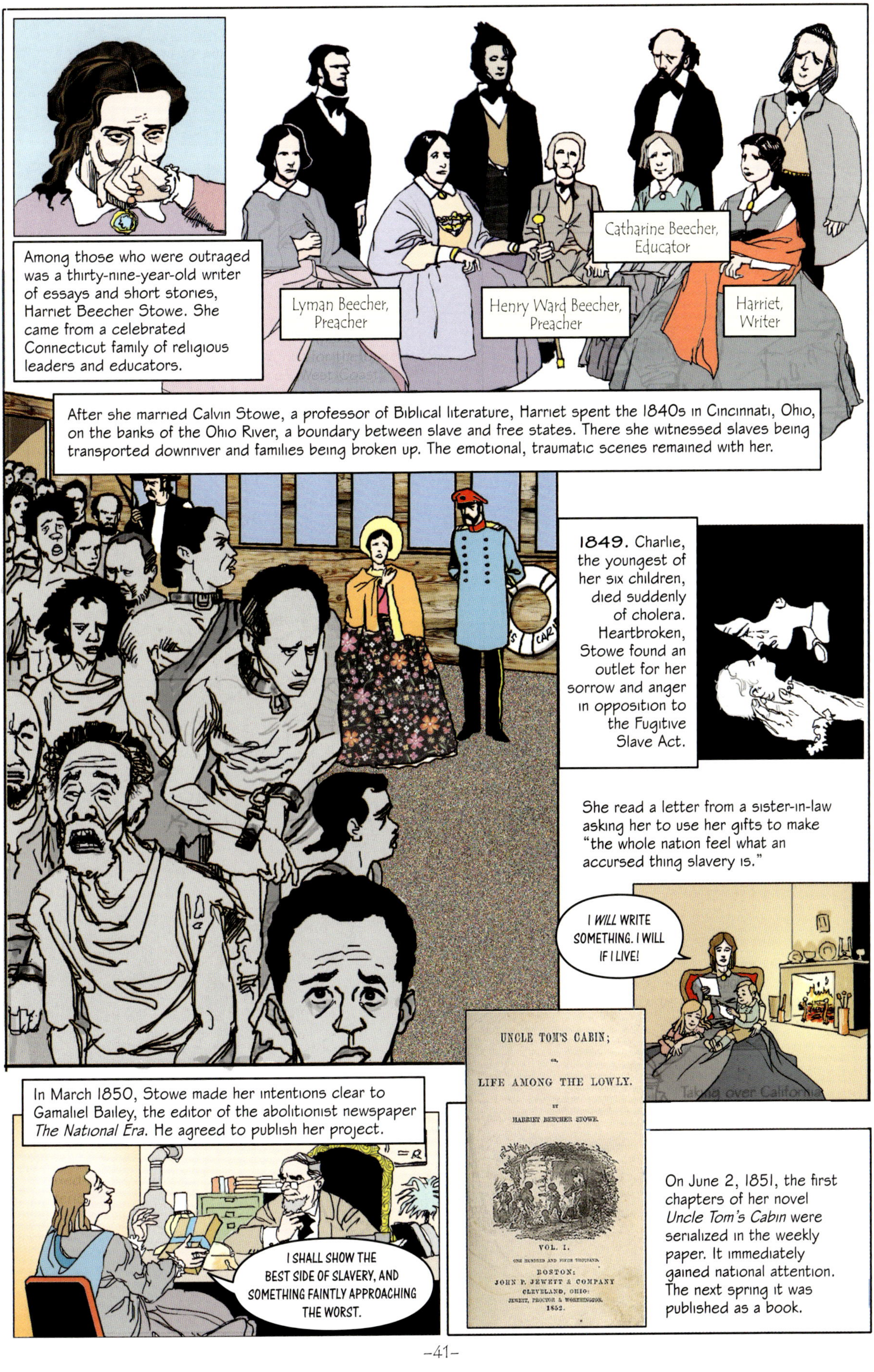

Among those who were outraged was a thirty-nine-year-old writer of essays and short stories, Harriet Beecher Stowe. She came from a celebrated Connecticut family of religious leaders and educators.
Lyman Beecher, Preacher
Henry Ward Beecher, Preacher
Catharine Beecher, Educator
Harriet, Writer
After she married Calvin Stowe, a professor of Biblical literature, Harriet spent the 1840s in Cincinnati, Ohio, on the banks of the Ohio River, a boundary between slave and free states. There she witnessed slaves being transported downriver and families being broken up. The emotional, traumatic scenes remained with her.
1849. Charlie, the youngest of her six children, died suddenly of cholera. Heartbroken, Stowe found an outlet for her sorrow and anger in opposition to the Fugitive Slave Act.
She read a letter from a sister-in-law asking her to use her gifts to make "the whole nation feel what an accursed thing slavery is."
I *WILL* WRITE SOMETHING. I WILL IF I LIVE!
In March 1850, Stowe made her intentions clear to Gamaliel Bailey, the editor of the abolitionist newspaper *The National Era*. He agreed to publish her project.
I SHALL SHOW THE BEST SIDE OF SLAVERY, AND SOMETHING FAINTLY APPROACHING THE WORST.
UNCLE TOM'S CABIN;
OR,
LIFE AMONG THE LOWLY.
BY
HARRIET BEECHER STOWE.
VOL. I.
BOSTON:
JOHN P. JEWETT & COMPANY
CLEVELAND, OHIO:
JEWETT, PROCTOR & WORTHINGTON.
1852.
On June 2, 1851, the first chapters of her novel *Uncle Tom's Cabin* were serialized in the weekly paper. It immediately gained national attention. The next spring it was published as a book.

A sprawling, panoramic, sentimental novel, *Uncle Tom's Cabin* introduced Americans to a variety of white and black characters living in the slave society along the Mississippi and Ohio rivers. In the opening scene, a Kentucky plantation owner makes a deal with a slave trader to settle unpaid debts.

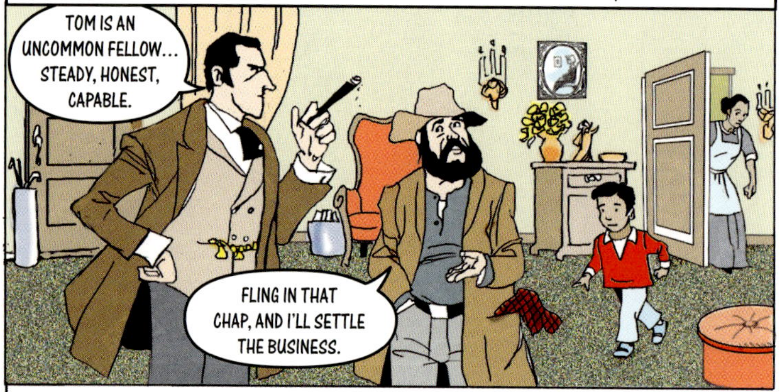
TOM IS AN UNCOMMON FELLOW... STEADY, HONEST, CAPABLE.
FLING IN THAT CHAP, AND I'LL SETTLE THE BUSINESS.

When Eliza, a house slave, overhears that her son, Harry, is about to be sold, she grabs him and runs to freedom.

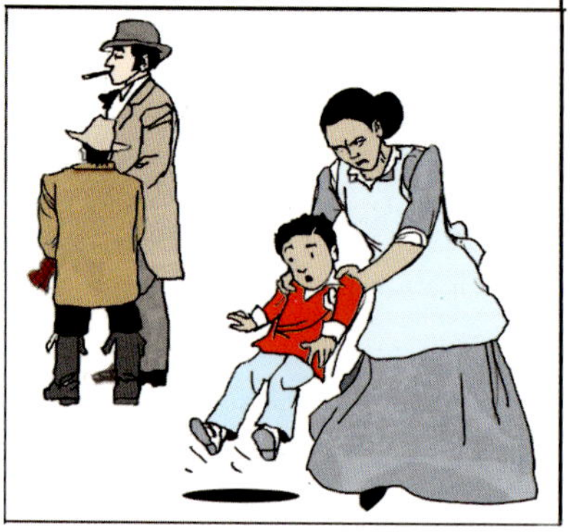

To increase sympathy for Eliza, Stowe speaks directly to her readers:

"If it were *your* Harry, mother, or your Willie, that were going to be torn from you by a brutal trader, tomorrow morning . . . how fast could *you* walk? How many miles could you make in those few brief hours, with the darling at your bosom, the sleepy head on your shoulder?"

In the most famous scene in the novel, Eliza reaches the banks of the Ohio River--and leaps from ice floe to ice floe to reach safety in the free state of Ohio, on the other side.

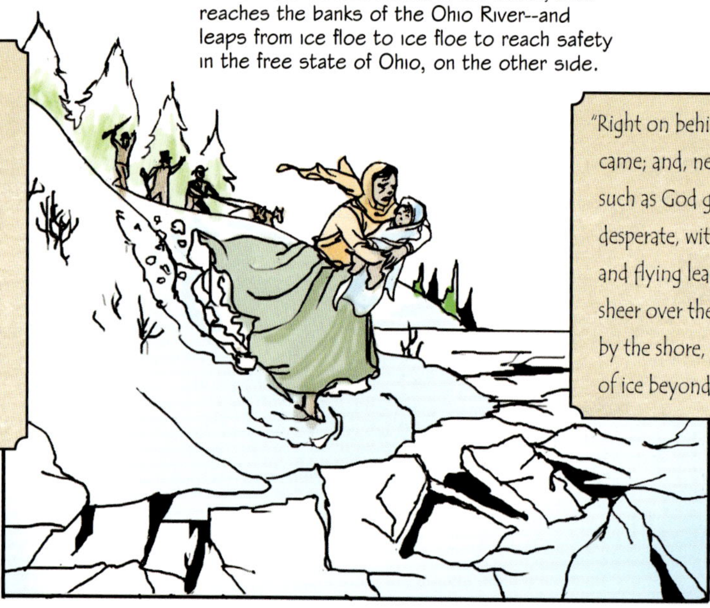

"Right on behind [her pursuers] came; and, nerved with strength such as God gives only to the desperate, with one wild cry and flying leap, she vaulted sheer over the turbid current by the shore, on to the raft of ice beyond."

Uncle Tom, however, is sold and transported down the Mississippi River, away from his wife and children. While aboard the riverboat, he saves Eva, the saintly young daughter of Augustine St. Clare, from drowning. St. Clare then buys Tom and brings him to the family's New Orleans home.

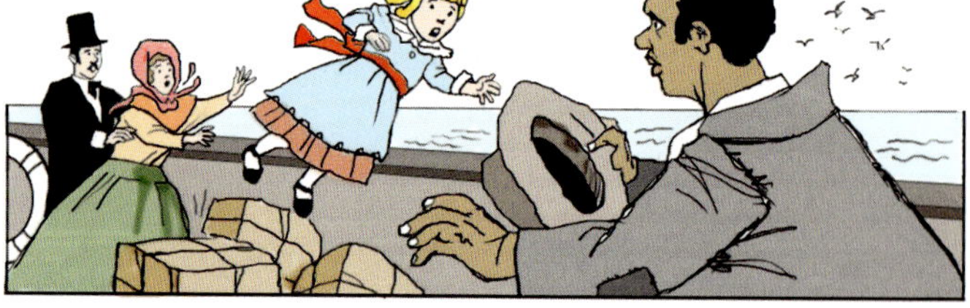

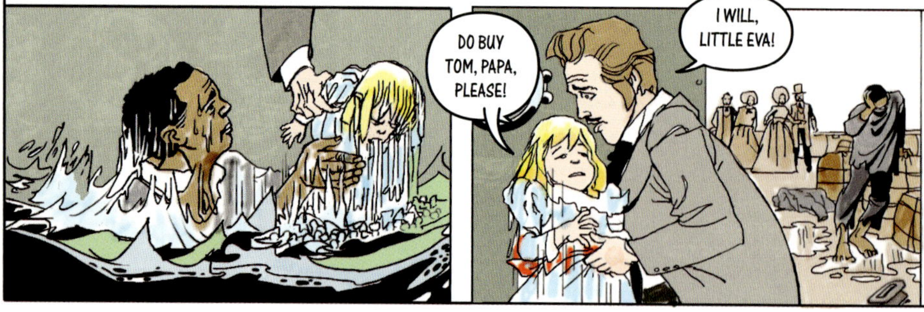
DO BUY TOM, PAPA, PLEASE!
I WILL, LITTLE EVA!

But when father and daughter both die two years later, he ends up in the hands of a sadistic planter.

Stowe wanted to portray the reality of slavery while not demonizing Southern white slave owners.

A) George Harris: *The runaway*

B) Topsy: *The slave girl*

C) Augustine St. Clare: *The slave owner*

D) Simon Legree: *The slave master*

E) Miss Ophelia: *The New England spinster*

F) Simeon and Rachel Halliday: *The Quaker abolitionists*

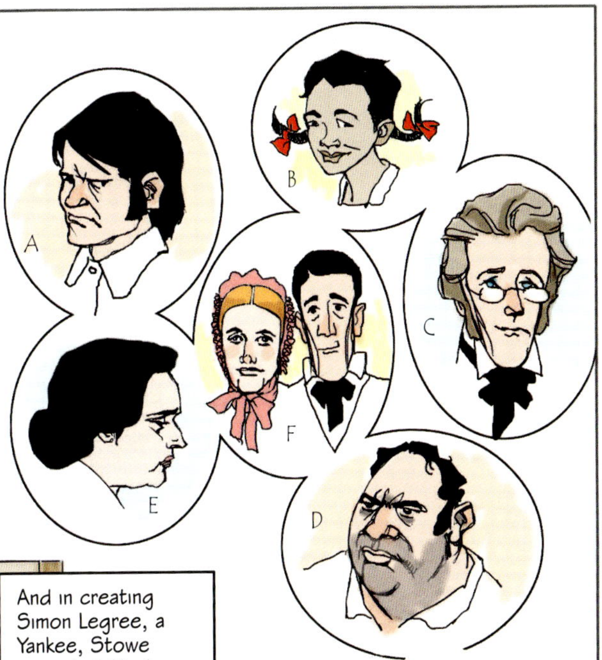
A
B
C
F
E
D

When Southerners complained that the novel was not a realistic portrayal of slavery, Stowe then wrote *A Key to Uncle Tom's Cabin*, a sourcebook of facts and documents to prove the truthfulness of her depiction--

--including the tragedy of families broken apart by death and slavery.

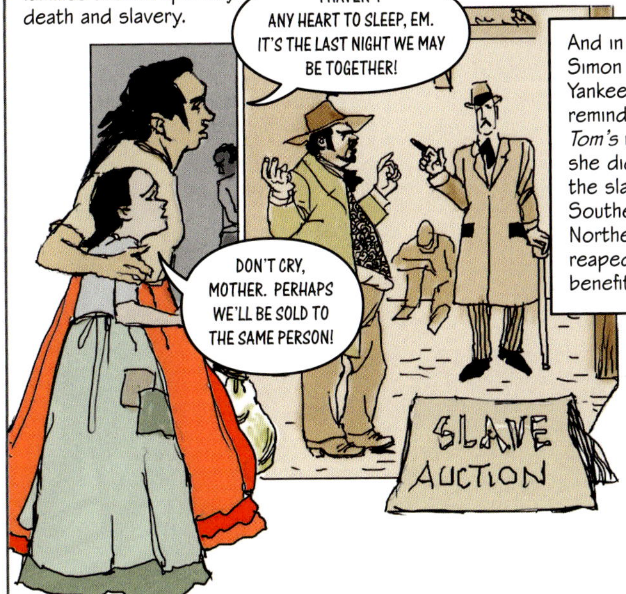
I HAVEN'T ANY HEART TO SLEEP, EM. IT'S THE LAST NIGHT WE MAY BE TOGETHER!
DON'T CRY, MOTHER. PERHAPS WE'LL BE SOLD TO THE SAME PERSON!
SLAVE AUCTION

And in creating Simon Legree, a Yankee, Stowe reminded *Uncle Tom's* readers that she did not blame the slave system on Southerners alone. Northerners also reaped a financial benefit from slavery.

As a woman from an evangelical Christian background, Stowe portrays slavery as a national sin, degrading slave and master alike.

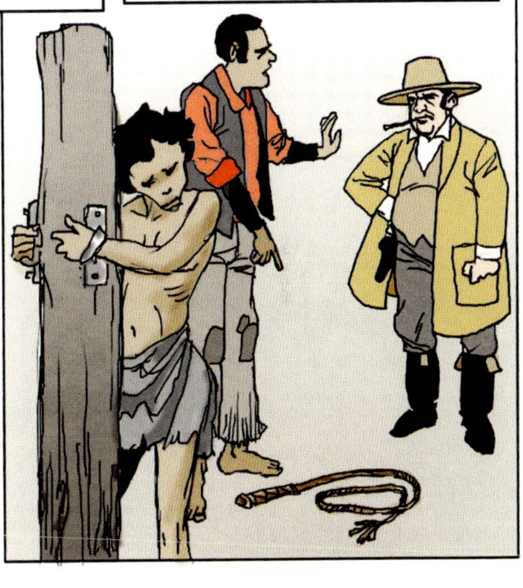

In the first year of publication alone, *Uncle Tom's Cabin* sold 300,000 copies in the United States (the equivalent of 3 million books today) and more than 2 million around the world. It was the bestselling American novel of the 19th century.

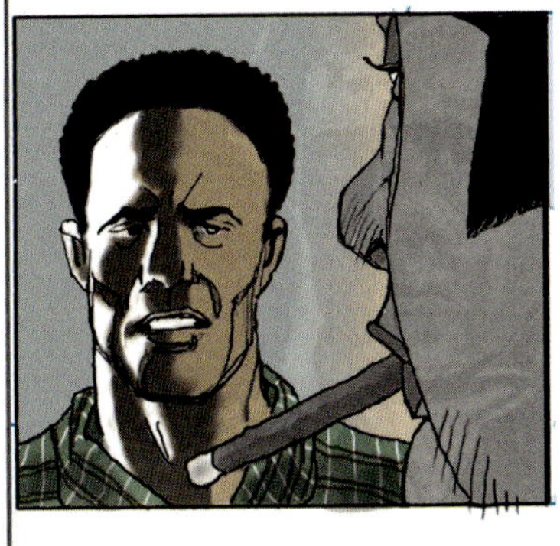

The White House, 1862. As a result of the book's popularity, Stowe had an opportunity to meet President and Mrs. Lincoln late that year. The details of their encounter have never been made clear.

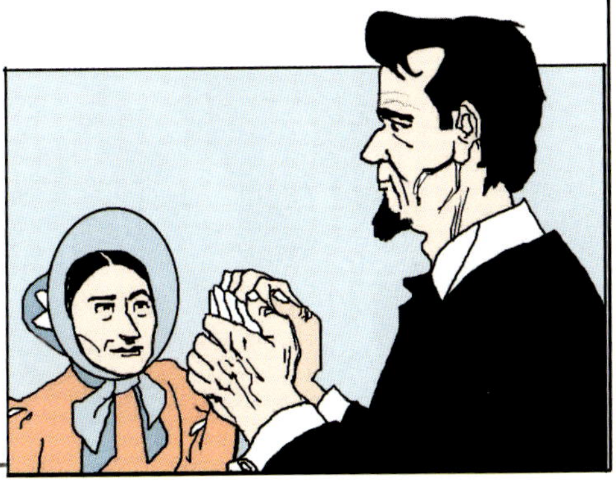

Uncle Tom's Cabin is a protest novel. Grounding her attack in religion and morality, Stowe succeeded in opening the eyes of the world to the cruelties of slavery. The melodramatic story allowed readers to identify with the characters and feel the full emotional impact of their suffering.

Over time, the figure of "Uncle Tom" became a symbol of black subjugation to the white man and the antithesis of black manhood. This interpretation is often linked to how the character was portrayed in the innumerable stage productions of the book. Others, however, see Tom as not only moral, but strong and unbending in the face of oppression.

The novel did not have enormous political impact. Most people, North and South, wanted the Compromise of 1850 to hold, and the Fugitive Slave Law stayed on the books. But by broadening the national conversation, Stowe helped lay the groundwork for slavery's eventual abolition.

EXCERPTS FROM *UNCLE TOM'S CABIN* "CONCLUDING REMARKS"

"The writer has only given a faint shadow, a dim picture, of the anguish and despair that are at this very moment riving thousands of hearts, shattering thousands of families, and driving a helpless and sensitive race to frenzy and despair... Nothing of tragedy can be written, can be spoken, can be conceived, that equals the frightful reality of scenes daily and hourly acting on our shores, beneath the shadow of American law, and the shadow of the cross of Christ.

"And now, men and women of America, is this a thing to be trifled with, apologized for, and passed over in silence? Farmers of Massachusetts, of New Hampshire, of Vermont, of Connecticut... is this a thing for you to countenance and encourage?... And you, mothers of America—you, who have learned by the cradles of your own children, to love and feel for all mankind... I beseech you, pity the mother who has all your affections, and not one legal right to protect, guide, or educate, the child of her bosom!"

The Kansas-Nebraska Act

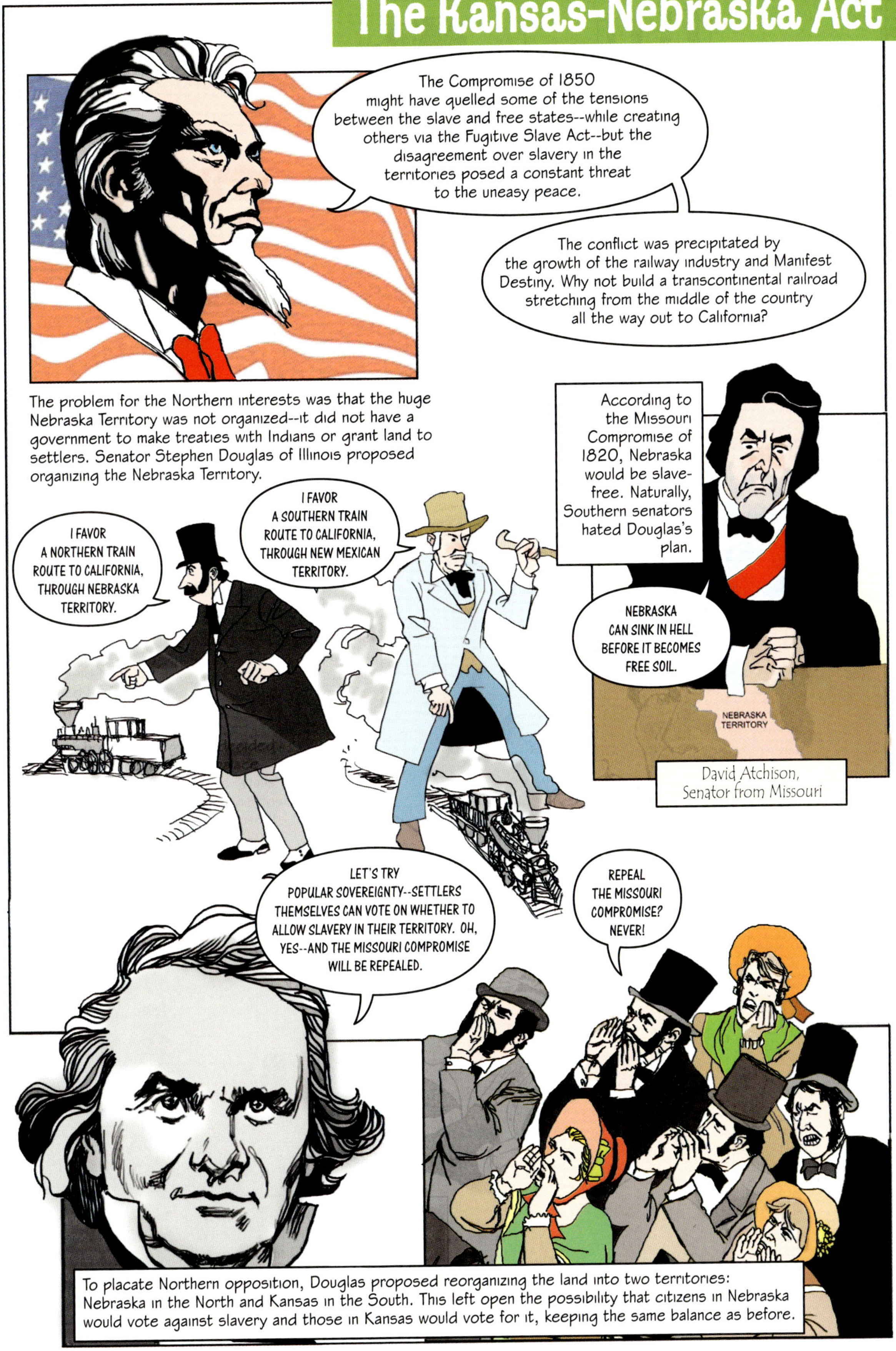

The Compromise of 1850 might have quelled some of the tensions between the slave and free states--while creating others via the Fugitive Slave Act--but the disagreement over slavery in the territories posed a constant threat to the uneasy peace.
The conflict was precipitated by the growth of the railway industry and Manifest Destiny. Why not build a transcontinental railroad stretching from the middle of the country all the way out to California?
The problem for the Northern interests was that the huge Nebraska Territory was not organized--it did not have a government to make treaties with Indians or grant land to settlers. Senator Stephen Douglas of Illinois proposed organizing the Nebraska Territory.
I FAVOR A NORTHERN TRAIN ROUTE TO CALIFORNIA, THROUGH NEBRASKA TERRITORY.
I FAVOR A SOUTHERN TRAIN ROUTE TO CALIFORNIA, THROUGH NEW MEXICAN TERRITORY.
According to the Missouri Compromise of 1820, Nebraska would be slave-free. Naturally, Southern senators hated Douglas's plan.
NEBRASKA CAN SINK IN HELL BEFORE IT BECOMES FREE SOIL.
NEBRASKA TERRITORY
David Atchison, Senator from Missouri
LET'S TRY POPULAR SOVEREIGNTY--SETTLERS THEMSELVES CAN VOTE ON WHETHER TO ALLOW SLAVERY IN THEIR TERRITORY. OH, YES--AND THE MISSOURI COMPROMISE WILL BE REPEALED.
REPEAL THE MISSOURI COMPROMISE? NEVER!
To placate Northern opposition, Douglas proposed reorganizing the land into two territories: Nebraska in the North and Kansas in the South. This left open the possibility that citizens in Nebraska would vote against slavery and those in Kansas would vote for it, keeping the same balance as before.

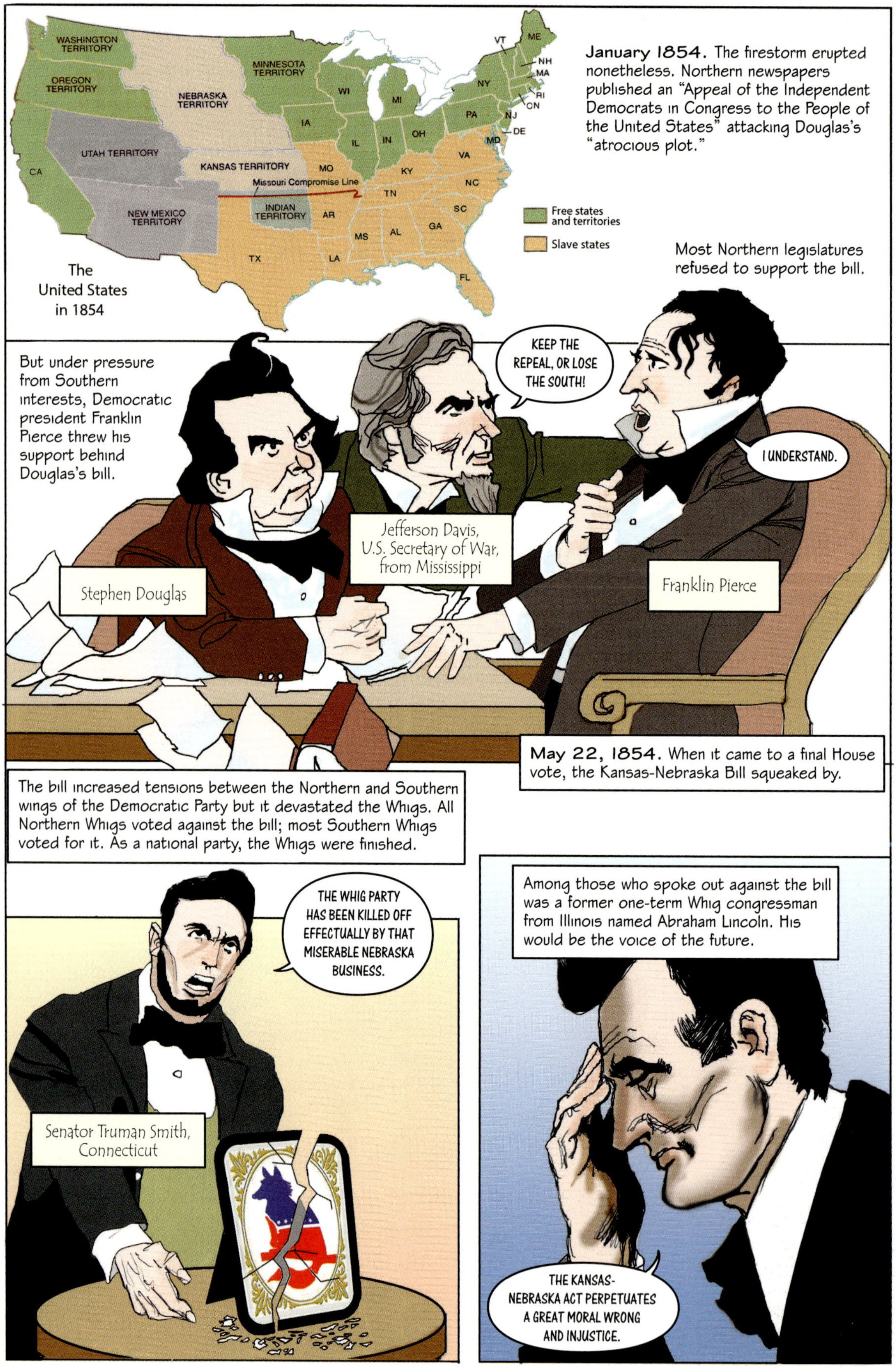
WASHINGTON TERRITORY
OREGON TERRITORY
NEBRASKA TERRITORY
MINNESOTA TERRITORY
UTAH TERRITORY
KANSAS TERRITORY
Missouri Compromise Line
INDIAN TERRITORY
NEW MEXICO TERRITORY
CA
WI
MI
IA
IL
IN
OH
NY
PA
VT
ME
NH
MA
RI
CN
NJ
DE
MD
MO
KY
VA
NC
TN
AR
SC
GA
AL
MS
LA
TX
FL
Free states and territories
Slave states
The United States in 1854
January 1854. The firestorm erupted nonetheless. Northern newspapers published an "Appeal of the Independent Democrats in Congress to the People of the United States" attacking Douglas's "atrocious plot."
Most Northern legislatures refused to support the bill.
But under pressure from Southern interests, Democratic president Franklin Pierce threw his support behind Douglas's bill.
KEEP THE REPEAL, OR LOSE THE SOUTH!
I UNDERSTAND.
Stephen Douglas
Jefferson Davis, U.S. Secretary of War, from Mississippi
Franklin Pierce
May 22, 1854. When it came to a final House vote, the Kansas-Nebraska Bill squeaked by.
The bill increased tensions between the Northern and Southern wings of the Democratic Party but it devastated the Whigs. All Northern Whigs voted against the bill; most Southern Whigs voted for it. As a national party, the Whigs were finished.
THE WHIG PARTY HAS BEEN KILLED OFF EFFECTUALLY BY THAT MISERABLE NEBRASKA BUSINESS.
Senator Truman Smith, Connecticut
Among those who spoke out against the bill was a former one-term Whig congressman from Illinois named Abraham Lincoln. His would be the voice of the future.
THE KANSAS-NEBRASKA ACT PERPETUATES A GREAT MORAL WRONG AND INJUSTICE.

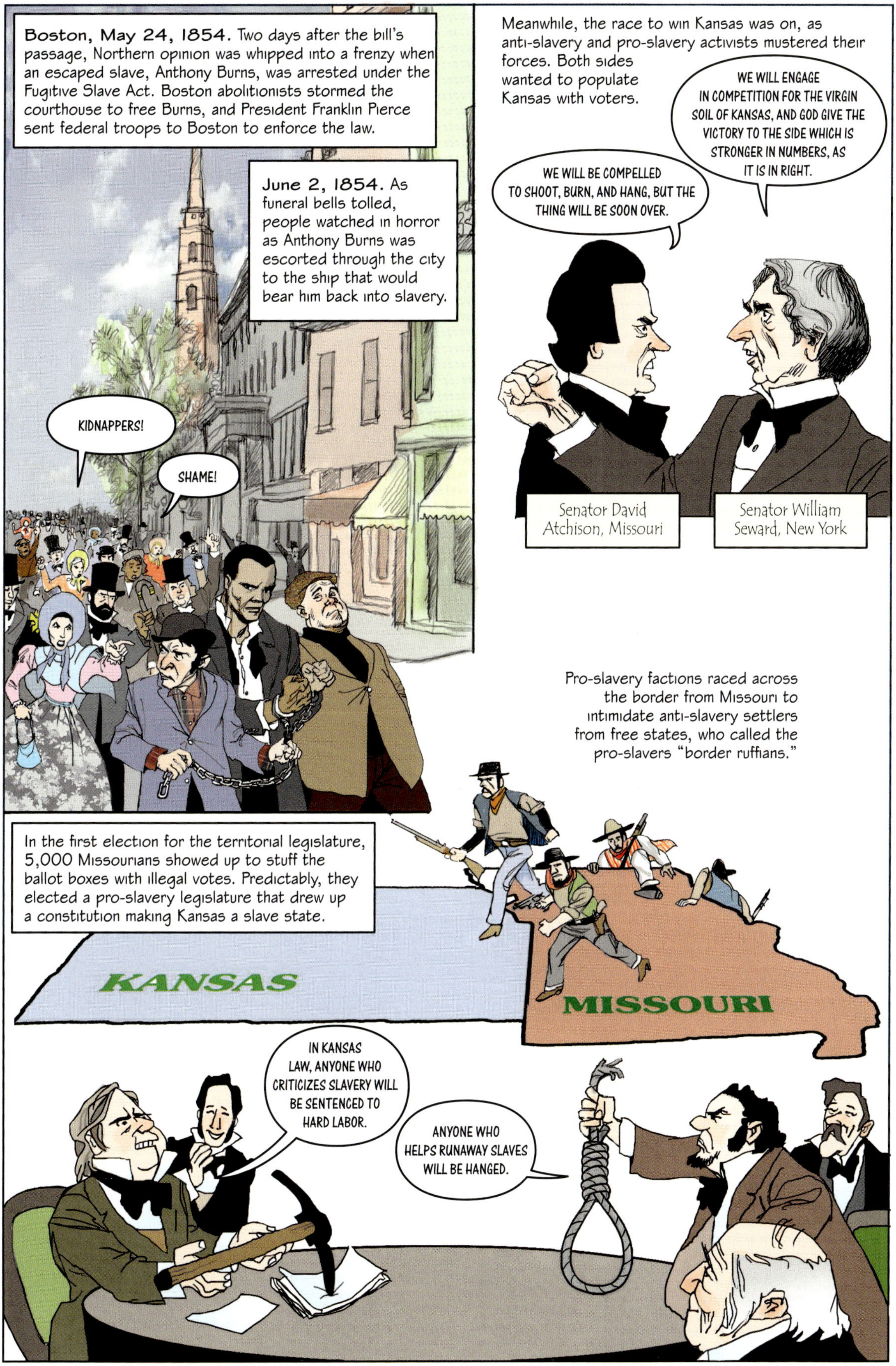
Boston, May 24, 1854. Two days after the bill's passage, Northern opinion was whipped into a frenzy when an escaped slave, Anthony Burns, was arrested under the Fugitive Slave Act. Boston abolitionists stormed the courthouse to free Burns, and President Franklin Pierce sent federal troops to Boston to enforce the law.
June 2, 1854. As funeral bells tolled, people watched in horror as Anthony Burns was escorted through the city to the ship that would bear him back into slavery.
KIDNAPPERS!
SHAME!
Meanwhile, the race to win Kansas was on, as anti-slavery and pro-slavery activists mustered their forces. Both sides wanted to populate Kansas with voters.
WE WILL ENGAGE IN COMPETITION FOR THE VIRGIN SOIL OF KANSAS, AND GOD GIVE THE VICTORY TO THE SIDE WHICH IS STRONGER IN NUMBERS, AS IT IS IN RIGHT.
WE WILL BE COMPELLED TO SHOOT, BURN, AND HANG, BUT THE THING WILL BE SOON OVER.
Senator David Atchison, Missouri
Senator William Seward, New York
Pro-slavery factions raced across the border from Missouri to intimidate anti-slavery settlers from free states, who called the pro-slavers "border ruffians."
In the first election for the territorial legislature, 5,000 Missourians showed up to stuff the ballot boxes with illegal votes. Predictably, they elected a pro-slavery legislature that drew up a constitution making Kansas a slave state.
KANSAS
MISSOURI
IN KANSAS LAW, ANYONE WHO CRITICIZES SLAVERY WILL BE SENTENCED TO HARD LABOR.
ANYONE WHO HELPS RUNAWAY SLAVES WILL BE HANGED.

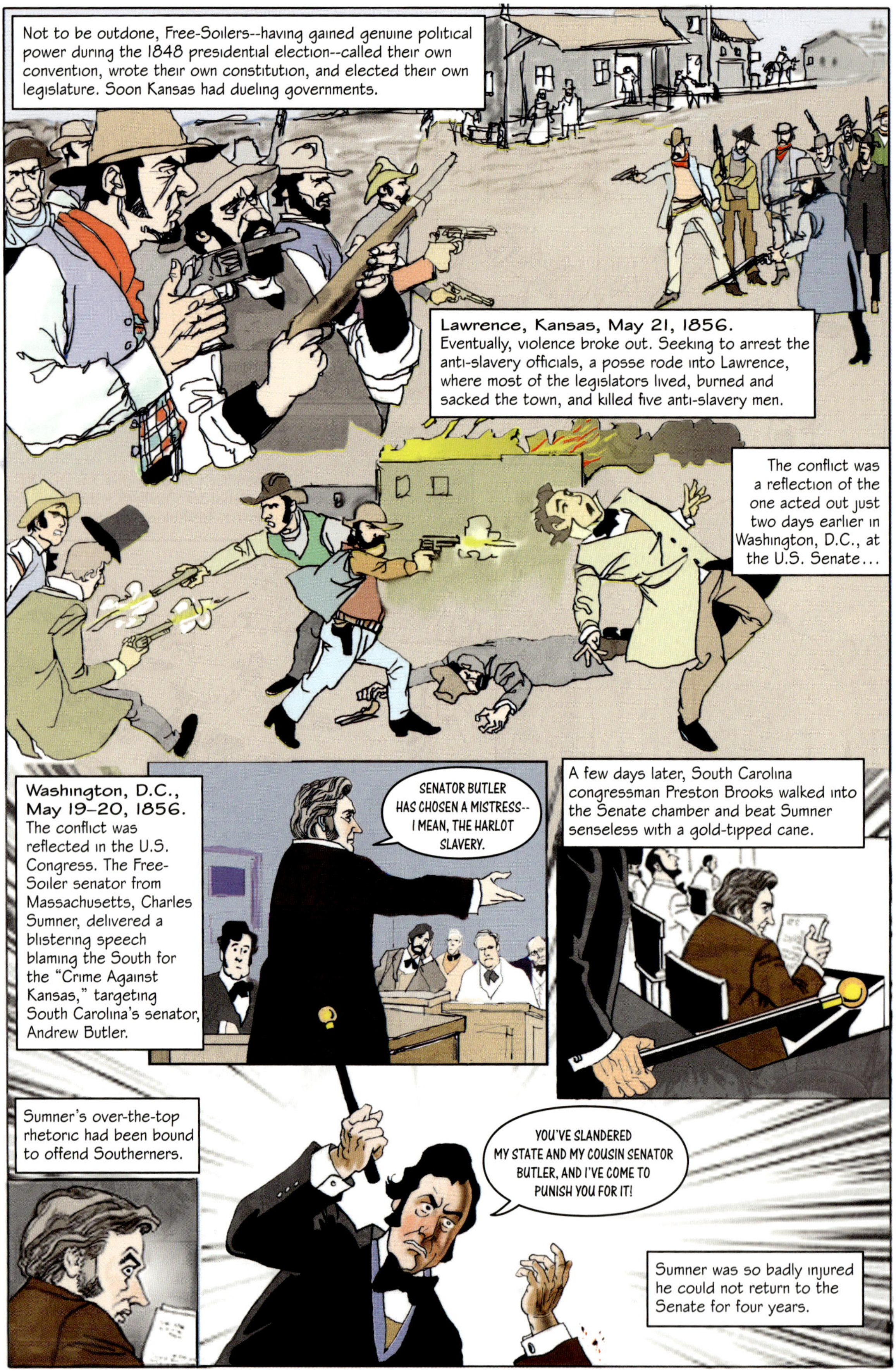
Not to be outdone, Free-Soilers--having gained genuine political power during the 1848 presidential election--called their own convention, wrote their own constitution, and elected their own legislature. Soon Kansas had dueling governments.
Lawrence, Kansas, May 21, 1856. Eventually, violence broke out. Seeking to arrest the anti-slavery officials, a posse rode into Lawrence, where most of the legislators lived, burned and sacked the town, and killed five anti-slavery men.
The conflict was a reflection of the one acted out just two days earlier in Washington, D.C., at the U.S. Senate...
Washington, D.C., May 19–20, 1856. The conflict was reflected in the U.S. Congress. The Free-Soiler senator from Massachusetts, Charles Sumner, delivered a blistering speech blaming the South for the "Crime Against Kansas," targeting South Carolina's senator, Andrew Butler.
SENATOR BUTLER HAS CHOSEN A MISTRESS-- I MEAN, THE HARLOT SLAVERY.
A few days later, South Carolina congressman Preston Brooks walked into the Senate chamber and beat Sumner senseless with a gold-tipped cane.
Sumner's over-the-top rhetoric had been bound to offend Southerners.
YOU'VE SLANDERED MY STATE AND MY COUSIN SENATOR BUTLER, AND I'VE COME TO PUNISH YOU FOR IT!
Sumner was so badly injured he could not return to the Senate for four years.

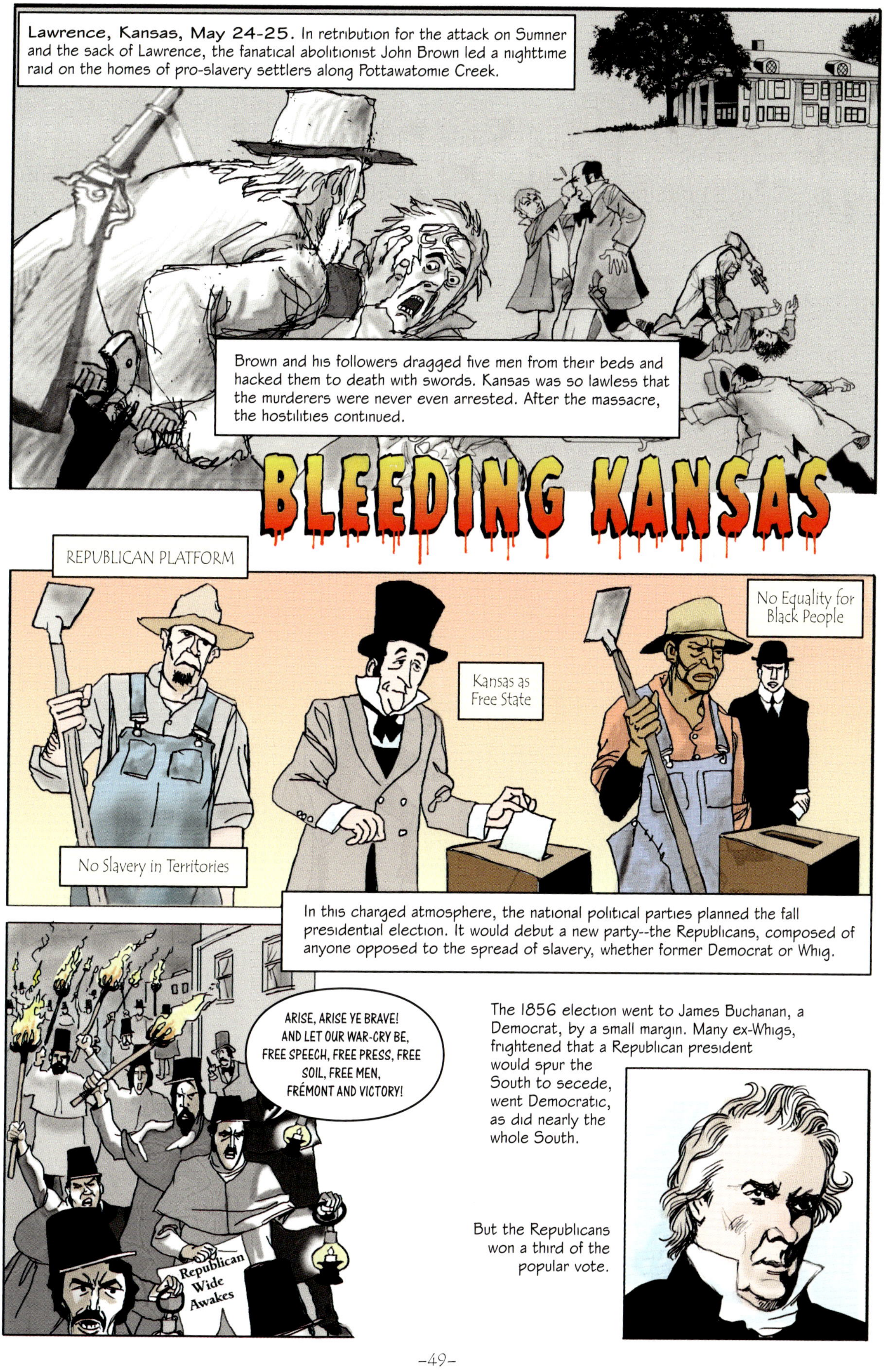

Lawrence, Kansas, May 24-25. In retribution for the attack on Sumner and the sack of Lawrence, the fanatical abolitionist John Brown led a nighttime raid on the homes of pro-slavery settlers along Pottawatomie Creek.
Brown and his followers dragged five men from their beds and hacked them to death with swords. Kansas was so lawless that the murderers were never even arrested. After the massacre, the hostilities continued.
BLEEDING KANSAS
REPUBLICAN PLATFORM
No Slavery in Territories
Kansas as Free State
No Equality for Black People
In this charged atmosphere, the national political parties planned the fall presidential election. It would debut a new party--the Republicans, composed of anyone opposed to the spread of slavery, whether former Democrat or Whig.
ARISE, ARISE YE BRAVE! AND LET OUR WAR-CRY BE, FREE SPEECH, FREE PRESS, FREE SOIL, FREE MEN, FRÉMONT AND VICTORY!
Republican Wide Awakes
The 1856 election went to James Buchanan, a Democrat, by a small margin. Many ex-Whigs, frightened that a Republican president would spur the South to secede, went Democratic, as did nearly the whole South.
But the Republicans won a third of the popular vote.

Indebted to Southerners, Buchanan supported the pro-slavery constitution for Kansas. Yet by 1858, Kansas citizens were overwhelmingly anti-slavery, and they voted against it. Kansas finally became a free state in 1861, after years of discord. By then, the Union had been torn asunder.

The Kansas-Nebraska Act divided the Nebraska territory into two smaller territories, mandated that popular sovereignty would resolve the question of slavery in each, and repealed the Missouri Compromise. The sectional conflict that followed destroyed the fragile accord formed by the Compromise of 1850.

The repeal and the lawlessness of the border ruffians convinced Northerners that the "Slave Power" would do anything to force slavery not just on Kansas, but on the whole country. The South, for its part, felt ever more threatened by the hostility of the North, the growing number of Free-Soilers, and the birth of the Republican Party.

The passage of the bill intensified the ferocity of the national debate, leading to violence on both sides, and sparked a civil war in Kansas that foretold the national civil war to come.

EXCERPT FROM THE KANSAS-NEBRASKA ACT

"That the Constitution, and all laws of the United States which are not locally inapplicable, shall have the same force and effect within the said Territory of Nebraska [and Kansas] as elsewhere within the United States, except the eighth section of the act preparatory to the admission of Missouri into the Union, approved March sixth, eighteen hundred and twenty, which, being inconsistent with the principle of non-intervention by Congress with slavery in the States and Territories, as recognized by the legislation of eighteen hundred and fifty, commonly called the Compromise Measures, is hereby declared inoperative and void; it being the true intent and meaning of this act not to legislate slavery into any Territory or State, nor to exclude it therefrom, but to leave the people thereof perfectly free to form and regulate their domestic institutions in their own way, subject only to the Constitution of the United States..."

Dred Scott v. Sandford

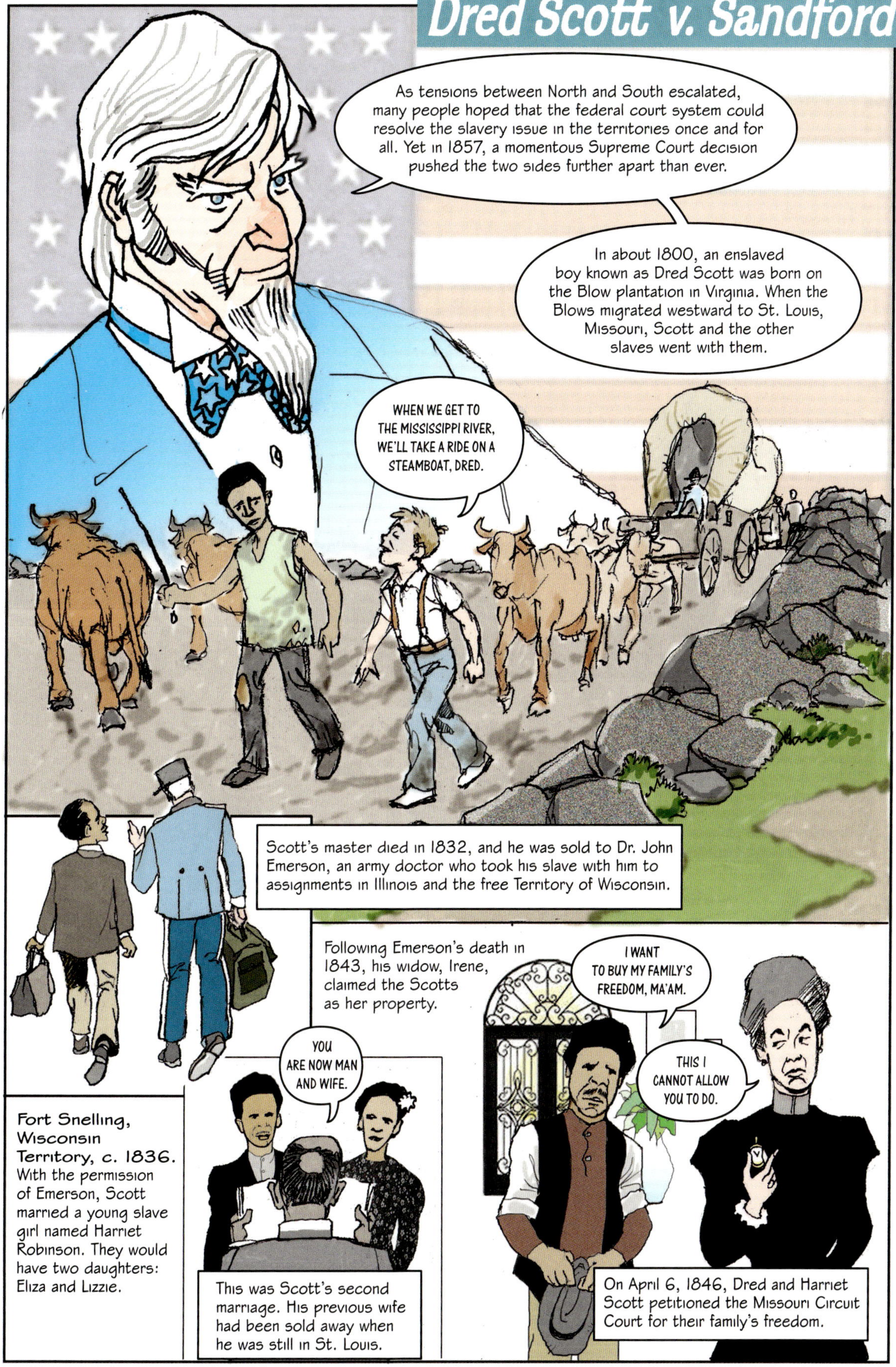
As tensions between North and South escalated, many people hoped that the federal court system could resolve the slavery issue in the territories once and for all. Yet in 1857, a momentous Supreme Court decision pushed the two sides further apart than ever.
In about 1800, an enslaved boy known as Dred Scott was born on the Blow plantation in Virginia. When the Blows migrated westward to St. Louis, Missouri, Scott and the other slaves went with them.
WHEN WE GET TO THE MISSISSIPPI RIVER, WE'LL TAKE A RIDE ON A STEAMBOAT, DRED.
Scott's master died in 1832, and he was sold to Dr. John Emerson, an army doctor who took his slave with him to assignments in Illinois and the free Territory of Wisconsin.
Fort Snelling, Wisconsin Territory, c. 1836. With the permission of Emerson, Scott married a young slave girl named Harriet Robinson. They would have two daughters: Eliza and Lizzie.
YOU ARE NOW MAN AND WIFE.
This was Scott's second marriage. His previous wife had been sold away when he was still in St. Louis.
Following Emerson's death in 1843, his widow, Irene, claimed the Scotts as her property.
I WANT TO BUY MY FAMILY'S FREEDOM, MA'AM.
THIS I CANNOT ALLOW YOU TO DO.
On April 6, 1846, Dred and Harriet Scott petitioned the Missouri Circuit Court for their family's freedom.

No one knows exactly why the Scotts decided to sue for freedom. Perhaps Dred had been counseled by members of the Blow family. Perhaps Harriet, who had joined the Second African Baptist Church of St. Louis, was persuaded by the Reverend John R. Anderson, who had bought his own freedom.

In Missouri, some slaves had won their freedom in court after proving they had lived in free territory.

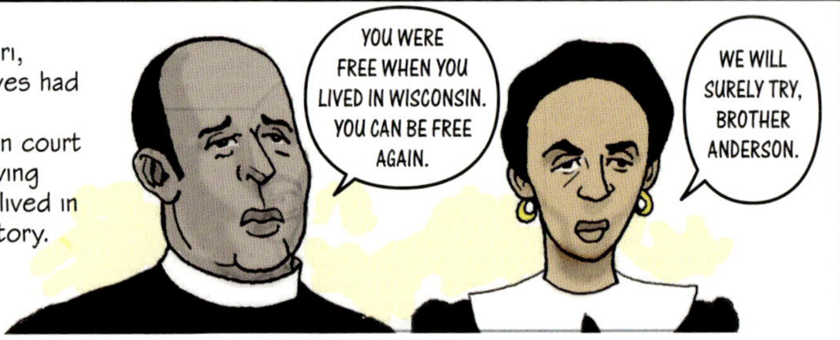
YOU WERE FREE WHEN YOU LIVED IN WISCONSIN. YOU CAN BE FREE AGAIN.
WE WILL SURELY TRY, BROTHER ANDERSON.

The complex case lasted 11 months. Dred and Harriet lost their suit, but in 1847 were granted a new trial, which they won in 1850. So, briefly, they were free.

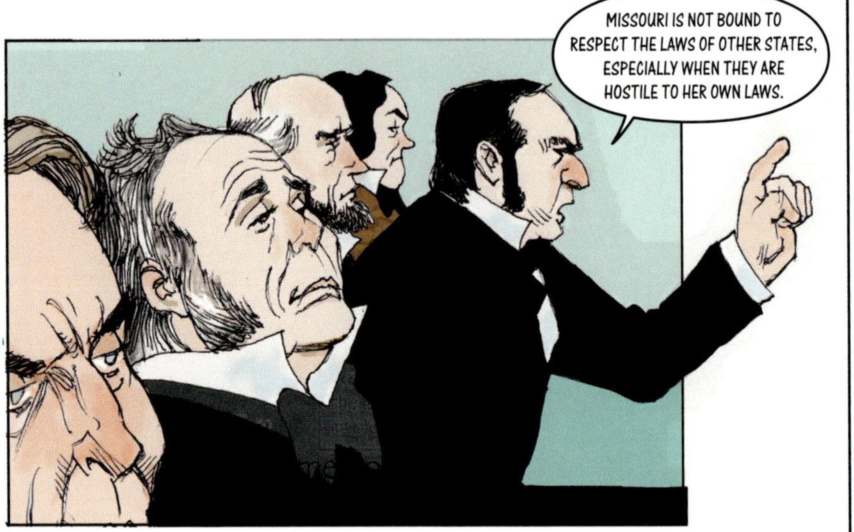
MISSOURI IS NOT BOUND TO RESPECT THE LAWS OF OTHER STATES, ESPECIALLY WHEN THEY ARE HOSTILE TO HER OWN LAWS.

March 22, 1852. When Mrs. Emerson appealed, the Missouri Supreme Court overturned the decision and the Scotts were returned to slavery.

Scott's lawyers appealed to lower federal courts, which upheld the Missouri Supreme Court's decision. Finally, they appealed to the highest court in the nation--the United States Supreme Court.

In the meantime, Mrs. Emerson had transferred ownership of the Scotts to her brother, John Sanford. The case on the Supreme Court's docket would be called *Scott v. Sandford* (a court clerk misspelled the name).

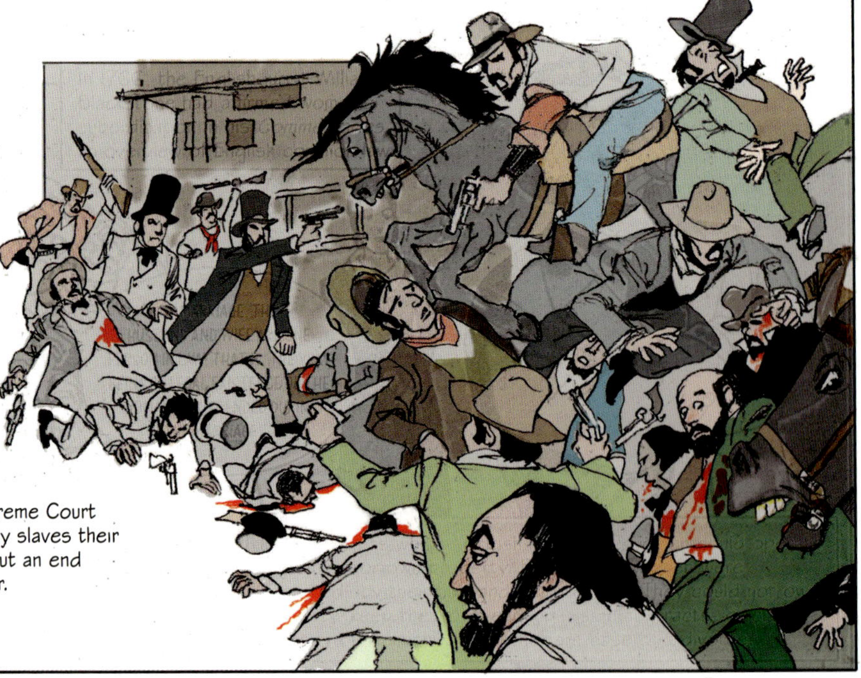

February 1856.
A lot had happened since Scott had first sued for freedom in 1846. The Compromise of 1850, with the attendant furor over the Fugitive Slave Law, and the bloody consequences of the Kansas-Nebraska Act of 1854, had greatly aggravated the conflict between pro-slavery and anti-slavery Americans. Like the Missouri Supreme Court, the pro-slavery Supreme Court was in no mood to grant any slaves their freedom. They wanted to put an end to freedom suits altogether.

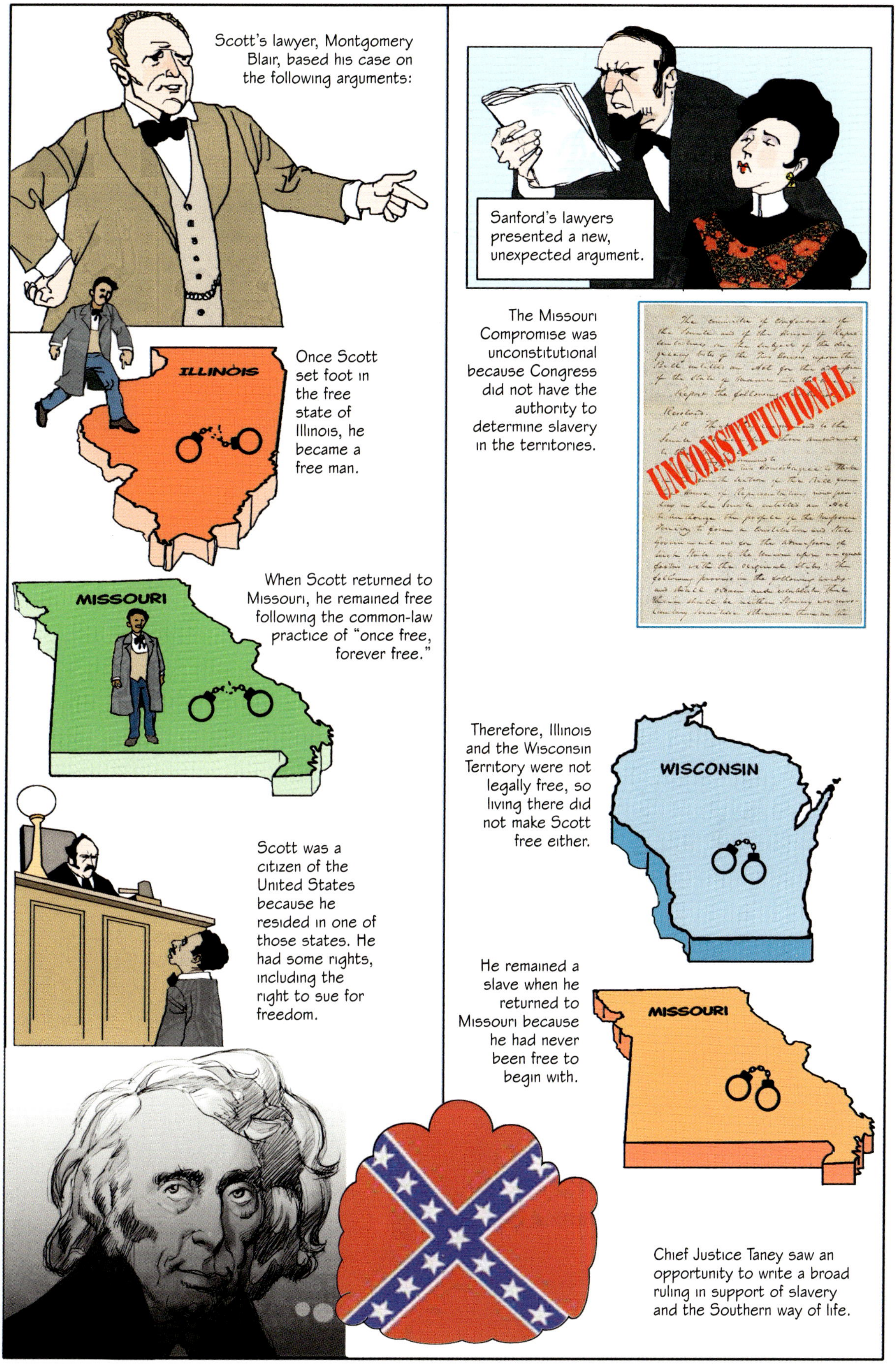
Scott's lawyer, Montgomery Blair, based his case on the following arguments:
ILLINOIS
Once Scott set foot in the free state of Illinois, he became a free man.
MISSOURI
When Scott returned to Missouri, he remained free following the common-law practice of "once free, forever free."
Scott was a citizen of the United States because he resided in one of those states. He had some rights, including the right to sue for freedom.
Sanford's lawyers presented a new, unexpected argument.
The Missouri Compromise was unconstitutional because Congress did not have the authority to determine slavery in the territories.
UNCONSTITUTIONAL
Therefore, Illinois and the Wisconsin Territory were not legally free, so living there did not make Scott free either.
WISCONSIN
He remained a slave when he returned to Missouri because he had never been free to begin with.
MISSOURI
Chief Justice Taney saw an opportunity to write a broad ruling in support of slavery and the Southern way of life.

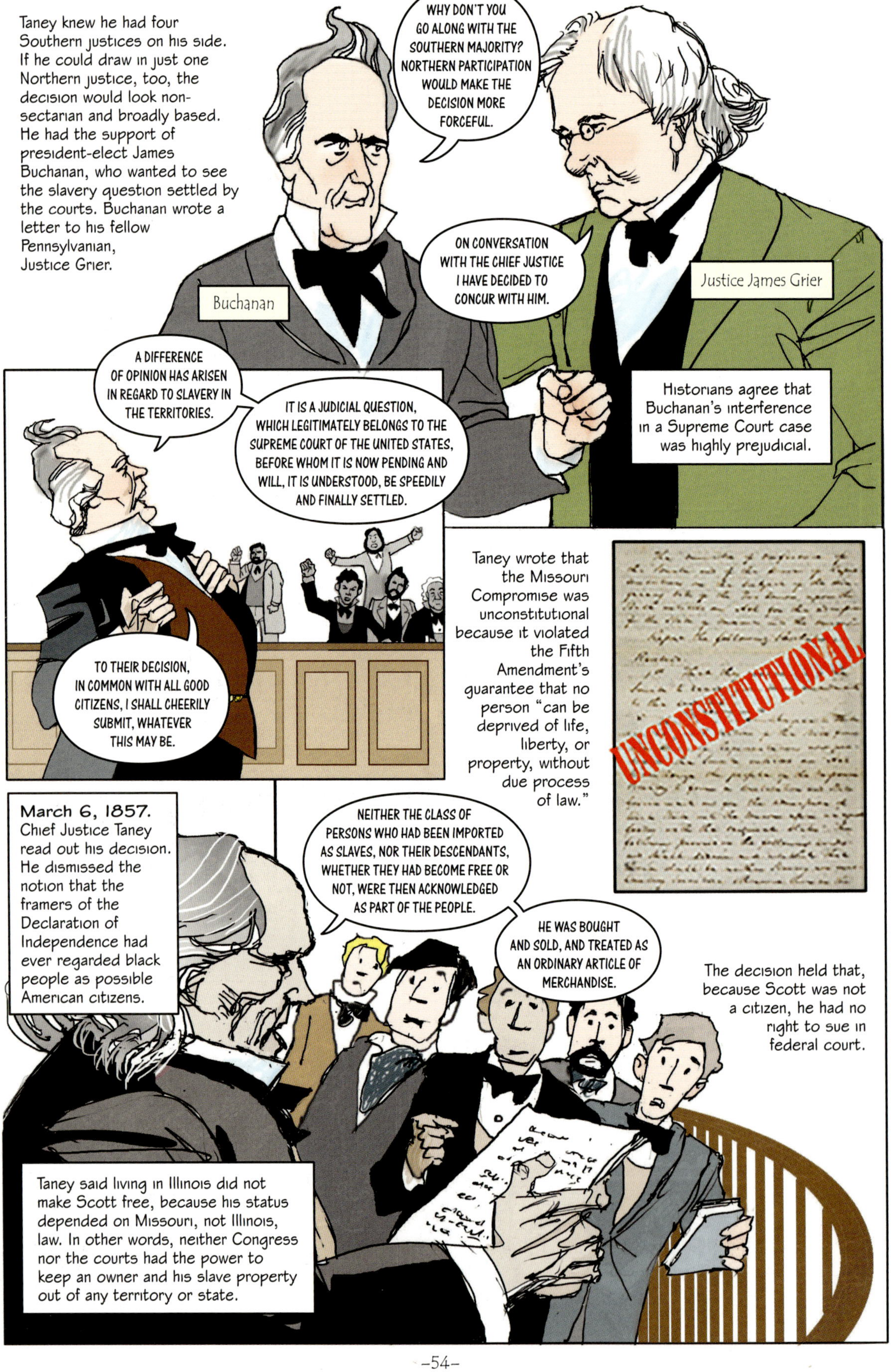
Taney knew he had four Southern justices on his side. If he could draw in just one Northern justice, too, the decision would look non-sectarian and broadly based. He had the support of president-elect James Buchanan, who wanted to see the slavery question settled by the courts. Buchanan wrote a letter to his fellow Pennsylvanian, Justice Grier.
WHY DON'T YOU GO ALONG WITH THE SOUTHERN MAJORITY? NORTHERN PARTICIPATION WOULD MAKE THE DECISION MORE FORCEFUL.
ON CONVERSATION WITH THE CHIEF JUSTICE I HAVE DECIDED TO CONCUR WITH HIM.
Buchanan
Justice James Grier
Historians agree that Buchanan's interference in a Supreme Court case was highly prejudicial.
A DIFFERENCE OF OPINION HAS ARISEN IN REGARD TO SLAVERY IN THE TERRITORIES.
IT IS A JUDICIAL QUESTION, WHICH LEGITIMATELY BELONGS TO THE SUPREME COURT OF THE UNITED STATES, BEFORE WHOM IT IS NOW PENDING AND WILL, IT IS UNDERSTOOD, BE SPEEDILY AND FINALLY SETTLED.
TO THEIR DECISION, IN COMMON WITH ALL GOOD CITIZENS, I SHALL CHEERILY SUBMIT, WHATEVER THIS MAY BE.
Taney wrote that the Missouri Compromise was unconstitutional because it violated the Fifth Amendment's guarantee that no person "can be deprived of life, liberty, or property, without due process of law."
UNCONSTITUTIONAL
March 6, 1857. Chief Justice Taney read out his decision. He dismissed the notion that the framers of the Declaration of Independence had ever regarded black people as possible American citizens.
NEITHER THE CLASS OF PERSONS WHO HAD BEEN IMPORTED AS SLAVES, NOR THEIR DESCENDANTS, WHETHER THEY HAD BECOME FREE OR NOT, WERE THEN ACKNOWLEDGED AS PART OF THE PEOPLE.
HE WAS BOUGHT AND SOLD, AND TREATED AS AN ORDINARY ARTICLE OF MERCHANDISE.
The decision held that, because Scott was not a citizen, he had no right to sue in federal court.
Taney said living in Illinois did not make Scott free, because his status depended on Missouri, not Illinois, law. In other words, neither Congress nor the courts had the power to keep an owner and his slave property out of any territory or state.

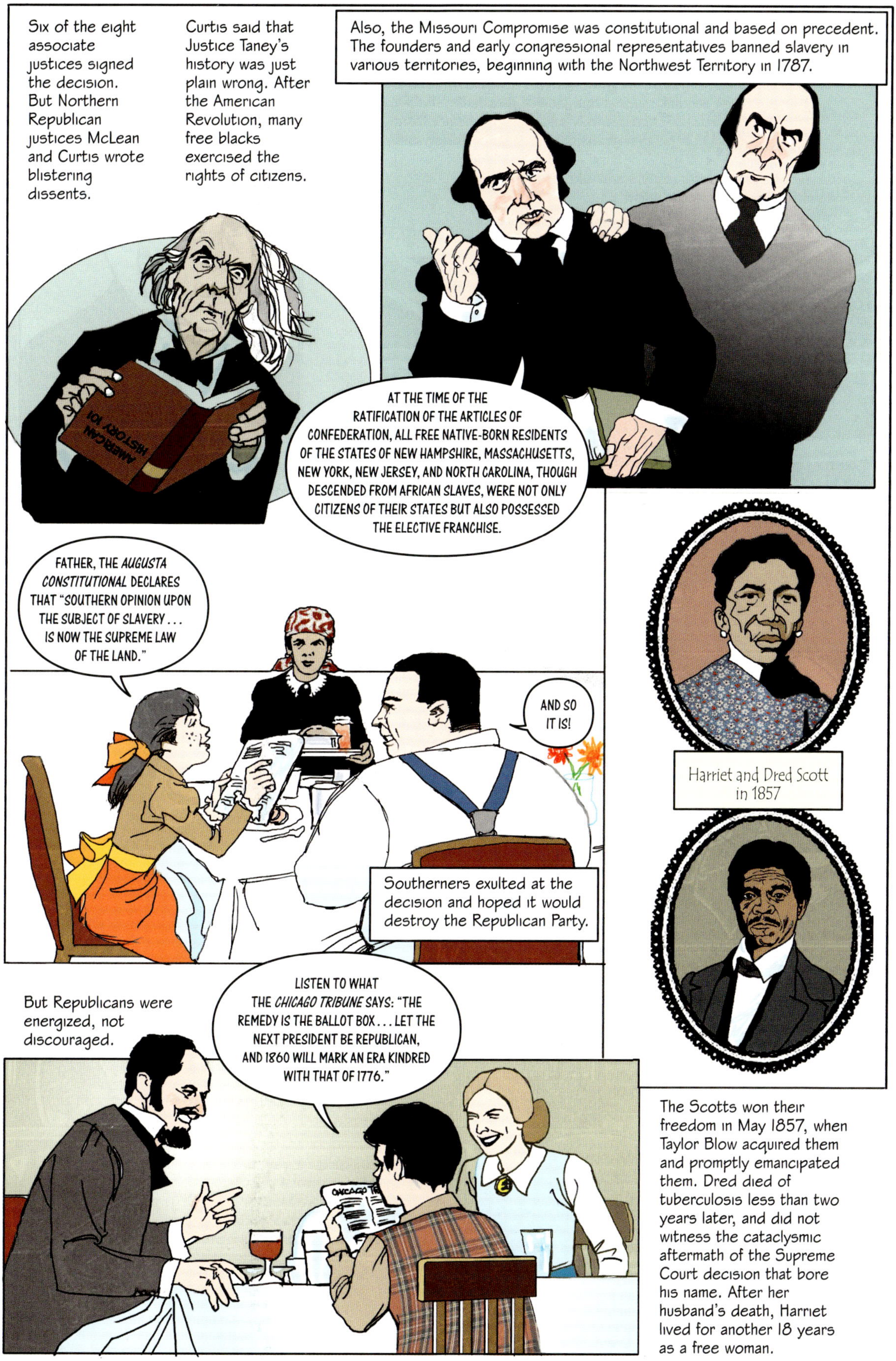
Six of the eight associate justices signed the decision. But Northern Republican justices McLean and Curtis wrote blistering dissents.
Curtis said that Justice Taney's history was just plain wrong. After the American Revolution, many free blacks exercised the rights of citizens.
Also, the Missouri Compromise was constitutional and based on precedent. The founders and early congressional representatives banned slavery in various territories, beginning with the Northwest Territory in 1787.
AMERICAN HISTORY 101
AT THE TIME OF THE RATIFICATION OF THE ARTICLES OF CONFEDERATION, ALL FREE NATIVE-BORN RESIDENTS OF THE STATES OF NEW HAMPSHIRE, MASSACHUSETTS, NEW YORK, NEW JERSEY, AND NORTH CAROLINA, THOUGH DESCENDED FROM AFRICAN SLAVES, WERE NOT ONLY CITIZENS OF THEIR STATES BUT ALSO POSSESSED THE ELECTIVE FRANCHISE.
FATHER, THE *AUGUSTA CONSTITUTIONAL* DECLARES THAT "SOUTHERN OPINION UPON THE SUBJECT OF SLAVERY . . . IS NOW THE SUPREME LAW OF THE LAND."
AND SO IT IS!
Southerners exulted at the decision and hoped it would destroy the Republican Party.
Harriet and Dred Scott in 1857
But Republicans were energized, not discouraged.
LISTEN TO WHAT THE *CHICAGO TRIBUNE* SAYS: "THE REMEDY IS THE BALLOT BOX . . . LET THE NEXT PRESIDENT BE REPUBLICAN, AND 1860 WILL MARK AN ERA KINDRED WITH THAT OF 1776."
The Scotts won their freedom in May 1857, when Taylor Blow acquired them and promptly emancipated them. Dred died of tuberculosis less than two years later, and did not witness the cataclysmic aftermath of the Supreme Court decision that bore his name. After her husband's death, Harriet lived for another 18 years as a free woman.

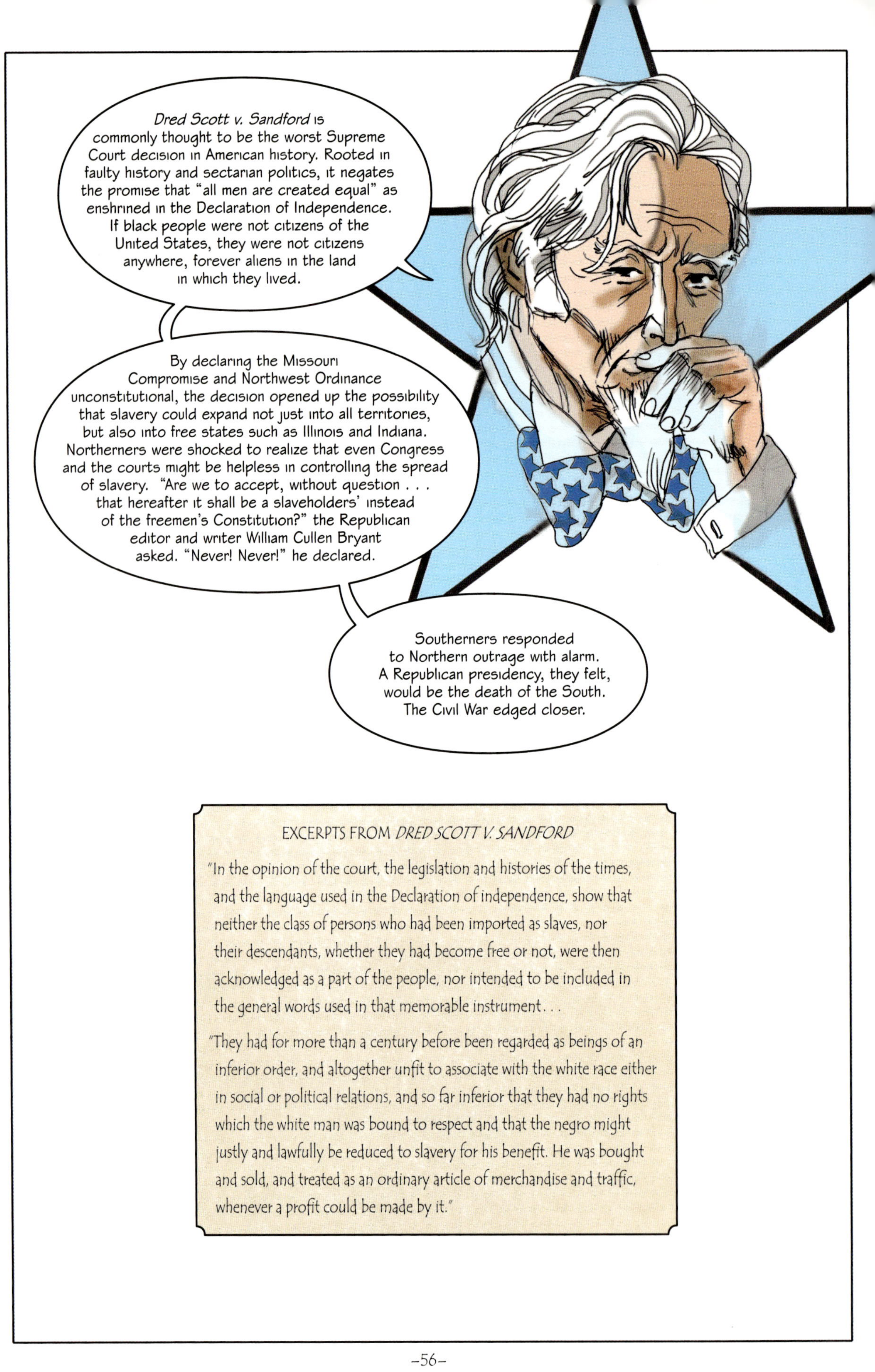
Dred Scott v. Sandford is commonly thought to be the worst Supreme Court decision in American history. Rooted in faulty history and sectarian politics, it negates the promise that "all men are created equal" as enshrined in the Declaration of Independence. If black people were not citizens of the United States, they were not citizens anywhere, forever aliens in the land in which they lived.
By declaring the Missouri Compromise and Northwest Ordinance unconstitutional, the decision opened up the possibility that slavery could expand not just into all territories, but also into free states such as Illinois and Indiana. Northerners were shocked to realize that even Congress and the courts might be helpless in controlling the spread of slavery. "Are we to accept, without question . . . that hereafter it shall be a slaveholders' instead of the freemen's Constitution?" the Republican editor and writer William Cullen Bryant asked. "Never! Never!" he declared.
Southerners responded to Northern outrage with alarm. A Republican presidency, they felt, would be the death of the South. The Civil War edged closer.

EXCERPTS FROM *DRED SCOTT V. SANDFORD*

"In the opinion of the court, the legislation and histories of the times, and the language used in the Declaration of independence, show that neither the class of persons who had been imported as slaves, nor their descendants, whether they had become free or not, were then acknowledged as a part of the people, nor intended to be included in the general words used in that memorable instrument. . .

"They had for more than a century before been regarded as beings of an inferior order, and altogether unfit to associate with the white race either in social or political relations, and so far inferior that they had no rights which the white man was bound to respect and that the negro might justly and lawfully be reduced to slavery for his benefit. He was bought and sold, and treated as an ordinary article of merchandise and traffic, whenever a profit could be made by it."

The "House Divided" Speech

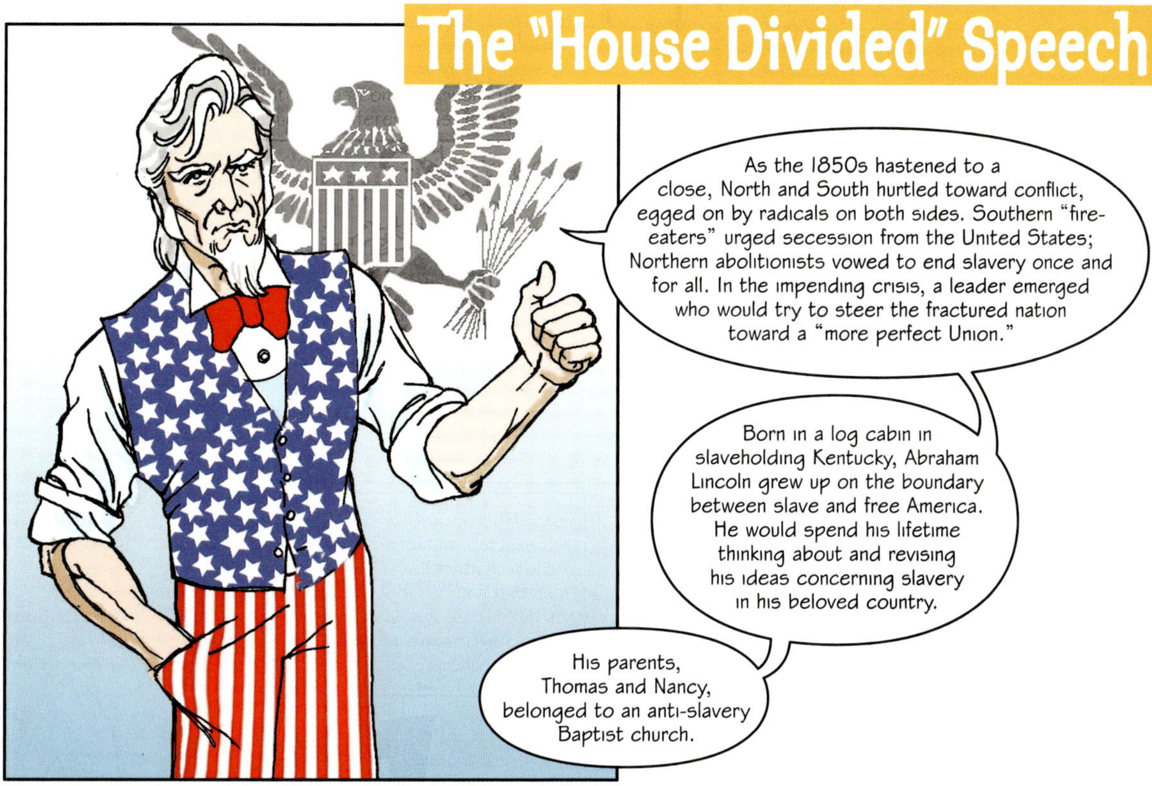
As the 1850s hastened to a close, North and South hurtled toward conflict, egged on by radicals on both sides. Southern "fire-eaters" urged secession from the United States; Northern abolitionists vowed to end slavery once and for all. In the impending crisis, a leader emerged who would try to steer the fractured nation toward a "more perfect Union."
Born in a log cabin in slaveholding Kentucky, Abraham Lincoln grew up on the boundary between slave and free America. He would spend his lifetime thinking about and revising his ideas concerning slavery in his beloved country.
His parents, Thomas and Nancy, belonged to an anti-slavery Baptist church.

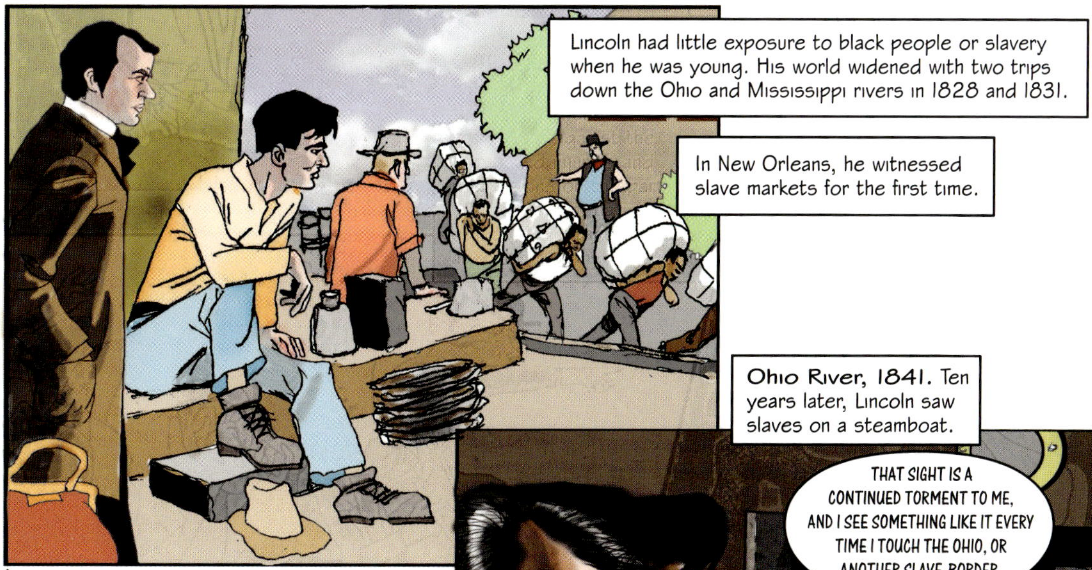
Lincoln had little exposure to black people or slavery when he was young. His world widened with two trips down the Ohio and Mississippi rivers in 1828 and 1831.
In New Orleans, he witnessed slave markets for the first time.

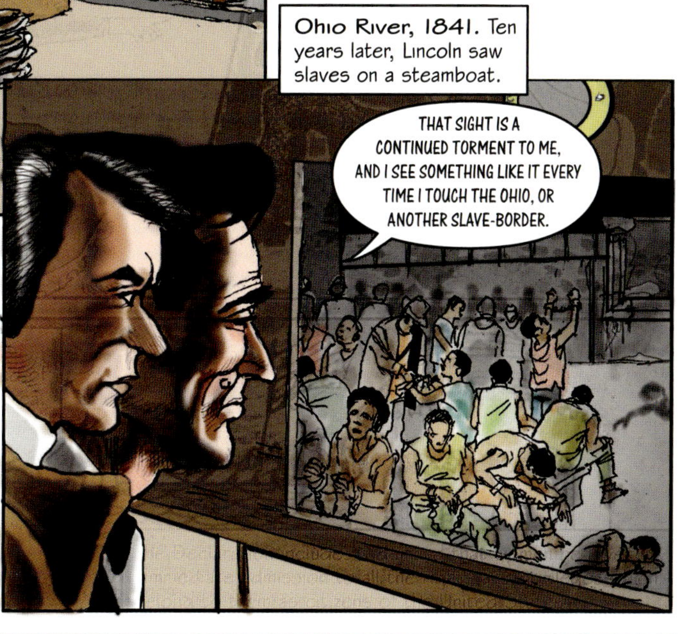
Ohio River, 1841. Ten years later, Lincoln saw slaves on a steamboat.
THAT SIGHT IS A CONTINUED TORMENT TO ME, AND I SEE SOMETHING LIKE IT EVERY TIME I TOUCH THE OHIO, OR ANOTHER SLAVE-BORDER.

In 1864, Lincoln would write, "I am naturally anti-slavery. If slavery is not wrong, nothing is wrong. I can not remember when I did not so think, and feel."

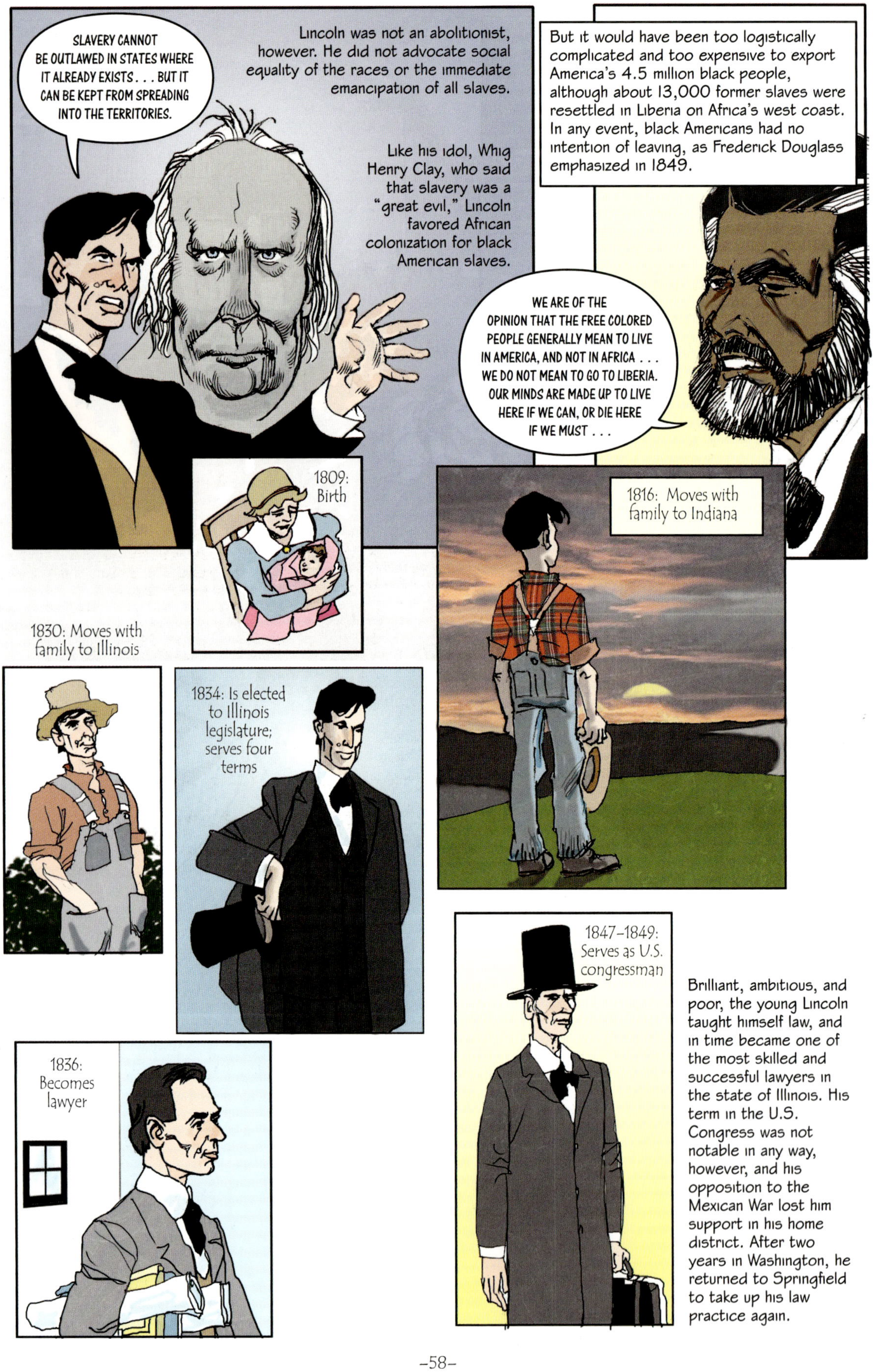
Lincoln was not an abolitionist, however. He did not advocate social equality of the races or the immediate emancipation of all slaves.
SLAVERY CANNOT BE OUTLAWED IN STATES WHERE IT ALREADY EXISTS . . . BUT IT CAN BE KEPT FROM SPREADING INTO THE TERRITORIES.
Like his idol, Whig Henry Clay, who said that slavery was a "great evil," Lincoln favored African colonization for black American slaves.
But it would have been too logistically complicated and too expensive to export America's 4.5 million black people, although about 13,000 former slaves were resettled in Liberia on Africa's west coast. In any event, black Americans had no intention of leaving, as Frederick Douglass emphasized in 1849.
WE ARE OF THE OPINION THAT THE FREE COLORED PEOPLE GENERALLY MEAN TO LIVE IN AMERICA, AND NOT IN AFRICA . . . WE DO NOT MEAN TO GO TO LIBERIA. OUR MINDS ARE MADE UP TO LIVE HERE IF WE CAN, OR DIE HERE IF WE MUST . . .
1809: Birth
1816: Moves with family to Indiana
1830: Moves with family to Illinois
1834: Is elected to Illinois legislature; serves four terms
1836: Becomes lawyer
1847–1849: Serves as U.S. congressman
Brilliant, ambitious, and poor, the young Lincoln taught himself law, and in time became one of the most skilled and successful lawyers in the state of Illinois. His term in the U.S. Congress was not notable in any way, however, and his opposition to the Mexican War lost him support in his home district. After two years in Washington, he returned to Springfield to take up his law practice again.

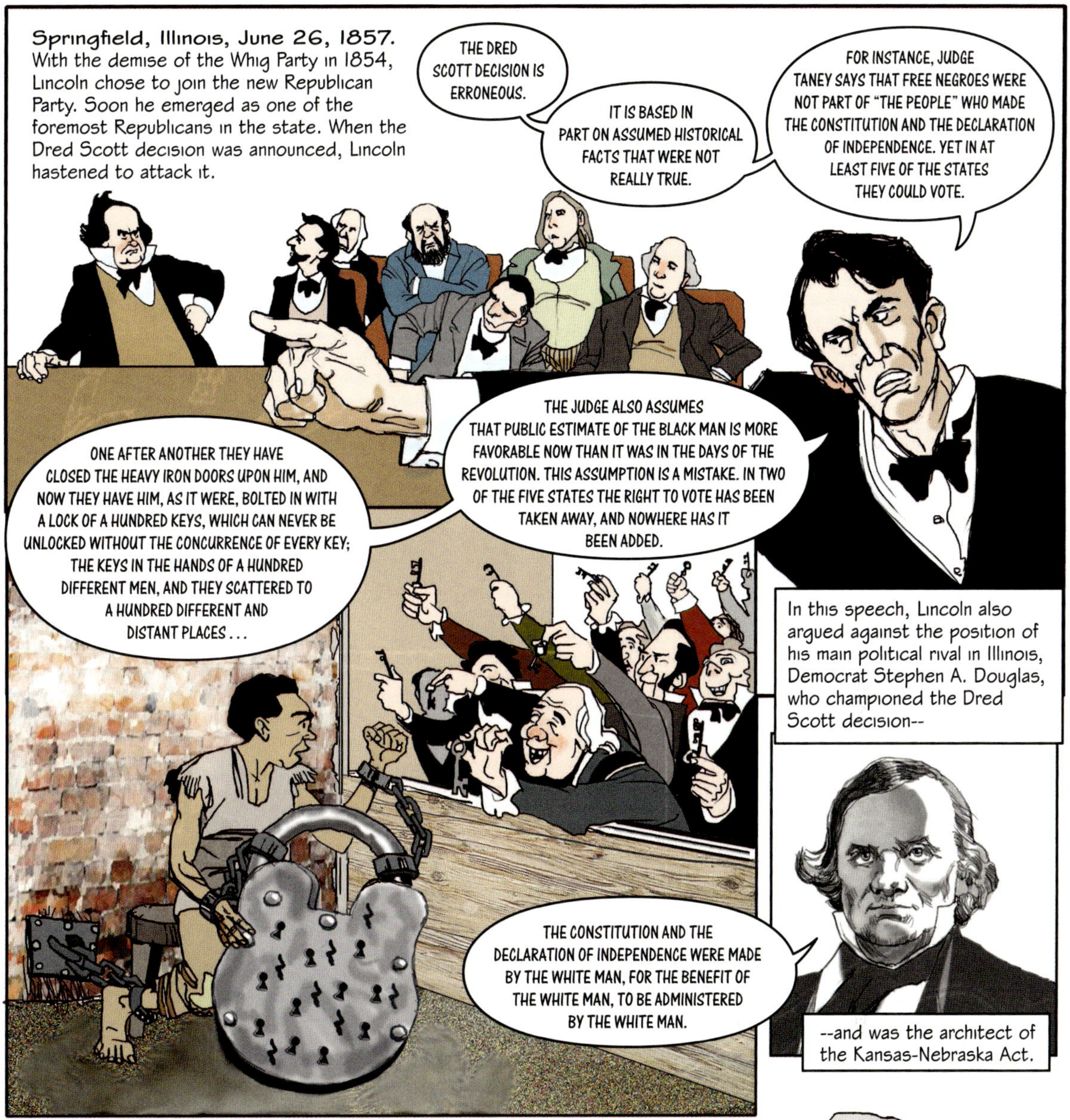
Springfield, Illinois, June 26, 1857. With the demise of the Whig Party in 1854, Lincoln chose to join the new Republican Party. Soon he emerged as one of the foremost Republicans in the state. When the Dred Scott decision was announced, Lincoln hastened to attack it.
THE DRED SCOTT DECISION IS ERRONEOUS.
IT IS BASED IN PART ON ASSUMED HISTORICAL FACTS THAT WERE NOT REALLY TRUE.
FOR INSTANCE, JUDGE TANEY SAYS THAT FREE NEGROES WERE NOT PART OF "THE PEOPLE" WHO MADE THE CONSTITUTION AND THE DECLARATION OF INDEPENDENCE. YET IN AT LEAST FIVE OF THE STATES THEY COULD VOTE.
THE JUDGE ALSO ASSUMES THAT PUBLIC ESTIMATE OF THE BLACK MAN IS MORE FAVORABLE NOW THAN IT WAS IN THE DAYS OF THE REVOLUTION. THIS ASSUMPTION IS A MISTAKE. IN TWO OF THE FIVE STATES THE RIGHT TO VOTE HAS BEEN TAKEN AWAY, AND NOWHERE HAS IT BEEN ADDED.
ONE AFTER ANOTHER THEY HAVE CLOSED THE HEAVY IRON DOORS UPON HIM, AND NOW THEY HAVE HIM, AS IT WERE, BOLTED IN WITH A LOCK OF A HUNDRED KEYS, WHICH CAN NEVER BE UNLOCKED WITHOUT THE CONCURRENCE OF EVERY KEY; THE KEYS IN THE HANDS OF A HUNDRED DIFFERENT MEN, AND THEY SCATTERED TO A HUNDRED DIFFERENT AND DISTANT PLACES . . .
In this speech, Lincoln also argued against the position of his main political rival in Illinois, Democrat Stephen A. Douglas, who championed the Dred Scott decision--
THE CONSTITUTION AND THE DECLARATION OF INDEPENDENCE WERE MADE BY THE WHITE MAN, FOR THE BENEFIT OF THE WHITE MAN, TO BE ADMINISTERED BY THE WHITE MAN.
--and was the architect of the Kansas-Nebraska Act.

Lincoln said, "In the hands of Taney and Douglas the Declaration . . . is assailed and sneered at . . . and torn till, if its framers could rise from their graves, they could not at all recognize it."

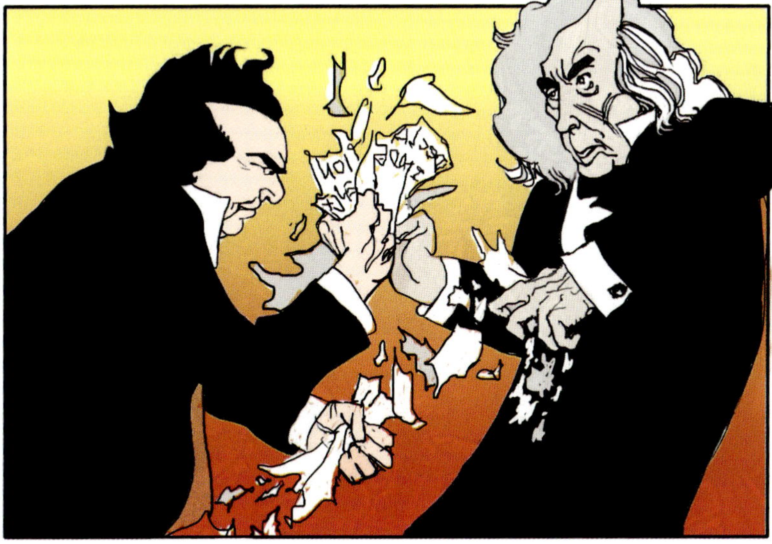

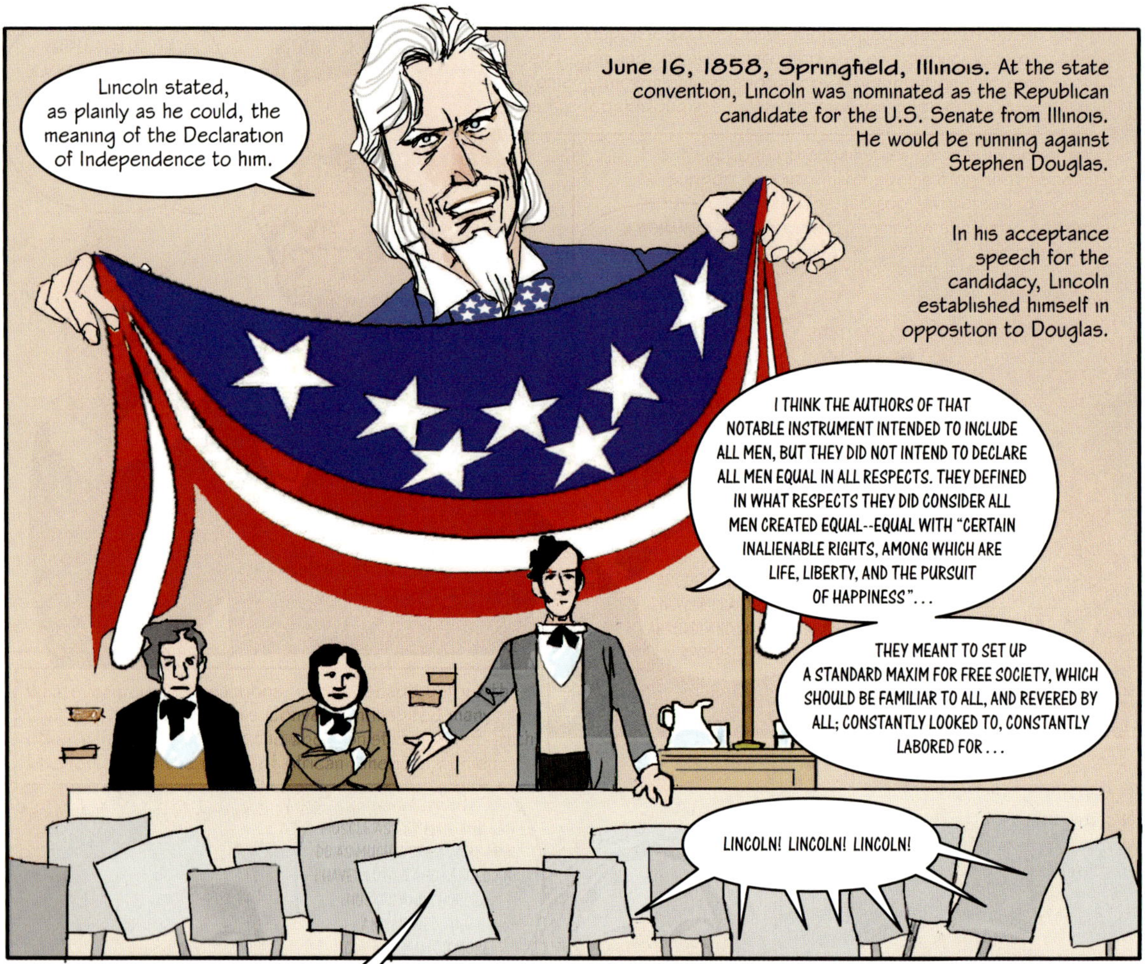
Lincoln stated, as plainly as he could, the meaning of the Declaration of Independence to him.
June 16, 1858, Springfield, Illinois. At the state convention, Lincoln was nominated as the Republican candidate for the U.S. Senate from Illinois. He would be running against Stephen Douglas.
In his acceptance speech for the candidacy, Lincoln established himself in opposition to Douglas.
I THINK THE AUTHORS OF THAT NOTABLE INSTRUMENT INTENDED TO INCLUDE ALL MEN, BUT THEY DID NOT INTEND TO DECLARE ALL MEN EQUAL IN ALL RESPECTS. THEY DEFINED IN WHAT RESPECTS THEY DID CONSIDER ALL MEN CREATED EQUAL--EQUAL WITH "CERTAIN INALIENABLE RIGHTS, AMONG WHICH ARE LIFE, LIBERTY, AND THE PURSUIT OF HAPPINESS"...
THEY MEANT TO SET UP A STANDARD MAXIM FOR FREE SOCIETY, WHICH SHOULD BE FAMILIAR TO ALL, AND REVERED BY ALL; CONSTANTLY LOOKED TO, CONSTANTLY LABORED FOR...
LINCOLN! LINCOLN! LINCOLN!

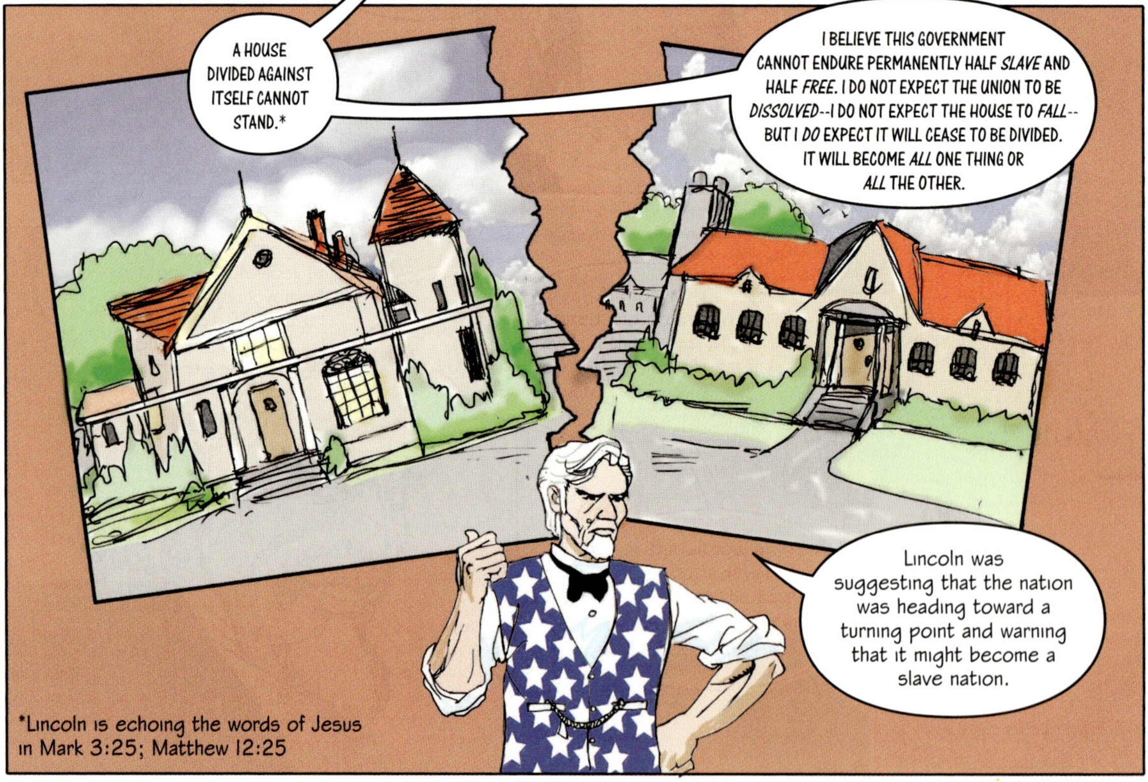
A HOUSE DIVIDED AGAINST ITSELF CANNOT STAND.*
I BELIEVE THIS GOVERNMENT CANNOT ENDURE PERMANENTLY HALF *SLAVE* AND HALF *FREE*. I DO NOT EXPECT THE UNION TO BE *DISSOLVED*--I DO NOT EXPECT THE HOUSE TO *FALL*--BUT I *DO* EXPECT IT WILL CEASE TO BE DIVIDED. IT WILL BECOME *ALL* ONE THING OR *ALL* THE OTHER.
Lincoln was suggesting that the nation was heading toward a turning point and warning that it might become a slave nation.
*Lincoln is echoing the words of Jesus in Mark 3:25; Matthew 12:25

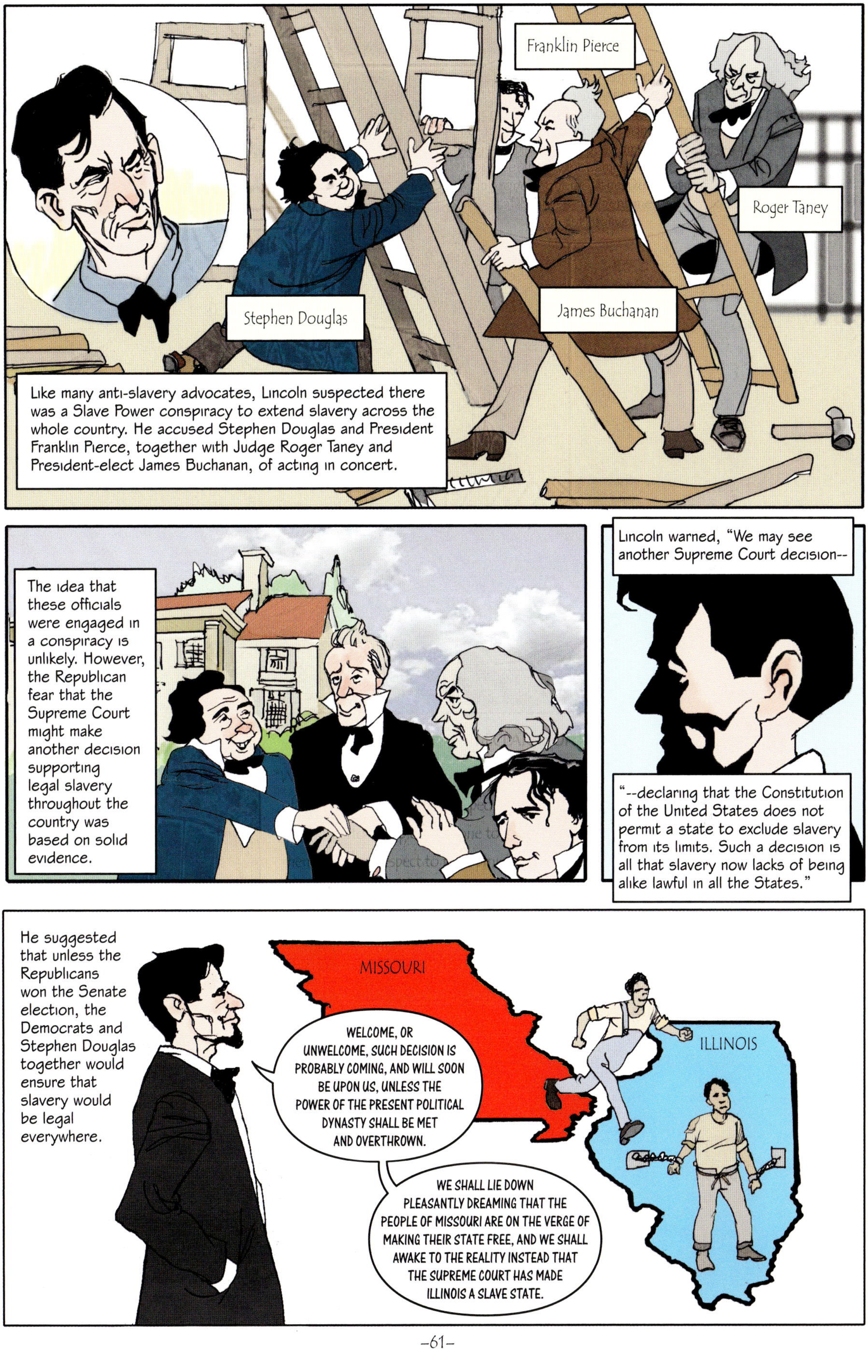

Franklin Pierce
Roger Taney
Stephen Douglas
James Buchanan
Like many anti-slavery advocates, Lincoln suspected there was a Slave Power conspiracy to extend slavery across the whole country. He accused Stephen Douglas and President Franklin Pierce, together with Judge Roger Taney and President-elect James Buchanan, of acting in concert.
The idea that these officials were engaged in a conspiracy is unlikely. However, the Republican fear that the Supreme Court might make another decision supporting legal slavery throughout the country was based on solid evidence.
Lincoln warned, "We may see another Supreme Court decision--
"--declaring that the Constitution of the United States does not permit a state to exclude slavery from its limits. Such a decision is all that slavery now lacks of being alike lawful in all the States."
He suggested that unless the Republicans won the Senate election, the Democrats and Stephen Douglas together would ensure that slavery would be legal everywhere.
MISSOURI
ILLINOIS
WELCOME, OR UNWELCOME, SUCH DECISION IS PROBABLY COMING, AND WILL SOON BE UPON US, UNLESS THE POWER OF THE PRESENT POLITICAL DYNASTY SHALL BE MET AND OVERTHROWN.
WE SHALL LIE DOWN PLEASANTLY DREAMING THAT THE PEOPLE OF MISSOURI ARE ON THE VERGE OF MAKING THEIR STATE FREE, AND WE SHALL AWAKE TO THE REALITY INSTEAD THAT THE SUPREME COURT HAS MADE ILLINOIS A SLAVE STATE.

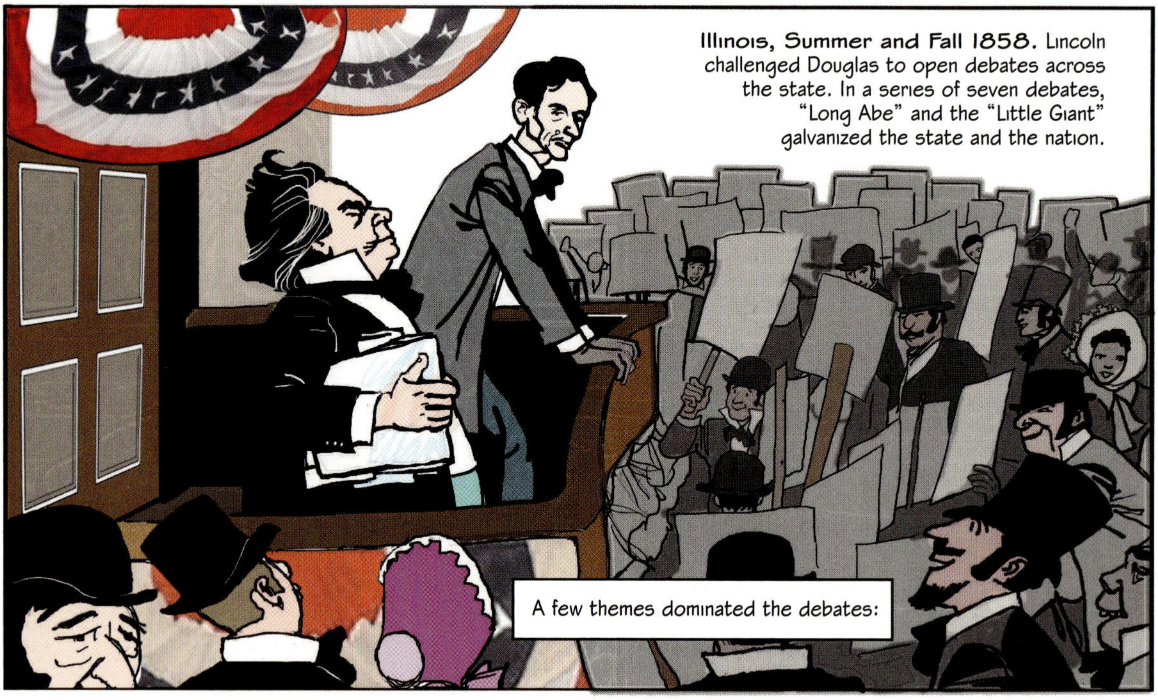
Illinois, Summer and Fall 1858. Lincoln challenged Douglas to open debates across the state. In a series of seven debates, "Long Abe" and the "Little Giant" galvanized the state and the nation.
A few themes dominated the debates:

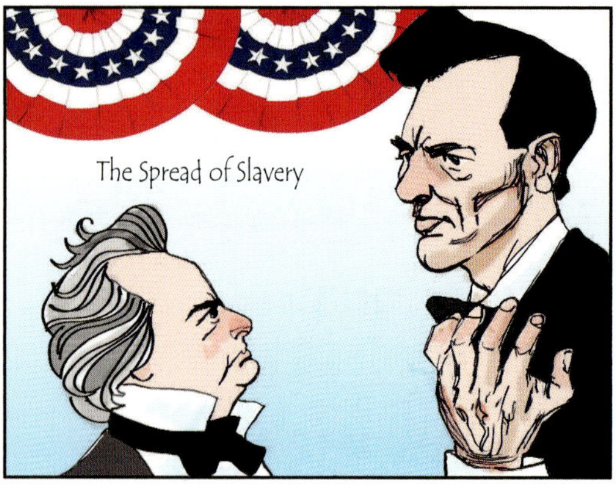
The Spread of Slavery

"Can the people of a United States Territory in any lawful way exclude slavery from their limits?" Lincoln asked his opponent.

"If the people of the Territory are opposed to slavery," Douglas countered, "they will elect members of the legislature who will adopt unfriendly legislation to it."

The topic then turned to racial equality. Douglas accused Lincoln and other so-called Black Republicans of advocating total social and political equality between blacks and whites, and interracial marriage.

"The Negro must always occupy an inferior position!" Douglas said.

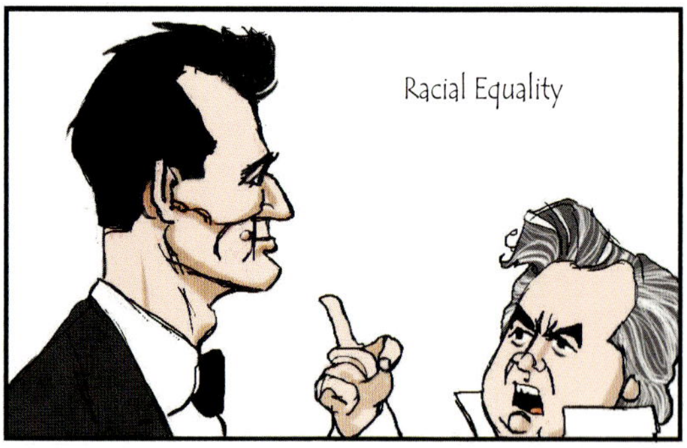
Racial Equality

Lincoln denied that he favored total equality between black and white people, but continued to support the idea that all men were entitled to the fruits of their labors:

"In the right to eat the bread, which his own hand earns, the black man is my equal and the equal of Judge Douglas and the equal of every living man."

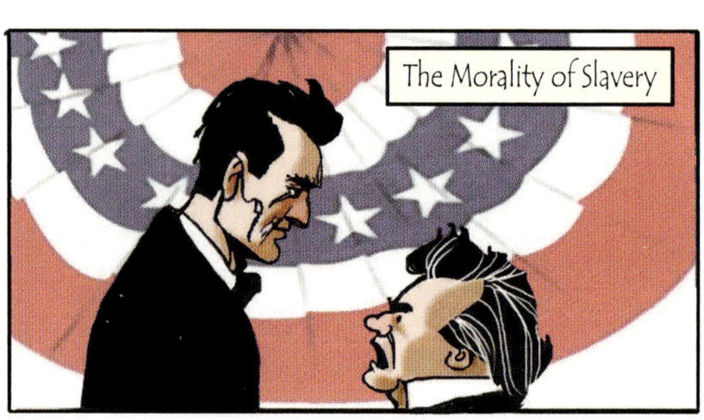
The Morality of Slavery

Douglas then said that the nation could continue to exist half slave and half free, as it had since its founding: "I don't care whether people vote up or vote down on slavery."

Lincoln strongly disagreed. "It is the eternal struggle between these two principles--right and wrong--throughout the world. The one is the common right of humanity, the other the divine right of kings. It is the same spirit that says, 'You toil and work and earn bread, and I'll eat it.'"

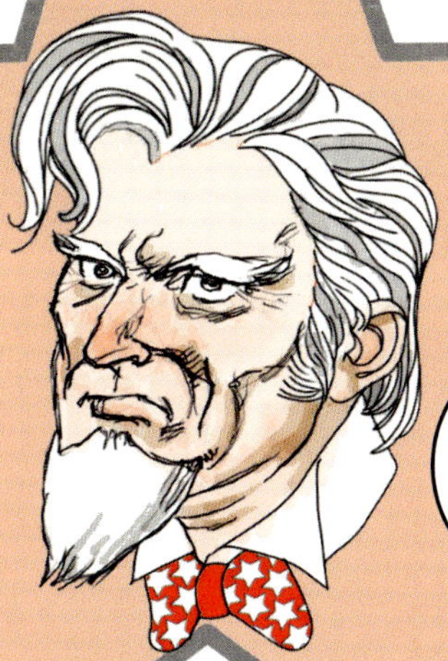
Historians have generally agreed that Lincoln won the debates, though he did not win the election. Votes in the state legislature (victory was not determined by direct popular vote) gave the victory to Douglas. But Lincoln's reputation as a moderate, eloquent Republican was secure. Throughout the North, the Republicans made great gains in the 1858 elections, at both the federal and state levels.
Harpers Ferry, Virginia, October 16, 1859. The nation was horrified when the fervent abolitionist John Brown led an armed attack of 21 men on the federal armory at Harpers Ferry. He was attempting to ignite a slave uprising. Instead, U.S. Army colonel Robert E. Lee and a company of U.S. Marines captured Brown, killing ten of his men.

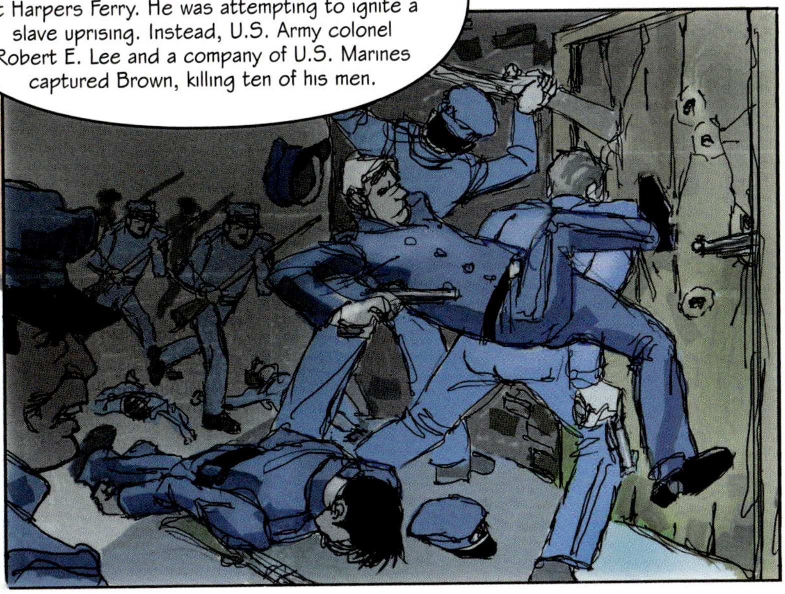

December 2, 1859. John Brown was unapologetic. Before being hanged for treason and murder, he wrote prophetically:

"I, John Brown, am now quite certain that the crimes of this guilty land will never be purged away but with blood. I had, as I now think, vainly flattered myself that without very much bloodshed it might be done."

Remembered as a martyr in much of the North, Brown was reviled in the South. Lincoln himself said that he agreed with Brown "in thinking slavery wrong" but could not excuse him for "violence, bloodshed, and treason."

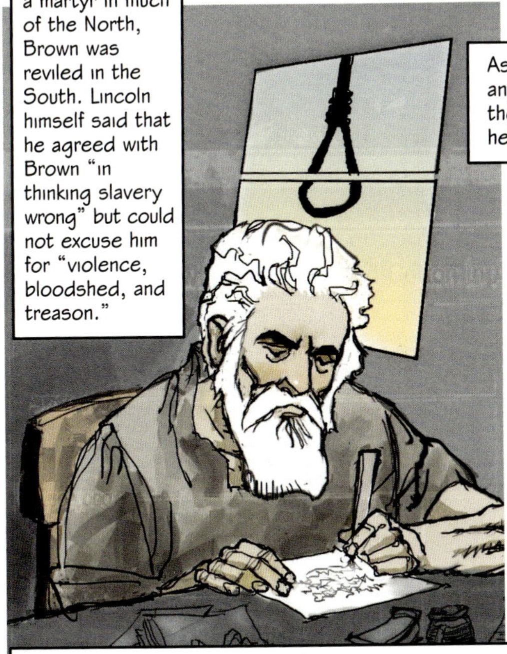

As Southern state legislatures funded militias to protect against any further abolitionist insurrections, secessionist fire-eaters beat the drums of disunion. In this incendiary environment, the nation held the 1860 presidential primaries.

The Republicans nominated Lincoln. The Democrats were torn between Southern pro-slavery and Northern popular-sovereignty factions, with J. C. Breckinridge and Stephen Douglas, respectively, being nominated. John Bell, a Tennessee senator and former secretary of war, was the nominee for the newly formed Constitutional Union.

Abraham Lincoln won the presidency, but as 1860 came to a close, dark times lay ahead, months before the newly elected president was to take office.

As Lincoln had foretold, the "house" of the United States was soon to be divided.

ELECTION RESULTS 1860

	ELECTORAL VOTE	POPULAR VOTE (%)
Abraham Lincoln (Republican)	180	1,865,593 (39.8)
J. C. Breckinridge	72	848,356 (18.1)
John Bell	39	592,906 (12.6)
Stephen Douglas	12	1,382.713 (29.5)

Abraham Lincoln delivered his "House Divided" speech at the start of his campaign for the U.S. Senate against Democrat Stephen A. Douglas. He wanted to stress his distance from Douglas, whose "popular sovereignty" doctrine would have allowed the extension of slavery into new states. Lincoln warned that the Dred Scott decision had demonstrated that the time for compromise was past; a united America could not and would not remain "half slave and half free."

EXCERPTS FROM ABRAHAM LINCOLN'S "A HOUSE DIVIDED" SPEECH

"Mr. President and Gentlemen of the Convention.

"If we could first know where we are, and *whither* we are tending, we could then better judge *what* to do, and how to do it. We are now far into the *fifth* year, since a policy was initiated with the *avowed* object and *confident* promise of putting an end to slavery agitation. Under the operation of that policy, that agitation has not only, *not* ceased, but has *constantly augmented*... In my opinion, it *will* not cease, until a *crisis* shall have been reached, and passed.

"A house divided against itself cannot stand." I believe this government cannot endure permanently half *slave* and half *free*. I do not expect the Union to be *dissolved*—I do not expect the house to *fall*—but I *do* expect it will cease to be divided. It will become *all* one thing or *all* the other. Either the *opponents* of slavery will arrest the further spread of it, and place it where the public mind shall rest in the belief that it is in the course of ultimate extinction; or its *advocates* will push it forward till it shall become alike lawful in *all* the States— *old* as well as *new*—*North* as well as *South*."

The Emancipation Proclamation

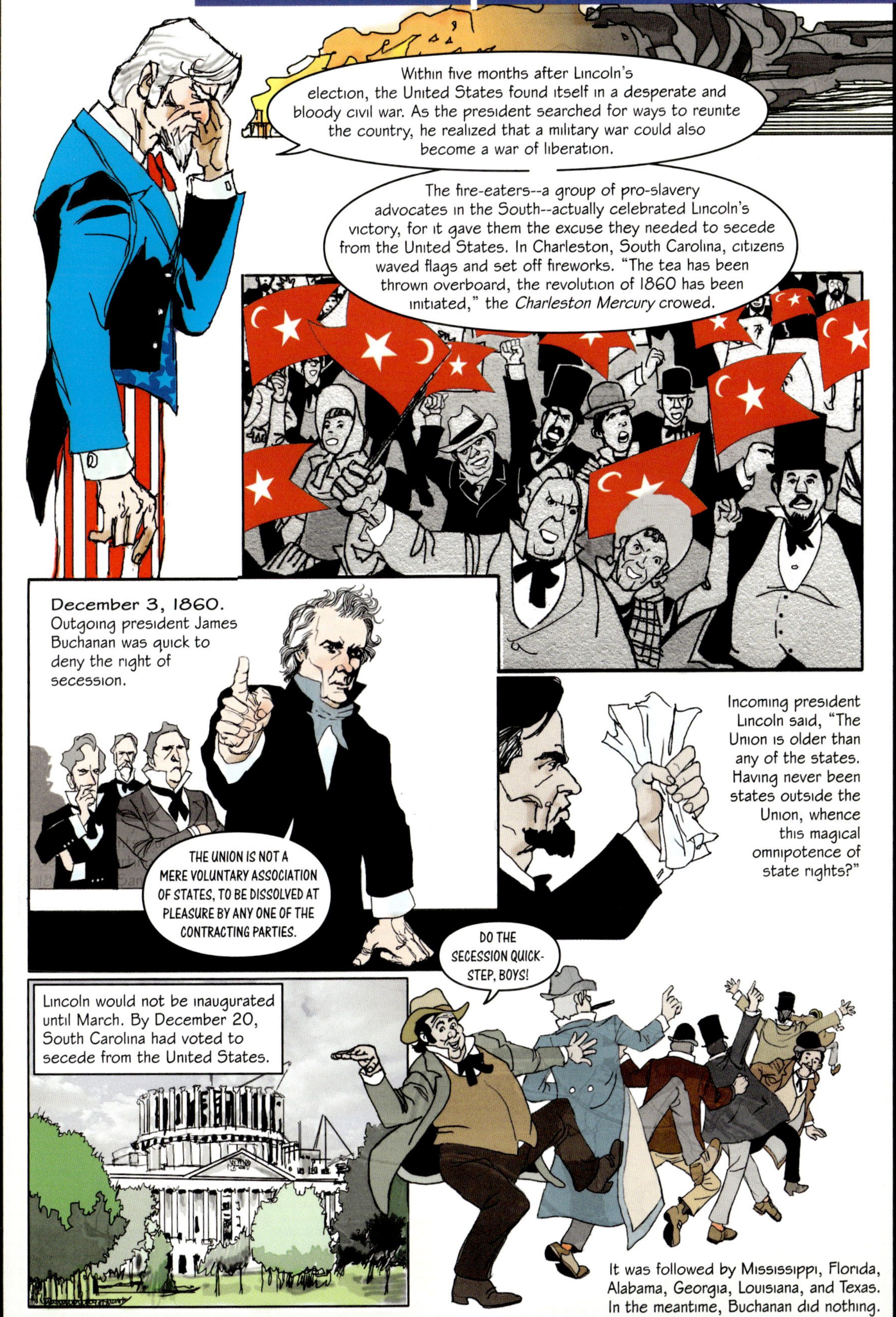
Within five months after Lincoln's election, the United States found itself in a desperate and bloody civil war. As the president searched for ways to reunite the country, he realized that a military war could also become a war of liberation.
The fire-eaters--a group of pro-slavery advocates in the South--actually celebrated Lincoln's victory, for it gave them the excuse they needed to secede from the United States. In Charleston, South Carolina, citizens waved flags and set off fireworks. "The tea has been thrown overboard, the revolution of 1860 has been initiated," the *Charleston Mercury* crowed.
December 3, 1860. Outgoing president James Buchanan was quick to deny the right of secession.
THE UNION IS NOT A MERE VOLUNTARY ASSOCIATION OF STATES, TO BE DISSOLVED AT PLEASURE BY ANY ONE OF THE CONTRACTING PARTIES.
Incoming president Lincoln said, "The Union is older than any of the states. Having never been states outside the Union, whence this magical omnipotence of state rights?"
Lincoln would not be inaugurated until March. By December 20, South Carolina had voted to secede from the United States.
DO THE SECESSION QUICK-STEP, BOYS!
It was followed by Mississippi, Florida, Alabama, Georgia, Louisiana, and Texas. In the meantime, Buchanan did nothing.

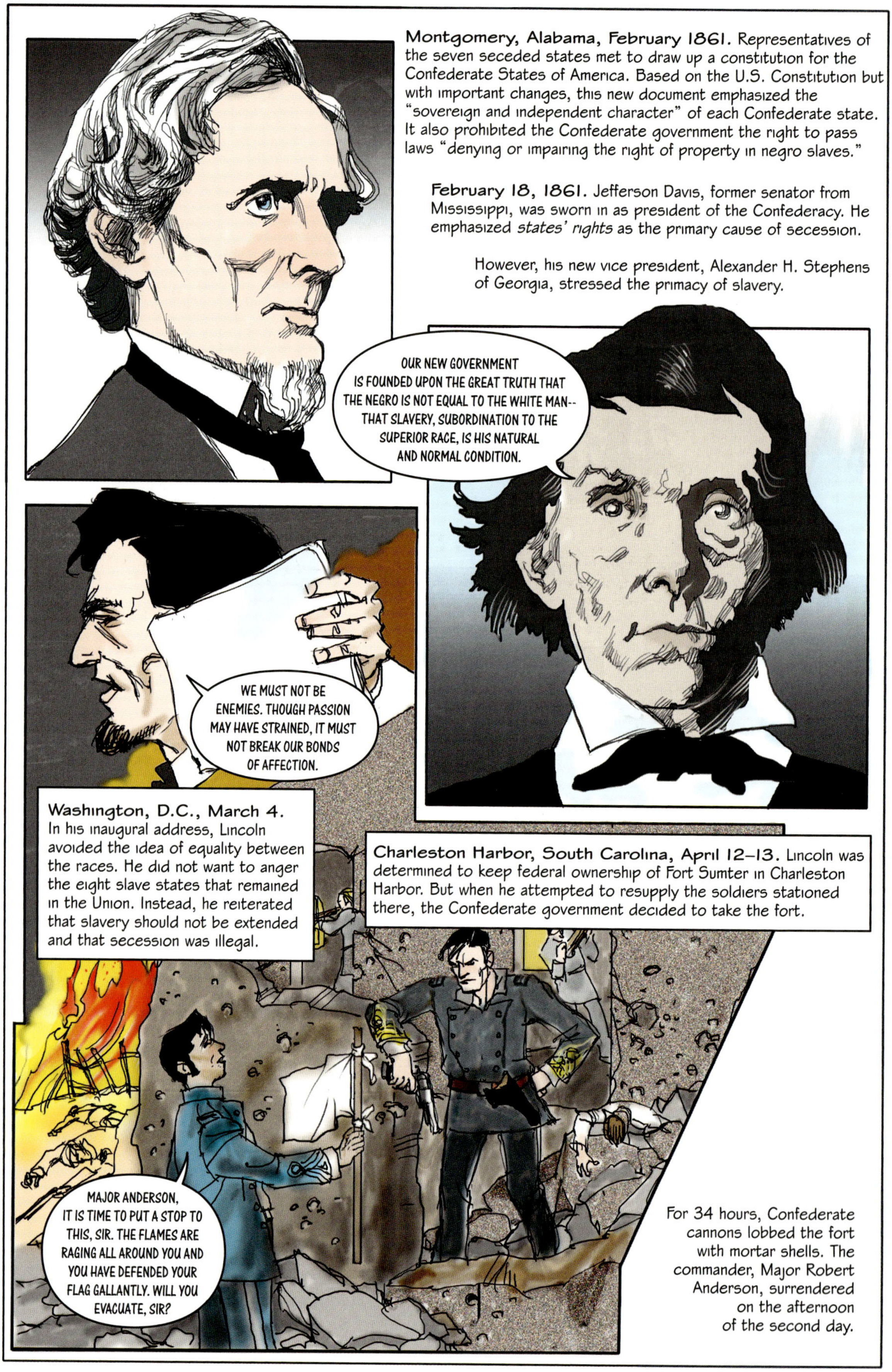
Montgomery, Alabama, February 1861. Representatives of the seven seceded states met to draw up a constitution for the Confederate States of America. Based on the U.S. Constitution but with important changes, this new document emphasized the "sovereign and independent character" of each Confederate state. It also prohibited the Confederate government the right to pass laws "denying or impairing the right of property in negro slaves."
February 18, 1861. Jefferson Davis, former senator from Mississippi, was sworn in as president of the Confederacy. He emphasized states' rights as the primary cause of secession.
However, his new vice president, Alexander H. Stephens of Georgia, stressed the primacy of slavery.
OUR NEW GOVERNMENT IS FOUNDED UPON THE GREAT TRUTH THAT THE NEGRO IS NOT EQUAL TO THE WHITE MAN-- THAT SLAVERY, SUBORDINATION TO THE SUPERIOR RACE, IS HIS NATURAL AND NORMAL CONDITION.
Washington, D.C., March 4. In his inaugural address, Lincoln avoided the idea of equality between the races. He did not want to anger the eight slave states that remained in the Union. Instead, he reiterated that slavery should not be extended and that secession was illegal.
WE MUST NOT BE ENEMIES. THOUGH PASSION MAY HAVE STRAINED, IT MUST NOT BREAK OUR BONDS OF AFFECTION.
Charleston Harbor, South Carolina, April 12–13. Lincoln was determined to keep federal ownership of Fort Sumter in Charleston Harbor. But when he attempted to resupply the soldiers stationed there, the Confederate government decided to take the fort.
MAJOR ANDERSON, IT IS TIME TO PUT A STOP TO THIS, SIR. THE FLAMES ARE RAGING ALL AROUND YOU AND YOU HAVE DEFENDED YOUR FLAG GALLANTLY. WILL YOU EVACUATE, SIR?
For 34 hours, Confederate cannons lobbed the fort with mortar shells. The commander, Major Robert Anderson, surrendered on the afternoon of the second day.

The consequences of the fall of Fort Sumter were immediate. First, in response to Lincoln's call for troops, 75,000 men enlisted in state militias across the North. Second, Virginia, Arkansas, Tennessee, and North Carolina seceded and joined the Confederacy. That left Delaware, Maryland, Kentucky, and Missouri as border states with populations that narrowly supported the Union--but maintained slavery. The western part of Virginia joined the Union as West Virginia in 1863.

WASHINGTON TERRITORY
DAKOTA TERRITORY
OREGON
MINN.
WIS.
MICH.
N.Y.
VT.
ME.
N.H.
MASS.
R.I.
CONN.
PA.
N.J.
DEL.
MD.
IOWA
NEBRASKA TERRITORY
NEVADA TERR.
UTAH TERRITORY
COLORADO TERRITORY
KANSAS
MO.
ILL.
IND.
OHIO
W.VA.
KY.
VA.
N.C.
TENN.
CALIF.
NEW MEXICO TERRITORY
INDIAN TERRITORY
ARK.
S.C.
MISS.
ALA.
GA.
TEXAS
LA.
FLA.
Union states
Confederate states
Border states. West Virginia became a state in 1863.

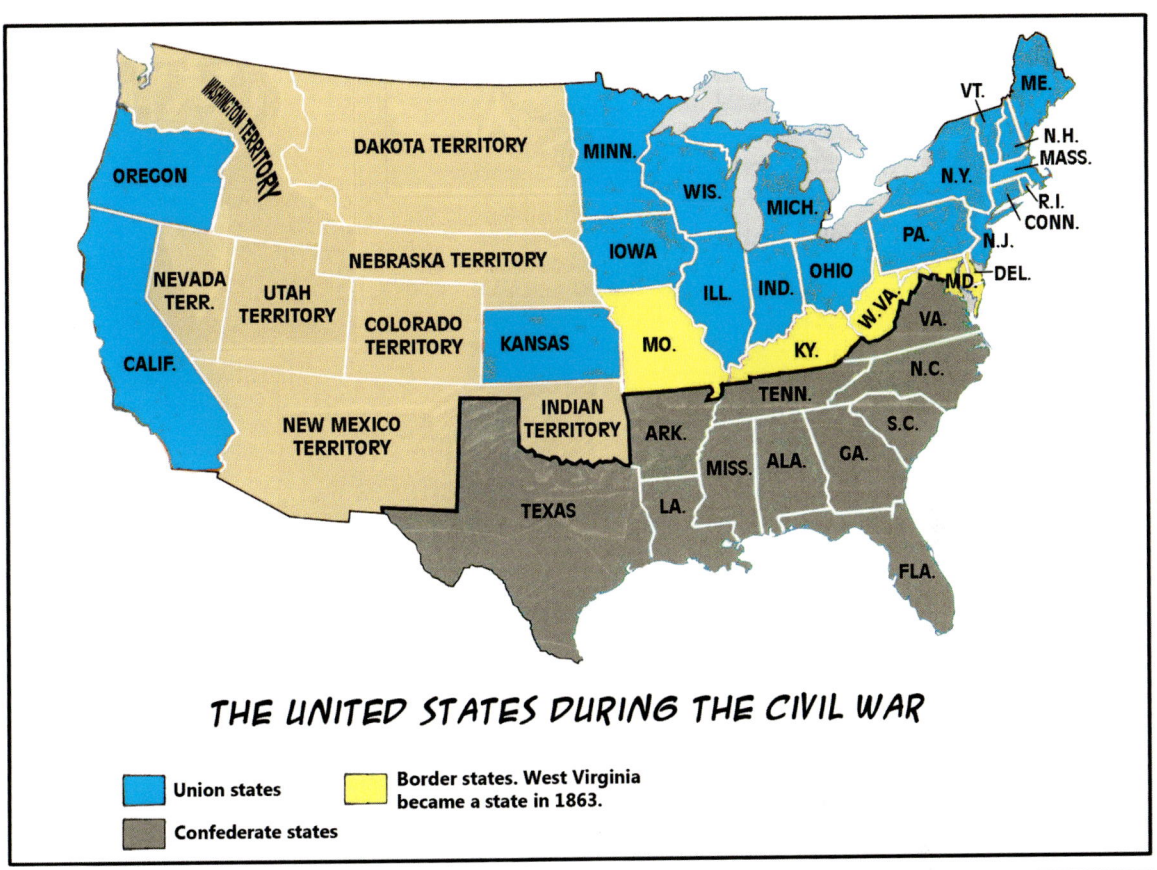

THE UNITED STATES DURING THE CIVIL WAR

THE NORTH	THE SOUTH
23 states	11 states
Pop. 22 million	Pop. 9 million
0.5 million slaves	3.5 million slaves
2 million in military	Less than 1 million in military
2/3 of railroads	1 train
9/10 of manufacturing	1 factory

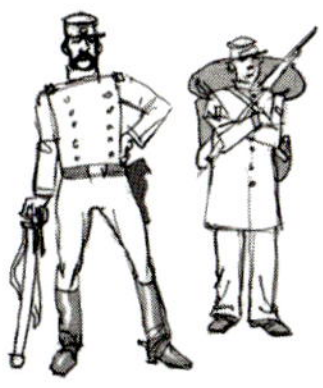

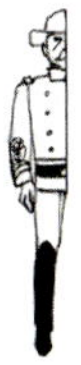

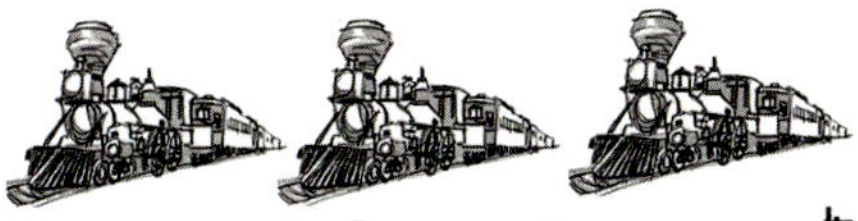

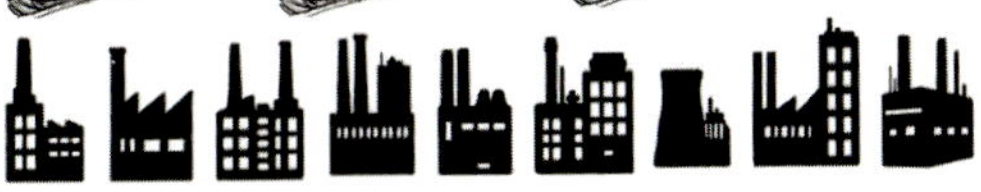

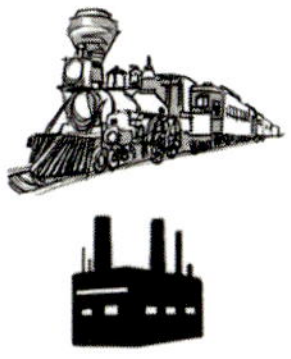

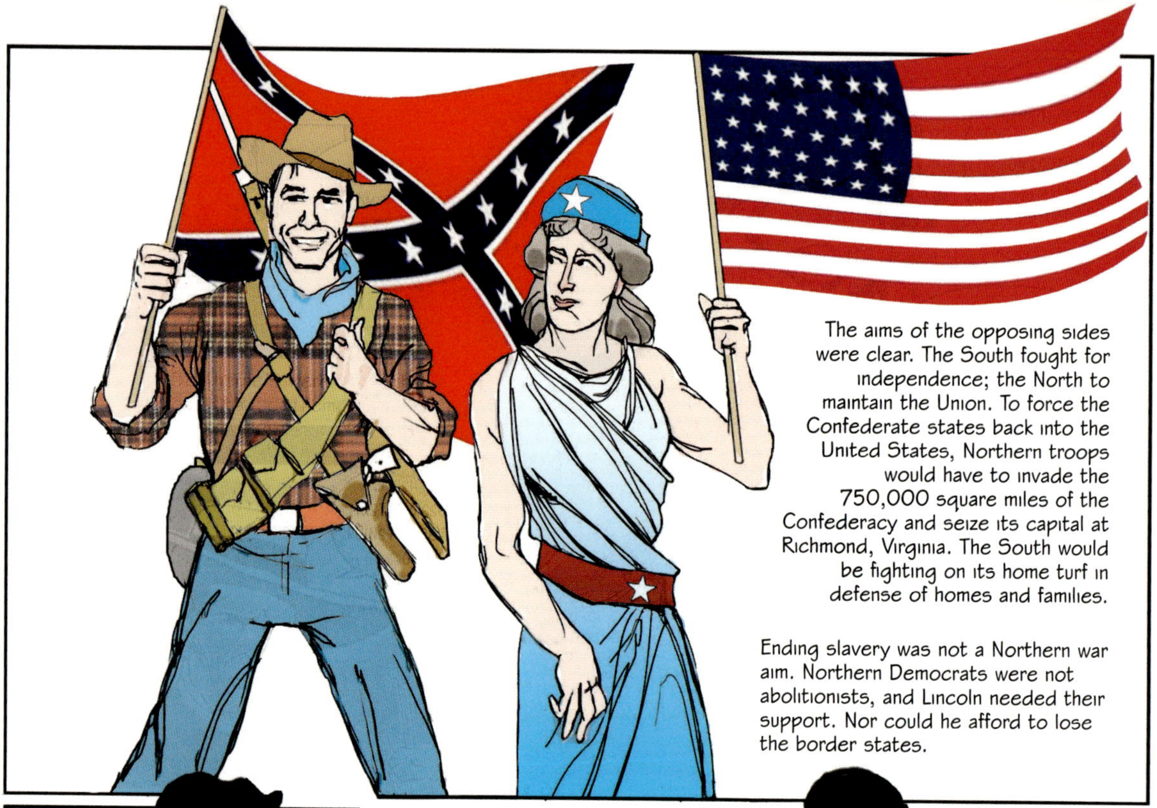

The aims of the opposing sides were clear. The South fought for independence; the North to maintain the Union. To force the Confederate states back into the United States, Northern troops would have to invade the 750,000 square miles of the Confederacy and seize its capital at Richmond, Virginia. The South would be fighting on its home turf in defense of homes and families.

Ending slavery was not a Northern war aim. Northern Democrats were not abolitionists, and Lincoln needed their support. Nor could he afford to lose the border states.

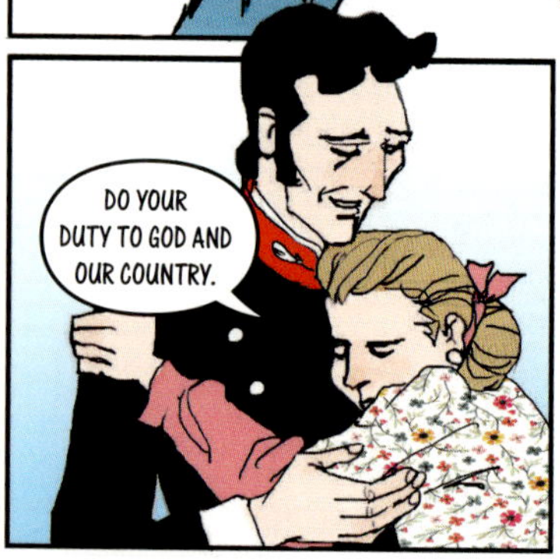
DO YOUR DUTY TO GOD AND OUR COUNTRY.

Each side had supreme confidence in its soldiers. Each side expected a quick victory.

Everyone was wrong. In July, the Union Army advanced to Manassas, Virginia, to a little creek called Bull Run. Spectators from Washington piled their carriages high with picnic baskets and set out for what they believed would be an entertaining afternoon.

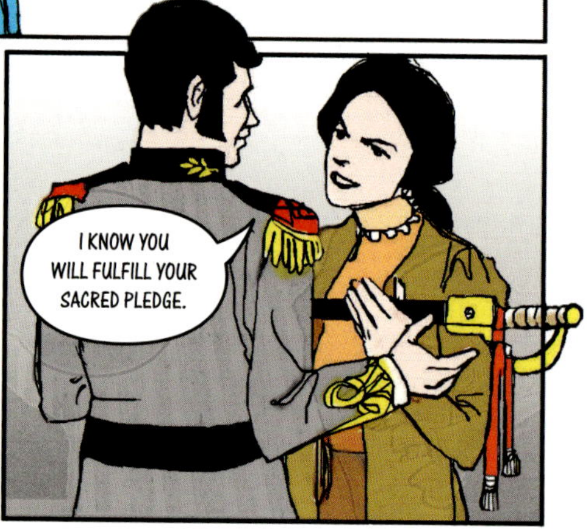
I KNOW YOU WILL FULFILL YOUR SACRED PLEDGE.

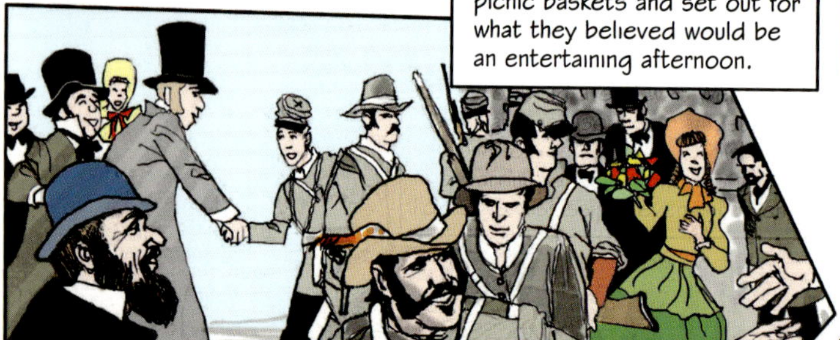

Inexperienced but resolute, the soldiers met in the first big battle of the war. At first, the Union offensive looked as if it might be successful.

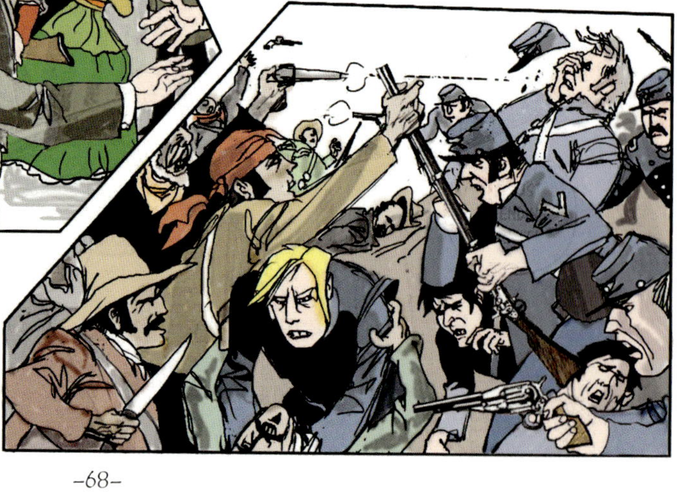

But when the Confederates counterattacked with fresh troops, the Northerners fell back and ordered a retreat.

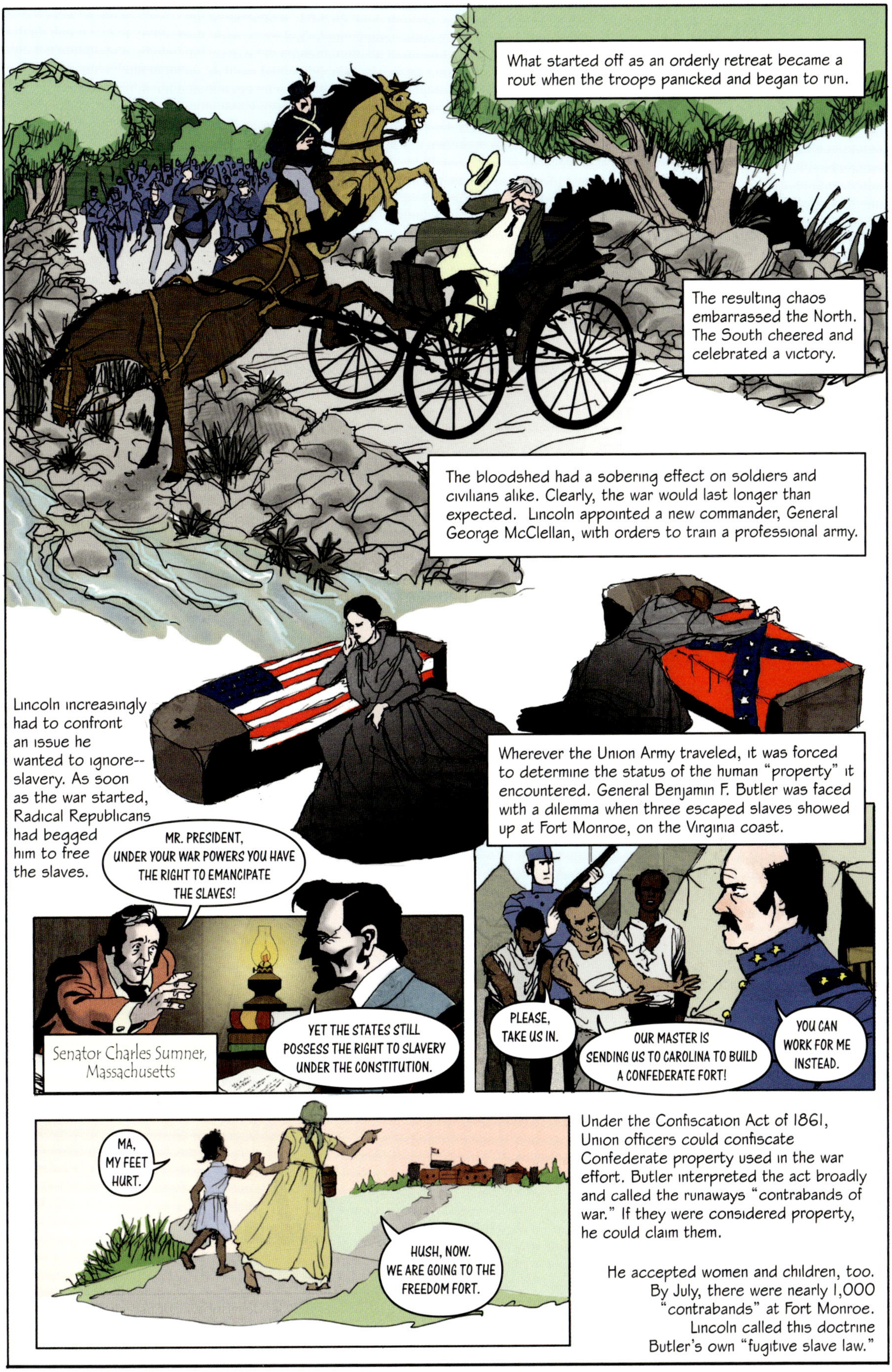
What started off as an orderly retreat became a rout when the troops panicked and began to run.
The resulting chaos embarrassed the North. The South cheered and celebrated a victory.
The bloodshed had a sobering effect on soldiers and civilians alike. Clearly, the war would last longer than expected. Lincoln appointed a new commander, General George McClellan, with orders to train a professional army.
Lincoln increasingly had to confront an issue he wanted to ignore--slavery. As soon as the war started, Radical Republicans had begged him to free the slaves.
MR. PRESIDENT, UNDER YOUR WAR POWERS YOU HAVE THE RIGHT TO EMANCIPATE THE SLAVES!
Senator Charles Sumner, Massachusetts
YET THE STATES STILL POSSESS THE RIGHT TO SLAVERY UNDER THE CONSTITUTION.
Wherever the Union Army traveled, it was forced to determine the status of the human "property" it encountered. General Benjamin F. Butler was faced with a dilemma when three escaped slaves showed up at Fort Monroe, on the Virginia coast.
PLEASE, TAKE US IN.
OUR MASTER IS SENDING US TO CAROLINA TO BUILD A CONFEDERATE FORT!
YOU CAN WORK FOR ME INSTEAD.
MA, MY FEET HURT.
HUSH, NOW. WE ARE GOING TO THE FREEDOM FORT.
Under the Confiscation Act of 1861, Union officers could confiscate Confederate property used in the war effort. Butler interpreted the act broadly and called the runaways "contrabands of war." If they were considered property, he could claim them.
He accepted women and children, too. By July, there were nearly 1,000 "contrabands" at Fort Monroe. Lincoln called this doctrine Butler's own "fugitive slave law."

The actual Fugitive Slave Law, however, had never been overturned, and some Union commanders continued to return escaped slaves to their owners.

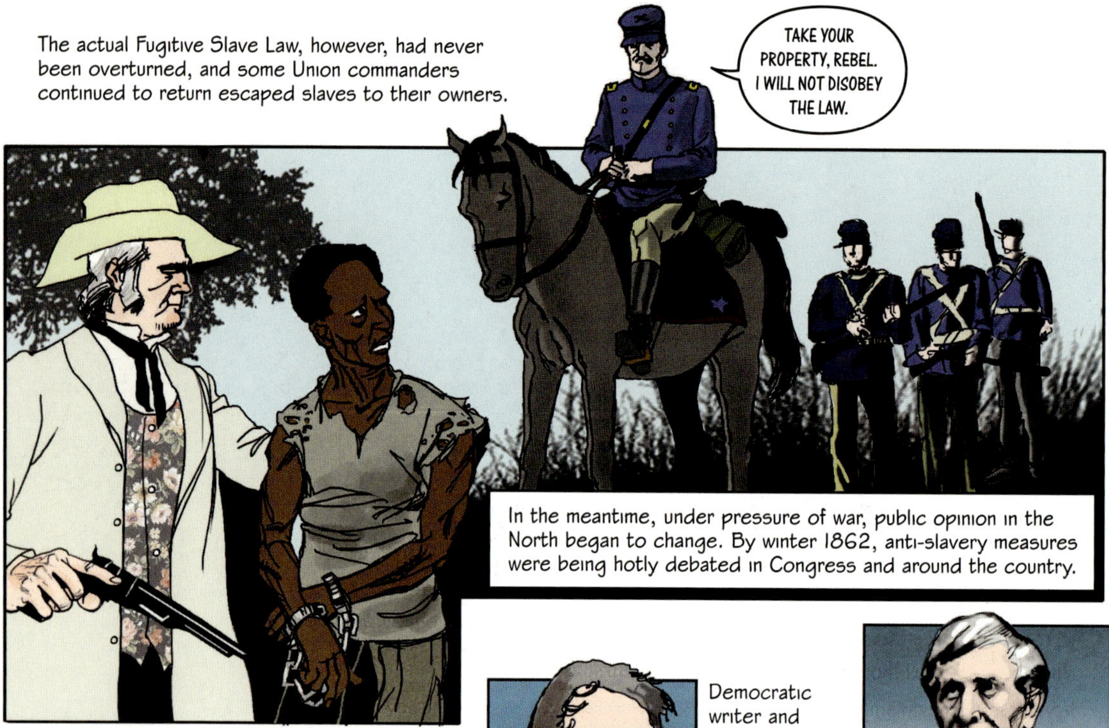
TAKE YOUR PROPERTY, REBEL. I WILL NOT DISOBEY THE LAW.
In the meantime, under pressure of war, public opinion in the North began to change. By winter 1862, anti-slavery measures were being hotly debated in Congress and around the country.

I believe that slavery is the sole cause of this rebellion and until this cause is removed and slavery abolished the rebellion will continue to exist.

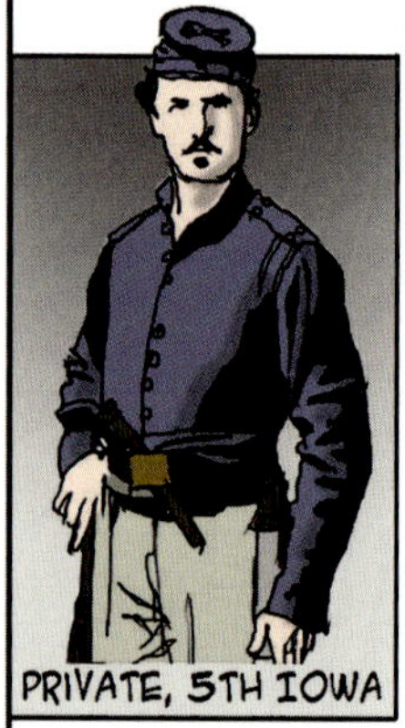
PRIVATE, 5TH IOWA

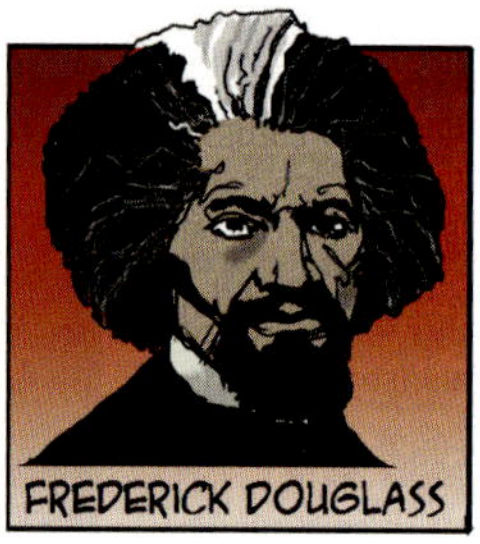
FREDERICK DOUGLASS

Sound policy, not less than humanity, demands the instant liberation of every slave in the rebel States.

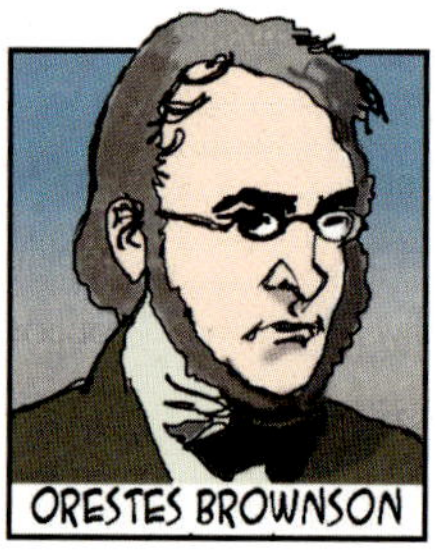
ORESTES BROWNSON

Democratic writer and editor: Emancipation is the only way to establish a permanent union of freedom.

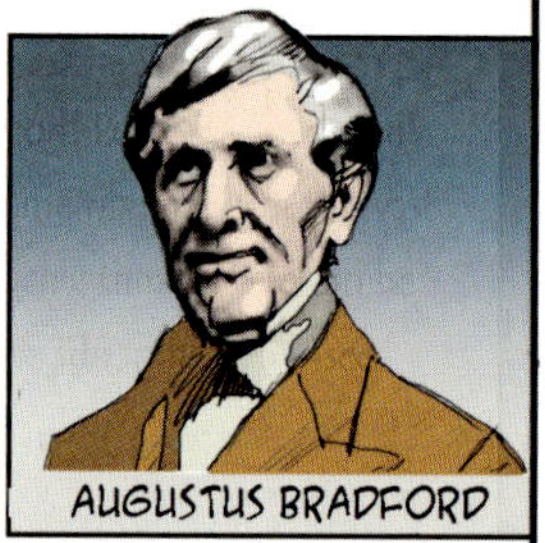
AUGUSTUS BRADFORD

Unionist governor of Maryland: Talk of abolition amounts to treason.

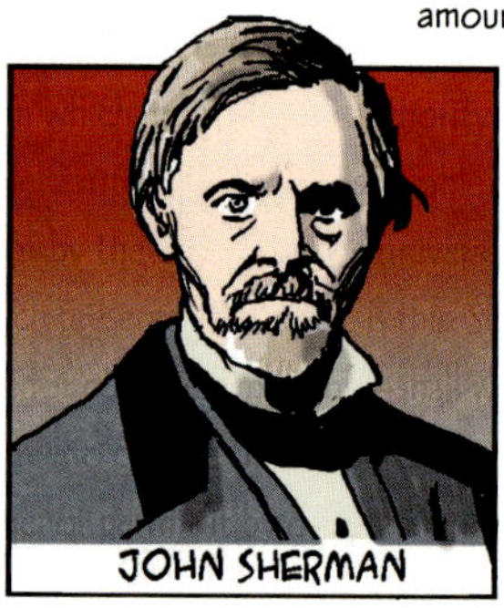
JOHN SHERMAN

Republican senator from Ohio: I am prepared to meet the broad issue of universal emancipation.

By summer 1862 the Union forces controlled the Mississippi River down to Vicksburg. But the struggle in Virginia was essentially at a stalemate.

BATTLE	CONFEDERATE WIN	UNION WIN
July 21, 1861 First Bull Run (Manassas), VA	X	
Feb. 16, 1862 Capture of Fort Donelson, TN		X
April 6-7, 1862 Battle of Shiloh, TN		X
May-June, 1862 Shenandoah Campaign, VA	X	
June 25-July 1, 1862 Seven Days Battles, VA	X	
Aug. 29-30 Second Bull Run (Manassas), VA	X	
Sept. 17, 1862 Battle of Antietam, MD		X
Dec. 13, 1862 Battle of Fredericksburg, VA	X	

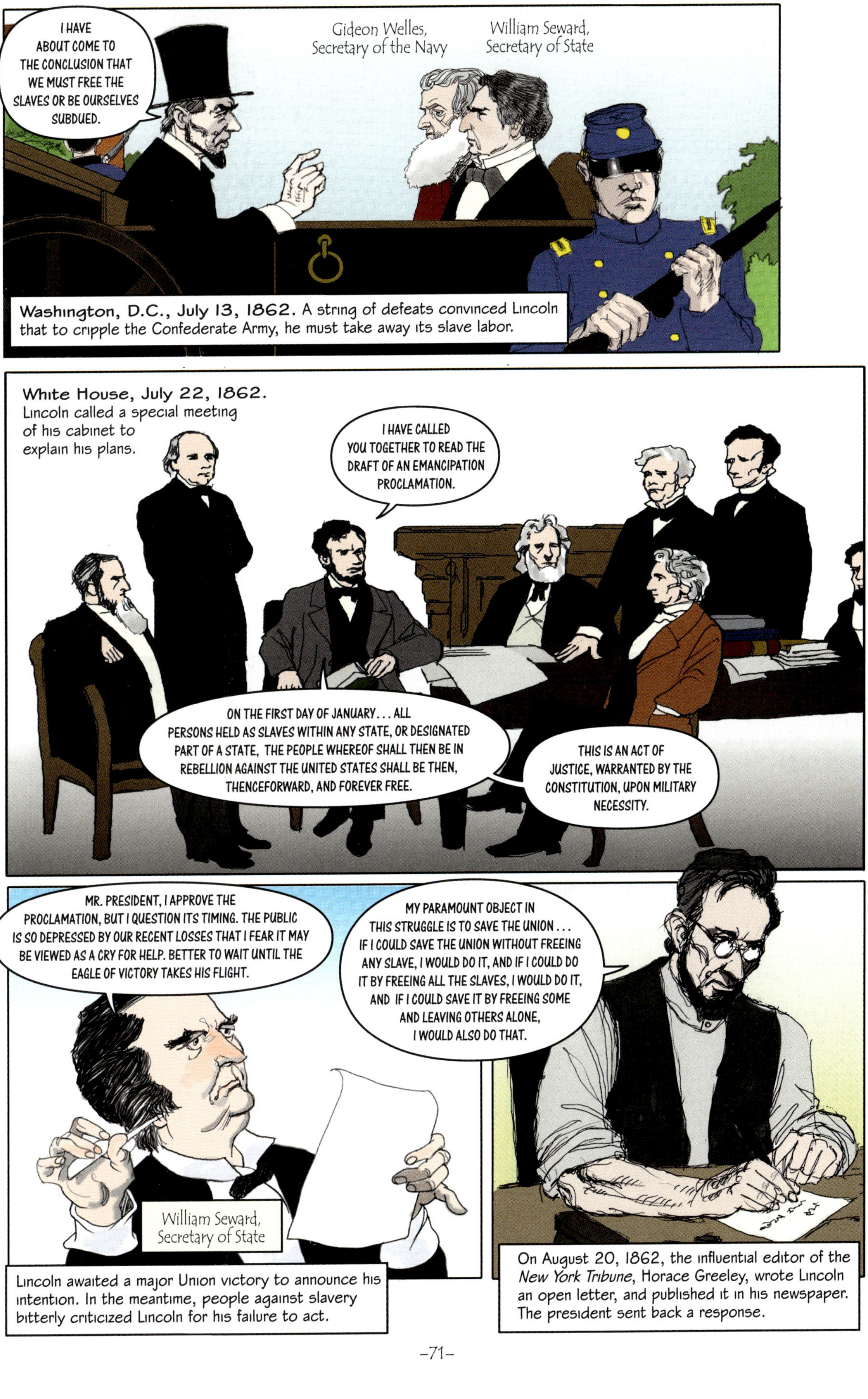
I HAVE ABOUT COME TO THE CONCLUSION THAT WE MUST FREE THE SLAVES OR BE OURSELVES SUBDUED.
Gideon Welles, Secretary of the Navy
William Seward, Secretary of State
Washington, D.C., July 13, 1862. A string of defeats convinced Lincoln that to cripple the Confederate Army, he must take away its slave labor.
White House, July 22, 1862. Lincoln called a special meeting of his cabinet to explain his plans.
I HAVE CALLED YOU TOGETHER TO READ THE DRAFT OF AN EMANCIPATION PROCLAMATION.
ON THE FIRST DAY OF JANUARY . . . ALL PERSONS HELD AS SLAVES WITHIN ANY STATE, OR DESIGNATED PART OF A STATE, THE PEOPLE WHEREOF SHALL THEN BE IN REBELLION AGAINST THE UNITED STATES SHALL BE THEN, THENCEFORWARD, AND FOREVER FREE.
THIS IS AN ACT OF JUSTICE, WARRANTED BY THE CONSTITUTION, UPON MILITARY NECESSITY.
MR. PRESIDENT, I APPROVE THE PROCLAMATION, BUT I QUESTION ITS TIMING. THE PUBLIC IS SO DEPRESSED BY OUR RECENT LOSSES THAT I FEAR IT MAY BE VIEWED AS A CRY FOR HELP. BETTER TO WAIT UNTIL THE EAGLE OF VICTORY TAKES HIS FLIGHT.
William Seward, Secretary of State
Lincoln awaited a major Union victory to announce his intention. In the meantime, people against slavery bitterly criticized Lincoln for his failure to act.
MY PARAMOUNT OBJECT IN THIS STRUGGLE IS TO SAVE THE UNION . . . IF I COULD SAVE THE UNION WITHOUT FREEING ANY SLAVE, I WOULD DO IT, AND IF I COULD DO IT BY FREEING ALL THE SLAVES, I WOULD DO IT, AND IF I COULD SAVE IT BY FREEING SOME AND LEAVING OTHERS ALONE, I WOULD ALSO DO THAT.
On August 20, 1862, the influential editor of the *New York Tribune*, Horace Greeley, wrote Lincoln an open letter, and published it in his newspaper. The president sent back a response.

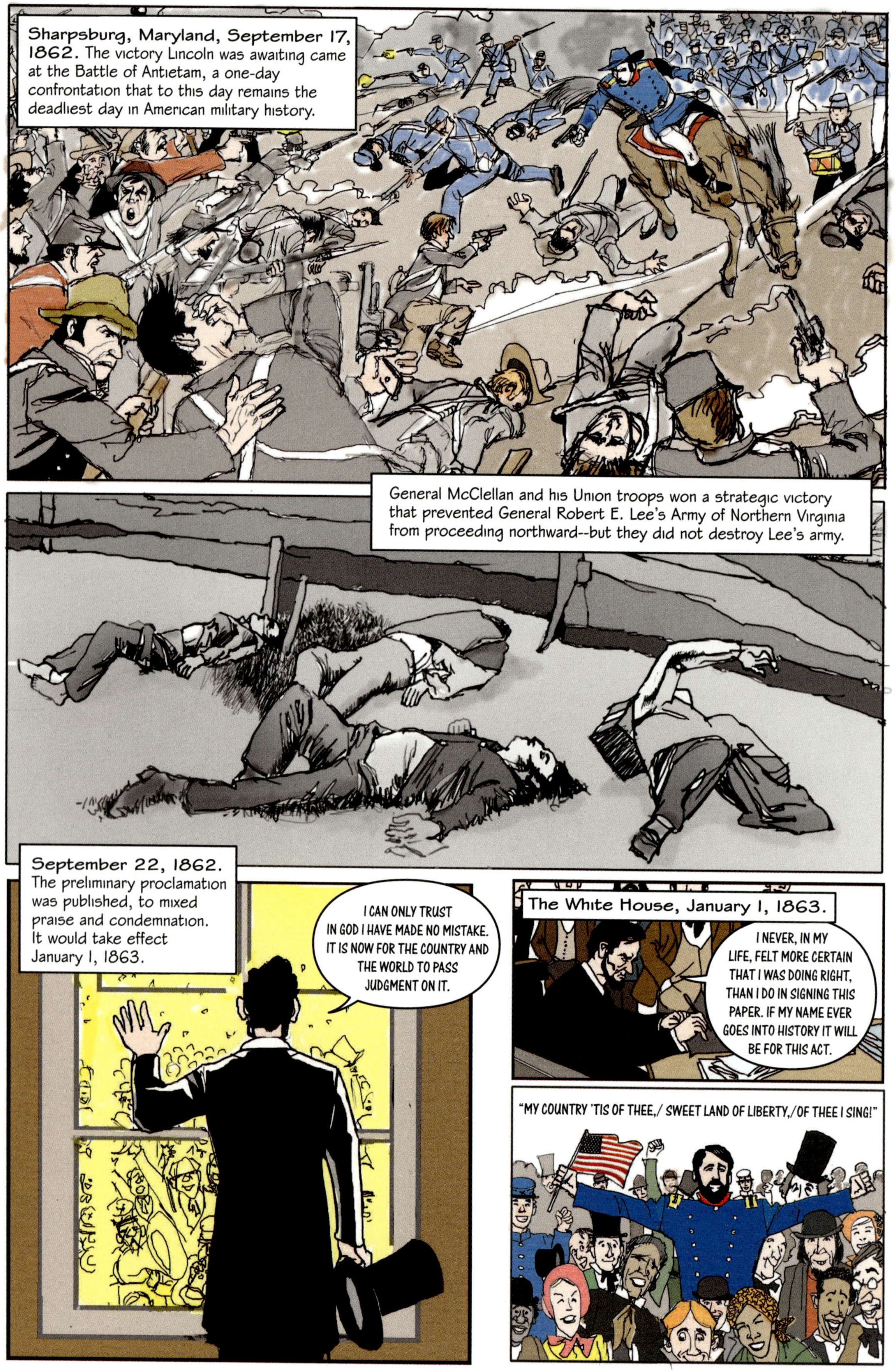
Sharpsburg, Maryland, September 17, 1862. The victory Lincoln was awaiting came at the Battle of Antietam, a one-day confrontation that to this day remains the deadliest day in American military history.
General McClellan and his Union troops won a strategic victory that prevented General Robert E. Lee's Army of Northern Virginia from proceeding northward--but they did not destroy Lee's army.
September 22, 1862. The preliminary proclamation was published, to mixed praise and condemnation. It would take effect January 1, 1863.
I CAN ONLY TRUST IN GOD I HAVE MADE NO MISTAKE. IT IS NOW FOR THE COUNTRY AND THE WORLD TO PASS JUDGMENT ON IT.
The White House, January 1, 1863.
I NEVER, IN MY LIFE, FELT MORE CERTAIN THAT I WAS DOING RIGHT, THAN I DO IN SIGNING THIS PAPER. IF MY NAME EVER GOES INTO HISTORY IT WILL BE FOR THIS ACT.
"MY COUNTRY 'TIS OF THEE,/ SWEET LAND OF LIBERTY,/OF THEE I SING!"

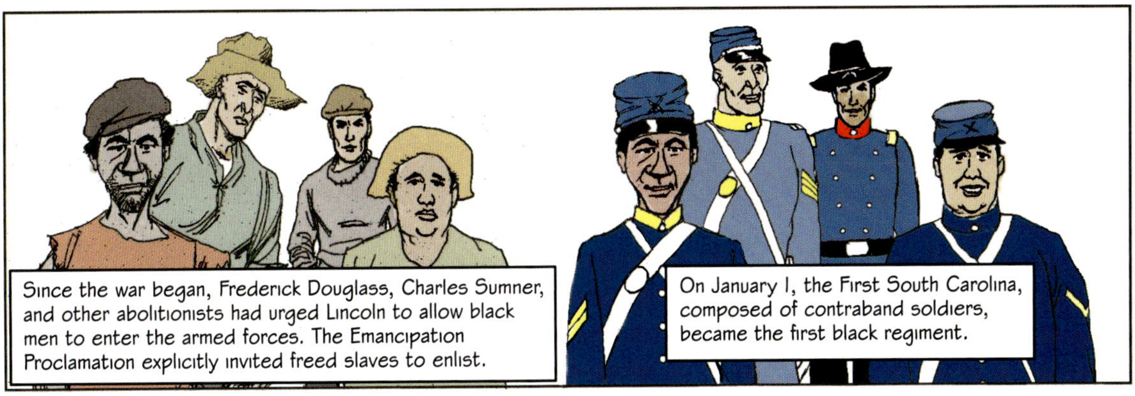
Since the war began, Frederick Douglass, Charles Sumner, and other abolitionists had urged Lincoln to allow black men to enter the armed forces. The Emancipation Proclamation explicitly invited freed slaves to enlist.
On January 1, the First South Carolina, composed of contraband soldiers, became the first black regiment.

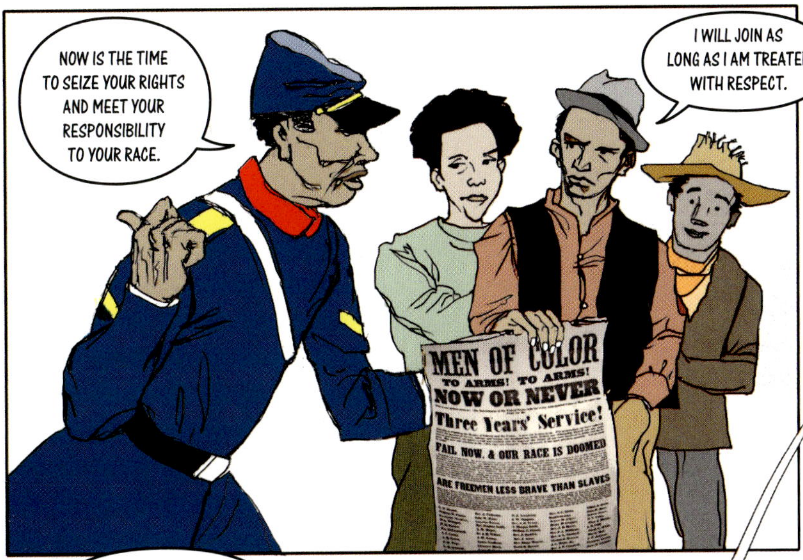
NOW IS THE TIME TO SEIZE YOUR RIGHTS AND MEET YOUR RESPONSIBILITY TO YOUR RACE.
I WILL JOIN AS LONG AS I AM TREATED WITH RESPECT.
MEN OF COLOR
TO ARMS! TO ARMS!
NOW OR NEVER
Three Years' Service!
FAIL NOW, & OUR RACE IS DOOMED
ARE FREEMEN LESS BRAVE THAN SLAVES

The governor of Massachusetts organized the first black regiment in the North, the 54th Massachusetts Infantry. Recruiters canvassed the North, looking for volunteers.

But black soldiers were paid less than white soldiers and did not receive the same benefits. Many white soldiers resented the presence of black troops.

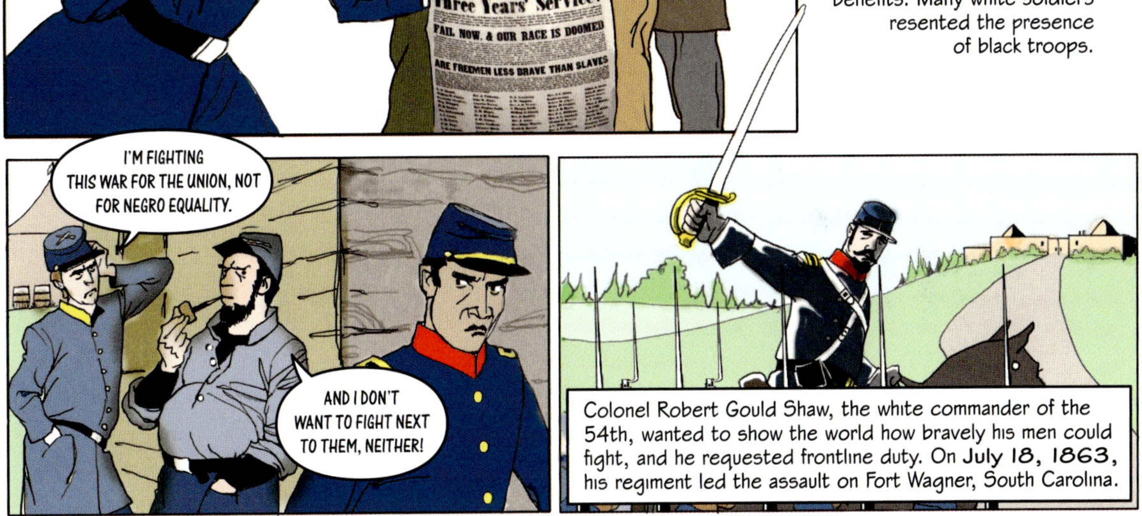
I'M FIGHTING THIS WAR FOR THE UNION, NOT FOR NEGRO EQUALITY.
AND I DON'T WANT TO FIGHT NEXT TO THEM, NEITHER!
Colonel Robert Gould Shaw, the white commander of the 54th, wanted to show the world how bravely his men could fight, and he requested frontline duty. On July 18, 1863, his regiment led the assault on Fort Wagner, South Carolina.

During the battle, the color guard was shot and Sergeant William H. Carney moved quickly to recover the fallen American flag. Even though he was wounded several times, Carney planted the colors on the parapet of the fort, then carried the flag back during the retreat.

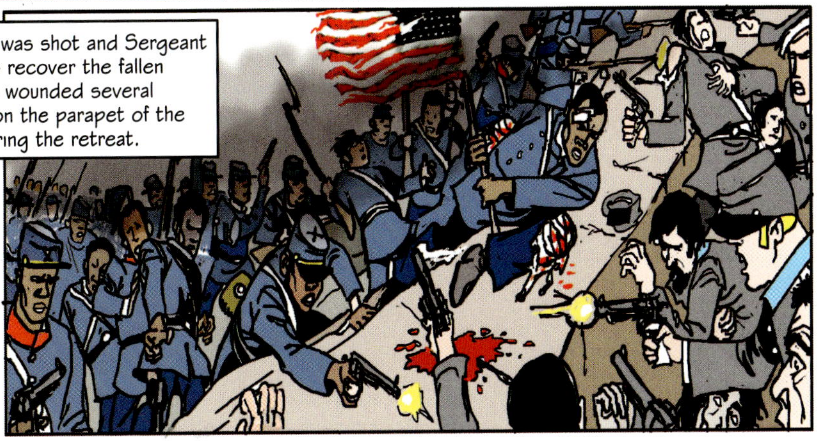

For his extraordinary bravery, Carney became the first black soldier to earn the Congressional Medal of Honor. General Ulysses S. Grant stated that "by arming the negro we have added a powerful ally." By war's end, more than 180,000 black soldiers had served in the Union Army, and nearly 30,000 in the navy.

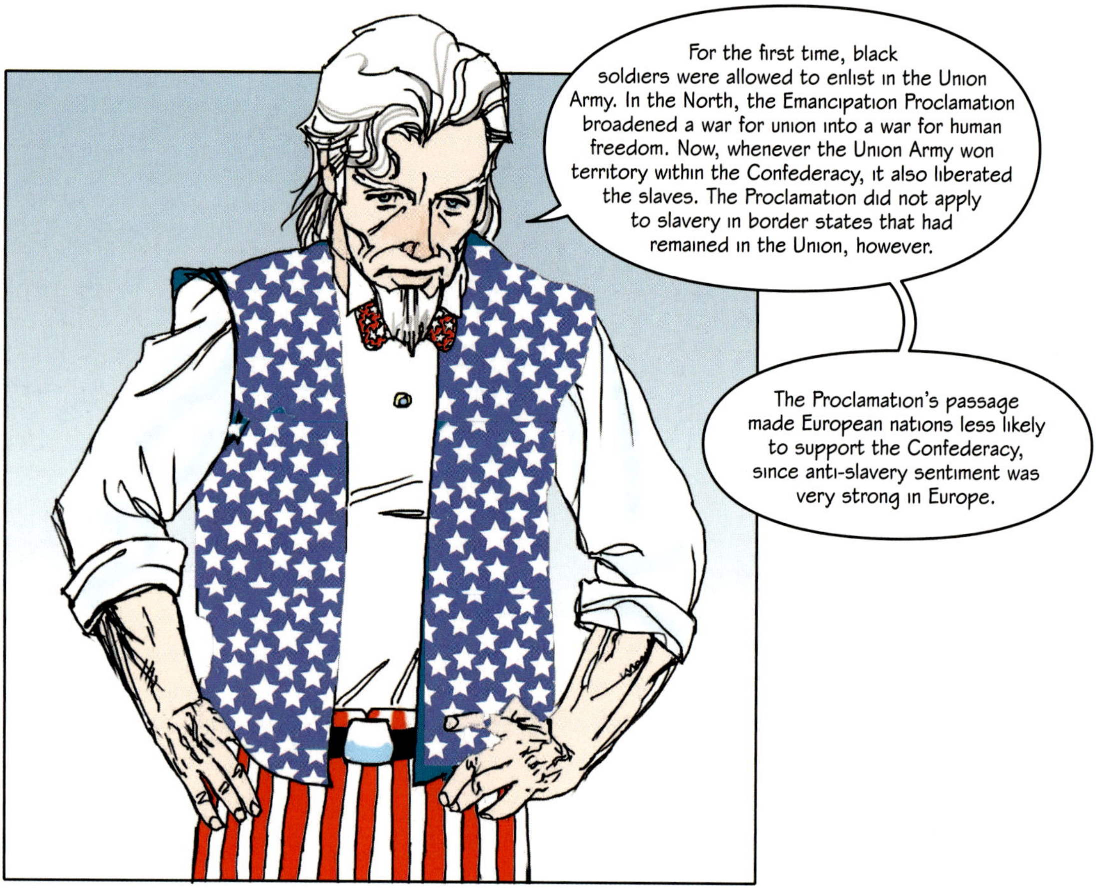
For the first time, black soldiers were allowed to enlist in the Union Army. In the North, the Emancipation Proclamation broadened a war for union into a war for human freedom. Now, whenever the Union Army won territory within the Confederacy, it also liberated the slaves. The Proclamation did not apply to slavery in border states that had remained in the Union, however.
The Proclamation's passage made European nations less likely to support the Confederacy, since anti-slavery sentiment was very strong in Europe.

EXCERPTS FROM THE EMANCIPATION PROCLAMATION

"Now, therefore I, Abraham Lincoln, President of the United States, by virtue of the power in me vested as Commander-in-Chief, of the Army and Navy of the United States in time of actual armed rebellion against the authority and government of the United States, and as a fit and necessary war measure for suppressing said rebellion, do, on this first day of January, in the year of our Lord one thousand eight hundred and sixty-three . . . order and declare that all persons held as slaves within said designated States [in the Confederacy], and parts of States, are, and henceforward shall be free; and that the Executive government of the United States, including the military and naval authorities thereof, will recognize and maintain the freedom of said persons.

"And I further declare and make known, that such persons of suitable condition, will be received into the armed service of the United States to garrison forts, positions, stations, and other places, and to man vessels of all sorts in said service.

"And upon this act, sincerely believed to be an act of justice, warranted by the Constitution, upon military necessity, I invoke the considerate judgment of mankind, and the gracious favor of Almighty God."

The Gettysburg Address

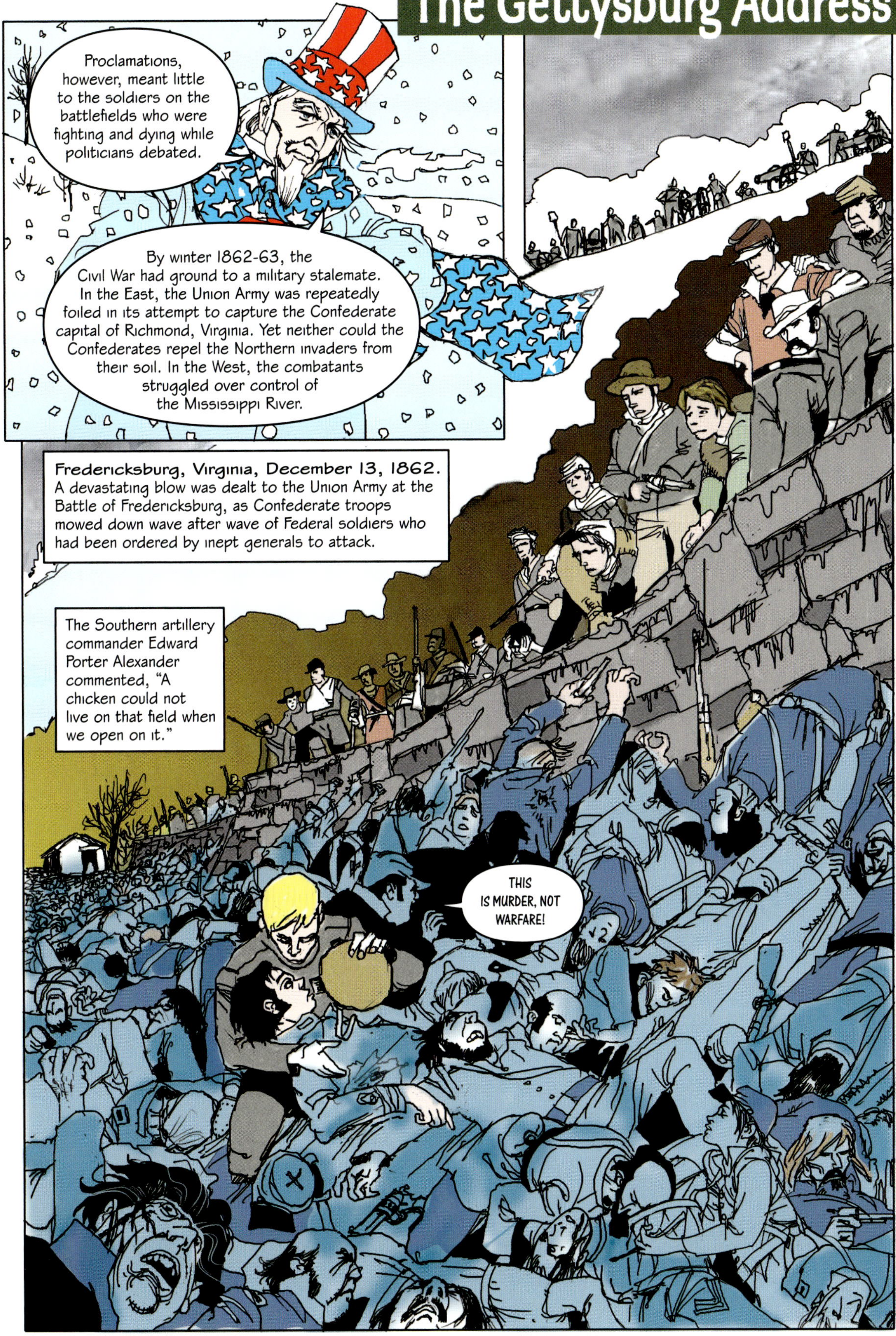
Proclamations, however, meant little to the soldiers on the battlefields who were fighting and dying while politicians debated.
By winter 1862-63, the Civil War had ground to a military stalemate. In the East, the Union Army was repeatedly foiled in its attempt to capture the Confederate capital of Richmond, Virginia. Yet neither could the Confederates repel the Northern invaders from their soil. In the West, the combatants struggled over control of the Mississippi River.
Fredericksburg, Virginia, December 13, 1862.
A devastating blow was dealt to the Union Army at the Battle of Fredericksburg, as Confederate troops mowed down wave after wave of Federal soldiers who had been ordered by inept generals to attack.
The Southern artillery commander Edward Porter Alexander commented, "A chicken could not live on that field when we open on it."
THIS IS MURDER, NOT WARFARE!

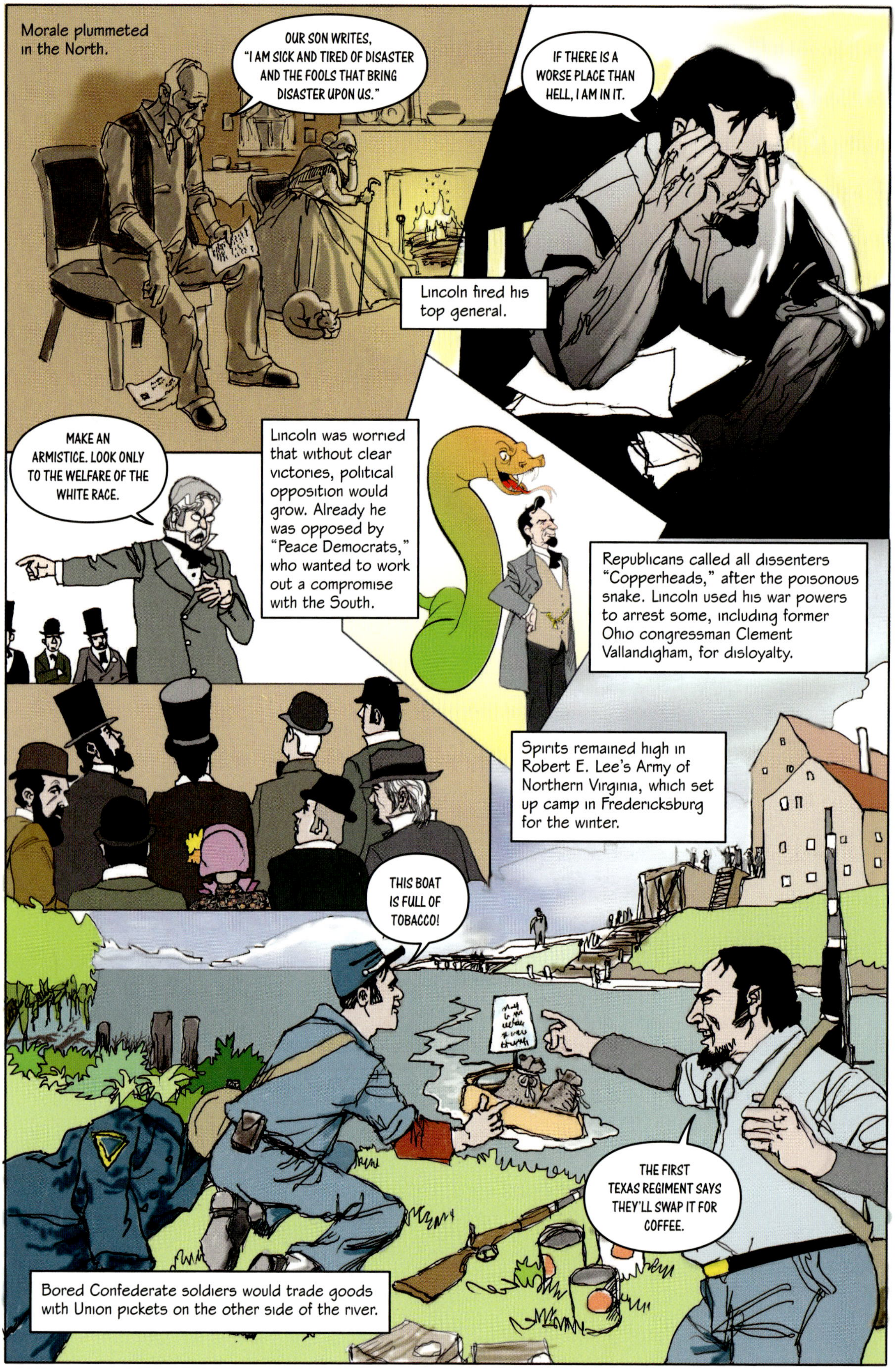
Morale plummeted in the North.
OUR SON WRITES, "I AM SICK AND TIRED OF DISASTER AND THE FOOLS THAT BRING DISASTER UPON US."
IF THERE IS A WORSE PLACE THAN HELL, I AM IN IT.
Lincoln fired his top general.
MAKE AN ARMISTICE. LOOK ONLY TO THE WELFARE OF THE WHITE RACE.
Lincoln was worried that without clear victories, political opposition would grow. Already he was opposed by "Peace Democrats," who wanted to work out a compromise with the South.
Republicans called all dissenters "Copperheads," after the poisonous snake. Lincoln used his war powers to arrest some, including former Ohio congressman Clement Vallandigham, for disloyalty.
Spirits remained high in Robert E. Lee's Army of Northern Virginia, which set up camp in Fredericksburg for the winter.
THIS BOAT IS FULL OF TOBACCO!
THE FIRST TEXAS REGIMENT SAYS THEY'LL SWAP IT FOR COFFEE.
Bored Confederate soldiers would trade goods with Union pickets on the other side of the river.

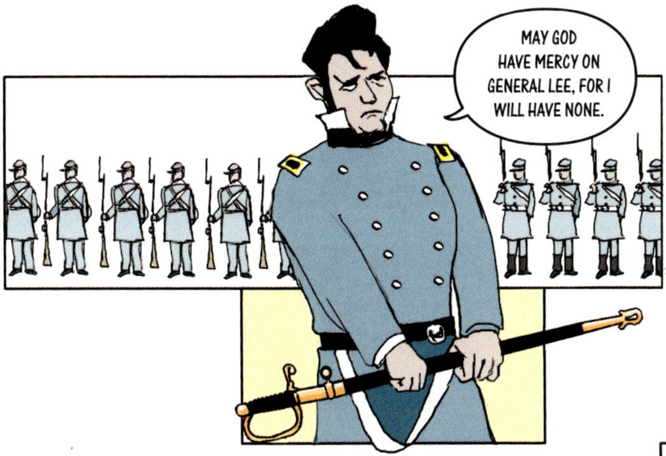
MAY GOD HAVE MERCY ON GENERAL LEE, FOR I WILL HAVE NONE.

In the spring of 1863, the armies were ready to make their move. Lincoln's new general, "Fighting" Joe Hooker, maneuvered his army of 120,000 to meet Lee's army of only 65,000.

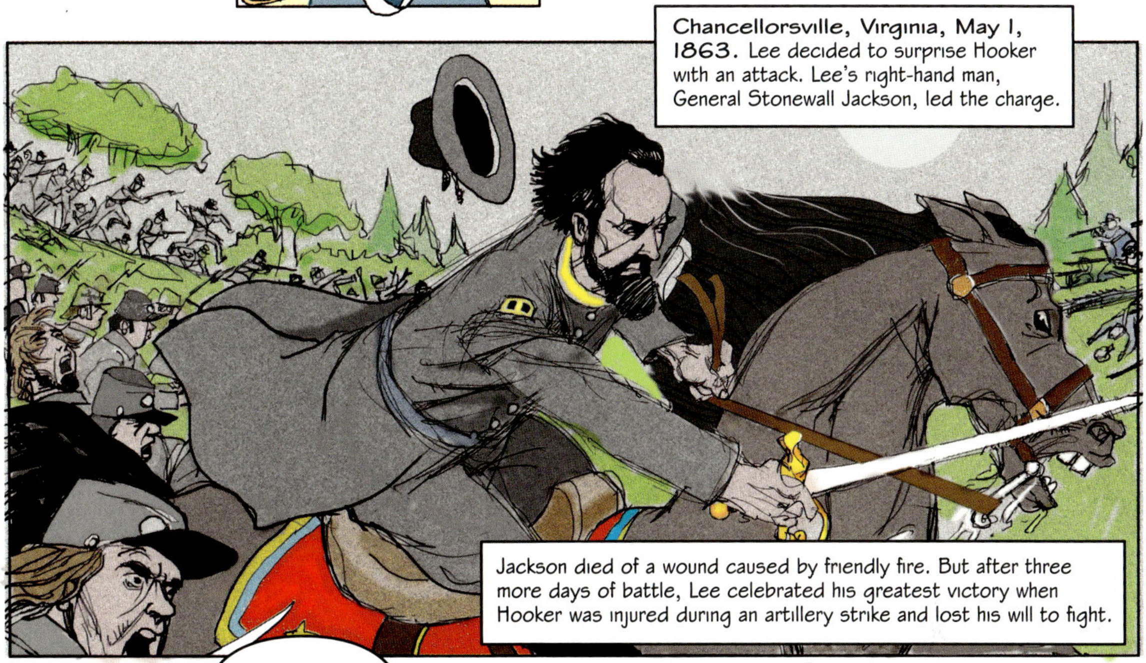
Chancellorsville, Virginia, May 1, 1863. Lee decided to surprise Hooker with an attack. Lee's right-hand man, General Stonewall Jackson, led the charge.
Jackson died of a wound caused by friendly fire. But after three more days of battle, Lee celebrated his greatest victory when Hooker was injured during an artillery strike and lost his will to fight.

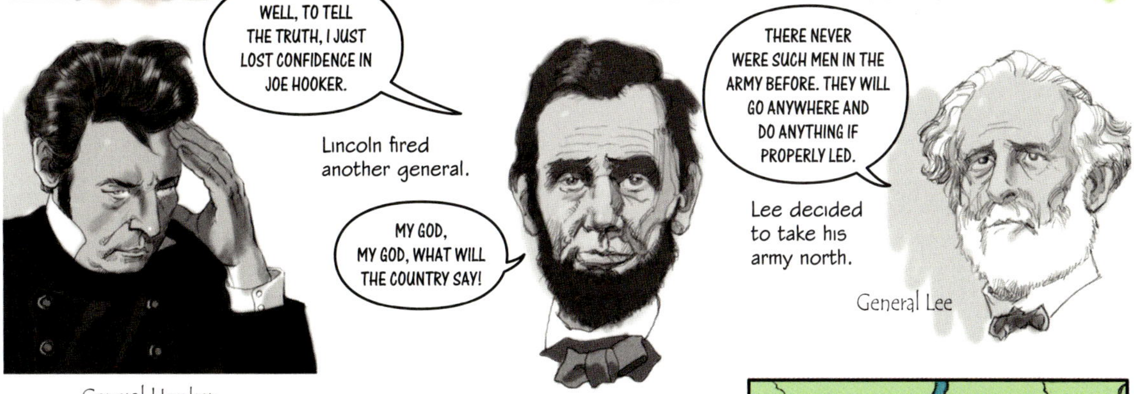
WELL, TO TELL THE TRUTH, I JUST LOST CONFIDENCE IN JOE HOOKER.
MY GOD, MY GOD, WHAT WILL THE COUNTRY SAY!
THERE NEVER WERE SUCH MEN IN THE ARMY BEFORE. THEY WILL GO ANYWHERE AND DO ANYTHING IF PROPERLY LED.

Lincoln fired another general.

Lee decided to take his army north.

General Lee

General Hooker

On May 18, in the Western Theater, General Grant and his Army of the Tennessee began what would become a six-week-long siege of Vicksburg, on the Mississippi River. With the destruction of the city's fortifications, the Federals would control the Mississippi and isolate Texas, Arkansas, and Louisiana from the rest of the Confederacy.

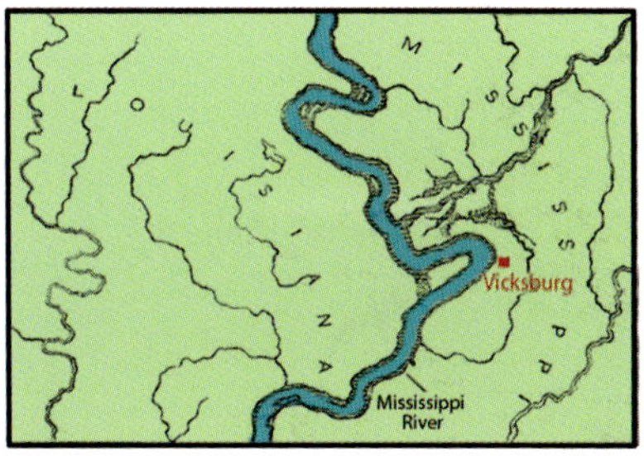
LOUISIANA
MISSISSIPPI
Vicksburg
Mississippi River

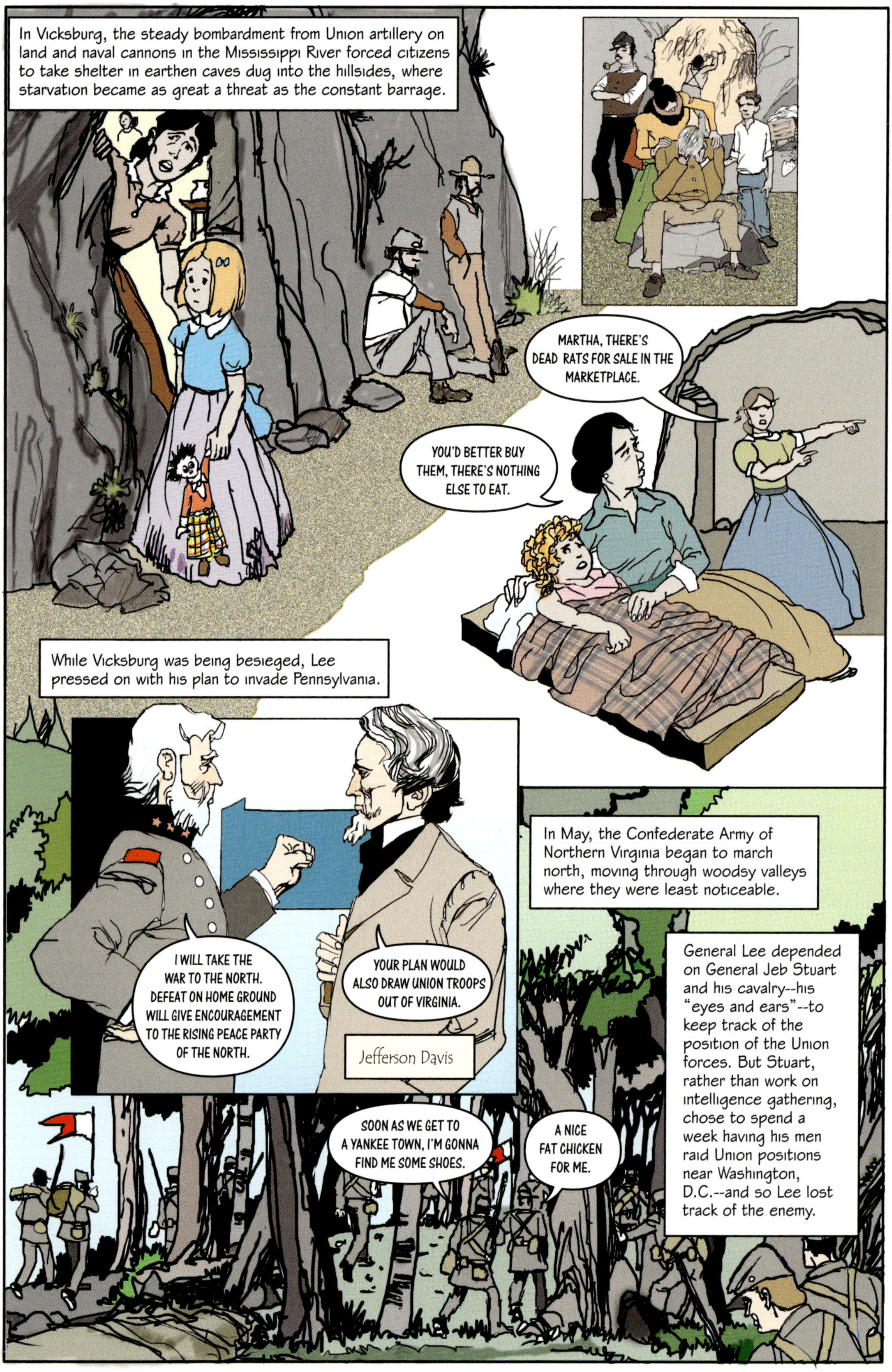
In Vicksburg, the steady bombardment from Union artillery on land and naval cannons in the Mississippi River forced citizens to take shelter in earthen caves dug into the hillsides, where starvation became as great a threat as the constant barrage.
MARTHA, THERE'S DEAD RATS FOR SALE IN THE MARKETPLACE.
YOU'D BETTER BUY THEM, THERE'S NOTHING ELSE TO EAT.
While Vicksburg was being besieged, Lee pressed on with his plan to invade Pennsylvania.
I WILL TAKE THE WAR TO THE NORTH. DEFEAT ON HOME GROUND WILL GIVE ENCOURAGEMENT TO THE RISING PEACE PARTY OF THE NORTH.
YOUR PLAN WOULD ALSO DRAW UNION TROOPS OUT OF VIRGINIA.
Jefferson Davis
In May, the Confederate Army of Northern Virginia began to march north, moving through woodsy valleys where they were least noticeable.
General Lee depended on General Jeb Stuart and his cavalry--his "eyes and ears"--to keep track of the position of the Union forces. But Stuart, rather than work on intelligence gathering, chose to spend a week having his men raid Union positions near Washington, D.C.--and so Lee lost track of the enemy.
SOON AS WE GET TO A YANKEE TOWN, I'M GONNA FIND ME SOME SHOES.
A NICE FAT CHICKEN FOR ME.

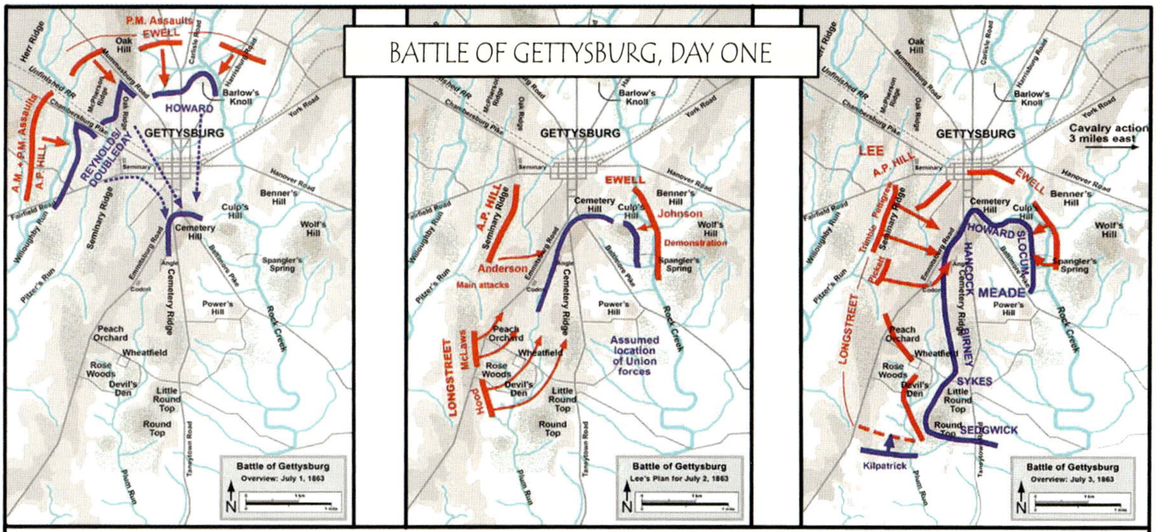
BATTLE OF GETTYSBURG, DAY ONE
P.M. Assaults
EWELL
A.M. + P.M. Assaults
A.P. HILL
REYNOLDS
DOUBLEDAY
HOWARD
GETTYSBURG
Oak Hill
Barlow's Knoll
Cemetery Hill
Culp's Hill
Wolf's Hill
Benner's Hill
Spangler's Spring
Power's Hill
Peach Orchard
Wheatfield
Rose Woods
Devil's Den
Little Round Top
Round Top
Seminary Ridge
Cemetery Ridge
Herr Ridge
Rock Creek
Battle of Gettysburg
Overview: July 1, 1863
EWELL
Johnson
Demonstration
A.P. HILL
Anderson
Main attacks
LONGSTREET
McLaws
Hood
Assumed location of Union forces
Battle of Gettysburg
Lee's Plan for July 2, 1863
Cavalry action 3 miles east
LEE
A.P. HILL
EWELL
LONGSTREET
Pickett
Trimble
Pettigrew
HOWARD
SLOCUM
HANCOCK
MEADE
BIRNEY
SYKES
SEDGWICK
Kilpatrick
Battle of Gettysburg
Overview: July 3, 1863

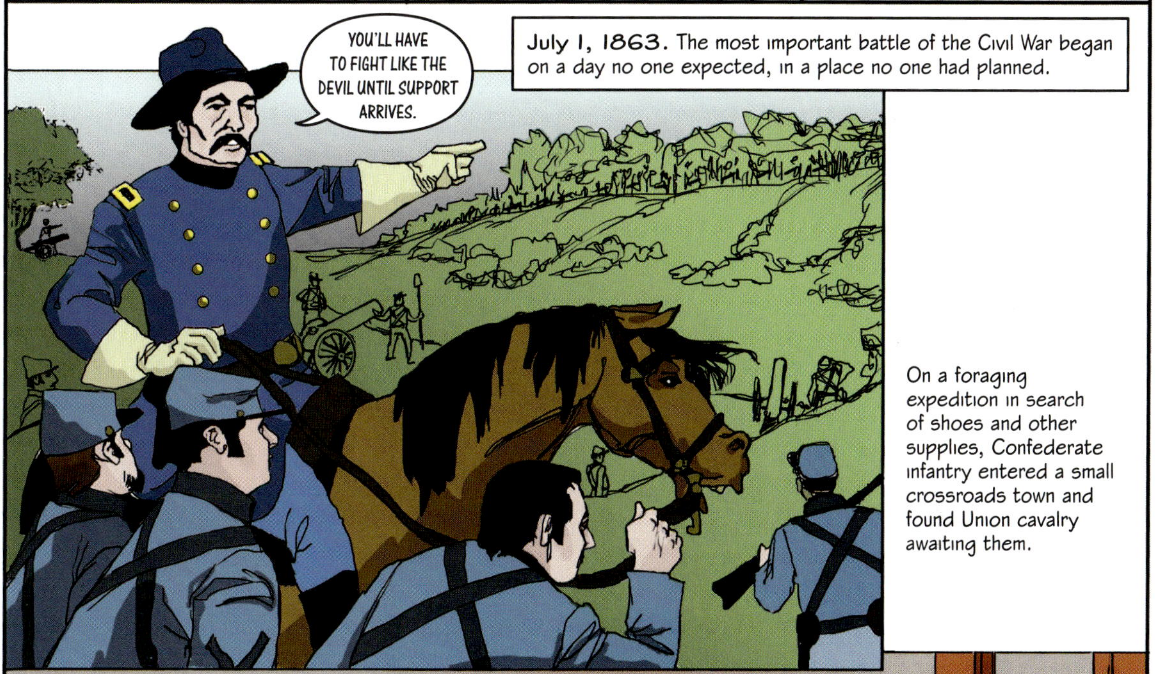
YOU'LL HAVE TO FIGHT LIKE THE DEVIL UNTIL SUPPORT ARRIVES.
July 1, 1863. The most important battle of the Civil War began on a day no one expected, in a place no one had planned.
On a foraging expedition in search of shoes and other supplies, Confederate infantry entered a small crossroads town and found Union cavalry awaiting them.

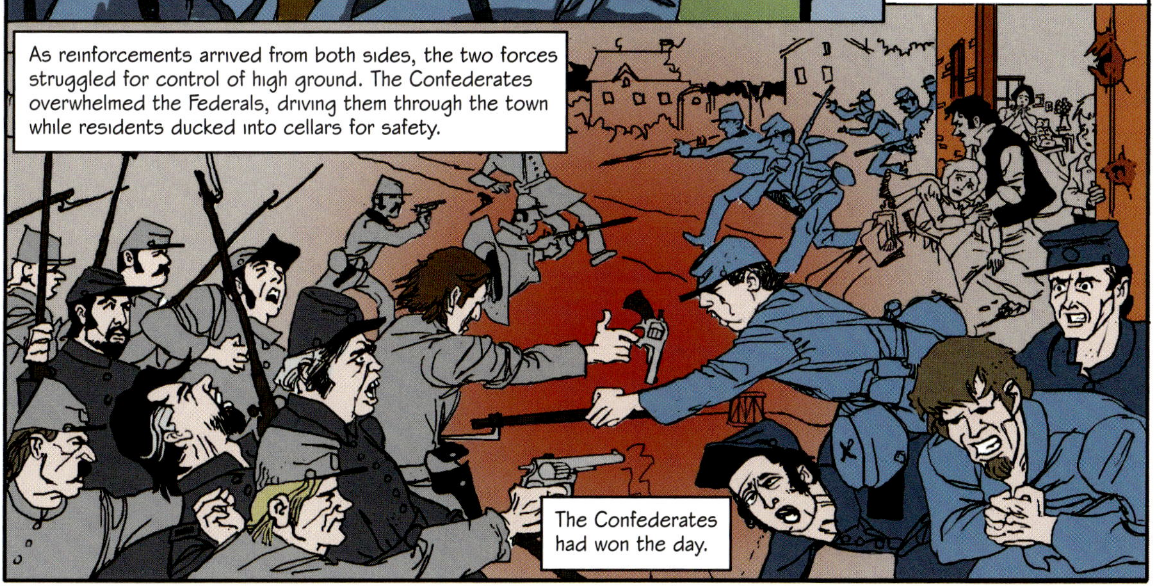
As reinforcements arrived from both sides, the two forces struggled for control of high ground. The Confederates overwhelmed the Federals, driving them through the town while residents ducked into cellars for safety.
The Confederates had won the day.

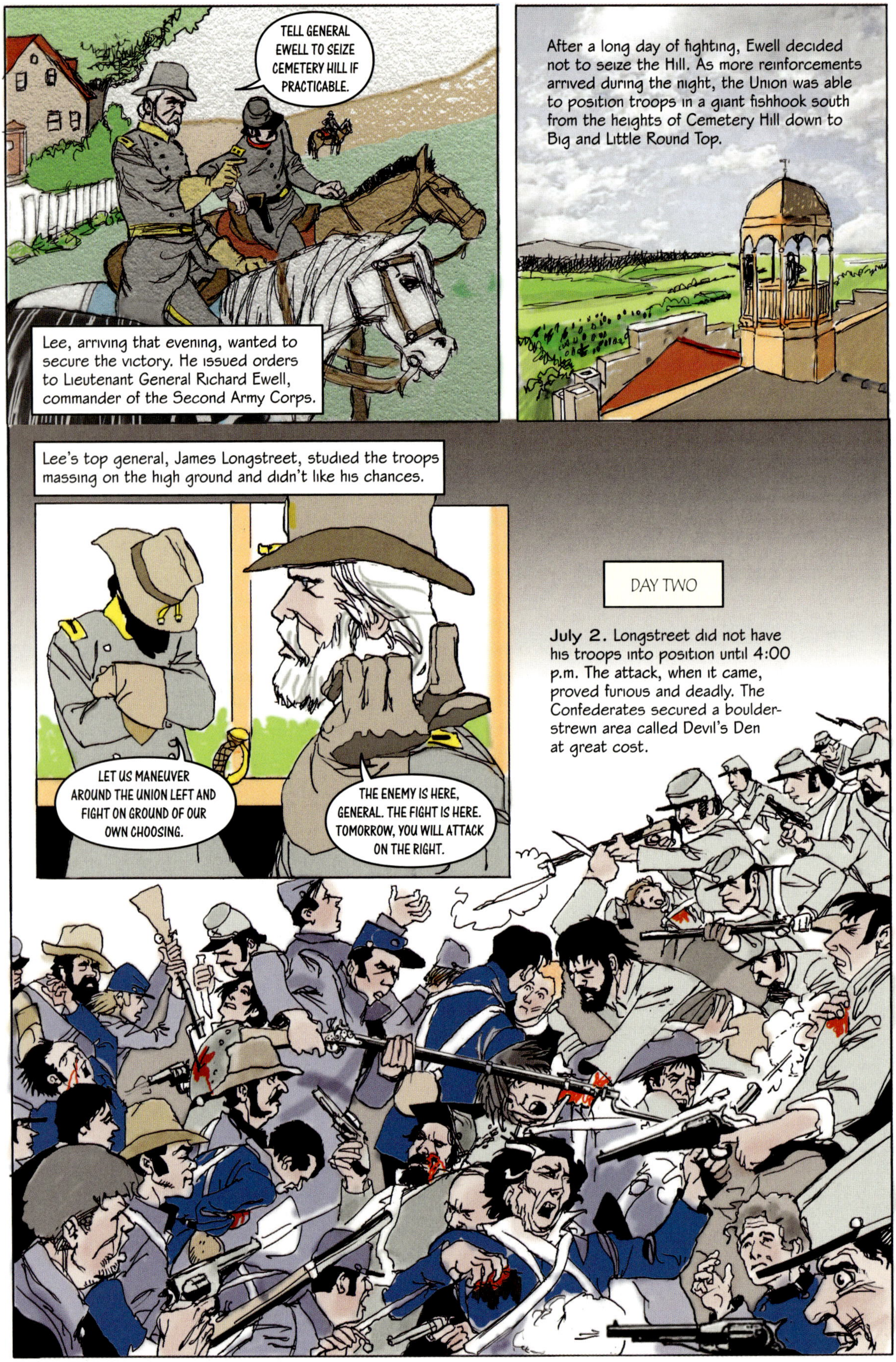
TELL GENERAL EWELL TO SEIZE CEMETERY HILL IF PRACTICABLE.
Lee, arriving that evening, wanted to secure the victory. He issued orders to Lieutenant General Richard Ewell, commander of the Second Army Corps.
After a long day of fighting, Ewell decided not to seize the Hill. As more reinforcements arrived during the night, the Union was able to position troops in a giant fishhook south from the heights of Cemetery Hill down to Big and Little Round Top.
Lee's top general, James Longstreet, studied the troops massing on the high ground and didn't like his chances.
LET US MANEUVER AROUND THE UNION LEFT AND FIGHT ON GROUND OF OUR OWN CHOOSING.
THE ENEMY IS HERE, GENERAL. THE FIGHT IS HERE. TOMORROW, YOU WILL ATTACK ON THE RIGHT.
DAY TWO
July 2. Longstreet did not have his troops into position until 4:00 p.m. The attack, when it came, proved furious and deadly. The Confederates secured a boulder-strewn area called Devil's Den at great cost.

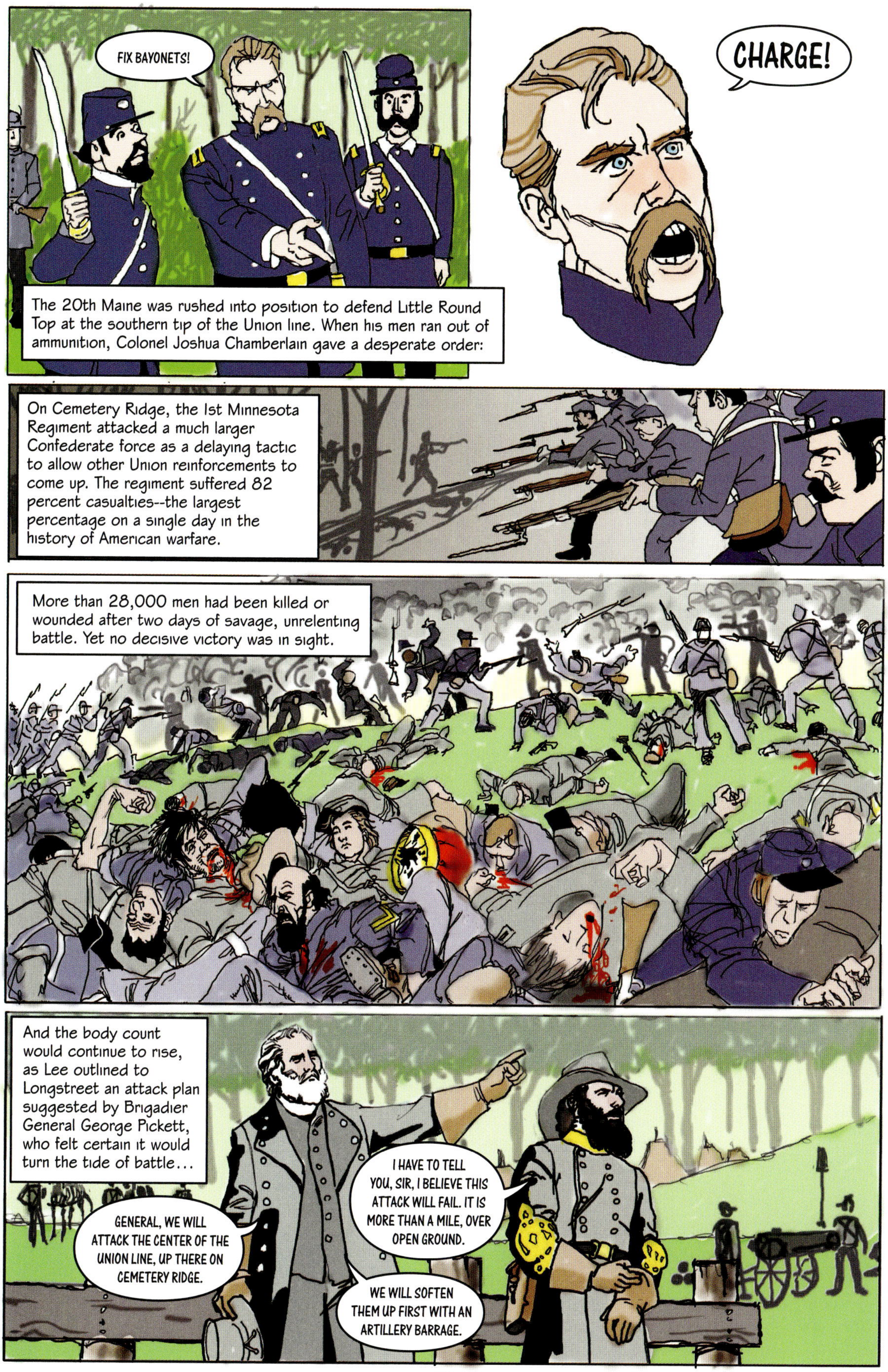
FIX BAYONETS!
The 20th Maine was rushed into position to defend Little Round Top at the southern tip of the Union line. When his men ran out of ammunition, Colonel Joshua Chamberlain gave a desperate order:
CHARGE!
On Cemetery Ridge, the 1st Minnesota Regiment attacked a much larger Confederate force as a delaying tactic to allow other Union reinforcements to come up. The regiment suffered 82 percent casualties--the largest percentage on a single day in the history of American warfare.
More than 28,000 men had been killed or wounded after two days of savage, unrelenting battle. Yet no decisive victory was in sight.
And the body count would continue to rise, as Lee outlined to Longstreet an attack plan suggested by Brigadier General George Pickett, who felt certain it would turn the tide of battle...
GENERAL, WE WILL ATTACK THE CENTER OF THE UNION LINE, UP THERE ON CEMETERY RIDGE.
WE WILL SOFTEN THEM UP FIRST WITH AN ARTILLERY BARRAGE.
I HAVE TO TELL YOU, SIR, I BELIEVE THIS ATTACK WILL FAIL. IT IS MORE THAN A MILE, OVER OPEN GROUND.

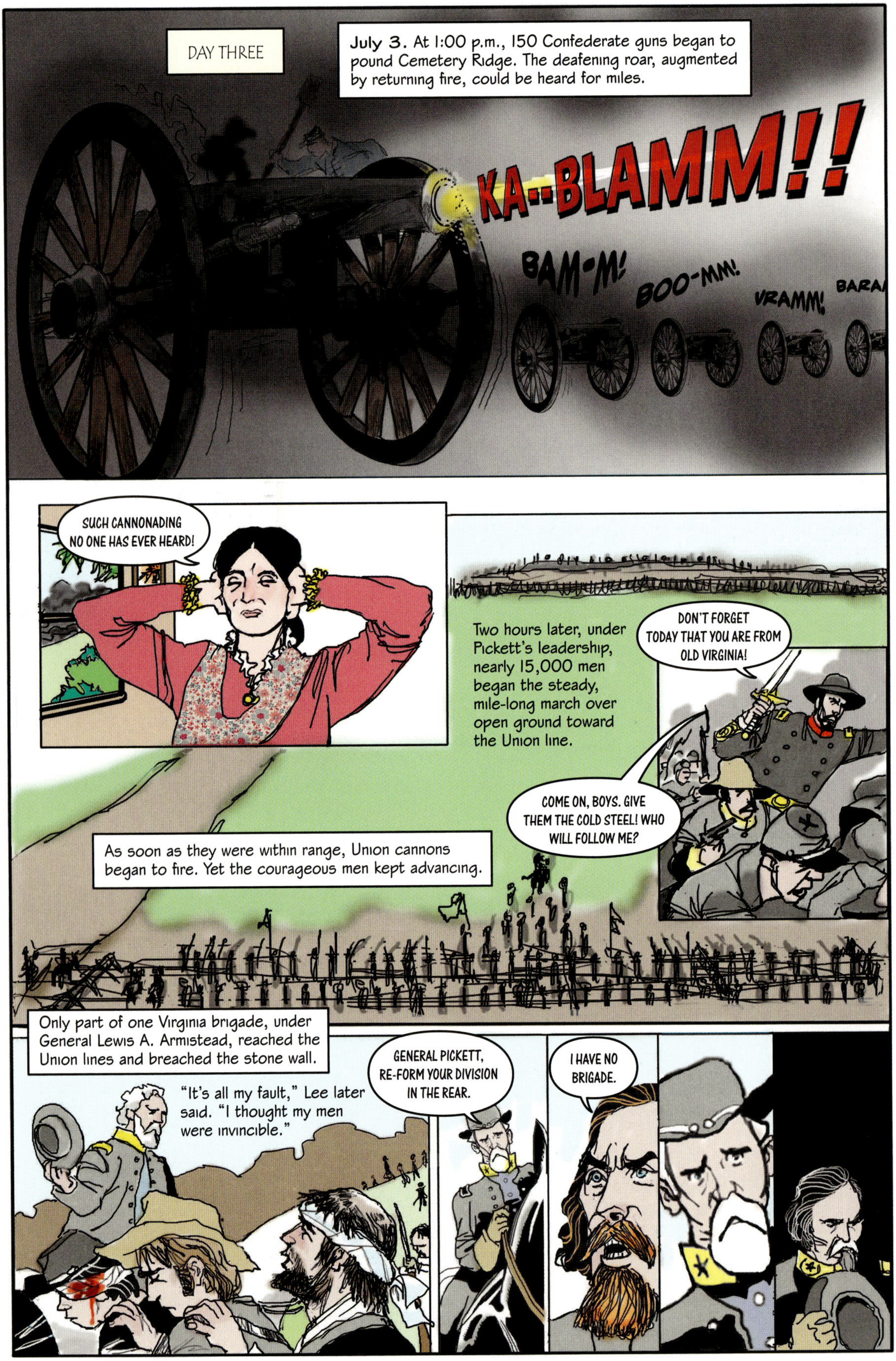
DAY THREE
July 3. At 1:00 p.m., 150 Confederate guns began to pound Cemetery Ridge. The deafening roar, augmented by returning fire, could be heard for miles.
KA--BLAMM!!
BAM-M!
BOO-MM!
VRAMM!
SUCH CANNONADING NO ONE HAS EVER HEARD!
Two hours later, under Pickett's leadership, nearly 15,000 men began the steady, mile-long march over open ground toward the Union line.
DON'T FORGET TODAY THAT YOU ARE FROM OLD VIRGINIA!
COME ON, BOYS. GIVE THEM THE COLD STEEL! WHO WILL FOLLOW ME?
As soon as they were within range, Union cannons began to fire. Yet the courageous men kept advancing.
Only part of one Virginia brigade, under General Lewis A. Armistead, reached the Union lines and breached the stone wall.
"It's all my fault," Lee later said. "I thought my men were invincible."
GENERAL PICKETT, RE-FORM YOUR DIVISION IN THE REAR.
I HAVE NO BRIGADE.

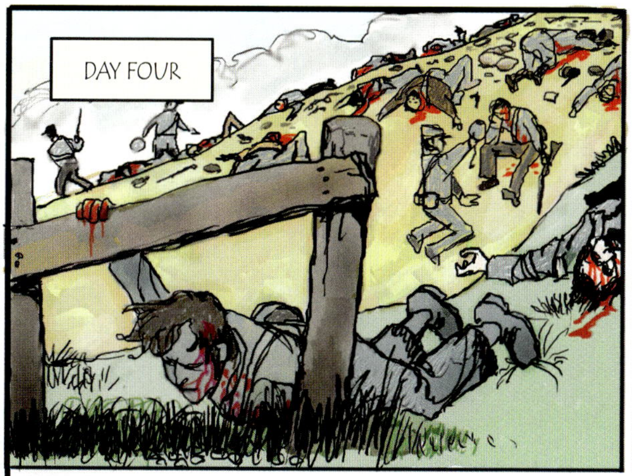
DAY FOUR

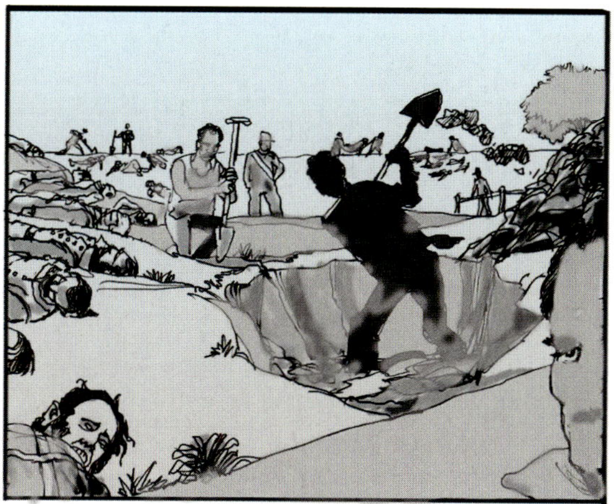

July 4. Through driving rain, a devastated Lee led the retreat back to the South. On the same day, the besieged city of Vicksburg surrendered to Ulysses S. Grant. The Confederacy had suffered a double blow. The war would continue--but the tide had turned.

From across the North, aid workers streamed in to tend the wounded . . . and bury the dead. Soldiers were interred where they fell. After the war, Confederates would be retrieved for Southern burial.

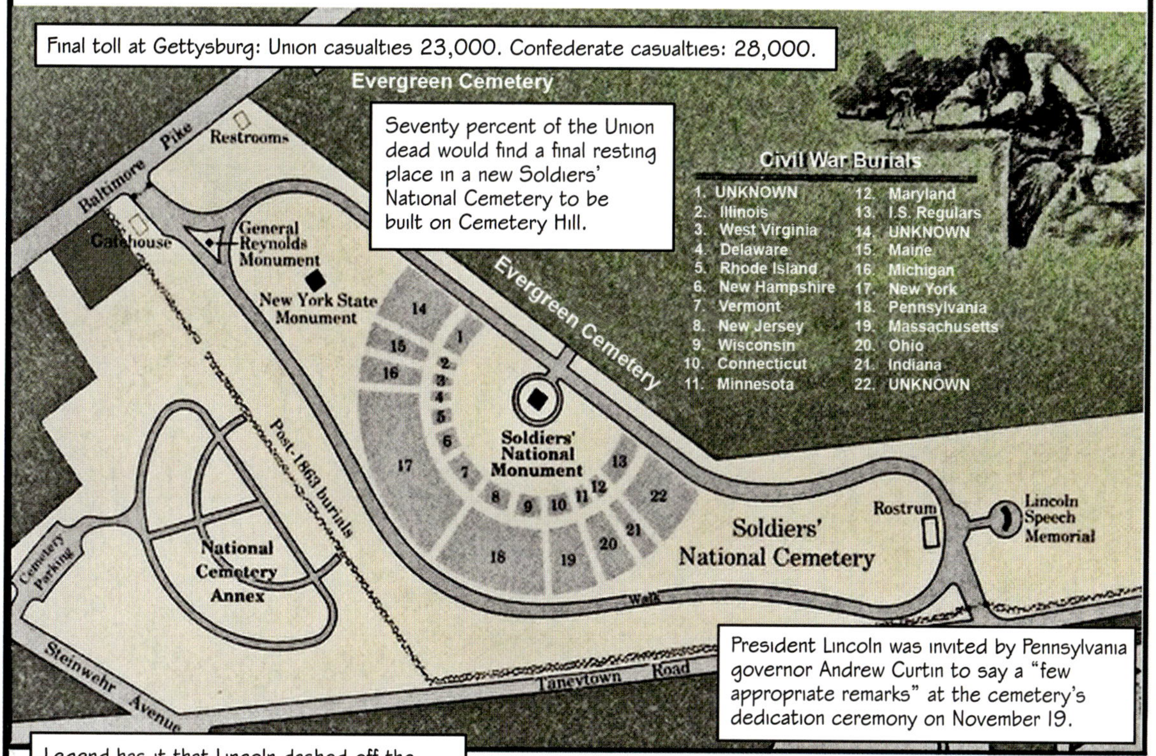
Final toll at Gettysburg: Union casualties 23,000. Confederate casualties: 28,000.
Seventy percent of the Union dead would find a final resting place in a new Soldiers' National Cemetery to be built on Cemetery Hill.
Evergreen Cemetery
Restrooms
Baltimore Pike
Gatehouse
General Reynolds Monument
New York State Monument
Evergreen Cemetery
Soldiers' National Monument
Post-1863 burials
National Cemetery Annex
Cemetery Parking
Rostrum
Lincoln Speech Memorial
Soldiers' National Cemetery
Walk
Steinwehr Avenue
Taneytown Road
Civil War Burials
1. UNKNOWN
2. Illinois
3. West Virginia
4. Delaware
5. Rhode Island
6. New Hampshire
7. Vermont
8. New Jersey
9. Wisconsin
10. Connecticut
11. Minnesota
12. Maryland
13. U.S. Regulars
14. UNKNOWN
15. Maine
16. Michigan
17. New York
18. Pennsylvania
19. Massachusetts
20. Ohio
21. Indiana
22. UNKNOWN
President Lincoln was invited by Pennsylvania governor Andrew Curtin to say a "few appropriate remarks" at the cemetery's dedication ceremony on November 19.

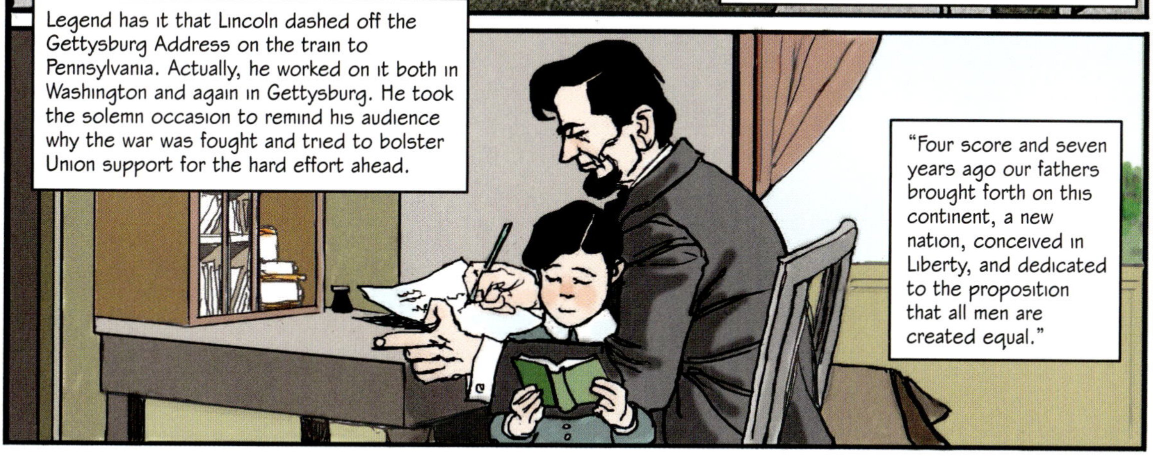
Legend has it that Lincoln dashed off the Gettysburg Address on the train to Pennsylvania. Actually, he worked on it both in Washington and again in Gettysburg. He took the solemn occasion to remind his audience why the war was fought and tried to bolster Union support for the hard effort ahead.
"Four score and seven years ago our fathers brought forth on this continent, a new nation, conceived in Liberty, and dedicated to the proposition that all men are created equal."

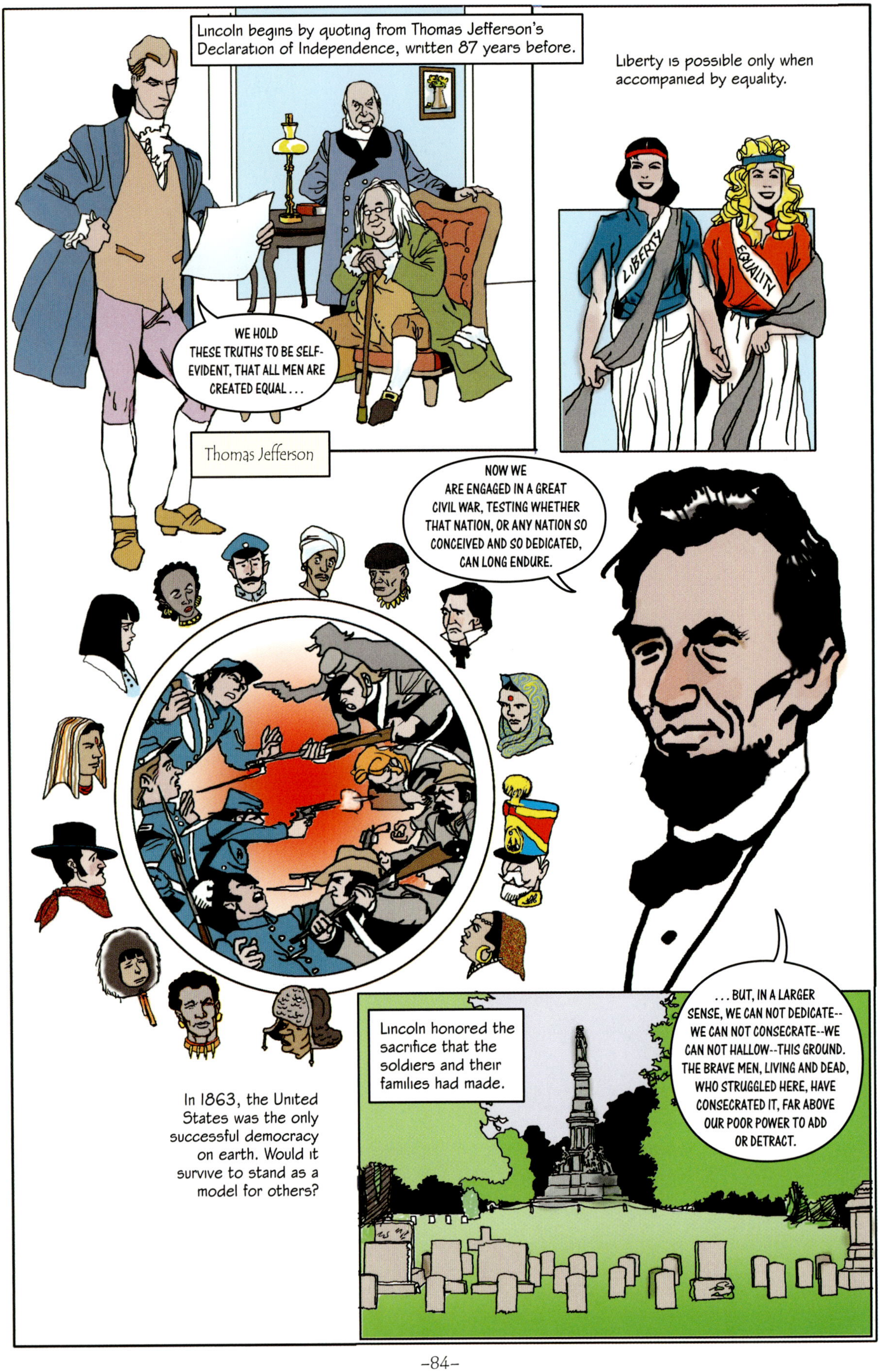
Lincoln begins by quoting from Thomas Jefferson's Declaration of Independence, written 87 years before.
WE HOLD THESE TRUTHS TO BE SELF-EVIDENT, THAT ALL MEN ARE CREATED EQUAL . . .
Thomas Jefferson
Liberty is possible only when accompanied by equality.
LIBERTY
EQUALITY
NOW WE ARE ENGAGED IN A GREAT CIVIL WAR, TESTING WHETHER THAT NATION, OR ANY NATION SO CONCEIVED AND SO DEDICATED, CAN LONG ENDURE.
In 1863, the United States was the only successful democracy on earth. Would it survive to stand as a model for others?
Lincoln honored the sacrifice that the soldiers and their families had made.
. . . BUT, IN A LARGER SENSE, WE CAN NOT DEDICATE--WE CAN NOT CONSECRATE--WE CAN NOT HALLOW--THIS GROUND. THE BRAVE MEN, LIVING AND DEAD, WHO STRUGGLED HERE, HAVE CONSECRATED IT, FAR ABOVE OUR POOR POWER TO ADD OR DETRACT.

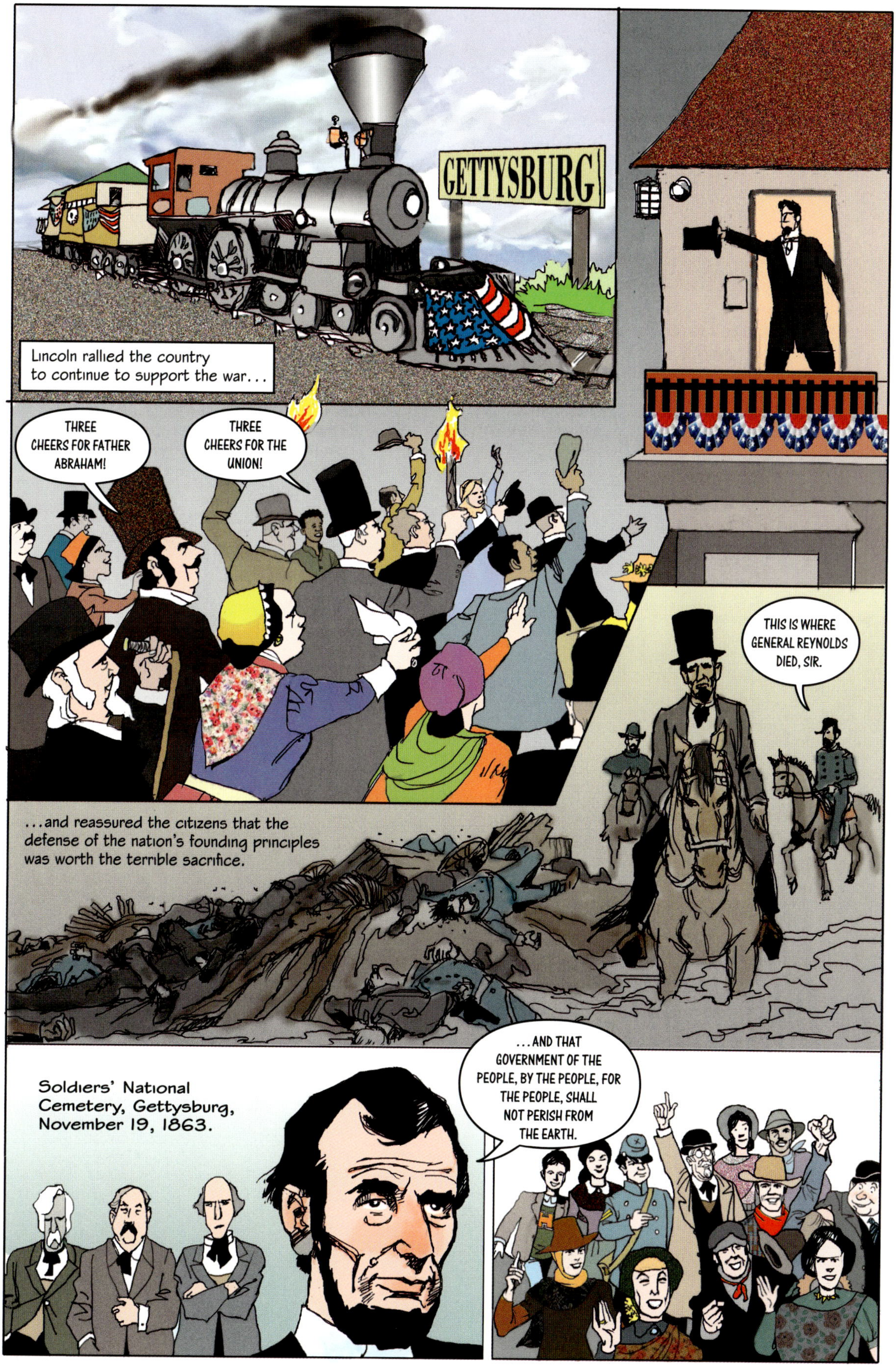
GETTYSBURG
Lincoln rallied the country to continue to support the war...
THREE CHEERS FOR FATHER ABRAHAM!
THREE CHEERS FOR THE UNION!
THIS IS WHERE GENERAL REYNOLDS DIED, SIR.
...and reassured the citizens that the defense of the nation's founding principles was worth the terrible sacrifice.
Soldiers' National Cemetery, Gettysburg, November 19, 1863.
...AND THAT GOVERNMENT OF THE PEOPLE, BY THE PEOPLE, FOR THE PEOPLE, SHALL NOT PERISH FROM THE EARTH.

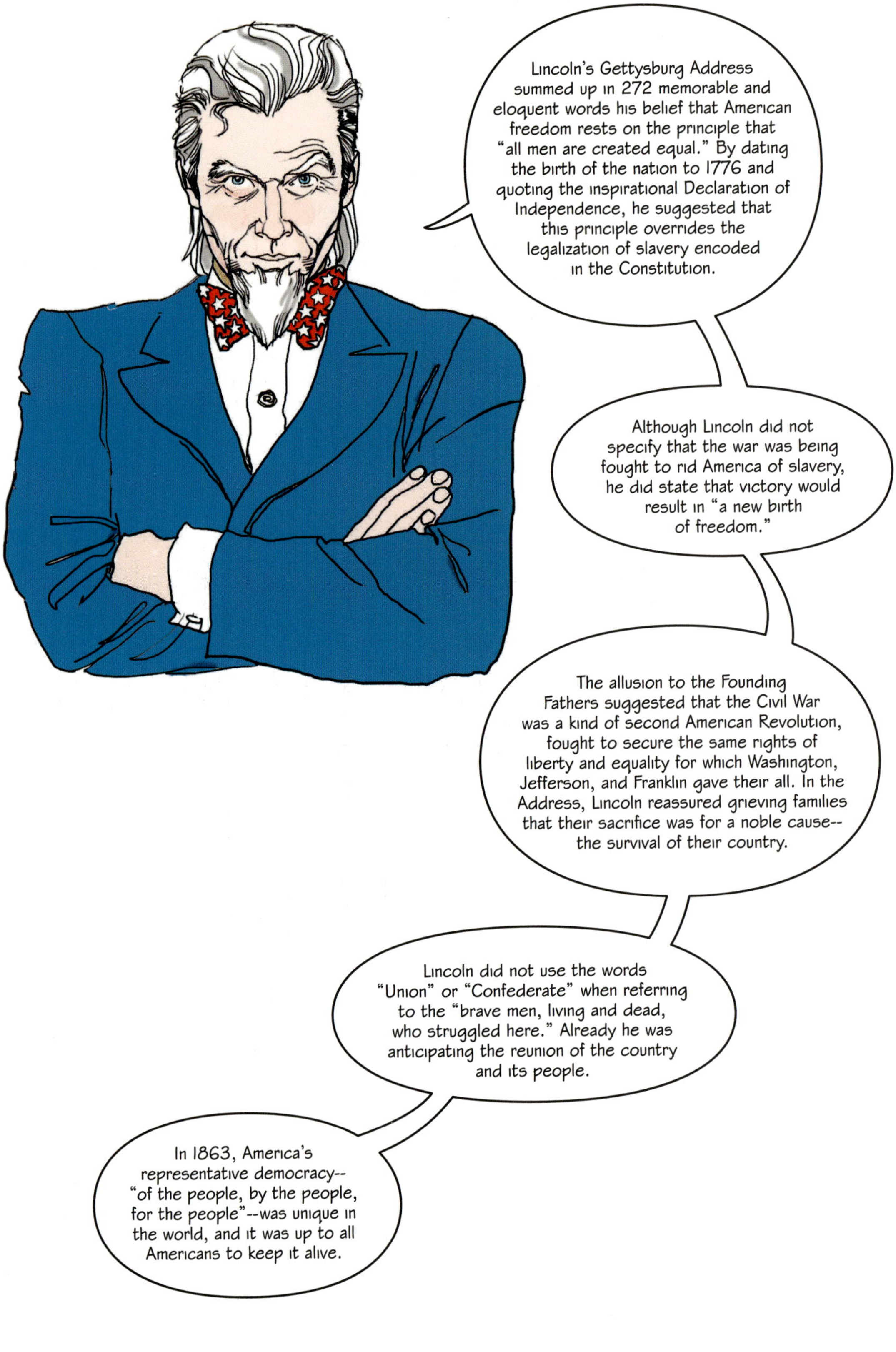
Lincoln's Gettysburg Address summed up in 272 memorable and eloquent words his belief that American freedom rests on the principle that "all men are created equal." By dating the birth of the nation to 1776 and quoting the inspirational Declaration of Independence, he suggested that this principle overrides the legalization of slavery encoded in the Constitution.
Although Lincoln did not specify that the war was being fought to rid America of slavery, he did state that victory would result in "a new birth of freedom."
The allusion to the Founding Fathers suggested that the Civil War was a kind of second American Revolution, fought to secure the same rights of liberty and equality for which Washington, Jefferson, and Franklin gave their all. In the Address, Lincoln reassured grieving families that their sacrifice was for a noble cause--the survival of their country.
Lincoln did not use the words "Union" or "Confederate" when referring to the "brave men, living and dead, who struggled here." Already he was anticipating the reunion of the country and its people.
In 1863, America's representative democracy--"of the people, by the people, for the people"--was unique in the world, and it was up to all Americans to keep it alive.

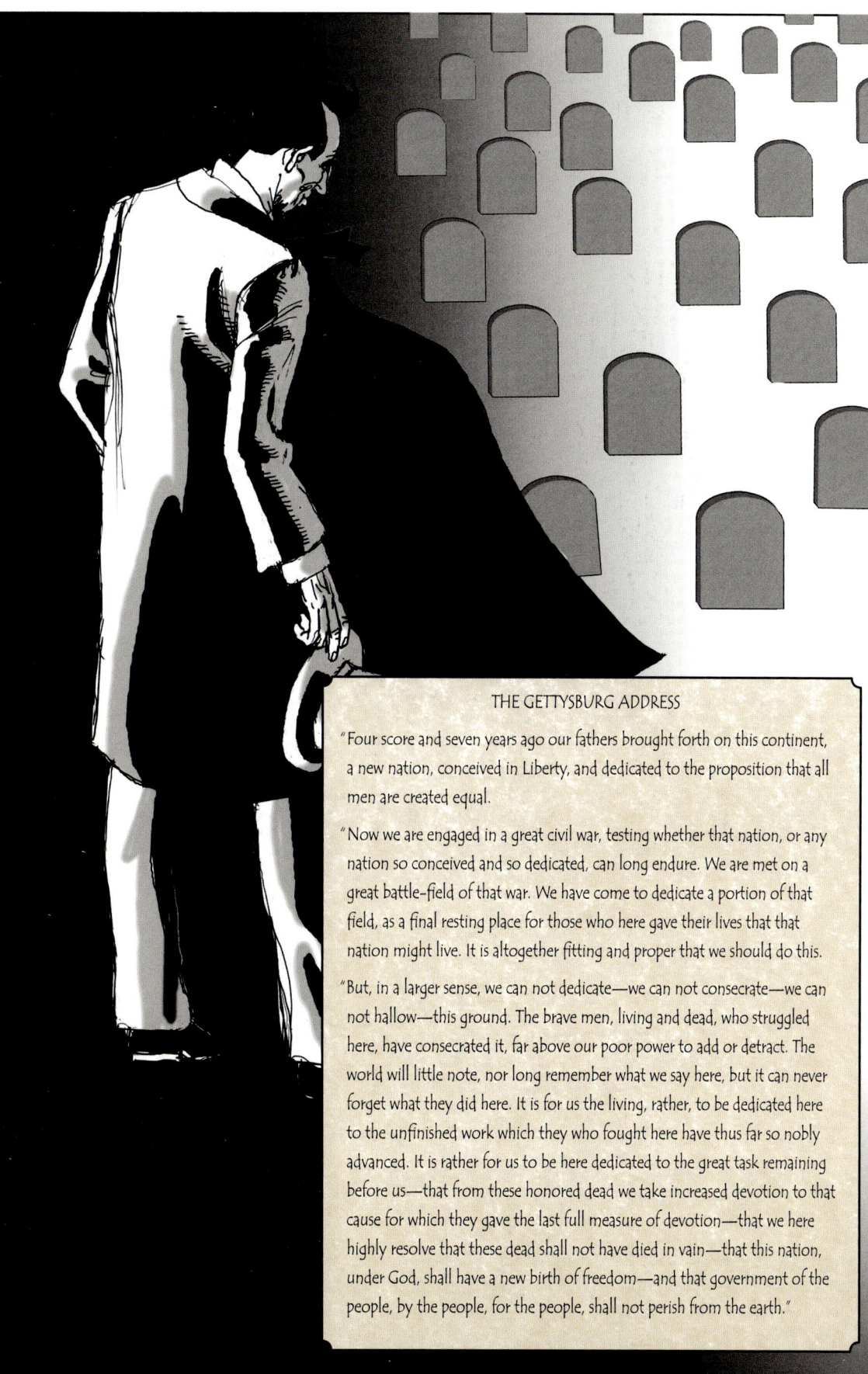

THE GETTYSBURG ADDRESS

"Four score and seven years ago our fathers brought forth on this continent, a new nation, conceived in Liberty, and dedicated to the proposition that all men are created equal.

"Now we are engaged in a great civil war, testing whether that nation, or any nation so conceived and so dedicated, can long endure. We are met on a great battle-field of that war. We have come to dedicate a portion of that field, as a final resting place for those who here gave their lives that that nation might live. It is altogether fitting and proper that we should do this.

"But, in a larger sense, we can not dedicate—we can not consecrate—we can not hallow—this ground. The brave men, living and dead, who struggled here, have consecrated it, far above our poor power to add or detract. The world will little note, nor long remember what we say here, but it can never forget what they did here. It is for us the living, rather, to be dedicated here to the unfinished work which they who fought here have thus far so nobly advanced. It is rather for us to be here dedicated to the great task remaining before us—that from these honored dead we take increased devotion to that cause for which they gave the last full measure of devotion—that we here highly resolve that these dead shall not have died in vain—that this nation, under God, shall have a new birth of freedom—and that government of the people, by the people, for the people, shall not perish from the earth."

Lincoln's Second Inaugural Address

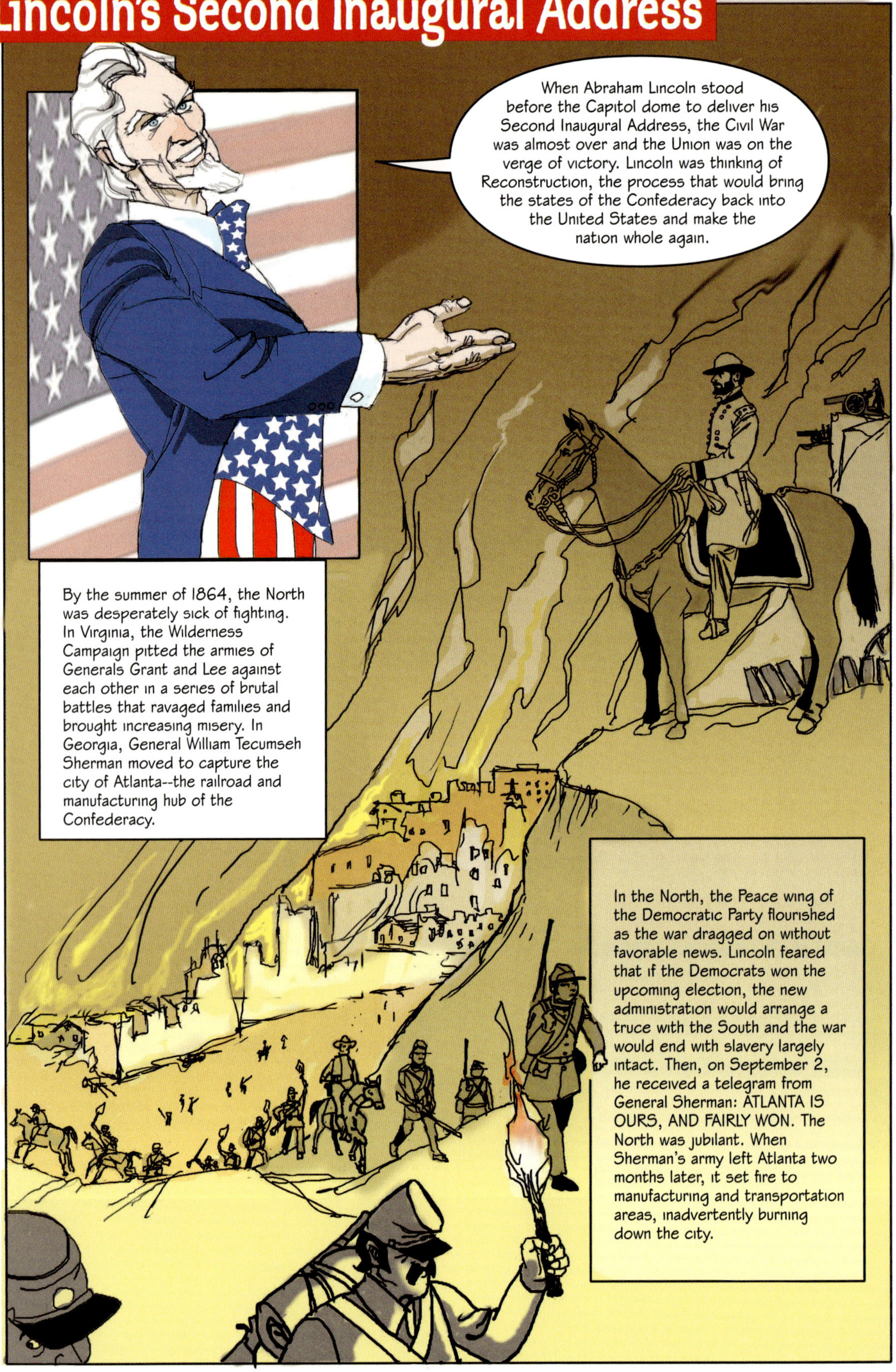

When Abraham Lincoln stood before the Capitol dome to deliver his Second Inaugural Address, the Civil War was almost over and the Union was on the verge of victory. Lincoln was thinking of Reconstruction, the process that would bring the states of the Confederacy back into the United States and make the nation whole again.
By the summer of 1864, the North was desperately sick of fighting. In Virginia, the Wilderness Campaign pitted the armies of Generals Grant and Lee against each other in a series of brutal battles that ravaged families and brought increasing misery. In Georgia, General William Tecumseh Sherman moved to capture the city of Atlanta--the railroad and manufacturing hub of the Confederacy.
In the North, the Peace wing of the Democratic Party flourished as the war dragged on without favorable news. Lincoln feared that if the Democrats won the upcoming election, the new administration would arrange a truce with the South and the war would end with slavery largely intact. Then, on September 2, he received a telegram from General Sherman: ATLANTA IS OURS, AND FAIRLY WON. The North was jubilant. When Sherman's army left Atlanta two months later, it set fire to manufacturing and transportation areas, inadvertently burning down the city.

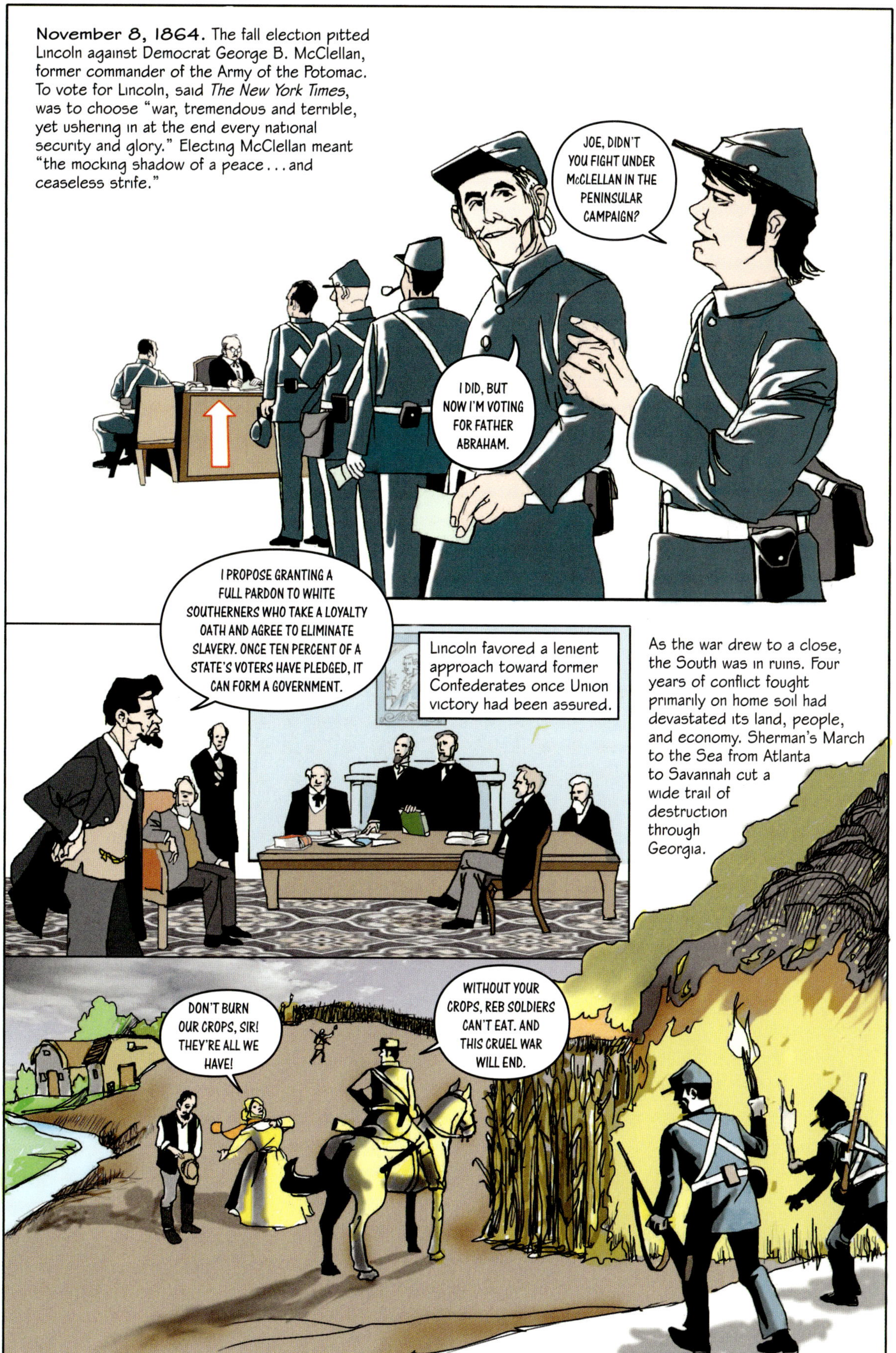
November 8, 1864. The fall election pitted Lincoln against Democrat George B. McClellan, former commander of the Army of the Potomac. To vote for Lincoln, said The New York Times, was to choose "war, tremendous and terrible, yet ushering in at the end every national security and glory." Electing McClellan meant "the mocking shadow of a peace . . . and ceaseless strife."
JOE, DIDN'T YOU FIGHT UNDER McCLELLAN IN THE PENINSULAR CAMPAIGN?
I DID, BUT NOW I'M VOTING FOR FATHER ABRAHAM.
I PROPOSE GRANTING A FULL PARDON TO WHITE SOUTHERNERS WHO TAKE A LOYALTY OATH AND AGREE TO ELIMINATE SLAVERY. ONCE TEN PERCENT OF A STATE'S VOTERS HAVE PLEDGED, IT CAN FORM A GOVERNMENT.
Lincoln favored a lenient approach toward former Confederates once Union victory had been assured.
As the war drew to a close, the South was in ruins. Four years of conflict fought primarily on home soil had devastated its land, people, and economy. Sherman's March to the Sea from Atlanta to Savannah cut a wide trail of destruction through Georgia.
DON'T BURN OUR CROPS, SIR! THEY'RE ALL WE HAVE!
WITHOUT YOUR CROPS, REB SOLDIERS CAN'T EAT. AND THIS CRUEL WAR WILL END.

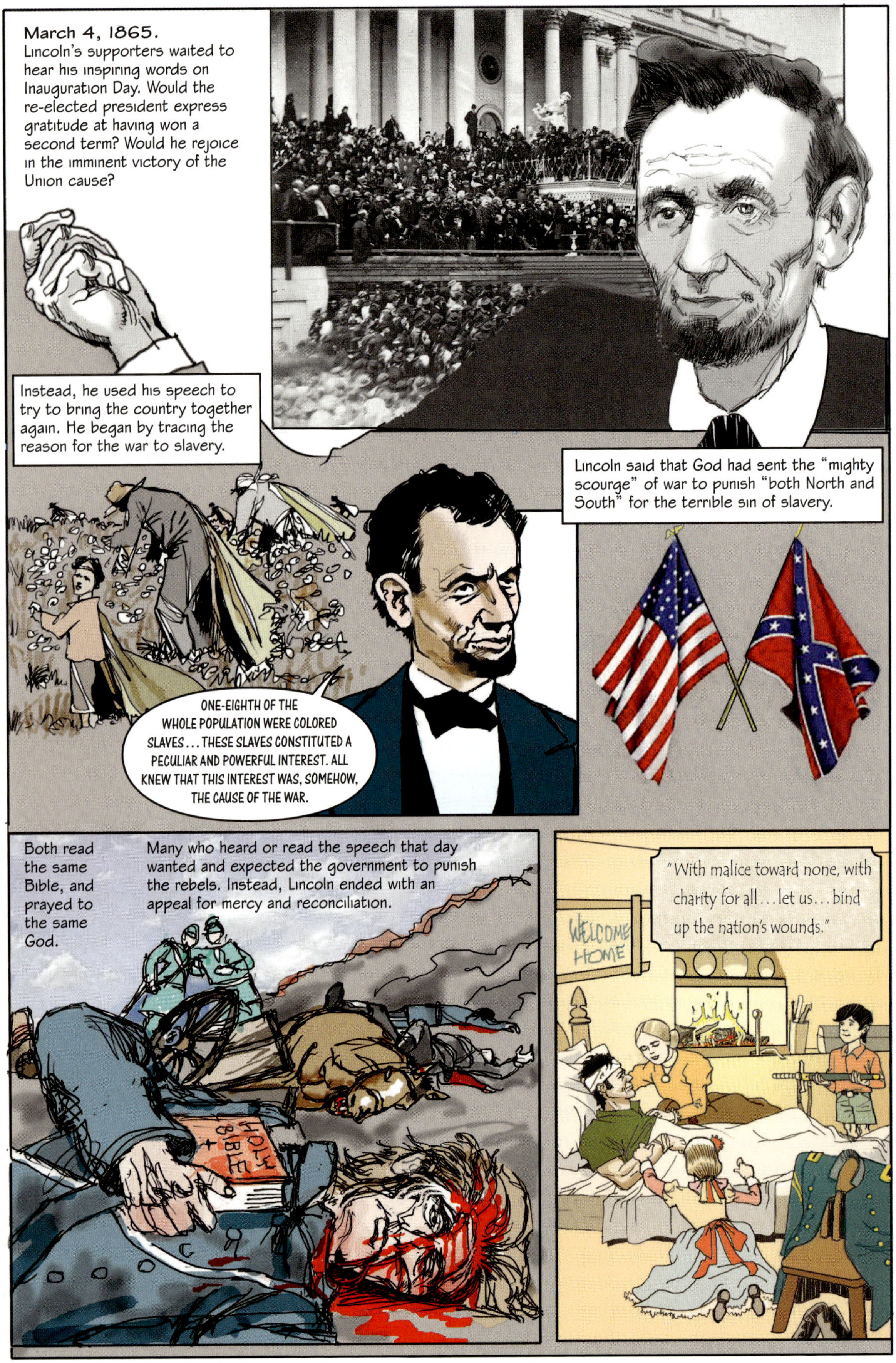
March 4, 1865.
Lincoln's supporters waited to hear his inspiring words on Inauguration Day. Would the re-elected president express gratitude at having won a second term? Would he rejoice in the imminent victory of the Union cause?
Instead, he used his speech to try to bring the country together again. He began by tracing the reason for the war to slavery.
ONE-EIGHTH OF THE WHOLE POPULATION WERE COLORED SLAVES . . . THESE SLAVES CONSTITUTED A PECULIAR AND POWERFUL INTEREST. ALL KNEW THAT THIS INTEREST WAS, SOMEHOW, THE CAUSE OF THE WAR.
Lincoln said that God had sent the "mighty scourge" of war to punish "both North and South" for the terrible sin of slavery.
Both read the same Bible, and prayed to the same God.
Many who heard or read the speech that day wanted and expected the government to punish the rebels. Instead, Lincoln ended with an appeal for mercy and reconciliation.
HOLY BIBLE
"With malice toward none, with charity for all . . . let us . . . bind up the nation's wounds."
WELCOME HOME

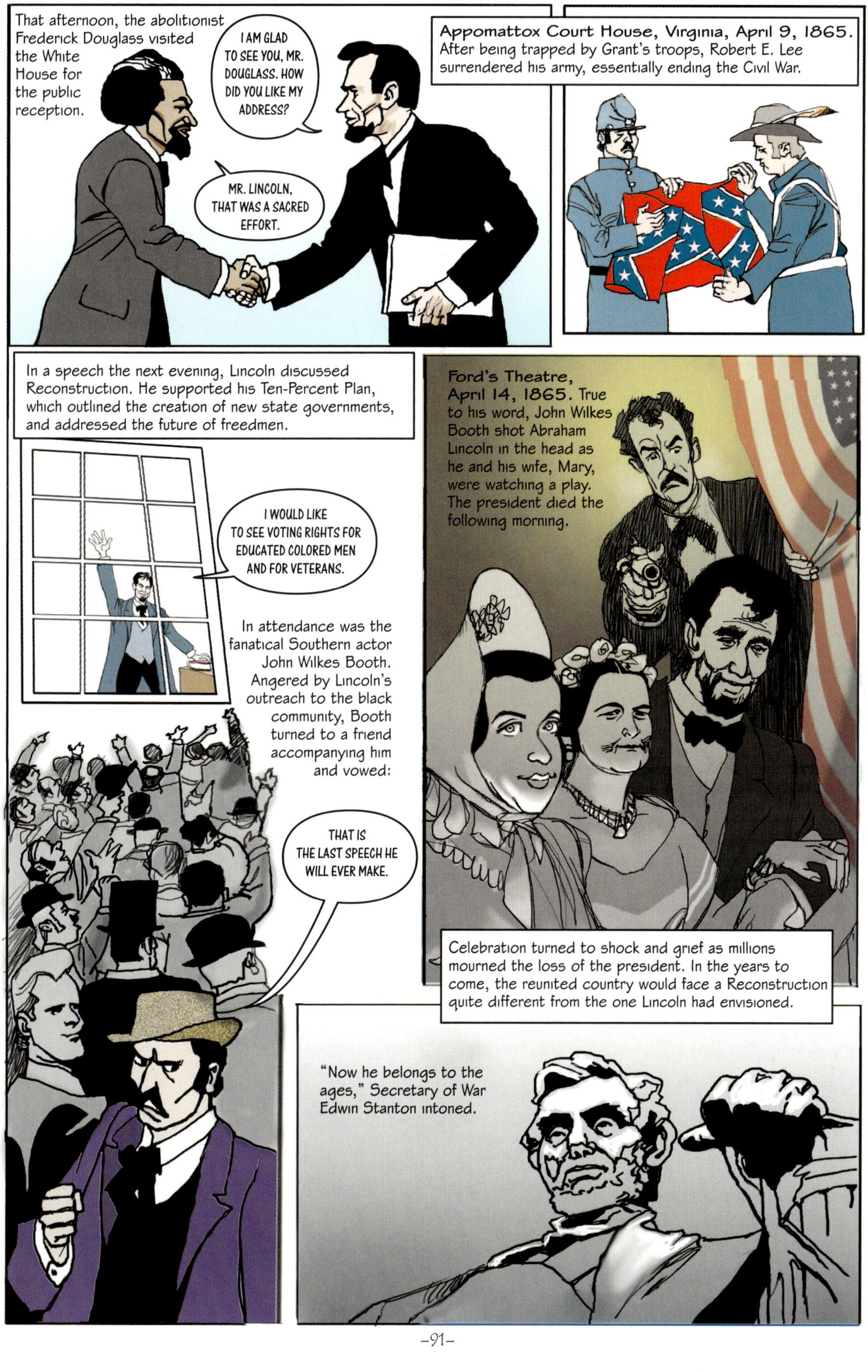

That afternoon, the abolitionist Frederick Douglass visited the White House for the public reception.
I AM GLAD TO SEE YOU, MR. DOUGLASS. HOW DID YOU LIKE MY ADDRESS?
MR. LINCOLN, THAT WAS A SACRED EFFORT.
Appomattox Court House, Virginia, April 9, 1865. After being trapped by Grant's troops, Robert E. Lee surrendered his army, essentially ending the Civil War.
In a speech the next evening, Lincoln discussed Reconstruction. He supported his Ten-Percent Plan, which outlined the creation of new state governments, and addressed the future of freedmen.
I WOULD LIKE TO SEE VOTING RIGHTS FOR EDUCATED COLORED MEN AND FOR VETERANS.
In attendance was the fanatical Southern actor John Wilkes Booth. Angered by Lincoln's outreach to the black community, Booth turned to a friend accompanying him and vowed:
THAT IS THE LAST SPEECH HE WILL EVER MAKE.
Ford's Theatre, April 14, 1865. True to his word, John Wilkes Booth shot Abraham Lincoln in the head as he and his wife, Mary, were watching a play. The president died the following morning.
Celebration turned to shock and grief as millions mourned the loss of the president. In the years to come, the reunited country would face a Reconstruction quite different from the one Lincoln had envisioned.
"Now he belongs to the ages," Secretary of War Edwin Stanton intoned.

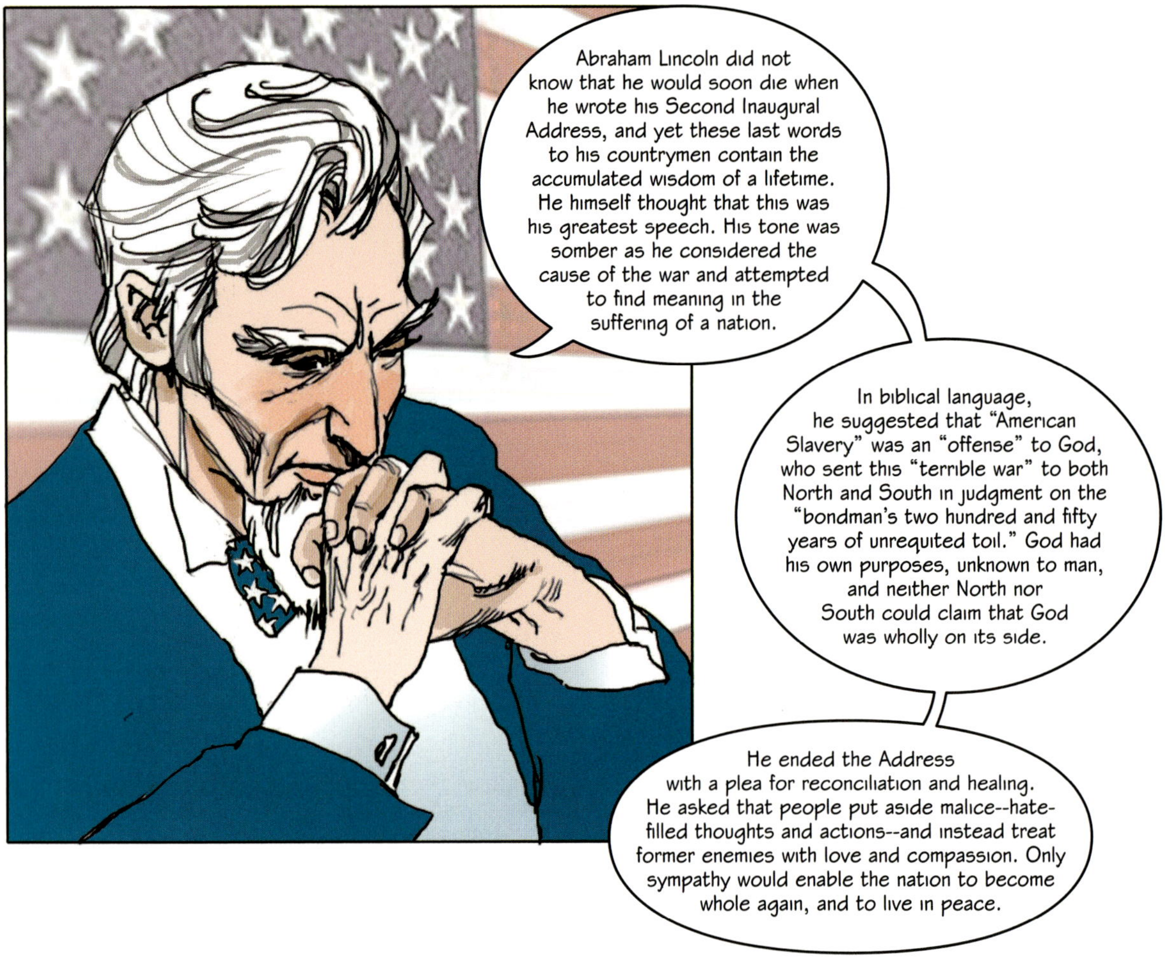
Abraham Lincoln did not know that he would soon die when he wrote his Second Inaugural Address, and yet these last words to his countrymen contain the accumulated wisdom of a lifetime. He himself thought that this was his greatest speech. His tone was somber as he considered the cause of the war and attempted to find meaning in the suffering of a nation.
In biblical language, he suggested that "American Slavery" was an "offense" to God, who sent this "terrible war" to both North and South in judgment on the "bondman's two hundred and fifty years of unrequited toil." God had his own purposes, unknown to man, and neither North nor South could claim that God was wholly on its side.
He ended the Address with a plea for reconciliation and healing. He asked that people put aside malice--hate-filled thoughts and actions--and instead treat former enemies with love and compassion. Only sympathy would enable the nation to become whole again, and to live in peace.

EXCERPT FROM LINCOLN'S SECOND INAUGURAL ADDRESS

"Fondly do we hope—fervently do we pray—that this mighty scourge of war may speedily pass away. Yet, if God wills that it continue, until all the wealth piled by the bond-man's two hundred and fifty years of unrequited toil shall be sunk, and until every drop of blood drawn with the lash, shall be paid by another drawn with the sword, as was said three thousand years ago, so still it must be said 'the judgments of the Lord, are true and righteous altogether.'

"With malice toward none; with charity for all; with firmness in the right, as God gives us to see the right, let us strive on to finish the work we are in; to bind up the nation's wounds; to care for him who shall have borne the battle, and for his widow, and his orphan—to do all which may achieve and cherish a just, and a lasting peace, among ourselves, and with all nations."

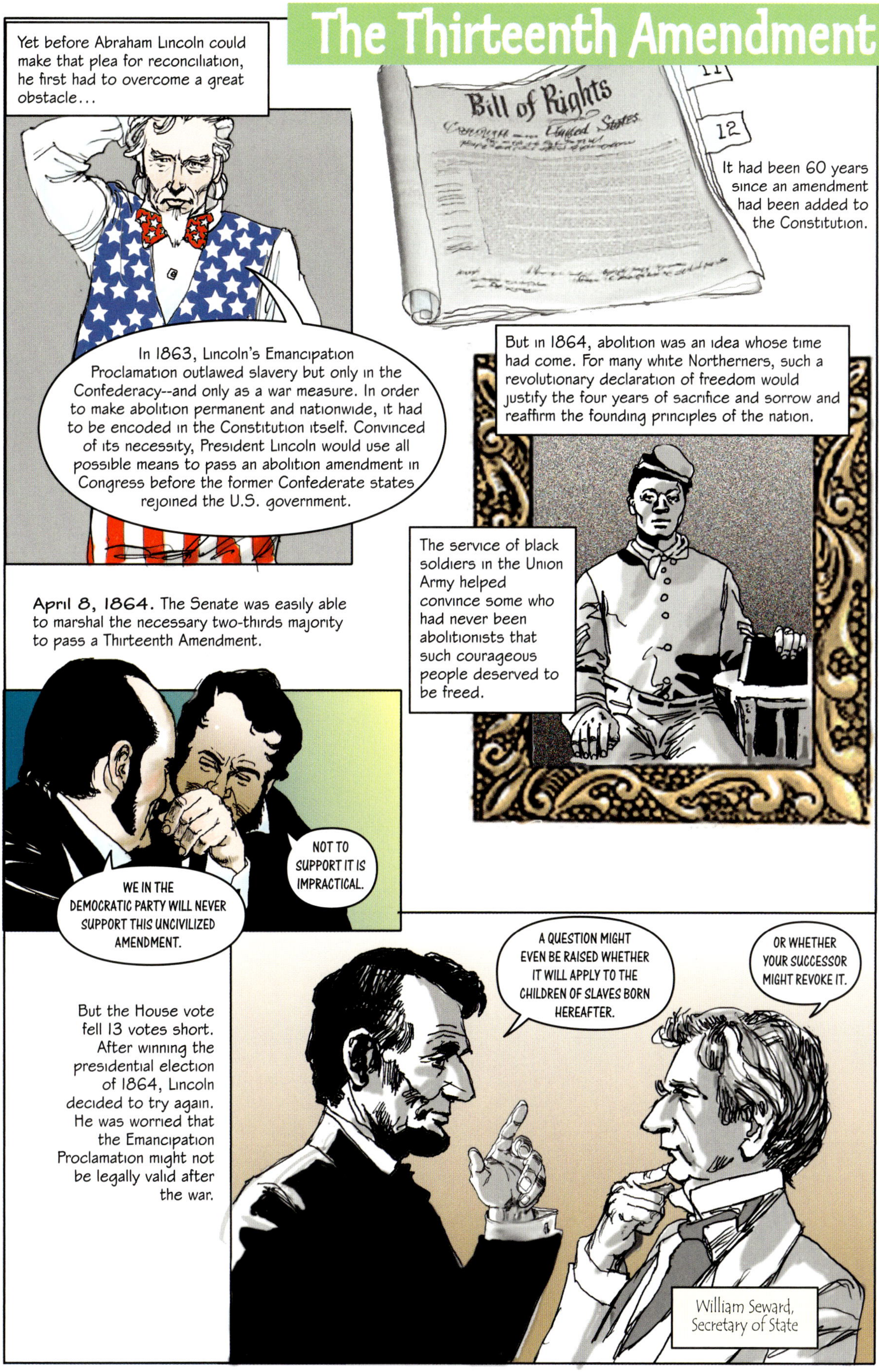
The Thirteenth Amendment
Yet before Abraham Lincoln could make that plea for reconciliation, he first had to overcome a great obstacle...
Bill of Rights
11
12
It had been 60 years since an amendment had been added to the Constitution.
In 1863, Lincoln's Emancipation Proclamation outlawed slavery but only in the Confederacy--and only as a war measure. In order to make abolition permanent and nationwide, it had to be encoded in the Constitution itself. Convinced of its necessity, President Lincoln would use all possible means to pass an abolition amendment in Congress before the former Confederate states rejoined the U.S. government.
But in 1864, abolition was an idea whose time had come. For many white Northerners, such a revolutionary declaration of freedom would justify the four years of sacrifice and sorrow and reaffirm the founding principles of the nation.
The service of black soldiers in the Union Army helped convince some who had never been abolitionists that such courageous people deserved to be freed.
April 8, 1864. The Senate was easily able to marshal the necessary two-thirds majority to pass a Thirteenth Amendment.
WE IN THE DEMOCRATIC PARTY WILL NEVER SUPPORT THIS UNCIVILIZED AMENDMENT.
NOT TO SUPPORT IT IS IMPRACTICAL.
But the House vote fell 13 votes short. After winning the presidential election of 1864, Lincoln decided to try again. He was worried that the Emancipation Proclamation might not be legally valid after the war.
A QUESTION MIGHT EVEN BE RAISED WHETHER IT WILL APPLY TO THE CHILDREN OF SLAVES BORN HEREAFTER.
OR WHETHER YOUR SUCCESSOR MIGHT REVOKE IT.
William Seward, Secretary of State

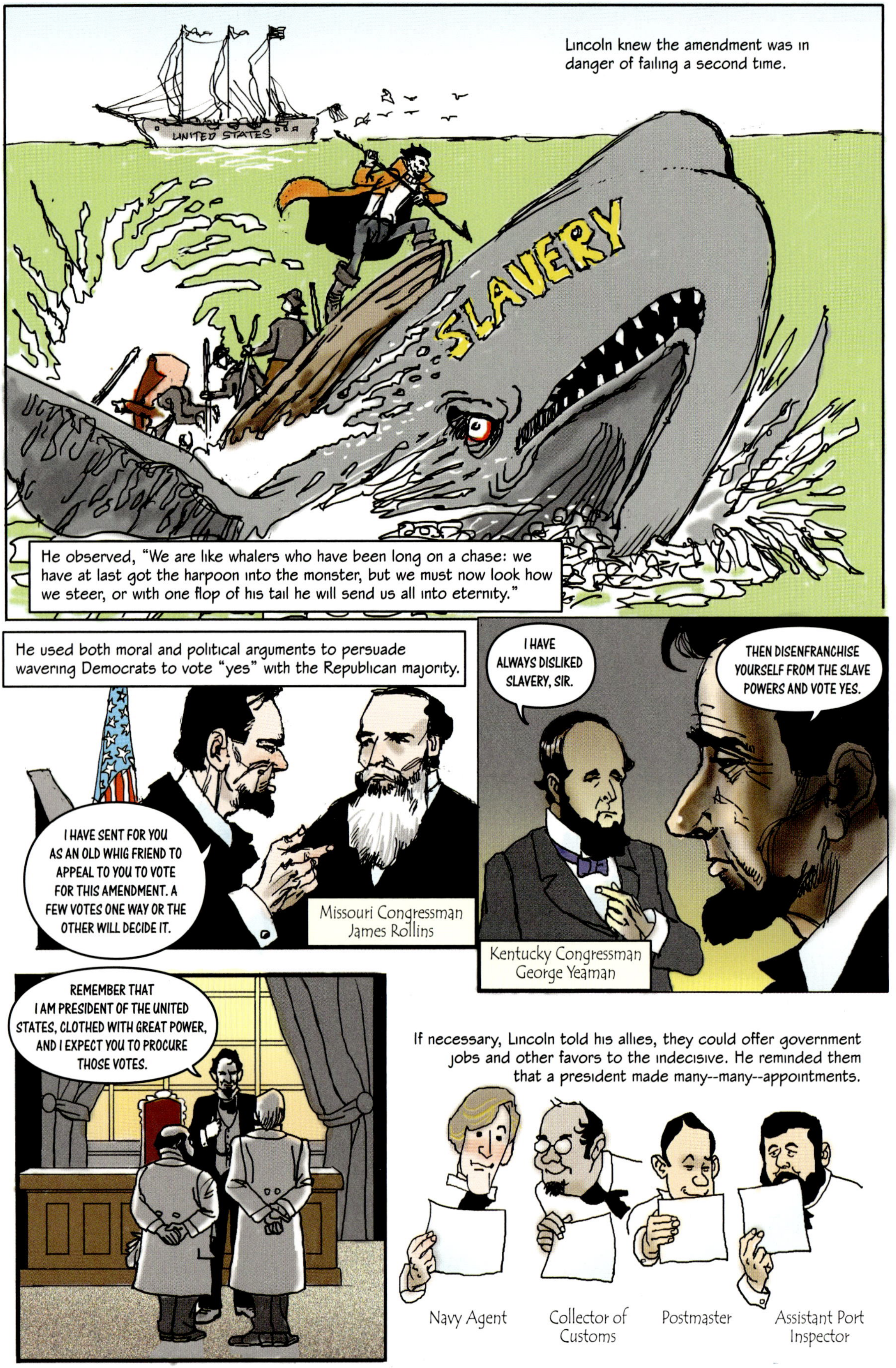
Lincoln knew the amendment was in danger of failing a second time.
UNITED STATES
SLAVERY
He observed, "We are like whalers who have been long on a chase: we have at last got the harpoon into the monster, but we must now look how we steer, or with one flop of his tail he will send us all into eternity."
He used both moral and political arguments to persuade wavering Democrats to vote "yes" with the Republican majority.
I HAVE SENT FOR YOU AS AN OLD WHIG FRIEND TO APPEAL TO YOU TO VOTE FOR THIS AMENDMENT. A FEW VOTES ONE WAY OR THE OTHER WILL DECIDE IT.
Missouri Congressman James Rollins
I HAVE ALWAYS DISLIKED SLAVERY, SIR.
THEN DISENFRANCHISE YOURSELF FROM THE SLAVE POWERS AND VOTE YES.
Kentucky Congressman George Yeaman
REMEMBER THAT I AM PRESIDENT OF THE UNITED STATES, CLOTHED WITH GREAT POWER, AND I EXPECT YOU TO PROCURE THOSE VOTES.
If necessary, Lincoln told his allies, they could offer government jobs and other favors to the indecisive. He reminded them that a president made many--many--appointments.
Navy Agent
Collector of Customs
Postmaster
Assistant Port Inspector

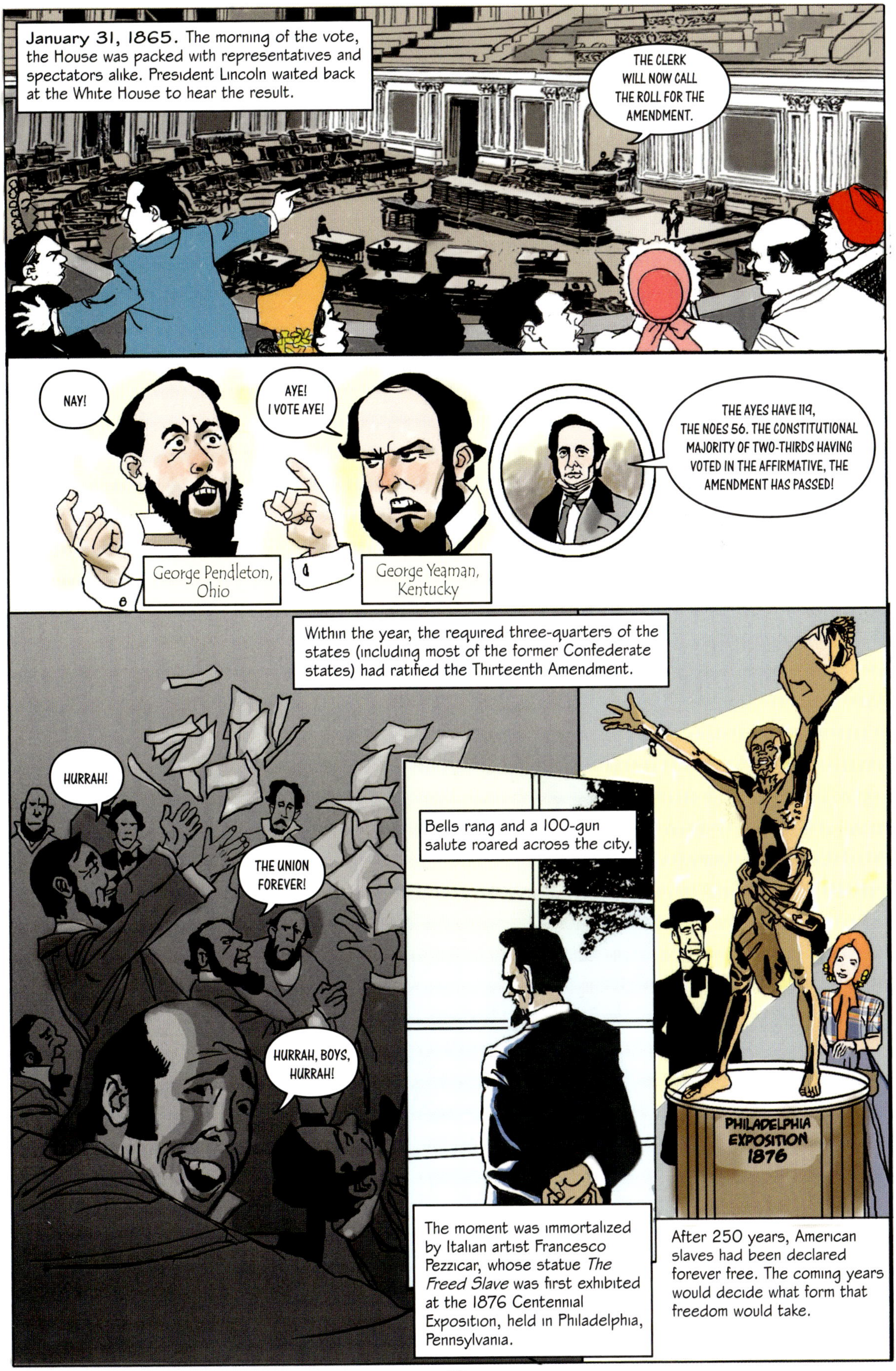
January 31, 1865. The morning of the vote, the House was packed with representatives and spectators alike. President Lincoln waited back at the White House to hear the result.
THE CLERK WILL NOW CALL THE ROLL FOR THE AMENDMENT.
NAY!
George Pendleton, Ohio
AYE! I VOTE AYE!
George Yeaman, Kentucky
THE AYES HAVE 119, THE NOES 56. THE CONSTITUTIONAL MAJORITY OF TWO-THIRDS HAVING VOTED IN THE AFFIRMATIVE, THE AMENDMENT HAS PASSED!
Within the year, the required three-quarters of the states (including most of the former Confederate states) had ratified the Thirteenth Amendment.
HURRAH!
THE UNION FOREVER!
HURRAH, BOYS, HURRAH!
Bells rang and a 100-gun salute roared across the city.
PHILADELPHIA EXPOSITION 1876
The moment was immortalized by Italian artist Francesco Pezzicar, whose statue *The Freed Slave* was first exhibited at the 1876 Centennial Exposition, held in Philadelphia, Pennsylvania.
After 250 years, American slaves had been declared forever free. The coming years would decide what form that freedom would take.

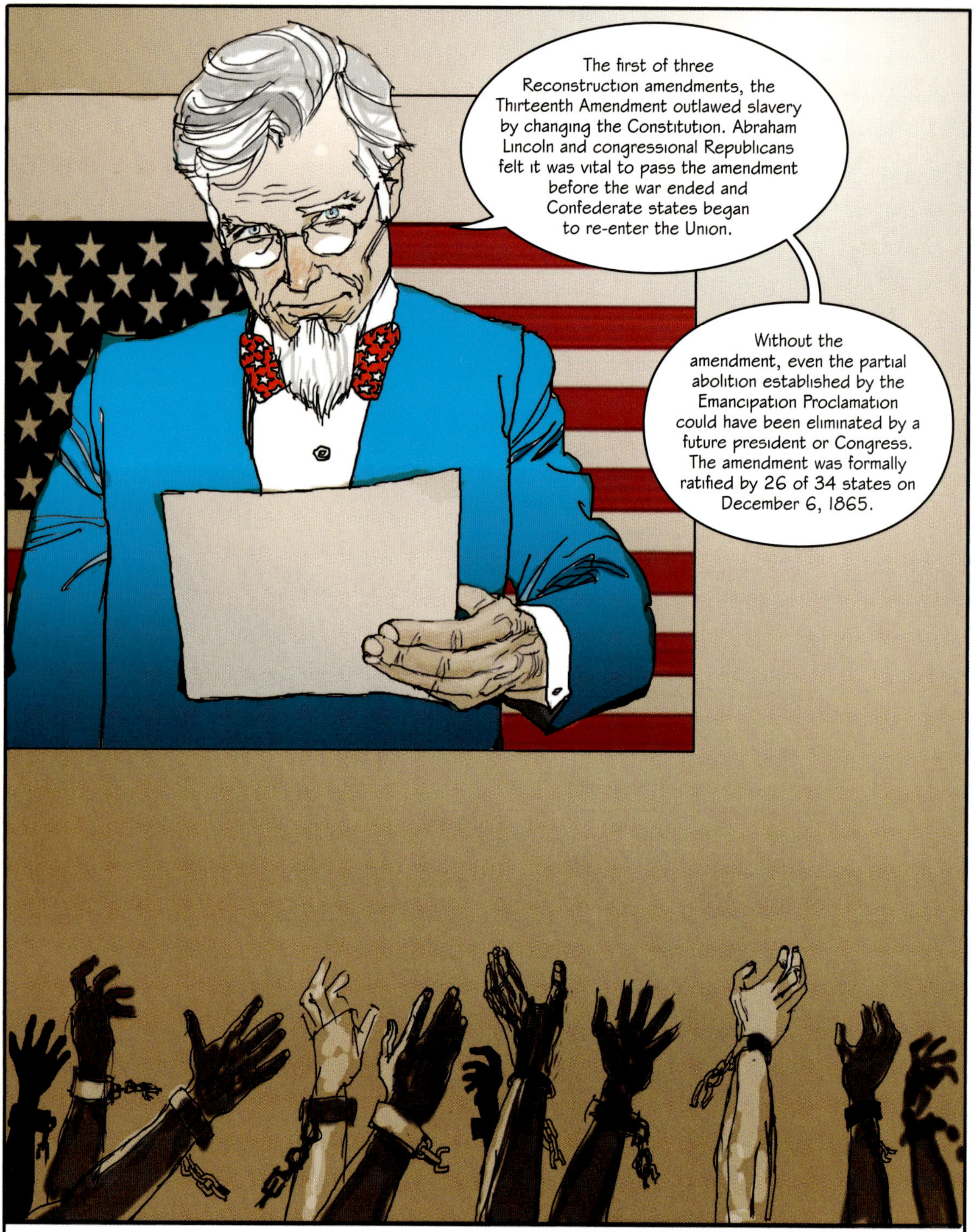
The first of three Reconstruction amendments, the Thirteenth Amendment outlawed slavery by changing the Constitution. Abraham Lincoln and congressional Republicans felt it was vital to pass the amendment before the war ended and Confederate states began to re-enter the Union.
Without the amendment, even the partial abolition established by the Emancipation Proclamation could have been eliminated by a future president or Congress. The amendment was formally ratified by 26 of 34 states on December 6, 1865.

THE THIRTEENTH AMENDMENT

"Section 1. Neither slavery nor involuntary servitude, except as a punishment for crime whereof the party shall have been duly convicted, shall exist within the United States, or any place subject to their jurisdiction.

"Section 2. Congress shall have power to enforce this article by appropriate legislation."

The Fourteenth Amendment

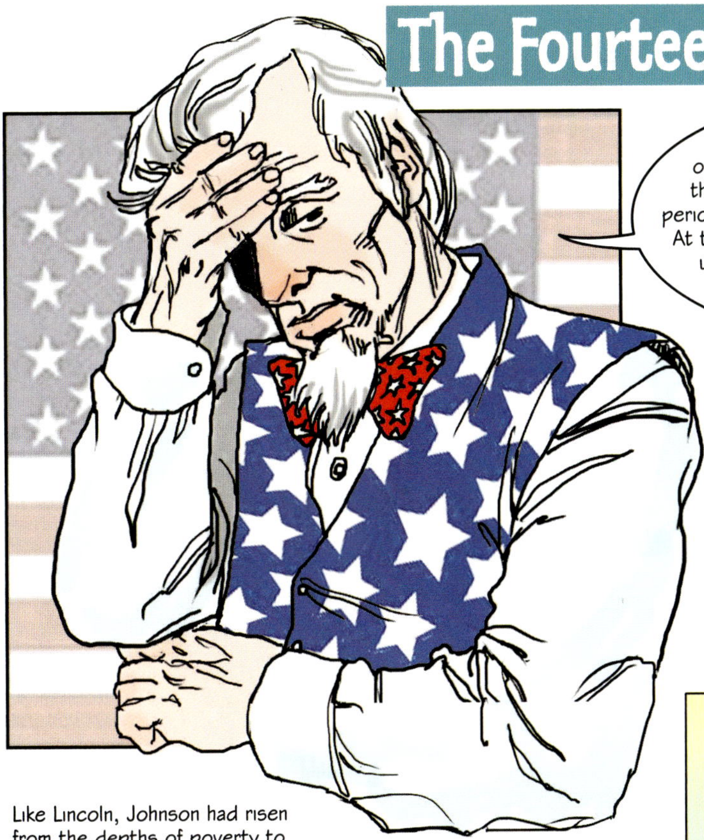
In the turmoil ushered in by the end of the Civil War and Abraham Lincoln's death, the South was agitated by an unprecedented period of social upheaval and economic uncertainty. At this critical time, it fell to Andrew Johnson, an untried and unprepared president, to steer the nation through the dangerous shoals of Reconstruction.

The most urgent question at the end of the war was how to bring the Confederate states back into the Union. As early as December 1863, President Lincoln had proposed a lenient Ten-Percent Plan whereby new state governments could be set up as soon as 10 percent of the population swore loyalty to the United States.

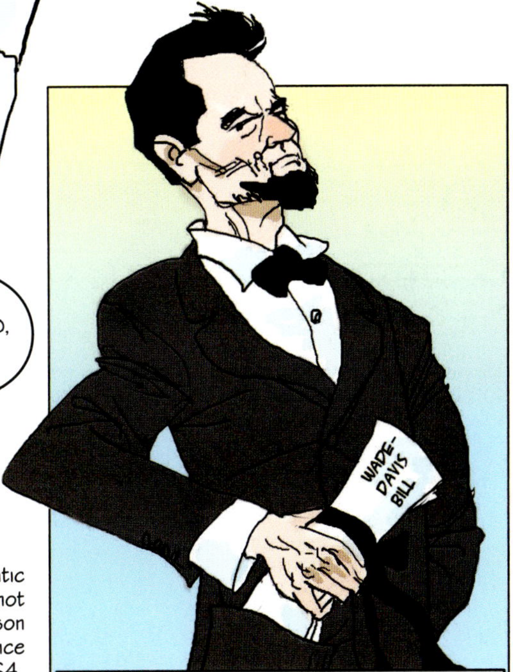
WADE-
DAVIS
BILL

Like Lincoln, Johnson had risen from the depths of poverty to become a successful politician--in Johnson's case, by championing small farmers in Tennessee against the planter elite.

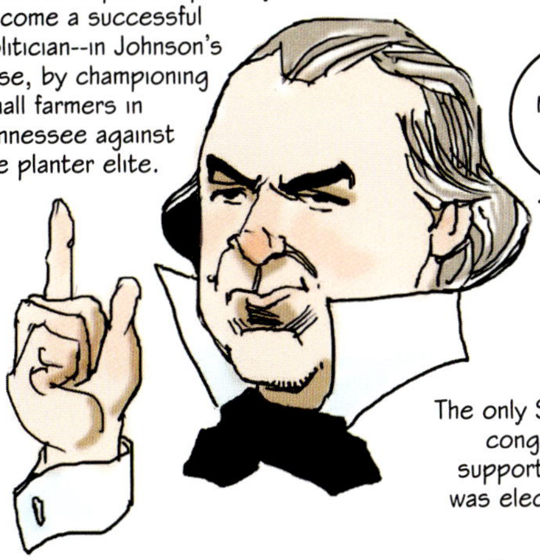
THE PLANTERS ARE NOTHING BUT A PAMPERED, BLOATED, CORRUPTED ARISTOCRACY.

The only Southern Democratic congressman who did not support secession, Johnson was elected as Lincoln's vice president in 1864.

In 1864, Radical Republicans passed the Wade-Davis Bill, which proposed a more stringent program requiring 50 percent of white men to swear loyalty. Lincoln quietly ignored the bill and it died the death of a pocket veto.

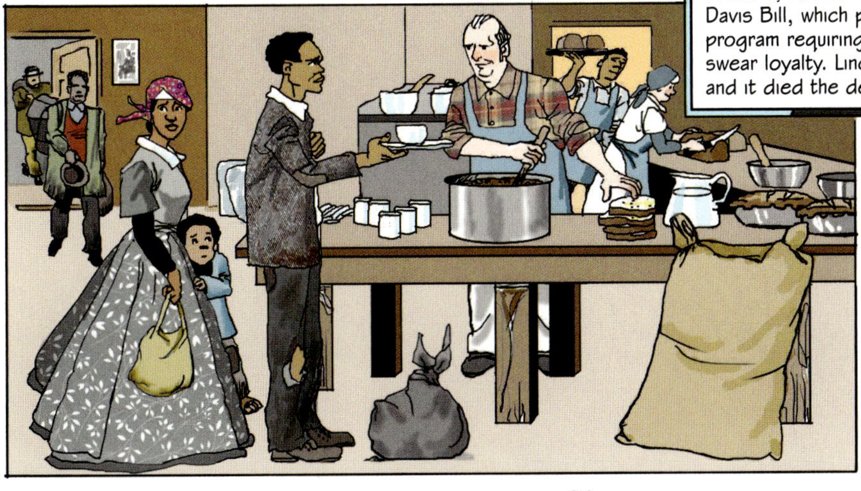

March 1865. Lincoln also set up a new agency of the War Department. The Freedmen's Bureau helped feed, clothe, educate, and settle the nearly 4 million former slaves. Northern teachers, reformers, and missionaries poured into the South to aid in whatever way they could.

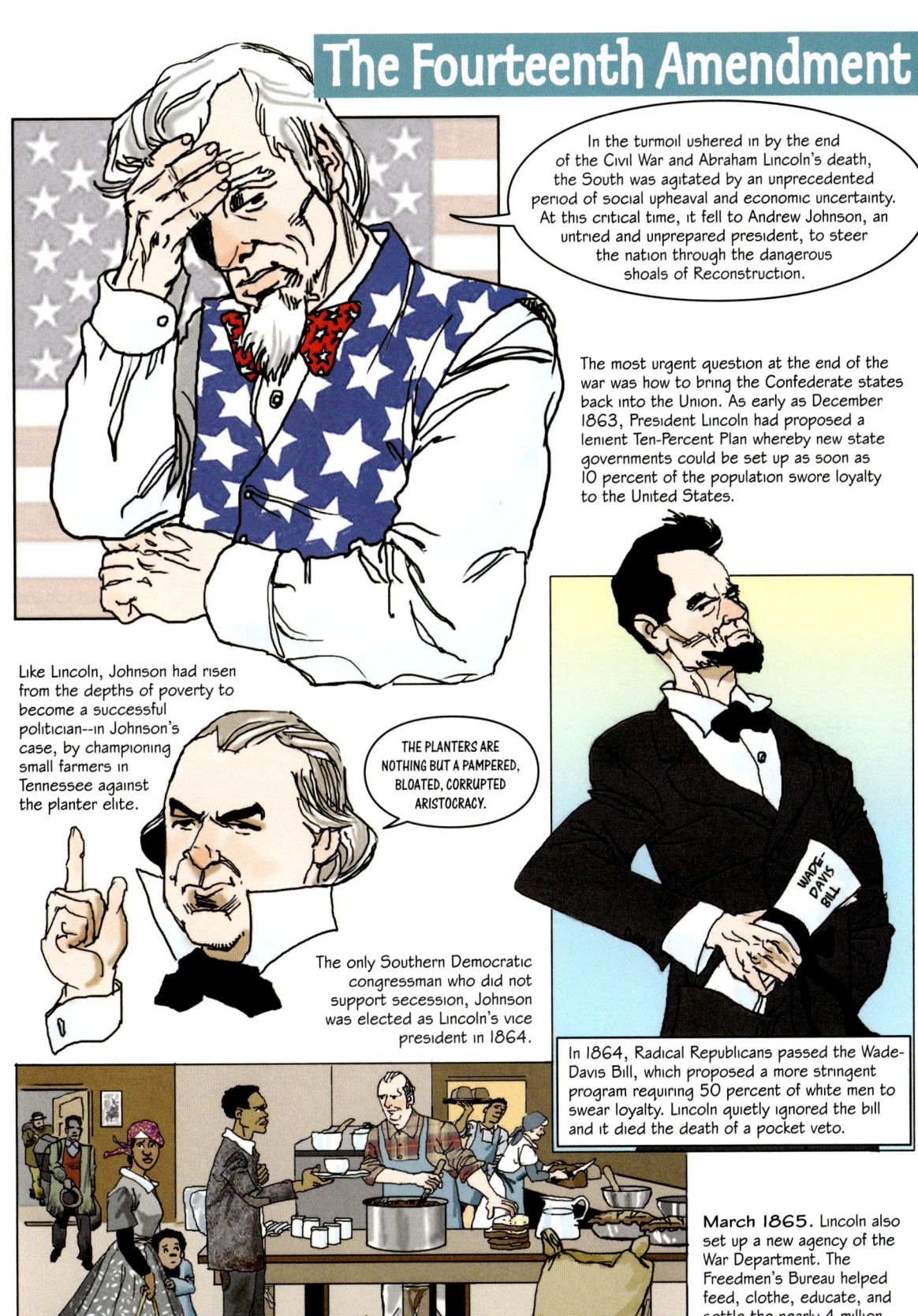

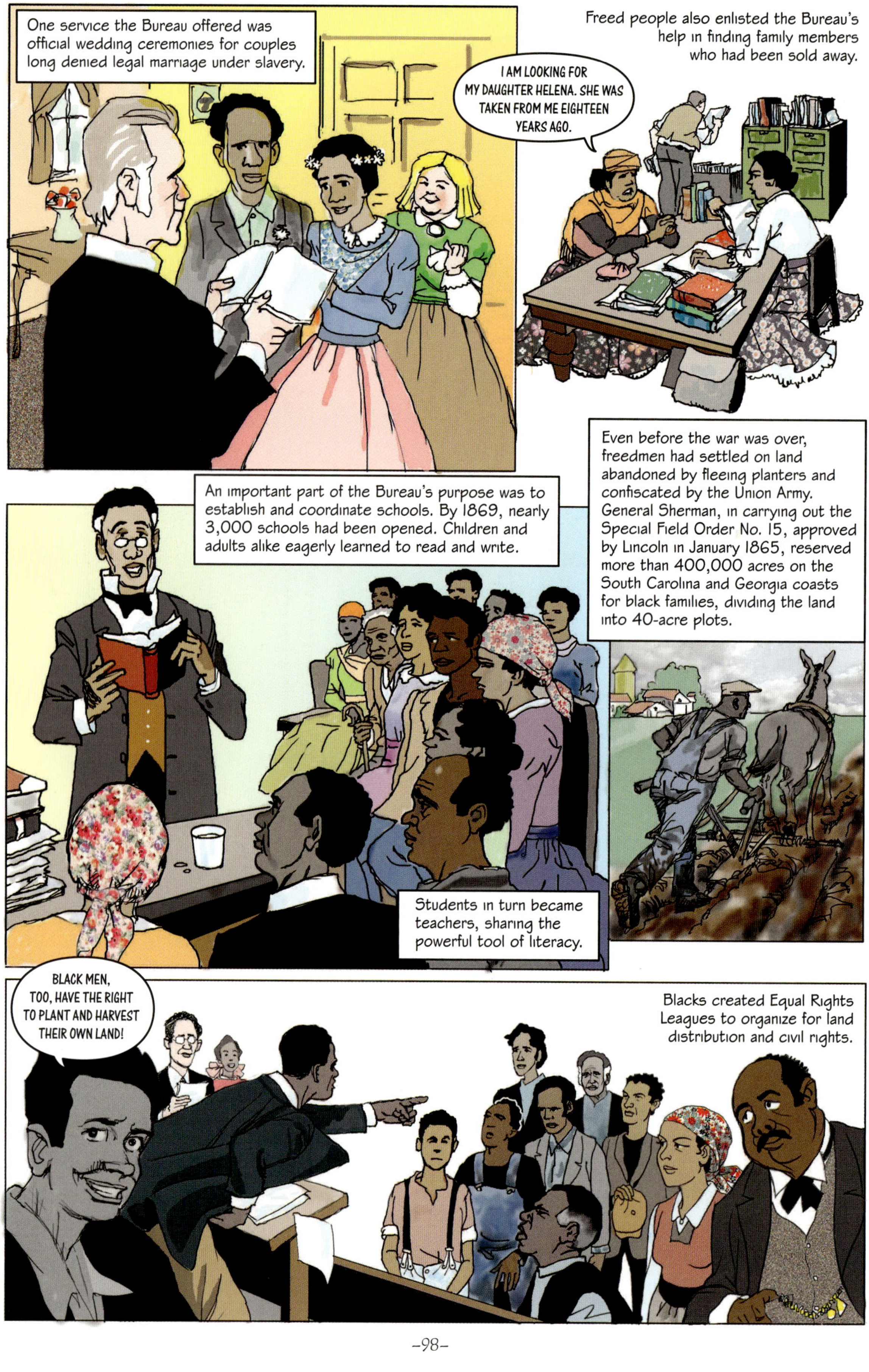
One service the Bureau offered was official wedding ceremonies for couples long denied legal marriage under slavery.
Freed people also enlisted the Bureau's help in finding family members who had been sold away.
I AM LOOKING FOR MY DAUGHTER HELENA. SHE WAS TAKEN FROM ME EIGHTEEN YEARS AGO.
An important part of the Bureau's purpose was to establish and coordinate schools. By 1869, nearly 3,000 schools had been opened. Children and adults alike eagerly learned to read and write.
Students in turn became teachers, sharing the powerful tool of literacy.
Even before the war was over, freedmen had settled on land abandoned by fleeing planters and confiscated by the Union Army. General Sherman, in carrying out the Special Field Order No. 15, approved by Lincoln in January 1865, reserved more than 400,000 acres on the South Carolina and Georgia coasts for black families, dividing the land into 40-acre plots.
BLACK MEN, TOO, HAVE THE RIGHT TO PLANT AND HARVEST THEIR OWN LAND!
Blacks created Equal Rights Leagues to organize for land distribution and civil rights.

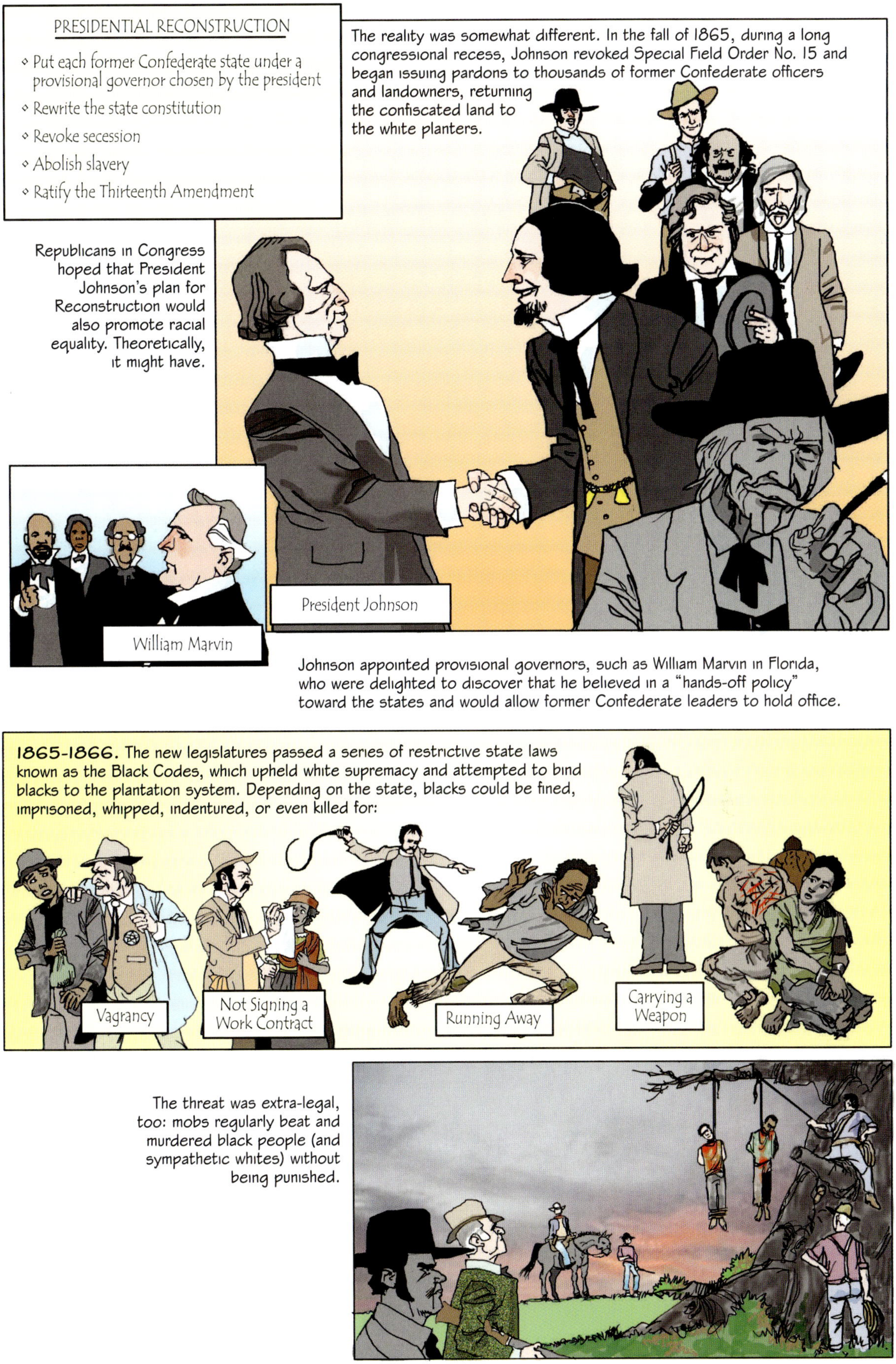
PRESIDENTIAL RECONSTRUCTION
◦ Put each former Confederate state under a provisional governor chosen by the president
◦ Rewrite the state constitution
◦ Revoke secession
◦ Abolish slavery
◦ Ratify the Thirteenth Amendment
The reality was somewhat different. In the fall of 1865, during a long congressional recess, Johnson revoked Special Field Order No. 15 and began issuing pardons to thousands of former Confederate officers and landowners, returning the confiscated land to the white planters.
Republicans in Congress hoped that President Johnson's plan for Reconstruction would also promote racial equality. Theoretically, it might have.
William Marvin
President Johnson
Johnson appointed provisional governors, such as William Marvin in Florida, who were delighted to discover that he believed in a "hands-off policy" toward the states and would allow former Confederate leaders to hold office.
1865-1866. The new legislatures passed a series of restrictive state laws known as the Black Codes, which upheld white supremacy and attempted to bind blacks to the plantation system. Depending on the state, blacks could be fined, imprisoned, whipped, indentured, or even killed for:
Vagrancy
Not Signing a Work Contract
Running Away
Carrying a Weapon
The threat was extra-legal, too: mobs regularly beat and murdered black people (and sympathetic whites) without being punished.

The *Chicago Tribune* thundered, "The men of the North will convert the state of Mississippi into a frog pond before they will allow such laws to disgrace one foot of soil in which the bones of our soldiers sleep and over which the flag of freedom waves."

Radical Republicans, led by Thaddeus Stevens of Pennsylvania, came back to Congress in December 1865 ready to battle the president over Reconstruction. At the heart of their disagreement was a fundamentally different idea of the future of black people in the former Confederacy.

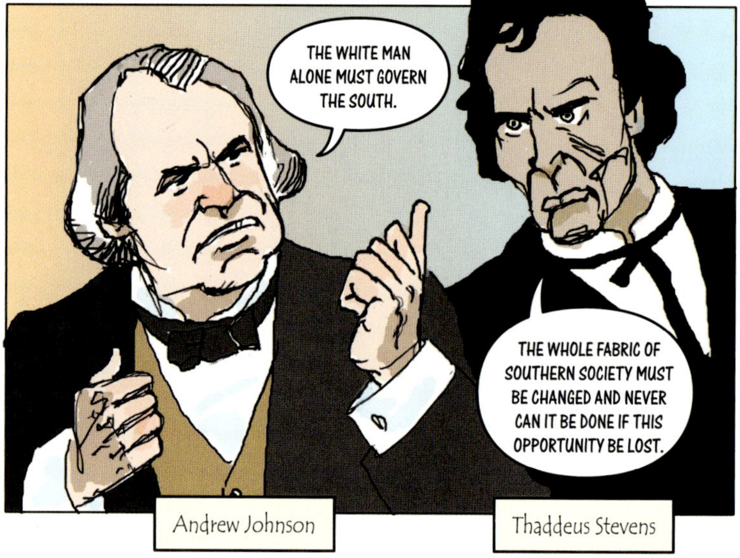
THE WHITE MAN ALONE MUST GOVERN THE SOUTH.
THE WHOLE FABRIC OF SOUTHERN SOCIETY MUST BE CHANGED AND NEVER CAN IT BE DONE IF THIS OPPORTUNITY BE LOST.
Andrew Johnson
Thaddeus Stevens

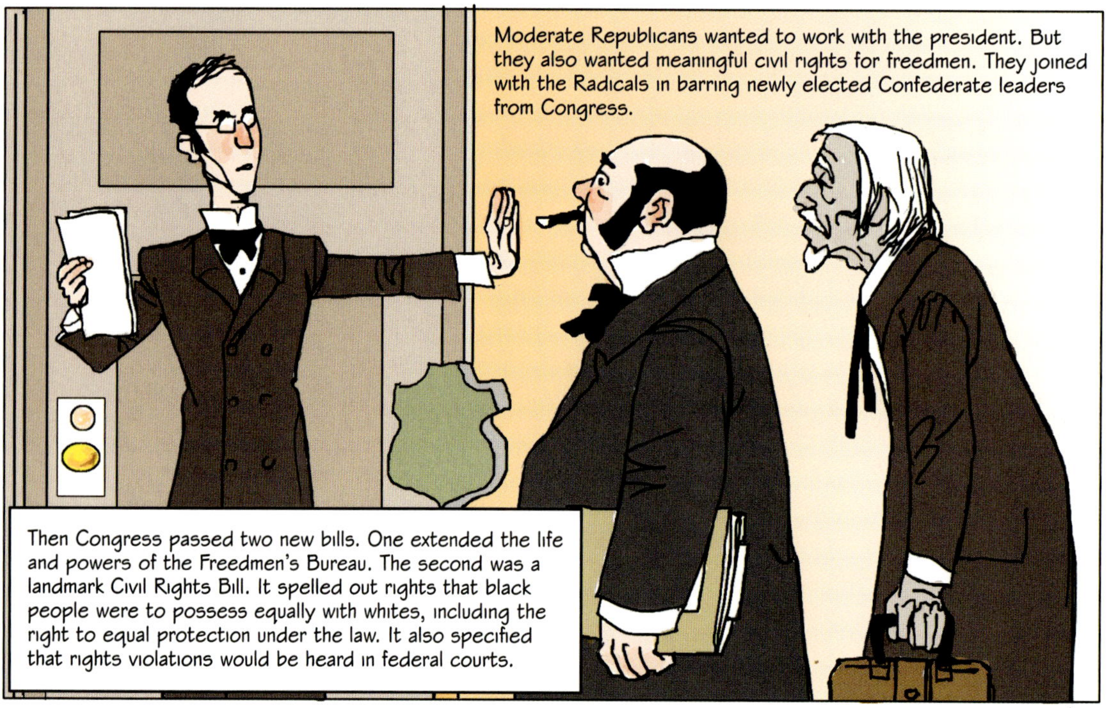
Moderate Republicans wanted to work with the president. But they also wanted meaningful civil rights for freedmen. They joined with the Radicals in barring newly elected Confederate leaders from Congress.
Then Congress passed two new bills. One extended the life and powers of the Freedmen's Bureau. The second was a landmark Civil Rights Bill. It spelled out rights that black people were to possess equally with whites, including the right to equal protection under the law. It also specified that rights violations would be heard in federal courts.

The Civil Rights Bill designated that everyone born in the United States was an American citizen.

But Johnson was not interested in granting civil rights to black people. He stubbornly vetoed both bills.

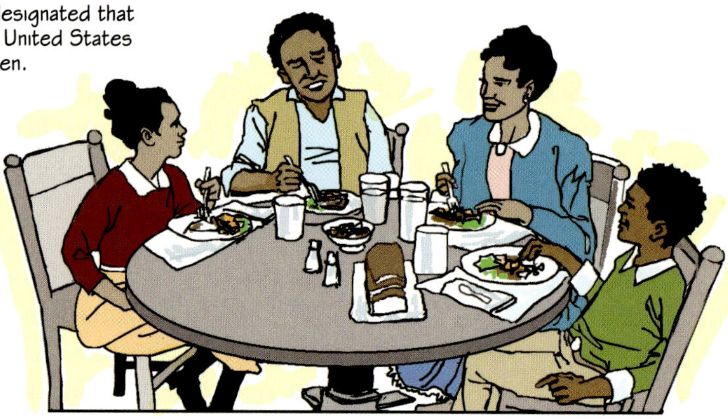

April 9, 1866. Congress overrode the president's veto, and the Civil Rights Bill became law . . . but Republicans decided the rights it defended were still not secure enough. They would write a new amendment to the Constitution.

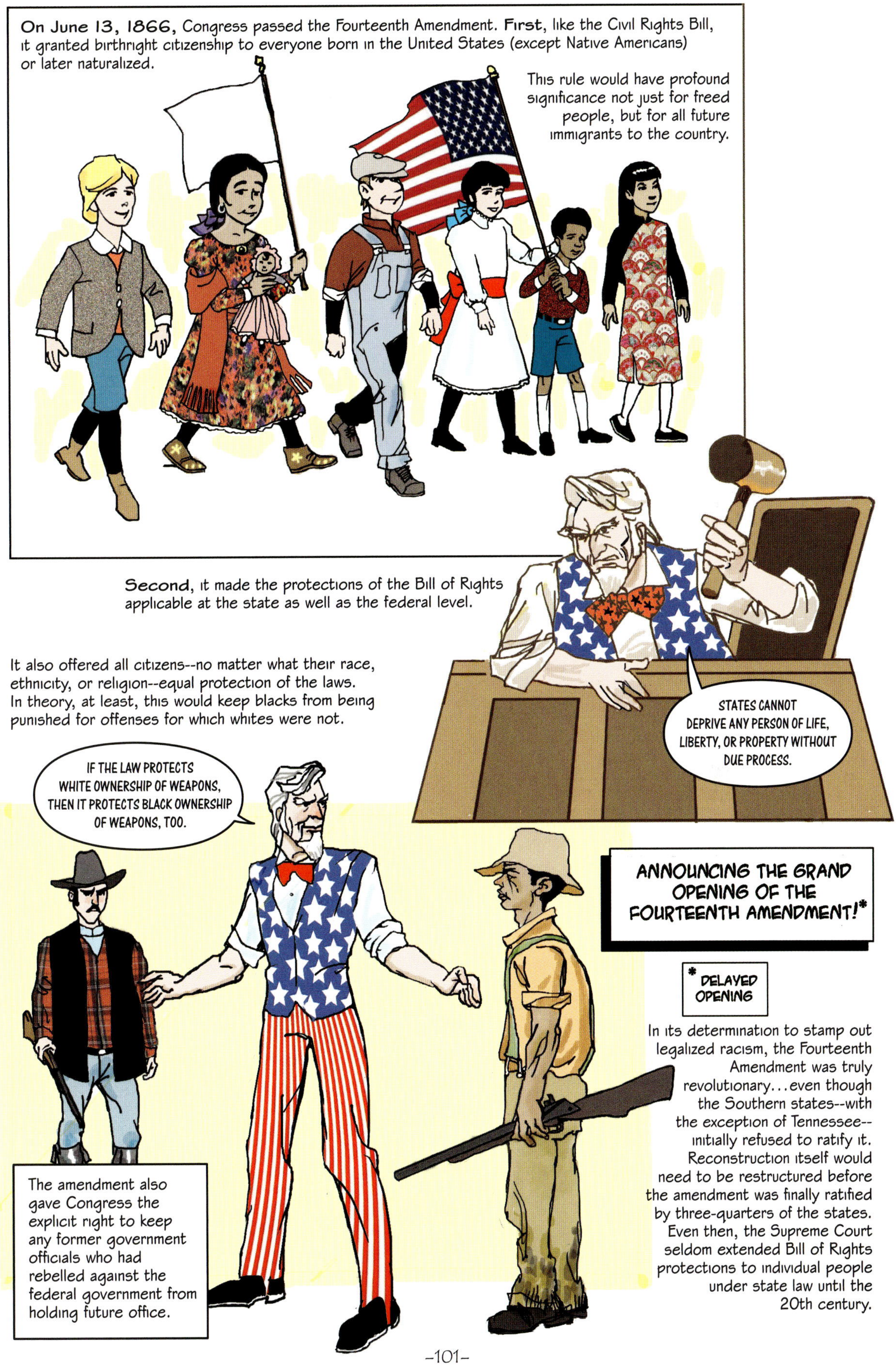
On June 13, 1866, Congress passed the Fourteenth Amendment. First, like the Civil Rights Bill, it granted birthright citizenship to everyone born in the United States (except Native Americans) or later naturalized.
This rule would have profound significance not just for freed people, but for all future immigrants to the country.
Second, it made the protections of the Bill of Rights applicable at the state as well as the federal level.
STATES CANNOT DEPRIVE ANY PERSON OF LIFE, LIBERTY, OR PROPERTY WITHOUT DUE PROCESS.
It also offered all citizens--no matter what their race, ethnicity, or religion--equal protection of the laws. In theory, at least, this would keep blacks from being punished for offenses for which whites were not.
IF THE LAW PROTECTS WHITE OWNERSHIP OF WEAPONS, THEN IT PROTECTS BLACK OWNERSHIP OF WEAPONS, TOO.
ANNOUNCING THE GRAND OPENING OF THE FOURTEENTH AMENDMENT!*
* DELAYED OPENING
In its determination to stamp out legalized racism, the Fourteenth Amendment was truly revolutionary. . . even though the Southern states--with the exception of Tennessee--initially refused to ratify it. Reconstruction itself would need to be restructured before the amendment was finally ratified by three-quarters of the states. Even then, the Supreme Court seldom extended Bill of Rights protections to individual people under state law until the 20th century.
The amendment also gave Congress the explicit right to keep any former government officials who had rebelled against the federal government from holding future office.

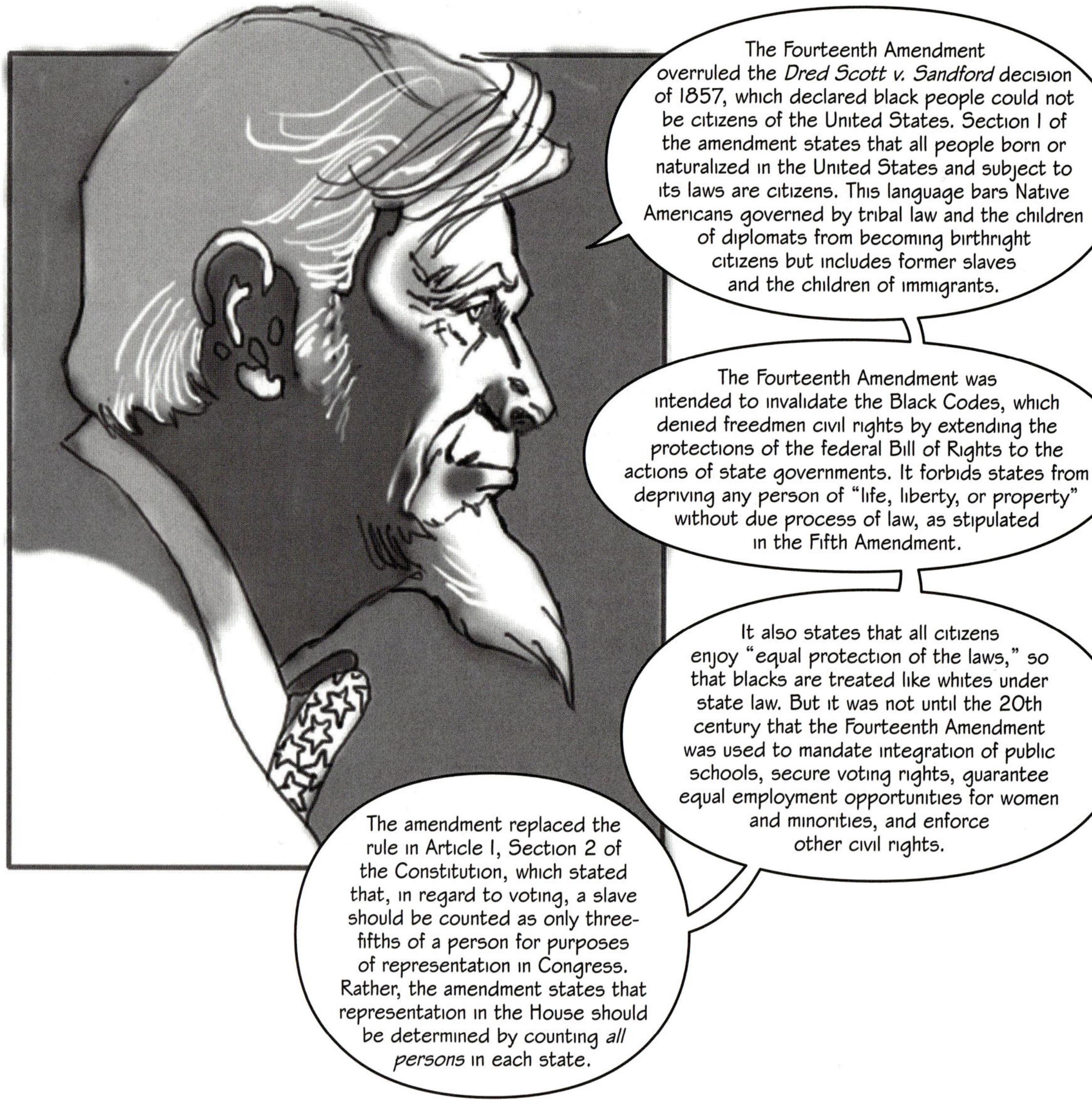
The Fourteenth Amendment overruled the *Dred Scott v. Sandford* decision of 1857, which declared black people could not be citizens of the United States. Section 1 of the amendment states that all people born or naturalized in the United States and subject to its laws are citizens. This language bars Native Americans governed by tribal law and the children of diplomats from becoming birthright citizens but includes former slaves and the children of immigrants.
The Fourteenth Amendment was intended to invalidate the Black Codes, which denied freedmen civil rights by extending the protections of the federal Bill of Rights to the actions of state governments. It forbids states from depriving any person of "life, liberty, or property" without due process of law, as stipulated in the Fifth Amendment.
It also states that all citizens enjoy "equal protection of the laws," so that blacks are treated like whites under state law. But it was not until the 20th century that the Fourteenth Amendment was used to mandate integration of public schools, secure voting rights, guarantee equal employment opportunities for women and minorities, and enforce other civil rights.
The amendment replaced the rule in Article 1, Section 2 of the Constitution, which stated that, in regard to voting, a slave should be counted as only three-fifths of a person for purposes of representation in Congress. Rather, the amendment states that representation in the House should be determined by counting *all persons* in each state.

THE FOURTEENTH AMENDMENT

"Section 1. All persons born or naturalized in the United States, and subject to the jurisdiction thereof, are citizens of the United States and of the State wherein they reside. No State shall make or enforce any law which shall abridge the privileges or immunities of citizens of the United States; nor shall any State deprive any person of life, liberty, or property, without due process of law; nor deny to any person within its jurisdiction the equal protection of the laws.

"Section 2. Representatives shall be apportioned among the several States according to their respective numbers, counting the whole number of persons in each State, excluding Indians not taxed. But when the right to vote at any election for the choice of electors for President and Vice President of the United States, Representatives in Congress, the Executive and Judicial officers of a State, or the members of the Legislature thereof, is denied to any of the male inhabitants of such State, being twenty-one years of age, and citizens of the United States, or in any way abridged, except for participation in rebellion or other crime, the basis of representation therein shall be reduced in the proportion which the number of such male citizens shall bear to the whole number of male citizens twenty-one years of age in such State..."

"The Fourteenth Amendment prohibits former military officers and federal and state officials who joined the Confederacy from again serving in the U.S. government. A two-thirds vote in Congress could exempt individuals from this rule. It also excused state and federal governments from having to pay debts incurred by the Confederacy or from compensating slave owners for the loss of their property.

"In Section 5, the amendment gives Congress the power to pass laws protecting civil rights.

THE FOURTEENTH AMENDMENT

"Section 3. No person shall be a Senator or Representative in Congress, or elector of President and Vice President, or hold any office, civil or military, under the United States, or under any State, who, having previously taken an oath, as a member of Congress, or as an officer of the United States, or as a member of any State legislature, or as an executive or judicial officer of any State, to support the Constitution of the United States, shall have engaged in insurrection or rebellion against the same, or given aid or comfort to the enemies thereof. But Congress may by a vote of two-thirds of each House remove such disability.

"Section 4. The validity of the public debt of the United States, authorized by law, including debts incurred for payment of pensions and bounties for services in suppressing insurrection or rebellion, shall not be questioned. But neither the United States nor any State shall assume or pay any debt or obligation incurred in aid of insurrection or rebellion against the United States, or any claim for the loss or emancipation of any slave; but all such debts, obligations and claims shall be held illegal and void.

"Section 5. The Congress shall have power to enforce, by appropriate legislation, the provisions of this article."

The Fifteenth Amendment

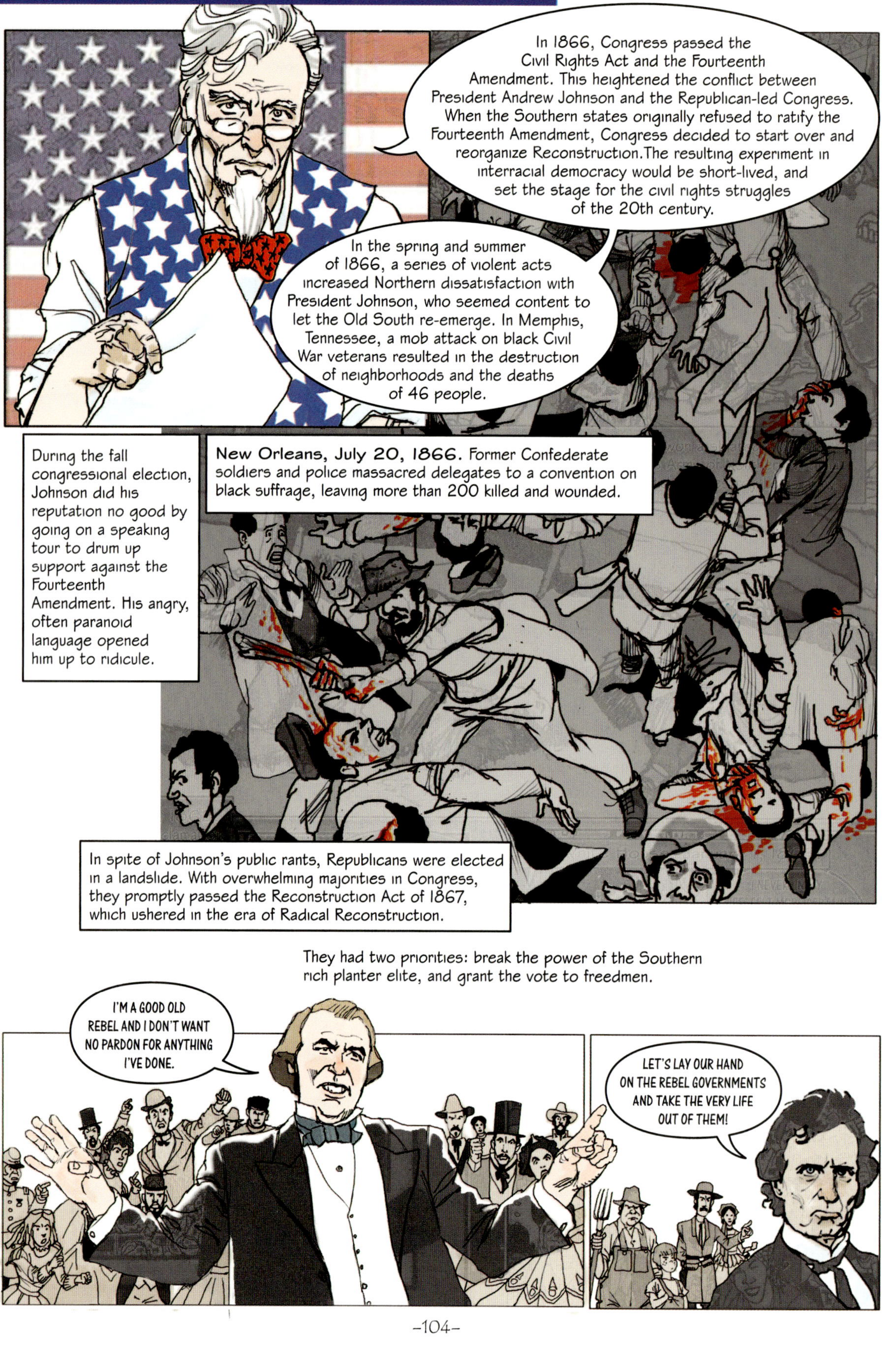

In 1866, Congress passed the Civil Rights Act and the Fourteenth Amendment. This heightened the conflict between President Andrew Johnson and the Republican-led Congress. When the Southern states originally refused to ratify the Fourteenth Amendment, Congress decided to start over and reorganize Reconstruction. The resulting experiment in interracial democracy would be short-lived, and set the stage for the civil rights struggles of the 20th century.
In the spring and summer of 1866, a series of violent acts increased Northern dissatisfaction with President Johnson, who seemed content to let the Old South re-emerge. In Memphis, Tennessee, a mob attack on black Civil War veterans resulted in the destruction of neighborhoods and the deaths of 46 people.
During the fall congressional election, Johnson did his reputation no good by going on a speaking tour to drum up support against the Fourteenth Amendment. His angry, often paranoid language opened him up to ridicule.
New Orleans, July 20, 1866. Former Confederate soldiers and police massacred delegates to a convention on black suffrage, leaving more than 200 killed and wounded.
In spite of Johnson's public rants, Republicans were elected in a landslide. With overwhelming majorities in Congress, they promptly passed the Reconstruction Act of 1867, which ushered in the era of Radical Reconstruction.
They had two priorities: break the power of the Southern rich planter elite, and grant the vote to freedmen.
I'M A GOOD OLD REBEL AND I DON'T WANT NO PARDON FOR ANYTHING I'VE DONE.
LET'S LAY OUR HAND ON THE REBEL GOVERNMENTS AND TAKE THE VERY LIFE OUT OF THEM!

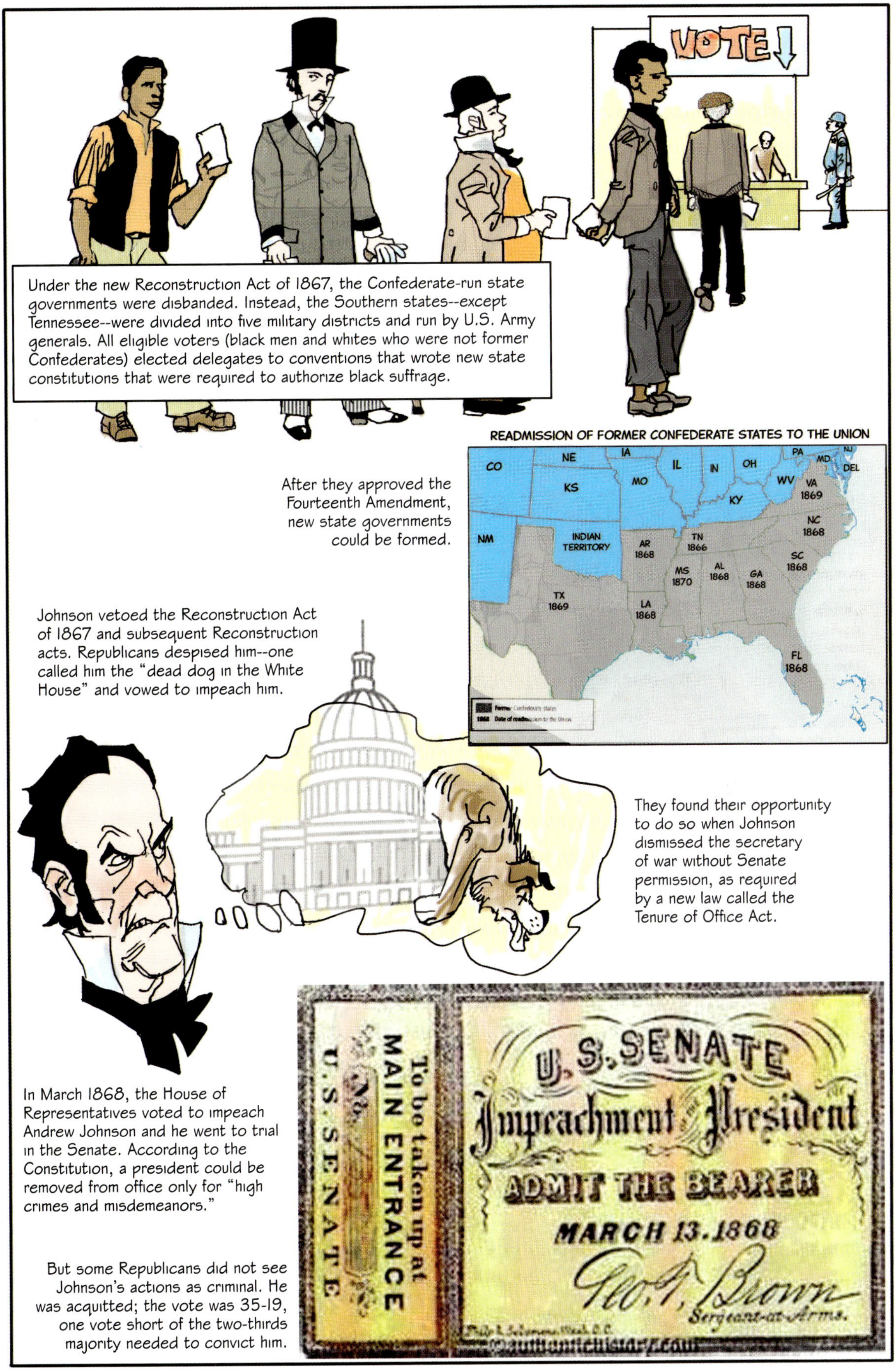
VOTE
Under the new Reconstruction Act of 1867, the Confederate-run state governments were disbanded. Instead, the Southern states--except Tennessee--were divided into five military districts and run by U.S. Army generals. All eligible voters (black men and whites who were not former Confederates) elected delegates to conventions that wrote new state constitutions that were required to authorize black suffrage.
READMISSION OF FORMER CONFEDERATE STATES TO THE UNION
CO
NE
IA
IL
IN
OH
PA
NJ
MD
DEL
KS
MO
KY
WV
VA 1869
NC 1868
NM
INDIAN TERRITORY
AR 1868
TN 1866
SC 1868
MS 1870
AL 1868
GA 1868
TX 1869
LA 1868
FL 1868
After they approved the Fourteenth Amendment, new state governments could be formed.
Johnson vetoed the Reconstruction Act of 1867 and subsequent Reconstruction acts. Republicans despised him--one called him the "dead dog in the White House" and vowed to impeach him.
They found their opportunity to do so when Johnson dismissed the secretary of war without Senate permission, as required by a new law called the Tenure of Office Act.
In March 1868, the House of Representatives voted to impeach Andrew Johnson and he went to trial in the Senate. According to the Constitution, a president could be removed from office only for "high crimes and misdemeanors."
But some Republicans did not see Johnson's actions as criminal. He was acquitted; the vote was 35-19, one vote short of the two-thirds majority needed to convict him.
To be taken up at
MAIN ENTRANCE
U.S. SENATE
U.S. SENATE
Impeachment President
ADMIT THE BEARER
MARCH 13.1868
Geo. T. Brown
Sergeant-at-Arms.

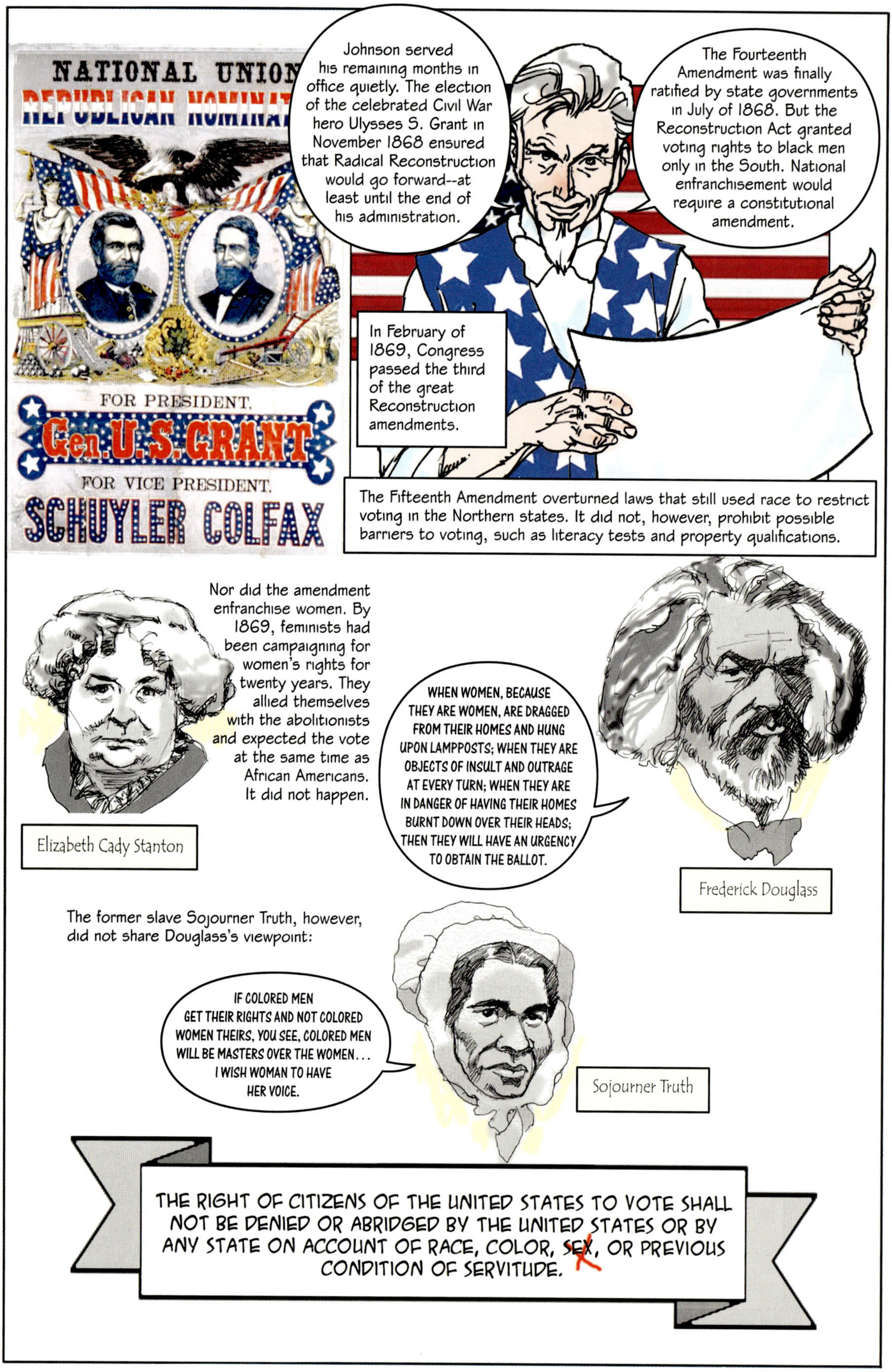
NATIONAL UNION
REPUBLICAN NOMINAT
FOR PRESIDENT.
Gen. U.S. GRANT
FOR VICE PRESIDENT.
SCHUYLER COLFAX
Johnson served his remaining months in office quietly. The election of the celebrated Civil War hero Ulysses S. Grant in November 1868 ensured that Radical Reconstruction would go forward--at least until the end of his administration.
The Fourteenth Amendment was finally ratified by state governments in July of 1868. But the Reconstruction Act granted voting rights to black men only in the South. National enfranchisement would require a constitutional amendment.
In February of 1869, Congress passed the third of the great Reconstruction amendments.
The Fifteenth Amendment overturned laws that still used race to restrict voting in the Northern states. It did not, however, prohibit possible barriers to voting, such as literacy tests and property qualifications.
Nor did the amendment enfranchise women. By 1869, feminists had been campaigning for women's rights for twenty years. They allied themselves with the abolitionists and expected the vote at the same time as African Americans. It did not happen.
Elizabeth Cady Stanton
WHEN WOMEN, BECAUSE THEY ARE WOMEN, ARE DRAGGED FROM THEIR HOMES AND HUNG UPON LAMPPOSTS; WHEN THEY ARE OBJECTS OF INSULT AND OUTRAGE AT EVERY TURN; WHEN THEY ARE IN DANGER OF HAVING THEIR HOMES BURNT DOWN OVER THEIR HEADS; THEN THEY WILL HAVE AN URGENCY TO OBTAIN THE BALLOT.
Frederick Douglass
The former slave Sojourner Truth, however, did not share Douglass's viewpoint:
IF COLORED MEN GET THEIR RIGHTS AND NOT COLORED WOMEN THEIRS, YOU SEE, COLORED MEN WILL BE MASTERS OVER THE WOMEN . . . I WISH WOMAN TO HAVE HER VOICE.
Sojourner Truth
THE RIGHT OF CITIZENS OF THE UNITED STATES TO VOTE SHALL NOT BE DENIED OR ABRIDGED BY THE UNITED STATES OR BY ANY STATE ON ACCOUNT OF RACE, COLOR, SEX, OR PREVIOUS CONDITION OF SERVITUDE.

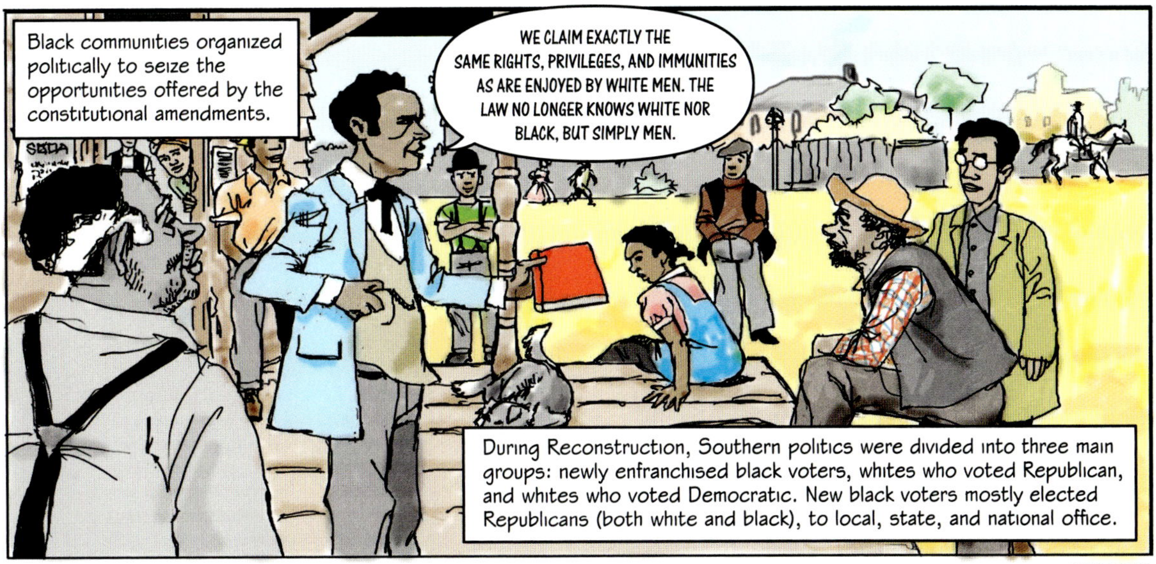
Black communities organized politically to seize the opportunities offered by the constitutional amendments.
WE CLAIM EXACTLY THE SAME RIGHTS, PRIVILEGES, AND IMMUNITIES AS ARE ENJOYED BY WHITE MEN. THE LAW NO LONGER KNOWS WHITE NOR BLACK, BUT SIMPLY MEN.
During Reconstruction, Southern politics were divided into three main groups: newly enfranchised black voters, whites who voted Republican, and whites who voted Democratic. New black voters mostly elected Republicans (both white and black), to local, state, and national office.

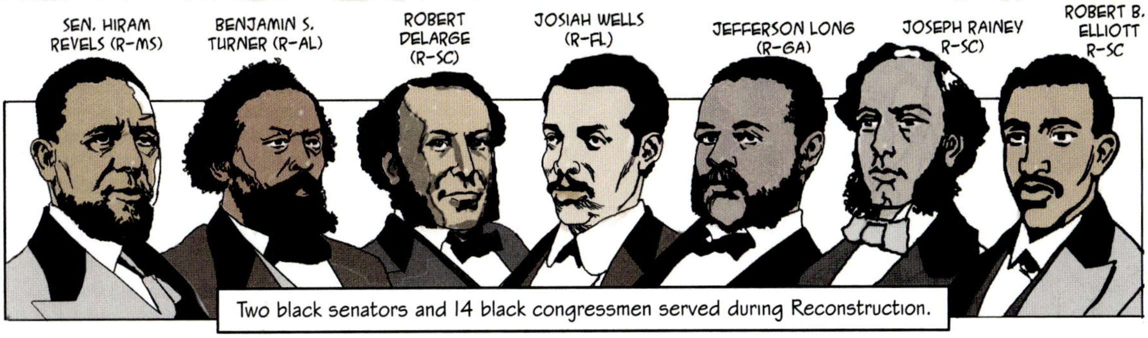
SEN. HIRAM REVELS (R-MS)
BENJAMIN S. TURNER (R-AL)
ROBERT DELARGE (R-SC)
JOSIAH WELLS (R-FL)
JEFFERSON LONG (R-GA)
JOSEPH RAINEY R-SC)
ROBERT B. ELLIOTT R-SC
Two black senators and 14 black congressmen served during Reconstruction.

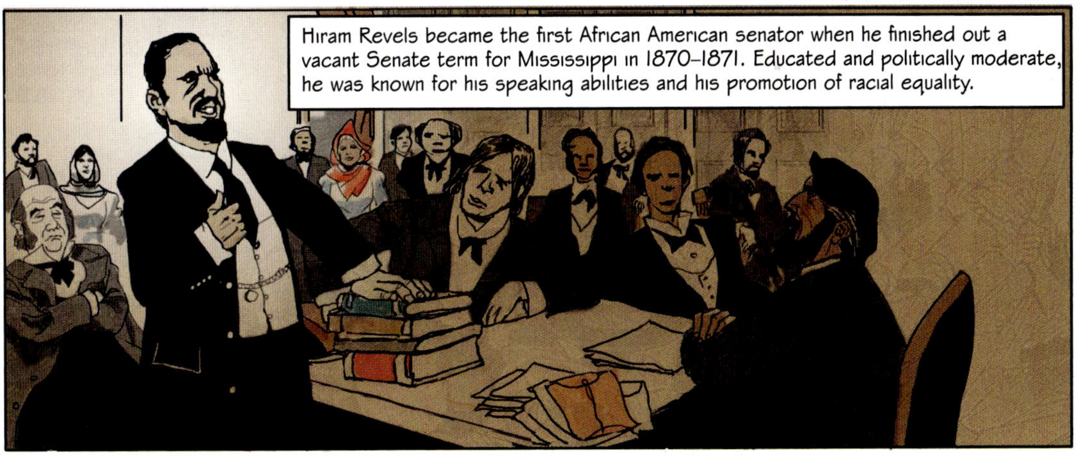
Hiram Revels became the first African American senator when he finished out a vacant Senate term for Mississippi in 1870–1871. Educated and politically moderate, he was known for his speaking abilities and his promotion of racial equality.

There were white Southern Republicans who had never supported secession, mostly small farmers and businessmen, and Northerners who went south seeking economic opportunity.

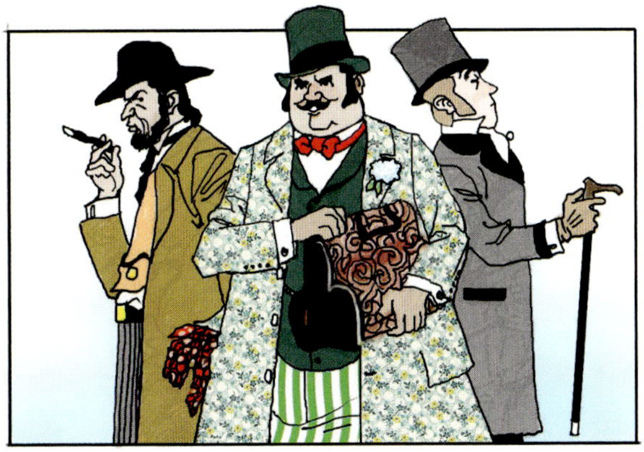

Conservative Southerners derisively called the Southern Republicans "scalawags" and the Northern opportunists "Carpetbaggers."

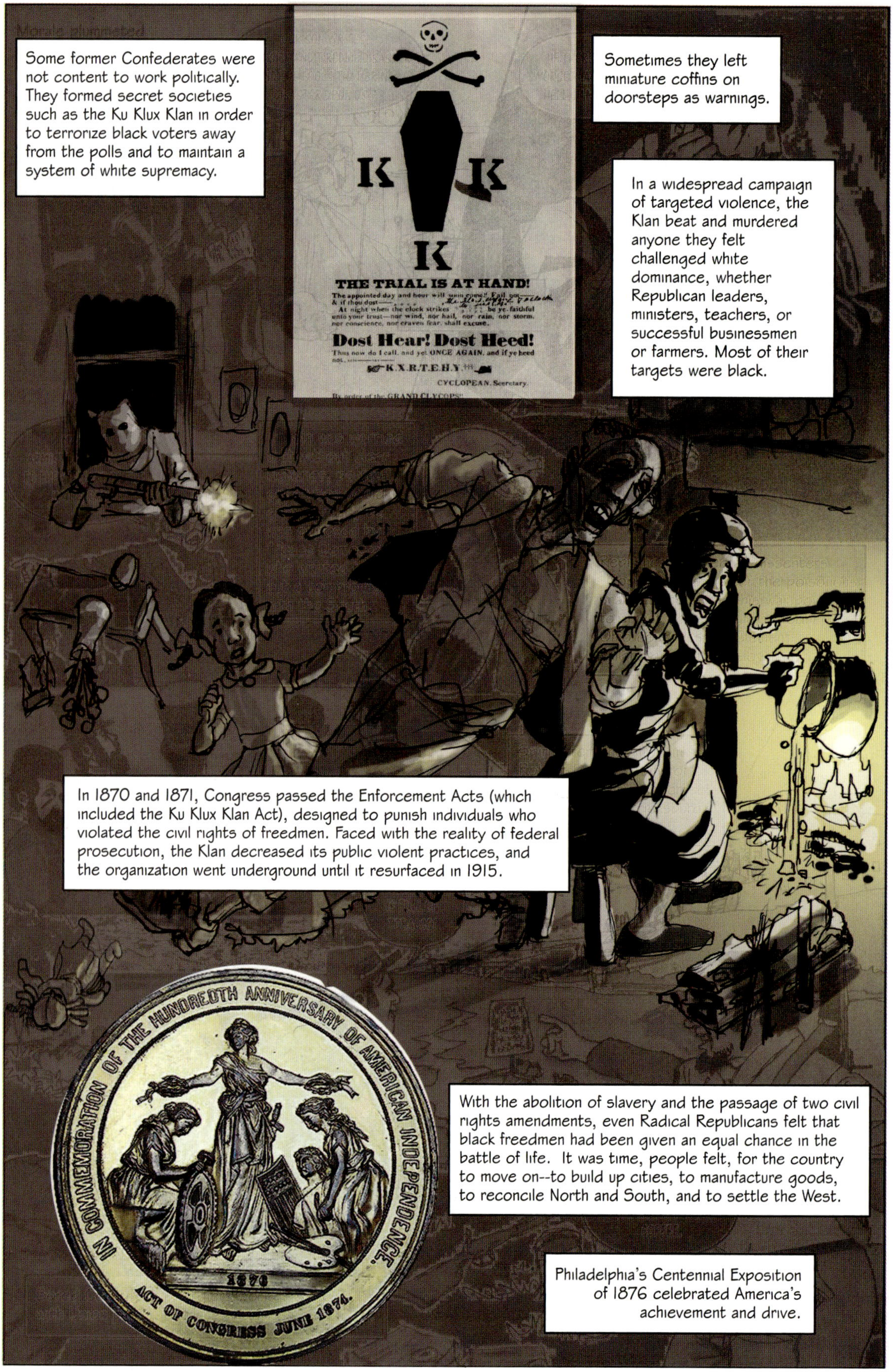
Some former Confederates were not content to work politically. They formed secret societies such as the Ku Klux Klan in order to terrorize black voters away from the polls and to maintain a system of white supremacy.
K K K
THE TRIAL IS AT HAND!
At night when the clock strikes be ye faithful unto your trust—nor wind, nor hail, nor rain, nor storm, nor conscience, nor craven fear, shall excuse.
Dost Hear! Dost Heed!
Thus now do I call, and yet ONCE AGAIN, and if ye heed not,
K.X.R.T.E.H.Y.
CYCLOPEAN, Secretary.
Sometimes they left miniature coffins on doorsteps as warnings.
In a widespread campaign of targeted violence, the Klan beat and murdered anyone they felt challenged white dominance, whether Republican leaders, ministers, teachers, or successful businessmen or farmers. Most of their targets were black.
In 1870 and 1871, Congress passed the Enforcement Acts (which included the Ku Klux Klan Act), designed to punish individuals who violated the civil rights of freedmen. Faced with the reality of federal prosecution, the Klan decreased its public violent practices, and the organization went underground until it resurfaced in 1915.
IN COMMEMORATION OF THE HUNDREDTH ANNIVERSARY OF AMERICAN INDEPENDENCE.
1876
ACT OF CONGRESS JUNE 1874.
With the abolition of slavery and the passage of two civil rights amendments, even Radical Republicans felt that black freedmen had been given an equal chance in the battle of life. It was time, people felt, for the country to move on--to build up cities, to manufacture goods, to reconcile North and South, and to settle the West.
Philadelphia's Centennial Exposition of 1876 celebrated America's achievement and drive.

Fall 1877. The disputed election of Rutherford B. Hayes in 1876 led to compromises with the Southern Democrats. Hayes, a Republican, won by one vote in the Electoral College only because he and his party agreed to withdraw federal troops from the rest of the occupied South.

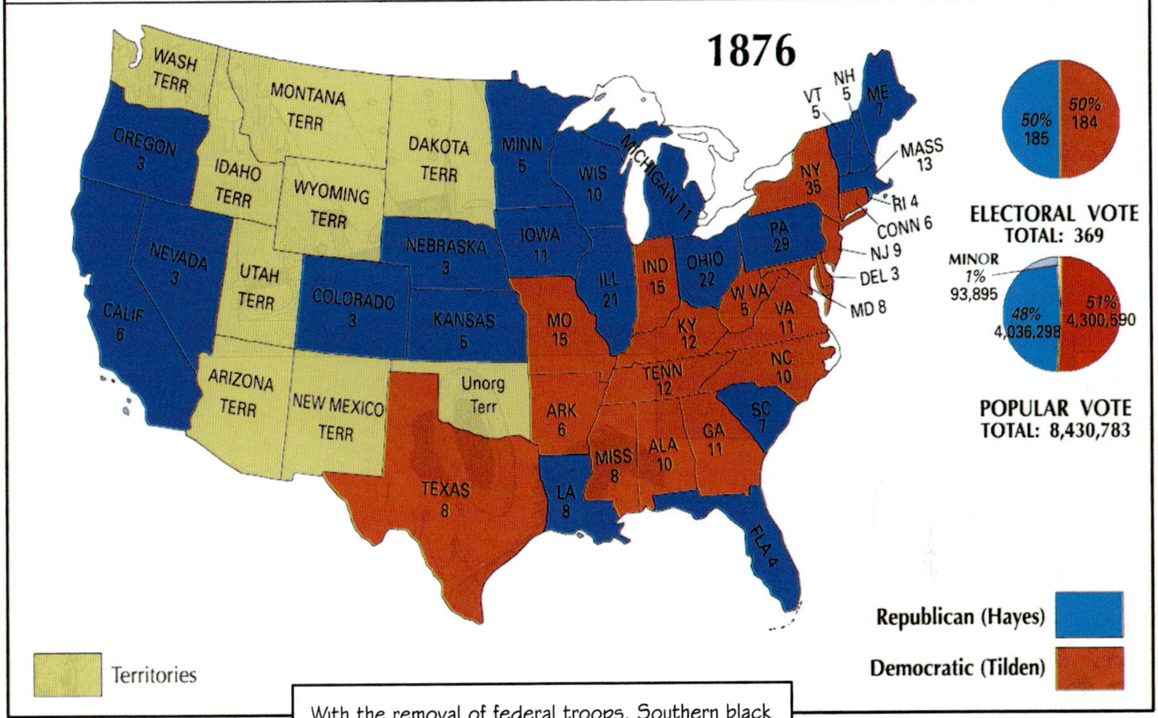
1876
WASH TERR
MONTANA TERR
DAKOTA TERR
OREGON 3
IDAHO TERR
WYOMING TERR
MINN 5
WIS 10
MICHIGAN 11
NEVADA 3
CALIF 6
UTAH TERR
COLORADO 3
NEBRASKA 3
KANSAS 5
IOWA 11
ILL 21
IND 15
OHIO 22
PA 29
NY 35
VT 5
NH 5
ME 7
MASS 13
RI 4
CONN 6
NJ 9
DEL 3
MD 8
W VA 5
VA 11
KY 12
MO 15
ARIZONA TERR
NEW MEXICO TERR
Unorg Terr
TEXAS 8
ARK 6
TENN 12
NC 10
SC 7
GA 11
ALA 10
MISS 8
LA 8
FLA 4
50% 185
50% 184
ELECTORAL VOTE
TOTAL: 369
MINOR 1% 93,895
48% 4,036,298
51% 4,300,590
POPULAR VOTE
TOTAL: 8,430,783
Republican (Hayes)
Democratic (Tilden)
Territories

With the removal of federal troops, Southern black citizens were left without protection from the federal government. Reconstruction was over.

As a result of Reconstruction, slaves had been freed and granted citizenship and voting rights. Newly free people were able to establish schools, churches, and political and community organizations of their own.

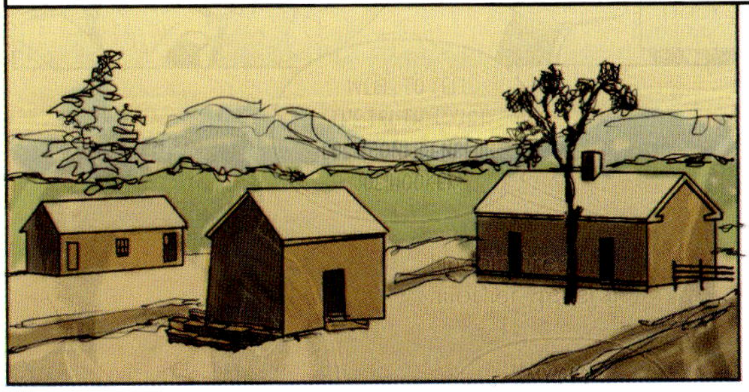

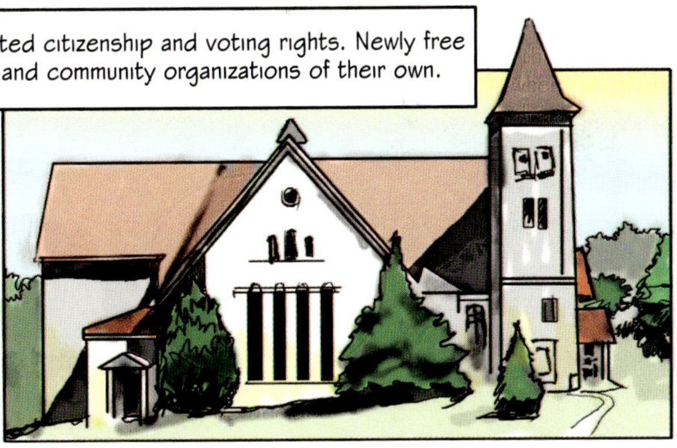

The failure of Reconstruction in 1877, however, led to the creation of a new set of laws that would disenfranchise and disempower blacks.

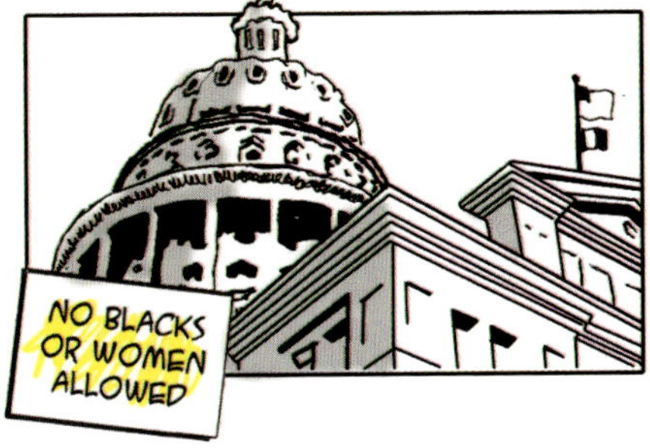
NO BLACKS OR WOMEN ALLOWED

Blanche Bruce, also a senator from Mississippi, was the first African American to serve a full term (1875–1881). He was born into slavery, the son of a black female slave and her white master, who educated Bruce and later freed him. Bruce was appointed to various U.S. government positions after leaving the Senate.

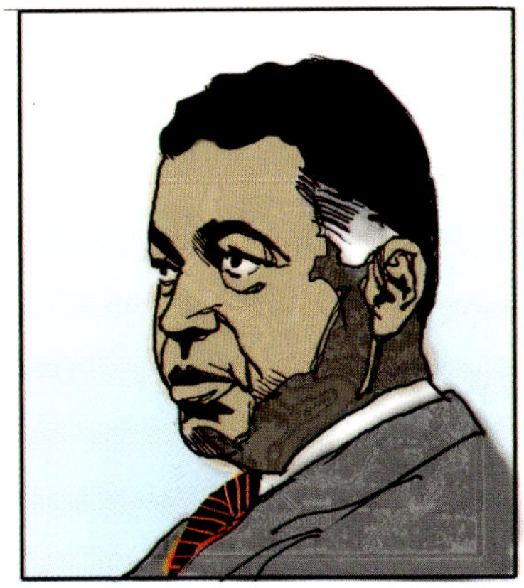

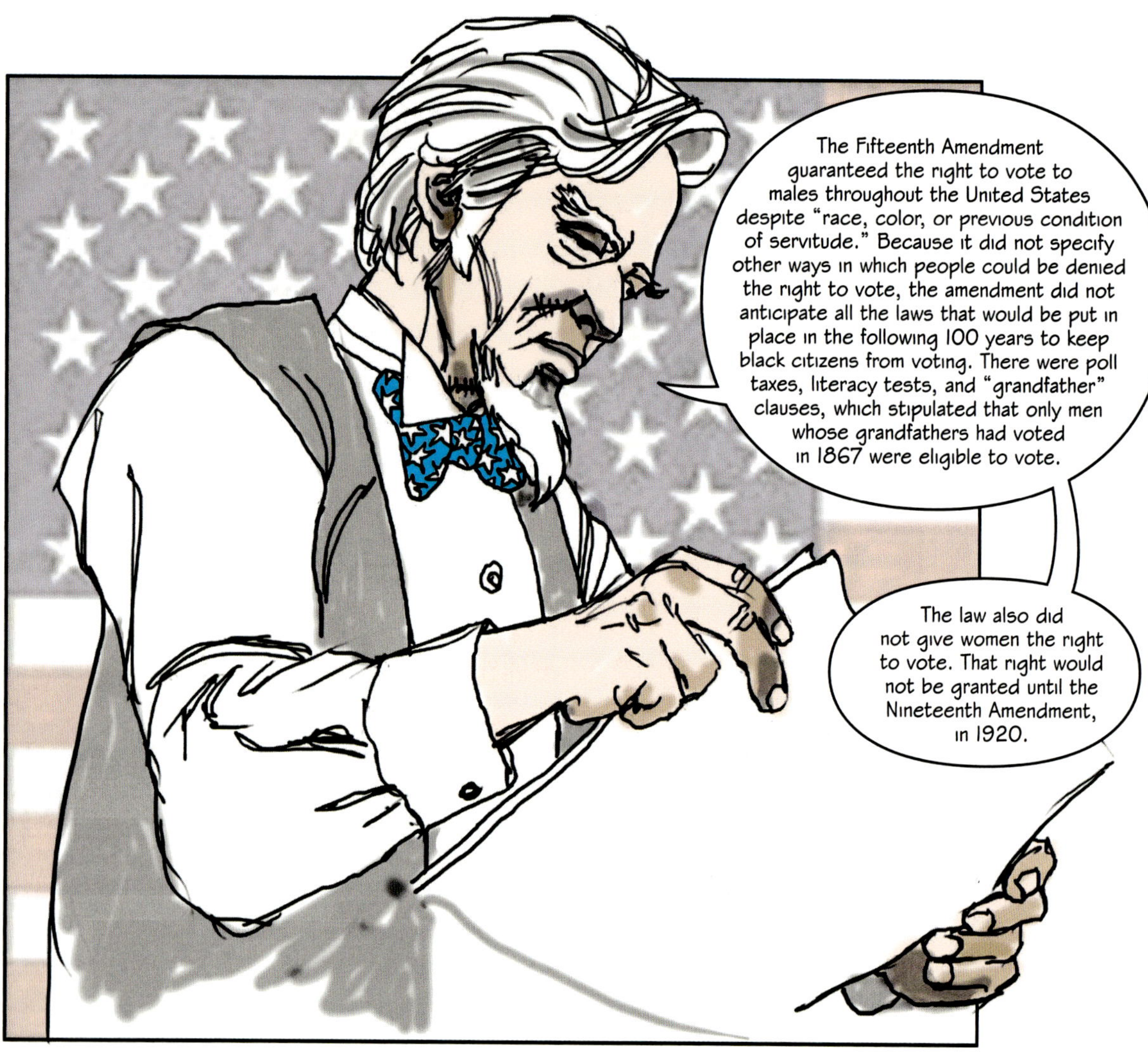
The Fifteenth Amendment guaranteed the right to vote to males throughout the United States despite "race, color, or previous condition of servitude." Because it did not specify other ways in which people could be denied the right to vote, the amendment did not anticipate all the laws that would be put in place in the following 100 years to keep black citizens from voting. There were poll taxes, literacy tests, and "grandfather" clauses, which stipulated that only men whose grandfathers had voted in 1867 were eligible to vote.
The law also did not give women the right to vote. That right would not be granted until the Nineteenth Amendment, in 1920.

THE FIFTEENTH AMENDMENT

"Section 1. The right of citizens of the United States to vote shall not be denied or abridged by the United States or any State on account of race, color, or previous condition of servitude.

"Section 2. The Congress shall have power to enforce this article by appropriate legislation."

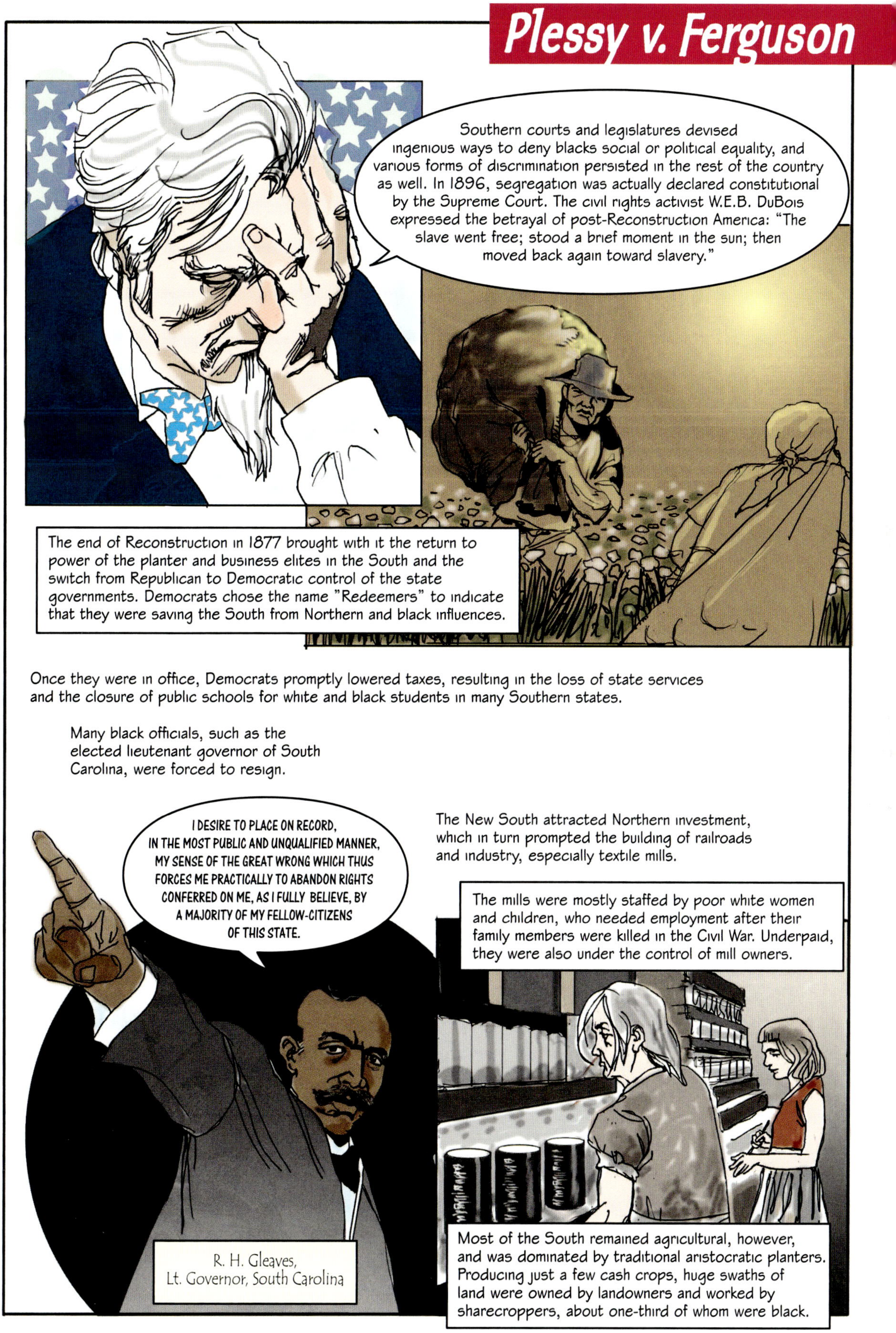
Plessy v. Ferguson
Southern courts and legislatures devised ingenious ways to deny blacks social or political equality, and various forms of discrimination persisted in the rest of the country as well. In 1896, segregation was actually declared constitutional by the Supreme Court. The civil rights activist W.E.B. DuBois expressed the betrayal of post-Reconstruction America: "The slave went free; stood a brief moment in the sun; then moved back again toward slavery."
The end of Reconstruction in 1877 brought with it the return to power of the planter and business elites in the South and the switch from Republican to Democratic control of the state governments. Democrats chose the name "Redeemers" to indicate that they were saving the South from Northern and black influences.
Once they were in office, Democrats promptly lowered taxes, resulting in the loss of state services and the closure of public schools for white and black students in many Southern states.
Many black officials, such as the elected lieutenant governor of South Carolina, were forced to resign.
I DESIRE TO PLACE ON RECORD, IN THE MOST PUBLIC AND UNQUALIFIED MANNER, MY SENSE OF THE GREAT WRONG WHICH THUS FORCES ME PRACTICALLY TO ABANDON RIGHTS CONFERRED ON ME, AS I FULLY BELIEVE, BY A MAJORITY OF MY FELLOW-CITIZENS OF THIS STATE.
R. H. Gleaves, Lt. Governor, South Carolina
The New South attracted Northern investment, which in turn prompted the building of railroads and industry, especially textile mills.
The mills were mostly staffed by poor white women and children, who needed employment after their family members were killed in the Civil War. Underpaid, they were also under the control of mill owners.
Most of the South remained agricultural, however, and was dominated by traditional aristocratic planters. Producing just a few cash crops, huge swaths of land were owned by landowners and worked by sharecroppers, about one-third of whom were black.

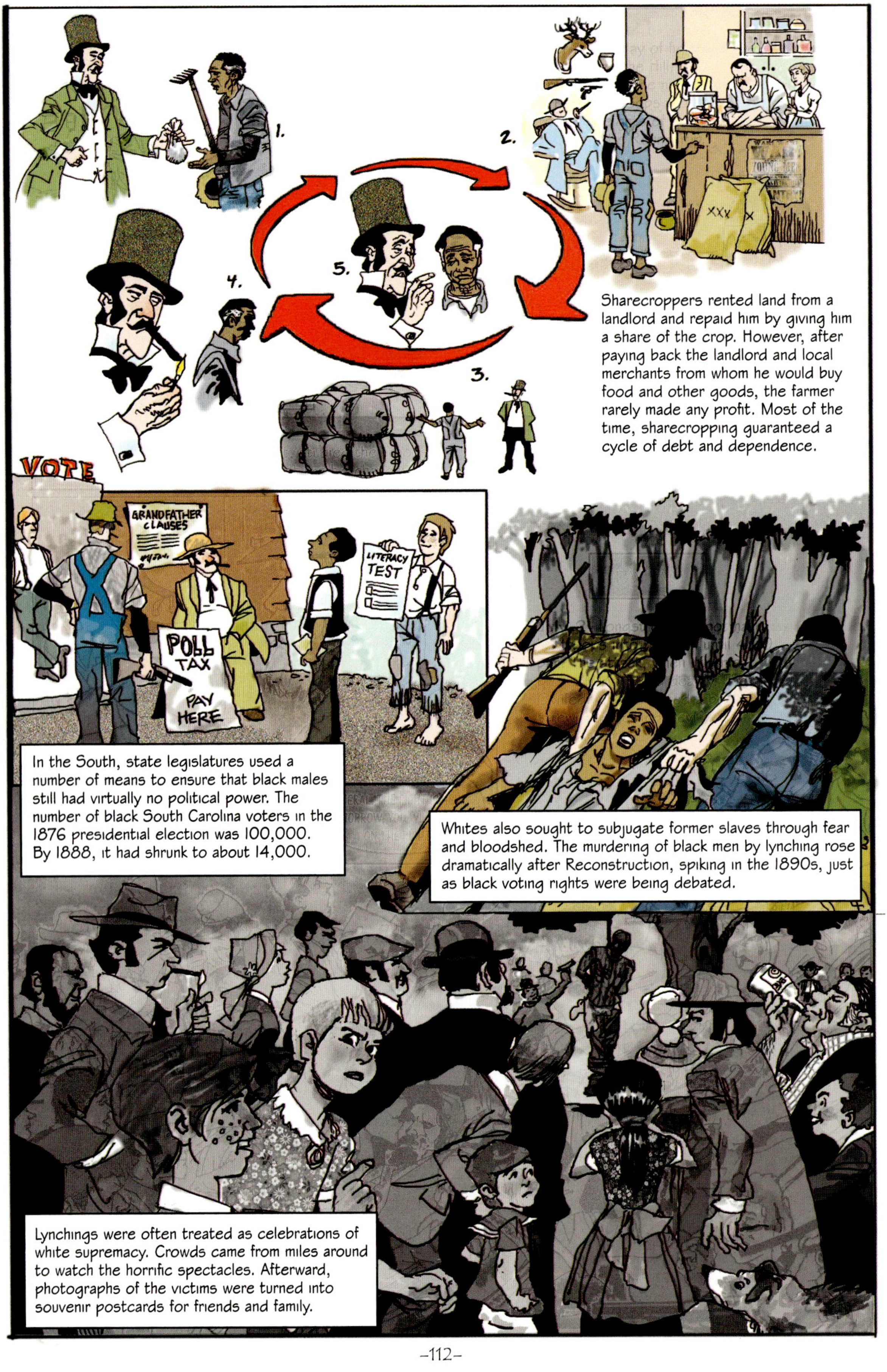
1.
2.
Sharecroppers rented land from a landlord and repaid him by giving him a share of the crop. However, after paying back the landlord and local merchants from whom he would buy food and other goods, the farmer rarely made any profit. Most of the time, sharecropping guaranteed a cycle of debt and dependence.
5.
4.
3.
VOTE
GRANDFATHER CLAUSES
LITERACY TEST
POLL TAX
PAY HERE
In the South, state legislatures used a number of means to ensure that black males still had virtually no political power. The number of black South Carolina voters in the 1876 presidential election was 100,000. By 1888, it had shrunk to about 14,000.
Whites also sought to subjugate former slaves through fear and bloodshed. The murdering of black men by lynching rose dramatically after Reconstruction, spiking in the 1890s, just as black voting rights were being debated.
Lynchings were often treated as celebrations of white supremacy. Crowds came from miles around to watch the horrific spectacles. Afterward, photographs of the victims were turned into souvenir postcards for friends and family.

Blacks were increasingly subject to a series of restrictive laws designed to separate them from white society and demean them as second-class citizens. After Reconstruction, Southern states hurried to pass segregation laws known as Jim Crow laws.

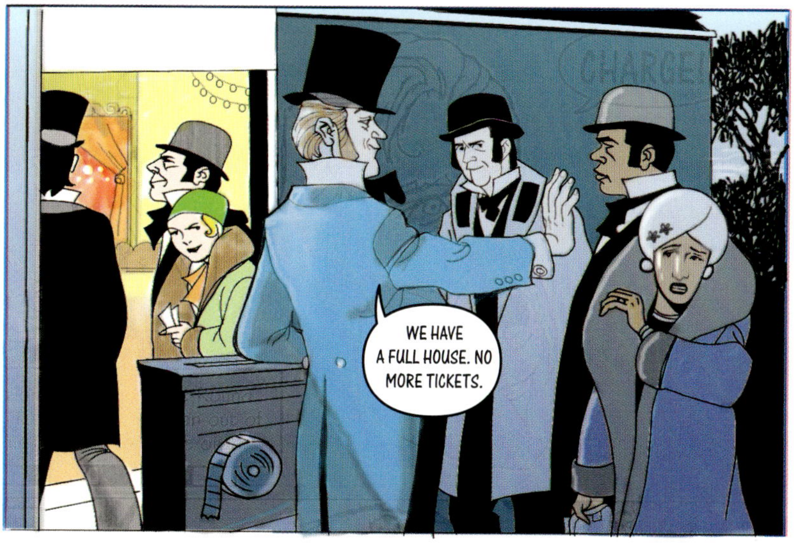
WE HAVE A FULL HOUSE. NO MORE TICKETS.

"Jim Crow" was a popular character in 19th-century minstrel shows, in which white performers in "blackface" mimicked slave music and songs. The silly, shuffling figure embodied racist stereotypes, and Jim Crow became a racist nickname for blacks.

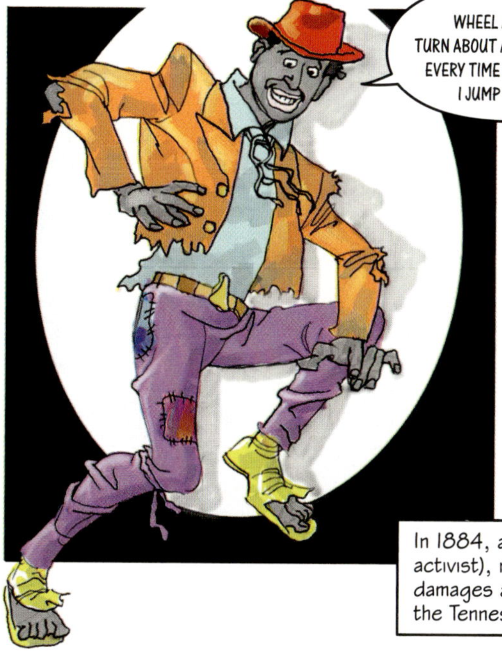
WHEEL ABOUT AND TURN ABOUT AND DO JEST SO-- EVERY TIME I WHEEL ABOUT I JUMP JIM CROW.

In the late 19th century, various modes of public transportation--railways, streetcars, and even subways--brought blacks and whites together in close proximity. In the post-Reconstruction era, one Southern state after another passed laws creating separate railcars for blacks and whites.

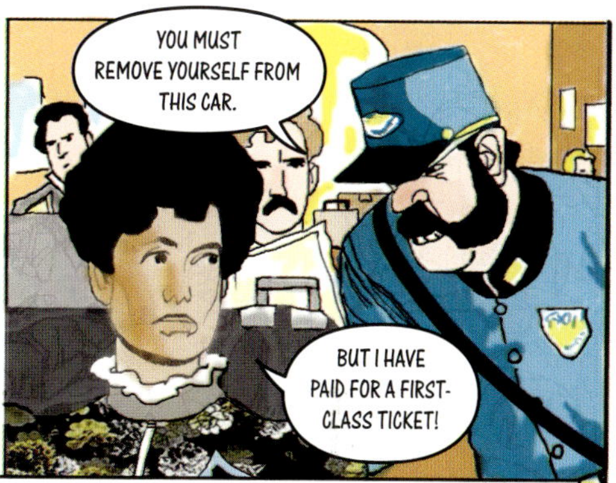
YOU MUST REMOVE YOURSELF FROM THIS CAR.
BUT I HAVE PAID FOR A FIRST-CLASS TICKET!

In 1884, a young teacher, Ida B. Wells (who later became an anti-lynching activist), refused to move to the "colored" train car. She won a verdict for damages against the Chesapeake & Ohio Railroad for $500. Two years later, the Tennessee Supreme Court reversed the lower court's ruling.

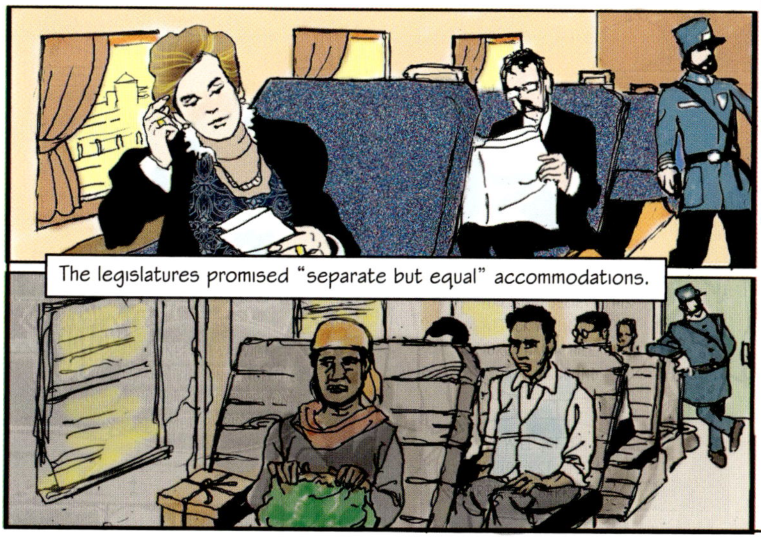

The legislatures promised "separate but equal" accommodations.

The disparity was not lost on Booker T. Washington, founder of Alabama's Tuskegee Normal and Industrial Institute (now known as Tuskegee University): "In every one of the Gulf states, the Negro is forced to ride in railroad cars that are inferior in every way to those given the white."

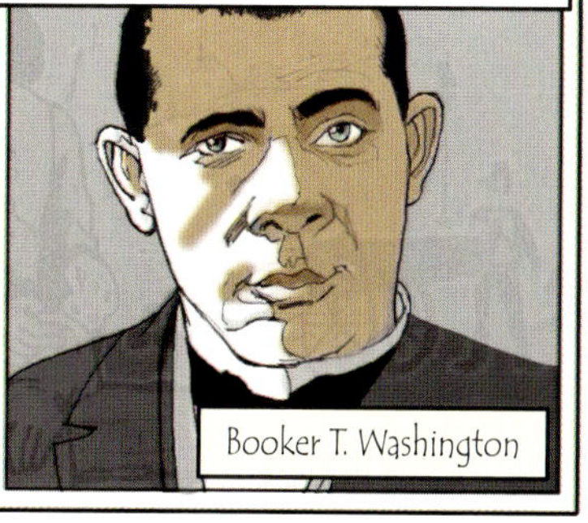

Booker T. Washington

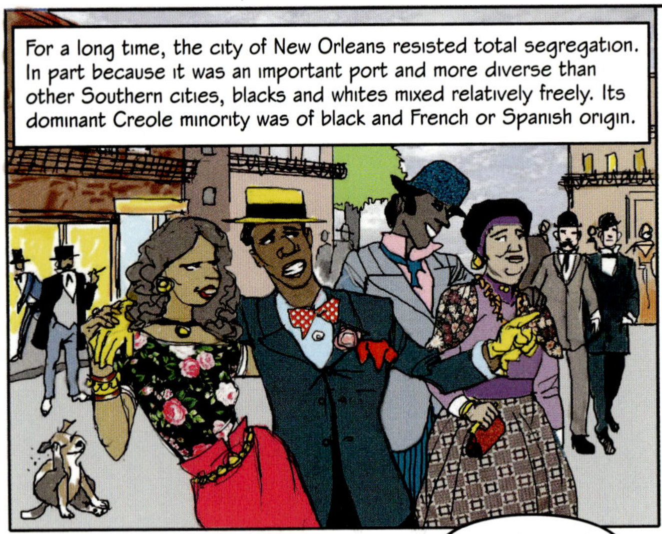
For a long time, the city of New Orleans resisted total segregation. In part because it was an important port and more diverse than other Southern cities, blacks and whites mixed relatively freely. Its dominant Creole minority was of black and French or Spanish origin.

But in 1890, as part of a political deal, the Louisiana legislature passed a bill establishing separate railcars for black and white citizens. Black newspapers rallied against the bill.

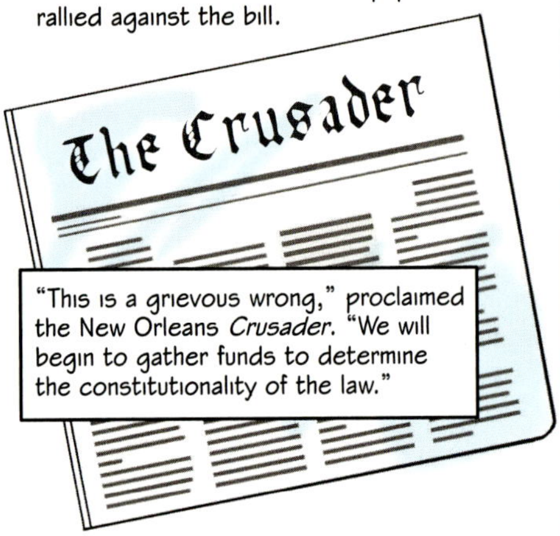
The Crusader
"This is a grievous wrong," proclaimed the New Orleans *Crusader*. "We will begin to gather funds to determine the constitutionality of the law."

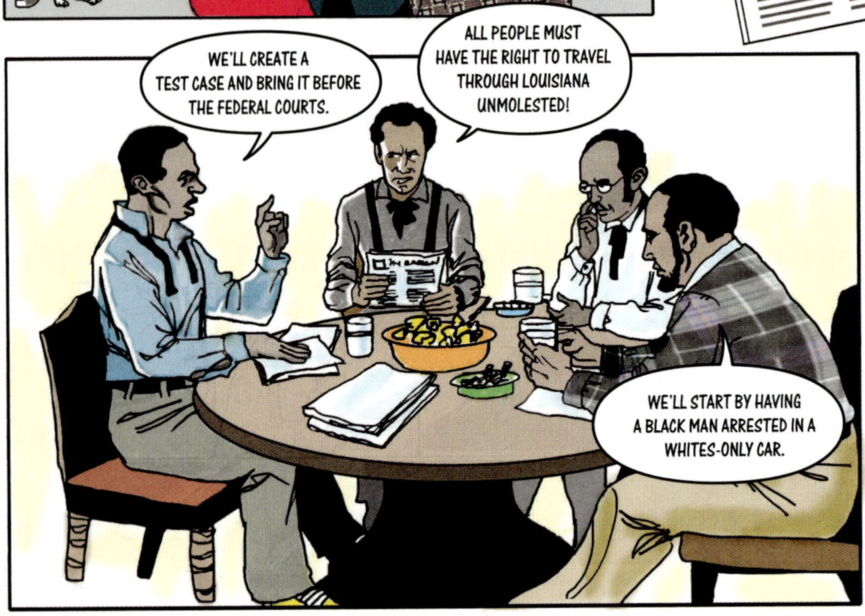
WE'LL CREATE A TEST CASE AND BRING IT BEFORE THE FEDERAL COURTS.
ALL PEOPLE MUST HAVE THE RIGHT TO TRAVEL THROUGH LOUISIANA UNMOLESTED!
WE'LL START BY HAVING A BLACK MAN ARRESTED IN A WHITES-ONLY CAR.

Opponents of the law, mostly Creole men, formed the Citizens' Committee to Test the Constitutionality of the Separate Car Act.

The Citizens' Committee arranged the arrest ahead of time with the East Louisiana Railroad, which, like many other railroad companies, did not want to spend the money for segregated cars.

The man who agreed to test the law was Homer Plessy, a 29-year-old shoemaker whose German grandfather had married a "free woman of color" some 60 years before. Since one of his eight great-grandparents was black, he was black by law.

During Reconstruction, the young Homer went to an integrated school, rode the streetcars freely, and voted in elections. Now he would make a bold move to recover his rights.

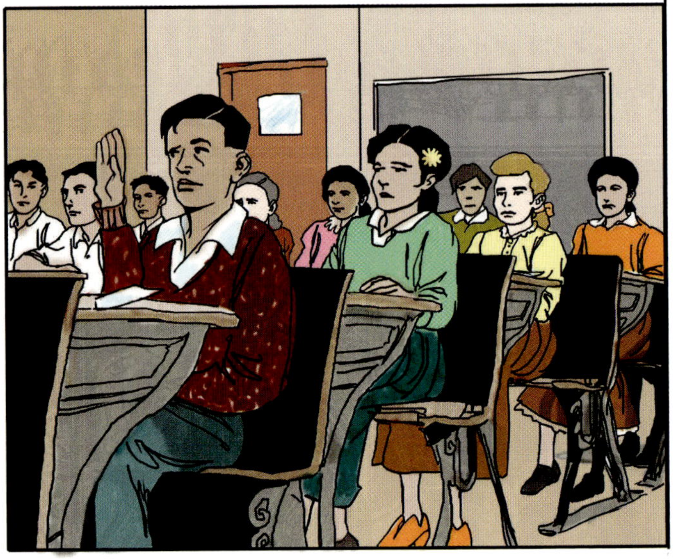

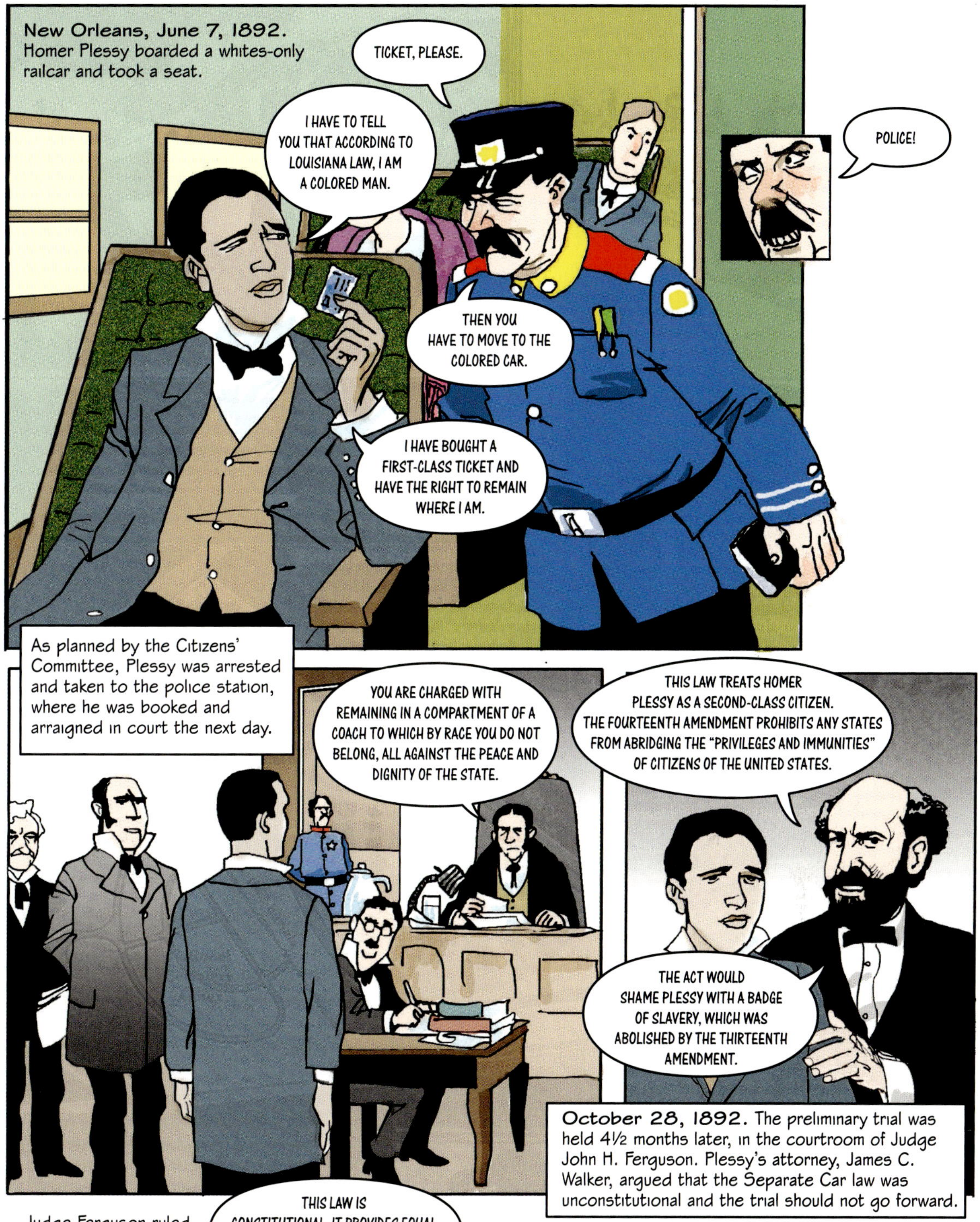
New Orleans, June 7, 1892.
Homer Plessy boarded a whites-only railcar and took a seat.
TICKET, PLEASE.
I HAVE TO TELL YOU THAT ACCORDING TO LOUISIANA LAW, I AM A COLORED MAN.
POLICE!
THEN YOU HAVE TO MOVE TO THE COLORED CAR.
I HAVE BOUGHT A FIRST-CLASS TICKET AND HAVE THE RIGHT TO REMAIN WHERE I AM.
As planned by the Citizens' Committee, Plessy was arrested and taken to the police station, where he was booked and arraigned in court the next day.
YOU ARE CHARGED WITH REMAINING IN A COMPARTMENT OF A COACH TO WHICH BY RACE YOU DO NOT BELONG, ALL AGAINST THE PEACE AND DIGNITY OF THE STATE.
THIS LAW TREATS HOMER PLESSY AS A SECOND-CLASS CITIZEN. THE FOURTEENTH AMENDMENT PROHIBITS ANY STATES FROM ABRIDGING THE "PRIVILEGES AND IMMUNITIES" OF CITIZENS OF THE UNITED STATES.
THE ACT WOULD SHAME PLESSY WITH A BADGE OF SLAVERY, WHICH WAS ABOLISHED BY THE THIRTEENTH AMENDMENT.
October 28, 1892. The preliminary trial was held 4½ months later, in the courtroom of Judge John H. Ferguson. Plessy's attorney, James C. Walker, argued that the Separate Car law was unconstitutional and the trial should not go forward.

Judge Ferguson ruled against Plessy.

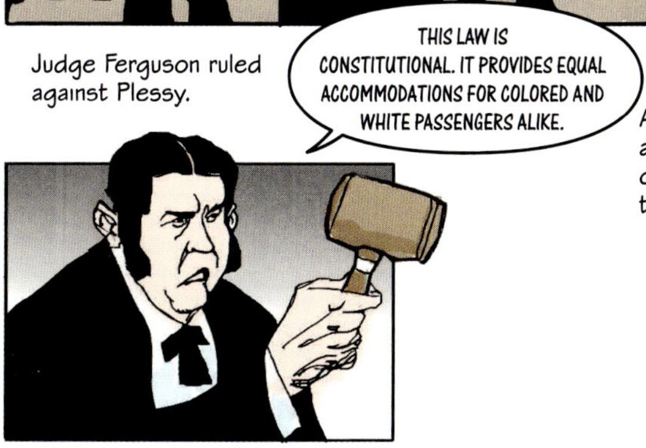
THIS LAW IS CONSTITUTIONAL. IT PROVIDES EQUAL ACCOMMODATIONS FOR COLORED AND WHITE PASSENGERS ALIKE.

As they had planned, the Citizens' Committee appealed to the Louisiana Supreme Court. When the court upheld Ferguson's decision, the Committee took the case to the United States Supreme Court.

The Northern attorney, author, and advocate of black rights Albion Tourgée argued the case before the Supreme Court. He feared that the court would not be sympathetic. Of the nine justices, only one, John M. Harlan, was known to be a liberal thinker.

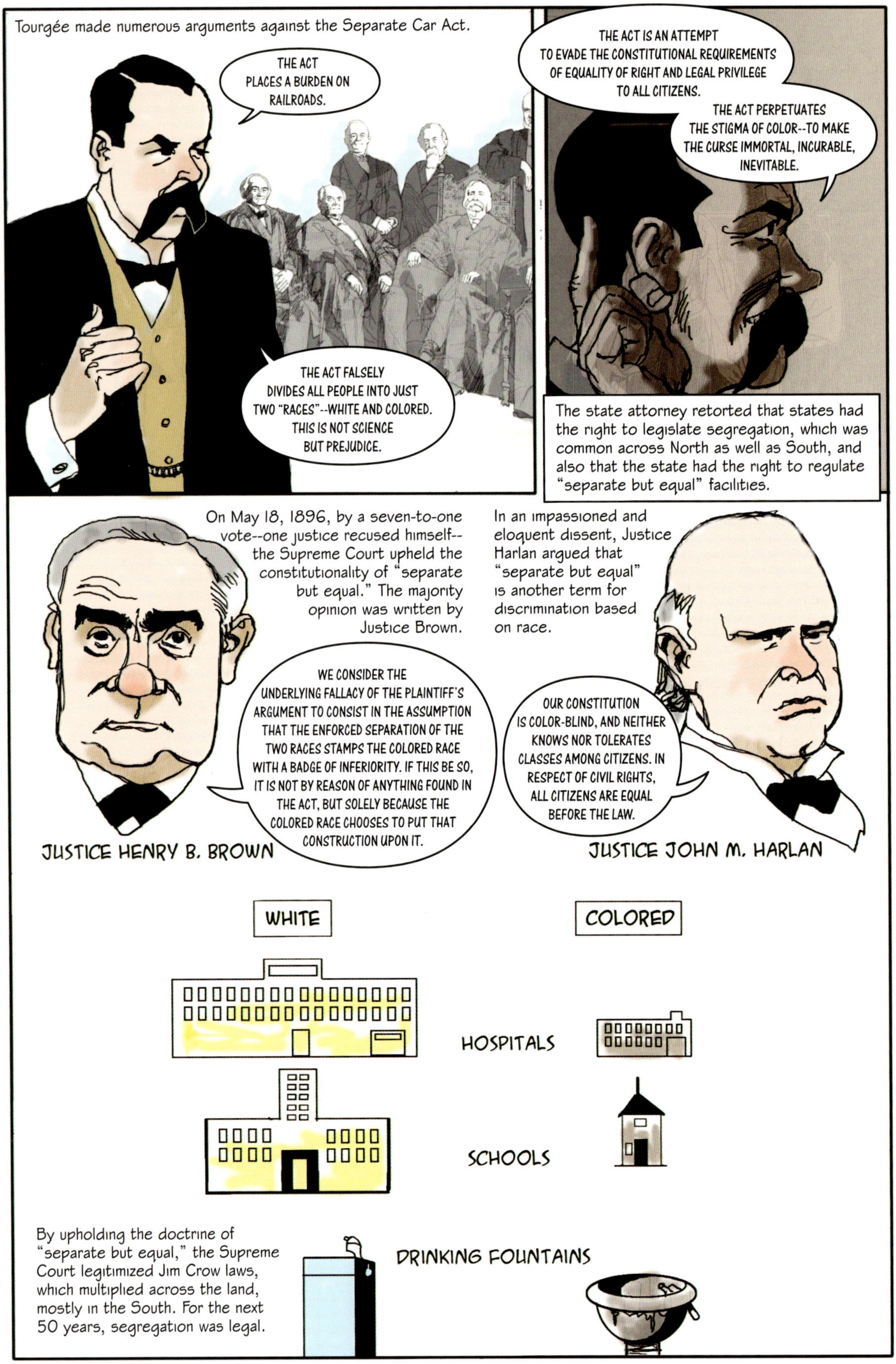
Tourgée made numerous arguments against the Separate Car Act.
THE ACT PLACES A BURDEN ON RAILROADS.
THE ACT FALSELY DIVIDES ALL PEOPLE INTO JUST TWO "RACES"--WHITE AND COLORED. THIS IS NOT SCIENCE BUT PREJUDICE.
THE ACT IS AN ATTEMPT TO EVADE THE CONSTITUTIONAL REQUIREMENTS OF EQUALITY OF RIGHT AND LEGAL PRIVILEGE TO ALL CITIZENS.
THE ACT PERPETUATES THE STIGMA OF COLOR--TO MAKE THE CURSE IMMORTAL, INCURABLE, INEVITABLE.
The state attorney retorted that states had the right to legislate segregation, which was common across North as well as South, and also that the state had the right to regulate "separate but equal" facilities.
On May 18, 1896, by a seven-to-one vote--one justice recused himself--the Supreme Court upheld the constitutionality of "separate but equal." The majority opinion was written by Justice Brown.
WE CONSIDER THE UNDERLYING FALLACY OF THE PLAINTIFF'S ARGUMENT TO CONSIST IN THE ASSUMPTION THAT THE ENFORCED SEPARATION OF THE TWO RACES STAMPS THE COLORED RACE WITH A BADGE OF INFERIORITY. IF THIS BE SO, IT IS NOT BY REASON OF ANYTHING FOUND IN THE ACT, BUT SOLELY BECAUSE THE COLORED RACE CHOOSES TO PUT THAT CONSTRUCTION UPON IT.
JUSTICE HENRY B. BROWN
In an impassioned and eloquent dissent, Justice Harlan argued that "separate but equal" is another term for discrimination based on race.
OUR CONSTITUTION IS COLOR-BLIND, AND NEITHER KNOWS NOR TOLERATES CLASSES AMONG CITIZENS. IN RESPECT OF CIVIL RIGHTS, ALL CITIZENS ARE EQUAL BEFORE THE LAW.
JUSTICE JOHN M. HARLAN
WHITE
COLORED
HOSPITALS
SCHOOLS
DRINKING FOUNTAINS
By upholding the doctrine of "separate but equal," the Supreme Court legitimized Jim Crow laws, which multiplied across the land, mostly in the South. For the next 50 years, segregation was legal.

After the Supreme Court ruling, Homer Plessy pleaded guilty in Judge Ferguson's courtroom and paid a $25 fine. He returned to a New Orleans where blacks were denied public education, public accommodations, and voting rights.

EXCERPTS FROM *PLESSY V. FERGUSON*

"The object of the [Fourteenth Amendment] was undoubtedly to enforce the absolute equality of the two races before the law, but, in the nature of things, it could not have been intended to abolish distinctions based upon color, or to enforce social, as distinguished from political, equality, or a commingling of the two races upon terms unsatisfactory to either . . .

"We consider the underlying fallacy of the plaintiff's argument to consist in the assumption that the enforced separation of the two races stamps the colored race with a badge of inferiority. If this be so, it is not by reason of anything found in the act, but solely because the colored race chooses to put that construction upon it . . . The argument also assumes that social prejudices may be overcome by legislation, and that equal rights cannot be secured to the negro except by an enforced commingling of the two races. We cannot accept this proposition. If the two races are to meet upon terms of social equality, it must be the result of natural affinities, a mutual appreciation of each other's merits, and a voluntary consent of individuals . . .

"Legislation is powerless to eradicate racial instincts or to abolish distinctions based upon physical differences, and the attempt to do so can only result in accentuating the difficulties of the present situation. If the civil and political rights of both races be equal, one cannot be inferior to the other civilly or politically. If one race be inferior to the other socially, the constitution of the United States cannot put them upon the same plane."

The Chinese Exclusion Act

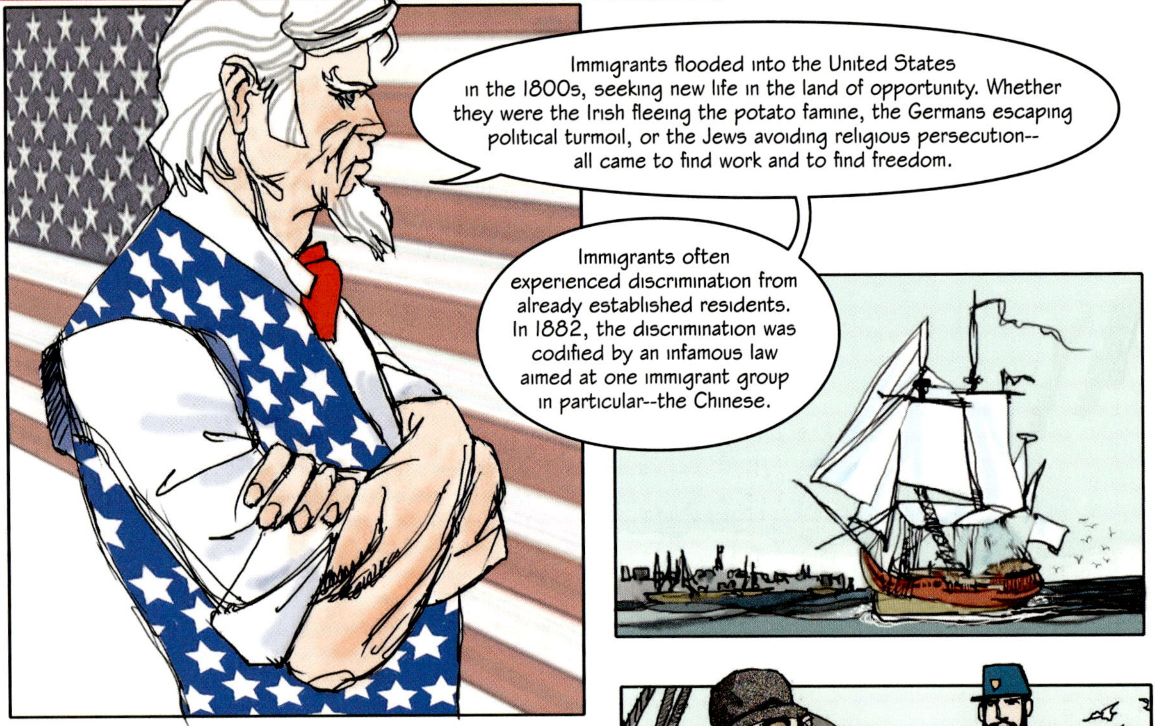

Immigrants flooded into the United States in the 1800s, seeking new life in the land of opportunity. Whether they were the Irish fleeing the potato famine, the Germans escaping political turmoil, or the Jews avoiding religious persecution--all came to find work and to find freedom.
Immigrants often experienced discrimination from already established residents. In 1882, the discrimination was codified by an infamous law aimed at one immigrant group in particular--the Chinese.

The relationship between China and the United States began with trade. In 1784, the American merchant ship the *Empress of China* sailed into the port of Canton in search of tea, silk, porcelain (also known as "china"), and other valuable goods.

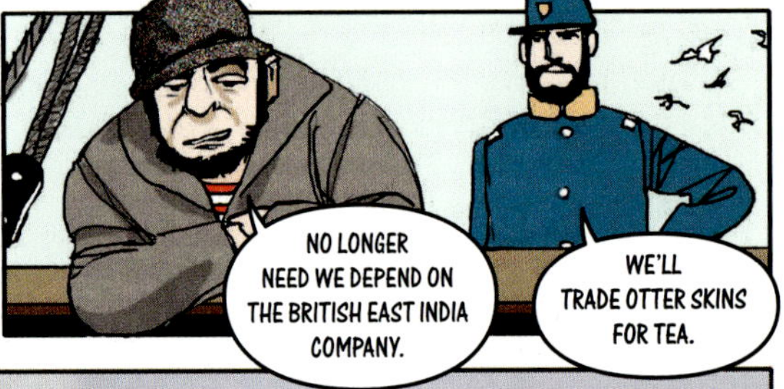

NO LONGER NEED WE DEPEND ON THE BRITISH EAST INDIA COMPANY.
WE'LL TRADE OTTER SKINS FOR TEA.

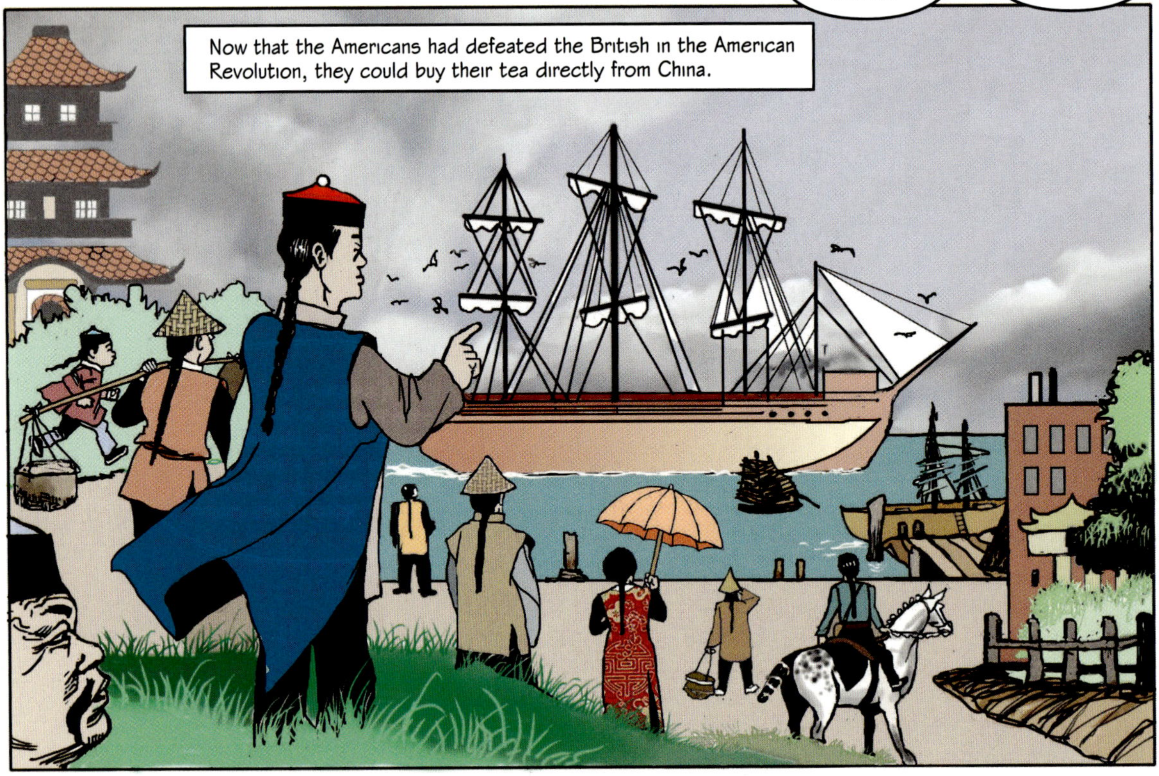

Now that the Americans had defeated the British in the American Revolution, they could buy their tea directly from China.

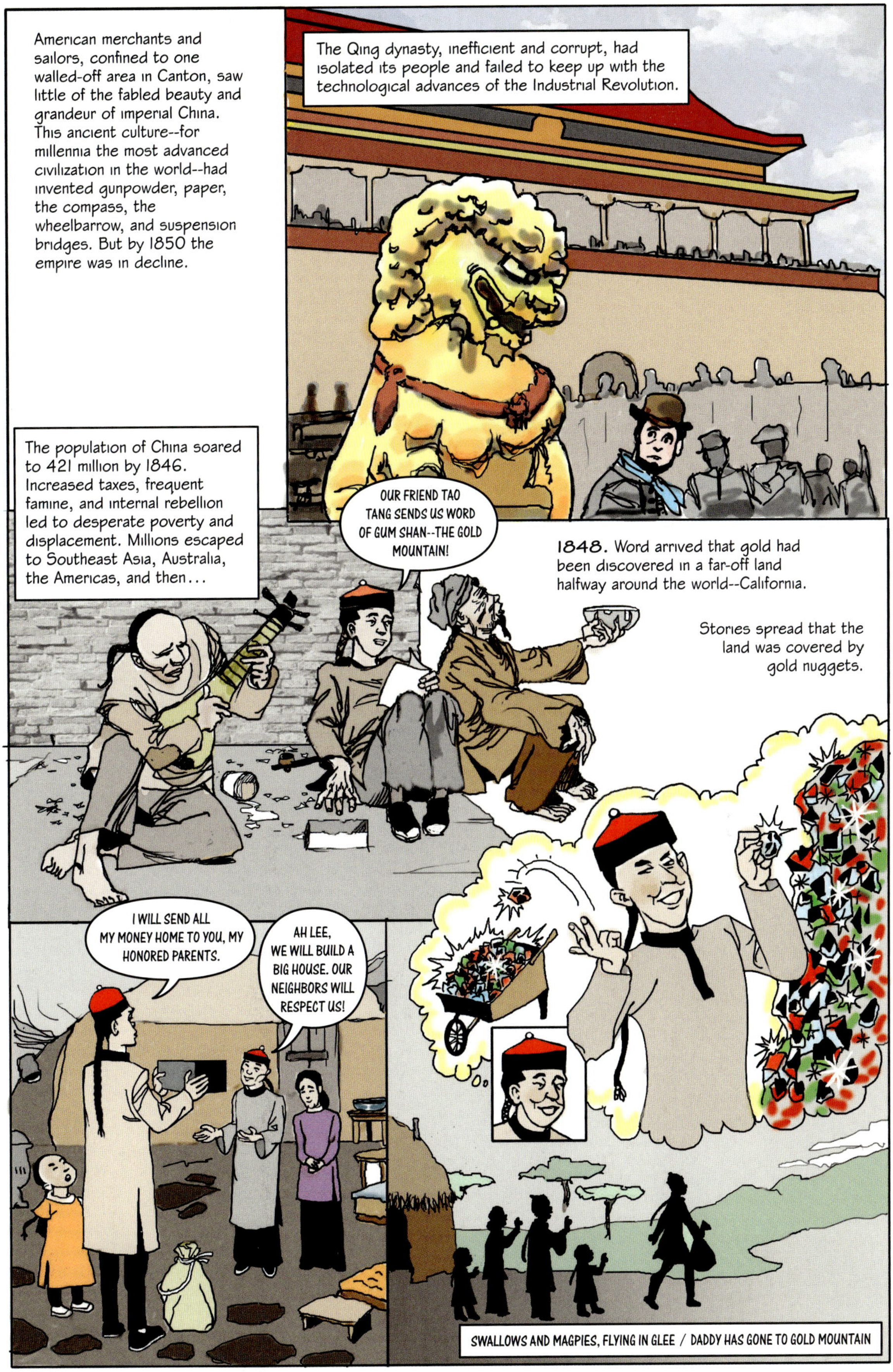
American merchants and sailors, confined to one walled-off area in Canton, saw little of the fabled beauty and grandeur of imperial China. This ancient culture--for millennia the most advanced civilization in the world--had invented gunpowder, paper, the compass, the wheelbarrow, and suspension bridges. But by 1850 the empire was in decline.
The Qing dynasty, inefficient and corrupt, had isolated its people and failed to keep up with the technological advances of the Industrial Revolution.
The population of China soared to 421 million by 1846. Increased taxes, frequent famine, and internal rebellion led to desperate poverty and displacement. Millions escaped to Southeast Asia, Australia, the Americas, and then...
OUR FRIEND TAO TANG SENDS US WORD OF GUM SHAN--THE GOLD MOUNTAIN!
1848. Word arrived that gold had been discovered in a far-off land halfway around the world--California.
Stories spread that the land was covered by gold nuggets.
I WILL SEND ALL MY MONEY HOME TO YOU, MY HONORED PARENTS.
AH LEE, WE WILL BUILD A BIG HOUSE. OUR NEIGHBORS WILL RESPECT US!
SWALLOWS AND MAGPIES, FLYING IN GLEE / DADDY HAS GONE TO GOLD MOUNTAIN

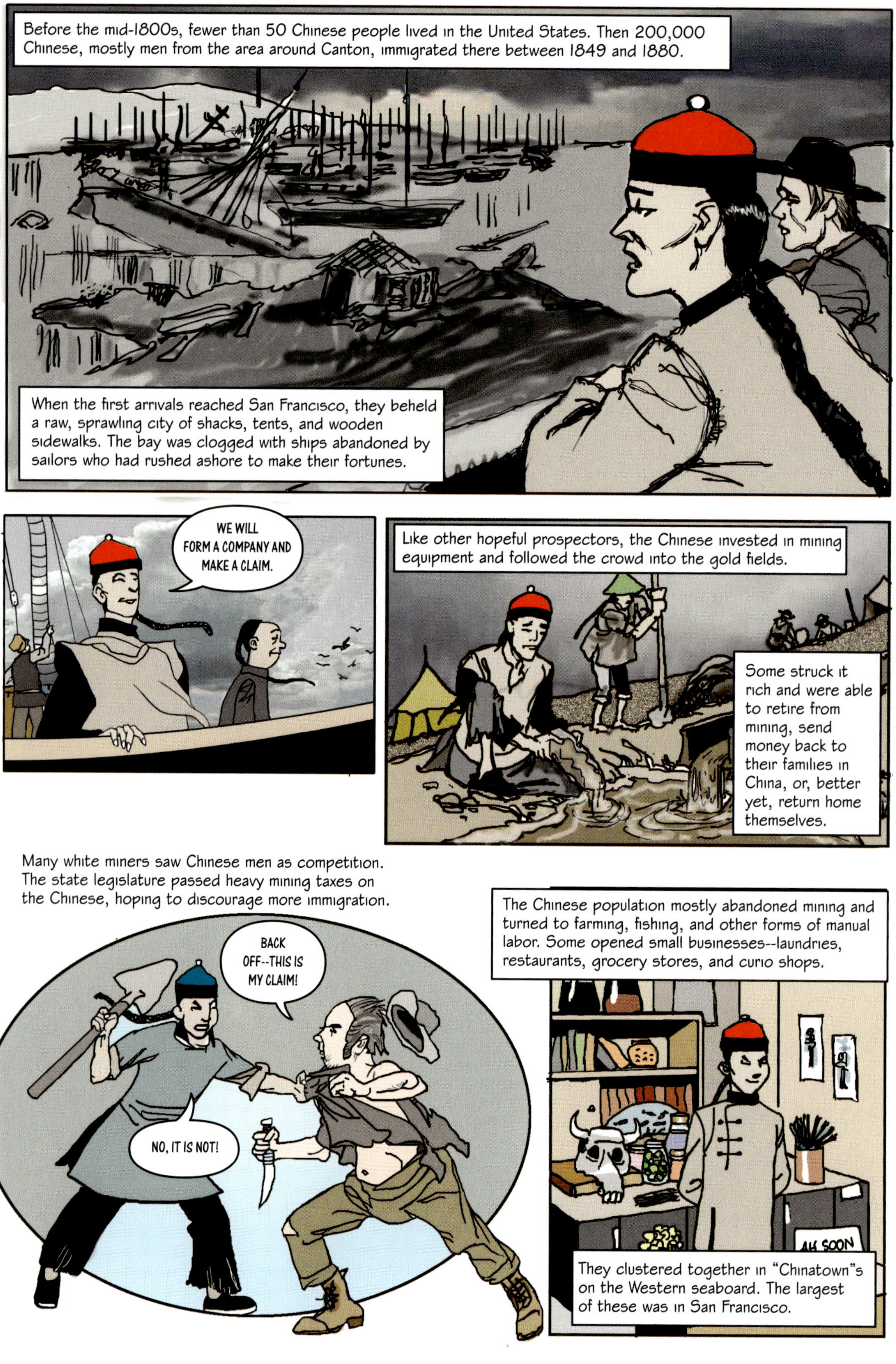
Before the mid-1800s, fewer than 50 Chinese people lived in the United States. Then 200,000 Chinese, mostly men from the area around Canton, immigrated there between 1849 and 1880.
When the first arrivals reached San Francisco, they beheld a raw, sprawling city of shacks, tents, and wooden sidewalks. The bay was clogged with ships abandoned by sailors who had rushed ashore to make their fortunes.
WE WILL FORM A COMPANY AND MAKE A CLAIM.
Like other hopeful prospectors, the Chinese invested in mining equipment and followed the crowd into the gold fields.
Some struck it rich and were able to retire from mining, send money back to their families in China, or, better yet, return home themselves.
Many white miners saw Chinese men as competition. The state legislature passed heavy mining taxes on the Chinese, hoping to discourage more immigration.
BACK OFF--THIS IS MY CLAIM!
NO, IT IS NOT!
The Chinese population mostly abandoned mining and turned to farming, fishing, and other forms of manual labor. Some opened small businesses--laundries, restaurants, grocery stores, and curio shops.
AH SOON
They clustered together in "Chinatown"s on the Western seaboard. The largest of these was in San Francisco.

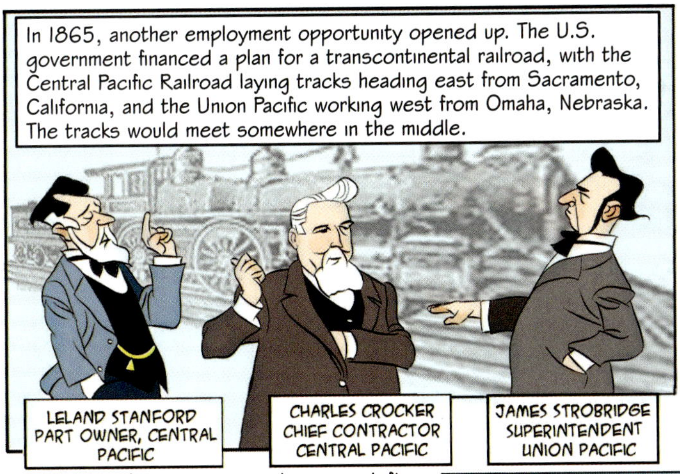
In 1865, another employment opportunity opened up. The U.S. government financed a plan for a transcontinental railroad, with the Central Pacific Railroad laying tracks heading east from Sacramento, California, and the Union Pacific working west from Omaha, Nebraska. The tracks would meet somewhere in the middle.
LELAND STANFORD PART OWNER, CENTRAL PACIFIC
CHARLES CROCKER CHIEF CONTRACTOR CENTRAL PACIFIC
JAMES STROBRIDGE SUPERINTENDENT UNION PACIFIC

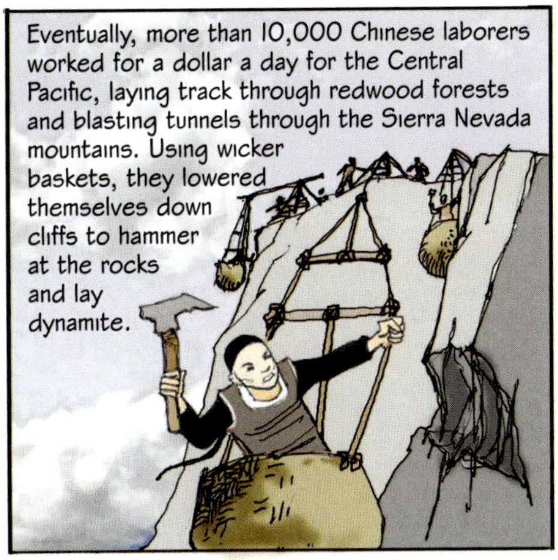
Eventually, more than 10,000 Chinese laborers worked for a dollar a day for the Central Pacific, laying track through redwood forests and blasting tunnels through the Sierra Nevada mountains. Using wicker baskets, they lowered themselves down cliffs to hammer at the rocks and lay dynamite.

During the frozen winters, when snowdrifts could reach 80 feet high, Chinese workers dug a maze of tunnels beneath the snow.

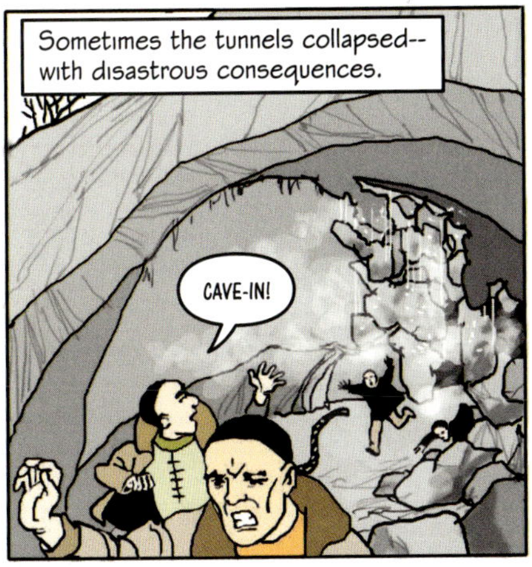
Sometimes the tunnels collapsed--with disastrous consequences.
CAVE-IN!

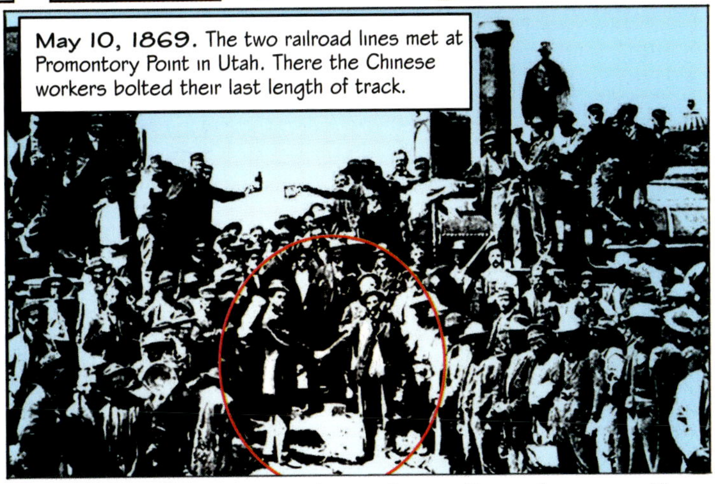
May 10, 1869. The two railroad lines met at Promontory Point in Utah. There the Chinese workers bolted their last length of track.

Yet when the official photograph was taken, no Chinese face was visible.

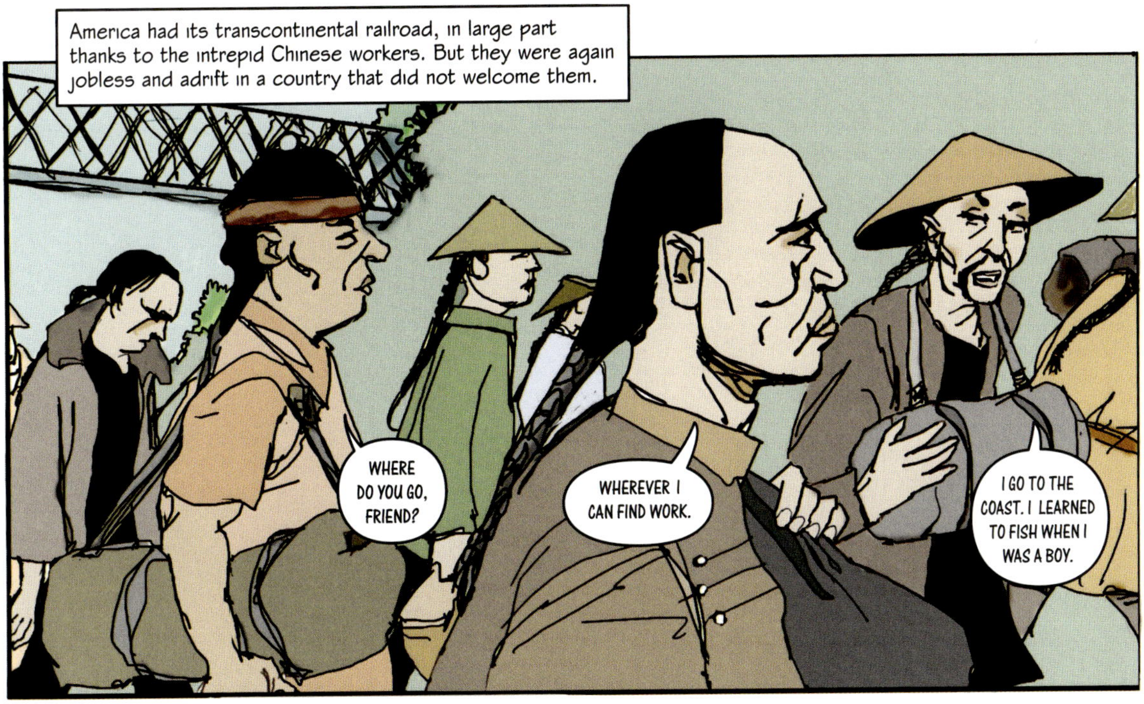
America had its transcontinental railroad, in large part thanks to the intrepid Chinese workers. But they were again jobless and adrift in a country that did not welcome them.
WHERE DO YOU GO, FRIEND?
WHEREVER I CAN FIND WORK.
I GO TO THE COAST. I LEARNED TO FISH WHEN I WAS A BOY.

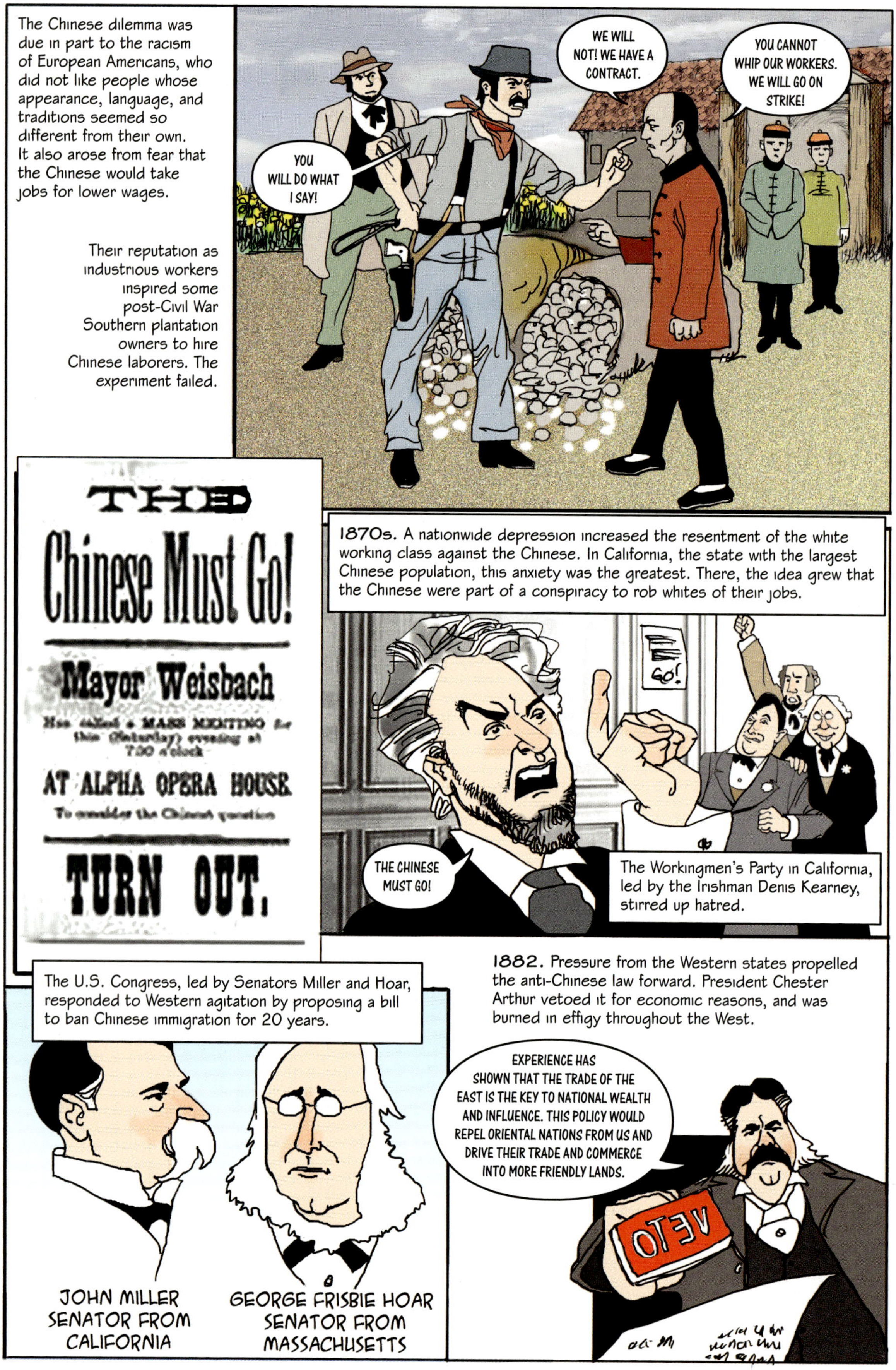
The Chinese dilemma was due in part to the racism of European Americans, who did not like people whose appearance, language, and traditions seemed so different from their own. It also arose from fear that the Chinese would take jobs for lower wages.
Their reputation as industrious workers inspired some post-Civil War Southern plantation owners to hire Chinese laborers. The experiment failed.
YOU WILL DO WHAT I SAY!
WE WILL NOT! WE HAVE A CONTRACT.
YOU CANNOT WHIP OUR WORKERS. WE WILL GO ON STRIKE!
THE Chinese Must Go!
Mayor Weisbach
AT ALPHA OPERA HOUSE
TURN OUT.
1870s. A nationwide depression increased the resentment of the white working class against the Chinese. In California, the state with the largest Chinese population, this anxiety was the greatest. There, the idea grew that the Chinese were part of a conspiracy to rob whites of their jobs.
GO!
THE CHINESE MUST GO!
The Workingmen's Party in California, led by the Irishman Denis Kearney, stirred up hatred.
The U.S. Congress, led by Senators Miller and Hoar, responded to Western agitation by proposing a bill to ban Chinese immigration for 20 years.
JOHN MILLER
SENATOR FROM CALIFORNIA
GEORGE FRISBIE HOAR
SENATOR FROM MASSACHUSETTS
1882. Pressure from the Western states propelled the anti-Chinese law forward. President Chester Arthur vetoed it for economic reasons, and was burned in effigy throughout the West.
EXPERIENCE HAS SHOWN THAT THE TRADE OF THE EAST IS THE KEY TO NATIONAL WEALTH AND INFLUENCE. THIS POLICY WOULD REPEL ORIENTAL NATIONS FROM US AND DRIVE THEIR TRADE AND COMMERCE INTO MORE FRIENDLY LANDS.
VETO

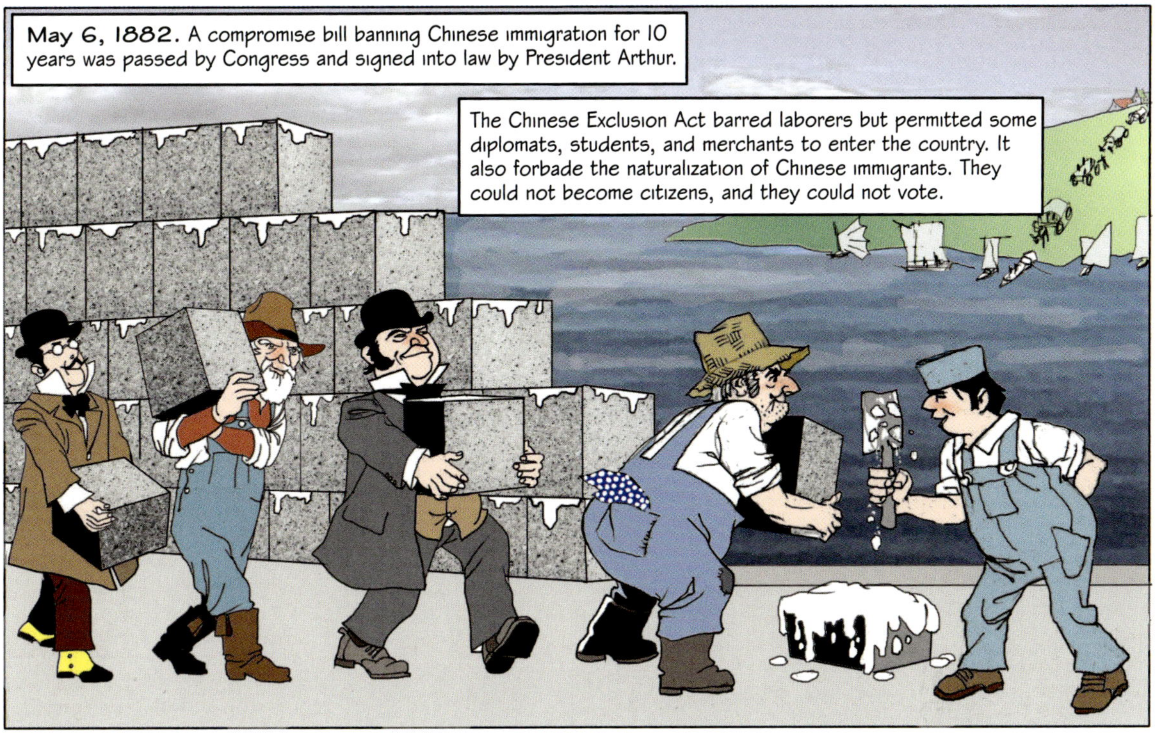
May 6, 1882. A compromise bill banning Chinese immigration for 10 years was passed by Congress and signed into law by President Arthur.
The Chinese Exclusion Act barred laborers but permitted some diplomats, students, and merchants to enter the country. It also forbade the naturalization of Chinese immigrants. They could not become citizens, and they could not vote.

In 1892, the Geary Act extended the Chinese Exclusion Act by 10 years and required all Chinese residents to carry photo identification. In 1902, this exclusion was made permanent.

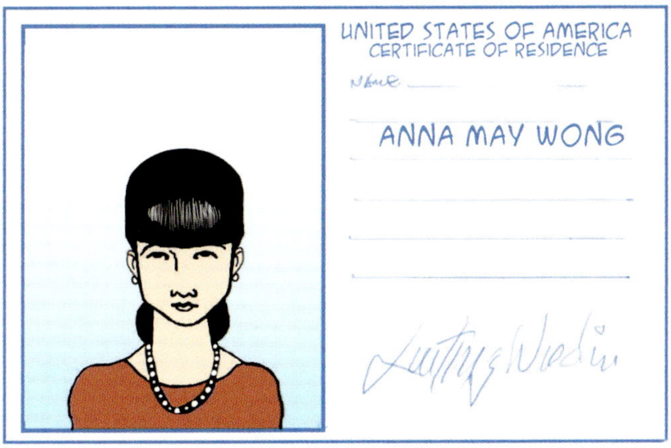
UNITED STATES OF AMERICA
CERTIFICATE OF RESIDENCE
ANNA MAY WONG

The Exclusion Act ushered in an era of anti-Chinese persecution known as the Driving Out. Throughout the West, mobs descended on Chinese communities, destroying homes and businesses and attacking people.

Rock Springs, Wyoming, September 26, 1885. White miners attacked a Chinese mining camp and massacred 28 people. Chinese residents fought back through political organizing and legal action--

--as in the case brought by California-born Wong Kim Ark when he was denied readmittance after visiting his family in China. In 1898, the Supreme Court affirmed that, according to the Fourteenth Amendment, Ark was an American citizen and could not be denied entry.

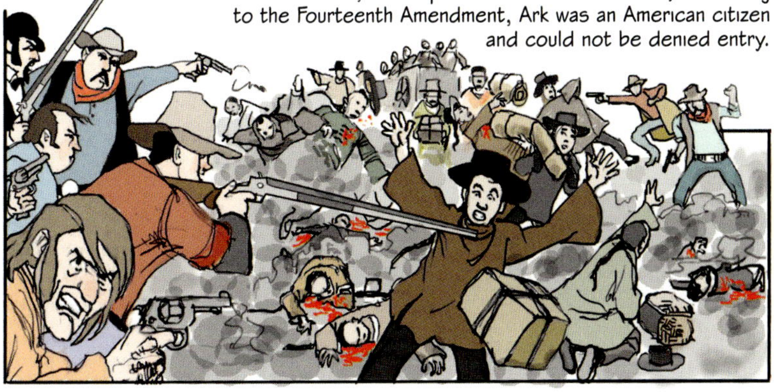

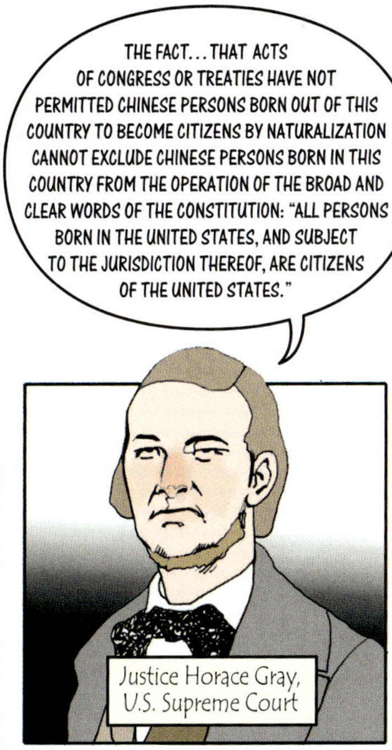
THE FACT... THAT ACTS OF CONGRESS OR TREATIES HAVE NOT PERMITTED CHINESE PERSONS BORN OUT OF THIS COUNTRY TO BECOME CITIZENS BY NATURALIZATION CANNOT EXCLUDE CHINESE PERSONS BORN IN THIS COUNTRY FROM THE OPERATION OF THE BROAD AND CLEAR WORDS OF THE CONSTITUTION: "ALL PERSONS BORN IN THE UNITED STATES, AND SUBJECT TO THE JURISDICTION THEREOF, ARE CITIZENS OF THE UNITED STATES."

Justice Horace Gray, U.S. Supreme Court

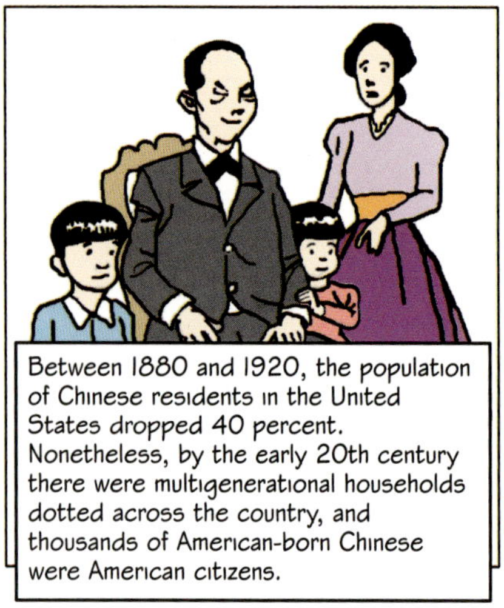
Between 1880 and 1920, the population of Chinese residents in the United States dropped 40 percent. Nonetheless, by the early 20th century there were multigenerational households dotted across the country, and thousands of American-born Chinese were American citizens.

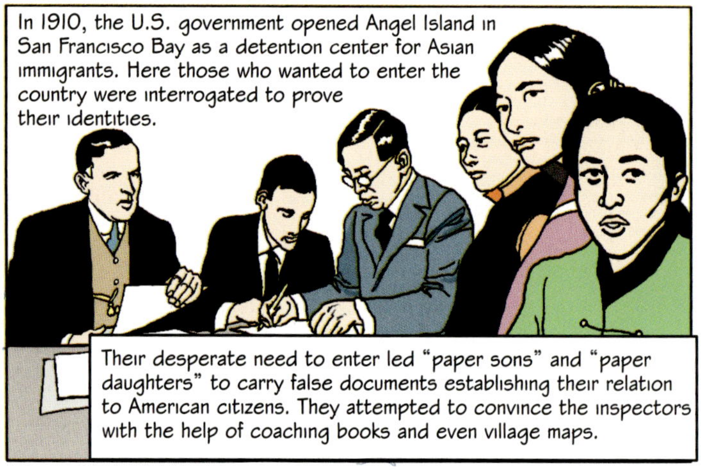
In 1910, the U.S. government opened Angel Island in San Francisco Bay as a detention center for Asian immigrants. Here those who wanted to enter the country were interrogated to prove their identities.
Their desperate need to enter led "paper sons" and "paper daughters" to carry false documents establishing their relation to American citizens. They attempted to convince the inspectors with the help of coaching books and even village maps.

Immigrants could be detained at Angel Island for months or even years. Homesick immigrants wrote poems on their barracks' walls.

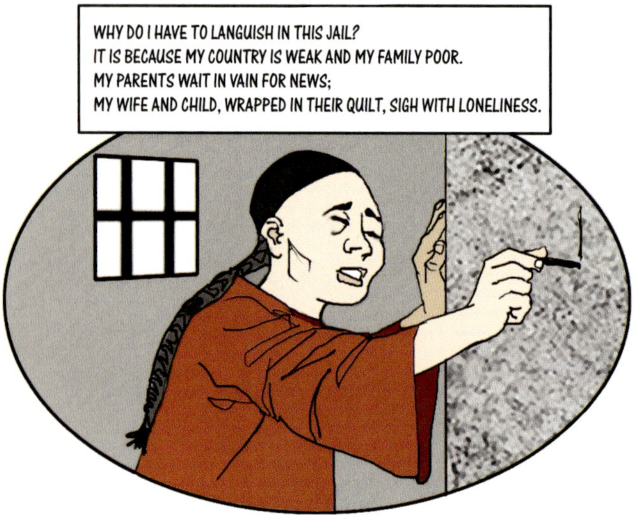
WHY DO I HAVE TO LANGUISH IN THIS JAIL?
IT IS BECAUSE MY COUNTRY IS WEAK AND MY FAMILY POOR.
MY PARENTS WAIT IN VAIN FOR NEWS;
MY WIFE AND CHILD, WRAPPED IN THEIR QUILT, SIGH WITH LONELINESS.

In the 1930s, when Japan invaded China, Chinese Americans urged their country to support China. After the Japanese bombed Pearl Harbor on December 7, 1941, the U.S. declared war against Japan and became China's ally. Nearly 20,000 Chinese American men served in the American military.

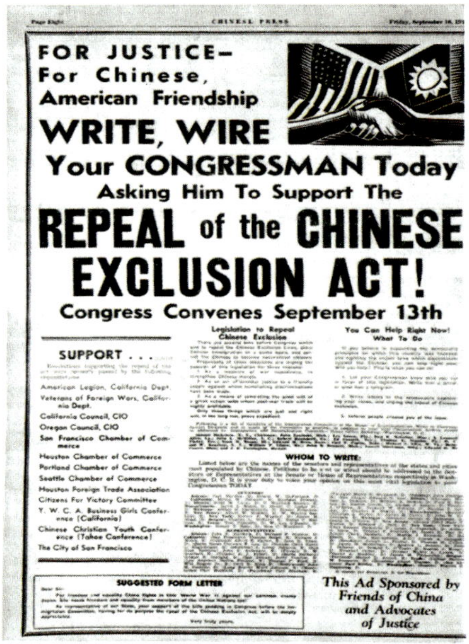

FOR JUSTICE—
For Chinese,
American Friendship

WRITE, WIRE
Your CONGRESSMAN Today
Asking Him To Support The
REPEAL of the CHINESE EXCLUSION ACT!
Congress Convenes September 13th

SUPPORT . . .

American Legion, California Dept.
Veterans of Foreign Wars, California Dept.
California Council, CIO
Oregon Council, CIO
San Francisco Chamber of Commerce
Houston Chamber of Commerce
Portland Chamber of Commerce
Seattle Chamber of Commerce
Houston Foreign Trade Association
Citizens For Victory Committee
Y. W. C. A. Business Girls Conference (California)
Chinese Christian Youth Conference (Tahoe Conference)
The City of San Francisco

Legislation to Repeal Chinese Exclusion

You Can Help Right Now! What To Do

WHOM TO WRITE:

SUGGESTED FORM LETTER

This Ad Sponsored by Friends of China and Advocates of Justice

December 17, 1943. In recognition of the new U.S.-China alliance, President Franklin D. Roosevelt signed a bill to repeal the Chinese Exclusion Act. Chinese could now immigrate, although the quota was set at 105 people per year. Just as important, Chinese could now become naturalized citizens.

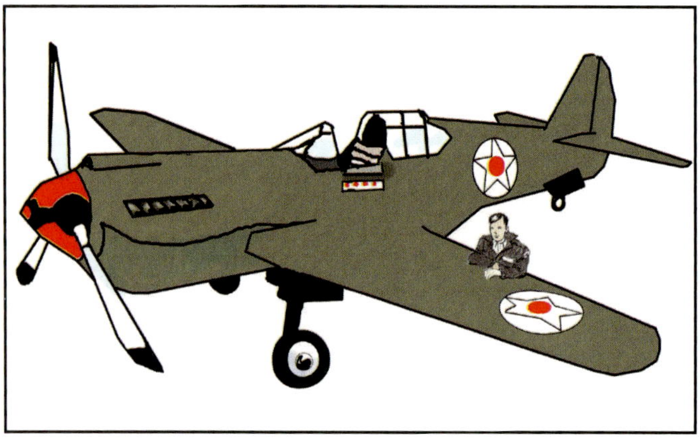

It would take more than 20 years for immigration quotas based on national origins to be eliminated.

The Chinese Exclusion Act barred the immigration of the Chinese into the United States based on both race and class. In addition, foreign-born Chinese could not become naturalized citizens. The Act served as a precedent for further 20th-century restrictive immigration laws that established quotas for international immigrant groups, favoring Northern Europeans.

The quotas were abolished by the Immigration and Naturalization Act, proposed by President John F. Kennedy in 1963 and signed into law by President Lyndon B. Johnson in 1965.

EXCERPTS FROM THE CHINESE EXCLUSION ACT

"An Act to execute certain treaty stipulations relating to Chinese.

"Whereas in the opinion of the Government of the United States the coming of Chinese laborers to this country endangers the good order of certain localities within the territory thereof: Therefore,

"Be it enacted by the Senate and House of Representatives of the United States of America in Congress assembled, that from and after the expiration of ninety days next after the passage of this act, and until the expiration of ten years next after the passage of this act, the coming of Chinese laborers to the United States be, and the same is hereby, suspended; and during such suspension it shall not be lawful for any Chinese laborer to come, or having so come after the expiration of said ninety days to remain within the United States.

"Section 2. That the master of any vessel who shall knowingly bring within the United States on such vessel, and land or permit to be landed, any Chinese laborer, from any foreign port or place, shall be deemed guilty of a misdemeanor, and on conviction thereof shall be punished by a fine of not more than five hundred dollars for each and every such Chinese laborer so brought, and maybe also imprisoned for a term not exceeding one year...

"Section 14. That hereafter no State court or court of the United States shall admit Chinese to citizenship; and all laws in conflict with this act are hereby repealed.

"Section 15. That the words 'Chinese laborers,' wherever used in this act shall be construed to mean both skilled and unskilled laborers and Chinese employed in mining.

"Approved, May 6, 1882."

The Dawes Severalty Act

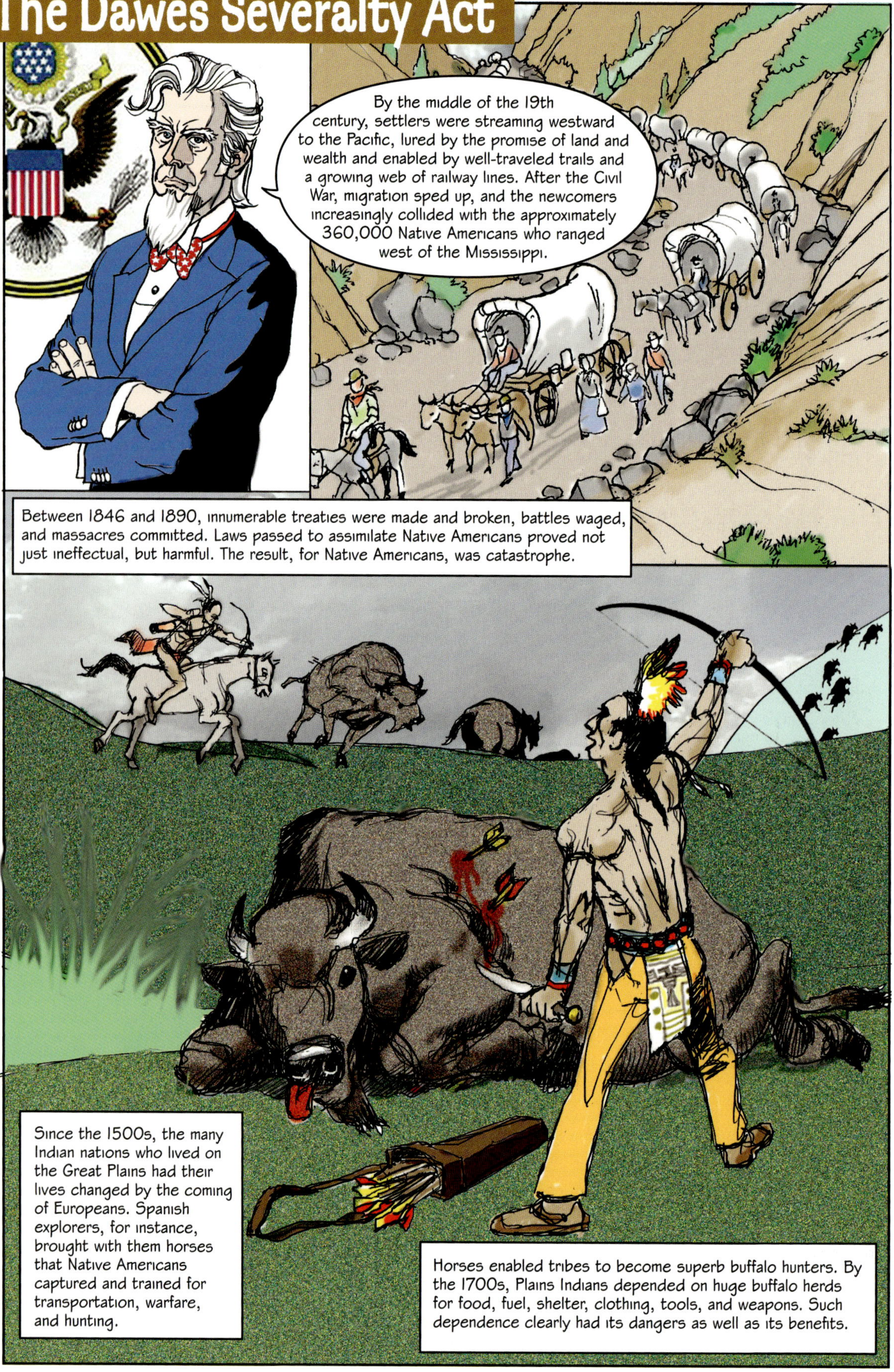

By the middle of the 19th century, settlers were streaming westward to the Pacific, lured by the promise of land and wealth and enabled by well-traveled trails and a growing web of railway lines. After the Civil War, migration sped up, and the newcomers increasingly collided with the approximately 360,000 Native Americans who ranged west of the Mississippi.
Between 1846 and 1890, innumerable treaties were made and broken, battles waged, and massacres committed. Laws passed to assimilate Native Americans proved not just ineffectual, but harmful. The result, for Native Americans, was catastrophe.
Since the 1500s, the many Indian nations who lived on the Great Plains had their lives changed by the coming of Europeans. Spanish explorers, for instance, brought with them horses that Native Americans captured and trained for transportation, warfare, and hunting.
Horses enabled tribes to become superb buffalo hunters. By the 1700s, Plains Indians depended on huge buffalo herds for food, fuel, shelter, clothing, tools, and weapons. Such dependence clearly had its dangers as well as its benefits.

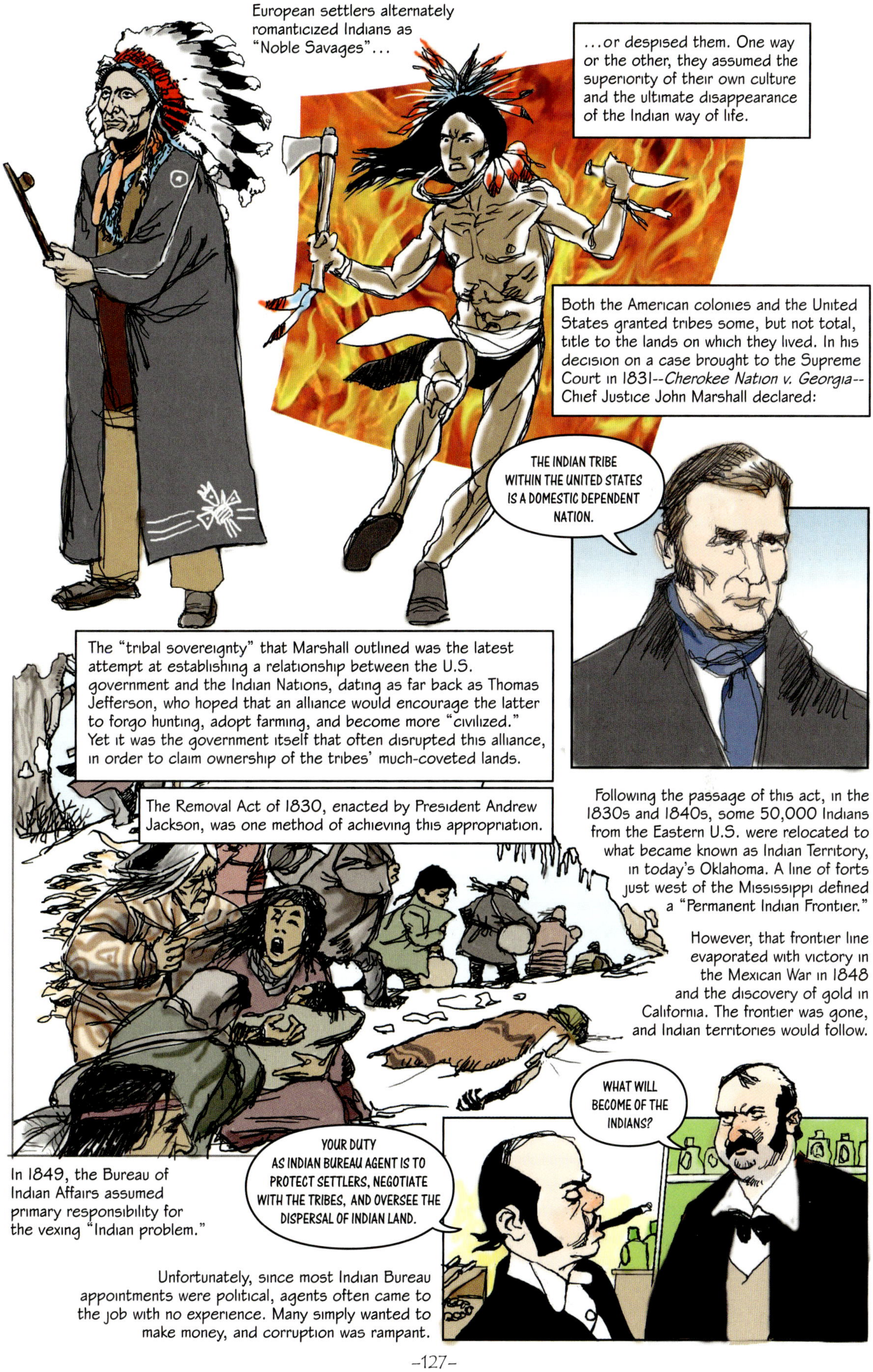
European settlers alternately romanticized Indians as "Noble Savages"...
...or despised them. One way or the other, they assumed the superiority of their own culture and the ultimate disappearance of the Indian way of life.
Both the American colonies and the United States granted tribes some, but not total, title to the lands on which they lived. In his decision on a case brought to the Supreme Court in 1831--*Cherokee Nation v. Georgia*--Chief Justice John Marshall declared:
THE INDIAN TRIBE WITHIN THE UNITED STATES IS A DOMESTIC DEPENDENT NATION.
The "tribal sovereignty" that Marshall outlined was the latest attempt at establishing a relationship between the U.S. government and the Indian Nations, dating as far back as Thomas Jefferson, who hoped that an alliance would encourage the latter to forgo hunting, adopt farming, and become more "civilized." Yet it was the government itself that often disrupted this alliance, in order to claim ownership of the tribes' much-coveted lands.
The Removal Act of 1830, enacted by President Andrew Jackson, was one method of achieving this appropriation.
Following the passage of this act, in the 1830s and 1840s, some 50,000 Indians from the Eastern U.S. were relocated to what became known as Indian Territory, in today's Oklahoma. A line of forts just west of the Mississippi defined a "Permanent Indian Frontier."
However, that frontier line evaporated with victory in the Mexican War in 1848 and the discovery of gold in California. The frontier was gone, and Indian territories would follow.
In 1849, the Bureau of Indian Affairs assumed primary responsibility for the vexing "Indian problem."
WHAT WILL BECOME OF THE INDIANS?
YOUR DUTY AS INDIAN BUREAU AGENT IS TO PROTECT SETTLERS, NEGOTIATE WITH THE TRIBES, AND OVERSEE THE DISPERSAL OF INDIAN LAND.
Unfortunately, since most Indian Bureau appointments were political, agents often came to the job with no experience. Many simply wanted to make money, and corruption was rampant.

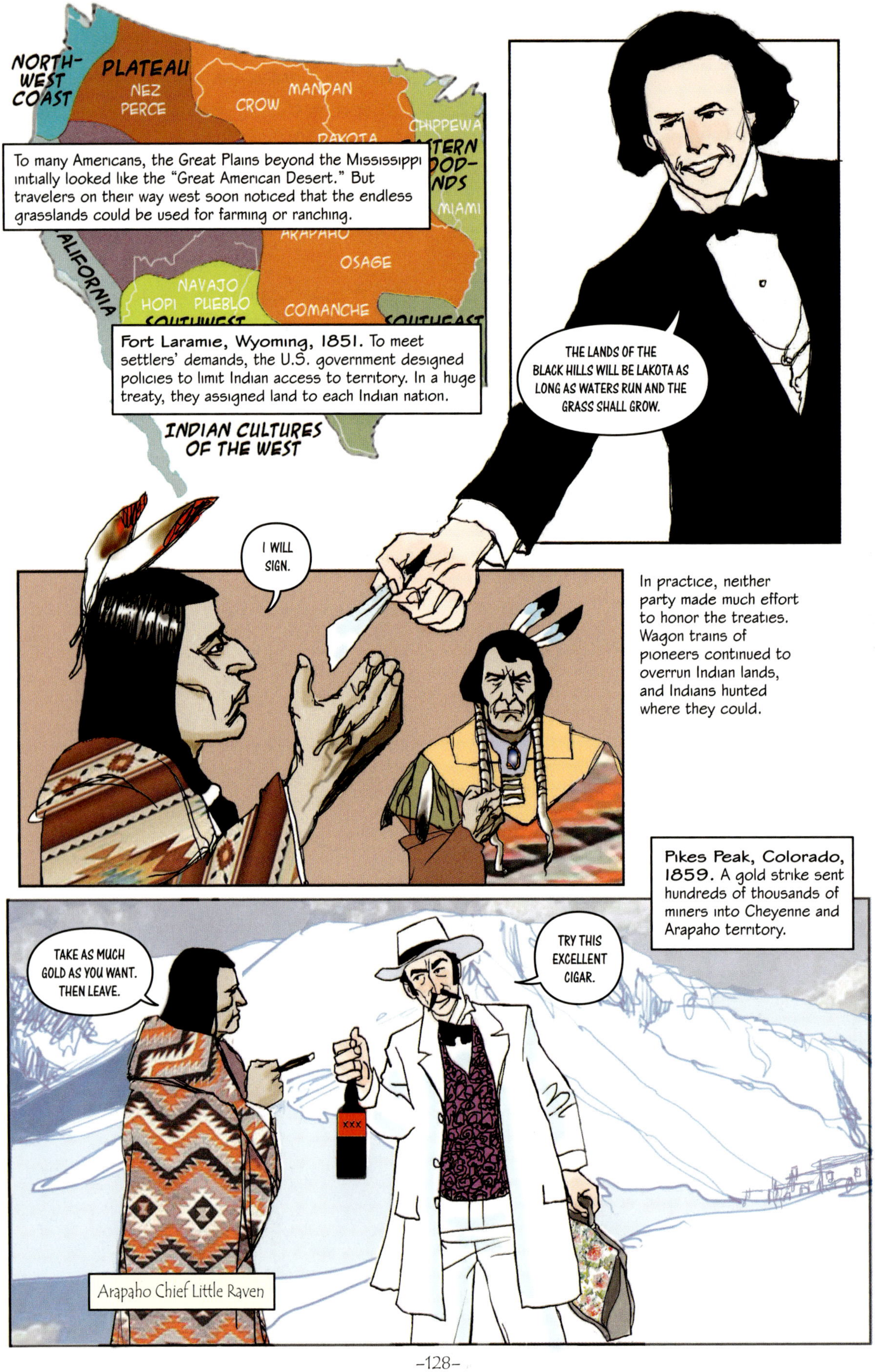
NORTH-WEST COAST
PLATEAU
NEZ PERCE
CROW
MANDAN
CHIPPEWA
MIAMI
CALIFORNIA
OSAGE
NAVAJO
HOPI
PUEBLO
COMANCHE
INDIAN CULTURES OF THE WEST
To many Americans, the Great Plains beyond the Mississippi initially looked like the "Great American Desert." But travelers on their way west soon noticed that the endless grasslands could be used for farming or ranching.
Fort Laramie, Wyoming, 1851. To meet settlers' demands, the U.S. government designed policies to limit Indian access to territory. In a huge treaty, they assigned land to each Indian nation.
THE LANDS OF THE BLACK HILLS WILL BE LAKOTA AS LONG AS WATERS RUN AND THE GRASS SHALL GROW.
I WILL SIGN.
In practice, neither party made much effort to honor the treaties. Wagon trains of pioneers continued to overrun Indian lands, and Indians hunted where they could.
Pikes Peak, Colorado, 1859. A gold strike sent hundreds of thousands of miners into Cheyenne and Arapaho territory.
TAKE AS MUCH GOLD AS YOU WANT. THEN LEAVE.
TRY THIS EXCELLENT CIGAR.
XXX
Arapaho Chief Little Raven

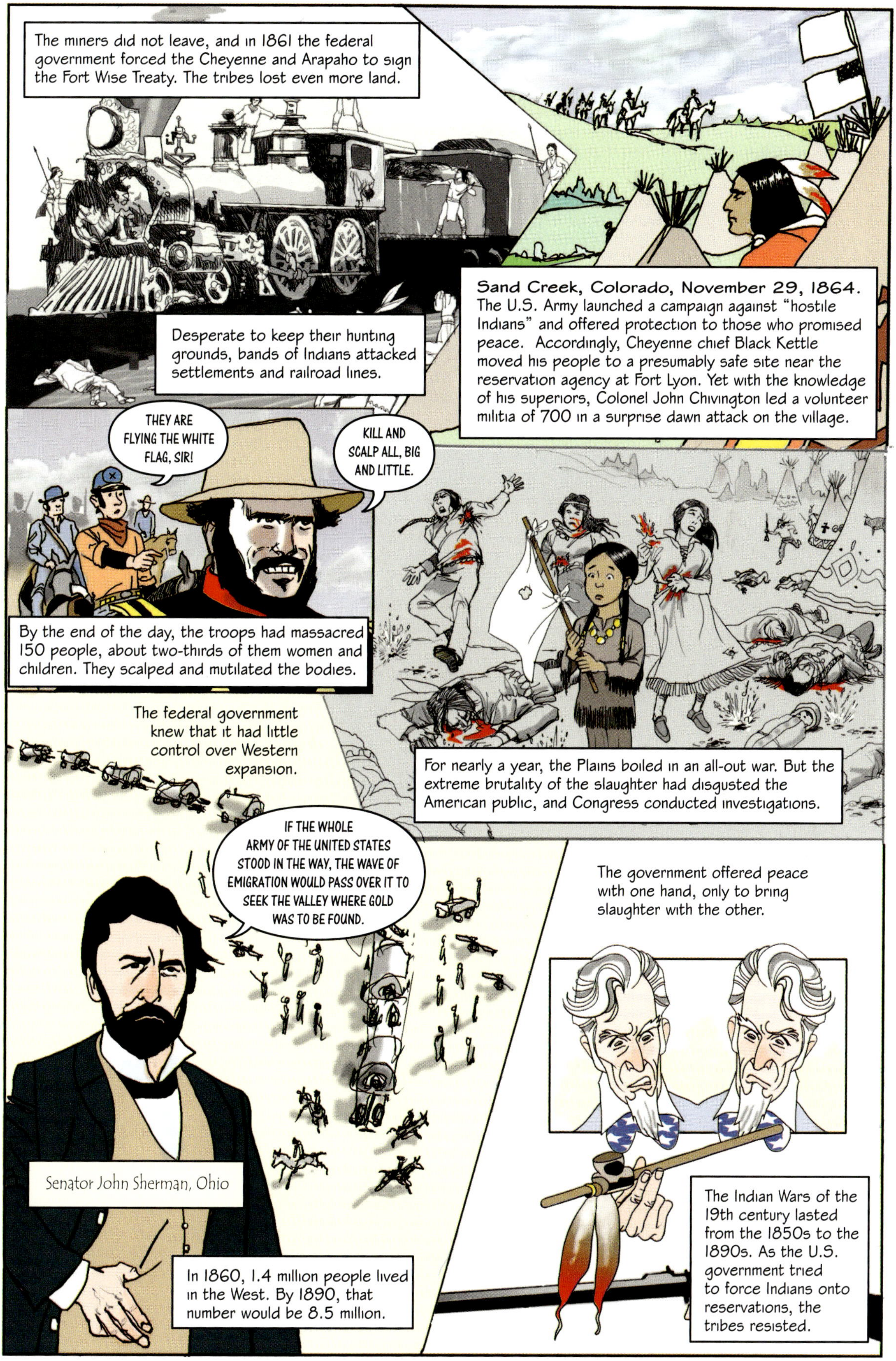
The miners did not leave, and in 1861 the federal government forced the Cheyenne and Arapaho to sign the Fort Wise Treaty. The tribes lost even more land.
Desperate to keep their hunting grounds, bands of Indians attacked settlements and railroad lines.
Sand Creek, Colorado, November 29, 1864. The U.S. Army launched a campaign against "hostile Indians" and offered protection to those who promised peace. Accordingly, Cheyenne chief Black Kettle moved his people to a presumably safe site near the reservation agency at Fort Lyon. Yet with the knowledge of his superiors, Colonel John Chivington led a volunteer militia of 700 in a surprise dawn attack on the village.
THEY ARE FLYING THE WHITE FLAG, SIR!
KILL AND SCALP ALL, BIG AND LITTLE.
By the end of the day, the troops had massacred 150 people, about two-thirds of them women and children. They scalped and mutilated the bodies.
For nearly a year, the Plains boiled in an all-out war. But the extreme brutality of the slaughter had disgusted the American public, and Congress conducted investigations.
The federal government knew that it had little control over Western expansion.
IF THE WHOLE ARMY OF THE UNITED STATES STOOD IN THE WAY, THE WAVE OF EMIGRATION WOULD PASS OVER IT TO SEEK THE VALLEY WHERE GOLD WAS TO BE FOUND.
Senator John Sherman, Ohio
In 1860, 1.4 million people lived in the West. By 1890, that number would be 8.5 million.
The government offered peace with one hand, only to bring slaughter with the other.
The Indian Wars of the 19th century lasted from the 1850s to the 1890s. As the U.S. government tried to force Indians onto reservations, the tribes resisted.

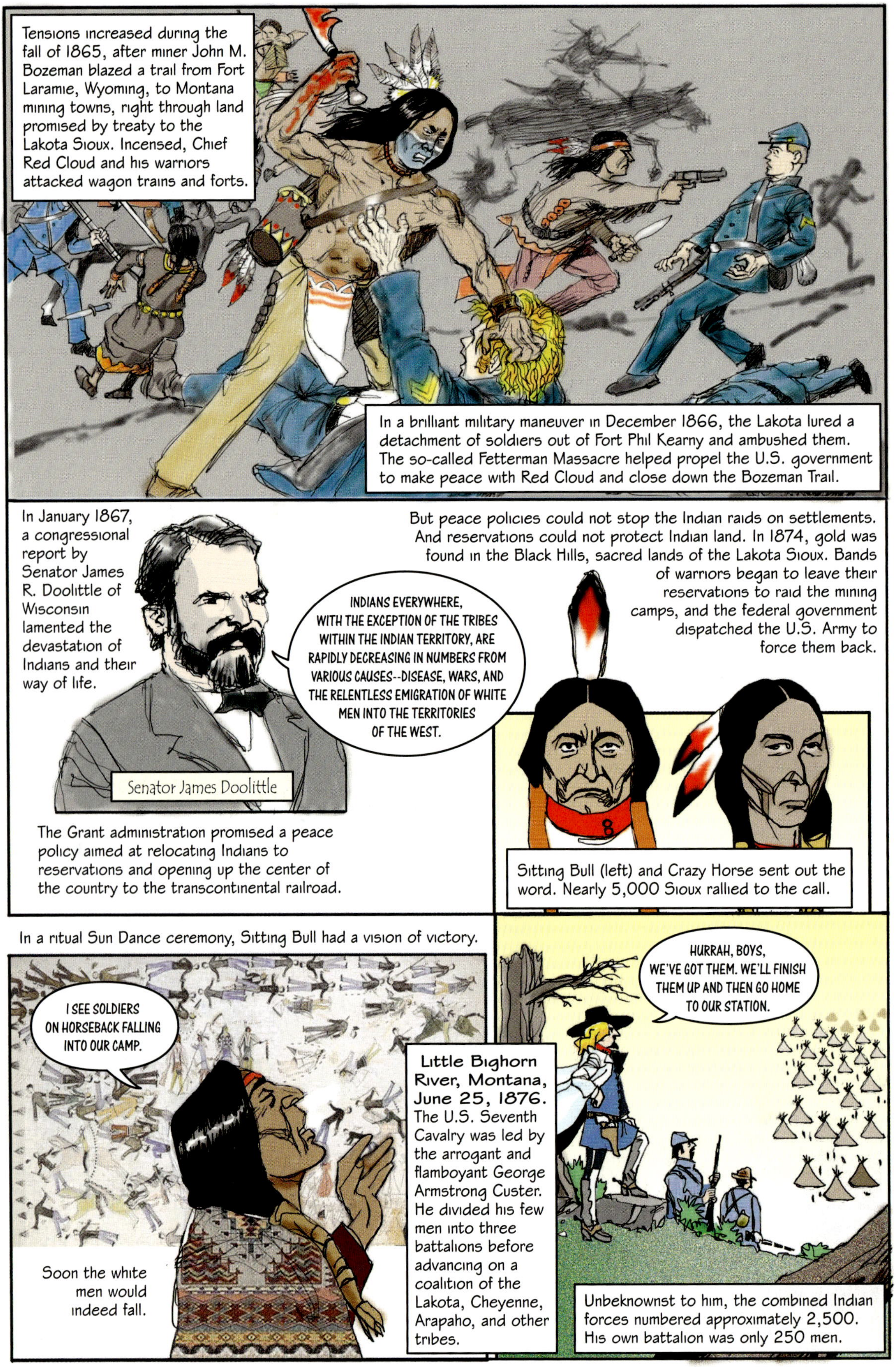

Tensions increased during the fall of 1865, after miner John M. Bozeman blazed a trail from Fort Laramie, Wyoming, to Montana mining towns, right through land promised by treaty to the Lakota Sioux. Incensed, Chief Red Cloud and his warriors attacked wagon trains and forts.
In a brilliant military maneuver in December 1866, the Lakota lured a detachment of soldiers out of Fort Phil Kearny and ambushed them. The so-called Fetterman Massacre helped propel the U.S. government to make peace with Red Cloud and close down the Bozeman Trail.
In January 1867, a congressional report by Senator James R. Doolittle of Wisconsin lamented the devastation of Indians and their way of life.
INDIANS EVERYWHERE, WITH THE EXCEPTION OF THE TRIBES WITHIN THE INDIAN TERRITORY, ARE RAPIDLY DECREASING IN NUMBERS FROM VARIOUS CAUSES--DISEASE, WARS, AND THE RELENTLESS EMIGRATION OF WHITE MEN INTO THE TERRITORIES OF THE WEST.
Senator James Doolittle
The Grant administration promised a peace policy aimed at relocating Indians to reservations and opening up the center of the country to the transcontinental railroad.
But peace policies could not stop the Indian raids on settlements. And reservations could not protect Indian land. In 1874, gold was found in the Black Hills, sacred lands of the Lakota Sioux. Bands of warriors began to leave their reservations to raid the mining camps, and the federal government dispatched the U.S. Army to force them back.
Sitting Bull (left) and Crazy Horse sent out the word. Nearly 5,000 Sioux rallied to the call.
In a ritual Sun Dance ceremony, Sitting Bull had a vision of victory.
I SEE SOLDIERS ON HORSEBACK FALLING INTO OUR CAMP.
Soon the white men would indeed fall.
Little Bighorn River, Montana, June 25, 1876. The U.S. Seventh Cavalry was led by the arrogant and flamboyant George Armstrong Custer. He divided his few men into three battalions before advancing on a coalition of the Lakota, Cheyenne, Arapaho, and other tribes.
HURRAH, BOYS, WE'VE GOT THEM. WE'LL FINISH THEM UP AND THEN GO HOME TO OUR STATION.
Unbeknownst to him, the combined Indian forces numbered approximately 2,500. His own battalion was only 250 men.

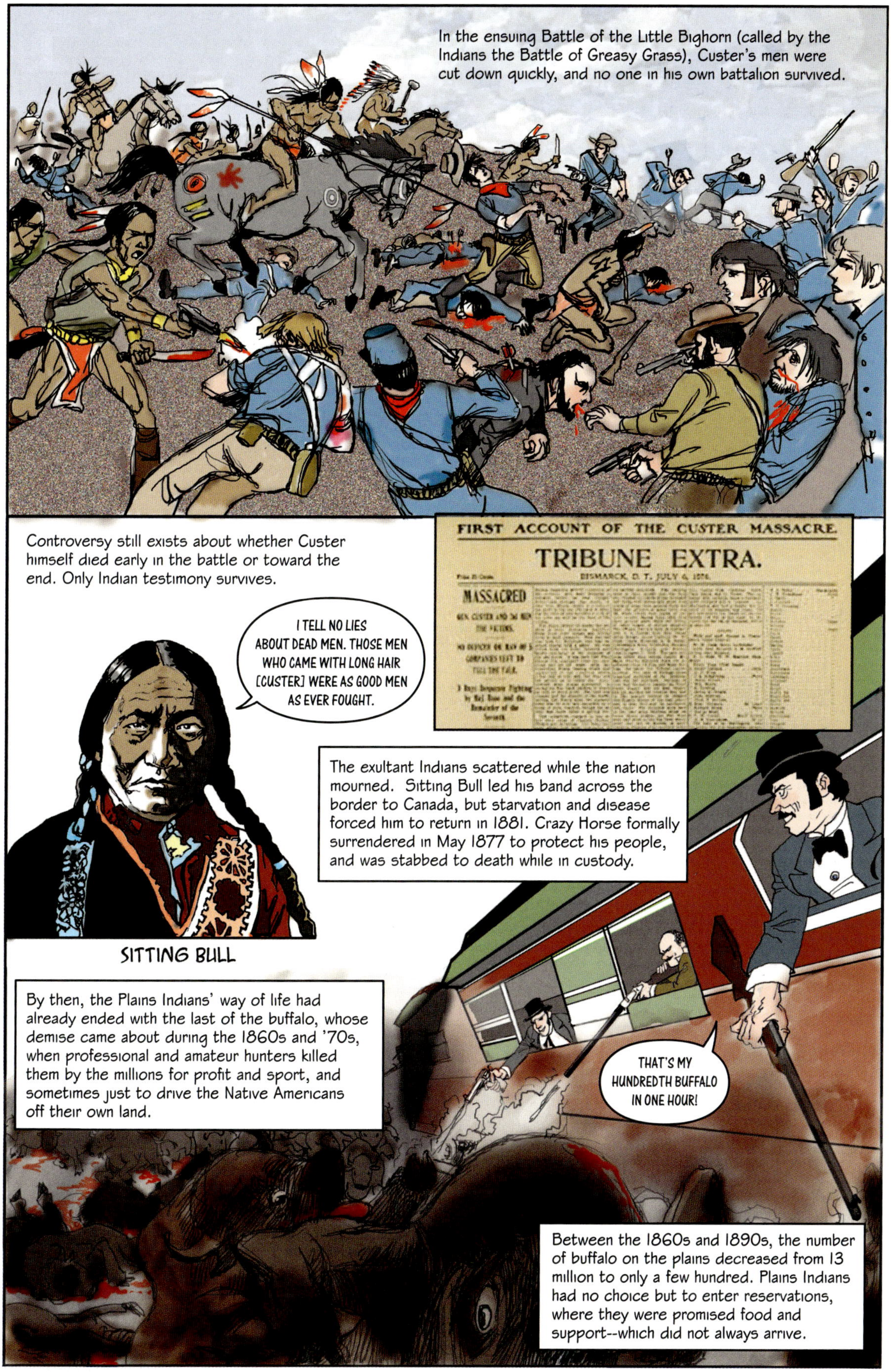
In the ensuing Battle of the Little Bighorn (called by the Indians the Battle of Greasy Grass), Custer's men were cut down quickly, and no one in his own battalion survived.
Controversy still exists about whether Custer himself died early in the battle or toward the end. Only Indian testimony survives.
FIRST ACCOUNT OF THE CUSTER MASSACRE.
TRIBUNE EXTRA.
MASSACRED
I TELL NO LIES ABOUT DEAD MEN. THOSE MEN WHO CAME WITH LONG HAIR [CUSTER] WERE AS GOOD MEN AS EVER FOUGHT.
The exultant Indians scattered while the nation mourned. Sitting Bull led his band across the border to Canada, but starvation and disease forced him to return in 1881. Crazy Horse formally surrendered in May 1877 to protect his people, and was stabbed to death while in custody.
SITTING BULL
By then, the Plains Indians' way of life had already ended with the last of the buffalo, whose demise came about during the 1860s and '70s, when professional and amateur hunters killed them by the millions for profit and sport, and sometimes just to drive the Native Americans off their own land.
THAT'S MY HUNDREDTH BUFFALO IN ONE HOUR!
Between the 1860s and 1890s, the number of buffalo on the plains decreased from 13 million to only a few hundred. Plains Indians had no choice but to enter reservations, where they were promised food and support--which did not always arrive.

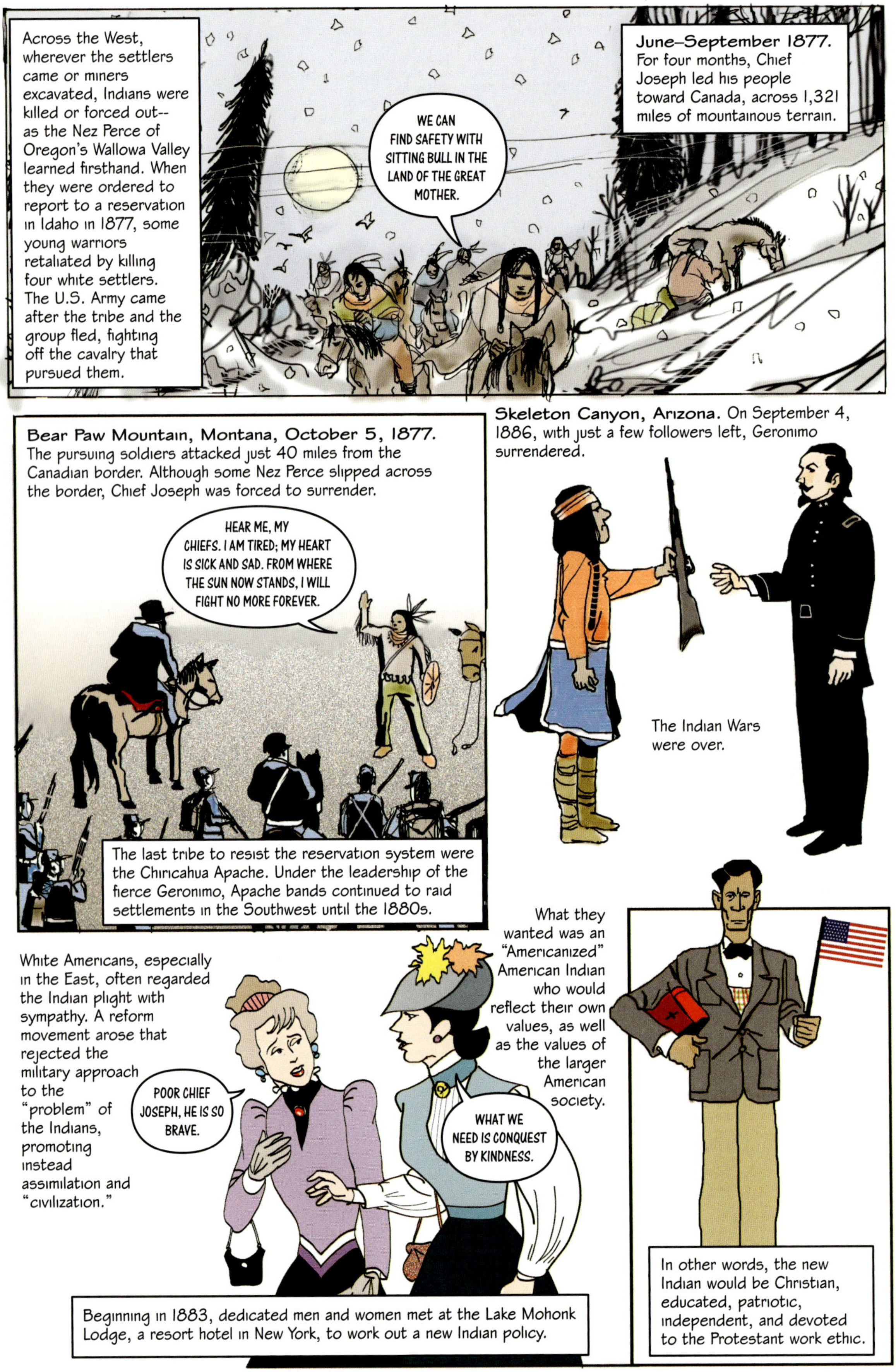
Across the West, wherever the settlers came or miners excavated, Indians were killed or forced out-- as the Nez Perce of Oregon's Wallowa Valley learned firsthand. When they were ordered to report to a reservation in Idaho in 1877, some young warriors retaliated by killing four white settlers. The U.S. Army came after the tribe and the group fled, fighting off the cavalry that pursued them.
WE CAN FIND SAFETY WITH SITTING BULL IN THE LAND OF THE GREAT MOTHER.
June–September 1877. For four months, Chief Joseph led his people toward Canada, across 1,321 miles of mountainous terrain.
Bear Paw Mountain, Montana, October 5, 1877. The pursuing soldiers attacked just 40 miles from the Canadian border. Although some Nez Perce slipped across the border, Chief Joseph was forced to surrender.
HEAR ME, MY CHIEFS. I AM TIRED; MY HEART IS SICK AND SAD. FROM WHERE THE SUN NOW STANDS, I WILL FIGHT NO MORE FOREVER.
The last tribe to resist the reservation system were the Chiricahua Apache. Under the leadership of the fierce Geronimo, Apache bands continued to raid settlements in the Southwest until the 1880s.
Skeleton Canyon, Arizona. On September 4, 1886, with just a few followers left, Geronimo surrendered.
The Indian Wars were over.
White Americans, especially in the East, often regarded the Indian plight with sympathy. A reform movement arose that rejected the military approach to the "problem" of the Indians, promoting instead assimilation and "civilization."
POOR CHIEF JOSEPH, HE IS SO BRAVE.
WHAT WE NEED IS CONQUEST BY KINDNESS.
What they wanted was an "Americanized" American Indian who would reflect their own values, as well as the values of the larger American society.
Beginning in 1883, dedicated men and women met at the Lake Mohonk Lodge, a resort hotel in New York, to work out a new Indian policy.
In other words, the new Indian would be Christian, educated, patriotic, independent, and devoted to the Protestant work ethic.

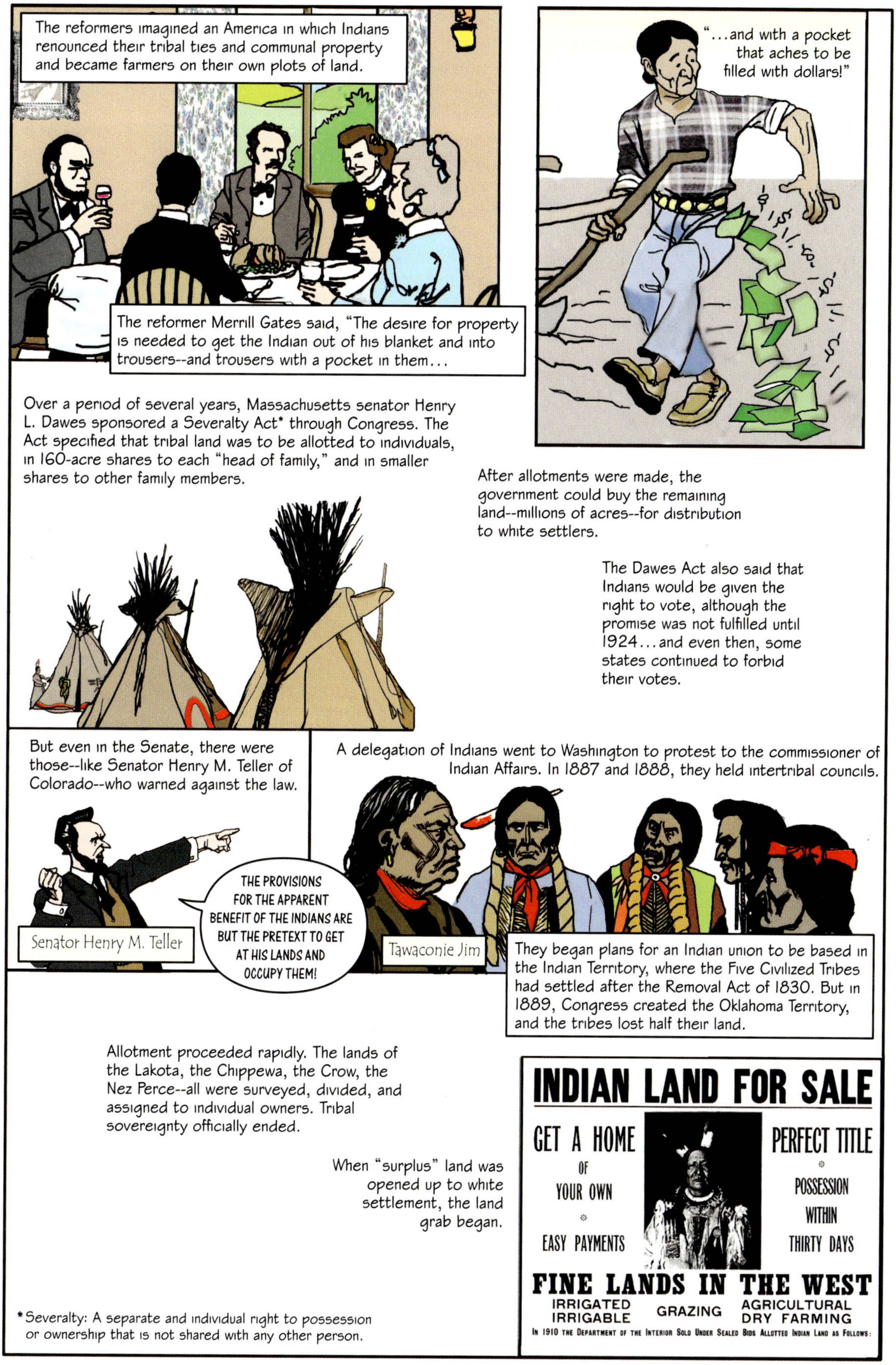
The reformers imagined an America in which Indians renounced their tribal ties and communal property and became farmers on their own plots of land.
The reformer Merrill Gates said, "The desire for property is needed to get the Indian out of his blanket and into trousers--and trousers with a pocket in them...
"...and with a pocket that aches to be filled with dollars!"
Over a period of several years, Massachusetts senator Henry L. Dawes sponsored a Severalty Act* through Congress. The Act specified that tribal land was to be allotted to individuals, in 160-acre shares to each "head of family," and in smaller shares to other family members.
After allotments were made, the government could buy the remaining land--millions of acres--for distribution to white settlers.
The Dawes Act also said that Indians would be given the right to vote, although the promise was not fulfilled until 1924...and even then, some states continued to forbid their votes.
But even in the Senate, there were those--like Senator Henry M. Teller of Colorado--who warned against the law.
Senator Henry M. Teller
THE PROVISIONS FOR THE APPARENT BENEFIT OF THE INDIANS ARE BUT THE PRETEXT TO GET AT HIS LANDS AND OCCUPY THEM!
A delegation of Indians went to Washington to protest to the commissioner of Indian Affairs. In 1887 and 1888, they held intertribal councils.
Tawaconie Jim
They began plans for an Indian union to be based in the Indian Territory, where the Five Civilized Tribes had settled after the Removal Act of 1830. But in 1889, Congress created the Oklahoma Territory, and the tribes lost half their land.
Allotment proceeded rapidly. The lands of the Lakota, the Chippewa, the Crow, the Nez Perce--all were surveyed, divided, and assigned to individual owners. Tribal sovereignty officially ended.
When "surplus" land was opened up to white settlement, the land grab began.
INDIAN LAND FOR SALE
GET A HOME OF YOUR OWN
EASY PAYMENTS
PERFECT TITLE
POSSESSION WITHIN THIRTY DAYS
FINE LANDS IN THE WEST
IRRIGATED IRRIGABLE
GRAZING
AGRICULTURAL DRY FARMING
IN 1910 THE DEPARTMENT OF THE INTERIOR SOLD UNDER SEALED BIDS ALLOTTED INDIAN LAND AS FOLLOWS:
*Severalty: A separate and individual right to possession or ownership that is not shared with any other person.

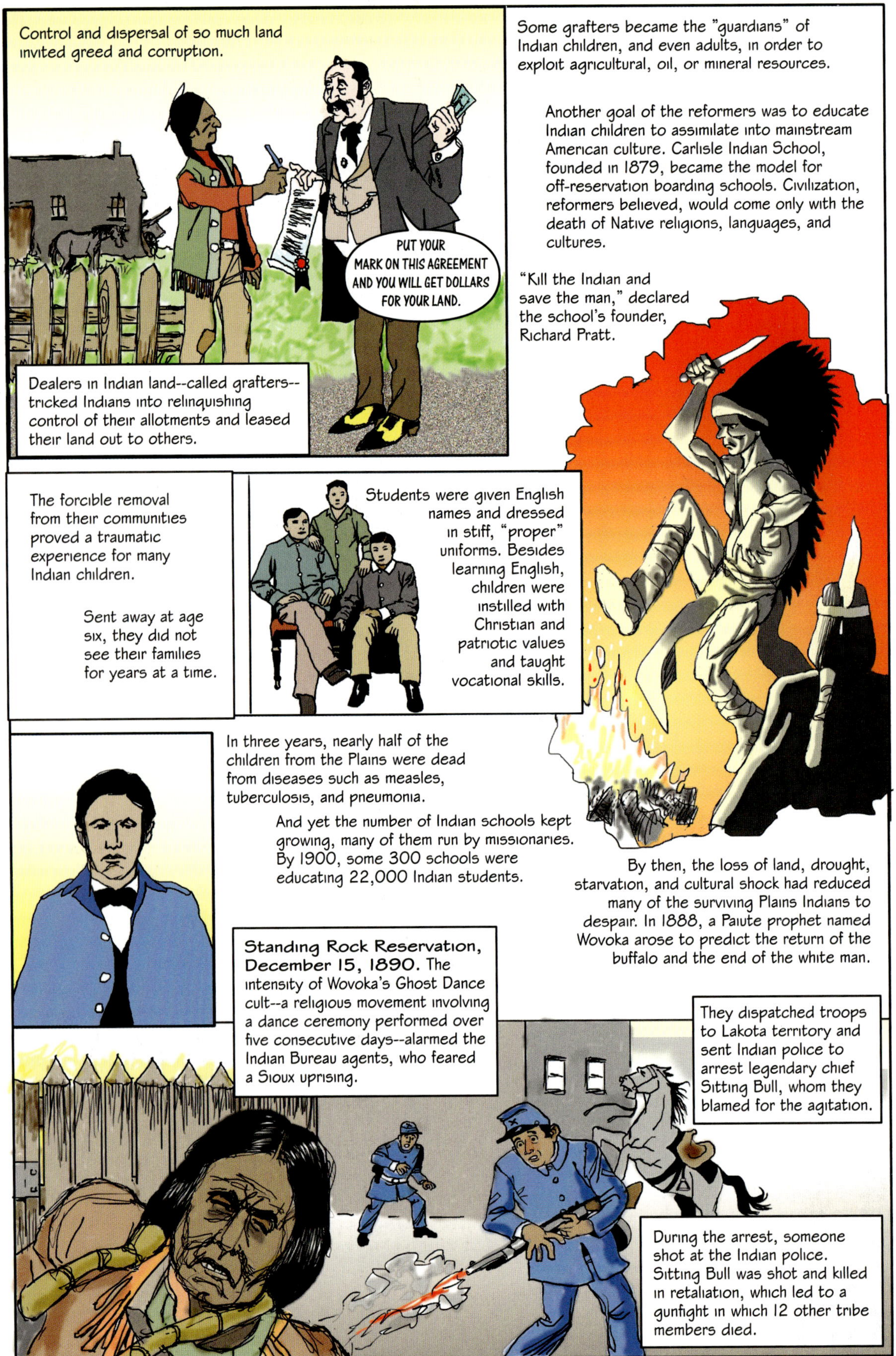
Control and dispersal of so much land invited greed and corruption.
PUT YOUR MARK ON THIS AGREEMENT AND YOU WILL GET DOLLARS FOR YOUR LAND.
Dealers in Indian land--called grafters--tricked Indians into relinquishing control of their allotments and leased their land out to others.
Some grafters became the "guardians" of Indian children, and even adults, in order to exploit agricultural, oil, or mineral resources.
Another goal of the reformers was to educate Indian children to assimilate into mainstream American culture. Carlisle Indian School, founded in 1879, became the model for off-reservation boarding schools. Civilization, reformers believed, would come only with the death of Native religions, languages, and cultures.
"Kill the Indian and save the man," declared the school's founder, Richard Pratt.
The forcible removal from their communities proved a traumatic experience for many Indian children.
Sent away at age six, they did not see their families for years at a time.
Students were given English names and dressed in stiff, "proper" uniforms. Besides learning English, children were instilled with Christian and patriotic values and taught vocational skills.
In three years, nearly half of the children from the Plains were dead from diseases such as measles, tuberculosis, and pneumonia.
And yet the number of Indian schools kept growing, many of them run by missionaries. By 1900, some 300 schools were educating 22,000 Indian students.
By then, the loss of land, drought, starvation, and cultural shock had reduced many of the surviving Plains Indians to despair. In 1888, a Paiute prophet named Wovoka arose to predict the return of the buffalo and the end of the white man.
Standing Rock Reservation, December 15, 1890. The intensity of Wovoka's Ghost Dance cult--a religious movement involving a dance ceremony performed over five consecutive days--alarmed the Indian Bureau agents, who feared a Sioux uprising.
They dispatched troops to Lakota territory and sent Indian police to arrest legendary chief Sitting Bull, whom they blamed for the agitation.
During the arrest, someone shot at the Indian police. Sitting Bull was shot and killed in retaliation, which led to a gunfight in which 12 other tribe members died.

Wounded Knee Creek, South Dakota, December 28, 1890. In their grief, some of Sitting Bull's followers joined another leader, Big Foot, who was trying to escape to safety. The Seventh Calvary--George Custer's unit--caught up with them.

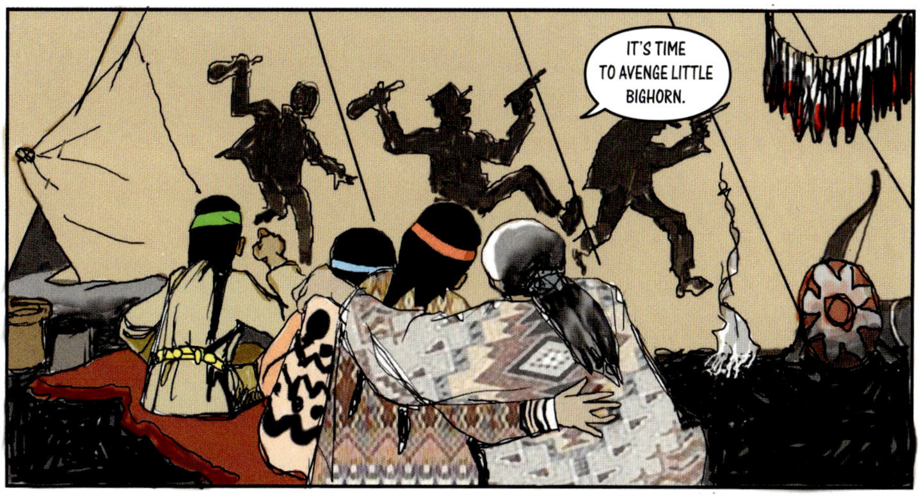
IT'S TIME TO AVENGE LITTLE BIGHORN.

December 29: The next morning, as the Sioux were being disarmed, a shot rang out, and the cavalry opened fire.

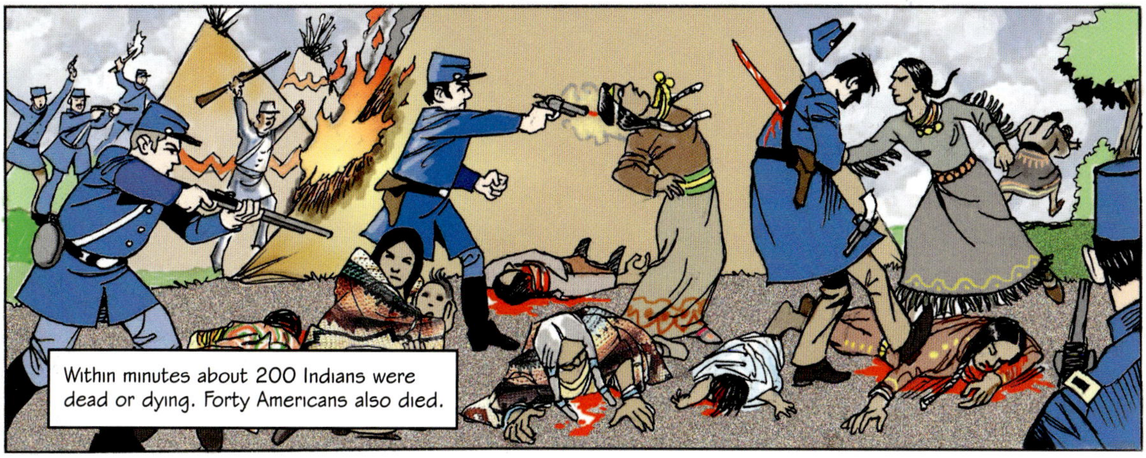
Within minutes about 200 Indians were dead or dying. Forty Americans also died.

For Americans, Wounded Knee symbolized the last of the frontier. It was also the final, irrevocable blow to the Indians' traditional way of life.

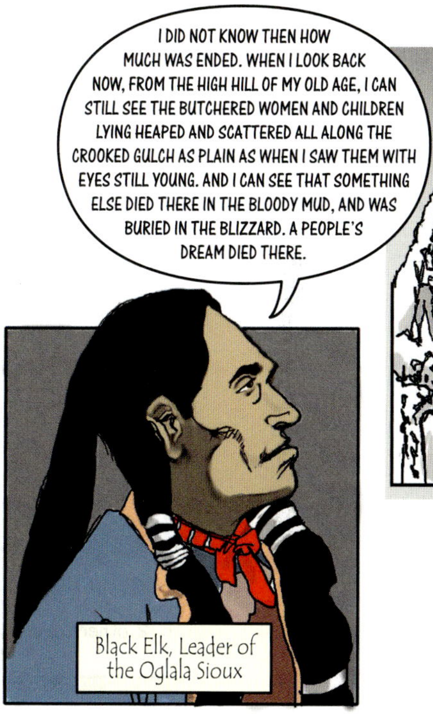
I DID NOT KNOW THEN HOW MUCH WAS ENDED. WHEN I LOOK BACK NOW, FROM THE HIGH HILL OF MY OLD AGE, I CAN STILL SEE THE BUTCHERED WOMEN AND CHILDREN LYING HEAPED AND SCATTERED ALL ALONG THE CROOKED GULCH AS PLAIN AS WHEN I SAW THEM WITH EYES STILL YOUNG. AND I CAN SEE THAT SOMETHING ELSE DIED THERE IN THE BLOODY MUD, AND WAS BURIED IN THE BLIZZARD. A PEOPLE'S DREAM DIED THERE.
Black Elk, Leader of the Oglala Sioux

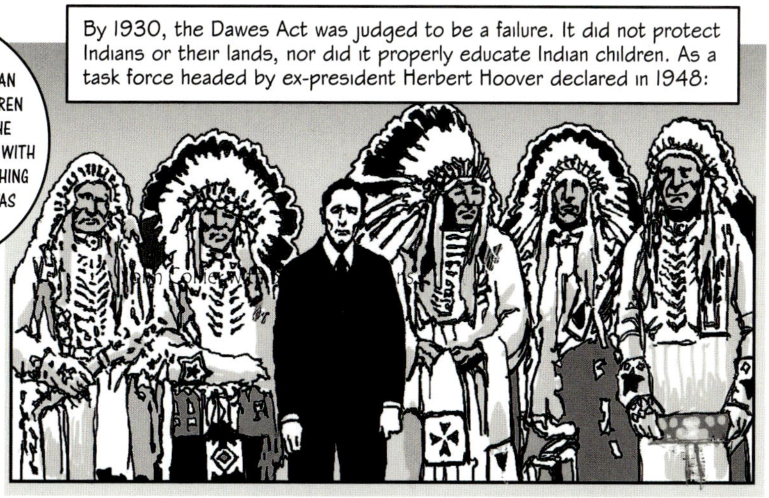
By 1930, the Dawes Act was judged to be a failure. It did not protect Indians or their lands, nor did it properly educate Indian children. As a task force headed by ex-president Herbert Hoover declared in 1948:

"The destruction of Indian tribal property, the liquidation of tribal organization and tribal property, and the hostility to all Indian ways and culture that characterized so much of government policy now appears to have been a mistake."

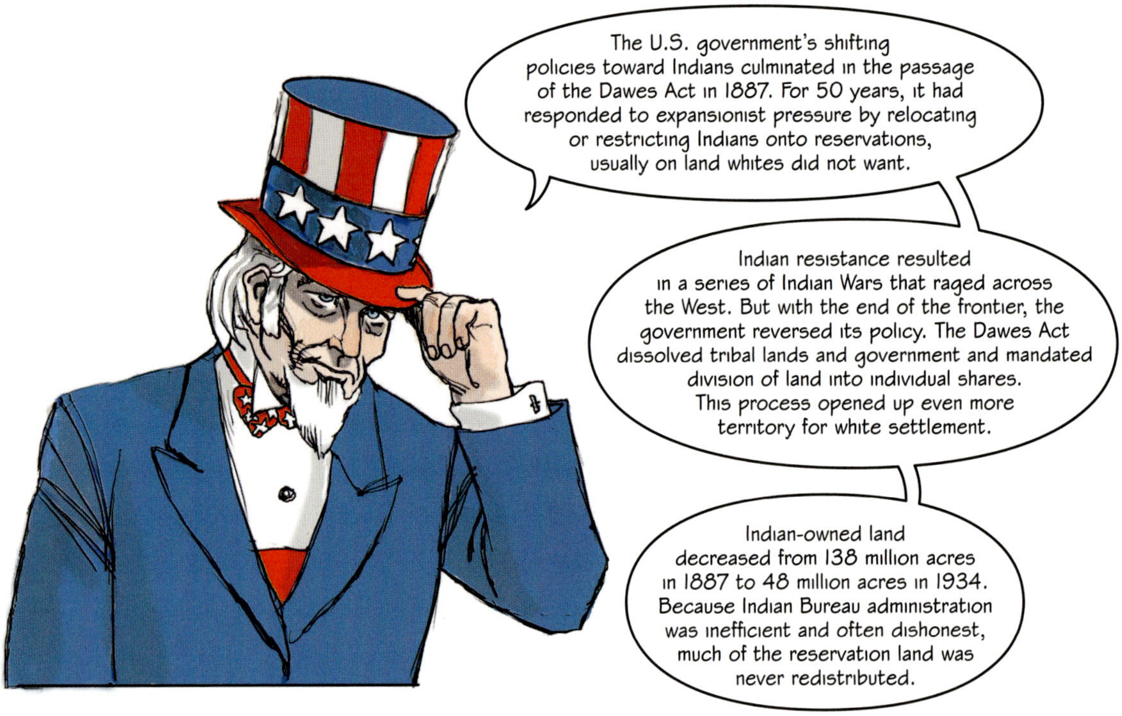
The U.S. government's shifting policies toward Indians culminated in the passage of the Dawes Act in 1887. For 50 years, it had responded to expansionist pressure by relocating or restricting Indians onto reservations, usually on land whites did not want.
Indian resistance resulted in a series of Indian Wars that raged across the West. But with the end of the frontier, the government reversed its policy. The Dawes Act dissolved tribal lands and government and mandated division of land into individual shares. This process opened up even more territory for white settlement.
Indian-owned land decreased from 138 million acres in 1887 to 48 million acres in 1934. Because Indian Bureau administration was inefficient and often dishonest, much of the reservation land was never redistributed.

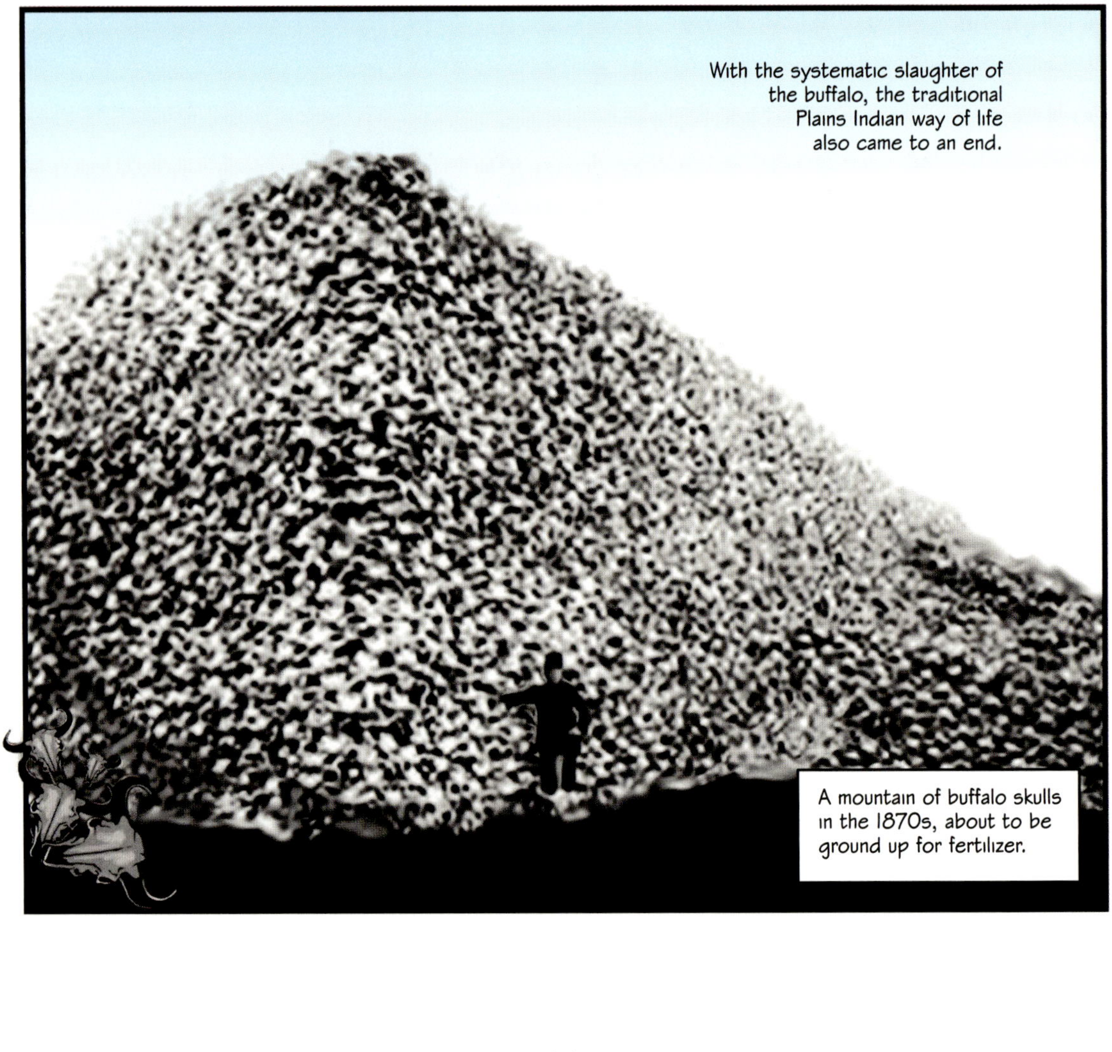
With the systematic slaughter of the buffalo, the traditional Plains Indian way of life also came to an end.
A mountain of buffalo skulls in the 1870s, about to be ground up for fertilizer.

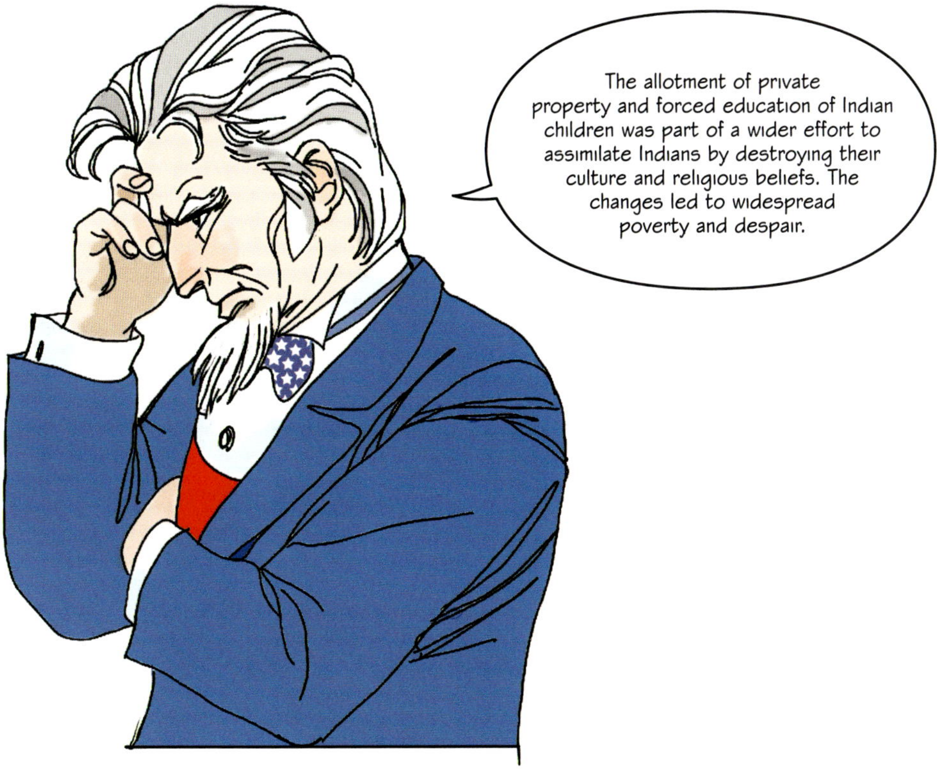
The allotment of private property and forced education of Indian children was part of a wider effort to assimilate Indians by destroying their culture and religious beliefs. The changes led to widespread poverty and despair.

EXCERPTS FROM THE DAWES ACT

"An Act to provide for the allotment of lands in severalty to Indians on the various reservations, and to extend the protection of the laws of the United States and the Territories over the Indians, and for other purposes.

"Be it enacted . . . that in all cases where any tribe or band of Indians has been, or shall hereafter be, located upon any reservation created for their use . . . the President of the United States be, and he hereby is, authorized, whenever in his opinion any reservation or any part thereof of such Indians is advantageous for agricultural and grazing purposes, to cause said reservation, or any part thereof, to be surveyed, or resurveyed if necessary, and to allot the lands in said reservation in severalty to any Indian located thereon in quantities as follows

"To each head of a family, one-quarter of a section;

"To each single person over eighteen years of age, one-eighth of a section . . .

"Section 5: . . . And provided further, that at any time after lands have been allotted to all the Indians of any tribe as herein provided, or sooner if in the opinion of the President it shall be for the best interests of said tribe, it shall be lawful for the Secretary of the Interior to negotiate with such Indian tribe for the purchase and release by said tribe . . . of such portions of its reservation not allotted as such tribe shall, from time to time, consent to sell, on such terms and conditions as shall be considered just and equitable between the United States and said tribe of Indians . . ."

White Man's Burden

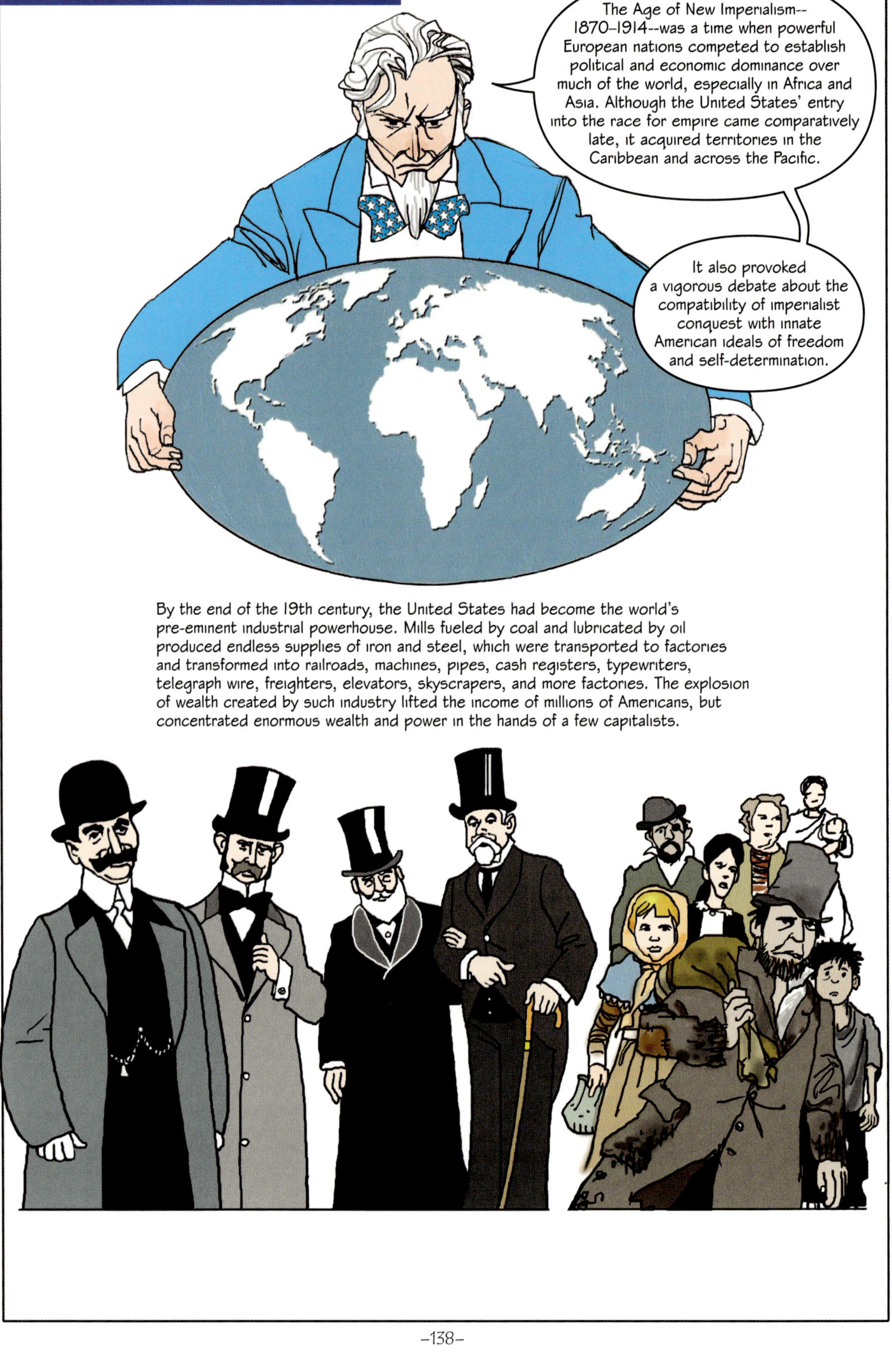
The Age of New Imperialism--1870–1914--was a time when powerful European nations competed to establish political and economic dominance over much of the world, especially in Africa and Asia. Although the United States' entry into the race for empire came comparatively late, it acquired territories in the Caribbean and across the Pacific.
It also provoked a vigorous debate about the compatibility of imperialist conquest with innate American ideals of freedom and self-determination.
By the end of the 19th century, the United States had become the world's pre-eminent industrial powerhouse. Mills fueled by coal and lubricated by oil produced endless supplies of iron and steel, which were transported to factories and transformed into railroads, machines, pipes, cash registers, typewriters, telegraph wire, freighters, elevators, skyscrapers, and more factories. The explosion of wealth created by such industry lifted the income of millions of Americans, but concentrated enormous wealth and power in the hands of a few capitalists.

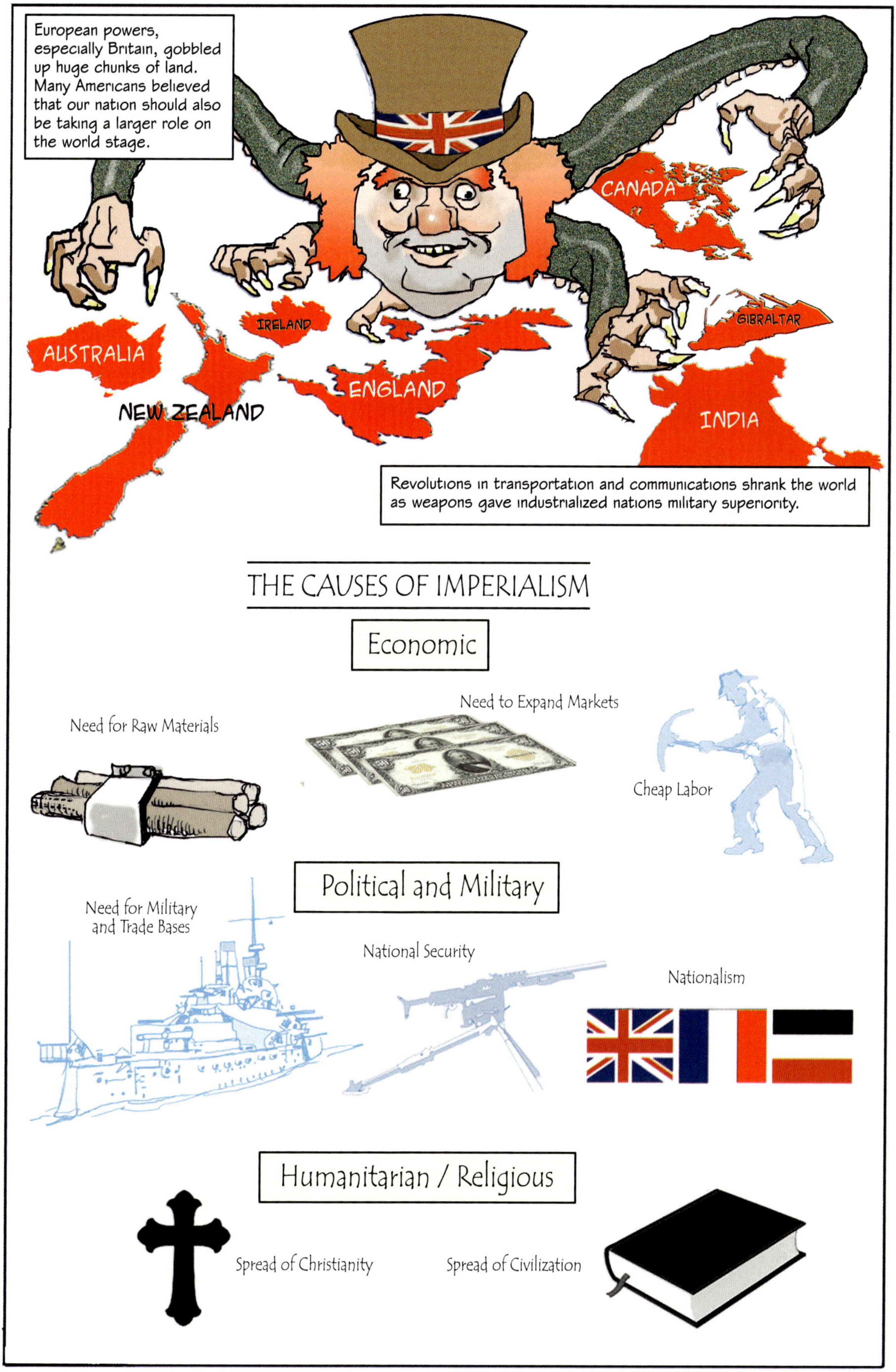
European powers, especially Britain, gobbled up huge chunks of land. Many Americans believed that our nation should also be taking a larger role on the world stage.
CANADA
IRELAND
GIBRALTAR
AUSTRALIA
ENGLAND
NEW ZEALAND
INDIA
Revolutions in transportation and communications shrank the world as weapons gave industrialized nations military superiority.
THE CAUSES OF IMPERIALISM
Economic
Need for Raw Materials
Need to Expand Markets
Cheap Labor
Political and Military
Need for Military and Trade Bases
National Security
Nationalism
Humanitarian / Religious
Spread of Christianity
Spread of Civilization

THEORY OF RACE ACCORDING TO SOCIAL DARWINISTS

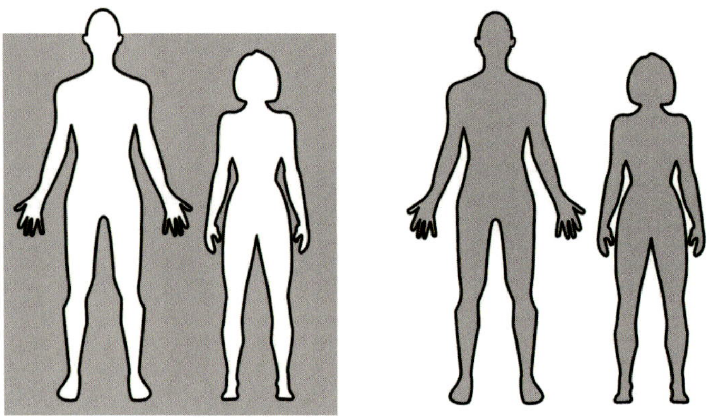

WHITE PEOPLE   INFERIOR PEOPLE

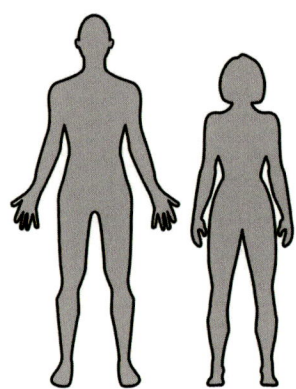

One justification for imperialism lay in the misuse of Charles Darwin's theory of evolution. In his *On the Origin of Species*, Darwin concluded that natural selection determined which species survived. Advocates of imperialism believed that some human races were superior to others and that it was natural for the weaker to be subordinate to the stronger.

The American frontier was gone. Yet as America watched the European powers, its own thirst for acquiring new territories was unquenchable. As noted by the up-and-coming politician Theodore Roosevelt, additional American expansion meant…

> NOT ONLY THE EXTENSION OF AMERICAN INFLUENCE AND POWER, BUT ALSO THE EXTENSION OF LIBERTY AND ORDER, AND THE BRINGING NEARER BY GIGANTIC STRIDES OF THE DAY WHEN PEACE SHALL COME TO THE WHOLE EARTH.

To many, American expansion overseas was the New Manifest Destiny.

Roosevelt was strongly influenced by Alfred Thayer Mahan, president of the Naval War College, who made a compelling case for foreign trade and the development of naval power. He quoted English Renaissance explorer Sir Walter Raleigh:

"For whosoever commands the sea commands the trade; whosoever commands the trade of the world commands the riches of the world, and consequently the world itself."

Mahan urged the United States to build a battle fleet, to acquire bases in the Caribbean and the Pacific, and to build a canal across Central America, from the Atlantic Ocean to the Pacific. By 1900, the U.S. had the third-largest navy in the world.

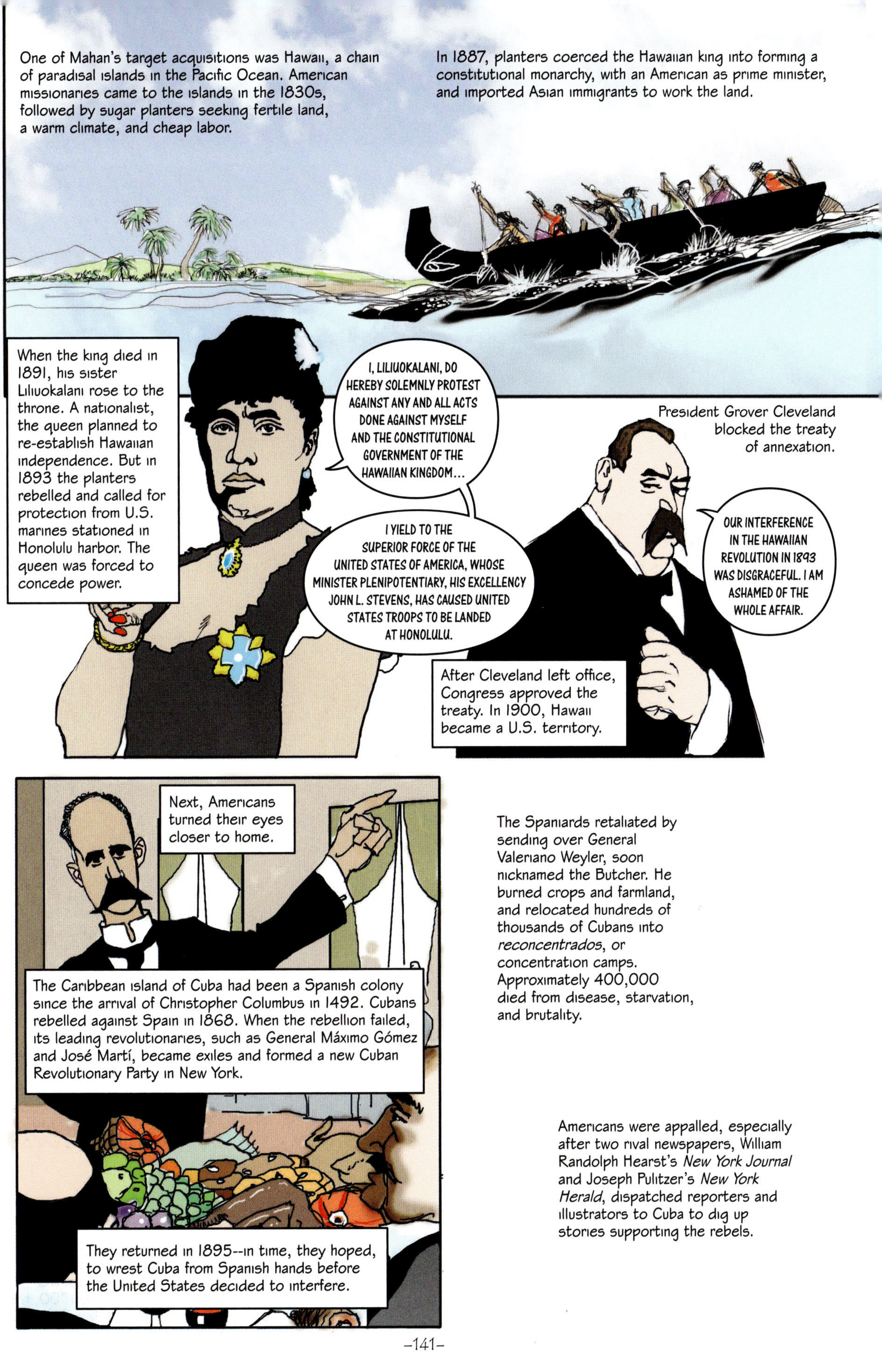
One of Mahan's target acquisitions was Hawaii, a chain of paradisal islands in the Pacific Ocean. American missionaries came to the islands in the 1830s, followed by sugar planters seeking fertile land, a warm climate, and cheap labor.
In 1887, planters coerced the Hawaiian king into forming a constitutional monarchy, with an American as prime minister, and imported Asian immigrants to work the land.
When the king died in 1891, his sister Liliuokalani rose to the throne. A nationalist, the queen planned to re-establish Hawaiian independence. But in 1893 the planters rebelled and called for protection from U.S. marines stationed in Honolulu harbor. The queen was forced to concede power.
I, LILIUOKALANI, DO HEREBY SOLEMNLY PROTEST AGAINST ANY AND ALL ACTS DONE AGAINST MYSELF AND THE CONSTITUTIONAL GOVERNMENT OF THE HAWAIIAN KINGDOM...
I YIELD TO THE SUPERIOR FORCE OF THE UNITED STATES OF AMERICA, WHOSE MINISTER PLENIPOTENTIARY, HIS EXCELLENCY JOHN L. STEVENS, HAS CAUSED UNITED STATES TROOPS TO BE LANDED AT HONOLULU.
President Grover Cleveland blocked the treaty of annexation.
OUR INTERFERENCE IN THE HAWAIIAN REVOLUTION IN 1893 WAS DISGRACEFUL. I AM ASHAMED OF THE WHOLE AFFAIR.
After Cleveland left office, Congress approved the treaty. In 1900, Hawaii became a U.S. territory.
Next, Americans turned their eyes closer to home.
The Caribbean island of Cuba had been a Spanish colony since the arrival of Christopher Columbus in 1492. Cubans rebelled against Spain in 1868. When the rebellion failed, its leading revolutionaries, such as General Máximo Gómez and José Martí, became exiles and formed a new Cuban Revolutionary Party in New York.
They returned in 1895--in time, they hoped, to wrest Cuba from Spanish hands before the United States decided to interfere.
The Spaniards retaliated by sending over General Valeriano Weyler, soon nicknamed the Butcher. He burned crops and farmland, and relocated hundreds of thousands of Cubans into *reconcentrados*, or concentration camps. Approximately 400,000 died from disease, starvation, and brutality.
Americans were appalled, especially after two rival newspapers, William Randolph Hearst's *New York Journal* and Joseph Pulitzer's *New York Herald*, dispatched reporters and illustrators to Cuba to dig up stories supporting the rebels.

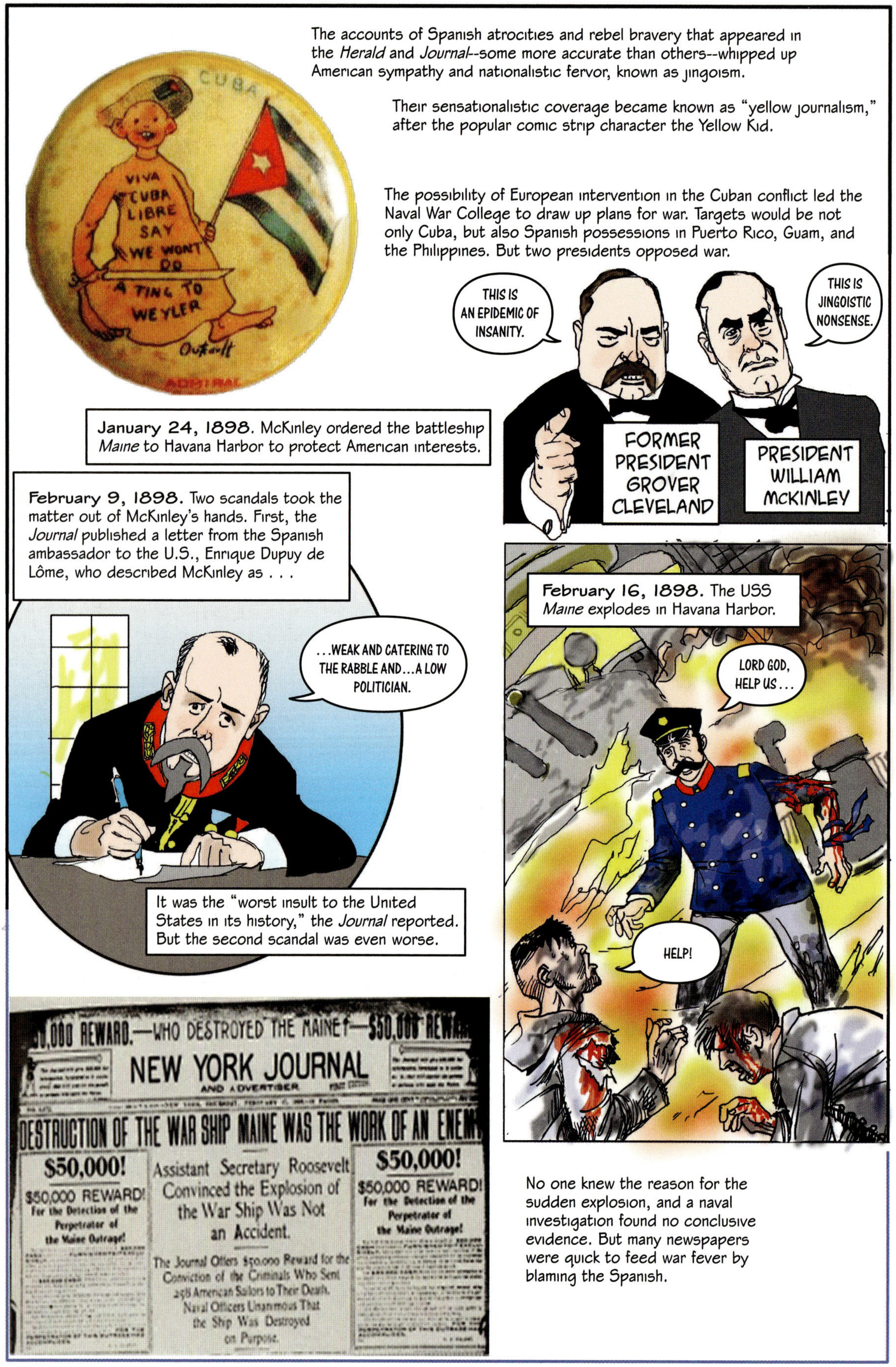
The accounts of Spanish atrocities and rebel bravery that appeared in the *Herald* and *Journal*--some more accurate than others--whipped up American sympathy and nationalistic fervor, known as jingoism.
Their sensationalistic coverage became known as "yellow journalism," after the popular comic strip character the Yellow Kid.
CUBA
VIVA CUBA LIBRE SAY WE WONT DO A TING TO WEYLER
Outcault
The possibility of European intervention in the Cuban conflict led the Naval War College to draw up plans for war. Targets would be not only Cuba, but also Spanish possessions in Puerto Rico, Guam, and the Philippines. But two presidents opposed war.
THIS IS AN EPIDEMIC OF INSANITY.
THIS IS JINGOISTIC NONSENSE.
FORMER PRESIDENT GROVER CLEVELAND
PRESIDENT WILLIAM MCKINLEY
January 24, 1898. McKinley ordered the battleship *Maine* to Havana Harbor to protect American interests.
February 9, 1898. Two scandals took the matter out of McKinley's hands. First, the *Journal* published a letter from the Spanish ambassador to the U.S., Enrique Dupuy de Lôme, who described McKinley as . . .
. . .WEAK AND CATERING TO THE RABBLE AND . . . A LOW POLITICIAN.
It was the "worst insult to the United States in its history," the *Journal* reported. But the second scandal was even worse.
February 16, 1898. The USS *Maine* explodes in Havana Harbor.
LORD GOD, HELP US . . .
HELP!
$50,000 REWARD.—WHO DESTROYED THE MAINE?—$50,000 REWARD
NEW YORK JOURNAL AND ADVERTISER
DESTRUCTION OF THE WAR SHIP MAINE WAS THE WORK OF AN ENEMY
$50,000! $50,000 REWARD! For the Detection of the Perpetrator of the Maine Outrage!
Assistant Secretary Roosevelt Convinced the Explosion of the War Ship Was Not an Accident.
The Journal Offers $50,000 Reward for the Conviction of the Criminals Who Sent 258 American Sailors to Their Death. Naval Officers Unanimous That the Ship Was Destroyed on Purpose.
$50,000! $50,000 REWARD! For the Detection of the Perpetrator of the Maine Outrage!
No one knew the reason for the sudden explosion, and a naval investigation found no conclusive evidence. But many newspapers were quick to feed war fever by blaming the Spanish.

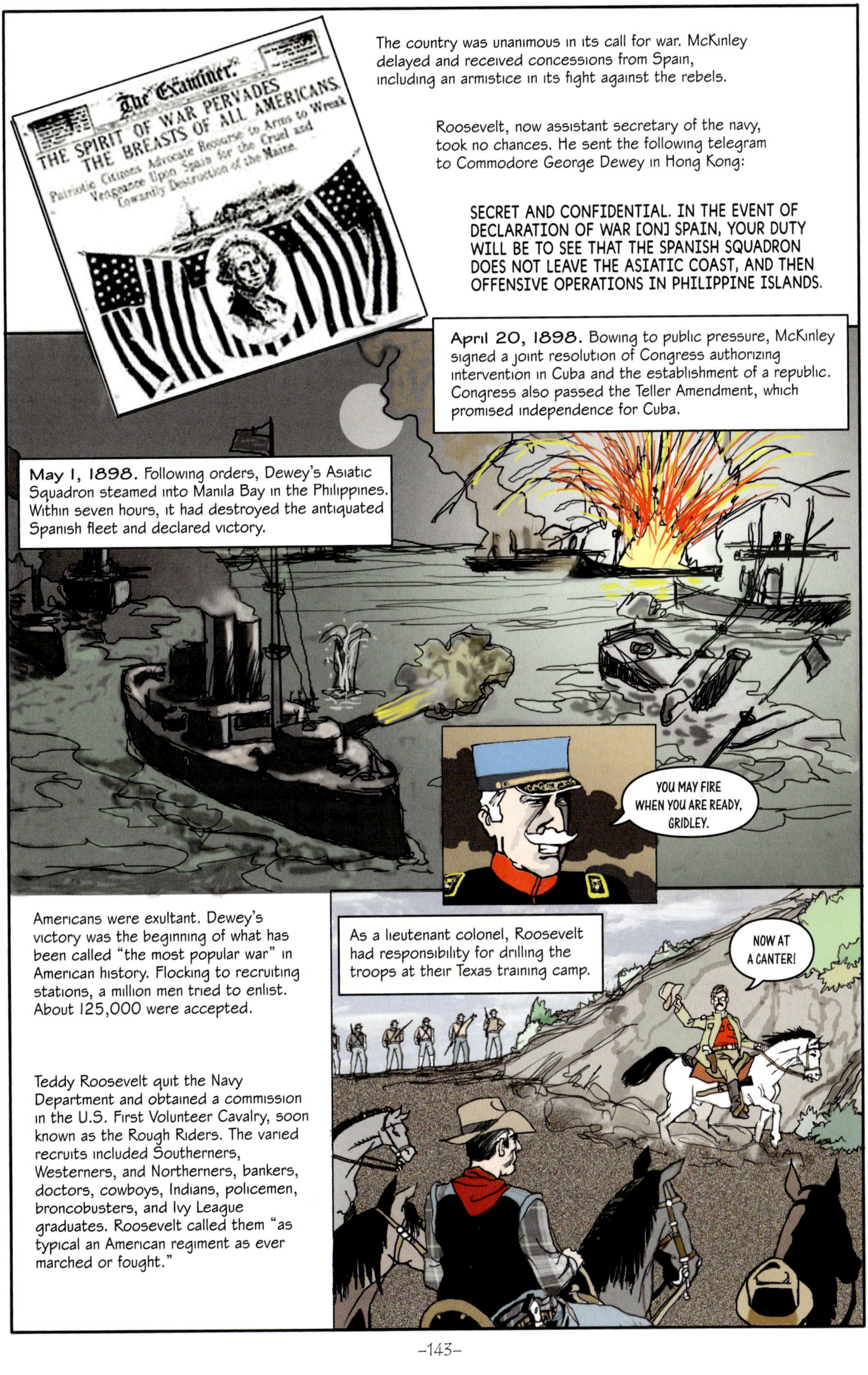
The Examiner.
THE SPIRIT OF WAR PERVADES THE BREASTS OF ALL AMERICANS.
Patriotic Citizens Advocate Recourse to Arms to Wreak Vengeance Upon Spain for the Cruel and Cowardly Destruction of the Maine.
The country was unanimous in its call for war. McKinley delayed and received concessions from Spain, including an armistice in its fight against the rebels.
Roosevelt, now assistant secretary of the navy, took no chances. He sent the following telegram to Commodore George Dewey in Hong Kong:
SECRET AND CONFIDENTIAL. IN THE EVENT OF DECLARATION OF WAR [ON] SPAIN, YOUR DUTY WILL BE TO SEE THAT THE SPANISH SQUADRON DOES NOT LEAVE THE ASIATIC COAST, AND THEN OFFENSIVE OPERATIONS IN PHILIPPINE ISLANDS.
April 20, 1898. Bowing to public pressure, McKinley signed a joint resolution of Congress authorizing intervention in Cuba and the establishment of a republic. Congress also passed the Teller Amendment, which promised independence for Cuba.
May 1, 1898. Following orders, Dewey's Asiatic Squadron steamed into Manila Bay in the Philippines. Within seven hours, it had destroyed the antiquated Spanish fleet and declared victory.
YOU MAY FIRE WHEN YOU ARE READY, GRIDLEY.
Americans were exultant. Dewey's victory was the beginning of what has been called "the most popular war" in American history. Flocking to recruiting stations, a million men tried to enlist. About 125,000 were accepted.
Teddy Roosevelt quit the Navy Department and obtained a commission in the U.S. First Volunteer Cavalry, soon known as the Rough Riders. The varied recruits included Southerners, Westerners, and Northerners, bankers, doctors, cowboys, Indians, policemen, broncobusters, and Ivy League graduates. Roosevelt called them "as typical an American regiment as ever marched or fought."
As a lieutenant colonel, Roosevelt had responsibility for drilling the troops at their Texas training camp.
NOW AT A CANTER!

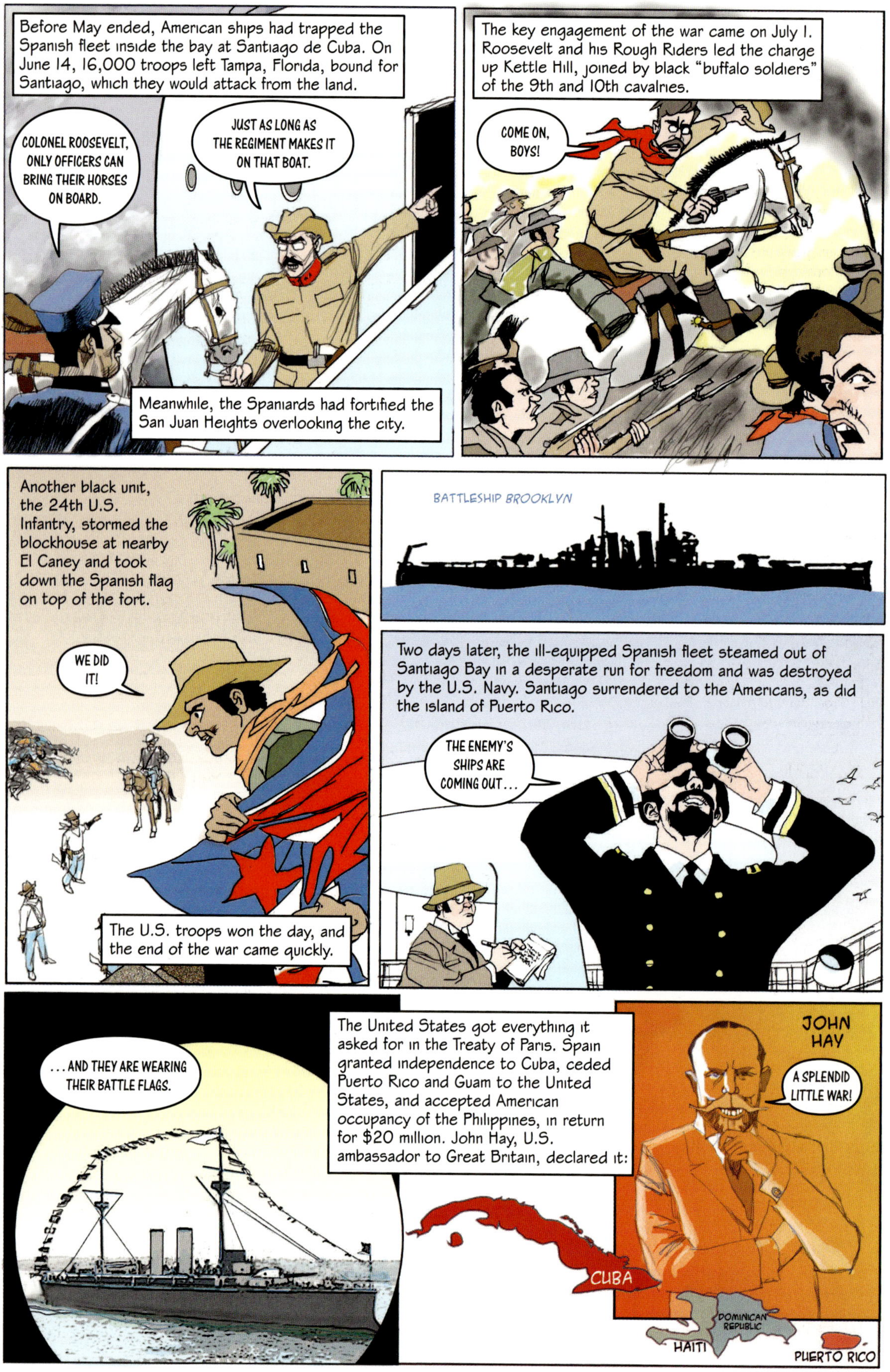
Before May ended, American ships had trapped the Spanish fleet inside the bay at Santiago de Cuba. On June 14, 16,000 troops left Tampa, Florida, bound for Santiago, which they would attack from the land.
COLONEL ROOSEVELT, ONLY OFFICERS CAN BRING THEIR HORSES ON BOARD.
JUST AS LONG AS THE REGIMENT MAKES IT ON THAT BOAT.
Meanwhile, the Spaniards had fortified the San Juan Heights overlooking the city.
The key engagement of the war came on July 1. Roosevelt and his Rough Riders led the charge up Kettle Hill, joined by black "buffalo soldiers" of the 9th and 10th cavalries.
COME ON, BOYS!
Another black unit, the 24th U.S. Infantry, stormed the blockhouse at nearby El Caney and took down the Spanish flag on top of the fort.
WE DID IT!
The U.S. troops won the day, and the end of the war came quickly.
BATTLESHIP BROOKLYN
Two days later, the ill-equipped Spanish fleet steamed out of Santiago Bay in a desperate run for freedom and was destroyed by the U.S. Navy. Santiago surrendered to the Americans, as did the island of Puerto Rico.
THE ENEMY'S SHIPS ARE COMING OUT...
...AND THEY ARE WEARING THEIR BATTLE FLAGS.
The United States got everything it asked for in the Treaty of Paris. Spain granted independence to Cuba, ceded Puerto Rico and Guam to the United States, and accepted American occupancy of the Philippines, in return for $20 million. John Hay, U.S. ambassador to Great Britain, declared it:
JOHN HAY
A SPLENDID LITTLE WAR!
CUBA
DOMINICAN REPUBLIC
HAITI
PUERTO RICO

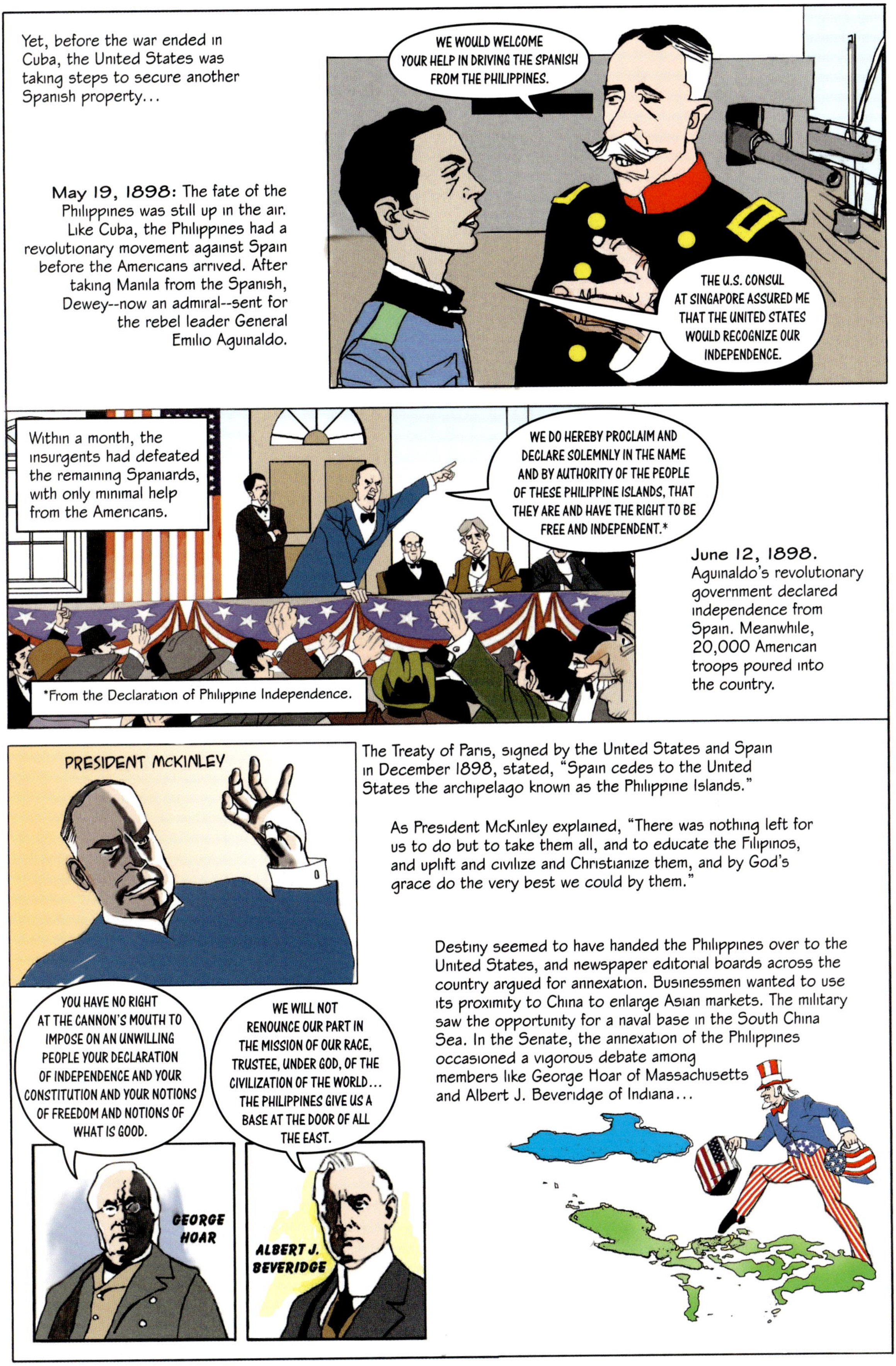
Yet, before the war ended in Cuba, the United States was taking steps to secure another Spanish property...
May 19, 1898: The fate of the Philippines was still up in the air. Like Cuba, the Philippines had a revolutionary movement against Spain before the Americans arrived. After taking Manila from the Spanish, Dewey--now an admiral--sent for the rebel leader General Emilio Aguinaldo.
WE WOULD WELCOME YOUR HELP IN DRIVING THE SPANISH FROM THE PHILIPPINES.
THE U.S. CONSUL AT SINGAPORE ASSURED ME THAT THE UNITED STATES WOULD RECOGNIZE OUR INDEPENDENCE.
Within a month, the insurgents had defeated the remaining Spaniards, with only minimal help from the Americans.
WE DO HEREBY PROCLAIM AND DECLARE SOLEMNLY IN THE NAME AND BY AUTHORITY OF THE PEOPLE OF THESE PHILIPPINE ISLANDS, THAT THEY ARE AND HAVE THE RIGHT TO BE FREE AND INDEPENDENT.*
June 12, 1898. Aguinaldo's revolutionary government declared independence from Spain. Meanwhile, 20,000 American troops poured into the country.
*From the Declaration of Philippine Independence.
PRESIDENT McKINLEY
The Treaty of Paris, signed by the United States and Spain in December 1898, stated, "Spain cedes to the United States the archipelago known as the Philippine Islands."
As President McKinley explained, "There was nothing left for us to do but to take them all, and to educate the Filipinos, and uplift and civilize and Christianize them, and by God's grace do the very best we could by them."
Destiny seemed to have handed the Philippines over to the United States, and newspaper editorial boards across the country argued for annexation. Businessmen wanted to use its proximity to China to enlarge Asian markets. The military saw the opportunity for a naval base in the South China Sea. In the Senate, the annexation of the Philippines occasioned a vigorous debate among members like George Hoar of Massachusetts and Albert J. Beveridge of Indiana...
YOU HAVE NO RIGHT AT THE CANNON'S MOUTH TO IMPOSE ON AN UNWILLING PEOPLE YOUR DECLARATION OF INDEPENDENCE AND YOUR CONSTITUTION AND YOUR NOTIONS OF FREEDOM AND NOTIONS OF WHAT IS GOOD.
WE WILL NOT RENOUNCE OUR PART IN THE MISSION OF OUR RACE, TRUSTEE, UNDER GOD, OF THE CIVILIZATION OF THE WORLD... THE PHILIPPINES GIVE US A BASE AT THE DOOR OF ALL THE EAST.
GEORGE HOAR
ALBERT J. BEVERIDGE

The debate also raged across the country. In June 1898, a group of critics formed the Anti-Imperialist League. They claimed that imperialism was essentially anti-American: "We maintain that governments derive their just powers from the consent of the governed."

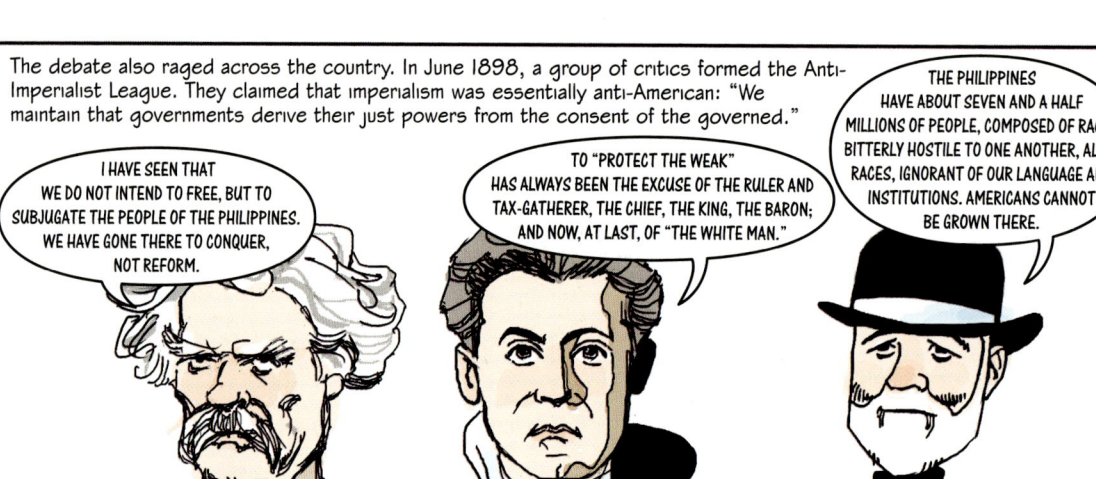

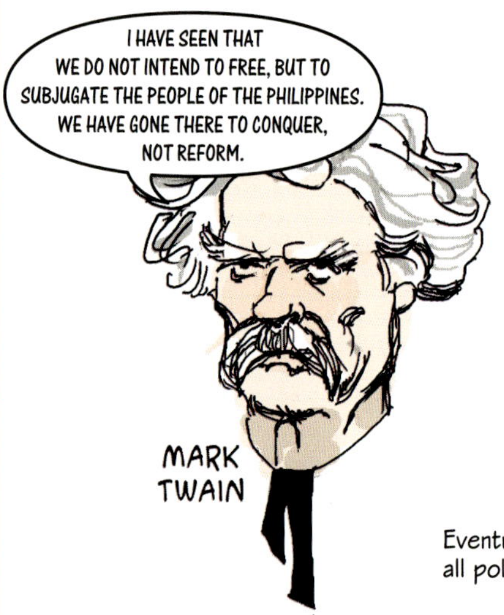
I HAVE SEEN THAT WE DO NOT INTEND TO FREE, BUT TO SUBJUGATE THE PEOPLE OF THE PHILIPPINES. WE HAVE GONE THERE TO CONQUER, NOT REFORM.
MARK TWAIN

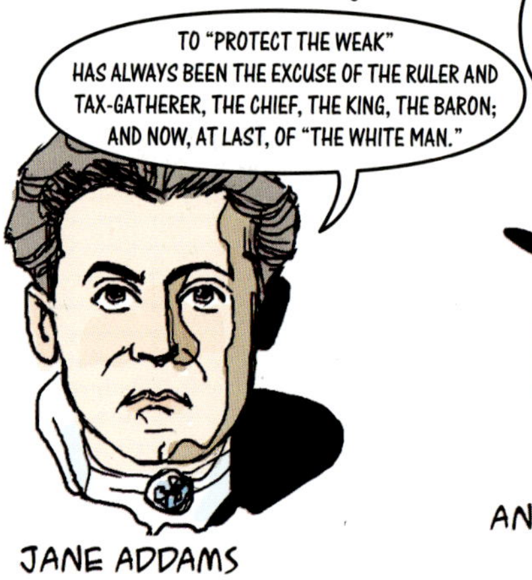
TO "PROTECT THE WEAK" HAS ALWAYS BEEN THE EXCUSE OF THE RULER AND TAX-GATHERER, THE CHIEF, THE KING, THE BARON; AND NOW, AT LAST, OF "THE WHITE MAN."
JANE ADDAMS

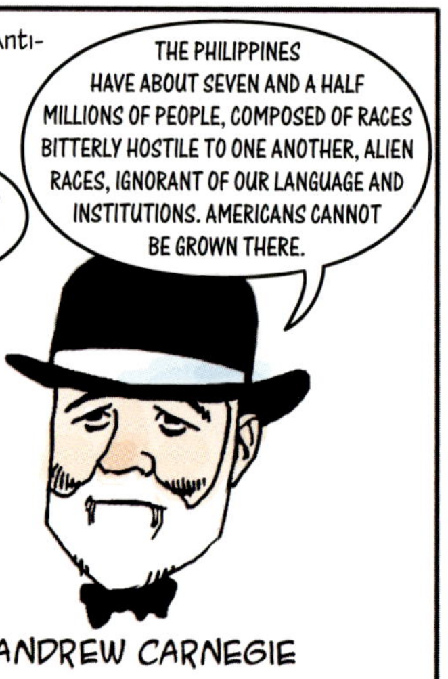
THE PHILIPPINES HAVE ABOUT SEVEN AND A HALF MILLIONS OF PEOPLE, COMPOSED OF RACES BITTERLY HOSTILE TO ONE ANOTHER, ALIEN RACES, IGNORANT OF OUR LANGUAGE AND INSTITUTIONS. AMERICANS CANNOT BE GROWN THERE.
ANDREW CARNEGIE

Eventually, the League would number about 50,000 people from all political parties and economic and social backgrounds.

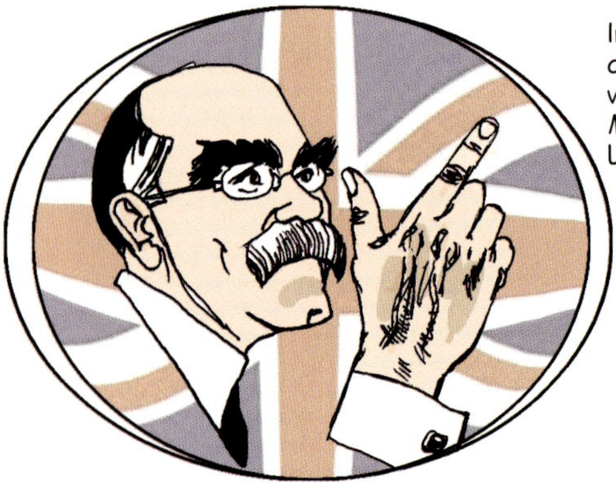

RUDYARD KIPLING

In February 1899, another voice was added to the mix--that of the British author Rudyard Kipling. A friend of soon-to-be-vice-president Theodore Roosevelt, he published a poem in *McClure's Magazine* entitled "The White Man's Burden: The United States and the Philippine Islands."

Kipling argued in favor of expansion, asserting that it was the responsibility of Western nations to share their superior culture through imperialist conquest.

Anti-imperialists thought the poem hypocritical, and black critics thought it racist. It inspired satirical cartoons and numerous parodies.

Many Americans welcomed the poem's claim that imperial conquest was actually a noble enterprise.

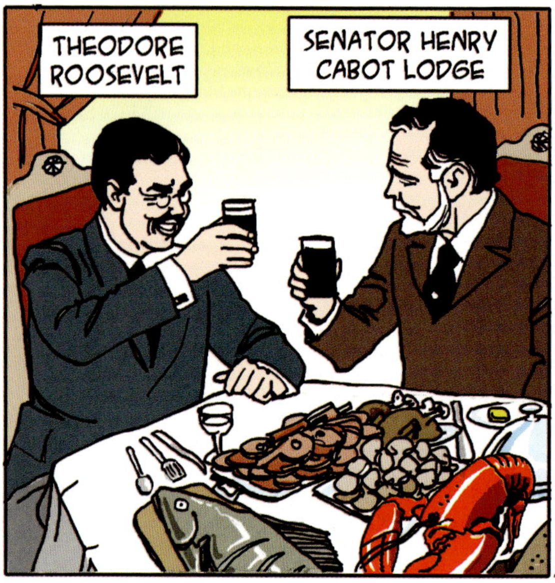
THEODORE ROOSEVELT
SENATOR HENRY CABOT LODGE

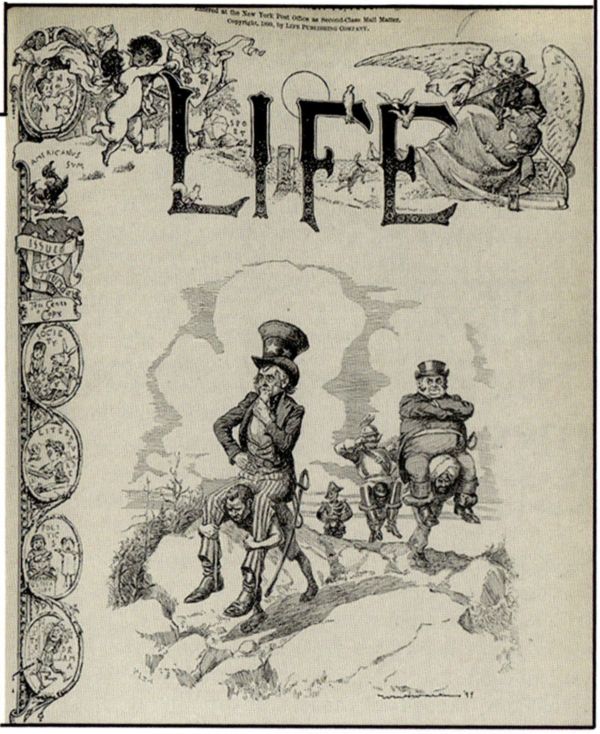
LIFE

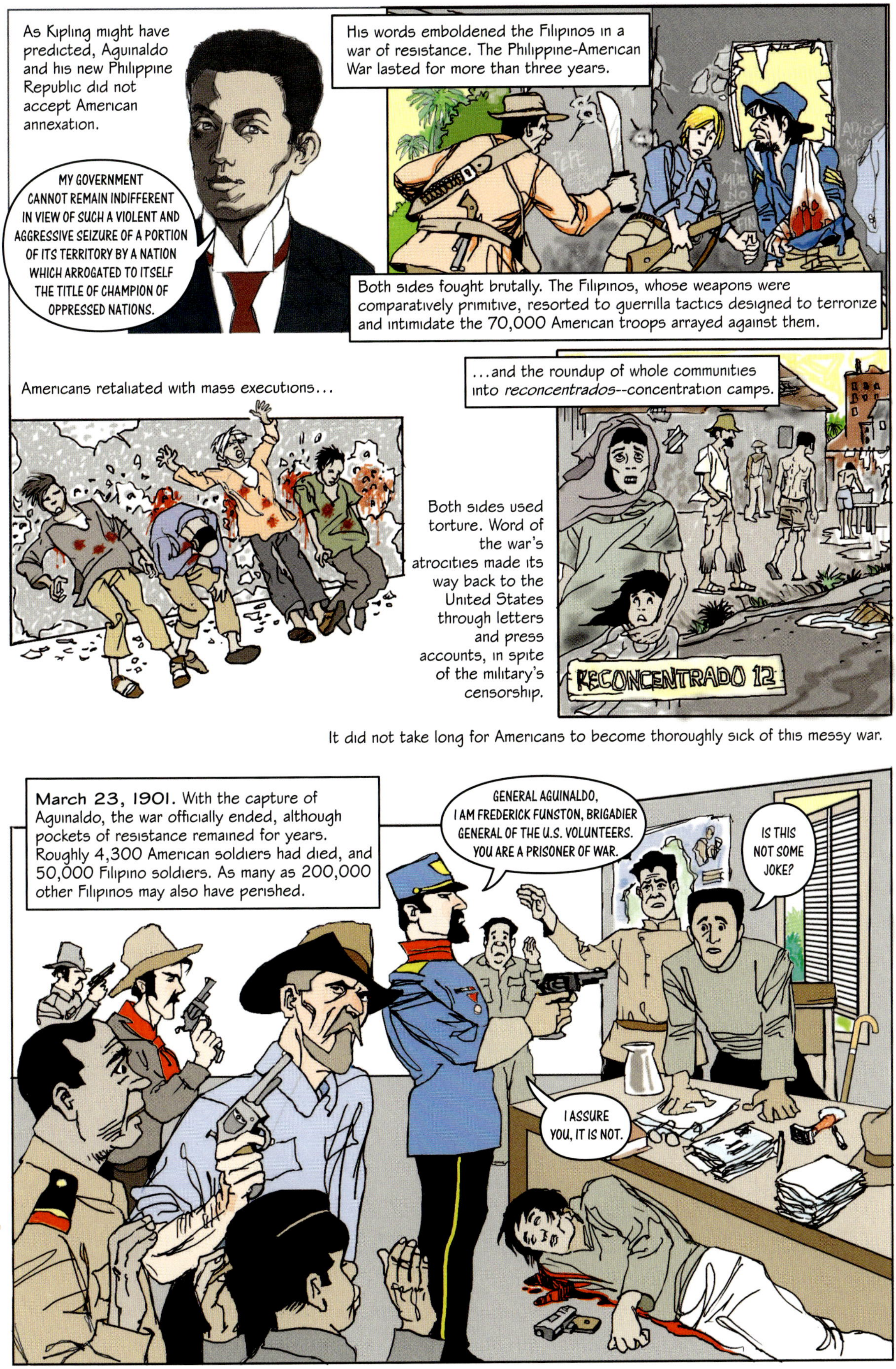
As Kipling might have predicted, Aguinaldo and his new Philippine Republic did not accept American annexation.
MY GOVERNMENT CANNOT REMAIN INDIFFERENT IN VIEW OF SUCH A VIOLENT AND AGGRESSIVE SEIZURE OF A PORTION OF ITS TERRITORY BY A NATION WHICH ARROGATED TO ITSELF THE TITLE OF CHAMPION OF OPPRESSED NATIONS.
His words emboldened the Filipinos in a war of resistance. The Philippine-American War lasted for more than three years.
Both sides fought brutally. The Filipinos, whose weapons were comparatively primitive, resorted to guerrilla tactics designed to terrorize and intimidate the 70,000 American troops arrayed against them.
Americans retaliated with mass executions...
...and the roundup of whole communities into *reconcentrados*--concentration camps.
Both sides used torture. Word of the war's atrocities made its way back to the United States through letters and press accounts, in spite of the military's censorship.
RECONCENTRADO 12
It did not take long for Americans to become thoroughly sick of this messy war.
March 23, 1901. With the capture of Aguinaldo, the war officially ended, although pockets of resistance remained for years. Roughly 4,300 American soldiers had died, and 50,000 Filipino soldiers. As many as 200,000 other Filipinos may also have perished.
GENERAL AGUINALDO, I AM FREDERICK FUNSTON, BRIGADIER GENERAL OF THE U.S. VOLUNTEERS. YOU ARE A PRISONER OF WAR.
IS THIS NOT SOME JOKE?
I ASSURE YOU, IT IS NOT.

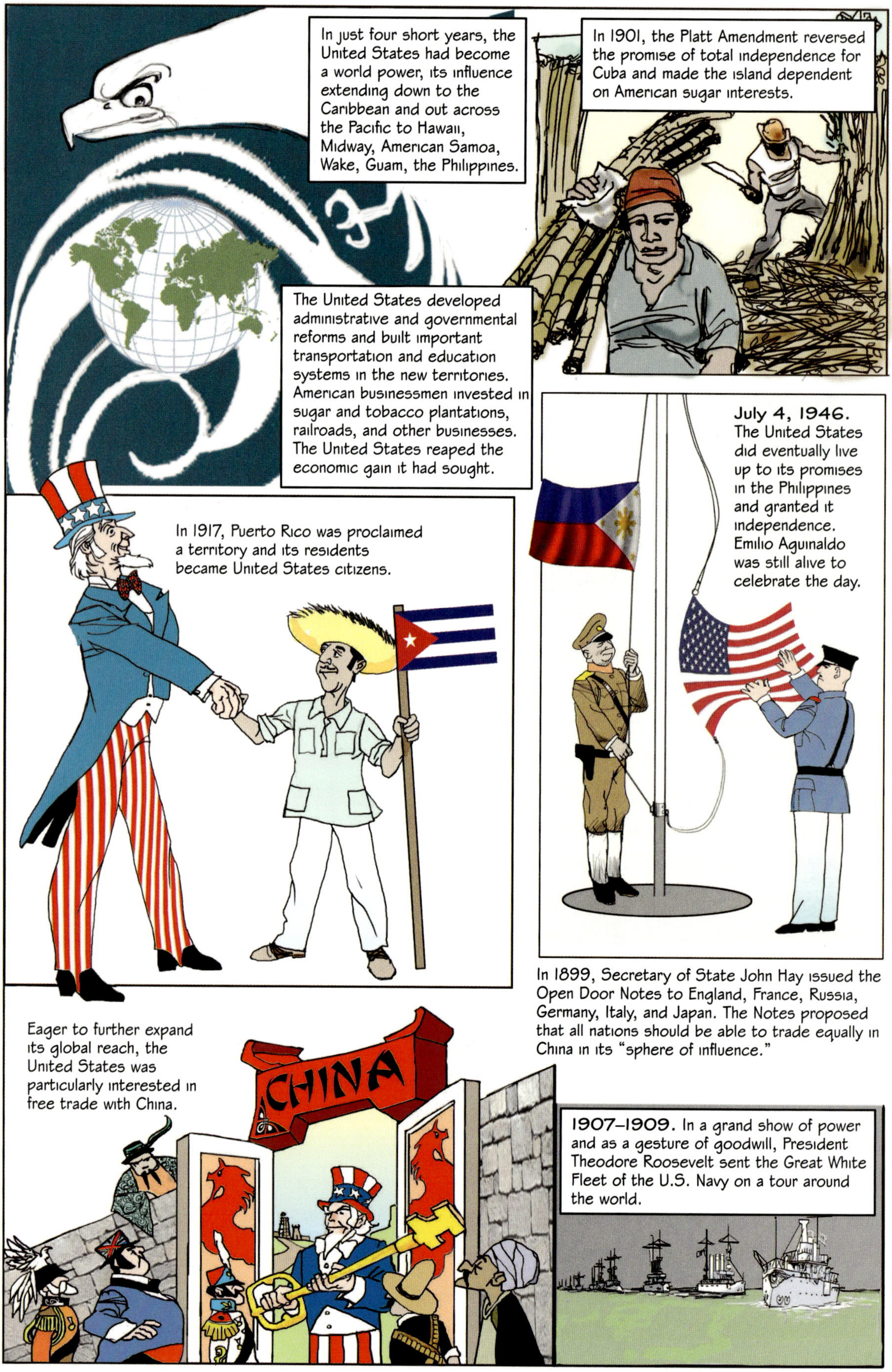
In just four short years, the United States had become a world power, its influence extending down to the Caribbean and out across the Pacific to Hawaii, Midway, American Samoa, Wake, Guam, the Philippines.
In 1901, the Platt Amendment reversed the promise of total independence for Cuba and made the island dependent on American sugar interests.
The United States developed administrative and governmental reforms and built important transportation and education systems in the new territories. American businessmen invested in sugar and tobacco plantations, railroads, and other businesses. The United States reaped the economic gain it had sought.
In 1917, Puerto Rico was proclaimed a territory and its residents became United States citizens.
July 4, 1946. The United States did eventually live up to its promises in the Philippines and granted it independence. Emilio Aguinaldo was still alive to celebrate the day.
Eager to further expand its global reach, the United States was particularly interested in free trade with China.
In 1899, Secretary of State John Hay issued the Open Door Notes to England, France, Russia, Germany, Italy, and Japan. The Notes proposed that all nations should be able to trade equally in China in its "sphere of influence."
CHINA
1907–1909. In a grand show of power and as a gesture of goodwill, President Theodore Roosevelt sent the Great White Fleet of the U.S. Navy on a tour around the world.

Rudyard Kipling's poem "The White Man's Burden," addressed to the American people, earned iconic status in its own day as an endorsement of imperialism. A belief in the superiority of Western society encouraged the conviction that the West had the right to rule and also, perhaps, an obligation to share its cultural and technological achievements. The poem makes explicit the underlying paternalism, even racism, of this idea. Yet it is also strangely idealistic in its message. Colonizers have a moral obligation to spread the blessings of civilization, no matter what the personal cost--even though the colonized may answer this sacrifice not with thanks, but with hate.

The United States came late to the imperialist game, in part because colonization seemed to contradict American ideals of freedom and self-determination for all people. The poem itself was met with praise from some, and scorn by others. Despite its ambivalence about imperialism, the nation proved most effective at securing overseas possessions in the Caribbean and the Pacific in a remarkably short period of time--and entered into a new role as a world power.

EXCERPTS FROM "THE WHITE MAN'S BURDEN"

"Take up the White Man's burden— / Send forth the best ye breed— / Go bind your sons to exile / To serve your captives' need; / To wait in heavy harness, / On fluttered folk and wild— / Your new-caught, sullen peoples, / Half-devil and half-child . . ."

"Take up the White Man's burden— / The savage wars of peace— / Fill full the mouth of Famine / And bid the sickness cease; / And when your goal is nearest / The end for others sought, / Watch sloth and heathen Folly / Bring all your hope to nought . . ."

"Take up the White Man's burden— / And reap his old reward: / The blame of those ye better, / The hate of those ye guard— / The cry of hosts ye humour / (Ah, slowly!) toward the light— / 'Why brought ye us from bondage, / Our loved Egyptian night?'"

The Mother of Exiles

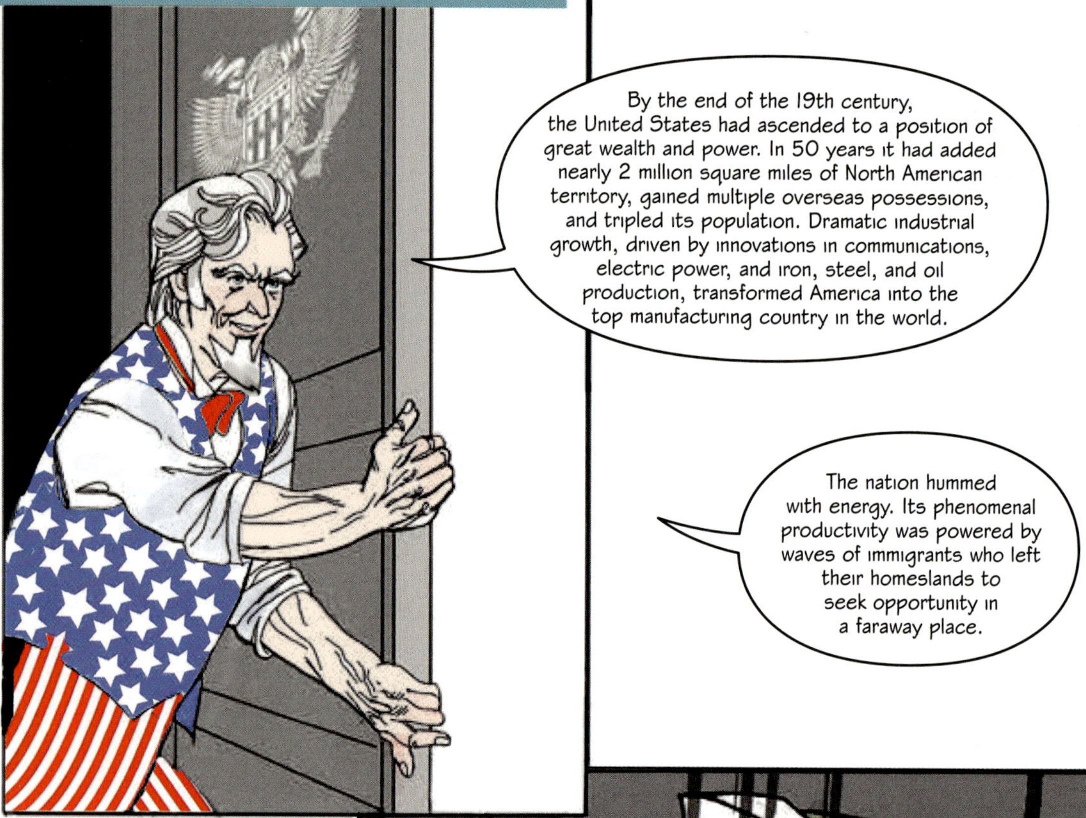
By the end of the 19th century, the United States had ascended to a position of great wealth and power. In 50 years it had added nearly 2 million square miles of North American territory, gained multiple overseas possessions, and tripled its population. Dramatic industrial growth, driven by innovations in communications, electric power, and iron, steel, and oil production, transformed America into the top manufacturing country in the world.
The nation hummed with energy. Its phenomenal productivity was powered by waves of immigrants who left their homelands to seek opportunity in a faraway place.

In 1865, two French patriots discussed erecting a memorial to American independence.

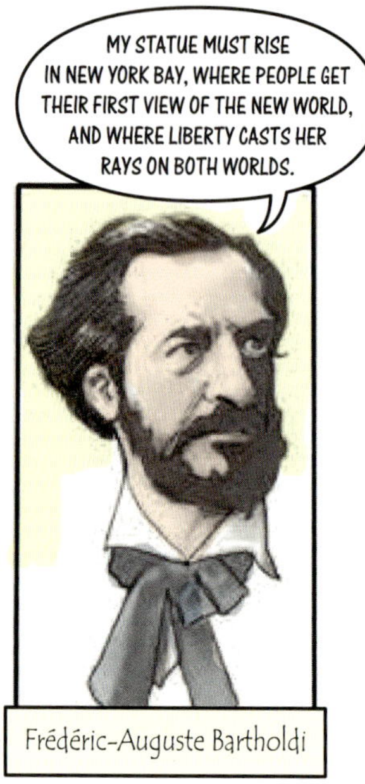
MY STATUE MUST RISE IN NEW YORK BAY, WHERE PEOPLE GET THEIR FIRST VIEW OF THE NEW WORLD, AND WHERE LIBERTY CASTS HER RAYS ON BOTH WORLDS.

Frédéric-Auguste Bartholdi

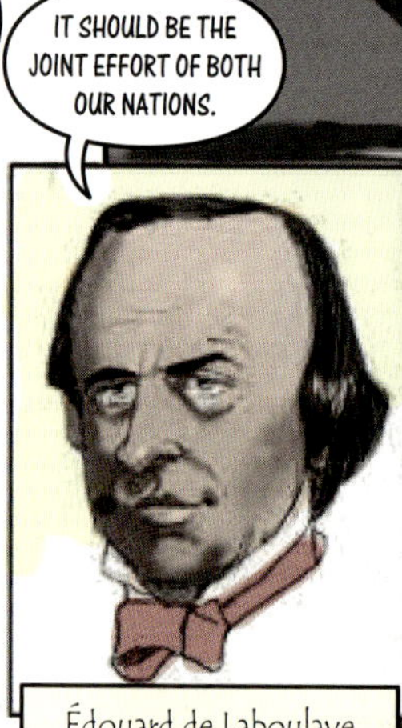
IT SHOULD BE THE JOINT EFFORT OF BOTH OUR NATIONS.

Édouard de Laboulaye

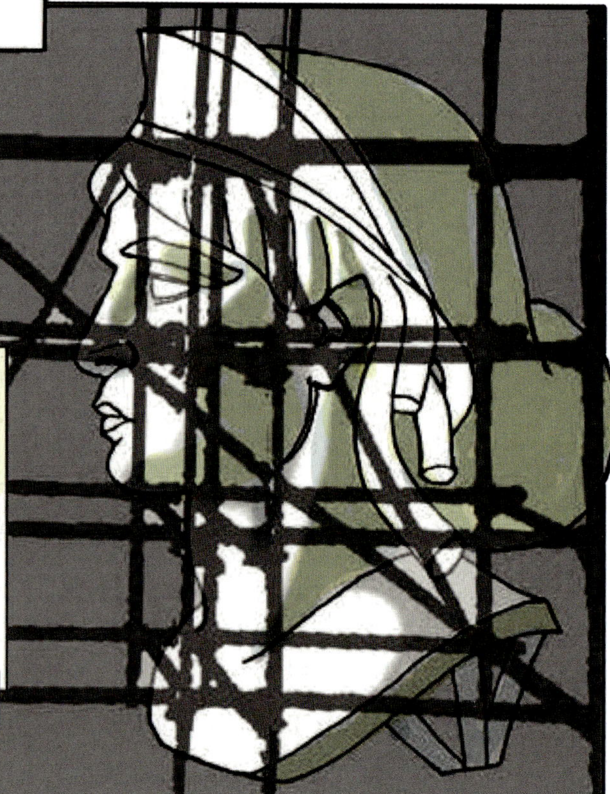

Their plan was to build the colossal sculpture of *Liberty Enlightening the World* in Paris and transport it to New York. The French would raise the money for the statue. Americans would finance the pedestal. It would take two decades of planning, fund-raising, and building before the creators' vision was realized.

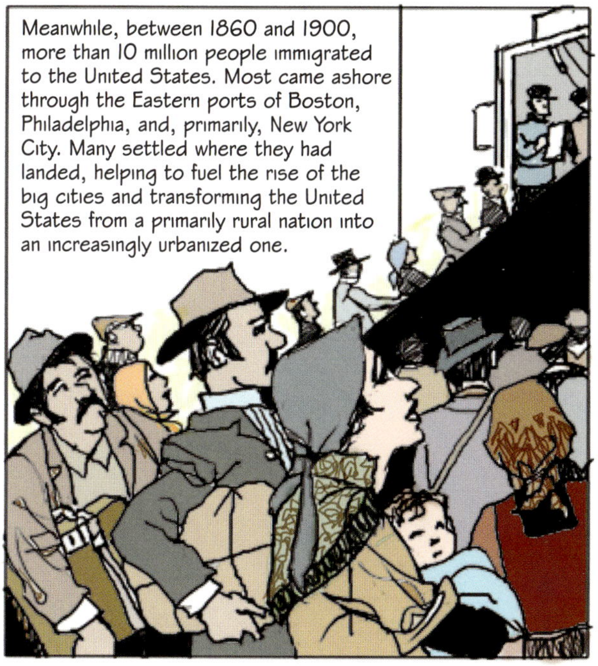
Meanwhile, between 1860 and 1900, more than 10 million people immigrated to the United States. Most came ashore through the Eastern ports of Boston, Philadelphia, and, primarily, New York City. Many settled where they had landed, helping to fuel the rise of the big cities and transforming the United States from a primarily rural nation into an increasingly urbanized one.

CHART OF EUROPEAN IMMIGRATION, 1860–1900

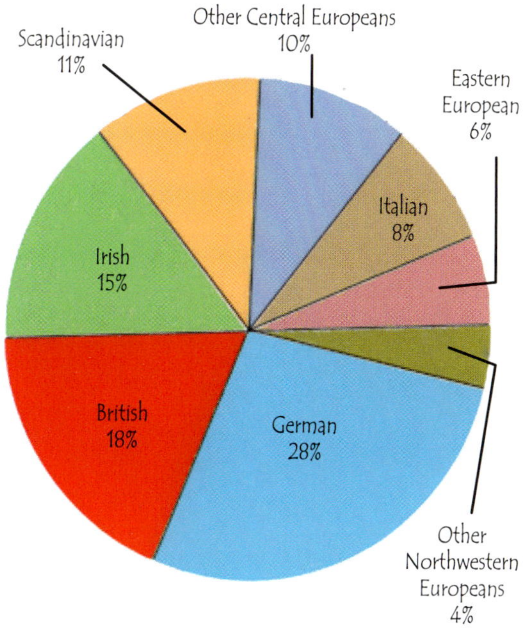
Scandinavian 11%
Other Central Europeans 10%
Eastern European 6%
Italian 8%
Irish 15%
British 18%
German 28%
Other Northwestern Europeans 4%

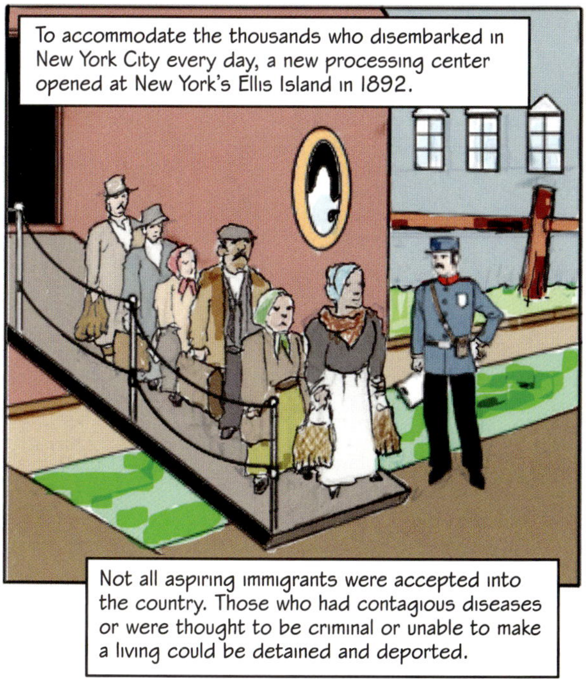
To accommodate the thousands who disembarked in New York City every day, a new processing center opened at New York's Ellis Island in 1892.
Not all aspiring immigrants were accepted into the country. Those who had contagious diseases or were thought to be criminal or unable to make a living could be detained and deported.

Most new urban dwellers crossed the sea from Europe. In the middle of the century, they came primarily from Northern Europe--Germany, Ireland, Britain, and Scandinavia. By the 1880s and 1890s, these were joined by the "new immigrants" from Southern, Central, and Eastern Europe.

Each ethnic group had specific reasons for making the hazardous journey. Russian Jews sought to escape the murderous pogroms of the czarist government. Poles fled political oppression and unemployment. Sicilian Italians sought to break away from crushing poverty. All wanted to make a fresh start for themselves and their families.

But for those who passed the inspection, the promise of America awaited.

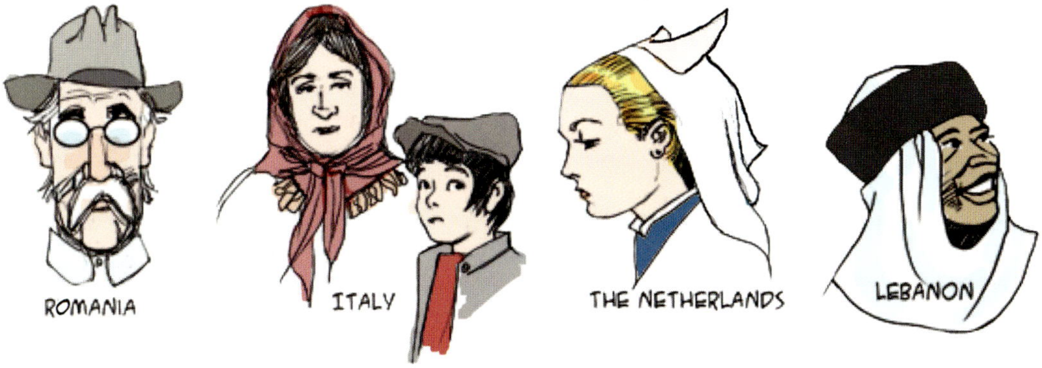
ROMANIA
ITALY
THE NETHERLANDS
LEBANON

Ethnic communities founded their own churches and synagogues, schools, newspapers, entertainment, and mutual-benefit societies to aid the newcomers. As parents became laborers, shopkeepers, factory workers, and domestic servants, children went to public or parochial schools and learned English.

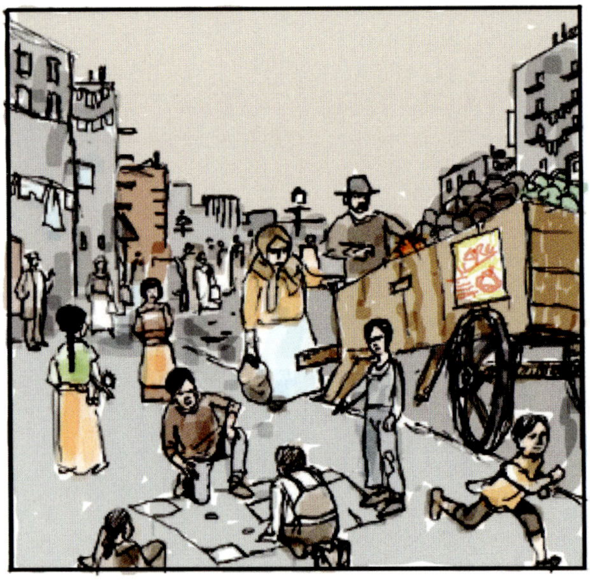

Often from small villages, the new arrivals could be overwhelmed by America's teeming, vibrant cities. Most settled in immigrant ghettos where their native languages were spoken. Old traditions helped ease the trials of living in an unfamiliar culture.

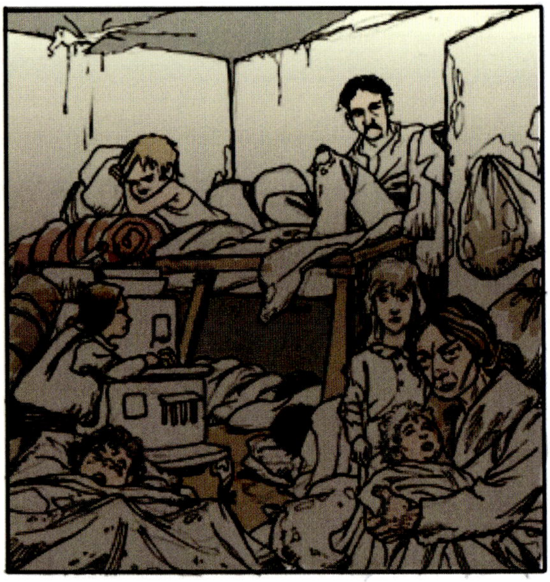

Still, life for the poorest of the poor could be wretched. They were packed into slums where violence and disease flourished and crime was rampant.

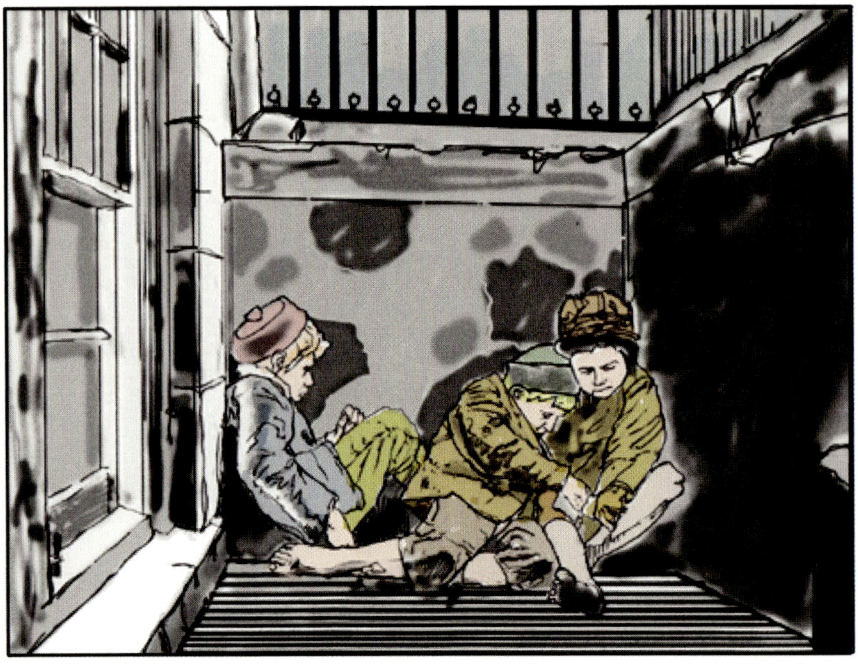

The Danish immigrant and journalist Jacob Riis, having seen this squalor during the 1880s, became determined to document the worst of the New York slums. He helped pioneer a form of flash photography that lit up the dark tenements and alleyways, revealing a world that the middle and upper classes knew little about.

By 1890, three-quarters of New York City's residents lived in tenements, often dark, damp, and airless, where whole families were squeezed into a few small rooms. Poor sanitation and contaminated water led to regular outbreaks of typhoid fever, cholera, and other diseases.

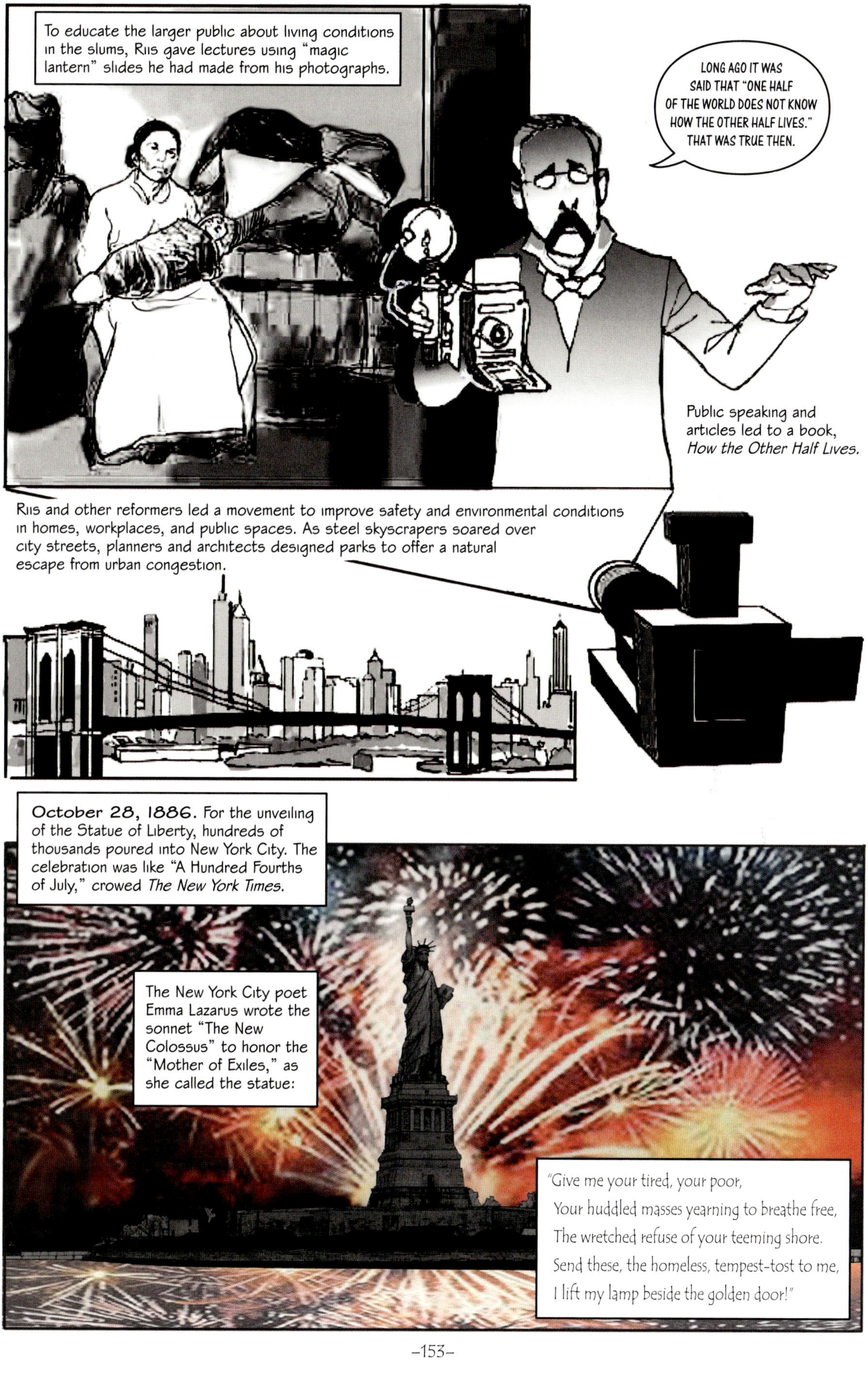
To educate the larger public about living conditions in the slums, Riis gave lectures using "magic lantern" slides he had made from his photographs.
LONG AGO IT WAS SAID THAT "ONE HALF OF THE WORLD DOES NOT KNOW HOW THE OTHER HALF LIVES." THAT WAS TRUE THEN.
Public speaking and articles led to a book, *How the Other Half Lives.*
Riis and other reformers led a movement to improve safety and environmental conditions in homes, workplaces, and public spaces. As steel skyscrapers soared over city streets, planners and architects designed parks to offer a natural escape from urban congestion.
October 28, 1886. For the unveiling of the Statue of Liberty, hundreds of thousands poured into New York City. The celebration was like "A Hundred Fourths of July," crowed *The New York Times.*
The New York City poet Emma Lazarus wrote the sonnet "The New Colossus" to honor the "Mother of Exiles," as she called the statue:
"Give me your tired, your poor,
Your huddled masses yearning to breathe free,
The wretched refuse of your teeming shore.
Send these, the homeless, tempest-tost to me,
I lift my lamp beside the golden door!"

UNCLE SAM is the most famous personification of the United States of America. Although Sam is rumored to have made his debut during the Revolutionary War, he probably stepped onto the American stage during the War of 1812.

Legend has it that his name derives from one Samuel Wilson, a meat-packer from Troy, New York, who was known locally as Uncle Sam. When Wilson supplied meat to American troops during the War of 1812, he stamped the initials "U.S." on every package—and soldiers began to associate the term "Uncle Sam" with the United States.

The Uncle Sam who serves as a symbolic representation of the nation owes his celebrity to two artists. In the middle of the 19th century, the editorial cartoonist Thomas Nast popularized what came to be the most familiar image of Uncle Sam, with his goatee, striped pants, and top hat. In the 20th century, the illustrator James Montgomery Flagg borrowed the image for a World War I and World War II army recruiting poster and created the most famous image of Uncle Sam ever.

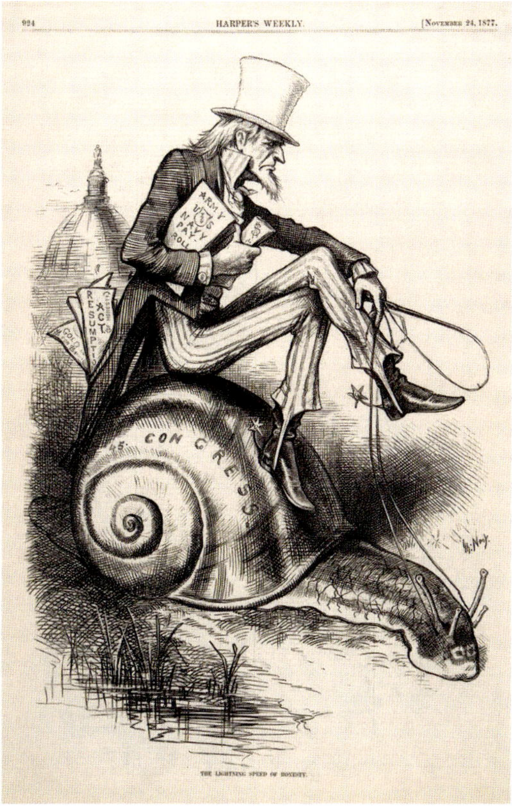
924
HARPER'S WEEKLY
[November 24, 1877.
CONGRESS

Thomas Nast

James Montgomery Flagg

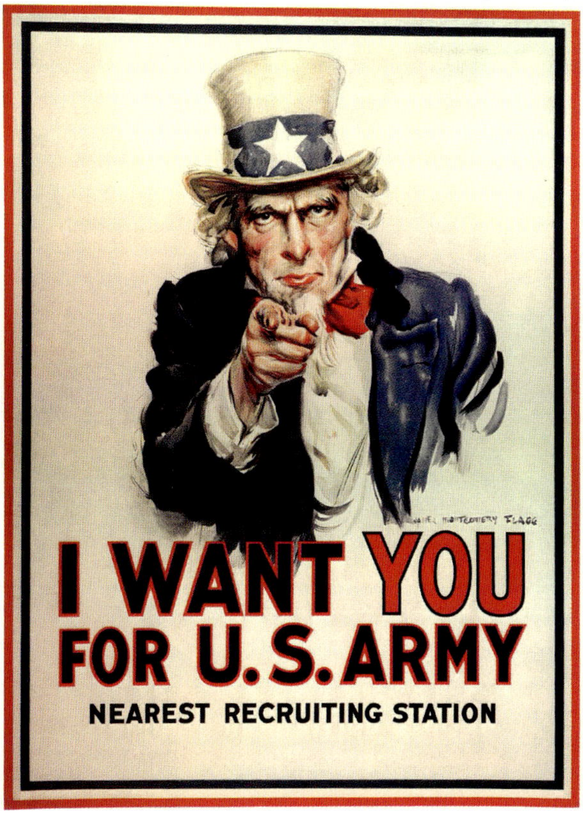
I WANT YOU
FOR U.S. ARMY
NEAREST RECRUITING STATION

So who is Uncle Sam? He is a protective uncle of the people. Over the years, he has been portrayed as just, fair, firm, enterprising, and wise. On Uncle Sam Day, designated by Congress in 1989 as September 13, President George H. W. Bush declared that "Uncle Sam recalls the pride and strength of the American people, as well as the freedom we enjoy... Today, the figure of Uncle Sam continues to remind us of the great risks and personal sacrifices endured by generations of Americans in the quest for liberty."

SUGGESTED READING

Aaronson, Marc. *The Real Revolution: The Global Story of American Independence.* New York: Clarion, 2005.
Alderman, Ellen, and Caroline Kennedy. *In Our Defense: The Bill of Rights in Action.* New York: Harper, 1992.
Ambrose, Stephen J. *Undaunted Courage: Meriwether Lewis, Thomas Jefferson, and the Opening of the American West.* New York: Simon & Schuster, 1996.
Beeman, Richard. *The Penguin Guide to the United States Constitution.* New York: Penguin, 2010.
Blumberg, Rhoda. *What's the Deal? Jefferson, Napoleon, and the Louisiana Purchase.* Washington, D.C.: National Geographic Society, 1998.
———. *The Incredible Journey of Lewis and Clark.* New York: HarperCollins, 1987.
Doherty, Kiernan. *Puritans, Pilgrims, and Merchants: Founders of the Northeastern Colonies.* Minneapolis, MN: The Oliver Press, 2000.
Ehle, John. *The Trail of Tears: The Rise and Fall of the Cherokee Nation.* New York: Anchor, 1988.
Ellis, Joseph. *Founding Brothers: The Revolutionary Generation.* New York: Knopf, 2001.
Faber, Doris and Harold Faber. *The Birth of a Nation.* New York: Scribner's, 1989.
Feelings, Tom. *The Middle Passage.* New York: Dial, 1996.
Fleming, Thomas J. *Liberty!: The American Revolution.* New York: Viking, 1997.
———. *The Louisiana Purchase.* Hoboken, New York: J. Wiley, 2003.
Greenblatt, Miriam. *War of 1812.* New York: Facts on File, 2003.
Hakim, Joy. *A History of Us.* Oxford University Press, Vols I-II. New York: Oxford University Press, 1993–2003.
Hartman, Gary R. *Landmark Supreme Court Cases.* New York: Checkmark Books, 2006.
Haynes, Charles C., Sam Chaltain and Susan M. Glisson. *First Freedoms: A Documentary History of First Amendment Rights in America.* Oxford, UK: Oxford University Press, 2006.
Heidler, David S. and Jeanne T. Heidler. *The War of 1812.* Westport, CT: The Greenwood Press, 2002.
Hennessey, Jonathan and Aaron McConnell. *The United States Constitution: A Graphic Adaptation.* New York: Hill and Wang, 2008.
Horton, James Oliver and Lois E. Horton. *Slavery and the Making of America.* Oxford, UK: Oxford University Press, 2005.
Kiernan, Denise and Joseph D'Agnese. *Signing Our Rights Away: The Fame and Misfortune of the Men Who Signed the Constitution.* Philadelphia: Quick Books, 2011.
———. *Signing Our Lives Away: The Fame and Misfortune of the Men Who Signed the Declaration of Independence.* Philadelphia: Quick Books, 2009.
King, Jonathan. *The Mayflower Miracle: The Pilgrim's Own Story of the Founding of America.* London: David & Charles, 1987.
Lewis, Anthony. *Freedom for the Thought that We Hate: A Biography of the First Amendment.* New York: Basic Books, 2007.
Lough, Loree. *Lord Baltimore: English Politician and Colonist.* New York: Chelsea House, 2000.
Mack, Stan. *Taxes, the Tea Party, and Those Revolting Rebels: A History in Comics of the American Revolution.* New York: NMB, 2012.
Marrin, Albert. *George Washington and the Founding of a Nation.* New York: Dutton, 2001.
———. *The War for American Independence: The Story of the American Revolution.* New York: Atheneum, 1988.
———. *The Struggle for a Continent: The French and Indian Wars, 1690–1760.* New York: Atheneum, 1987.
———. *1812: The War Nobody Won.* New York: Atheneum, 1985.
McCullough, David. *1776.* New York: Simon & Schuster, 2005.
Miller, John, ed. *The Complete History of American Slavery.* San Diego, CA: Greenhaven Press, 2001.
Molotsky, Irvin. *The Flag, the Poet and the Song: The Story of the Star-Spangled Banner.* New York: Dutton, 2001.
Monk, Linda R. *The Constitution: The Words We Live By: Your Annotated Guide to the Constitution.* New York: Hyperion, 2004.
Our Documents: 100 Milestone Documents from the National Archives. New York: Oxford University Press, 2003.
Philbrick, Nathaniel. *Mayflower.* New York: Penguin, 2006.
Rakove, Jack N. *The Annotated U.S. Constitution and Declaration of Independence.* Cambridge, MA: Harvard University Press, 2009.
Rediker, Marcus. *The Slave Ship.* New York: Viking, 2007.
Sgroi, Peter. *The Living Constitution: Landmark Supreme Court Decisions.* New York: Julian Messner, 1987.
Stewart, Mark. *The Indian Removal Act.* Minneapolis, MN: Compass Point Books, 2007.
Werner, Kirk D., ed. *The American Revolution.* San Diego, CA: Greenhaven Press, 2000.
Zinn, Howard. *A People's History of the United States: 1492-Present.* New York: HarperCollins, 2003.

SUGGESTED WEBSITES AND MULTIMEDIA

Slavery and the Making of America. WNET, 2005. DVD.
National Constitution Center: www.constitutioncenter.org
www.ushistory.org, 1995–2013.
American Masters: www.pbs.org
American Experience: www.pbs.org
Architect of the Capitol: www.aoc.gov

The Library of Congress: www.loc.gov
National Archives: www.archives.gov
The History Channel: www.history.com
The Gilder Lehrman Institute for American History: www.gilderlehrman.org

ACKNOWLEDGMENTS

To Howard Zimmerman, who first imagined that a graphic history of the most important documents of American history could be both fun and educational. His leadership and editorial expertise have been invaluable and we are most grateful for his friendship and advice.

To Russell Motter, whose encyclopedic knowledge of American history has informed the project from start to finish. Thank you, Russell, for your careful, detailed notes on each chapter and for your suggestions on revision.

To Richard Amari, book designer par excellence, who has been dedicated and creative in his interpretation of picture and words.

To Steven Roman, whose patience, professionalism and editorial skills made this book possible. His ability to juggle the many tasks necessary to prepare a book for publication proved essential.

And to Hill and Wang's former publisher, Thomas LeBien, who had the vision and courage to create the American Documents series and allow students to learn about American history in a friendlier environment.

A NOTE ABOUT THE AUTHOR AND THE ILLUSTRATOR

RUTH ASHBY is the author of more than thirty books for children and young adults. A former book editor, she teaches English at Portledge School in Locust Valley, New York. She earned her undergraduate degree in English at Yale University and a master's degree in Enlgish literature at the University of Michigan.

ERNIE COLÓN is the illustrator of the *New York Times* bestseller *The 9/11 Report: A Graphic Adaptation*, *Che*, and *Anne Frank* (all published by Hill and Wang). He has worked at Marvel and at DC Comics, where he oversaw the production for *Green Lantern*, *Wonder Woman*, *Blackhawk*, and *The Flash*. For many years he illustrated *Richie Rich* and *Casper the Friendly Ghost* for Harvey Comics.

A NOTE ABOUT THE EDITORIAL CONSULTANT

RUSSELL MOTTER teaches U.S. history and African American studies at 'Iolani School in Honolulu, Hawaii. He holds a master's degree in history from the University of Hawaii and has done graduate work at Rice University and Columbia University.

ALSO AVAILABLE

The Great American Documents

VOLUME I: 1620–1830

ACRONYMS DICTIONARY

FIRST EDITION

A GUIDE TO ALPHABETIC DESIGNATIONS, CONTRACTIONS AND INITIALISMS:

Association, Aerospace, Business, Electronic, Governmental, International, Labor, Military, Public Affairs, Scientific, Societies, Technical, Transportation, United Nation.

PRICE $10.00

GALE RESEARCH COMPANY
BOOK TOWER · DETROIT 26, MICHIGAN

COPYRIGHT 1960 BY: GALE RESEARCH COMPANY
LIBRARY OF CONGRESS CATALOG CARD NUMBER: 60-10869

PRINTED IN UNITED STATES OF AMERICA

CONTENTS

FOREWORD **4**

INTRODUCTION **5**

    HISTORICAL BACKGROUND

    DEVELOPMENT OF THE WORD

    HOW IT CAME ABOUT

    DEFINITION

    OFFICIAL SANCTION

    CURRENT USAGE

    STYLE

    PRONUNCIATION

HOW TO USE THIS BOOK **8**

    SCOPE OF THIS BOOK

    HOW TO USE THIS BOOK

    DESCRIPTION OF LISTINGS

ACRONYMS **11**

FOREWORD

This is the first edition of ACRONYMS DICTIONARY, a guide to alphabetic designations, contractions, initialisms, etc.

In recent years the use of acronyms has been rapidly increasing and the editors of this book hope it will provide a source of information for librarians, editors, writers, businessmen, educators, government officials, and research workers.

Future editions of this book are planned, and comments from readers concerning errors of omission or comission will be welcome. Other suggestions concerning scope, content, and arrangement of this book will likewise be appreciated. Forms for reporting such items have been provided in the back of this book.

In addition to the acronym entries, an introduction describing the development and current usage of the acronym has been provided on pages 5 to 9. To our knowledge this is the only study on acronyms and we hope it will be useful to our readers and particularly to students of word usage.

Before using this book please refer to page 9 which tells how to use the book and describes the arrangement of entries.

Gale Research Company

INTRODUCTION

HISTORICAL BACKGROUND

The use of acronyms is not new. Through recorded history man has shortened words to make them easier to say or to write. In Caesar's day, the term SPQR - Senatus Populusque Romanus, for Senate and People of Rome, was used.

The characteristic American penchant for brevity appears to have taken root early in the country's development. Perhaps the earliest abbreviation known is O.K. which appeared in the first dictionaries published in America. This word "okay" is supposed to have derived from the term Olk Kinderhook, a New York political organization of the period, or more likely, from the peculiar yankee expression Oll Korrect.

The 19th century was a particularly rich one in the evolution of the acronym in the popular American idiom. As the frontier moved westward, the names of the railroads prominent in the movement tended to be popularly referred to by the abbreviations for their names, as for example-B&O for Baltimore and Ohio, C&O for the Chesapeake and Ohio railroad, and Katy for Missouri, Kansas and Texas lines. Other popular and by now universally accepted acronyms developed during the century include TB for tuberculer bacillus (tuberculosis) and QT for quiet or subrosa. H. L. Mencken referred to acronyms in "The American Language" as the "characteristic American habit of reducing complete concepts to starkist abbreviations."

DEVELOPMENT OF THE WORD ACRONYM

While the use of acronyms is as old as recorded time, the word "acronym" is a relatively new entry into modern language use. Comprised of the Greek term "akros," meaning tip, and "onyma," meaning name, the word appears to have been used first in the February 1943 issue of "American Notes and Queries." It appears later in other periodicals related to language usage including "Word Study," G.C. Merriam Company, May 1947, and "American Speech," Vol. 23, 1948.

The term acronym first received dictionary recognition in the Random House "American College Dictionary" 1947 edition. Funk & Wagnall's 1950 dictionary supplement describes acronyms as "telescope words" and in more recent years most other dictionaries have incorporated the term.

HOW THEY CAME ABOUT

Toward the close of the 19th century, with the accretion in the number of federal boards, commissions and departments, abbreviations of official titles were used. The trend continued during World War I and in the second decade of the 20th century a number of commercial companies and enterprises, recognized the commercial advantage of consumer identification of company products or services with the acronym as an effective mnemonic device. In this era, Alcoa for Aluminum Company of America, and Nabisco for National Biscuit Company were born.

The phenomenon was not restricted to commercial organizations. A considerable number of associations, professional societies, federations and labor unions also came to be popularly known by their acronyms, as for example - NAM, NEA, ALA, CIO and AF of L. The use of acronyms came into very widespread practice during the New Deal with its conglomeration of new "alphabet agencies."

It was during World War II that the most expressive military acronym came into being -- GI. Here was a term which humorously embraced everything for which the all-knowing and all-powerful government was the sponsor. Even including the military personnel themselves who came to be known as GI's, or "government issue."

Because of its addiction to acronyms, the Navy found itself in an embarrassing position late in 1941. At that time the Commander-in-Chief of the U.S. Fleet was known as CINCUS, pronounced "sink-us." Needless to say, the name was changed on December 8.

On another occasion, when it compiled a storehouse of truncated words used during the war, the Navy got into more hot water. A 1945 editorial in a Washington newspaper ridiculed the Navy for its plethora of "oink" sounds. Among others there was OINC, or officer-in-charge. This, the newspaper said, was "talking like ungracious pigs." With tongue in cheek, the newspaper commented further that the Germans had been practicing such "agglutination" of words for many years "and see what happened to them."

In modern times many organizations have deliberately adopted a name which may readily be reduced to an acronym capable of easy pronunciation and bearing mnemonic features. Thereafter the term very often becomes widely known and is identified with the organization as a complete title. One illustration is CARE - Cooperative for American Remittances to Everywhere (originally Europe).

DEFINITION

Webster's, (G.C. Merriam Company) defines an acronym as a word formed by the initial letters of successive parts of a compound term, such as ASDIC, Thorndike-Barnhart's "Comprehensive Desk Dictionary," says that an acronym is a word formed from the first letters of syllables of other words, such as UNESCO. Funk & Wagnall's describes it as a word composed of the initial letters of a series of words, such as ENIAC, the initial syllables and letters, such as radar, or the first plus the final syllables of words, such as motel. Bergen and Cornelia Evans in their book "A Dictionary of Contemporary American Usage" (Random House), define acronyms as acrostic words formed from the initial letters of other words, or from first letters or syllables of succeeding parts of a compound term, or from initial letters plus final letters of the final part of a compound term.

There are instances where a special effort has been made to devise an acronym then find words to fit. One of these, the Evans feel, is WAVES, Woman Accepted for Voluntary Emergency Service. Others try to create euphony, such as LANTCOM for Atlantic Command, still others a special meaning such as calling women Coast Guard Reservists SPARS from the Coast Guard motto "Semper PARatus" -- Always Ready. A recent usage has been the creation of acronyms from the names of entertainers to designate their production firms, e.g., Desilu, Gomalco, and Roncom.

No doubt the Russians will claim credit for the invention of the acronym because they have long used what we now call acronyms. Their secret police was first called CHEKA, then VECHEKA, soon followed by GPU and OGPU, then NKGB switched to NKVD, followed by MVD, more recently by MGB and now KBG. No effort is made to put down the Russian words in the Cyrillic alphabet, unintelligible to Americans, but all these acronyms simply boil down to State Security Police.

High U.S. officials have helped bring forth acronyms and make them popular in use and acceptance. During the Korean War in 1952, the then Secretary of State Dean Acheson apologized to the British for bombing North Korean power plants without first consulting our Allies. He explained there was a "snafu" (situation normal, all fouled up).

The word gained added prominence in 1954 when Franklin D. Roosevelt, Jr. was campaigning for office in New York State. A sign painter got confused and inserted "lieutenant governor" for "attorney general" as the designation for the office Roosevelt sought. A New York newspaper headlined the incident "snafu."

Also in 1952, the then Secretary of Defense Robert A. Lovett frankly advocated "initialese." However, he said he abandoned the idea of abbreviating secretary of defense to SOD. He felt "this would require the most careful enunciation in order not to be acceptably accurate as a description of the secretary."

STYLE

In the past there has been little uniformity in the style of acronyms with respect to capitalization and use of periods or spaces. However, in its latest edition, the Government Printing Office Style Manual arbitrarily sets the style for "coined words." It prefers to set off acronyms according to these paraphrased rules: 1) omit periods in names of scientific, technical and industrial groups that have adopted definite forms and do not use punctuation; 2) use periods between initials that are part of a proper name or composed of a contraction of initials or numbers, such as U.S. and U.S.S.R.; 3) omit periods and spaces after initials used as shortened names of government agencies and other organized bodies except where specifically designated otherwise 4) when only the first letter of each word in a term is used to make up the symbol, use all capital letters, such as MAG for Military Advisory Group; 5) when proper names are used in shortened form and contain more than the first letter of each word, use capital and lowercase letters, such as Pepco for Potomac Electric Power Company; 6) in common-noun combinations made of more than the first letter of lowercased words, use all lowercase, such as loran for long-range-navigation.

However, the most recent trend is to write acronyms using all capitals without periods and spaces at all. As one newspaperman commented, it is best to use an acronym without using periods. He added that "this is much more satisfactory, a great deal neater and provides more uniformity."

PRONUNCIATION

There is no standard pattern in the pronunciation of acronyms. Frequently persons within the same organization will insist on pronouncing them in different ways. Some persons stress pronouncing acronyms as if they were complete words wherever possible. Others try to say most of them as individual letters.

Because of variations in usage, the editors of this book have made no effort to list pronounciations of acronyms. For one thing, both the acronym and its pronounciation often change rapidly. For another, it is largely a matter of personal preference. No standard has been set--or seems likely to be.

SCOPE OF THIS BOOK

In addition to acronyms of federal agencies, military organizations, titles and expressions, this book lists the myriad aerospace and communications-electronics terms, many of them interrelated with federal agencies. It also contains acronyms of thousands of associations, societies, federations, unions and other non-profit organizations in the U.S. Corporations, universities and transportation facilities known by acronyms are seldom listed because usage is generally restricted to relatively limited geographic areas, likewise no attempt is made to list acronyms of state and local government agencies, associations and other terms in limited use.

Nearly any company or corporation name can be reduced to an acronym. For instance, the Union Carbide Corporation could be referred to as UCC, but seldom is. On the other hand, it is probably more common to call the General Electric Company GE, than not. And the largest corporation in the world, General Motors, is most frequently referred to as GM.

Some persons may call Eastern Air Lines EAL, but that is not common usage. As a matter of fact, the firm's own advertising advises you to fly "Eastern." However, such airlines as Trans-World or Pan-American are normally referred to as TWA and Pan-Am.

Often the New York Central Railroad is dubbed NYC, but the Pennsylvania is more frequently called Penn or Pennsy than PRR. In many cases, ship lines also use special words to refer to themselves.

In almost any area a college or university is known by its acronym to students and perhaps faculty and neighbors. Nearby newspapers will probably refer to it by its acronym in headline treatment--one of the big boosters of the terms.

Some persons, for instance, may refer to Carnegie, or Case, Institute of Technology as CIT. But it is more common to say Carnegie Tech and Case. The two giant institutions of University of Michigan and Minnesota, among others, may be called UofM or UM in the locality, nearly everyone else knows them simply as Michigan and Minnesota.

Therefore, only those commercial and institutional acronyms that are known nationally are listed in this volume.

Military ranks are generally avoided in this work, as are educational degrees because not all schools use the same ones, they change from time to time and only a very few are commonly used. Acronyms of such specialized nature that they are used only in a particular field are also not listed. Examples are common abbreviations, shortened forms of Christian names and little-known foreign, business or military terms. Others not listed include stock exchange, musical and mathematical symbols, Roman numerals, Greek or radio alphabets, civil air and private railroad car markings, proofreader's marks, geographic directions or locations. Only acronyms of national or international scope are contained in this book.

HOW TO USE THIS BOOK

Listings are organized in alphabetical order according to acronym. If the acronym applies to more than one title or term, the others are listed step-by-step below the first in alphabetical order with the acronym being listed only once.

When an acronym refers to an organization it may be followed by the notation NC. This means "name changed to" and the new name is then listed. MW means "merged with" and is followed by the name of the successor organization or perhaps a new name. DF means "defunct" and indicates the organization is no longer in existance. If the acronym is no longer in use, it is noted as OB for "obsolete."

DESCRIPTION OF LISTINGS

To make entries easier to read and locate, all acronyms listed in this volume are printed in capital letters. This does not necessarily mean, however, that each should be written that way. The section on style offers a guide as to how to write acronyms. Common nouns have been capitalized to indicate the letters comprising the acronym.

All acronyms are American, except where specifically designated "United Nations," "International," "German" or some other nationality.

US and UN are used throughout the book to mean United States or United Nations. Only at the appropriate alphabetical listing are they spelled out as part of a word group. Where necessary to show their distinction from forces of other nations, the acronym US precedes some military designations.

In instances where the branch of service is not clearly shown, or where military titles and terms apply to one branch only, they are designated "Army," "Navy," "Air Force," "Marine Corps" or "Coast Guard," the five separate branches of the US armed forces. When an acronym is used in more than one branch of the service or throughout the Department of Defense, it is designated "Military" unless such terms as "armed services" or "armed forces" are included in the title.

Due to constant change, some obsolete acronyms may be included in this book without being so noted. Others may just be coming into use. It is impossible to make a work of this type completely correct, but the editors have made every effort to be as accurate as possible. The publisher will welcome comments from readers concerning omissions or errors. Forms for this purpose have been provided in the back of this book. Future editions of this book are planned and other comments concerning scope, content and arrangement will be appreciated.

MEMORANDUM

ACRONYMS

A	Army
AA	Alcoholics Anonymous
	American Airlines
	Arlington Annex (Navy)
	Antiaircraft (Military)
	Aviatsionnaya Armiya (Russian - air army)
AAA	Allied Artists of America
	American Academy of Advertising
	American Academy of Allergy
	American Accordionists Association
	American Accounting Association
	American Angus Association
	American Anthropological Association
	American Arbitration Association
	American Association of Anatomists
	American Automobile Association
	Antiaircraft Artillery (Military)
	Appraisers Association of America
	Archives of American Art
AAAA	American Association of Advertising Agencies
	Army Aviation Association of America
	Associated Actors and Artistes of America
AAACE	American Association of Agricultural College Editors
AAAE	American Association of Airport Executives
AAAIS	Antiaircraft Artillery Information Service (Military)
AAAL	American Academy of Arts and Letters
AAAN	Affiliated Advertising Agencies Network
	American Academy of Applied Nutrition
AAAS	American Academy of Arts and Science
	American Association of Advancement of Science
AAASS	American Association for the Advancement of Slavic Studies
AAAUS	Association of Average Adjusters of the U.S.
AAB	Aircraft Accident Board (Military)
	American Association of Bioanalysts
	Antiaircraft Balloon (Military)
	Army Air Base (OB)
AABB	American Association of Blood Banks
AABC	Accrediting Association of Bible Colleges
	American Amateur Baseball Congress
AABGA	American Association of Botanical Gardens and Arboretums
AABM	Association of American Battery Manufacturers
AABTM	American Association of Baggage Traffic Managers
AAC	Aeronautical Advisory Council
	Aeronautical Approach Chart (Military)
	Alaska Air Command (Air Force)
	American Alpine Club
	American Alumni Council
	Antiaircraft Common (Navy)
	Army Air Corps (OB)
	Association of American Colleges
	Automotive Advertisers Council
AACBC	American Association of College Baseball Coaches
AACC	American Association of Cereal Chemists
	American Association of Clinical Chemists
	American Association of Commercial Colleges

ACRONYMS

AACC	Association for Aid of Crippled Children
AACCP	American Association of Colleges of Chiropody-Podiatry
AACE	American Association of Cost Engineers
AACI	American Association for Conservation Information
AACM	American Academy of Compensation Medicine
AACP	American Academy for Cerebral Palsy
	American Association of Colleges of Pharmacy
	American Association of Commerce Publications
	American Association of Correctional Psychologists
AACPR	American Association for Cleft Palate Rehabilitation
AACR	American Association for Cancer Research
AACRAO	American Association of Collegiate Registrars & Admissions Officers
AACS	Airways and Air Communications Service (Air Force)
	Army Airways Communications Systems (OB)
AACSB	American Association of Collegiate Schools of Business
AACTE	American Association of Colleges for Teacher Education
AADA	Advanced Air Depot Area (Air Force)
	Antiaircraft Defended Area (Military)
AADE	American Association of Dental Examiners
AADM	American Academy of Dental Medicine
AADS	American Association of Dental Schools
AAE	American Association of Endodontists
	American Association of Engineers
	Army Aviation Engineers
AAEA	American Agricultural Editors Association
AAF	American Air Filter Company, Inc.
	American Architectural Foundation
	American Astronautical Federation
	Army Airfield
	Army Air Forces (OB)
AAFAS	Army Air Forces Aid Society (OB)
AAFC	Army Air Forces Center (OB)
	Association of Advertising Film Companies
AAFCE	Allied Air Force, Central Europe
AAFCO	Association of American Feed Control Officials
	Association of American Fertilizer Control Officials
AAFCWF	Army and Air Force Central Welfare Fund
AAFEMPS	Army and Air Force Exchange and Motion Picture Service
AAFES	Army and Air Force Exchange Service
AAFH	Academy of American Franciscan History
AAFIS	Army Air Forces Intelligence School (OB)
AAFM	American Association of Feed Microscopists
AAFMTO	Army Air Force Headquarters, Mediterranean Theatre of Operations (OB)
AAFNE	Allied Air Force, Northern Europe
AAFP	American Association of Film Producers
AAFPOA	Army Air Forces, Pacific Ocean Areas (OB)
AAFPS	Army and Air Force Postal Service
AAFRC	American Association of Fund-Raising Counsel
AAFSAT	Army Air Forces School of Applied Tactics (OB)
AAFSE	Allied Air Force, Southern Europe
AAFTAC	Army Air Forces Tactical Center (OB)
AAFTAD	Army Air Forces Training Aids Division (OB)
AAFTC	Army Air Forces Training Command (OB)
AAFTTC	Army Air Forces Technical Training Command (OB)
AAFWB	Army and Air Force Wage Board

ACRONYMS

AAG .... Air Adjutant General (Air Force)
              Association of American Geographers
AAGBA .... American Angora Goat Breeders' Association
AAGC .... American Association for Gifted Children
AAGP .... American Academy of General Practice
AAGR .... Air-to-Air Gunnery Range (Air Force)
AAGS .... All-America Gladiolus Selections
AAGUS .... American Association of Genito-Urinary Surgeons
AAHA .... American Animal Hospital Association
              American Association of Hospital Accountants
              Awaiting Action of Higher Authority (Military)
AAHD .... American Academy of the History of Dentistry
AAHM .... American Association for the History of Medicine
AAHPER ...... American Association for Health, Physical Education and Recreation
AAHPhA ...... American Animal Health Pharmaceutical Association
AAHQ .... Allied Air Headquarters (OB)
AAI .... African-American Institute
              Agricultural Ammonia Institute
              Allied Armies in Italy (OB)
              American Association of Immunologists
AAIA .... Association on American Indian Affairs
AAIB .... American Association of Instructors of the Blind
AAIC .... Allied Air Intelligence Center (Military)
AAID .... American Academy of Implant Dentures
              American Association of Industrial Dentists
AAIE .... American Association of Industrial Editors
              American Association of Industrial Engineers
AAIIP .... Alfred Adler Institute for Individual Psychology
AAIN .... American Association of Industrial Nurses
AAJC .... American Association of Junior Colleges
AAL .... Aid Association for Lutherans
AALA .... American Auto Laundry Association
AALGCSU ..... American Association of Land-Grant Colleges and State Universities
AALL .... American Association of Law Libraries
AALS .... Association of American Law Schools
              Association of American Library Schools
AALT .... American Association of Library Trustees
AAM .... Air-to-Air-Missile
              American Academy of Microbiology
              American Association of Museums
AAMA .... American Academy of Medical Administrators
AAMC .... American Association of Marriage Counselors
              American Association of Medical Clinics
              Association of American Medical Colleges
AAMD .... American Association on Mental Deficiency
              Association of Art Museum Directors
AAMG .... Antiaircraft Machine Gun (Military)
AAMGA .... American Association of Managing General Agents
AAMI .... American Association of Machinery Importers
              Association of Allergists for Mycological Investigation
AAMIH .... American Association for Maternal and Infant Health
AAML .... Arctic Aero Medical Laboratory (Air Force)
AAMMC .... American Association of Medical Milk Commissions
AAMRL .... American Association of Medical Record Librarians
AAMS .... American Air Mail Society

ACRONYMS

AAMVA	American Association of Motor Vehicle Administrators
AAN	American Academy of Neurology
	American Association of Nurserymen
AANA	American Association of Nurse Anesthetists
AANO	Albanian-American National Organization
AANR	American Association of Newspaper Representatives
AANS	American Academy of Neurological Surgery
AAO	Academy of Applied Osteopathy
	American Academy of Organ
	American Association of Orthodontists
AAOC	American Association of Osteopathic Colleges
	Antiaircraft Operations Center (Military)
AAODC	American Association of Oilwell Drilling Contractors
AAOG	American Association of Obstetricians and Gynecologists
AAONMS	Ancient Accepted Order of the Nobles of the Mystic Shrine
AAOO	American Academy of Ophthalmology and Otolaryngology
AAOP	American Academy of Oral Pathology
AAOS	American Academy of Orthopaedic Surgeons
AAOT	American Association of Orthoptic Technicians
AAP	Academy of American Poets
	American Academy of Pediatrics
	American Academy of Periodontology
	Association for the Advancement of Psychoanalysis
	Association for the Advancement of Psychotherapy
	Association of American Physicians
AAPA	American Amateur Press Association
	American Association of Physical Anthropologists
	American Association of Port Authorities
AAPB	American Association of Pathologists and Bacteriologists
AAPC	Advertising Agency Production Club of New York
AAPCC	American Association of Psychiatric Clinics for Children
AAPCM	Association of American Playing Card Manufacturers
AAPCO	Association of American Pesticide Control Officials
AAPE	American Academy of Physical Education
AAPG	American Association of Petroleum Geologists
AAPHD	American Association of Public Health Dentists
AAPIU	Allied Aerial Photographic Interpretation Unit
AAPL	American Artists Professional League
	American Association of Petroleum Landmen
AAPOR	American Association for Public Opinion Research
AAPS	American Association of of Plastic Surgeons
	Association of American Physicians and Surgeons
AAPSS	American Academy of Political and Social Science
AAPT	American Association of Physics Teachers
	Association of Asphalt Paving Technologists
AAPTO	American Association of Passenger Traffic Officers
AAQM	Acting Assistant Quartermaster (Marine Corps)
AAR	Aircraft Accident Record (Military)
	Association of American Railroads
	Automotive Affiliated Representatives
AARD	American Academy of Restorative Dentistry
AARDCO	Association of American Railroad Dining Car Officers
AARS	American Association of Railroad Superintendents
	American Association of Railway Surgeons
	Army Aircraft Repair Ship

- 14 -

ACRONYMS

AART .... American Association for Rehabilitation Therapy
AARTA .... American Association of Railroad Ticket Agents
AAS .... All-America Selections (Hotriculture)
              American Antiquarian Society
              American Astronomical Society
              Army Air Service (OB)
              Arnold Air Society
              Association for Asian Studies
AASA .... American Association of School Administrators
AASB .... American Association of Small Business
AASDJ .... American Association of Schools and Departments of Journalism
AASE .... Association for Applied Solar Energy
AASG .... Association of American State Geologists
AASGP .... Association of American Soap and Glycerine Producers
AASHO .... American Association of State Highway Officials
AASL .... American Association of School Librarians
              American Association of State Libraries
AASLH .... American Association for State and Local History
AASND .... American Association for Study of Neoplastic Diseases
AASO .... Association of American Ship Owners
AASP&RC ..... American Association of Sheriffs Posses and Riding Clubs
AASR .... Ancient and Accepted Scottish Rite
AASRE .... American Association of Schools Religious Education
AASS .... American Association for Social Security
AAST .... American Association for Surgery of Trauma
AATA .... American Automobile Touring Alliance
AATC .... Antiaircraft Training Center (Navy)
AATCC .... American Association of Textile Chemists and Colorists
AATF .... American Association of Teachers of French
AATG .... American Association of Teachers of German
AATI .... American Association of Teachers of Italian
AATP .... American Academy of Tuberculosis Physicians
AATPA .... American Association of Traveling Passenger Agents
AATS .... American Association of Theological Schools
AATT .... American Association for Textile Technology
AAT&TC ...... Antiaircraft Training Test Center (Navy)
AAU .... Amateur Athletic Union of the United States
              Association of American Universities
AAUN .... American Association for the United Nations
AAUP .... American Association of University Professors
AAUTI .... American Association of University Teachers of Insurance
AAUW .... American Association of University Women
AAVN .... American Association of Veterinary Nutritions
AAVRPHS ..... American Association for Vital Records and Public Health Statistics
AAVSO .... American Association of Variable Star Observers
AAW .... Advertising Association of the West
AAWB .... American Association of Workers for the Blind
AAWM .... American Association of Women Ministers
AAZPA .... American Association of Zoological Parks & Aquariums
AB .... Able-Bodied Seaman (Navy)
              Aeronautical Board (Air Force)
              Air Base (Air Force)
ABA .... Air Brake Association
              American Badminton Association
              American Bakers Association

- 15 -

ACRONYMS

ABA .... American Bandmasters Association
American Bankers Association
American Bantam Association
American Bar Association
American Berkshire Association
American Booksellers Association
Ayrshire Breeders' Association
ABAA .... Antiquarian Booksellers Association of America
ABATU .... Advanced Base Aviation Training Unit (Navy)
ABBA .... American Brahman Breeders Association
ABBB .... Association of Better Business Bureaus
ABC .... American Beagle Club
American Beveren Club
American Bowling Congress
American Brahma Club
American, British, Canadian plans (OB)
American Broadcasting Company
Atomic, Biological and Chemical Warfare
Audit Bureau of Circulations
Automotive Booster Clubs International
ABCB .... American Bottlers of Carbonated Beverages
ABCCTC ...... Advanced Base Combat Communication Training Center (Navy)
ABCD .... Advanced Base Construction Depot (Navy)
Awaiting Bad Conduct Discharge (Military)
ABCFM .... American Board of Commissioners for Foreign Missions
ABD .... Advanced Base Depot (Military)
Advanced Base Dock (Navy)
ABDA .... American-British-Dutch-Australian command (OB-World War II)
ABDACOM .... Advanced Base Depot Area Command (Navy)
ABDAFLOAT ... American-British-Dutch-Australian Naval operational command (WW II)
ABDAIR ...... American-British-Dutch-Australian Air operational command (WW II)
ABDARM ...... American-British-Dutch-Australian Army operational command (WW II)
ABEA .... American Broncho-Esophagological Association
ABEC .... Annular Bearing Engineers Committee
ABF .... Aircraft Battle Force (Navy)
American Beekeeping Federation
ABFM .... American Board of Foreign Missions
ABG .... Air Base Group (Navy)
ABGP .... Air Base Group (Air Force)
ABI .... American Butter Institute
ABIM .... American Board of International Missions
ABJS .... Association of Bone and Joint Surgeons
ABLA .... Amateur Bicycle League of America
American Business Law Association
ABMA .... American Boiler Manufacturers Association
Army Ballistic Missile Agency
ABMAC .... American Bureau for Medical Aid to China
ABMC .... American Battle Monuments Commission
ABMD .... Air Ballistic Missile Division (Air Force)
ABMS .... American Bureau of Metal Statistics
ABMU .... American Baptist Missionary Union
ABNINF ...... Airborne Infantry (Military)
ABNM .... American Board of National Missions
ABO .... American Board of Ophthalmology
American Board of Otolaryngology

ACRONYMS

A (bomb)	Atom Bomb
ABO	Association of Buying Offices
ABP	Associated Business Publications
ABPA	Advanced Base Personnel Administration (Navy)
ABPC	American Book Publishers Council
ABPG	Advanced Base Proving Ground (Navy)
ABPO	Advanced Base Personnel Officer (Navy)
ABPU	Advanced Base Personnel Unit (Navy)
ABR	Amphibian Boat Reconnaissance Aircraft (Navy)
ABRB	Advanced Base Receiving Barracks (Navy)
ABRD	Advanced Base Repair Depot (Navy)
	Advanced Base Reshipment Depot (Navy)
ABS	Air Base Squadron (Air Force)
	American Bible Society
	American Bryological Society
	American Bureau of Shipping
ABSAP	Airborne Search and Attack Plotter (Navy)
ABSD	Advanced Base Sectional Dock (Navy)
	Advanced Base Supply Depot (Navy)
ABTF	Airborne Task Force (Military)
ABTPA	American Bridge, Tunnel and Turnpike Association
ABTU	Advanced Base Torpedo Unit (Navy)
	Advanced Base Training Unit (Navy)
	Air Bombers Training Unit (Navy)
ABWA	American Business Writing Association
	Associated Business Writers of America
ABWG	Air Base Wing (Air Force)
AC	Admiral Commanding (Navy)
	Air Corps (OB)
	Aircraft
	Alaskan Command (Military)
	Allis Chalmers
	Alternating Current
	Amphibious Corps (Military)
	Architect of the Capitol
	Atlantic Congress
	Aviation Cadet (Military)
ACA	Aero Club of America
	Alaska Coastal Airlines
	American Camping Association
	American Canoe Association
	American Carnivals Association
	American Cemetery Association
	American Collectors Association
	American College of Allergists
	American College of Anesthesiologists
	American College of Apothecaries
	American Communications Association
	American Composers Alliance
	American Congregational Association
	American Correctional Association
	American Corriedale Association
	American Cryptogram Association
	American Crystallographic Association
	Associated Chiropodists of America

ACA	Association Canado-Americaine
	Association of Correctional Administrators
	Physically on board Awaiting Combat Assignment (Navy)
ACAC	Allied Container Advisory Committee (Military)
	Association of College Admissions Counselors
ACAD	American Conference of Academic Deans
ACAF	Amphibious Corps, Atlantic Fleet
ACAN	Army Command and Administrative Network
ACAPA	American Concrete Agricultural Pipe Association
ACAS	Association of Casualty Accountants and Statisticians
ACB	Advertising Checking Bureau
	Airmen Classification Battery (Air Force Personnel Test)
	Association of the Customs Bar
ACBA	American Charbray Breeders Association
ACBB	American Council for Better Broadcasts
ACBL	American Contract Bridge League
ACBS	Accrediting Commission for Business Schools
ACC	Administrative Committee on Coordination (United Nations)
	Air Center Commander (Navy)
	Air Control Center (Navy)
	Air Coordination Committee (Military)
	Allied Control Commission (OB)
	Allied Control Council (OB)
	American Conference of Cantors
	American Craftsmen's Council
	Army Chemical Center
ACCA	Ad Hoc Crypto-coordination Agency (Military)
	American Clinical and Climatological Association
	American Correctional Chaplains' Association
ACCC	American Council of Christian Churches
ACCCA	American Catholic Correctional Chaplains Association
ACCCE	Association of Consulting Chemists and Chemical Engineers
ACCCF	American Concert Choir and Choral Foundation
ACCCI	American Coke and Coal Chemicals Institute
ACCE	American Chamber of Commerce Executives
ACCL	American Council of Christian Laymen
ACCP	American College of Chest Physicians
ACD	American College of Dentists
ACE	Allied Command, Europe (Military)
	American Cinema Editors (Association)
	American Council on Education
	Aviation Construction Engineers (Military)
ACEF	Asian Cultural Exchange Foundation
ACEI	Association for Childhood Education International
ACEJ	American Council on Education for Journalism
ACEN	Assembly of Captive European Nations /(Navy)
ACEORP	Automotive and Construction Equipment Overhaul and Repair Plant
ACEP	American Council for Emigres in the Professions
ACEPD	Automotive and Construction Equipment Parts Depot (Navy)
ACF	Alternate Communications Facility (Military)
	American Car and Foundry
	American Culinary Federation
	Association of Consulting Foresters
ACFN	American Committee for Flags of Necessity
ACFO	American College of Foot Orthopedists

ACRONYMS

ACFR	Advisory Council on Federal Reports
ACG	Airborne Coordinating Group (Military)
	American College of Gastroenterology
ACGA	American Cranberry Growers Association
ACGC	American Checkered Giant Club
ACGIH	American Conference of Governmental Industrial Hygienists
ACGM	Aircraft Carrier General Memorandum (Navy)
ACHA	American Catholic Historical Association
	American College Health Association
	American College of Hospital Administrators
ACI	Air Combat Information
	Air Combat Intelligence (Navy)
	Air-Controlled Interception
	Alloy Casting Institute
	American Carpet Institute
	American Concrete Institute
ACIATE	American Council on Industrial Arts Teacher Education
ACIC	Aeronautical Chart and Information Center (Air Force)
	Allied Captured Intelligence Center (OB)
	Auxiliary Combat Information Center (Navy)
ACIL	American Council of Independent Laboratories
ACIO	Air Combat Intelligence Office (r) (Navy)
ACIWLP	American Committee for International Wild Life Protection
ACJ	American Council for Judaism
ACL	Allowable Cabin Load (Air Force)
	American Classical League
	American Committee for Liberation
	Association of Cinema Laboratories
ACLA	American Country Life Association
ACLANT	Allied Command Atlantic (Military)
ACLS	American Council of Learned Societies
ACLU	American Civil Liberties Union
	American College of Life Underwriters
ACM	Air Court-Martial (Air Force)
	American Campaign Medal (Military)
	Association for Computing Machinery
ACMA	American Certified Morticians Association
ACME	Advisory Council on Medical Education
	Association of Consulting Management Engineers
ACMF	Air Corps Medical Forces (OB)
	Allied Central Mediterranean Forces (OB)
	American Corn Millers Federation
ACMI	American Cotton Manufacturers Institute
ACMP	Amateur Chamber Music Players
ACMT	American College of Medical Technologists
	American Commission on Ministerial Training
ACN	American Council on Nato
ACNA	Advisory Council on Naval Affairs
ACNO	Assistant Chief of Naval Operations
ACNOT	Assistant Chief of Naval Operations (Transportation)
ACO	American Academy of Optometry
ACOA	American Committee on Africa
ACOG	Aircraft on Ground (Military)
	American College of Obstetricians and Gynecologists
ACOHA	American College of Hospital Administrators

- 19 -

ACRONYMS

ACOOG	American College of Osteopathic Obstetricians and Gynecologists
ACOS	American College of Osteopathic Surgeons
ACP	Allied Communications Publication (Military)
	American College of Physicians
	Animal Care Panel
	Anti-Comintern Pact (OB)
	Association of Correctional Psychologists
ACPA	American Capon Producers Association
	American Catholic Psychological Association
	American College Personnel Association
	American Concrete Pipe Association
	Asbestos-Cement Products Association
ACPC	American Christian Palestine Committee
ACPE	American Council on Pharmaceutical Education
ACPF	Amphibious Corps, Pacific Fleet
ACPMR	American Congress of Physical Medicine and Rehabilitation
ACPRA	American College Public Relations Association
ACQT	Aviation Cadet Qualification Test (Military)
ACR	Aircraft Control Room (Navy)
	Airfield Control Radar (Air Force)
	American Academy in Rome
	American College of Radiology
ACRA	American Collegiate Retailing Association
ACRC	Air Compressor Research Council
ACRI	American Cocoa Research Institute
ACRL	Association of College and Research Libraries
ACRR	American Council on Race Relations
ACRW	American Council of Railroad Women
ACS	Alaska Communication System (Military)
	American Camellia Society
	American Cancer Society
	American Carnation Society
	American Ceramic Society
	American Chemical Society
	American College of Surgeons
	Assistant Chief of Staff (Military)
ACSA	Association of Collegiate Schools of Architecture
AC/SAF	Assistant Chief of Staff, Air Force
ACSC	Air Command and Staff College (OB - now Command and Staff College)
	Asssociation of Casualty and Surety Companies
ACSEA	Air Command, Southeast Asia (OB)
ACSF	Attack Carrier Striking Force (Navy)
ACSI	Assistant Chief of Staff, Intelligence (Military)
ACSM	American Congress on Surveying and Mapping
ACSMA	American Cloak and Suit Manufacturers Association
ACSN	Association of Collegiate Schools of Nursing
ACSOC	Acoustical Society of America
ACSRC	Assistant Chief of Staff for Reserve Components (Military)
ACSSAVO	Association of Chief State School Audio-Visual Officers
ACSSN	Association of Colleges and Secondary Schools for Negroes
ACST	Army Clerical Speed Test
ACT	Air Control Team (Military)
	Aviation Classification Test (Navy)
ACTA	Aircoach Transport Association
ACTG	Advance Carrier Training Group (Navy)

ACRONYMS

ACTH . . . . Adrenocorticotropic Hormone
ACTION . . . . . . American Council to Improve our Neighborhoods
ACTL . . . . American College of Trial Lawyers
ACTM . . . . Association of Cotton Textile Merchants of New York
ACTOR . . . . Askania Cine-Theodolite Optical-Tracking Range
ACTREP . . . . Activities Report (Shipping)
ACTSECNAV . . . Acting Secretary of the Navy
ACU . . . . American Congregational Union
                 Association of College Unions
ACUE . . . . American Committee of United Europe
ACUHO . . . . . . Association of College and University Housing Officers
ACVAFS . . . . . . American Council of Voluntary Agencies for Foreign Service
ACVC . . . . American Council of Venture Clubs
ACVP . . . . American College of Veterinary Pathologists
AC&W . . . . Air Communications and Weather (Military)
ACW . . . . Air Control and Warning (Military)
                 Alternating Continuous Waves (Radio)
                 American Chain of Warehouses (Association)
ACWA . . . . Amalgamated Clothing Workers of America
ACWC . . . . Advisory Committee on Weather Control
AC&WS . . . . Aircraft Control and Warning Stations (Military)
ACYD . . . . Association of Cotton Yarn Distributors
AD . . . . Active Duty (Military)
                 Air Defense (Military)
                 Air Depot (Military)
                 Airdrome
                 Anno Domini (In the Year of Our Lord)
                 Aviatsionnaya Diviziya (Russian - air division)
ADA . . . . Air Defense Area (Military)
                 American Dairy Association
                 American Dehydrators Association
                 American Dental Association
                 American Dermatological Association
                 American Diabetes Association
                 American Dietetic Association
                 Americans for Democratic Action
ADAA . . . . American Dental Assistants Association
ADARCO . . . . . . Advise Date of Reporting in Compliance with These Orders (Military)
ADAVAL . . . . . . Advise Availability (Military)
ADC . . . . Aid to Dependent Children
                 Aide-de-Camp (Military)
                 Air Defense Command (Air Force)
                 Air Development Center (Air Force)
                 Alaska Defense Command (Military)
ADCC . . . . Air Defense Control Center (Military)
                 American Devon Cattle Club
ADCI . . . . American Die Casting Institute
ADCOM . . . . . . Administrative Command (Military)
ADCOMINPAC . . Administrative Command, Minecraft, Pacific Fleet
ADCOMPHIBSPAC . . Administrative Command, Amphibious Forces, Pacific Fleet /Comm.
ADCOMSUBORDCOMPHIBSPAC . . Admin. Command, Amphib. Forces, Pacific Flt., Subordinate
ADCON . . . . . . Advise all Concerned (Navy)
ADCONSEN . . . With the Advice and Consent of the Senate (Military)
ADDC . . . . Air Defense Direction Center (Military)
                 Association of Desk and Derrick Clubs of North America

ACRONYMS

ADDL .... Aircraft Dummy Deck Landing (Navy)
ADDU .... Additional Duty (Military)
ADEP .... Air Depot (Military)
ADF .... Air Direction Finder (Military)
ADFC .... Air Defense Filter Center (Military)
ADFI .... American Dog Feed Institute
ADHA .... American Dental Hygienists' Association
ADHCA .... Advise this Headquarters of Complete Action (Military)
ADI .... Air Distribution Institute
            Alien Declared Intention
            American Documentation Institute
ADINTELCEN... Advanced Intelligence Center (Navy)
ADIS .... Air Defense Integrated System (Military)
ADIV .... Air Division (Air Force)
ADIZ .... Air Defense Identification Zone (Military)
ADL .... Anti-Defamation League of B'nai B'rith
ADLS .... Air Dispatch Letter Service (Navy)
ADMA .... American Drug Manufacturers' Association
            Aviation Distributors and Manufacturers Association
ADMI .... American Dry Milk Institute
ADMINO ...... Administrative Orders (Military)
ADMRA .... American and Delaine-Merino Record Association
ADOGA .... American Dehydrated Onion and Garlic Association
ADP .... Academy of Denture Prosthetics
            Air Defense Position (Military)
            Airport Development Program
ADR .... Aircraft Direction Room (Navy)
ADROBN ...... Airdrome Battalion (Military)
ADS .... Air Defense Sector (Military)
            American Dahlia Society
            American Denture Society
            American Dialect Society
ADSA .... American Dairy Science Association
ADSEC .... Advanced Section (Military)
ADSM .... American Defense Service Medal
ADTA .... American Dental Trade Association
ADTIC .... Artic-Desert-Tropic Information Center (Air Force)
ADVHED ...... Advanced Headquarters (Navy)
ADVON .... Advanced Echelon (Military)
            Advanced Operations Unit (Navy)
ADW .... Air Defense Warning (Military)
ADWKP .... Air Defense Warning Key Point (Military)
A&E .... Armament & Electronics (Air Force)
AE .... Air Explorer (Senior Boy Scout)
AEA .... Actors' Equity Association
            Adult Education Association of the U.S.A.
            American Economic Association
            American Education Association
            American Enterprise Association
            American Export Airlines
            Artists Equity Association
            Automotive Electric Association
AEAF .... Allied Expeditionary Air Force (OB)
AEC .... Atomic Energy Commission
AECP .... Airman's Education and Commissioning Program (Air Force)

ACRONYMS

```
AECTR . . . . . . . American Emergency Committee for Tibetan Refugees
AED . . . . . . . . Associated Equipment Distributors (Association)
AEDC . . . . . . . Arnold Engineering Development Center (Air Force)
AEDD . . . . . . . Air Engineering Development Division (Air Force)
AEF . . . . . . . . Advertising Educational Foundation
                   Allied Expeditionary Force (OB)
                   American Economic Foundation
                   American Expeditionary Forces (OB)
                   Aviation Engineer Force (Military)
AEHL . . . . . . . Army Environmental Health Laboratory
AEI . . . . . . . . Acrylic Eye Illustrator (Medical)
                   Air Express International
AEJ . . . . . . . . Association for Education in Journalism
AEL . . . . . . . . Aeronautical Engine Laboratory (Navy)
                   Animal Education League
AEO . . . . . . . . Air Engineer Officer (Navy)
AEOP . . . . . . . Amend Existing Orders Pertaining to (Military)
AEOS . . . . . . . Ancient Egyptian Order of Sciots, Supreme Pyramid
AEPEM . . . . . . Association of Electronic Parts and Equipment Manufacturers
AER . . . . . . . . Abbreviated Effectiveness Report (Military)
                   Airman Effectiveness Report (Air Force)
                   Army Emergency Relief
AERA . . . . . . . American Educational Research Association
                   Automotive Engine Rebuilders Association
AEROF . . . . . . Aerological Officer (Navy)
AERNO . . . . . . Aeronautical Equipment Reference Number (Military)
AES . . . . . . . . American Electrochemical Society
                   American Electroencephalographic Society
                   American Electroplaters Society
                   American Entomological Society
                   American Epidemiological Society
                   American Epilepsy Society
                   American Ethnological Society
                   American Eugenics Society
                   Audio Engineering Society
AESC . . . . . . . American Engineering Standards Committee
AETA . . . . . . . American Educational Theatre Association
AETS . . . . . . . Association for the Education of Teachers in Science
AEU . . . . . . . . American Ethical Union
AEW . . . . . . . . Airborne Early Warning (Military)
AEWC . . . . . . . Airborne Early Warning and Control (Military)
AEWTU . . . . . . Airborne Early Warning Training Unit (Military)
AF . . . . . . . . . Air Force
                   America's Future
                   Army Force
                   Asiatic Fleet (OB)
                   Audio Frequency
                   Automatic Following (Military radar)
AFA . . . . . . . . Actors' Fund of America
                   Advertising Federation of America
                   Air Force Association
                   Allergy Foundation of America
                   Amateur Fencing Association
                   American Federation of Arts
                   American Federation of Astrologers
```

ACRONYMS

AFA	American Forestery Association
	American Foundrymen's Association
	American Fracture Association
	Armed Forces Act
	Army Flight Activity
	Association of Federal Architects
AFAB	Air Force Academy Board
AFAC	Air Force Armament Center
AFAFC	Air Force Accounting and Finance Center
AFAPO	Air Force Property Accountable Officer
AFAS	Air Force Aid Society
	American Fine Arts Society
AFASE	Association for Applied Solar Energy
AFB	Air Force Base
	Air Force Bulletin
	American Foundation for the Blind
AFBF	American Farm Bureau Federation
AFBMA	Anti-Friction Bearing Manufacturers Association
AFBU	Air Force Base Unit
AFC	Air Force Council (advisory board to USAF)
	Air Force Cross
	American Finance Conference
	Army Finance Center
	Automatic Frequency Control
AFCA	American Football Coaches Association
	Armed Forces Chemical Association
AFCC	Air Force Combat Command (OB)
AFCCE	Association of Federal Communications Consulting Engineers
AFCE	Armed Forces Chemical Association
	Automatic Flight Control Equipment (Military)
AFCEA	Armed Forces Communications and Electronics Association
AFCENT	Air Forces, Central Europe
AFCI	American Foot Care Institute
AFCM	Association of First Class Mailers
AFCO	Air Force Contracting Officer
	American Furnace Company
AFCOS	Armed Forces Courier Service
AFCR	American Federation for Clinical Research
AFCRC	Air Force Cambridge Research Center
AFCS	Active Federal Commissioned Service (Military)
AFD	Air Force Depot
	Association of Food Distributors
AFDCB	Armed Forces Disciplinary Control Board
AFDCCO	Air Force Departmental Catalog Coordinating Office
AFDEA	American Funeral Directors and Embalmers Association
AFDO	Assistant Fighter Director Office (Navy)
AFDOUS	Association of Food and Drug Officials of the United States
AFEA	American Farm Economic Association
	American Film Export Association
AFEB	Armed Forces Epidemiological Board
AFES	Armed Forces Examining Station
AFF	Army Field Forces (OB- now U.S. Continental Army Command)
AFFA	Air Freight Forwarders Association
AFFD	Air Force Finance Division
AFFE	Army Forces Far East

ACRONYMS

AFFS - AFORD

AFFS	American Federation of Film Societies
AFFTC	Air Force Flight Test Center
AFGE	American Federation of Government Employees
AFGIS	Aerial Free Gunnery Instructions School (s) (Navy)
AFGM	American Federation of Grain Millers
AFGU	Aerial Free Gunnery Unit (Navy)
AFGWUNA	American Flint Glass Workers Union of North America
AFH	Air Force Hospital
	American Foundation for Homoeopathy
AFHA	Armed Forces Hostess Association
AFHF	American Foot Health Foundation
AFHQ	African Force Headquarters (OB)
	Allied Force Headquarters (OB)
AFHU	American Friends of Hebrew University
AFHW	American Federation of Hosiery Workers
AFI	Air Filter Institute
	Armed Forces Institute (Also known as USAFI)
AFIA	American Foreign Insurance Association
AFII	American Federation of International Institutes
AFIP	Air Forces Information Program
	Armed Forces Institute of Pathology
AFIR	Air Force Installations Representative
AFIRO	Air Force Installations Representative Officer
AFIS	Armed Forces Information School
AFIT	Air Force Institute of Technology (OB - now Institute of Technology)
AFJKT	Air Force Job Knowledge Test
AFL	Aeromedical Field Laborabory (Air Force)
	Air Force Letter
	American Federation of Labor
	Association for Family Living
AFLA	Amateur Fencers League of America
	American Foreign Law Association
AFL-CIO	American Federation of Labor and Congress of Industrial Organizations
AFM	Air Force Manual
	Air Force Museum
	American Federation of Musicians
AFMA	American Feed Manufacturers Association
	American Fur Merchants Association
	Armed Forces Management Association
AFMDC	Air Force Materiel Development Center
	Air Force Missile Development Center
AFME	American Friends of the Middle East
AFMED	Allied Forces, Mediterranean
AFMFP	Aircraft Fleet Marine Force Pacific
AFMH	American Foundation for Mental Hygiene
AFML	Armed Forces Medical Library
AFMS	Air Force Medical Service
	American Federation of Mineralogical Societies
AFMSC	Air Force Medical Specialist Corps
AFNORTH	Allied Forces, Northern Europe
AFO	Atlantic Fleet Organization
AFOAE	Air Force Office of Atomic Energy
AFOB	American Foundation for Overseas Blind
AFOQT	Air Force Officer Qualifying Test
AFORD	Air Force Overseas Replacement Depot (OB)

ACRONYMS

AFORG	Air Force Overseas Replacement Group (OB)
AFOSCR	Air Force Organization Status Change Report
AFOSR	Air Force Office of Scientific Research
AFOUAR	Air Force Outstanding Unit Award Ribbon
AFP	Air Force Pamphlet
	Associated Fantasy Publishers
AFPC	Air Force Procurement Circular
	Armed Forces Policy Council
AFPE	American Foundation for Pharmaceutical Education
	American Foundation for Political Education
AFPG	Air Force Personnel Processing Group
AFPH	American Federation of the Physically Handicapped
AFPI	Air Force Procurement Instructions
	American Forest Products Industries
AFPP	Air Force Procurement Procedures
AFPR	Air Force Plant Representative
AFPS	Armed Forces Press Service
AFPTRC	Air Force Personnel and Training Research Center
AFPU	Air Force Postal Unit
AFQT	Armed Forces Qualification Test
AFQTVA	Armed Forces Qualification Test, Verbal Arithmetic sub-test
AFR	Air Force Regulation
AFRA	American Farm Research Association
AFRB	Air Force Retiring Board
AFRBA	Armed Forces Relief and Benefit Association
AFRC	Air Force Records Center
AFRCTC	Air Force Reserve Combat Training Center
AFRES	Air Force Reserve
AFRESM	Armed Forces Reserve Medal
AFRO	Air Force Reserve Orders
AFROIC	Air Force Resident Officer-in-Charge
AFROTC	Air Force Reserve Officers Training Corps
AFRP	American Foundation of Religion and Psychiatry
AFRS	Armed Forces Radio Service
AFRSTC	Air Force Reserve Specialist Training Center
AFRTS	Armed Forces Radio and Television Service
AFS	Air Force Specialty
	Air Force Station
	American Feline Society
	American Fern Society
	American Field Service
	American Fisheries Society
	American Folklore Society
	American Foundrymen's Society
AFSA	American Flight Strips Association
	American Foreign Service Association
	Armed Forces Security Agency (OB)
AFSBO	American Federation of Small Business Organizations
AFSC	Air Force Service Command (OB)
	Air Force Specialty Code
	Air Force Supply Catalog
	American Federation of Soroptimist Clubs
	American Friends Service Committee
	Armed Forces Staff College
AFSCC	Air Force Special Communications Center

ACRONYMS

AFSCC	Armed Forces Supply Control Center
AFSCME	American Federation of State, County and Municipal Employees
AFSMAAG	Air Force Section, Military Assistance Advisory Group
AFSN	Air Force Serial Number
	Air Force Stock Number
AFSOUTH	Allied Forces, Southern Europe
AFSS	Air Force Service Statement
AFSU	Auxiliary Ferry Service Unit (Navy)
AFSUB	Army Air Forces Anti-Submarine Command (OB)
AFSWA	Assistant Secretary of War for Air (OB)
AFSWC	Air Force Special Weapons Center
AFSWP	Armed Forces Special Weapons Project (OB - see DASA)
AFT	Air Freight Terminal
	American Federation of Teachers
AFTC	American Fair Trade Council
AFTE	American Federation of Technical Engineers
AFTM	American Foundation for Tropical Medicine
AFTRA	American Federation of Television and Radio Artists
AFTRC	Air Force Training Command (OB)
AFU	American Fraternal Union
AFUS	Air Force of the United States (OB)
	Armed Forces of the United States
AFV	Armored Fighting Vehicle (Marine Corps)
	Armored Force Vehicle (Military)
AFVA	Air Force Visual Aid
AFWAR	Air Force personnel on duty with Army
AFWB	Air Force Welfare Board
AFWESPAC	Army Forces, Western Pacific (OB)
AFWL	Armed Forces Writers' League
AFWN	Air Force personnel on duty with Navy
AFWOFS	Air Force Weather Observing and Forecasting System
AFWST	Armed Forces Women's Selection Test
AG	Adjutant General (Military)
	Air-to-Ground (Air Force)
	Air Group (Military)
	Anti-Gas (Military)
	Armed Guard (Military)
	Arresting Gear and Barriers (Navy)
	Artists Guild
	Attorney General
AGA	Abrasive Grain Association
	American Gas Association
	American Gastroenterological Association
	American Gastroscopic Society
	American Genetic Association
	American Goiter Association
	Automatic Gain Control (Radar)
AGARD	Advisory Group for Aeronautical Research and Development (Military)
AGAS	Aviation Gasoline (Navy)
AGAUS	Adjutants General Association of United States
AGBA	American Galloway Breeders' Association
AGBAD	Alexander Graham Bell Association for the Deaf
AGBU	Armenian General Benevolent Union of America
AGC	Adjutant General's Corps (Army)
	American Grassland Council

ACRONYMS

AGC	Armed Guard Center (Military)
	Associated General Contractors of America
AGCC	American Guernsey Cattle Club
AGCO	Air-Ground Cooperation Officer (OB - Military)
AGCT	Army General Classification Test
AGCTS	Armed Guard Center Training School (Military)
AGD	Adjutant General's Department (Army)
AGDA	American Gasoline Dealers Association
AGE	Amarillo Grain Exchange
AGEP	Advisory Group on Electronic Parts (Military)
AG&ES	American Gas & Electric System
AGF	Army Ground Forces (OB)
AGFRTS	Air and Ground Forces Resources and Technical Staff (OB - Military)
AGGR	Air-to-Ground Gunnery Range (Air Force)
AGI	American Geographical Institute
AGIC	Air-Ground Information Center (Air Force)
AGIO	Armed Guard Inspection Officer (Military)
AGIS	Armed Guard Inspection Service (Military)
AGIT-PROP	Agitation and Propaganda (Military)
AGL	Airborne Gun Laying (Air Force)
AGLC	Air-Ground Liaison Code (Air Force)
AGLO	Air Ground Liaison Officer (Marine Corps)
AGLT	Airborne Gun Laying for Turrets (Air Force)
AGM	Air-to-Ground Missile
	American Guild of Music
AGMA	American Gear Manufacturers Association
	American Guild of Musical Artists
AGMSA	American Gem and Mineral Suppliers Association
AGN	Articles for the Government of the Navy
AGO	Adjutant General's Office (Army)
	Air Gunnery Officer (Military)
	American Guild of Organists
AGOS	Air-Ground Operations School (Air Force)
	Air-Ground Operations Section (Military)
	Air-Ground Operations System
	Aviation Gunnery Officers School (Navy)
AGP	Aircraft Grounded for lack of Parts (Military)
AGPA	American Group Psychotherapy Association
AGPI	Automatic Ground Position Indicator (Military)
AGRS	American Graves Registration Service (Military)
AGS	Airborne Gunsight (Air Force)
	Allied Geographic Section (OB)
	American Gem Society
	American Geographical Society
	American Geriatrics Society
	American Gloxinia Society
	American Goat Society
	American Gynecological Society
	Armed Guard School (Navy)
	Army General Staff
	Automatic Gain Stabilization (Military)
AGSM	American Gold Star Mothers
AGSPW	Association of Girl Scout Professional Workers
AGTA	Airline Ground Transportation Association
AGTOA	American Greyhound Track Operators Association

ACRONYMS

AGU	American Geophysical Union
AGVA	American Guild of Variety Artists
AGW	Allowable Gross (takeoff) Weight (Air Force)
AGWAR	Adjutant General, War Department (OB)
AH	Army Hospital
AHA	Adirondack Historical Association
	American Heart Association
	American Hereford Association
	American Historical Association
	American Hospital Association
	American Hotel Association
	American Humane Association
	American Hypnotherapy Association
AHAUS	Amateur Hockey Association of the U.S.
AHC	American Horticultural Council
	Appaloosa Horse Club
AHCA	American Hockey Coaches Association
AHCRA	Arabian Horse Club Registry of America
AHDGA	American Hot Dip Galvanizers Association
AHE	Association for Higher Education
AHEA	American Home Economics Association
AHF	American Heritage Foundation
	American Hobby Federation
	Associated Health Foundation
AHFI	Associated Health Foundation, Inc.
AHI	American Honey Institute
	Animal Health Institute
AHIL	Association of Hospital and Institutional Librarians
AHLA	American Home Lighting Institute
AHLMA	American Home Laundry Manufacturers Association
AHM	Appalachian Hardwood Manufacturers
AHMA	American Hardware Manufacturers Association
AHNA	Accredited Home Newspapers of America
AHP	Allied Hydrographic Publication
AHQ	Air Headquarters (OB)
	Army Headquarters
AHS	Agricultural History Society
	American Hearing Society
	American Helicopter Society
	American Horticultural Society
AHSA	American Hampshire Sheep Association
	American Horse Shows Association
AHSS	Association of Home Study Schools
AHST	Association of Highway Steel Transporters
AI	Airborne Intercept (Military)
	Air Inspector (Air Force)
	Air Installations (Air Force)
	Alteration and Improvement program (Military)
	Anti-Icing (Military)
	Aptitude Index
	Arctic Institute (Military)
	Astrologers International
AIA	Aerospace Industries Association
	Aircraft Industries Association of America
	American Institute of Accountants (NC - American Inst. of CPA)

ACRONYMS

AIA	American Institute of Actuaries (MW - Society of Actuaries)
	American Institute of Architects
	American Insurance Association
	American International Academy
	American International Association (for Economic and Social Development)
	Archaeological Institute of America
	Association of Industrial Advertisers
	Association of Insurance Attorneys
AIAA	American Industrial Arts Association
	Association of International Advertising Agencies
AIAE	Associate Institute of Automobile Engineers
AIAESD	American International Association for Economics and Social Development
AIB	American Institute of Baking
	American Institute of Banking
AIBA	American Industrial Bankers Association
	Association of International Border Agencies
AIBNRM	American Institute of Bolt, Nut and Rivet Manufacturers
AIBS	American Institute of Biological Sciences
AIC	Advanced Intelligence Center (Navy)
	Aircraft in Commission (Military)
	Allied Intelligence Committee, London (OB - Military)
	American Institute of Chemists
	American Institute of Cooperation
	Ammunition Identification Code
	Army Industrial College (OB)
AICA	American Institute of Commemorative Art
	American-International Charolais Association
AICBM	Anti-Intercontinental Ballistic Missile
AICCP	Association of Interstate Commerce Commission Practitioners
AICE	American Institute of Chemical Engineers
	American Institute of Consulting Engineers
AICF	America-Israel Cultural Foundation
AIChE	American Institute of Chemical Engineers
AICO	Action Information Control Officer (Navy)
AICPA	American Institute of Certified Public Accountants
AICPOA	Advanced Intelligence Center, Pacific Ocean Area (Navy)
AID	American Institute of Decorators
AIDC	American Industrial Development Council
AIEC	American Indian Ethnohistorical Conference
AIEE	American Institute of Electrical Engineers
AIER	American Institute of Economic Research
AIF	Air Intelligence Force (Navy)
	Atomic Industrial Forum
AIFD	American Institute of Food Distribution
AIFR	American Institute of Family Relations
AIFS	Advanced Instruction Flying School (Navy)
AIGA	American Institute of Graphic Arts
AIH	American Institute of Homeopathy
AIHA	American Industrial Hygiene Association
AIHP	American Institute of History of Pharmacy
AIHS	American Irish Historical Society
AIIE	American Institute of Industrial Engineers
AIL	American Institute of Laundering
	Art Institute of Light
	Aviation Instrument Laboratory (Navy)

ACRONYMS

AILC	Association of Life Insurance Counsel
AIM	American Institute of Management
AIMACO	Air Material Computer (Air Force)
AIMBW	American Institute of Men's and Boys' Wear
AIMMPE	American Institute of Mining, Metallurgical and Petroleum Engineers
AIMO	Audibly Instructed Manufacturing Operations (Military)
AIMU	American Institute of Marine Underwriters
AIN	American Institute of Nutrition
AINA	Arctic Institute of North America
AINL	Association of Immigration and Nationality Lawyers
AINO	Assistant Inspector of Naval Ordnance
AINTSEC	Air Intelligence Section (OB)
AIO	Action Information Organization
	Allied Interrogating Organization (OB)
AIOA	American Iron Ore Association
AIOW	Association of Independent Optical Wholesalers
AIP	American Institute of Parliamentarians
	American Institute of Physics
	American Institute of Planners
AIPD	Associated Industrial Photographic Dealers
AIPE	American Institute of Park Executives
	American Institute of Plant Engineers
AIPR	American Institute of Pacific Relations
	Association of International Publishers Representatives
AIR	American Institute of Refrigeration
AIRA	Air Attache (Air Force)
AIRAF	Aircraft, Asiatic Fleet (OB)
AIRARMUNIT	Aircraft, Armament Unit (Navy)
AIRASDEVLANT	Aircraft Anti-Submarine Development Detachment, Atlantic Fleet
AIRBASECOM	Air Base Commander (Military)
AIRBATFORPAC	Aircraft Battle Force, Pacific Fleet
AIRBM	Anti-Intermediate Range Ballistic Missile
AIRC	Association of International Relations Clubs
AIRCENT	Allied Air Forces, Central Europe
AIRDEFCOM	Air Defense Commander (Military)
AIREA	American Institute of Real Estate Appraisers
AIREIO	Air Electrical Officer (Navy)
AIRENGPROPACCOVERHAUL	Airplane Engine, Propellor and Accessory Overhaul (Navy)
AIREO	Air Engineer Officer (Navy)
AIREPDN	Aircraft Repair Division (Military)
AIREVACWING	Air Evacuation Wing (Military)
AIRFERONS	Naval Air Ferry Squadrons (OB)
AIRFMFPAC	Aircraft, Fleet Marine Force, Pacific
AIRFORWARD	Shore-Based Air Force, Forward Area, Central Pacific (OB - Navy)
AIRHC	Alaska International Rail and Highway Commission (Government Agency)
AIRIS	Air Store Issuing Ship (Navy)
AIRLANT	Air Forces, Atlantic Fleet
AIRLO	Air Liaison Officer (Military)
AIRMG	Aircraft, Machine Gunner (Navy)
AIRNORSOLS	Aircraft, Northern Solomons (OB - Navy)
AIRNORTH	Allied Air Forces, Northern Europe
AIROPS	Air Operations (Military)
AIRPAC	Air Forces, Pacific Fleet
AIRPAC (ADV)	Air Forces Pacific Advanced (OB - Navy)
AIRPAC (PEARL)	Air Forces Pacific, Pearl Harbor (OB - Navy)

ACRONYMS

```
AIRPACSUBCOMFORD . . Air Forces Subordinate Command, Forward Area (OB - Navy)
AIRSCOFORPAC . Aircraft Scouting Force, Pacific Fleet
AIRSOPAC . . . . . Aircraft, South Pacific Force (OB - Navy)
AIRSOUTH . . . . . Allied Air Forces, Southern Europe
AIRSOWESPAC . . Aircraft Southwest Pacific Force (OB - Navy)
AIRTRAINRON . . Air Training Squadron (Navy)
AIRTRANSRON . . Air Transport Squadron (OB - Navy)
AIRTRANSRONLANT . Air Transport Squadron, Atlantic (OB - Navy)
AIRTRANSRONPAC . . Air Transport Squadron, Pacific (OB - Navy)
AIRTRANSRONWESTCO . . Air Transport Squadron, West Coast (OB - Navy)
AIRXRS . . . . . . American Industrial Radium and X-Ray Society
AIS . . . . . . . . Air Intelligence Service (Military)
                    American Iris Society
                    Army Intelligence School (OB)
AISC . . . . . . . American Institute of Steel Construction
AISE . . . . . . . Association of Iron and Steel Engineers
AISI . . . . . . . American Iron and Steel Institute
                    America-Italy Society, Inc.
AISS . . . . . . . American Institute for Imported Steel
AIT . . . . . . . . Advanced Individual Training (Military)
                    Automatic Information Test (Military)
AITC . . . . . . . Action Information Training Center (Military)
AIW . . . . . . . . International Union, Allied Industrial Workers of America
AIWPHSA . . . . . American Institute of Wholesale Plumbing and Heating Supply Associations
A/J . . . . . . . . Anti-Jamming (radar)
AJ . . . . . . . . Associate Justice (U.S. Supreme Court)
AJA . . . . . . . . American Jewish Archives
AJC . . . . . . . . American Jewish Committee
                    American Jewish Congress
AJCC . . . . . . . American Jersey Cattle Club
AJHS . . . . . . . American Jewish Historical Society
AJLA . . . . . . . Association of the Junior Leagues of America
AJPC . . . . . . . American Jewish Periodical Center
                    American Jewish Physicians' Committee
AJRC . . . . . . . American Junior Red Cross
AJS . . . . . . . . American Judicature Society
AKA . . . . . . . . Also Known As
AKC . . . . . . . . American Kennel Club
AKF . . . . . . . . American-Korean Foundation
AKFM . . . . . . . Association of Knitted Fabrics Manufacturers
AL . . . . . . . . Allegheny Ludlum Steel Corp.
                    American League of Professional Baseball Clubs
                    American Legion
                    Astronomical League
ALA . . . . . . . . Amalgamated Lithographers of America
                    American Landrace Association
                    American Laryngological Association
                    American Legion Auxiliary
                    American Library Association
ALACP . . . . . . American League for Abolition of Capital Punishment
ALAMCABCO . . . All American Cable Company
ALBA . . . . . . . American Lawn Bowling Association
                    American Leather Belting Association
ALBM . . . . . . . Air-Launched Ballistic Missile (Military)
ALBUS . . . . . . All Bureaus (Navy)
```

ACRONYMS

ALC .... American Langshan Club
American Life Convention
ALCA .... American Leather Chemists Association
ALCEA .... Air Line Communication Employees Association
ALCO .... Airlift Liaison Coordination Officer (Military)
American Locomotive Company
ALCOA .... Aluminum Company of America
ALCOM ...... Alaska Command (Military)
A dispatch to All Commands in an area (Navy)
ALCORCEN .... Air Logistics Coordination Center (Military)
ALCU .... Altocumulus (Military)
ALD .... At a Later Date (Military)
ALDA .... Air Line Dispatchers Association
Allied Linens and Domestics Association
ALEAA .... American Lithuanian Engineers and Architects Association
ALES .... American Labor Education Service
ALG .... Advanced Landing Ground (Air Force)
ALGCU .... Association of Land Grant Colleges and Universities
ALGM .... Air-Launched Guided Missile (Military)
ALHA .... American Labor Health Association
ALI .... Agricultural Limestone Institute
American Ladder Institute
American Law Institute
Automotive Lift Institute
ALIC .... Association of Life Insurance Counsel
ALIMDA ...... Association of Life Insurance Medical Directors of America
ALITALIA ..... Italian International Airline (Aerolinee Italiane Internazionali)
ALL .... Augustana Luther League
ALM .... American Leprosy Missions
ALMA .... American Lace Manufacturers Association
ALNAV .... Communication directed to All Navy and Marine Corps activities
ALNAVSTA .... Letter to All Naval Stations
ALLNAVSTAS ... All Naval Stations
ALO .... Air Liaison Officer (Marine Corps)
Allied Liaison Office (OB)
American Liaison Office (OB)
ALOA .... Amalgamated Lace Operatives of America
Amalgamated Lithographers of America
Assembly of Librarians of the Americas
Associated Locksmiths of America
ALP .... Air Liaison Party (OB - Military)
Allied Logistic Publication (Military)
Ambulance Loading Post (Military)
American Labor Party
ALPA .... Air Line Pilots Association
ALPEC .... Ammunition Loading Production Engineering Center (Army)
ALPO .... Association of Lunar and Planetary Observers
ALR .... American Law Reports
ALROS .... American Laryngological, Rhinological and Otological Society
ALSA .... American Law Student Association
ALSEAFRON ... Alaskan Sea Frontier (Navy)
ALSEC .... Alaskan Sector (Navy)
ALST .... Alaska Standard Time
ALST .... Altostratus (Military)
ALSTACON .... Letter to All Stations, Continental United States (Navy)

- 33 -

ACRONYMS

ALTA — AME

ALTA	Airline Traffic Association
	Association of Local and Territorial Airlines
ALUSLO	U.S. Naval Liaison Officer
ALUSNA	U.S. Naval Attache
ALUSNOB	U.S. Naval Observer
A&M	Agricultural & Mechanical
AM	Amplitude Modulation
	Ante Meridian (Forenoon)
AMA	Academy of Model Aeronautics
	Acoustical Materials Association
	Aero Medical Association
	Air Materiel Area (Air Force)
	American Machinery Association
	American Management Association
	American Marketing Association
	American Medical Association
	American Ministerial Association
	American Monument Association
	American Motel Association
	American Motorcycle Association
	American Municipal Association
	American Mutual Alliance (Insurance association)
	Automobile Manufacturers Association
AMAA	Adhesives Manufacturers Association of America
	Armenian Missionary Association of America
	Army Mutual Aid Association
AMADA	Archery Manufacturers and Dealers Association
AMAFA	Air Mass and Frontal Analysis (weather)
AMAI	Arena Managers Association, Inc.
AMAS	American Military Assistance Staff
AMATC	Air Materiel Armament Test Center
AMB	Airways Modernization Board
AMBBA	Associated Master Barbers and Beauticians of America
AMC	Air Mail Center (Navy)
	Air Materiel Command (Air Force)
	Aircraft Manufacturers Council
	American Maritime Cases
	American Mining Congress
	American Mothers Committee
	American Motors Corp.
	American Music Conference
	Appalachian Mountain Club
	Army Medical Center
AMCA	Air Moving and Conditioning Association
	American Mosquito Control Association
	Associated Male Choruses of America
AMCBMC	Air Materiel Command Ballistic Missile Center (Air Force)
AMC&BW	Amalgamated Meat Cutters and Butcher Workmen
AMCBWNA	Amalgamated Meat Cutters and Butcher Workmen of North America
AMCON	American Consul
AMCONREPO . .	American Consular Reporting Officer
AMCS	Association of Military Colleges and Schools
AMD	Air Movement Designator (Military)
AMDA	Airlines Medical Directors Association
AME	African Methodist Episcopal

- 34 -

ACRONYMS

AME . . . . Aviation Medical Examiner (Military)
AMEDS . . . . Army Medical Service
AMER . . . . American Middle East Relief
AMERIND . . . . . American Indian
AMEROSE . . . . . American Committee of OSE
AMF . . . . Air Materiel Force (Air Force)
                  American Machine and Foundry Company
AMFA . . . . Association Medicale Franco-Americaine
AMFEUR . . . . . . Air Materiel Force, Europe
AMFIE . . . . Association of Mutual Fire Insurance Engineers
AMG . . . . Aircraft Machine Gunner (Navy)
                  Allied Military Government
                  Automatic Magnetic Guidance
AMGOT . . . . . . Allied Military Government (OB)
AMGRA . . . . . . American Milk Goat Record Association
AMHA . . . . American Motor Hotel Association
AMHS . . . . American Material Handling Society
AMI . . . . American Meat Institute
                  American Military Institution
                  Association of Medical Illustrators
AMIA . . . . American Mutual Insurance Alliance
AMICO . . . . American Measuring Instrument Company
AMIND . . . . American Indian
AML . . . . Aeromedical Laboratory
                  Aeronautical Materials Laboratory (Navy)
                  Allied Military Liaison (OB)
                  American Mail Line
AMM . . . . Anti-Missile Missile
AMMI . . . . American Merchant Marine Institute
AMMLA . . . . . . American Merchant Marine Library Association
AMMO . . . . Ammunition
AMMTR . . . . . . Antimissile Missile Test Range (Military)
AMNH . . . . American Museum of Natural History
AMO . . . . Aircraft Material Officer (Navy)
AMOCO . . . . . . American Oil Company
AMORC . . . . . . Ancient Mystical Order Rosae Crucis (Rosicrucian Order)
AMOS . . . . Ancient Mystic Order of Samaritans
AMP . . . . Air Mail Pioneers
AMPA . . . . American Manganese Producers Association
                  American Manganese Producers Association
                  Associated Motion Picture Advertisers
                  Association of Motion Picture Advertisers
AMPAS . . . . Academy of Motion Picture Arts and Sciences
AMPHFORLANT . Amphibious Force, Atlantic (Navy)
AMPHFORMED . . Amphibious Force, Mediterranean (Navy)
AMPHFORPAC . . Amphibious Force, Pacific (Navy)
AMPHIBFOR . . . . Amphibious Forces (Navy)
AMPHIBFORCENPAC . . Amphibious Forces, Central Pacific (Navy)
AMPP . . . . Association of Motion Picture Producers
AMPS . . . . Army Mine Planter Service
AMR . . . . Airman Military Record (Air Force)
                  Atlantic Missile Range
AMRA . . . . American Metal Repair Association
AMRI . . . . Association of Missile and Rocket Industries
AMRL . . . . Army Medical Research Laboratory

ACRONYMS

AMS	Agricultural Marketing Service
	American Mathematical Society
	American Meteor Society
	American Meteorological Society
	American Microscopical Society
	American Museum of Safety
	American Musicological Society
	Army Map Service
	Association of Messenger Services
AMSA	Adhesives Manufacturers Association of America
AMSAM	Anti-Missile Surface-to-Air Missile
AMSC	Allied Military Staff Conference (OB)
	Army Medical Specialist Corps
AMSCO	Army Medical Supply Control Officer
AMSGS	Army Medical Service Graduate School
AMSI	Atlantic Merchant Shipping Instructions
AMSO	Ammunition Shipment Order (Military)
AMSOC	American Miscellaneous Society
AMSS	American Milking Shorthorn Society
	Army Medical Service School
AMSTAN	American Radiator and Standard Sanitary Corp.
AMSUS	Association of Military Surgeons of the United States
AMT	American Medical Technologists
AMTANK	Amphibious Tank (Military)
AMTDA	American Machine Tool Distributors Association
AMTEA Corp.	American Machine Tool Export Associates
AMTI	Airborne Moving Target Indicator (Military)
AMTRAC	Amphibious Tractor (Military)
AMU	American Malacological Union
	Atomic Mass Unit
AMUUS	Association of Marine Underwriters of the U.S.
AMVETS	American Veterans of World War II and Korea
AMWA	American Medical Women's Association
	American Medical Writers' Association
AN	Army-Navy
ANA	American Nature Association
	American Neurological Association
	American Numismatic Association
	American Nurses Association
	Association of National Advertisers
ANADP	Association of North American Directory Publishers
ANC	Arlington National Cemetery
	Army Nurse Corps
ANCA	American National Cattlemen's Association
	Armenian National Council of America
ANCAM	Association of Newspaper Classified Advertising Managers
ANCR	Aircraft Not Combat Ready (Military)
ANCXF	Allied Naval Commander Expeditionary Forces (OB)
ANDB	Air Navigation Development Board
ANDUS	Anglo-Dutch-United States (OB - World War II)
ANEEG	Army, Navy, Electronics Evaluation Group
ANF	American Nurses' Foundation
ANFE	Aircraft Not Fully Equipped (Military)
ANG	Air National Guard
	American Newspaper Guild

ACRONYMS

ANGAU . . . . . . Australia-New Guinea Administrative Unit (OB - World War II)
ANGUS . . . . . . Air National Guard of the United States
ANHA . . . . American Nursing Home Association
ANHS. . . . . American Natural Hygiene Society
ANJSB . . . . Army-Navy Joint Specifications Board (OB)
ANMB . . . . Army-Navy Munitions Board (OB)
ANMC . . . . Assistant Navy Mail Clerk
ANO . . . . Above Named Officer (Military)
ANPA. . . . . American Newspaper Publishers Association
ANPB . . . . Army-Navy Petroleum Board (OB)
ANPD. . . . . Aircraft Nuclear Propulsion Department (Navy)
ANPP. . . . . Association of Negro Press Photographers
ANPPPC . . . . . . Army-Navy Petroleum Pool, Pacific Coast (OB)
ANRAC. . . . . . . Aids Navigation Radio Control (Military)
ANRC. . . . . American National Red Cross
ANS. . . . . American Name Society
                 American Nuclear Society
                 American Numismatic Society
ANSCOL. . . . . . Army-Navy Staff College (OB)
ANSIA . . . . Army-Navy Shipping Information Agency (OB)
ANSO . . . . Assistant Naval Stores Officer
ANSS . . . . American Nature Study Society
ANTA. . . . . American National Theatre and Academy
ANTS . . . . Advanced Naval Training School
ANTU. . . . . Air Navigation Training Unit (Navy)
ANU . . . . Army and Navy Union
ANWC . . . . American Newspaper Women's Club
ANZAC . . . . . . Australia-New Zealand Army Corps
ANZUS. . . . . . . Australia-New Zealand-United States Treaty (OB - now part of SEATO)
AO . . . . Administration Office (Military)
                 Airdrome Officer (Air Force)
                 American Optical Company
AOA . . . . American Optometric Association
                 American Ordnance Association
                 American Orthopaedic Association
                 American Osteopathic Association
AOAC . . . . Association of Official Agricultural Chemists
AOAO . . . . American Osteopathic Academy of Orthopedics
AOB. . . . . Advanced Operational Base (Military)
AOC . . . . Air Officer Commanding (Marine Corps)
                 Airport Operators Council
                 Aviation Officer Candidate (Navy)
AOCA . . . . American Osteopathic College of Anesthesiologists
AOCM . . . . Aircraft Out of Commission for Maintenance (Military)
AOCP. . . . . Aircraft Out of Commission for Parts (Military)
AOCPR . . . . American Osteopathic College of Proctology
AOCR. . . . . American Osteopathic College of Radiology
AOCS. . . . . American Oil Chemists' Society
AODRA. . . . . . . American Oxford Down Record Association
AOF. . . . . Ancient Order of Foresters
AOH . . . . Ancient Order of Hibernians in America
AOHA . . . . American Osteopathic Hospital Association
AOIL . . . . Aviation Oil (Navy)
AOL. . . . . Absent-Over-Leave (Navy)
AOM . . . . Army of Occupation Medal

ACRONYMS

```
AOM  . . . . . . . . Association of Operative Millers
AOMP . . . . . . . Artisans Order of Mutual Protection
AOND . . . . . . . Administrative Office, Navy Department
AOO  . . . . . . . . Aviation Ordnance Officer (Navy)
AOPA . . . . . . . Aircraft Owners and Pilots Association
AOQ  . . . . . . . . Aviation Officers' Quarters (Navy)
AOR  . . . . . . . . Air Operations Room (Navy)
AOS  . . . . . . . . American Ophthalmological Society
                     American Orchid Society
                     American Oriental Society
                     American Otological Society
AOSA . . . . . . . Association of Official Seed Analysts
AOSC . . . . . . . Association of Oilwell Servicing Contractors
AOSEA. . . . . . . American Office Supply Exporters Association
AOSPS. . . . . . . American Otorhinologic Society for Plastic Surgery
AOTA . . . . . . . American Occupational Therapy Association
AOTC . . . . . . . Aviation Officers Training Corps (Navy)
AOTE . . . . . . . Amphibious Operational Training Element (Navy)
AOU  . . . . . . . . American Ornithologists' Union
AP   . . . . . . . . . Aerial Port
                     Aiming Point (Military)
                     Air Police (Air Force)
                     Airport
                     Air Position (Military)
                     Air Publication (Military)
                     Armor Piercing (Military)
                     Associated Press
                     Atlantic and Pacific Tea Company
                     Atomic Powered
                     Aviapolk (Russian - air regiment)
                     Aviation Pilot (Navy)
APA  . . . . . . . . Agricultural Publishers Association
                     American Pharmaceutical Association
                     American Philological Association
                     American Photoengravers Association
                     American Podiatry Association
                     American Poultry Association
                     American Protestant Association
                     American Psychiatric Association
                     American Psychoanalytic Association
                     American Psychological Association
                     American Psychotherapy Association
                     American Pulpwood Association
                     Appropriation Purchases Account
                     Association of Port Authorities
                     Association for the Protection of the Adirondacks
APAC . . . . . . . Air Pollution Control Association
APART. . . . . . . Alliance of Pan American Round Tables
APB  . . . . . . . . All Points Bulletin (Police call)
APBA . . . . . . . American Power Boat Association
APBE . . . . . . . Association for Professional Broadcasting Education
APC  . . . . . . . . Aeronautical Planning Chart (Military)
                     American Parents Committee
                     American Power Conference
                     Armor-Piercing Capped (Military)
```

ACRONYMS

APC . . . . Armored Personnel Carrier (Military)
              Aspirin "all purpose capsules"
              Associated Pimiento Canners
APCA . . . . Air Pollution Control Association
              American Planning and Civic Association
APCCLA . . . . . . Aviation Petroleum Coordinating Committee, Latin America (OB)
APCI . . . . Association of Pulp Consumers, Inc.
APCM . . . . Asiatic-Pacific Campaign Medal
APCO . . . . Associated Police Communications Officers
APCS . . . . Air Photographic and Charting Service (Air Force)
APD . . . . Air Procurement District (Air Force)
APEL . . . . Aeronautical Photographic Experimental Laboratory (Navy)
APERS . . . . Antipersonnel (bomb or mine)
APF . . . . American Progress Foundation
              Association of Pacific Fisheries
APG . . . . Aberdeen Proving Ground (Army)
              Air Proving Ground (Air Force)
              Army Planning Group
APGA . . . . American Personnel and Guidance Association
APGG . . . . Air Proving Ground Center (Air Force)
APH . . . . American Printing House for the Blind
APHA . . . . American Polled Hereford Association
              American Protestant Hospital Association
              American Public Health Association
APHF . . . . American Poultry and Hatchery Federation
APHS . . . . American Poultry Historical Society
API . . . . Air Position Indicator (Military)
              American Petroleum Institute
              American Potash Institute
              Americans for Progressive Israel
              Archconfraternity of Prayer for the Conversion of Israel
              Armor-Piercing Incendiary (Military)
APIC . . . . Army Photointerpretation Center
              Army Planning Group
APICS . . . . American Production and Inventory Control Society
APID . . . . Army Photo Interpretation Detachment
APIT . . . . Armor-Piercing Incendiary Tracer (Military)
APJA . . . . Appliance Parts Jobbers Association
APLA . . . . American Patent Law Association
              Aviation Pilot, Airship (Navy)
APM . . . . Air Provost Marshal (Air Force)
              Assistant Paymaster (Marine Corps)
APMA . . . . Absorbent Paper Manufacturers Association
              Advance Payment of Mileage Authorized (Military)
              Automatic Phonograph Manufacturers Association   /(Military)
APMALTA . . . . . Advance Payment of Monetary Allowance in Lieu of Trans. Authorized
APMI . . . . American Power Metallurgy Institute
APMR . . . . Association for Physical and Mental Rehabilitation
APO . . . . Area Petroleum Office (r) (Military)
              Army Post Office
APOD . . . . Aerial Port of Debarkation (Air Force)
APOPA . . . . Association of Private Office Personnel Agencies
APOTA . . . . Automatic Positioning of Telemetering Antenna
APP . . . . Army Procurement Procedure
APPA . . . . American Paper and Pulp Association

APPA	American Psychopathological Association
	American Public Power Association
APPAC	Aviation Petroleum Products Allocation Committee (OB)
APPACL	Aviation Petroleum Products Allocation Committee, London (OB)
APPM	Association of Publication Production Managers
APPMSA	American Pulp and Paper Mill Superintendents Association
APPR	Army Package Power Reactor
APR	Air Pictorial Service (NC - Air Photographic and Charting Service)
	Association of Publishers Representatives
APRA	Aircraft Production Resources Agency
	American Public Relations Association
	Automotive Parts Rebuilders Association
APRCAS	All Purpose Rocket for Collecting Atmospheric Soundings (Navy)
APRI	Air Priority (Military)
APRL	Army Prosthetics Research Laboratory
APRO	Aerial Phenomena Research Organization
APRS	American Performing-Rights Society
APS	Academy of Political Science
	American Peace Society
	American Pediatric Society
	American Peony Society
	American Philatelic Society
	American Philosophical Society
	American Physical Society
	American Physiological Society
	American Phytopathological Society
	American Polar Society
	American Proctologic Society
	American Psychosomatic Society
	Army Postal Service
APSA	American Political Science Association
AP&SC	Army Port and Service Command
APSQ	Advance Payment of Subsistence and Quarters (Military)
APSS	Associated Public School Systems
APT	Airman Proficiency Test (Air Force)
	Armor-Piercing Tracer (Military)
APTA	American Physical Therapy Association
APTPDA	Advance Payment of Travel Per Diem Authorized (Military)
APTW	Asiatic-Pacific Theater of War
APU	Army Postal Unit
APUC	Area Production Urgency Committee (OB)
APWA	American Public Welfare Association
	American Public Works Association
APWI	Air Prisoner of War Interrogation (Air Force)
AQE	Airman Qualifying Examination (Air Force)
AR	Amphibian Reconnaissance (Military)
	Army
	Army Regulations
	Army Reserve
	Assembly and Repair (Navy)
ARA	American Radio Association
	Artists' Representatives Association
	American Rheumatism Association
ARAE	American Retail Association Executives
ARAMCO	Arabian-American Oil Company

ACRONYMS

ARBA – ARO

ARBA	American Rabbit Breeders Association
	American Road Builders Association
ARBBA	American Railway Bridge and Building Association
ARC	Agricultural Relations Council
	Agricultural Research Center (Agriculture Department)
	Air Reserve Center
	American National Red Cross
	American Red Cross (See American National Red Cross)
	American Rehabilitation Committee
	Ames Research Center (National Aeronautics and Space Administration)
ARCB	Association of Reserve City Bankers
ARCI	Aid Refugee Chinese Intellectuals
	American Railway Car Institute
ARCO	Aircraft Resources Control Office (Navy)
ARCS	Air Resupply and Communication Service (OB - Air Force)
ARCT	Army Radio Code Aptitude Test
ARCUS	Associated Retail Confectioners of the U.S.
ARD	Air Reserve District (Air Force)
	Association of Research Directors
ARDA	American Railway Development Association
ARDC	Air Research and Development Command (Air Force)
	American Racing Drivers Club
AREA	American Railway Engineering Association
	Association of Records Executives and Administrators
AREFS	Air Refueling Squadron (Air Force)
ARF	Advertising Research Foundation
	American Rehabilitation Foundation
	American Retail Federation
	American Rose Foundation
	Armour Research Foundation
	Arthritis and Rheumatism Foundation
ARFC	Air Reserve Flying Center (Air Force)
ARFCW	Athletic and Recreation Federation of College Women
ARGCA	American Rice Growers Cooperative Association
ARGMA	Army Rocket and Guided Missile Agency
ARI	Agricultural Research Institute
	Air Conditioning and Refrigeration Institute
	American Rayon Institute
ARIA	Adult Reading Improvement Association
ARIB	Asphalt Roofing Industry Bureau
ARKLA	Arkansas Louisiana Gas Company
ARL	Association of Research Libraries
ARLNO	Army Liaision Officer
ARMA	Army Attache
ARMEA	American Railway Magazine Editors Association
ARMH	Academy of Religion and Mental Health
ARMI	American Rack Merchandisers Institute
ARMISH	U.S. Military Mission with the Iranian Army
ARMMA	American Railway Master Mechanics' Association
ARNA	Army with Navy
	Association of Radio-Television News Analysts
ARNG	Army National Guard
ARNMD	Association for Research in Nervous and Mental Disease
ARO	Airborne Range Only (Military)
	Air Radio Officer (Navy)

ARO	Association for Research in Ophthalmology
AROU	Aviation Repair and Overhaul Unit (Navy)
ARP	Air Raid Precautions
ARPA	Advanced Research Projects Agency (Military)
ARPC	Annual Report Producers Council
ARPU	American Racing Pigeon Union
ARR	Air Regional Representative (Air Force)
ARRC	Air Reserve Records Center (Air Force)
ARRL	Aeronautical Radio and Radar Laboratory (Navy)
	American Radio Relay League
ARRS	American Roentgen Ray Society
ARRUS	Arrived Within Continental Limits of US (Navy)
ARS	Agricultural Research Service
	Air Regulating Squadron (Navy)
	Air Rescue Service (Air Force)
	American Radium Society
	American Recreation Society
	American Repair Service
	American Rocket Society
	American Rose Society
	Army Relief Society
ARSA	Allied Railway Supply Association
ARSBA	American Rambouillet Sheep Breeders Association
ARSD	Aviation Repair Supply Depot (Navy)
ARSTS	Air Reserve Specialist Training Squadron (Air Force)
ART	Arithmetic Reading Test (Military)
ARTCC	Air Route Traffic Control Center
ARTL	Awaiting Result of Trial (Military)
ARTP	Air Reserve Technician Program (Air Force)
ARTU	Automatic Range Tracking Unit (Military)
ARTY	Artillery (Army)
ARU	Air Reserve Unit (Air Force)
	American Railway Union
ARUG	Air Reserve Unit General Training (Air Force)
ARUSNP	Air Reserve Unit General Training Nonpay (Air Force)
ARUSP	Air Reserve Unit General Training Pay (Air Force)
ARVIDA	Arthur Vining Davis Corporation
ARVSG	Air Reserve Volunteer Support Group
ARW	Air-Conditioning and Refrigeration Wholesalers
	Air-Raid Warning
ARWA	American Right of Way Association
ARWC	Army War College
AS	Air Service (OB)
	Air Staff (Air Force)
	Air Station (Military)
	Antisubmarine (Military)
	Aviaeskadra (Russian - air squadron)
ASA	Acoustical Society of America
	Actuarial Society of America (MW - Society of Actuaries)
	Amateur Softball Association of America
	American Sightseeing Association
	American Society for Abrasives
	American Society for Aesthetics
	American Society of Agronomy
	American Society of Anesthesiologists

ACRONYMS

ASA	American Soybean Association
	American Standards Association
	American Statistical Association
	American Stockyards Association
	American Studies Association
	American Sunbathing Association
	American Surgical Association
	Anthroposophical Society in America
	Army Security Agency
	Assistant Secretary of the Army
	Associated Stenotypists of America
	Atomic Security Agency (Army)
	Aviation Supply Annex (Navy)
ASAC	Air Service Area Command (OB)
	American Society of Arms Collectors
ASACMA	Assistant Secretary of the Army Civil and Military Affairs
ASAE	American Society of Agricultural Engineers
	American Society of Association Executives
ASofAF	Assistant Secretary of the Air Force
ASAFM	Assistant Secretary of the Army Financial Management
ASAGAD	American Society for Advancement of General Anesthesia in Dentistry
ASAHC	American Society of Architectural Hardware Consultants
ASALOG	Assistant Secretary of the Army Logistics
ASAMPE	Allied States Association of Motion Picture Exhibitors
ASAP	American Society of Animal Production
	Anti-Submarine Attack Plotter (Navy)
	As Soon As Possible (Military)
ASAS	Army Security Agency School
ASATTU	Anti-Submarine Attack Teacher Training Unit (Navy)
ASBA	American Shorthorn Breeders Association
	American Southdown Breeders' Association
	Association of Ship Brokers and Agents
ASBC	American Society Biological Chemists
	American Society of Brewing Chemists
ASBCA	Armed Services Board of Contract Appeals
ASBE	American Society of Bakery Engineers
	American Society of Body Engineers
ASBO	Association of School Business Officials of the U.S.
ASBPA	American Shore and Beach Preservation Association
ASC	Aeronautical Systems Center (Air Force)
	Air Service Command (OB - Air Force)
	Air Support Control (Navy)
	American Silk Council
	American Society of Cinematographers
	American Society of Criminology
	Associated Sandblasting Contractors
ASCA	American School Counselor Association
	American Standard Chinchilla Association
ASCAP	American Society of Composers, Authors and Publishers
ASCCA	Automobile Seat Cover Association of America
ASCD	Association for Supervision and Curriculum Development
ASCE	American Society of Civil Engineers
ASCH	American Society of Church History
ASCI	American Society for Clinical Investigation
ASCL	American Sugar Cane League of the USA

ACRONYMS

ASCLU	American Society of Chartered Life Underwriters
ASCM	Association of Sprocket Chain Manufacturers
ASCO	Association of Schools and Colleges of Optometry
ASCP	American Society of Clinical Pathologists
ASCR	American Society of Chiropodical Roentgenology
ASCS	American Society of Corporate Secretaries
ASCU	Air Support Control Units (Navy)
ASD	Artillery Spotting Division (Military)
	Association of Steel Distributors
	Aviation Supply Depot
ASDA	American Seafood Distributors Association
	American Stamp Dealers' Association
ASDC	American Society of Dentistry for Children
ASDE	Airport Surface Detection Equipment (Military)
	American Society of Danish Engineers
ASDEVLANT	Anti-Submarine Development Detachment, Atlantic Fleet
ASDIC	Allied Submarine Devices Investigation Committee (World War I)
ASDJ	American Society of Disk Jockeys
ASE	Airborne Search Equipment (Military)
	Aircraft Stores Establishment (Navy)
	All-Steel Equipment, Inc.
	American Stock Exchange
ASEA	American Society of Engineers and Architects
ASEBS	Association of Senior Engineers of the Bureau of Ships
ASEE	American Society for Engineering Education
ASEF	Association of Stock Exchange Firms
ASEP	American Society for Experimental Pathology
ASESA	Armed Services Electro-Standards Agency
ASESB	Armed Services Explosives Safety Board
ASETC	Armed Services Electron Tube Committee
ASF	Alaskan Sea Frontier (Navy)
	American-Scandinavian Foundation
	Army Service Forces (OB)
	Association of State Foresters
	Automotive Safety Foundation
ASFA	American Steel Foundrymen's Association
ASFDO	Anti-Submarine Fixed Defenses Officer (Navy)
ASFMRA	American Society of Farm Managers and Rural Appraisers
ASFS	American Seamen's Friend Society
ASFSA	American School Food Service Association
ASFTRNTRARONPAC	Auxiliary Service Force, Transition Training Squadron, Pacific (Navy)
ASG	Aeronautical Standards Group (Military)
	Air Service Group (OB - Air Force)
ASGA	Advertising Specialty Guild of America
ASGS	Assistant Secretary of the General Staff (Army)
ASHA	American School Health Association
	American Social Hygiene Association
	American Speech and Hearing Association
ASHAE	American Society of Heating and Air Conditioning Engineers
ASHBA	American Saddle Horse Breeders Association
ASHF	American Swedish Historical Foundation
ASHG	American Society of Human Genetics
ASHP	American Society of Hospital Pharmacists
ASHPS	American Scenic and Historic Preservation Society
ASHRAE	American Society of Heating, Refrigerating and Air-Conditioning Engineers

- 44 -

ACRONYMS

ASHS	American Society for Horticultural Science
ASI	American Specification Institute
	American Swedish Institute
ASIA	American Society of Industrial Auctioneers
	American Stone Importers Association
ASID	American Society of Industrial Designers
ASIH	American Society of Ichthyologists and Herpetologists
ASIL	American Society of International Law
ASIM	American Society of Insurance Management
ASIS	American Society for Industrial Security
ASJA	Assistant Staff Judge Advocate (Air Force)
ASJSA	American Society of Journalism School Administrators
ASLA	American Society of Landscape Architects
ASLI	American Savings and Loan Institute
ASLO	American Society of Limnology and Oceanography
ASLRA	American Short Line Railroad Association
ASM	Air-To-Surface Missile
	American Society of Mammalogists
	American Society for Metals
ASMA	American Ski Manufacturers' Association
	American Society of Music Arrangers
ASME	American Society of Mechanical Engineers
ASMMA	American Supply and Machinery Manufacturers Association
ASMP	American Society of Magazine Photographers
ASMPA	Armed Services Medical Procurement Agency
ASMPE	American Society of Motion Picture Engineers
ASMRO	Armed Services Medical Regulating Office
ASMT	American Society of Medical Technologists
ASN	American Society of Naturalists
	Army Serial Number
ASNA	Advertising Specialty National Association
ASNE	American Society of Naval Engineers
	American Society of Newspaper Editors
ASNLH	Association for the Study of Negro Life and History
ASO	Air Signal Officer (Navy)
	Assistant Secretary's Office (Navy)
ASOA	Avicultural Society of America
ASOL	American Symphony Orchestra League
ASOP	Aviation Supply Office Philadelphia (Navy)
ASOR	American Schools of Oriental Research
ASOS	American Society of Oral Surgeons
	American Sociological Society
	Assistant Supervisor of Shipbuilding (Navy)
ASP	American Society of Parasitologists
	American Society of Photogrammetry
	Ammunition Supply Point (Military)
	Anti-Submarine Patrol (Military)
ASPA	American Society for Personnel Administration
	American Society for Public Administration
ASPB	American Society of Professional Biologists
	Armed Services Petroleum Board
ASPC	American Sheep Producers Council
	American Shetland Pony Club
ASPCA	American Society for Prevention of Cruelty to Animals
ASPDA	Association of State Planning and Development Agencies

ASPET - ASTIA ACRONYMS

ASPET . . . . American Society for Pharmacology and Experimental Therapeutics
ASPH . . . . Association of Schools of Public Health
ASPO . . . . American Society of Planning Officials
ASPP . . . . American Society of Polar Philatelists
ASPPA . . . . Armed Services Petroleum Purchasing Agency
ASPPR. . . . . Association of Sugar Producers of Puerto Rico
ASPR . . . . American Society for Psychical Research
             Armed Services Procurement Regulation
ASPRS. . . . . American Society of Plastic and Reconstructive Surgery
ASPSPOM . . . . . American Society for the Preservation of Sacred, Patriotic & Operatic Music
ASQC. . . . . American Society for Quality Control
ASQDE. . . . . . . American Society of Questioned Document Examiners
ASR . . . . Airport Surveillance Radar (Military)
             Air-Sea Rescue (Military)
             American Society of Rocketry
             Association of Southeastern Railroads
             Available Supply Rate (Military)
ASRA . . . . American Shropshire Registry Association
ASRBA . . . . American Satin Rabbit Breeders Association
ASRDL . . . . Army Signal Research and Development Laboratory
ASRE . . . . American Society of Refrigerating Engineers
ASREC . . . . American Society of Real Estate Counselors
ASRI. . . . . Aluminum Smelters Research Institute
ASRM . . . . American Society of Range Management
ASROC . . . . Anti-Submarine Rocket (assisted missile)
ASRS . . . . Anglo-Soviet Recognition Signals (OB)
ASSA . . . . American Society for the Study of Arteriosclerosis
ASSBT. . . . . American Society of Sugar Beet Technologists
ASSCI. . . . . American Section of the Societe de Chimie Industrielle
ASSE . . . . American Society of Safety Engineers
             American Society of Sanitary Engineering
ASSERON . . . . . Army Service Squadron (OB)
ASSH . . . . American Society for Surgery of the Hand
AS&SL . . . . All Ships and Stations Letter (Navy)
ASSRON . . . . . . Air Service Support Squadron (OB)
ASSS . . . . American Society for the Study of Sterility
             American Suffolk Sheep Society
ASST . . . . American Society for Steel Treating
ASSU . . . . American Sunday School Union
AST . . . . Association for Student Teaching
ASTA . . . . American Seed Trade Association
             American Society of Travel Agents
             American Spice Trade Association
             American String Teachers Association
             American Surgical Trade Association
ASTD . . . . American Society of Training Directors
ASTDLHS. . . . . . Association of State and Territorial Directors of Local Health Services
ASTE . . . . American Society of Tool Engineers
ASTEC . . . . Antisubmarine Technical Evaluation Center (Military)
ASTHO . . . . Association of State and Territorial Health Officers
ASTM . . . . American Society for Testing Materials
ASTMH . . . . American Society of Tropical Medicine and Hygiene
ASTND . . . . Association of State and Territorial Nutrition Directors
ASTHO . . . . Association of State and Territorial Health Officers
ASTIA. . . . . Armed Services Technical Information Agency

- 46 -

ACRONYMS

ASTM	American Society of Testing Materials
ASTMH	American Society of Tropical Medicine and Hygiene
ASTP	Army Specialized Training Program
ASTRP	Army Specialized Training Reserve Program
ASTSECNAV	Assistant Secretary of the Navy
ASTSECNAVAIR	Assistant Secretary of the Navy for Air
ASofTT	American Society of Traffic and Transportation
ASTU	Air Support Training Units (Navy)
	Army Specialized Training Unit
ASU	Aircraft Scheduling Unit
	American Snowshoe Union
ASUUS	Amateur Skating Union of US
ASV	Airborne Radar for detecting Surface Vessels (Navy)
	Angle Stop Valve
ASW	Anti-Submarine Warfare (Military)
	Assistant Secretary of War (OB)
ASWA	American Society of Women Accountants
	American Steel Warehouse Association
ASWO	Air Stations Weekly Orders (Navy)
ASWORG	Anti-Submarine Warfare Operations Research Group (Navy)
ASWTC	Anti-Submarine Warfare Training Center (Navy)
ASWTRACEN	Anti-Submarine Warfare Training Center (Navy)
ASWTU	Anti-Submarine Warfare Training Unit (Navy)
ASWU	Anti-Submarine Warfare Unit (Navy)
ASXT	American Society of X-Ray Technicians
ASYA	American Stock Yards Association
ASYMCA	Association of Secretaries Young Men's Christian Associations
ASZ	American Society of Zoologists
AT	Advanced Trainer (OB - Air Force)
	Antitank (Military)
ATA	Advertising Typographers Association of America
	Air Transport Association
	Amateur Trapshooting Association
	American Taxicab Association
	American Teachers Association
	American Title Association
	American Topical Association
	American Transit Association
	American Tree Association
	American Trucking Associations
	American Tunaboat Association
	Army Transportation Association
	Association for Academic Travel Abroad
ATAA	Air Transport Association of America
ATABW	American Trade Association for British Woolens
ATAD	Absent on Temporary Additional Duty (Navy)
	Air Technical Analysis Division (Navy)
ATAE	American Trade Association Executives (now ASAE)
ATAF	Allied Tactical Air Force
ATAM	Automotive Trade Association Managers (Association)
ATAR	Antitank Aircraft Rocket (Military)
ATAS	Academy of Television Arts and Sciences
	Association of Telephone Answering Services
ATB	Amphibious Training Base (Navy)
ATC	Air Traffic Control (Military)

ACRONYMS

ATC	Air Training Command (Air Force)
	Air Transport Command (MW - Military Air Transport Service)
	Airport Traffic Control
	Army Training Center
ATCA	Associated Traffic Clubs of America
ATCC	Atlantic Division, Transport Control Center (Military)
	Atlantic Transportation Terminal Command (Army)
ATCCL	Allied Tanker Coordinating Committee in London (OB - shipping)
ATCCW	Allied Tanker Coordinating Committee in Washington (OB - shipping)
ATCLO	Amphibious Training Command Liaison Officer (Navy)
ATCMU	Associated Third Class Mail Users
ATCO	Air Traffic Coordinating Officer (Military)
ATCOM	Atoll Commander (Military)
ATCOR	Air Traffic Coordinator (Military)
ATCOREU	Air Traffic Coordinator Europe (Military)
ATCORUS	Air Transport Coordinator for the United States (Military)
ATCS	Air Traffic Communication Stations (Military)
ATD	Actual Time of Departure
ATDS	Air Tactical Data System (Marine Corps)
ATE	Administration of Territories, Europe (OB)
	Associated Telephone Exchanges
ATEA	American Technical Education Association
ATERM	Air-to-Air Gunnery Range (Navy)
ATF	Air Task Force (Air Force)
	American Type Founders, Inc.
ATFAC	American Turpentine Farmers Association Cooperative
ATFP	Alliance of Television Film Producers
ATG	Accordion Teachers' Guild
	Air-to-Ground (Military)
ATI	Air Technical Intelligence (Air Force)
	Asbestos Textile Institute
ATIC	Air Technical Intelligence Center (Air Force)
ATIS	Adirondack Trail Improvement Society
	Allied Translation and Intelligence Section (OB)
ATL	American Tariff League
	Awaiting Trial (Military)
ATLA	American Theological Library Association
ATM	Associated Tobacco Manufacturers
ATMA	American Textile Machinery Association
ATMU	Aircraft Torpedo Maintenance Unit (Navy)
ATO	Assisted Take-off
ATOA	American Tung Oil Association
ATOMDEF	Atomic Defense (Military)
ATOMDEV	Atomic Device (Military)
ATORP	Anti-Torpedo (Navy)
	Atomic Torpedo (Military)
ATP	Allied Tactical Publication (Military)
	Army Training Program
ATPAM	Association of Theatrical Press Agents and Managers
ATPI	American Textbook Publishers Institute
ATPM	Association of Teachers of Preventive Medicine
ATR	Aircraft Trouble Report
	Aviation Training Record (Navy)
ATRAN	Automatic Terrain Recognition and Navigation (Military)
ATRC	Air Training Command (OB - Air Force)

ACRONYMS

ATRON — AVS

ATRON	Atlantic Squadron (OB – Navy)
ATS	Aeronautical Training Society
	Air Tactical School (OB – Air Force)
	American Temperance Society
	American Therapeutic Society
	American Trudeau Society
	Army Transport Service (MW – Military Sea Transport Service)
ATSC	Air Technical Service Command (OB – Air Force)
AT&T	American Telegraph and Telephone Company
ATT	Army Training Test
ATTA	American Tin Trade Association
ATTC	Atlantic Transportation Terminal Command (Army)
	Aviation Technical Training Center (Navy)
ATU	Advanced Training Unit (Navy)
ATW	American Theatre Wing
ATWA	American Travel Writers Association
ATWS	Automatic Track While Scanning (radar)
AU	Air University (Air Force)
	Army Unit
	Associated Universities
AUA	Allied Underwear Association
	American Urological Association
	Associated Unions of America
AUBBER	Associated University Bureaus of Business and Economic Research
AUBV	Air University Board of Visitors
AUDREY	Automatic Digit Recognition
AUEC	Association of University Evening Colleges
AUGU	Augmenting Unit (Navy)
AUL	Air University Library (Air Force)
AUM	Air-to-Underwater Missile
	Junior Order United American Mechanics
AUP	Air University Press
AURA	Association of Universities for Research in Astronomy
AUS	Army of the United States (OB)
AUSA	Association of the United States Army
AUU	Association of Urban Universities
AV	American Viewpoint
	Audio-Visual
AVA	American Vocational Association
AVATI	Asphalt and Vinyl Asbestos Tile Institute
AVBAD	Army Aviation Badge
AVC	American Veterans Committee
	Association of Vitamin Chemists
	Automatic Volume Control
AVCAD	Aviation Cadet (Navy)
AVCS	Assistant Vice Chief of Staff (Military)
AVDA	American Venereal Disease Association
AVE	Automatic Volume Expansion
AVG	American Volunteer Group
AVGAS	Aviation Gasoline (Military)
AVL	Associated Veterinary Laboratories
AVMA	American Veterinary Medical Association
AVPA	American Veneer Package Association
AVRO	A. V. Roe Ltd.
AVS	American Vacuum Society

ACRONYMS

AW .... Air Warning (Military)
            Articles of War (Military)
            Automatic Weapons (Military)
AWA .... Aluminum Wares Association
            American Warehousemen's Association
            American Watch Association
            American Waterfowl Association
            American Women's Association
            Aviation Writers Association
AWAS .... American Waldensian Aid Society
AWC .... Air War College (OB - Air Force - see War College)
            American Watershed Council
            American Wool Council
            Army War College (OB - see U.S. Army War College)
AWCO .... Area Wage and Classification Office (Civil Service)
AWCS .... Air Weapons Control System
AWD .... Air Warfare Division (Navy)
AWDA .... Automotive Warehouse Distributors Association
AWDMA ...... Aluminum Window and Door Manufacturers Association
AWFI .... American Wood Fabric Institute
AWG .... American Wire Gauge
AWH .... American Women's Hospitals
AWI .... Animal Welfare Institute
            Architectural Woodwork Institute
A&WI .... Atlantic and West Indies (Navy)
AWIU .... Aluminum Workers International Union
AWL .... Absent With Leave (Military)
AWM .... American War Mothers
AWMA .... Aluminum Window Manufacturers Association
            American Walnut Manufacturers Association
AWMPA ...... Association of Women of the Motion Picture Industry
AWO .... American Waterways Operators
AWOL .... Absent Without Official Leave (Military)
AWPA .... American Wood Preservers Association
AWR .... Association of Western Railways
AWRNCO ..... Aircraft Warning Company (Marine Corps)
AWRT .... American Women in Radio and Television
AWS .... Air Weapon Systems (Air Force)
            Air Weather Service (Air Force)
            American Welding Society
AWSA .... American Water Ski Association
AWTAO ...... Association of Water Transportation Accounting Officers
AWTE .... Association for World Travel Exchange
AWVS .... American Women's Voluntary Services
AWWA .... American Water Works Association
AWWI .... American Wash and Wear Institute
AWWPA ...... American Wire Weavers Protective Association
AXP .... Allied Exercise Publication (Military)
AY .... Allied Youth
AYD .... Association of Yarn Distributors
AYH .... American Youth Hostels
AYWS .... (North American) Association of Youth Work Secretaries
AZC .... American Zionist Council
AZI .... American Zinc Institute

ACRONYMS

B

BA	Blind Approach (Flying)
	British Army
	Bureau of Accounts (Treasury Department)
	Bureau of Apprenticeship (Labor Department)
BAATC	Bay Area Army Terminal Center
BABS	Blind Approach Beacon System (Flying)
	Blind Approach Beam System (Flying)
BAC	British Air Commission (OB)
	Bureau of Air Commerce
	Business Advisory Council
BACC	British-American Coordinating Committee (OB)
BACU	Battle Area Control Unit (OB - Military)
BAD	Berlin Airlift Device (Military)
	British Admiralty Delegation (OB)
BADA	Base Air Depot Area (Air Force)
BAFCOM	Basic Armed Forces Communication Plan
BAGRCD	Bureau of Aeronautics General Representative, Central District (Navy)
BAGRED	Bureau of Aeronautics General Representative, Eastern District (Navy)
BAGRWD	Bureau of Aeronautics General Representative, Western District (Navy)
BAI	Bureau of Animal Industry (Agriculture Department)
BAL	Base Authorization List (Air Force)
BALLWIN	Ballistic Winds (Military)
BALSPACON	Balance of Space to Space Control agencies (Military)
BAMC	Brooke Army Medical Center
BAMO	Bureau of Aeronautics Material Officer (Navy)
BAMRO	Bureau of Aeronautics Maintenance Repair Officer (Navy)
BAMRRO	Bureau of Aeronautics Maintenance Resident, Representative Office (Navy)
BAMS	Broadcast to Allied Merchant Ships (OB)
BAO	Budget and Accounting Officer (Military)
BAQ	Bachelor Airmen's Quarters (Air Force)
	Basic Allowance for Quarters (Military)
BAR	Browning Automatic Rifle (Military)
	Bureau of Aeronautics Representative (Navy)
BARB	British Angular Rate Bombsight
BARR	Bureau of Aeronautics Resident Representative (Navy)
BART	Brooklyn Army Terminal
BAS	Basic Airspeed (Flying)
	Basic Allowance for Subsistence (Military)
BASEC	Base Section (Military)
BASEFOR	Base Force (Military)
BASIC (English)	British-American Scientific International Commercial English
BASO	Base Accountable Supply Officer (Air Force)
BASOPS	Base Operations (Military)
BAT	Blind Approach Training (Air Force)
BATCRULANT	Battleships and Cruisers, Atlantic Fleet
BATCRUPAC	Battleships and Cruisers, Pacific Fleet
BATDIV	Battleship Division (Navy)
BATFOR	Battle Force (Navy)
BATLANT or BATSHIPSLANT	Battleships, Atlantic Fleet
BATM	Bureau of Air Traffic Management
BATPAC or BATSHIPSPAC	Battleships, Pacific Fleet
BATSHIP	Battleships, Battleforce (Navy)
BATSHIPSBATFORPAC	Battleships, Battle Force, Pacific Fleet

BAWA	Burley Auction Warehouse Association
BB	Blood Bank
BBA	Bermuda Benevolent Association
	Big Brothers of America
BBAA	Bridal and Bridesmaids Apparel Association
BBC	British Broadcasting Corporation
BBDO	Batten, Barton, Durstine and Osborn
BBIA	Billiard and Bowling Institute of America
BBII	Brass and Bronze Ingot Institute of America
BBSA	Bridge and Building Supply Association
BBSI	Beauty and Barber Supply Institute
BBW	B'nai B'rith Women
BBYO	B'nai B'rith Youth Organization
BC	Battery Commander (Military)
	Before Christ
	Bomber Command (OB - Air Force)
	Bureau of Consultation (Federal Trade Commission)
	Bureau of Customs
BCA	Billiard Congress of America
	Boys' Clubs of America
BCCUS	Belgian Chamber of Commerce in the United States
BCD	Bad Conduct Discharge (Military)
BCDA	Biscuit and Cracker Distributors Association
BCDD	Base Construction Depot Detachment (Navy)
BCG	Bacillus Calmette-Guerin anti-tuberculosis vaccine
BCI	Bituminous Coal Institute
	Bureau of Contract Information
BCMAA	Biscuit and Cracker Manufacturers Association
BCMR	Board for Correction of Military Records
BCR	Bituminous Coal Research
BCRA	Bureau Centrale de Reseignements et d'Action (Free French)
BCT	Basic Combat Training (Military)
BCTD	Building and Construction Trades Department (AFL-CIO)
BCWIU	Bakery and Confectionery Workers' International Union of America
BDA	Bomb Damage Assessment (Military)
BDGC	Bad conduct Disc., Gen. Court-Martial after confinement in prison (Navy)
BDGI	Bad conduct Disc., Gen. court martial, Immediate (Navy)
BDGP	Bad conduct Disc., Gen. court martial, after violation of Probation (Navy)
BDHCA	Belgian Draft Horse Corporation of America
BDI	Bearing Deviation Indicator (Navy - Sonar)
	Bureau of Dairy Industry (Agriculture Department)
BDLTEA	Burley and Dark Leaf Tobacco Export Association
BDA	Bomb Damage Assessment (Military)
BDSA	Business and Defense Services Administration
BDSI	Bad conduct Discharge, Sentence of summary court martial, Immediate
BDSP	Bad conduct Discharge, Summary court martial, after violation of Probation
BE	Bureau of Economics (Federal Trade Commission)
	Bureau of Engraving
BEA	Barn Equipment Association
	British European Airways
BEAA	Business Education Administrators Association
BEART	Beaver Army Terminal
BEC	Bureau of Employees Compensation
	Business Electronics Computer (used in training)
BEFT	Bureau of Education for Fair Trade

ACRONYMS

BEMA	Bakery Equipment Manufacturers Association
BENA	Belgian Engineers in North America
BENELUX	Belgium, Netherlands, Luxembourg
BEP	Bureau of Engraving and Printing (Treasury Department)
BEPOC	Burrough's Electrographic Printer-plotter for Ordnance Computing
BERF	Business Education Research Foundation
BERSEAPAT	Bering Sea Patrol (Navy)
BES	Bureau of Employment Security (Labor Department)
BEW	Board of Economic Warfare (OB)
BF	Belgian Fourragere (Military)
	Brought Forward (Military)
BFC	Bureau of Foreign Commerce (Commerce Department)
BFCU	Bureau of Federal Credit Unions (Social Security Administration)
BFI	Business Forms Institute
BFM	Basic Field Manual (Army)
BFO	Beat Frequency Oscillator
BFUP	Board of Fire Underwriters of the Pacific
BG	Battle Group (Military)
BGA	Barre Granite Association
BGFE	Boston Grain and Flour Exchange
BGFRS	Board of Governors, Federal Reserve System
BGPP	Beneficiary Government Production Program (OB)
BHC	Better Heating-Cooling Council
BHO	Branch Hydrographic Office (Navy)
BHP	Brake Horsepower
BHQ	Brigade Headquarters (Military)
BHRI	Brewers Hop Research Institute
BI	Background Investigation (Military)
	Bermuda Islands
	Bureau of Investigation (Federal Trade Commission)
BIA	Bee Industries Association
	Bicycle Institute of America
	Braille Institute of America
	Bureau of Indian Affairs (Interior Department)
	Bureau Issues Association
BIB	Baby Incendiary Bomb (Military)
BIEM	Bureau Internationale de L'Edition Mecanique
BIF	Bombardier's Information File (Air Force)
BIM	Basic Industrial Materials program (Navy)
BINAC	Binary Automatic Computer
BIO	Branch Intelligence Officer (Navy)
BIOWAR	Biological Warfare
BIPAD	Bureau of Independent Publishers and Distributors
BIS	Bank for International Settlement
	Board of Inspection and Survey (Navy)
BIW	Battle Injury or Wound (Military)
BJCEB	British Joint Communications-Electronics Board
BJM	Bluejacket's Manual (Navy)
BJSM	British Joint Staff Mission (OB)
BJU	Beach Jumper Unit (Army)
BL	Bill of Lading (Military)
	Bombline (Military)
	Bureau of Litigation (Federal Trade Commission)
BLADING	Bill of Lading (Military)
BLE	Brotherhood of Locomotive Engineers

Acronym	Meaning
BLFE	Brotherhood of Locomotive Firemen and Enginemen
BLIMPHEDRON	Blimp Maintenance Squadron (Navy)
BLIMPRON	Blimp Squadron (Navy)
BLM	Bureau of Land Management (Interior Department)
BLO	Bombardment Liaison Officer (Navy)
	British Liaison Officer (Military)
BLS	Bureau of Labor Standards (Labor Department)
	Bureau of Labor Statistics
BLT	Battalion Landing Team (Army)
BL&T	Blind Loaded and Traced (Military)
BLTI	Better Lawn and Turf Institute
BM	Bench Mark (Military)
	Boston and Maine Railroad
	Bureau of Mines (Interior Department)
	Bureau of the Mint
BMD	Base Maintenance Division (Navy)
BME	Brotherhood of Marine Engineers
BMEA	Building Material Exhibitors Association
BMEC	Ball Manufacturers Engineers Committee
BMEP	Brake Mean Effective Pressure
BMETO	Ballistic Missiles European Task Organization (Military)
BMEWS	Ballistic Missile Early Warning System (Military)
BMG	Browning Machine Gun (Military)
BMI	Barley and Malt Institute
	Battelle Memorial Institute
	Book Manufacturers Institute
	Broadcast Music Incorporated
BMMA	Beverage Machinery Manufacturers Association
BMNT	Beginning Morning Nautical Twilight (Military)
BMPIUA	Bricklayers, Masons and Plasterers International Union of America
BMRC	Brookhaven Medical Research Center
BMTS	Basic Military Training School
BMU	Beachmaster Unit (Army)
BMW	Bayerische Motoren Werke (German automobile)
BMWE	Brotherhood of Maintenance of Way Employees
BN	Brazilian Navy
	Bureau of Narcotics
BNA	Brazil Nut Association
BNAS	British Naval Air Service
BNF	Brand Names Foundation
BNHQ	Battalion Headquarters (Marine Corps)
BNHSC	Boston National Historic Sites Commission (government agency)
BNL	Brookhaven National Laboratory
BNLO	British Naval Liaison Officer
BNP	Bureau of Naval Personnel Publications
BNPCL	Bureau of Naval Personnel Circular Letters
BNW	Bureau of Naval Weapons
B&O	Baltimore and Ohio Railroad
BO	Base Order (Military)
	Blackout
	Body Odor
BOAC	British Overseas Airways Corporation
BOASI	Bureau of Old-Age and Survivors Insurance (Social Security Administration)
BOB	Bureau of the Budget
BOCA	Building Officials Conference of America

ACRONYMS

BODU . . . . Bureau of Ordnance Design Unit (Navy)
BOI . . . . Basis of Issue (Military)
BOM . . . . Bureau of Mines
BOMCOM . . . . . Bomber Command (OB - Army)
BOMID . . . . Branch Office Military Intelligence Division (OB)
BOMREP . . . . . . Bombing Report (Military)
BOMRON . . . . . Bombing Squadron (Navy)
BOQ . . . . Bachelor Officers' Quarters (Military)
BORM . . . . Bureau of Raw Materials for American Vegetable Oils and Fats Industries
BORU . . . . Boat Operating and Repair Unit (Navy)
BOSOX . . . . Boston Red Sox (baseball team)
BOU . . . . Boat Operating Unit (Navy)
BP . . . . Base Pay (Military)
            Base Point (Military)
            Beach Party (Military)
            Bureau of Prisons
BPA . . . . Biological Photographic Association
            Bonneville Power Administration
            Bureau of Public Assistance (Social Security Administration)
            Business Publications Audit of Circulation
BPAA . . . . Bowling Proprietors' Association of America
BPAC . . . . Better Packaging Advisory Council
BPB . . . . Base Planning Board (Military)
BPD . . . . Bureau of the Public Debt (Treasury Department)
BPFILO . . . . British Pacific Fleet Intelligence Liaison Officer
BPO . . . . Base Post Office (Military)
BPOE . . . . Benevolent and Protective Order of Elks
BPR . . . . Bridge Plotting Room (Navy)
            Bureau of Public Roads
BPS . . . . Biophysical Society
BPWC . . . . International Federation of Business and Professional Women (Clubs)
BPWMA . . . . . . Buff and Polishing Wheel Manufacturers Association
B&Q . . . . Barracks and Quarters (Army)
BQM . . . . Base Quartermaster (Marine Corps)
BR . . . . Briefing Room (Military)
            Bureau of Reclamation (Interior Department)
BRA . . . . Building Renovating Association
BRAB . . . . Building Research Advisory Board
BRAL . . . . Bureau de Renseignements et d'Action, Londres (Free French)
BRANE . . . . Bombing Radar Navigation Equipment (Military)
BRASO . . . . Branch Aviation Supply Office (Navy)
BRCA . . . . Brotherhood Railway Carmen of America
BRDA . . . . Boxboard Research and Development Association
BRF . . . . Brain Research Foundation
BRI . . . . Building Research Institute
BRL . . . . Bomb Release Line (Military)
BRLG . . . . Bomb, Radio, Longitudinal, Generator-powered
BRO . . . . British Routing Office
BRR . . . . Bridge Receiving Room (Navy)
BRSA . . . . Brotherhood of Railroad Signalmen of America
BRT . . . . Brotherhood of Railroad Trainmen
BRU . . . . Boat Repair Unit (Navy)
BRUSA . . . . British-United States Agreement (on communications circuits)
BS . . . . Battle Star (Military)
            Battleship Squadron (Navy)

Acronym	Meaning
BS	British Standard
BSA	Bibliographical Society of America
	Botanical Society of America
	Boy Scouts of America
BSC	Balkan Supply Center (OB – Military)
	Beltsville Space Center (National Aeronautics and Space Administration)
	Burley Stabilization Corporation
BSCBA	Brown Swiss Cattle Breeders' Association of the U.S.A.
BSDF	Beet Sugar Development Foundation
BSDL	Boresight Datum Line (Military)
BSE	Base Support Equipment (Air Force)
BSERBN	Base Service Battalion (Marine Corps)
BSI	British Solomon Islands
	Building Stone Institute
BSM	Bronze Star Medal (Military)
BSMCP	Blue Shield Medical Care Plans
BSO	Base Supply Officer (Navy)
	Bomb Safety Officer (Navy)
BSU	Base Service Unit (Navy)
BT	Basic Trainer (OB – Air Force)
BTC	Basic Training Center (Military)
BTCA	Basic Tables of Commissioning Allowances (OB – Navy)
B of TCC	Board of Trade of the City of Chicago
BTE	British Troops in Egypt (OB – World War II)
BTGCA	Burley Tobacco Growers Cooperative Association
B of TKC	Board of Trade of Kansas City
BTMA	Boat Trailer Manufacturers Association
BTO	Bombing Through Overcast (Military)
	Branch Transportation Officer (Military)
BTU	British Thermal Unit(s)
BU	Base Unit (Air Force)
BUAER	Bureau of Aeronautics (MW – Bureau of Naval Weapons)
BUCO	Buildup Control Office
BUDOCKS	Bureau of Yards and Docks (Navy)
BUMED	Bureau of Medicine and Surgery (Navy)
BUNAV	Bureau of Navigation (OB – Navy)
BUORD	Bureau of Ordnance (MW – Bureau of Naval Weapons)
BUPERS	Bureau of Naval Personnel (Navy)
BUPS	Beacon, Ultra Portable "S" band (Navy)
BUSANDA	Bureau of Supplies and Accounts (Navy)
BUSCI	British-United States Convoy Instructions (OB)
BUSHIPS	Bureau of Ships (Navy)
BUSRA	British-United States Routing Agreement (Shipping)
BUT	Bureau of University Travel
BVA	Blinded Veterans Association
BVI	Better Vision Institute
BVRR	Bureau of Veterans' Reemployment Rights (Labor Department)
BW	Bendix-Westinghouse Automotive Air Brake Company
	Biological Warfare
B&W	Black and White (film)
BW	Borg-Warner Corporation
B&W	Bread and Water
BWAA	Bowling Writers' Association of America
BWC	Board of War Communications (OB)
BWGMSB	Bright Wire Goods Manufacturers Service Bureau

ACRONYMS

BWI . . . . British West Indies (OB - see Federated West Indies)
BWP . . . . Basic War Plan (Navy)
BWTA . . . . Boston Wool Trade Association
BX . . . . Base Exchange (Air Force)
BYC . . . . Brewers Yeast Council
BYPU . . . . Baptist Young People's Union

C

CA . . . . Capital Airlines
                Charge d'Affaires (State Department Foreign Service)
                Civil Affairs (Military)
                Civil Authorities (Military)
                Clerical Aptitude Test (Military)
                Combat Aircrew or Aircrewman (Military)
                Commandant Assistant (Coast Guard)
                Convening Authority (Navy)
CAA . . . . Catholic Art Association
                Chief of Army Aviation
                Civil Aeronautics Administration (OB - see Federal Aviation Agency)
                Civil Aeronautics Authority (OB)
                Collectors of American Art
CAAA . . . . College Art Association of America
CAAAA . . . . Chicago Area Agricultural Advertising Association
CAAF . . . . Chief, Army Air Forces (OB)
                Combined Allied Air Forces (OB)
CAAN . . . . Continental Advertising Agency Network
CAAWTS . . . . . . Civil Aviation Authority--War Training Service (OB)
CAB . . . . Civil Aeronautics Board
                Civil Aeronautics Bulletin
                Civil Air Branch (Air Force)
CABMA . . . . College Athletic Business Managers Association
CABRA . . . . Copper and Brass Research Association
CAC . . . . Catholic Anthropological Conference
                Chief of Air Corps (OB)
                Coast Artillery Corps (OB - Army)
                Combat Air Crew (Military)
                Commander Air Center (Navy)
CACA . . . . Citizens Association for the Care of Animals
CACR . . . . Council for Agricultural and Chemurgic Research
CACS . . . . Continental Airways and Communications Service (Air Force)
CACW . . . . Chinese-American Composite Wing (OB - Air Force)
CAD . . . . Civil Affairs Division (Military)
CADC . . . . Combined Administrative Committee (OB - Military)
CADF . . . . Central Air Defense Force (Air Force)
CADO . . . . Central Air Documents Office (OB - Air Force)
CADRC . . . . Combined Air Documents Research Center (OB - Military)
CAE . . . . Continental Aviation and Engineering Corporation
CAF . . . . Clerical, Administrative and Fiscal (OB - Civil Service Employee)
CAFAC . . . . Commander All Forces, Aruba-Curacao (Navy)
CAFAF . . . . Commander Amphibious Force Atlantic Fleet
C of AFCH . . . . . Chief of Air Force Chaplains
CAFT . . . . Consolidated Advance Field Teams (Navy)
CAG . . . . Carrier Air Group (Navy)
                Composers-Authors Guild

ACRONYMS

CAG	Concert Artists Guild
CAGA	Catholic Actors Guild of America
	Church Architectural Guild of America
CAI	Canvas Awning Institute
CAID	Convention of American Instructors of the Deaf
CAIP	Catholic Association for International Peace
CAIRC	Caribbean Air Command (Air Force)
CALF	Combined Allied Land Forces (OB)
CALTECH	California Institute of Technology
CAM	Christian Amendment Movement
	Commercial Air Movement (Military)
CAMA	Civil Aviation Medical Association
CAMG	Civil Affairs/Military Government (Military)
CAMSI	Canadian, American Merchant Shipping Instructions
CANAIRDEF	Canadian Air Defense command hdqts.
CANAIRDIV	Canadian Air Division headquarters (Allied Air Forces in Europe)
CANAIRHED	Canadian Air Force Headquarters
CANAIRLIFT	Canadian Air Transport command headquarters
CANAIRLON	Canadian Air member, joint staff London
CANAIRMAT	Canadian Air Materiel command headquarters
CANAIRPEG	Canadian 14th Air training group headquarters Winnipeg
CANAIRTAC	Canadian Tactical Air command headquarters
CANAIRTRAIN	Canadian Air Training command headquarters
CANAIRVAN	Canadian 12th Air defense group headquarters, Vancouver
CANCON	Canadian Control system (for convoys in Canadian Coastal Zone)
CANF	Combined Allied Naval Forces (OB)
CANFSWPA	Combined Allied Naval Forces, Southwest Pacific Area (OB)
CANFSWPAOPPlan	Combined Allied Naval Forces, S.W.Pac.Ocean Area Operating Plan
CANSERVCOL	Canadian Services College
CANUKUS	Canada-United Kingdom-United States agreement
CANUKUS JCECS	Canadian-UK - U.S. Joint Communications-Electronics Committees
CAO	Civil Affairs Officer (Navy)
CAP	Catapult and Arresting-Gear Pool (Navy)
	Civil Air Patrol (Air Force)
	Combat Air Patrol (Military)
	Current Assessment Plan (Military)
CAPCP	Civil Air Patrol Coastal Patrol
CAPP	Conference of Actuaries in Public Practice
CAPUC	Coordinating Area Production Urgency Committee (OB)
CARAIRGROUP	Carrier Air Group (Navy)
CAR DIV	Carrier Division (Navy)
CARE	Cooperative for American Remittances to Everywhere
CARIBCOM	Caribbean Command (Military)
CARIBSEAFRON	Caribbean Sea Frontier (Navy)
CARP	Computed Air Release Point (used in connection with paradropping)
CARPAC	Carriers, Pacific Fleet (Navy)
CAR TASK FOR	Carrier Task Force (Navy)
CARTRANSRON	Carrier Transport Squadron (Navy)
CARTU	Combat Aircrew Refresher Training Unit (Navy)
CAS	Calibrated Airspeed (Flying)
	Casualty Actuarial Society
	Chief of Air Staff (Marine Corps)
	Civil Affairs Section (Military)
CASA	Chinese Art Society of America
CASC	Council for Advancement of Small Colleges

ACRONYMS

CASCO........Canadian Australian Line
CASCP........Caribbean Area Small Craft Project (Navy)
CASCU........Commander Aircraft Support Control Unit (Navy)
CASD.........Carrier Aircraft Service Detachment (Marine Corps)
             Carrier Aircraft Service Division (Navy)
CASDIV.......Carrier Aircraft Service Division (Navy)
CASE.........Commission on Accreditation of Service Experiences
CASF.........Composite Air Strike Force (Air Force)
CASL.........Committee of American Steamship Lines
CASU.........Carrier Aircraft Service Unit (Navy)
             Combat Aircraft Service Unit (Navy)
CASUM........Civil Affairs Summary (Navy)
CASW.........Church Association for Seamen's Work
CASWO........Confidential and Secret Weekly Orders (to Naval Air Stations)
CAT..........Carburetor Air Temperature (Flying)
CATCUSAF.....Commander Amphibious Training Command United States Atlantic Fleet
CATOR........Combined Air Transport Operations Room (Air Force)
CATRALA......Car and Truck Renting and Leasing Association
CATS.........Civil Affairs Training School (Navy)
CATU.........Combat Aircrew Training Unit (Navy)
CAVEA........Catholic Audio-Visual Educators Association
CAVU.........Ceiling and Visibility Unlimited
CB...........Center of Buoyancy
C (bomb).....Cobalt Bomb
CB...........Census Bureau (Commerce Department)
             Children's Bureau (Social Security Administration)
             Construction Battalion (Navy)
             Control Branch (Military)
CBA..........Catholic Biblical Association of America
             Catholic Broadcasters Association
             Christian Booksellers Association
             Consumer Bankers Association
CBAA.........Conservative Baptist Association of America
             Corset and Brassiere Association of America
CBALS........Carrier Borne Air Liaison Section (Navy)
CBBI.........Cast Bronze Bearing Institute
CBC..........Canadian Broadcasting Company
             Contraband Control (Navy)
CBCC.........Conviction by Civil Court (Military)
CBD..........Construction Battalion Detachment (Navy)
CBDNA........College Band Directors National Association
CBE..........Council for Basic Education
CBEA.........Catholic Business Education Association
CBI..........Carbonated Beverage Institute of America
CB&I.........Chicago Bridge & Iron Company
CBI..........China-Burma-India (OB - World War II theater of operations)
             Coffee Brewing Institute
CBJO.........Coordinating Board of Jewish Organizations
CBLFA........Corn Belt Livestock Feeders Association
CBLO.........Chief Bombardment Liaison Officer (Navy)
CBLS.........Carrier Borne Air Liaison Section (Navy)
CBM..........Certified Ballast Manufacturers
             Continental Ballistic Missile
CBMC.........Corregidor-Bataan Memorial Commission (government agency)
CBMU.........Construction Battalion Maintenance Unit (Navy)

CBO	Coding Board Officer (Navy)
CBR	California Bearing Ratio
	Chemical Biological and Radiological warfare
CBRA	Copper and Brass Research Association
CBRD	Construction Battalion Replacement Depot (Navy)
CBRS	Chiropody Bibliographical Research Society
CBS	Columbia Broadcasting System
CBT	Cincinnati Board of Trade
C of C	Chamber of Commerce
C/C	Change of Course (Flying)
CC	Channel Command (Military - refers to English Channel)
	Chrysler Corporation
	Cirrocumulus (Military)
	Combat Command (Army)
	Common Carrier
	Construction Corps (Navy)
	Control Center (Military)
	Cubic Centimeter
CCA	California Central Airlines
	Carrier-Controlled Approach (Navy)
	Cash Clothing Allowance (Military)
	Circuit Court of Appeals
	Clown Club of America
	Comics Code Authority
	Committee for Conventional Armaments
	Consumers Cooperative Association
	Corduroy Council of America
CCAC	Combined Civil Affairs Committee (OB - Military)
CCAC/L	Combined Civil Affairs Committee, London Subcommittee (OB - Military)
CCAC/S	Combined Civil Affairs Committee, Supply Subcommittee (OB - Military)
CCAF	Chinese Communist Air Force
CCAO	Chief Civil Affairs Officer (Navy)
CCAR	Central Conference of American Rabbis
CCATNA	Combined Committee on Air Training in North America (OB - Military)
CCB	Close Control Bombing (Air Force)
	Combined Communications Board (OB - Military)
	Contraband Control Base (Navy)
CCBP	Combined Communications Board Publications (OB - Military)
CCC	Catholic Civics Clubs of America
	Chief Cable Censor (Navy)
	Civilian Conservation Corps (DF)
	Combined Coordinating Committee (OB - Military)
	Commodity Credit Corporation
	Continental Can Company
CCCA	Classic Car Club of America
CCCC	Conference on College Composition and Communication
CCCO	Central Committee for Conscientious Objectors
CCCP	Council on Cooperative College Projects
CCD	Central Commissioning Detail (Navy)
CCDA	Commercial Chemical Development Association
CCF	Christian Children's Fund
	Common Cold Foundation
CCFA	Cancer Cytology Foundation of America
CCGA	California Cactus Growers Association
CCGD	Commander Coast Guard District

ACRONYMS

C of CH	Chief of Chaplains (Army)
CCH	Citizenship Clearing House
	Commerce Clearing House
CCI	Calcium Chloride Institute
	Cotton Council International
CCIA	Consumer Credit Insurance Association
CCIT	Comite Consultatif Internationale Telegraphique (French)
CCJ	Conference of Chief Justices
CCJO	Consultative Council of Jewish Organizations
CCL	Communications Circular Letter (Navy)
CCLS	Court of Claims
CCLSR	Court of Claims Reports
CCM	Combat Cargo Mission (Air Force)
	Combined Cipher Machine (Military)
	Combined Coding Machine (Military)
CCMA	Card Clothing Manufacturers Association
CCMCC	Continuing Committee on Muslim-Christian Cooperation
CCMLO	Chief Chemical Officer (Army)
CCN	Contract Change Notification (Military)
CCNR	Citizens Committee on Natural Resources
CCNRA	Central Council of National Retail Associations
CCNSC	Cancer Chemotherapy National Service Center
CCNY	College of the City of New York
CCO	Convoy Control Officer (Navy)
CCPA	Court of Customs and Patent Appeals
CCPO	Central Civilian Personnel Office (Military)
CCR	Combat Crew (Air Force)
	Commission on Civil Rights
CCRC	Combat Crew Replacement Center (Air Force)
CCS	Catholic Committee on Scouting
	Church of Christ, Scientist
	Combined Chiefs of Staff (OB - Military)
	Committee for Collective Security
CCSC	Civil Affairs Staff Center (OB - Military)
CCSF	Commander Caribbean Sea Frontier (Navy)
CCSFI	Canned Chop Suey Foods Industry
CCT	Communications Control Team (Military)
CCTA	Coordination Committee on Technical Assistance (OAS)
CCTS	Combat Crew Training School (Air Force)
CCU	Catholic Central Union
	Council on Christian Unity
	Croatian Catholic Union of USA
CCUA	Catholic Central Union of America
CCUN	Collegiate Council for the United Nations
CCUS	Chamber of Commerce of the United States
CCZA	Canadian Coastal Zone Atlantic
CCZP	Canadian Coastal Zone Pacific
CD (film)	Camouflage Detection Film (Military)
CD	Civil Defense
	Coastal Defense (Marine Corps)
	Coastal Defense (radar for detecting surface vessels)
	Commerce Department
	Confidential Document (Military)
	Conning Director (Navy)
CDA	Catholic Daughters of America

ACRONYMS

CDC	Caribbean Defense Command (er) (Military)
	Commissioners of District of Columbia
	Continental Dorset Club
CDCA	Chefs de Cuisine Association of America
CDD	Certificate of Disability for Discharge (Military)
CDFAB	California Dried Fig Advisory Board
CDGA	California Date Growers Association
CDI	Classified Defense Information (Military)
CDO	Command Duty Officer (Navy)
CDOA	Car Department Officers' Association
CDRA	Civil Defense Research Associates
CDS	Central Distribution System publications (Navy)
	Climatological Data Sheet (Air Force)
	Commander, Destroyer Squadron (Navy)
CDSA	Country Dance Society of America
CDT	Central Daylight Time
CDU	Coastal Defense radar for detecting U-boats
CE	Chief Engineer (Navy)
	Circular Error (Military)
	Civil Engineer (Navy)
	Combustion Engineering (Navy)
	Common Era
C-E	Communications-Electronics (Military)
CE	Corps of Engineers (Army)
CEA	Catholic Economic Association
	Church Evangelism Association
	Circular Error Average (Military)
	College English Association
	Commodity Exchange Authority (Agriculture Department)
	Conservation Education Association
	Correctional Education Association
	Council of Economic Advisers
CEAPD	Central Air Procurement District (Air Force)
CEASD	Conference of Executives of American Schools for the Deaf
CEBAR	Chemical, Biological, Radiological warfare
CEC	Central Economic Committee (OB)
	Civil Engineer Corps (Navy)
CECO	Chandler Evans Corporation
CECS	Communications-Electronics Coordinating Section (Military)
CED	Committee for Economic Development
CEEA	Catholic Educational Exhibitors Association
CEF	Captain commanding Escort Forces (Navy)
	Corps Expeditionaire Francais (OB - World War II)
	Creative Education Foundation
CEFCTU	Central European Federation of Christian Trade Unions
CEI	Communication Electronic Instructions (Military)
CEIP	Carnegie Endowment for International Peace
CEL	Constitutional Educational League
CEMA	Conveyor Equipment Manufacturers Association
	Council for the Encouragement of Music and the Arts
CEMF	Counter-Electromotive Force (Military)
CENCATS	Central Pac.Combat Air Transport Service
CENDRAFT	Central Drafting Officer (Navy)
C of ENGRS	Chief of Engineers (Army)
CENPACFOR	Central Pacific Forces (Navy)

ACRONYMS

CENTCOM — C&GS

CENTCOM	Central Pacific Communications Instructions (Navy)
CENTPACBACOM	Central Pacific Base Command (Navy)
CEO	Casualty Evacuation Officer (Navy)
CEOINC	Civil Engineer, Officer-in-Charge (Navy)
CEP	Circular Error Probability (Military)
	Conference on Economic Progress
CERMET	Ceramic Material Bonded to Metal (Military)
CES	Comparative Education Society
CESF	Commander Eastern Sea Frontier (Navy)
CESI	Council for Elementary Science International
CEWA	Combined Economic Warfare Agencies (OB – World War II)
CF	Carry Forward
C of F	Chief of Finance (Army)
CF	Coastal Frontier (Army)
	Conservation Foundation
	Counterfire (Military)
CFA	Circus Fans Association of America
	Commission on Fine Arts (government agency)
	Cowl-Flap Angle (Air Force)
CFAC	Citizens Foreign Aid Committee
CFC	Central Fire-Control (Military)
	Controlled Force Circulation boilers (Navy)
CFDA	Cooperative Food Distributors of America
CFE	California Fruit Exchange
	Contractor-Furnished Equipment (Military)
CFG	Camp Fire Girls
CFLN	Comite Francais Liberation Nationale (OB – World War II)
CFM	Christian Family Movement
	Cubic Feet per Minute
CFR	Code of Federal Relations
	Committee on Friendly Relations Among Foreign Students
	Contact Flight Rules (flying)
	Council on Foreign Relations
CFS	Cystic Fibrosis Society
CFSSB	Central Flight Status Selection Board (Air Force)
CFTMA	Caster and Floor Truck Manufacturers Association
CFU	Croatian Fraternal Union of America
CG	Cargo Glider (Military)
	Center of Gravity
	Coast Guard
	Commanding General (Army and Marine Corps)
C of G	Convenience of the Government (Military)
CGA	Coast Guard Academy
	Coast Guard Auxiliary
	Compressed Gas Association
CGAAF	Commanding General Army Air Forces (OB)
CGAB	Coast Guard Air Base
CGAS	Coast Guard Air Station
CGC	Coast Guard Cutter
CGD	Coast Guard District
CGL	Coast Guard League
CGMB	Commanding General, Marine Base
CGOB	Coast Guard Operating Base
CGOS	Combat Gunnery Officers School (OB – Army Air Forces)
C&GS	Coast & Geodetic Survey

- 63 -

ACRONYMS

CGS	Commission on Government Security
CGSC	Command and General Staff College (Army)
C&GSS	Command & General Staff School (Army)
CGTFL	California Grape and Tree Fruit League
CGTM	Command Guided Tactical Missile
CGTS	Coast Guard Training Station
CGYD	Coast Guard Yard
CH	Chain Home (Flying)
	Compass Heading
CHA	Catholic Hospital Association of United States and Canada
CHACOM	Chain of Command (Military)
CHB	Cargo Handling Battalion (Military)
	Chain Home Beamed (Flying)
CHC	Chaplain Corps, U.S. Air Force (now mostly called "Chaplaincy")
CHCW	Conference for Health Council Work
CHEL	Chain Home Extra Low (Flying)
CHIAA	Crop-Hail Insurance Actuarial Association
CHICOM	Chinese Communist
CHISOX	Chicago White Sox (baseball team)
CHL	Chain Home Low (Flying)
CHNAVAIRSHIPTRA	Chief of Naval Airship Training
CHNAVMIS	Chief, U.S. Naval Mission
CHOP	Change of Operational Control
CHORI	Chief of Office of Research and Inventions (OB - Navy)
CHQ	Corps Headquarters (Army)
CHSM	China Service Medal (Military)
CHT	Cylinder-Head Temperature
CI	Combustion Institute
	Cost Inspector (Military)
	Counter Intelligence (Military)
CIA	Central Intelligence Agency
	China Institute of America
	Cigar Institute of America
	Controllers Institute of America
	Cork Institute of America
	Correctional Industries Association
	Cotton Importers Association
	Cotton Insurance Association
CIAA	Coordinator of Inter-American Affairs
CIAC	Council for Inter-American Cooperation
CIB	Central Intelligence Board
CIC	Combat Information Center (Military)
	Combined Intelligence Committee (OB - Military)
	Commander-in-Chief (Air Force)
	Counter Intelligence Corps (Army)
CICU	Cirrocumulus
CID	Council for Independent Distribution
	Criminal Investigation Division (Army)
CIDEM	Inter-American Music Center (Centro Interamericano de Musica)
CIEG	Committee for International Economic Growth
CIEP	Committee on Intl. Exchange of Persons
CIF	Cost, Insurance and Freight
CIG	Counter Intelligence Group (Military)
CIGS	Chief of Imperial General Staff (United Kingdom)
CIIC	Counter Intelligence Interrogation Center (Military)

ACRONYMS

CIIUAP . . . . Commission on Increased Industrial Use of Agricultural Products
CIM . . . . Communications Improvement Memorandum (Military)
CIMC . . . . Committee for International Municipal Cooperation
CIMS . . . . Communications Instructions for Merchant Ships (Navy)
CINC . . . . Commander-in-Chief (Military)
CINCAF . . . . . . Commander-in-Chief, Allied Forces
         Commander-in-Chief, Asiatic Fleet (OB)
CINCAFMED . . . Commander-in-Chief, Allied Forces, Mediterranean
CINCAFPAC . . . Commander-in-Chief, Army Forces in the Pacific
CINCAIREASTLANT . . Air Commander-in-Chief, Eastern Atlantic area
CINCAL . . . . . . Commander-in-Chief, Alaskan Command
CINCALAIRCENEUR . . Commander-in-Chief, Allied Air Forces, Central Europe
CINCBPF . . . . . . Commander-in-Chief, British Pacific Fleet
CINCCAIRIB . . . Commander-in-Chief, Caribbean
CINCEASTLANT . Commander-in-Chief, Eastern Atlantic Area
CINCENT . . . . . Commander-in-Chief, Allied Forces, Central Europe
CINCEUR . . . . . Commander-in-Chief, Europe
CINCFE . . . . . . Commander-in-Chief, Far East
CINCHAN . . . . . Allied Commander-in-Chief, Channel
CINCLANT . . . . Commander-in-Chief, Atlantic
CINCLANTFLT . . Commander-in-Chief, Atlantic Fleet
CINCMAIRCHAN . . Allied Maritime Air Commander-in-Chief, Channel
CINCMED . . . . . Commander-in-Chief, Mediterranean
CINCNE . . . . . . Commander-in-Chief, Northeast Command
CINCNELM . . . . Commander-in-Chief, Naval Forces Eastern Atlantic and Mediterranean
CINCNOREUR . . Commander-in-Chief, Northern Europe
CINCNORTH . . . Commander-in-Chief, Allied Forces, Northern Europe
CINCPAC . . . . . Commander-in-Chief, Pacific Forces
CINCPACAF . . . Commander-in-Chief, Pacific Air Forces
CINCPAC-CINCPOA . . Commander-in-Chief, Pacific Fleet and Pacific Ocean Areas
CINCPACFLT . . . Commander-in-Chief, Pacific Fleet
CINCPACHEDPEARL . . Commander-in-Chief, Pacific Fleet Headquarters, Pearl Harbor
CINCPOA . . . . . Commander-in-Chief, Pacific Ocean Areas
CINCPOAHEDPEARL . . Commander-in-Chief, Pacific Ocean Areas Headquarters, Pearl Harbor
CINCSAC . . . . . Commander-in-Chief, Strategic Air Command
CINCSOUTH . . . Commander-in-Chief, Allied Forces, Southern Europe
CINCTAC . . . . . Commander-in-Chief, Tactical Air Command
CINCUS . . . . . . Commander-in-Chief, US Fleet (OB)
CINCUSAFE . . . Commander-in-Chief, US Air Forces in Europe
CINCUSAREUR . . Commander-in-Chief, US Army in Europe
CINCWESTLANT . Commander-in-Chief, Western Atlantic Area
CINE . . . . Committee on International Non-theatrical Events
CINFO . . . . Chief of Information (Army)
CIO . . . . Combat Intelligence Officer (Military)
         Congress of Industrial Organizations (MW- AFL-CIO)
CIOA . . . . Center for Information on America
CIOS . . . . Combined Intelligence Operations Section (OB)
CIP . . . . Catholic Institute of the Press
CIPC . . . . Combined Intelligence Priorities Committee (OB)
CIPHONY . . . . . Cipher and Telephony Equipment (Military)
CIPM . . . . Council for International Progress in Management
CIPRA . . . . Cast Iron Pipe Research Association
CIR . . . . Commission on Intergovernmental Relations
CIRES . . . . Communication Instructions for Reporting Enemy Sightings (Navy)
CIRF . . . . Corn Industries Research Foundation

ACRONYMS

CIS	Central Instructor School (Air Force)
	Cost Inspection Service (Navy)
CISA	Council for Independent School Aid
CISPI	Cast Iron Soil Pipe Institute
CIU	Coopers' International Union of North America
CIVCLO	Civilian Clothing (Navy)
CIW	Carnegie Institution of Washington
CJ	Chief Justice (various supreme courts)
CJBT	Costume Jewelry Board of Trade of New York
CJFWF	Council of Jewish Federations and Welfare Funds
CJSS	Conference on Jewish Social Studies
CJTF	Commander Joint Task Force (Military)
CKA	Catholic Knights of America
CL	Carload
CLA	Catholic Library Association
	Christian Labor Association of the United States of America
	College Language Association
CLAC	Combined Liberated Areas Committee (OB)
CLAS	Catholic Ladies' Aid Society
CLC	Catholic Ladies of Columbia
CLE	Chicago Livestock Exchange
CLL	Chief of Legislative Liaison (Military)
CLLA	Commercial Law League of America
CLMA	Clothing Monetary Allowance (Military)
CLR	Council on Library Resources
CLS	Canon Law Society of America
	Counsular Law Society
CLSC	Chautauqua Literary and Scientific Circle
CLTCLANT	Commander Fleet Operational Training Command, Atlantic Fleet
CLTE	Commissioned Loss To Enlisted status revocation of appointment (Navy)
CLU	Chartered Life Underwriter
CLUSA	Continental Limits, United States of America (Navy)
	Cooperative League of the USA
CM	Centimeter
	Construction and Machinery (Navy)
	Controlled Mine field (Military)
	Countermeasure (Military)
	Countermortar (Military)
	Court-Martial (Military)
CMA	Casket Manufacturers Association of America
	Christian and Missionary Alliance
	Clothespin Manufacturers of America
	Clothing Manufacturers Association of the U.S.
	Colorado Mining Association
	Confederate Memorial Association
	Corps Maintenance Area (Army)
	Court of Military Appeals
	Crucible Manufacturers Association
CMAA	Cigar Manufacturers Association of America
	Club Managers Association of America
	Cocoa Merchants Association of America
	Comics Magazine Association of America
CMAIISS	Clothing Monetary Allowance, Initial issue (Military)
CMAS	Clothing Monetary Allowance, Standard (Military)
CMC	Combined Meterological Committee (OB)

ACRONYMS

CMC — CNC

CMC	Commandant of the Marine Corps
CMCC	Conference of Mutual Casualty Companies
CM&D	Counter Measures and Deception (Military radar)
CMEA	Central Medical Establishment, Aviation (OB- Air Force)
	Council for Middle Eastern Affairs
CMF	Chocolate Milk Foundation
	Court-Martial Forfeiture (Military)
CMH	Chief of Military History (Army)
	Congressional Medal of Honor (see Medal of Honor)
CMI	Can Manufacturers Institute
CMIA	Coal Mining Institute of America
	Cultivated Mushroom Institute of America
CMIU	Cigar Makers' International Union
CMLC	Chemical Corps (Army)
CMLCENCOM	Chemical Corps Engineering Command (Army)
CMLCMATCOM	Chemical Corps Materiel Command (Army)
CMLCRDCOM	Chemical Corps Research and Development Command (Army)
CMLCTNGCOM	Chemical Corps Training Command (Army)
CMMR	Confirmed and Made a Matter of Record (Military)
CMO	Controlled Materials Officer (OB - Navy)
	Court Martial Orders (Navy)
CMP	Controlled Materials Plan (OB - War Production Board)
	Corps of Military Police (OB - Army - see Military Police Corps)
CMPA	Corrugated Metal Pipe Association
CMPAA	Certified Milk Producers Association of America
CMPHE	Conference of Municipal Public Health Engineers
CMRA	Chemical Market Research Association
CMS	College Music Society
CMSCI	Council of Mechanical Specialty Contracting Industries
CMTC	Civilian Military Training Camp (OB)
	Combined Military Transportation Committee (OB)
CN	Commonwealth Nation
	Compass North
	Cuban Navy
CNA	Canadian Northwest Atlantic area
	Chief of Naval Air
CNAADTRA	Chief of Naval Air Advanced Training
CNAB	Commander Naval Air Bases
CNABTRA	Chief of Naval Air Basic Training
CNAINTERMTRA	Chief of Naval Air Intermediate Training (OB - see CNAADTRA)
CNAOT	Chief of Naval Air Operational Training
CNAPRIMTRA	Chief of Naval Air Primary Training (OB - see CNARFSTRA)
CNAPT	Chief of Naval Air Primary Training
CNARESTRA	Chief of Naval Air Reserve Training
CNARFSTRA	Chief of Naval Air Primary Training
CNAS	Civil Navigation Aids System
CNAT	Chief of Naval Air Training
CNATE	Chief of Naval Airship Training and Experimentation
CNATECLTA	Commander, Naval Air Technical Training Lighter-Than-Air
CNATECHTRA	Chief of Naval Air Technical Training
CNATRA	Chief of Naval Air Training
CNAVANTRA	Chief of Naval Air Advanced Training
CNB	Commander, Naval Base
CNC	Chief Naval Censor
	Chief of Naval Communications

ACRONYMS

CNDO	Chief Navy Disbursing Officer
CNE	Canadian National Exposition
CNF	Commander Naval Forces
CNG	Commander Northern Group (Navy)
CNGB	Chief, National Guard Bureau
CNI	Chief of Naval Intelligence
CNLA	Council on National Library Associations
CNM	Chief of Naval Material
CNO	Chief of Naval Operations (see OPNAV)
CNOB	Commander, Naval Operating Base
CNP	Chief of Naval Personnel
CNR	Canadian National Railways
	Change(s) to Navy Regulations
	Chief of Naval Research
CNS	Canadian Naval Service
	Congress of Neurological Surgeons
	Control Net System (chiefly British)
CNT	Celestial Navigation Trainer (Military)
CNTP	Committee for a National Trade Policy
CNTS	Chief, Naval Transportation Service
C&O	Chesapeake & Ohio Railway
CO	Combined Operations (Military)
	Commanding Officer (Military)
	Communications Officer (Navy)
COA	California Olive Association
	Comptroller of the Army
COAC	Commanding Officer, Atlantic Coast (Military)
COAIREVACRON	Commanding Officer, Air Evacuation Squadron (Navy)
COB	Committee of combined Boards (OB)
COBT	Chicago Open Board of Trade
COC	Chief of Chaplains (Navy)
COCEEE	Committee on Captured Enemy Electronics Equipment (OB)
COD	Cash On Delivery
CODAN	Coded Weather Analysis (Navy)
CODCAVE	Committee on Decentralization of Controls After V-E Day (OB)
CODIS	Completed Discharge (Navy)
COEBG	Commission on Organization of the Executive Branch of the Government
COEL	Chain Overseas Extremely Low (Flying)
COF	Catholic Order of Foresters
COFRON	Coastal Frontier (Coast Guard)
COFT	Commander Fleet Train (Navy)
COG	Commander of the Guard (Military)
	Convenience of the Government (Military)
COGARD	United States Coast Guard
COHAMA	Cohn-Hall-Marx Company
COHQ	Combined Operations Headquarters (OB)
COI	Communication Operation Instructions (Military)
COIC	Combined Operational Intelligence Center (Navy)
COL	Chain Overseas Low (Flying)
COLANFORASCU	Commanding Officer, Landing Force Air Support Control Unit (Navy)
COLOD	Completed Loading (Navy)
COM	Commissioned Officers Mess (Navy)
COMAIR	Commander Aircraft (Navy)
	Commander Air Forces (Navy)
COMAIRCENT	Commander Allied Air Forces, Central Europe

ACRONYMS

COMAIRCENTLANT – COMSERFORSOPACSUBCOM

COMAIRCENTLANT .. Air Commander, Central Atlantic subarea (Military)
COMAIRLANT .. Commander Air Force, Atlantic Fleet
COMAIRNORECHAN .. Air Commander, Northeast subarea Channel (Military)
COMAIRNORLANT ... Air Commander, Northern Atlantic subarea (Military)
COMAIRNORTH . Commander Allied Air Forces, Northern Europe
COMAIRPAC ... Commander Air Force, Pacific Fleet
COMAIRPLYMCHAN .. Air Commander, Plymouth subarea Channel (Military)
COMAIRSOUTH . Commander Allied Air Forces, Southern Europe
COMALAIRNOREUR .. Commander, Allied Air Force, Northern Europe
COMALNAVNOREUR . Commander, Allied Naval Forces, Northern Europe
COMAT ...... Commodore Air Train (Navy)
COMATS ...... Commander Military Air Transport Service
COMBASFRANCE .... Commander Ports and Bases, France
COMTBRON ... Commander Motor Torpedo Boat Squadron (Navy)
COMEXDIV .... Commander Experimental Division (Navy)
COMFAIR ..... Commander Fleet Air (Navy)
COMFOURATAF . Commander, Fourth Allied Tactical Air Force, Central Europe
COMICEDEFOR . Commander, Iceland Defense Force (Military)
COMINTERN ... Communist International
COMJEF ...... Commander, Joint Expeditionary Force (Military)
COMMCEN .... Communication Center (Military)
COMNAB ..... Commander, Naval Air Bases
COMNAVFE ... Commander, Naval Forces, Far East
COMPAF...... Commander, Pacific Air Force
COMGEN .... Commanding General (Army and Marine Corps)
COMGENPOA .. Commanding General, Army Forces, Pacific Ocean Areas (OB)
COMGENMED .. Commanding General, Army Forces, Mediterranean Theatre of Op)
COMGENTEN .. Commanding General, Tenth Army (OB)
COMGREPAT .. Commander Greenland Patrol (Navy)
COMHAWSEAFRON .. Commander Hawaiian Sea Frontier (Navy)
COMIN ...... Commander Minecraft (Navy)
COMINCH .... Commander-in-Chief, US Fleet
COMINDIV .... Commander Minecraft Division (Navy)
COMINFORM .. Communist Information
COMINGRP.... Commander Mine Group (Navy)
COMIN GRPOK . Commander Mine Group Okinawa (Navy)
COMINLANT... Commander Mine Force, Atlantic Fleet
COMINPAC.... Commander Minecraft, Pacific Fleet
COMINST..... Communications Instructions (Navy)
COMLO ...... Combined Operations Material Liaison Officer (OB)
COMMCEN .... Communications Center (Military)
COMNAV..... Navy Command (part of North American Air Defense command)
COMNAVEASTLANTMED .. Commander Naval Forces Eastern Atlantic and Mediterranean
COMNAVJAP .. Commander Naval Activities Japan
COMNAVNAW . Commander Naval Forces, Northwest African Waters
COMNAVZOR .. Commander Naval Forces Azores
COMO .... Communications Officer (Navy)
COMPATPLANEREPRONSPAC .. Command Patrol Plane Replacement Squadrons Pacific (Navy)
COMPGENDEC . Comptroller General Decisions (Military)
COMPHIBFOR .. Commander Amphibious Force (Navy)
COMRATS ..... Commuted Rations (Navy)
COMPRON or COMPORON .. Composite Squadron (Navy)
COMROUTE.... Commander-in-Chief, US Fleet, Convoy and Routing Section
/Command (Navy)
COMSEAFRON .. Commander Sea Frontier (Navy)
COMSERFORSOPACSUBCOM .. Commander Service Force South Pacific Subordinate

- 69 -

ACRONYMS

COMSTS	Commander Military Sea Transport Service
COMTBFLOT	Commander Motor Torpedo Boat Flotilla (Navy)
COMTBRONTRACENT	Commander Motor Torpedo Boat Squadron Training Center (Navy)
COMTRAN	Commercial Translater
COMUSBASFRANCE	Commander US Ports and Bases, France
COMTWOATAF	Commander, Second Allied Tactical Air Force
COMZ	Communications Zone (Military)
CONAB	Commanding Officer, Naval Advanced Base
	Commanding Officer, Naval Air Base
CONAC	Continental Air Command (Air Force)
CONAD	Continental Air Defense command (Military)
CONAIR	Commanding Officer, Naval Air Wing
CONALT	Construction and repair, Alteration (Coast Guard)
CONAS	Commanding Officer, Naval Air Station
CONELRAD	Control of Electromagnetic Radiation
CONFBUL	Confidential Bulletin (Navy)
CONFMOD	Confidential-Modified handling authorized (Military)
CONHYDROLANT	Confidential Hydrographic office reports Atlantic (Navy)
CONNORPAC	Commander Naval Forces, Northern Pacific
CONROUTE	Convoy and Routing Section (Navy)
CONTRAIL	Condensation Trail (in the air)
CONUS	Continental United States (Military)
CONVAIR	Consolidated-Vultee Aircraft (OB - now official name of firm)
COPE	Committee on Political Education (AFL-CIO)
COPL	Committee for Oil Pipe Lines
COPP	Combined Operations Pilotage Party (OB)
COPSI	Council of Profit Sharing Industries
COR	Combat Operations Report (Military)
CORA	Conditioned Reflex Analogue
C of Ord	Chief of Ordnance (Army)
CORD	Coordinating of Research and Development (Navy)
CORE	Congress on Racial Equality
COREP	Combined Overload Repair Control (Navy)
CORTDIV	Escort Division (Navy)
COS	Cash-On-Shipment
	Chief of Staff (Marine Corps)
	Civilian Occupational Specialty
	Clinical Orthopaedic Society
COSD	Combined Operations Supply Depot (OB)
COSIDA	College Sports Information Directors of America
COSMD	Combined Operations Signal Maintenance Depot (OB)
COSMO	Combined Operations Signal Maintenance Officer (OB)
	Cosmopolitan Associates
COSO	Combined Operations Signal Officer (OB)
COSSAC	Chief of Staff, Supreme Allied Command
COSU	Combined Operations Scout Unit (OB)
COTA	Confirming telephone or message authority of
COTC	Commander Fleet Operational Training Command
COTCPACSUBCOM	Commander Fleet Operational Training Comm. Pacific Subordinate Comm.
COTP	Captain of the Port (Coast Guard)
COUSNAB	Commander of US Naval Advanced Base
COUSS	Commanding Officer, US Ship
CP	Command Post (Military)
	Communication Personnel (Marine Corps)
	Copilot

ACRONYMS

CPA	Catholic Press Association
	Certified Public Accountant
	Civilian Production Administration (OB)
CPAA	Cultured Pearl Association of America
CPAB	Cling Peach Advisory Board
CPAD	Central Pay Accounts Division (Navy)
CPAGA	California Prune and Apricot Growers Association
CPB	Contractors Pump Bureau
CPC	Chief Pay Clerk (Navy)
	Chief Planning and Control staff (Coast Guard)
	College Placement Council
	Crafts, Protective and Custodial (OB - Civil Service job classification)
CPCU	Chartered Property and Casualty Underwriter
CPD	Central Procurement Division (Marine Corps)
	Civilian Personnel Division (Military)
CPEA	College Physical Education Association
CPFF	Cost Plus Fixed Fee
CPG	College Publishers Group
CPHV	Conference of Public Health Veterinarians
CPI	Chief of Public Information (OB - Military)
	Clay Pipe Institute
	Consumer Price Index
	Crop Protection Institute
CPL	Civilian Personnel Letter
CPL&D	Civilian Personnel Letters and Dispatches
CPLIA	Contracting Plasterers' and Lathers' International Association
CPM	Combat air Patrol Mssion (Air Force)
CPO	Civilian Personnel Officer
CPOCT	Committee to Protect Our Children's Teeth
CPOSMA	Conference of Presidents and Officers of State Medical Associations
CPP	Children's Plea for Peace
CPPA	Classroom Periodical Publishers Association
	Coated and Processed Paper Association
CPPC	Clifton Precision Products, Inc.
CPR	Civilian Personnel Regulation
CPRA	Chemical Public Relations Association
CPRB	Combined Production and Resources Board (OB)
CPRC	Civilian Payroll Circular
CPS	Combined Staff Planners (OB)
	Cycles Per Second
CPSA	Catholic Poetry Society of America
CPTF	Central Plains Turfgrass Foundation
CPU	Church Peace Union
CPX	Command Post Exercise (Military)
CQ	Charge of Quarters (Military)
CQI&R	Cent. Qualifications Inventory & Referral System (Army Ordnance)
CQTU	Carrier Qualification Training Unit (Navy)
C/R	Certificate of Retirement (Military)
CR	Change Release (Military)
	Combat Reserve (Military)
	Commendation Ribbon (Military)
C&R	Construction and Repair (Coast Guard)
	Convoy and Routing (Navy)
CR	Crossroads
CRA	California Redwood Association

ACRONYMS

CRAB	California Raisin Advisory Board
CRACC	Communication and Radar Assignment Coordinating Committee (OB)
CRAF	Civil Reserve Air Fleet
CRAG	Carrier Replacement Air Group (Navy)
CRB	Cab Research Bureau
CRBA	Christian Record Benevolent Association
CRC	Central Requirements Committee (Military)
	Combined Rubber Committee (OB)
	Control and Reporting Center (Military)
	Copy Research Council
CRCPI	Coordinating Research Council of the Petroleum Industry
CRD	Chief of Research and Development (Army)
CRDF	Canadian Radio-Direction Finding or finder
	Cathode-Ray Direction Finding (radar)
CREWTAF	Crew Training Air Force (OB)
CRF	Cryptographic Repair Facility (Military)
CRFUSAIC	Central Records Facility, US Army Intelligence Center
CRI	Committee for Reciprocity Information
CRIME	Censorship Records and Information, Middle East (Military)
CRIS	Council for Religion in Independent Schools
CRM	Counter Radar Missile
CRMA	Commercial Refrigerator Manufacturers Association
CRMB	Combined Raw Materials Board (OB)
CRO	Cathode Ray Oscilloscope
	Civilian Repair Organization, Aircraft (Navy)
CROP	Christian Rural Overseas Program
CRP	Creative Protein
CRPL	Central Radio Propagation Laboratory (Military)
CRPM	Combined Registered Publication Memoranda (OB)
	Communication Registered Publication Memoranda (Military)
CRS	Catholic Renascence Society
CRSI	Concrete Reinforcing Steel Institute
CRT	Cathode Ray Tube
	Combat Readiness Training (Military)
CRUBATFOR	Cruisers, Battle Force (Navy)
CRUITSTA	Recruiting Station (Navy)
CRULANTFLT	Cruisers, Atlantic Fleet
CRUPACFLT	Cruisers, Pacific Fleet
CRUSCOFOR	Cruiser Scouting Force (Navy)
CRUSCORON	Cruiser Scouting Squadron (Navy)
CRWO	Coding Room Watch Officer (Navy)
C/S	Call Signal
	Certificate of Service (Military)
C of S	Chief of Staff (Military)
CS	Cirrostratus
	Close Support (Military)
	Coaling Station (Navy)
	Commissary Store (Navy)
	Community Service
	Contract Surgeon
	Current Series
CSA	Central Supply Association
C of SA	Chief of Staff, U.S. Army
CSA	Commercial-Service Authorization (Military)
	Community Service Activities (AFL-CIO)

ACRONYMS

CSA . . . . Confederate States of America (OB)
            Confederate States Army (OB)
            Consular Shipping Adviser
            Correctional Service Associates
CSAA . . . . Child Study Association of America
CSAB . . . . Combined Shipping Adjustment Board (OB)
C/SAF . . . . Chief of Staff, Air Force
CSBA . . . . Columbia Sheep Breeders' Association of America
CSC . . . . Civil Service Commission
            Civilian Screening Center (Military)
            Combined Shipbuilding Committee (OB)
            Command and Staff College (Air Force)
C-SCAN . . . . . . Viewing Cathode-Ray Screen (Air Force)
CSCC . . . . Council of State Chambers of Commerce
C-SCOPE . . . . . Cathode-Ray Screen (Air Force)
CSDIC . . . . Combined Services Detailed Interrogation Center (OB)
CSF . . . . Caribbean Sea Frontier (Navy)
CSFPSC . . . . . . Commander, Subordinate Command, Service Force, Pacific Fleet
CSG . . . . Combat Service Group (Military)
            Council of State Governments
CSHS . . . . Chief Superintendent of Hydrographic Supplies (Navy)
CSI . . . . Construction Specifications Institute
            Correct Seating Institute
CSIGO . . . . Chief Signal Officer (Army)
CSLEA . . . . Center for the Study of Liberal Education for Adults
CSM . . . . Close-Support Mission (Air Force)
            Council of the Southern Mountains
CSMA . . . . Chemical Specialties Manufacturers Association
CSO . . . . Communication Standing Order (Military)
CSOP . . . . Commission to Study the Organization of Peace
CSP . . . . Chaplain Service Personnel (Air Force)
            Combined Staff Planners (OB)
            Communications Security Publication (Military)
CSPA . . . . Catholic School Press Association
            Clay Sewer Pipe Association
            Columbia Scholastic Press Association
CSPM . . . . Communication Security Publication Memorandum (Military)
CSPPHLD . . . . . . Conference of State and Provincial Public Health Laboratory Directors
CSS . . . . Commodity Stabilization Service
CSSA . . . . Clothing and Small Stores Account (Navy)
            Crop Science Society of America
CSSCO . . . . Office of the Chief of Staff, Staff Communications Office (Army)
CSSE . . . . Conference of State Sanitary Engineers
CSSF . . . . Clothing and Small Stores Fund (Navy)
CST . . . . Central Standard Time
CSTA . . . . Cloak and Suit Trucking Association
CSWE . . . . Council on Social Work Education
C of T . . . . Chief of Transportation (Army)
CT . . . . Combat Team (Military)
            Communications Technician (Military)
            Crosstrail (Military)
CTA . . . . Chemical Toilet Association
CTAF . . . . Crew Training Air Force (OB)
CTAUA . . . . Catholic Total Abstinence Union of America
CTB . . . . Commercial Traffic Bulletin (Military)

- 73 -

ACRONYMS

CTC	Carbon Tetrachloride
	Combined Training Center (OB)
CTCC	Continental Division, Transport Control Center (Air Force)
CTCLS	Court of Claims
CTD	Commander Transportation Division (Navy)
CTDA	Custom Tailors and Designers Association of America
CTE	Commander Task Element (Military)
CTF	Commander Task Force (Military)
CTG	Commander Task Group (Military)
CTI	Cooling Tower Institute
CTMA	Cutting Tool Manufacturers Association
CTMC	Collapsible Tube Manufacturers Council
CTO	Courier Transfer Officer (Military)
CTS	Courier Transfer Station (Military)
CTTC	Chanute Technical Training Center (Air Force)
CTU	Combat Training Unit
	Commander Task Unit (Military)
CU	Consumers Union of United States
CUD	Craft Union Department (AFL-CIO)
CUMMFU	Complete Utter Monumental Military Foul Up
CUNA	Credit Union National Association
CUPA	College and University Personnel Association
CUSARROTC	Chief, US Army Reserve and ROTC Affairs
CUSRPG	Canada-US Regional Planning Group
CVS	Committee on Valuation of Securities
CW	Chemical Warfare
	Continuous Wave (radio symbol for code transmission)
CWA	Canadian Western Approaches
	Chinese Women's Association
	Communications Workers of America
CWBC	Credit Women's Breakfast Clubs of North America
CWC	Country Women's Council of U.S.A.
CWCA	Civil War Centennial Association
CWCC	Civil War Centennial Commission (government agency)
CWDWD	Committee for World Development and World Disarmament
CWLA	Child Welfare League of America
CWMAA	Clock and Watch Manufacturers Association of America
CWMTU	Cold Weather Material Test Unit (Military)
CWO	Communications Watch Officer (Navy)
CWS	Chemical Warfare Service (OB - Army - see Chemical Corps)
CWSF	Commander Western Sea Frontier (Navy)
CWV	Catholic War Veterans of the U.S.A.
CWVA	Catholic War Veterans Ladies Auxiliary
CYA	Carded Yarn Association
	Catholic Youth Adoration Society
CYO	Catholic Youth Organization
CYSA	Combed Yarn Spinners Association
CZ	Canal Zone
	Combat Zone (Army)
CZG	Canal Zone Government

D

D of A	Daughters of America
DA	Defense Aid (OB - Lendlease)

ACRONYMS DA - DC

DA	Delayed Action (bomb or shell fuze)
	Department of Agriculture
	Department of the Army
	Direct Action (bomb or shell fuze)
	District Attorney
	Double Acting
DAA	Durene Association of America
DAA&AM	Defense Aid Aircraft and Aeronautical Material (OB - Lend Lease)
DABLC	Director, Advanced Base Logistics Control (Navy)
DABOA	Director, Advanced Base Office, Atlantic (Navy)
DABOP	Director, Advanced Base Office, Pacific (Navy)
DAC	National Society, Daughters of the American Colonists
	Defenders of the American Constitution
DACAN	Standing Group Distribution and Accounting Agency, NATO
DACOR	Diplomatic and Consular Officers, Retired
DAF	Demonstration Air Force (OB)
	Department of the Air Force
DAF&E	Defense Aid Facilities and Equipment (OB - Lend Lease)
DAFS	Duty Air Force Specialty
DAGO	District Aviation Gas Office (Navy)
DAI	Death from Accidental Injuries (Military)
DAL	Delta Air Lines
DALVP	Delay enroute Authorized as ordinary Leave Provided it does not interfere /with reporting date
DAMRW	Director of Aircraft Maintenance and Repair Washington (Navy)
DAO	District Accounting Office (r) (Navy)
	District Aviation Office (r) (Navy)
	Division Ammunition Officer (Military)
DAO&OS	Defense Aid Ordnance and Ordnance Stores (OB - Lend Lease)
DAR	Daily Activity Report (Military)
	National Society, Daughters of the American Revolution
DAS	Director (ate) of Administrative Services (Air Force)
DASA	Defense Atomic Support Agency (Military)
DASD	Department of the Army Shipping Document
DAT	Director (ate) of Advanced Technology (Air Force)
DATA	Defense Air Transportation Administration (Military)
DATO	Disbursing and Transportation Office (Military)
DAT&OV	Defense Aid Tanks and Other Vehicles (OB - Lend Lease)
DAV	Disabled American Veterans
DAVA	Disabled American Veterans Auxiliary
DAVI	Department of Audio-Visual Instruction
DAWG	Dynamic Air War Game (Military)
D/B	Deposit Book (Military)
DB	Depth Bomb (Military)
	Disciplinary Barracks (Military)
D&B	Dun & Bradstreet
DBA	Doing Business As
DBH	Division Beachhead (Army)
DBSO	District Base Service Office (Navy)
DBW	Differential Ballistic Wind
D of C	Daughters of the Confederacy
DC	Deck Court (Navy)
	Defense Counsel (Military)
	Dental Corps (Military)
	Department of Commerce
	Depth Charge (Military)

DC	Direct Current
	Disciples of Christ
	District of Columbia
DCA	Defense Contre Avion (French)
DC/AS	Deputy Chief of Air Staff (OB)
DCB	Defense Communications Board (Military)
DCC	District Communications Center (Navy)
DCCAO	Deputy Chief Civil Affairs Officer (Military)
DCE	Director (ate) of Civil Engineering (Air Force)
DCG	Deputy Commanding General
DCGO	District Coast Guard Officer
DCH	District Chaplain (Navy)
DCMA	Dry Color Manufacturers Association
DCNO	Deputy Chief of Naval Operations
DCNOA	Deputy Chief of Naval Operations, Administration
DCNOAIR	Deputy Chief of Naval Operations, Air
DCNOFOR	Deputy Chief of Naval Operations, Fleet Operations and Readiness
DCNS	Deputy Chief of Naval Staff (Marine Corps)
DCO	District Camouflage Office (r) (Navy)
	District Clothing Office (r) (Navy)
	District Communications Office (r) (Navy)
DCOME	Director of Combined Operations Middle East (OB)
DCP	Director of Civilian Personnel (Navy)
DCPB	Departmental Civilian Personnel Branch (Navy)
DCPO	Director (ate) of Civilian Personnel Office (Air Force)
	District Civilian Personnel Office (r) (Navy)
DCRO	District Civil Readjustment Office (r) (Navy)
DCS	Deputy Chief of Staff (Military)
DC of SA	Deputy Chief of Staff, Army
DC/SAF	Deputy Chief of Staff, Air Force
DCS/C	Deputy Chief of Staff, Comptroller (Air Force)
DCS/D	Deputy Chief of Staff, Development (Air Force)
DCSLOG	Deputy Chief of Staff for Logistics (Army)
DCS/M	Deputy Chief of Staff, Materiel (Air Force)
DCS/O	Deputy Chief of Staff, Operations (Air Force)
DCSOPS	Deputy Chief of Staff for Military Operations (Army)
DCS/P	Deputy Chief of Staff, Personnel (Air Force)
DCSPER	Deputy Chief of Staff for Personnel (Army)
DCS/PR	Deputy Chief of Staff, Plans and Research (Air Force)
DCSPR	Deputy Chief of Staff for Plans and Research (Army)
DCT	Department of Classroom Teachers (of the NEA)
DCW	National Society, Daughters of Colonial Wars
DD	Department of Defense
	Dishonorable Discharge (Military)
D/D	Donation on Discharge (see DONISCH)
DD	Double Drift (as used in a navigator's log)
DDA	Dental Dealers of America
DDALV	Days' Delay enroute Authorized Chargeable as Leave (Military)
D (Day)	Day set for assault by land forces
DDD	Deadline Delivery Date (Military)
	Diesel Direct Drive (Navy) /(Navy)
DDGC	Dishonorable Discharge, General court martial, after confinement in prison
DDGI	Dishonorable Discharge, General court martial, Immediate (Navy)
DDGP	Dishonorable Discharge, General court martial, after violation of Probation
DDO	Destroyers, Disbursing Office (Navy) /(Navy)

ACRONYMS

DDO - DFT

DDO	District Dental Office (r) (Navy)
DDP	Director (ate) of Development Planning (Air Force)
DDT	Dichloro-Diphenyl-Trichloroethane (insect killer)
DDTO	District Domestic Transportation Office (r) (Navy)
DE	Date of Entry or Date of Extension (Military)
	Deflection Error (Military)
	Department of Education
DEAL	Detachment Equipment Authorization List (Military)
DECA	Distributive Education Clubs of America
DECON	Decontaminate (Military)
DEDD	Diesel Electric Direct Drive (Navy)
DEFSEC	Defense Sector (Navy)
DEG & DEP	Degaussing and Deperming (Navy)
DEMA	Diesel Engine Manufacturers Association
DEML	Detached Enlisted Men's List (Military)
DEMO	Demolition (Military)
DEMOB	Demobilization (Military)
DEO	District Engineer Officer (Army)
DEPERM STA	Deperming and Flashing Station (Navy)
DERAX	Detection and Range (early name for radar)
DEROS	Date Eligible for Return from Overseas (Military)
DESAF	Destroyers, Asiatic Fleet (OB - Navy)
DESBATFOR	Destroyer Battle Force (Navy)
DESCOFOR	Destroyer Scouting Force (Navy)
DESCRUPAC	Destroyers/Cruisers, Pacific Fleet
DESDIV	Destroyer Division (Navy)
DESEFF	Deserter's Effects (Military)
DESFLOT	Destroyer Flotilla (Navy)
DESIG NAP	Designated as Naval Aviation Pilot (Marine Corps)
DESILU	Desi-Lucille Arnaz Company
DESLANT	Destroyers, Atlantic Fleet
DESO	District Educational Service Officer (Navy)
DESOIL	Diesel Oil (Navy)
DESP	Department of Elementary School Principals (of the NEA)
DESPAC	Destroyers, Pacific Fleet
DESREP	Destroyer Repair (Navy)
	Destroyer Representative (Navy)
DESRON	Destroyer Squadron (Navy)
DESSOWESPAC	Destroyers, Southwest Pacific Fleet
DEW	Distant Early Warning (radar picket line)
DF	Defensive Fire (Military)
	Direction Finder (radio)
	Disposition Form (Military)
DFA	Drop Forging Association
DFAC	Dried Fruit Association of California
DFC	Distinguished Flying Cross (Military)
DFCO	Duty Flying Control Officer (Navy)
DFI	Decorative Fabrics Institute
DFING	Radio Direction-Finding (Military)
DFPA	Daughters of Founders and Patriots of America
	Douglas Fir Plywood Association
DFR	Dropped From Roll (Military)
DFSB	Defense Force Section Base (Navy)
DFSR	Director (ate) of Flight Safety Research (Air Force)
DFT	Director, Fleet Training

ACRONYMS

DG — DIVCOM

DG	Degaussing (Navy)
	Distinguished Graduate (Military)
DGD	Diesel Geared Drive (Navy)
DGI	Date Growers' Institute
DGMG	Diesel-Geared-Motor Geared (Navy)
DGO	Degaussing Officer (Navy)
DGRO	Degaussing Range Officer (Navy)
DGTO	Degaussing Technical Officer (Navy)
DGWO	Degaussing Wiping Officer (Navy)
DGZ	Desired Ground Zero (bombing)
DHE	Department of Home Economics (of the NEA)
DHEW	Department of Health, Education and Welfare
DHIRS	District Headquarters Induction and Recruiting Station (Marine Corps)
DHO	District Historical Office (r) (Navy)
DHPA	Degree of Honor Protective Association
DHQ	Division Headquarters (Military)
DI	Department of the Interior
	Director(ate) of Installations (Air Force)
	Discomforture Index (weather - OB - see THI)
	District Inspector (Navy)
	Drill Instructor (Marine Corps)
DIA	Date of Initial Appointment (Military)
DIC	Dairy Industry Committee
	Detailed Interrogation Center (Navy)
DICAB	Directive Coordinated and Approved by Budget director (Air Force)
DICBM	Defense Intercontinental Ballistic Missile
DID	Daily Intelligence Digest (Military) /(Navy)
DI/DES	Vessels Disposed of by sinking, burning, abandoning or other Destruction
DIF	Direction Finder (radio)
	Duty Involving Flying (Military)
DI/FLC	Vessels in forward areas transferred to State Dept. Foreign Liquidation Corp.
DIFOT	Duty Involving Operational or Training Flights (Air Force)
DIFOTECH	Duty Involving Operational or Training Flights as a Technical observer (AF)
DIFOTINS	Duty Involving Operational or Training Flights under Instruction (AF)
DIFOTRELAS	Duty Involving Operational or Training Flights as his own Relief (AF)
DIIO	District Industrial Incentive Office (r) (Navy)
DIM	District Industrial Manager (Navy)
DINA	Direct Noise Amplifier (airborne radar transmitter)
DINO	Deputy Inspector of Naval Ordnance
DIO	District Intelligence Office (r) (Navy)
	Duty Intelligence Officer (Air Force)
DIR	Depot Inspection and Repair (Navy)
DIRLANTDOCKS	Director, Atlantic Division, Bureau of Yards and Docks (Navy)
DIRNAVHIST	Director of Naval History
DIRNSA	Director, National Security Agency
DIRO	District Industrial Relations Officer (OB - Navy)
DIRPACDOCKS	Director, Pacific Division, Bureau of Yards and Docks (Navy)
DIS	Dwarf Iris Society
DISA	Dairy Industries Supply Association
DI/SAL	Vessels Disposed of by Sale through Navy Material Redistribution Agency
DI/SCP	Vessels Disposed of by Scrapping (Navy)
DITC	Disability Insurance Training Council
DI/TES	Vessels Disposed of by using as targets and Tests (Navy) /(Navy)
DI/TRN	Vessels Transferred to other Govt. Agencies and miscellaneous activities
DIVCOM	Division Commander (Navy)

ACRONYMS

DI/WSA ...... Vessels transf. to War Shipping Admin.-Maritime Commission for Disposition /(Navy)
DJ .... Department of Justice
           Disc Jockey
DL .... Department of Labor
           Destroyer Leader (Navy)
DLC .... Disaster Loan Corp.
DLCA .... Dairymen's League Cooperative Association
DLF .... Development Loan Fund
DLNC .... Deputy Local Naval Commander
DLO .... District Legal Office(r) (Navy)
DLRO .... District Labor Relations Office(r) (Navy)
DLT .... Deck Landing Training (Navy)
DLTS .... Deck Landing Training School (Navy)
DMA .... Dental Manufacturers of America
DMAA .... Direct Mail Advertising Association
DMB .... Defense Mobilization Board
DME .... Distance-Measuring Equipment
DMEA .... Defense Minerals Exploration Administration (Interior Department)
DMIAA .... Diamond Manufacturers and Importers Association of America
DMO .... District Marine Officer
           District Material Officer (Navy)
           District Medical Officer (Navy)
DMP .... Director(ate) of Military Personnel (Air Force)
           Disarmed Military Personnel
DMPI .... Desired Mean Point of Impact
DMR .... Defective Materiel Report (Air Force)
DMZ .... Demilitarized Zone
DN .... Department of the Navy
DNB .... Deutches Nachrichtenburo (German news agency)
DNC .... Democratic National Committee
           Director of Naval Communications (OB)
DNI .... Director of Naval Intelligence
DNOP .... Director of Naval Officer Procurement
DNRH .... Director of Naval Records and History
DNTS .... Director Naval Transportation Service (OB)
DO .... Defense Order
           Dental Officer (Navy)
           Disbursing Officer (Navy)
           Duty Officer (Military)
DOA .... Dead on Arrival
           Disabled Officers Association
DOB .... Date of Birth (Military)
DOCA .... Date of Current Appointment (Military)
DOCE .... Date of Current Enlistment (Military)
DOCG .... Date of rank in Current Grade (Military)
DOD .... Department of Defense
           Died of Disease (Military)
DODMPRC ..... Department of Defense Military Personnel Records Center
DODR&E ...... Department of Defense Research & Engineering division
DOE .... Date of Enlistment (Military)
DOF .... Defenders of Furbearers
DOKK .... Dramatic Order Knights of Khorassan
DOL .... Detached Officer's List (Army)
DOLOA .... Dog Owners League of America
DOO .... District Ordnance Office(r) (Navy)

DOP	Detachment of Patients (Military)
DOPF	Duty directed in Order is being Performed For (Military)
DORAN	Doppler Range and Navigation (electronic)
DOS	Date of Separation (Military)
DOT	Dependent Overseas Territory
	Dictionary of Occupational Titles
DOV	Disbursing Officer's Voucher (Navy)
DOVAP	Doppler Velocity and Position (electronic)
DOW	Died of Wounds (Military)
DP	Deep Penetration (Air Force)
D of P	Degree of Pocahontas
DP	Department of the Pacific (Marine Corps)
D/P	Detained Pay (Military)
DP	Direction of the President
	Displaced Person
	Distribution Point (Military)
	Double Purpose gun (Military)
DPB	Defense Policy Board
DPC	Defense Plants Corporation
DPD	Director, Personnel Department (Marine Corps)
	District Port Director (Navy)
DPG	Date of Permanent Grade (Military)
DPI	Department of Public Information (United Nations)
DPIO	District Public Information Office(r) (Navy)
DPLO	District Postal Liaison Officer (Navy)
DPM	Designated for Prompt Mobilization (Military)
DPMC	Director of Personnel Marine Corps
DPO	Development Planning Objective
	District Personnel Office(r) (Navy)
	District Postal Office(r) (Navy)
DPP	Director(ate) of Personnel Planning (Air Forces)
DPPO	District Publications and Printing Office (Navy)
DPPT	Director(ate) of Personnel Procurement and Training (Air Force)
DPRO	District Public Relations Office(r) (Navy)
DPTO	District Property Transportation Office(r) (Navy)
DPUO	Duty directed is being Performed for Unit issuing Order (Military)
DPWO	District Public Works Office(r) (Navy)
DQM	Depot Quartermaster (Marine Corps)
DQP	Depot Quartermaster, Philadelphia (Marine Corps)
DQPH	Depot Quartermaster, Pearl Harbor (Marine Corps)
D/R	Date of Rank (Military)
DR or D/R	Dead Reckoning
D/R	Directional Radio
	Dispatch Rider (Marine Corps)
DRA	Dead Reckoning Analyzer
	Dude Ranchers' Association
DRC	Division of Rehabilitation Counseling (of the APGA)
DRD	Director(ate) of Research and Development (Air Force)
	Documentary Research Division (Air Force)
DRE	Department of Rural Education (of the NEA)
	Director(ate) of Research and Engineering (Military)
DRMF	Damon Runyon Memorial Fund for Cancer Research
DRMO	District Records Management Officer (Navy)
DROS	Date Returned from Overseas (Military)
DRP	Dead Reckoning Plotter

ACRONYMS

DRT . . . . Daughters of the Republic of Texas
　　　　　　　　　 Dead Reckoning Tracer
DRU . . . . Demolition Research Unit (Navy)
DS . . . . Date of Service (Military)
D of S . . . . Daughters of Scotia
　　　　　　　　　 Day of Supply (Military)
DS . . . . Delphian Society
　　　　　　　　　 Department of State
D of S . . . . Depot of Supplies (Marine Corps)
D/S . . . . Detached Service (Army)
DS . . . . Direct Support (Military)
DSA . . . . Division Service Area (Army)
DSC . . . . Defense Supply Corporation
　　　　　　　　　 Distinguished Service Cross (Army)
DSCP . . . . Division Supply Control Point (Army)
DSI . . . . Dairy Society International
　　　　　　　　　 Distilled Spirits Institute
DSIA . . . . Diaper Service Institute of America
DSM . . . . Direction de Service de Securite Militaire (France)
　　　　　　　　　 Distinguished Service Medal (Military)
DSO . . . . District Security Office(r) (Navy)
　　　　　　　　　 District Service Office(r) (Navy)
　　　　　　　　　 District Supply Office(r) (Navy)
DSS . . . . Director(ate) of Statistical Services (Air Force)
DSSO . . . . District Ships Service Office(r) (Navy)
DSW . . . . Director of Special Weapons (Army)
D of SW . . . . . . Director of Stores Washington (Navy)
DT . . . . Dental Technician (Military)
　　　　　　　　　 Department of Treasury
DTG . . . . Date-Time Group (Military)
DTO . . . . District Training Office(r) (Navy)
　　　　　　　　　 District Transportation Office(r) (Navy)
DU . . . . Diagnosis Undetermined
　　　　　　　　　 Ducks Unlimited (Conservation Association)
DUC . . . . Distinguished Unit Citation (Military)
DUCE . . . . Distinguished Unit Citation Emblem (Military)
DUCON . . . . . . Duty Connected (Military)
DUDAT . . . . . . Due Date
DUE . . . . Distinguished Unit Emblem (Military)
DUFLY . . . . Duty involving Flying (Military)
DUFLYTECH . . . . Duty involving Flying as a Technical observer (Military)
DUFLYTECHNAV . . Duty involving Flying as a Technical observer non-pilot Navigator
DUKW . . . . Amphibious Truck (Military)
DURBI . . . . Directory of University Research Bureaus and Institutes
DUVCW . . . . . . Daughters of Union Veterans of the Civil War
DV . . . . Distinguished Visitor (Military)
DVFR . . . . Defense Visual Flight Rules
DWA . . . . Died of Wounds resulting from Action with enemy (Military)
DWBO . . . . District War Bond Office (r) (OB - Navy)
DWPO . . . . District War Plans Office(r) (Navy)
DYNA-SOAR . . . Dynamic Soaring (space flight)
DZ . . . . Drop Zone (Military)
DZA . . . . Drop Zone Area (Military)

E

EA	Enemy Aircraft
EAA	Ecuadorean-American Chamber of Commerce
	Encyclopedia of American Associations
	Engineers and Architects Association
EABN	Engineer Aviation Battalion (Military)
EAC	Eastern Air Command (OB)
	European Advisory Commission (OB)
	Exhibitors Advisory Council
EAD	Extended Active Duty (Military)
EADF	Eastern Air Defense Force (Air Force)
EAGA	Episcopal Actors' Guild of America
EAME	Europe-Africa-Middle East
EAMECM	European-African-Middle-Eastern Campaign Medal (Military)
EANA	Esperanto Association of North America
EAPAUS	Employment Agencies Protective Association of the U.S.
EAPD	Eastern Air Procurement District (Air Force)
EAS	Equivalent Airspeed
EASTAF	Eastern Transport Air Force
EASTCO	East Coast (Navy)
EASTCON	Eastern Sea Frontier Control local of shipping in Gulf of Maine (Navy)
EASTLANT	Eastern Atlantic Area (Navy)
EASTLANTMEDCOM	Eastern Atlantic and Mediterranean Command (Military)
EASTOMP	East-Ocean Meeting Point (Shipping)
EASTSEAFRON	Eastern Sea Frontier (Navy)
EAT	Earliest Arriving Time
	Earliest Arrival Time
EATI	Equipment and Tool Institute
EAUTC	Engineer Aviation Unit Training Center (Military)
EBMA	Elastic Braid Manufacturers Association
EBSR	Eye-Bank for Sight Restoration
EC	Engineering Construction (Military)
	Extension Course
ECA	Economic Cooperation Administration (OB - now Mutual Security Agency)
ECAB	Employees' Compensation Appeals Board (Labor Department)
ECAD	European Civil Affairs Division (OB - Military)
ECAFE	Economic Commission for Asia and the Far East (United Nations)
ECC	Emergency Conservation Committee
	European Coordinating Committee
ECCM	Electronic Counter-Countermeasure(s) (Military)
ECE	Economic Commission for Europe (United Nations)
ECGAI	Education Council of the Graphic Arts Industry
ECHO	Enteric Cytopathogenic Human Orphan (medicine)
ECI	Electronic Communications Inc.
	Extension Course Institute (Air Force)
ECL	Equipment Component List (Military)
ECLA	Economic Commission for Latin America (United Nations)
ECLC	Emergency Civil Liberties Committee
ECM	Electric Coding (or Cipher) Machine (Military)
	Electronic Counter Measures (Military)
ECO	Economic Cooperation Organization
ECOSOC	Economic and Social Council (United Nations)
ECP	Engineering Change Proposed (Military)
ECPD	Engineers Council for Professional Development

ACRONYMS

ECS – ELNA

ECS	Electrochemical Society
ECSA	European Communications Security Agency (Military)
ED	Eastern District (Navy)
	Extra Duty (Military)
EDC	Eastern Defense Command (Army)
EDCMR	Effective Date of Change of Morning Report (OB)
EDCSA	Effective Date of Change of Strength Accountability (Military)
EDD	Eastern Development Division (Air Force)
EDDC	East Coast Distribution Center (Naval Publications)
EDFR	Effective Date of Federal Recognition (Military)
EDFTCA	Eastern Dark-Fired Tobacco Growers Association
EDO	Engineering Duties Only (Military)
EDP	Electronic Data Processing
EDRT	Effective Date of Relief from Training (Military)
EDS	Estimated Date of Separation (Military)
EDSA	Effective Date of change in Station Assignment (Military)
EDT	Eastern Daylight Time
	Effective Date of Training (Military)
EE	Electronics Engineering division (Coast Guard)
EEC	European Economic Community
EEG	Electroencephalography
EEI	Edison Electric Institute
	Environmental Equipment Institute
	Essential Elements of Information (Military)
EENT	End Evening Nautical Twilight
	Eye, Ear, Nose and Throat
EE&RM	Elementary Electrical and Radio Material training school (Navy)
EET	Education Equivalency Test (Military)
EF	Elevation Finder (Military)
EFD	Excused From Duty (Military)
EFL	Educational Facilities Laboratories
EFLA	Educational Film Library Association
EF&LTC	Enemy Fuels and Lubricants Technical Committee (Military)
EFM	Expeditionary Force Message (Military)
EFMA	Evangelical Foreign Missions Association
EFMI	Elastic Fabric Manufacturers Institute
EFTS	Elementary Flying Training School (Navy)
EG	Escort Group (Navy)
	Expert Gunner (Military)
EGT	Exhaust-Gas Temperature
EHA	Economic History Association
EHF	Extremely High Frequency
EHV	Extra High Voltage
EIA	Electronic Industries Association
	Envelope Institute of America
E-IB	Export-Import Bank
EIL	Explosives Investigation Laboratory
EIT	Electrical Information Test (Military)
EJI	Expansion Joint Institute
EJMA	Educational Jewelry Manufacturers Association
EKG	Electrocardiogram (medicine)
EL	Education Level (Military)
ELLA	European Long Lines Agency (Military)
ELM	Eastern Atlantic and Mediterranean (Military)
ELNA	Esperanto League for North America

ELRIC	Employers Labor Relations Information Committee
ELSB	Edge Lighted Status Board (Navy)
ELTC	Enlisted Loss to Commissioned status (Navy)
ELTW	Enlisted Loss to Warrant status (Navy)
EM	Education Manual (Military)
	Enlisted Man or Men (Military)
EMA	Evaporated Milk Association
EMAA	Envelope Manufacturers Association
EMCCC	European Military Communicati
EMF	Electromotive Force
	Excerpta Medica Foundation
EMIDEC	EMI Data Electronic Computer (made by EMI Industries – Great Britain)
EMG	Executive Mansion and Grounds (Executive Office of the President)
EML	Equipment Modification List (Military)
EMR	Enlisted Manning Report (Air Force)
EMSA	Electron Microscope Society of America
EMT	Emergency Medical Tag (Military)
ENC	Enlistment Cancelled (Navy)
ENIAC	Electronic Numerical Integrator and Computer
EO	Executive Order (Military)
EOA	Effective On or About (Military)
EOCI	Electric Overhead Crane Institute
EOD	Date of Entering Office (Military)
	Entry on Duty (Military)
	Explosive Ordnance Disposal (Military)
EODP	Engineering Order Delayed for Parts
EOP	Executive Office of the President
EOR	Explosive Ordnance Reconnaissance (Military)
EOS	Eligible for Overseas Service (Military)
EOSO	Escort Oilers Supervising Officer (Navy)
EOU	Enemy Objective Unit (OB – Military)
EP	Engineer Personnel (Marine Corps)
	Entrucking Point (Military)
EPA	Employee Plan Administrators
EPAA	Educational Press Association of America
	Employing Printers Association of America
EPC	End Products Committee (OB – War Production Board)
EPCO	Engine Parts Coordinating Office (Navy)
EPD	Earliest Practicable Date (Military)
	Eastern Procurement Division (Navy)
	Eastern Production District (Navy)
EPEAA	Employing Photo-Engravers Association of America
EPLA	Electronics Precedence List Agency (Military)
EPR	Engineer Photographic and Reproduction (Marine Corps)
EPTE	Existed Prior to Entry (Military)
ER	Effectiveness Report (Military)
	Emergency Rescue
E&R	Engineering and Repair Department (Navy)
ER	Expert Rifleman (Military)
ERA	Electric Railroaders Association
ERB	Equipment Review Board (Military)
ERC	Enlisted Reserve Corps (Army)
ERFA	European Radio Frequency Agency
ERICR	Eleanor Roosevelt Institute for Cancer Research
ERMA	Electronic Recording Machine Accounting

ACRONYMS

ERO – EUM

ERO	Emergency Repair Overseer (Navy)
ERP	European Recovery Program (OB)
ERPC	Eastern Railroads Presidents Conference
ERSA	Electronic Research Supply Agency (Navy)
ES	Econometric Society
	Eligible for Separation (Military)
	Endocrine Society
ESA	Ecological Society of America
	Electrolysis Society of America
	Engineers and Scientists of America
	Entomological Society of America
	Euthanasia Society of America
ESAR	Electronically Steerable Array Radar (Military)
ESAWC	Evaluation Staff, War College (Air Force)
ESC	Economic and Social Council (United Nations)
ESCA	Executive Stewards' and Caterers' Association
ESCARFOR	Escort Carrier Force (Navy)
ESCORDIV	Escort Division (Navy)
ESCORON	Escort Scouting Squadron (Navy)
ESCORTFIGHTRON	Escort Fighter Squadron (Navy)
ESF	Eastern Sea Frontier (Navy)
ESHU	Emergency Ship Handling Unit (Navy)
ESM	Escort Mission (Military)
ESMA	Engraved Stationery Manufacturers Association
ESMRI	Engraved Stationery Manufacturers Research Institute
ESO	Educational Services Office (r) (Navy)
ESOA	Epiphyllum Society of America
ESP	Extrasensory Perception /competent Written Orders in advance
ESPWO	Exigencies of the Service having been such as to Preclude the issuance of
ESS	Educational Services Section (Navy)
ESSO	Standard Oil
EST	Eastern Standard Time
	Enlistment Screening Test (Military)
ESTAR	Estimated Arrival Date
ESU	English-Speaking Union of the United States
ETA	Estimated Time of Arrival
ETC	Estimated Time of Completion
	European Travel Commission
ETD	Estimated Time of Departure
ETE	Estimated Time Enroute
ETF	Eastern Task Force (Navy)
ETI	Electric Tool Institute
	Estimated Time of Interception
ETN	Eastern Technical Net (Air Force)
	Equipment Table Nomenclature (Military)
ETO	European Theater of Operations (OB)
ETOUSA	European Theater of Operations United States Army (OB)
ETR	Estimated Time of Return
ETRA	Estimated Time to Reach Altitude
ETS	Expiration Term of Service (Army)
ETSP	Entitled to Severance Pay (Military)
ETTA	Evangelical Teacher Training Association
EUA	Eastern Underwriters Association
EUCOM	European Command (Military)
EUM	European-Mediterranean (Military)

EURAILPASS	European Railway Passenger (ticket)
EURAL	European Air Lines
EURATOM	European Atomic Energy Community
EUROMART	European Common Market
EUSA	Eighth US Army
EUSAR	Eighth US Army Rear
EVA	Escort Vessel Administration (Navy)
EVM	Evacuation Mission (Air Force)
EW	Electronic Warfare
	Enlisted Woman or Women (Military)
EWA	Education Writers Association
EWAS	Economic Warfare Analysis Section (OB - Navy)
EWD	Economic Warfare Division (OB - Navy)
EWHA	Eastern Women's Headwear Association
EWMC	Eli Whitney Metrology Center
EWR	Early-Warning Radar
EWSC	Electric Water Systems Council
EWT	Eastern War Time (OB)
EXDIV	Experimental Division (Navy)
EXIM	Export-Import Bank
EXO	Executive Officer (Military)
EXOS	Executive Office of the Secretary (Navy)
EXPDIVUNIT	Experimental Diving Unit (Navy)
EXSTA	Experimental Station (Navy)

F

F	Fahrenheit
FA	Family Allowance (Military)
F/A	Field Activities
FA	Field Artillery (Military)
	Folklore Americas
	Friendly Aircraft
FAA	Federal Aviation Agency
	Fleet Air Arm
	Foreman's Association of America
	Foundation for American Agriculture
	Fraternal Actuarial Association
FAAA	First Allied Airborne Army (OB - World War II)
FAAS	Fellow of the American Association for the Advancement of Science
FAAG	First Advertising Agency Group
FAB	Fleet Air Base
	For'ca Aerea Brasileira (Brazilian Air Force)
FABU	Fleet Air Base Unit
FAC	Federal Aviation Commission (OB)
	Forward Air Controller (Military)
	Frequency Allocation Committee (OB - Military)
FAD	Fleet Air Detachment
FAETUA	Fleet Airborne Electronics Unit, Atlantic
FAETUP	Fleet Airborne Electronics Unit, Pacific
FAGAIRTRANS	First Available Government Air Transportation (Navy)
FAGT	First Available Government Transportation (Military)
FAI	Federation Aeronautique Internationale
FAIR	Fleet Air Wing
FAIRSHIPWING	Fleet Airship Wing

ACRONYMS

FAIRWEST PAC..	Fleet Air Wing, Western Pacific Area
FAIRWING	Fleet Air Wing
F&AM........	Free and Accepted Masons
FAMA........	Fire Apparatus Manufacturers Association
FAMBSA	Farmers and Manufacturers Beet Sugar Association
FAMU........	Fleet Aircraft Maintenance Unit (Navy)
FANNIE MAE ..	Federal National Mortgage Association
FAO.........	Fleet Administration Office
	Food and Agriculture Organization (United Nations)
FAP	Frequency Allocation Panel (Military)
FAPG	Fleet Air Photographic Group (Navy)
	Forward America Publishing Guild
FAPRON......	Fleet Air Photo Squadron (Navy)
FAR	Foreign Agricultural Relations office
FAS	Federation of American Scientists
	Foreign Agriculture Service
	Free Alongside (Navy)
FASA	Fleet Airships, Atlantic
FASEB........	Federation of American Societies for Experimental Biology
FASP	Fleet Airships, Pacific
FASRON	Fleet Aircraft Service Squadron
FASRON	Fleet Air Service Squadron
FASTP........	Foreign Area Specialist Training Program (Military)
FASTULANT....	Fleet Ammunition Ship Training Unit, Atlantic
FASTUPAC.....	Fleet Ammunition Ship Training Unit, Pacific
FATU	Fleet Air Tactical Unit
FAW.........	Fleet Air Wing
FB	Fighter Bomber (Military)
	Film Bulletin
	Free Baptist
	Fumigation and Bath (Military)
FBA	Federal Bar Association
FBI..........	Federal Bureau of Investigation
FBLA........	Future Business Leaders of America
FBM.........	Fleet Ballistic Missile
FBMP	Fleet Ballistic Missile Program (Navy)
FBP	Fleet Boat Pool
FBRL.........	Final Bomb Release Line
FC	Ferrying Command (OB - Air Force)
	Fighter Command (OB - Air Force)
	Finance Corps (Army)
F/C	Flight Certificate (Air Force)
FC	Fractocumulus
FCA	Farm Credit Administration
	Fire Control Area (Military)
	Flight Control Assemblies (Navy)
FCB	Facility Clearance Board (OB - War Production Board)
FCBA	Federal Communications Bar Association
FCC	Federal Communications Commission
	Fighter Control Center (Military)
	Florida Citrus Commission
FCCA	Farmers Cinchilla Cooperative of America
FCCUS	French Chamber of Commerce of the United States
FCE	Fleet Civil Engineer
FCF	Free China Fund for Medical and Refugee Aid

Acronym	Meaning
FCI	Fluid Controls Institute
FCIC	Federal Crop Insurance Corporation
FCMSBR	Federal Coal Mine Safety Board of Review
FCMV	Fuel Consuming Motor Vehicle (Military)
FCNL	French Committee of National Liberation (OB - free French)
FCO	Flag Communications Officer (Navy)
	Flying Control Officer (Military)
FCP	Fire Control Personnel (Marine Corps)
FCPC	Fair Campaign Practices Committee
FCPG	Federation of Catholic Physicians' Guilds
FCR	Fire Controlman, Range-finder operator (Navy)
FCRAA	Folding Chair Rental Association of America
FCS	Farmer Cooperative Service (Agriculture Department)
	Federal Catalog System
	Fighter Command School (OB - Air Force)
FCSA	Forest Conservation Society of America
FCSC	Foreign Claims Settlement Commission
FCST	Federal Council for Science and Technology
FCSU	First Catholic Slovak Union
FCUSA	Finance Center, US Army
FD	Fighter Direction (Navy)
	Finance Department (OB - Army)
	Fire Department
FDA	Food and Drug Administration
FDAS	Field Depot Aviation Squadron (Air Force)
FDATC	Flying Division, Air Training Command (Air Force)
FDC	Fire Direction Center (Military)
	Forward Direction Center (Air Force)
FDD	Floating Drydock (Navy)
FDIC	Federal Deposit Insurance Corporation
	Fire Department Instructors Conference
FDO	Fighter Director Officer (Military)
FDP	Foreign Duty Pay (Military)
FE	Far East
	Fighter Escort (Air Force)
F/E	Flight Engineer (Air Force)
	Fraudulent Enlistment (Military)
FEA	Foreign Economic Administration
FEAF	Far East Air Force (OB)
FEALOGFOR	Far East Air Logistics Force (OB)
FEAMCOM	Far East Air Materiel Command (OB)
FEB	Flying Evaluation Board (Air Force)
FEC	Far East Command (OB - Military)
	Office of Foreign Economic Coordination
	Free Europe Committee
FECB	Far East Combined Bureau (OB - World War II)
FEE	Foundation for Economic Education
FEF	Foundry Educational Foundation
FEI	Farm Equipment Institute
FEIA	Flight Engineers' International Association
FEMA	Farm Equipment Manufacturers Association
	Fire Equipment Manufacturers Association
	Flavoring Extract Manufacturers' Association of US
FEPC	Farm Employment Practices Committee (OB)
FES	Federal Extension Service (Agriculture Department)

ACRONYMS

```
FETC .........Federal Excise Tax Council
FEWA .........Farm Equipment Wholesalers Association
FF ...........Farm Foundation
F of F........Field of Fire (Military)
FF ...........Ford Foundation
              Fragrance Foundation
              French Fourragere (Military)
FFA ..........For Further Assignment (Military)
              Future Farmers of America
FFAC .........Forest Farmers Association Cooperative
FFAR .........Folding-Fin Air Rocket
              Forward-Fighting Aerial Rocket
FFAUS ........Federation of French Alliances in the US
FFC ..........Farmers Federation Cooperative
              Federal Facilities Corp. (government agency)
FFCB .........Federal Farm Credit Board (Farm Credit Administration)
FFDO .........Force Fighter Director Officer (Navy)
FFES .........Food Facilities Engineering Society
FFF ..........Farm Film Foundation
FFI ..........Forces Francaises de l'Interieur (OB - Maguis)
              Frozen Food Institute
FFMC .........Federal Farm Mortgage Corporation
FFP ..........Fleet Frequency Plans
FFV ..........First Families of Virginia
FFVA .........Florida Fruit and Vegetable Association
FG ...........Forgotten Generation (Association)
FGAA .........Federal Government Accountants Association
FGJA .........Flat Glass Jobbers Association
FGO ..........Flag Gunnery Officer (Navy)
FGS ..........Friends of the Golden State
FGTSA ........Fur Garment Traveling Salesmen's Association
FHA ..........Farmers Home Administration
              Federal Housing Administration
              Fine Hardwoods Association
              Future Homemakers of America
FHLBB ........Federal Home Loan Bank Board
FHP ..........Friction Horsepower
FI ...........Fighter Interceptor (Military)
FIA ..........Factory Insurance Association
              Flatware Importers Association
FIAT .........Fabbrica Italiana Automobile Torino (Italian automobile)
              Field Information Agency Technical (OB - Military)
FIC ..........Federation of Insurance Counsel
FICA .........Federal Insurance Contributions Act
FIDO .........Fog, Intensive Dispersal of (Military)
FIGA .........Fretted Instrument Guild of America
FIGHT RON ....Fighter Squadron (Navy)
FILCEN .......Filter Center (Military)
FINEBEL ......France, Italy, Netherland, Belgium and Luxemburg (economic agreement)
FINO .........Finance Officer (Army)
FINSUPSCOL ...Finance and Supply School (Coast Guard)
FIO ..........Fleet Intelligence Officer
FIRAV ........First Available (Military)
FIRETRAC .....Firing Error Trajectory Recorder and Computer
FIRSTASKFLT ..First Task Fleet
```

FIS	Fighter-Interceptor Squadron (Air Force)
FIT	Forward Inspection Team (Military)
FITA	Federation of International Travel Agencies
FIU	Forward Interpretation Unit (Army)
FIUS	Flax Institute of the US
FL	Focal Length
FLAK	Flugzeugabwehrkanone (Ger.-"Cannon to ward off--defend against airplane attacks")
FLC	Foreign Liquidation Commission
FLI	Flight Leader Identification (Military)
FLICON	Flight Control (Military)
FLOA	Federal Licensed Officers Association
FLOG	Fleet Logistics air wing
FLOZ	Fluid Ounce
FLPA	Foreign Language Press of America
FLS	Family Location Service
FLSA	Fair Labor Standards Act
FLTACT	Fleet Activities
FLTCERT	Flight Certificate (Military)
FLTGUNSCH	Fleet Gunnery School
FLTLOSCAP	Fleet Liaison Officer, Supreme Commander Allied Powers (OB)
FLTSERVSCOL	Fleet Service School
FLTSOUNDSCOL	Fleet Sound School
FLTTRACEN	Fleet Training Center
FLYTAF	Flying Training Air Force (OB)
FM	Field Manual (Military)
	Field Music (Marine Corps)
F/M	Foreign Mission
FM	Frequency Modulation
FMA	Food Merchandisers of America
	Forging Manufacturers Association
FMACC	Foreign Military Assistance Coordinating Committee
FMASC	Foreign Military Assistance Steering Committee
FMAW	First Marine Aircraft Wing
FMB	Federal Maritime Board
FMBSA	Farmers and Manufacturers Beet Sugar Association
FMCS	Federal Mediation and Conciliation Service
FMEA	Flour Millers Export Association
FMFIC	Federation of Mutual Fire Insurance Companies
FMFPAC	Fleet Marine Force, Pacific Ocean Areas
FMG	Flakmessgerat (German - antiaircraft gun-laying radar)
FMI	Frequency Modulation Inter-city relay broadcasting
FMMA	Floor Machine Manufacturers Association
FMO	Fleet Maintenance Office (r)
	Fleet Medical Officer
FMPC	Federation of Motion Picture Councils
FMRA	Foreign Media Representatives Association
FMRS	Federal Mediation and Reconciliation Service
FMS	Federal Mediation Service
	Field Music School (Marine Corps)
	Financial Management System
FMSI	Friction Materials Standards Institute
FN	Flight Nurse (Air Force)
FNA	Following Named Airmen (Air Force)
FNB	Food and Nutrition Board
FNGDA	Farmers National Grain Dealers Association

ACRONYMS

FNH.	Flashless, Nonhygroscopic (flashless gunpowder – Military)
FNMA	Federal National Mortgage Association (AKA – Fannie Mae)
FNO	Following Named Officers (Military)
FNOA	Following Named Officers and Airmen
FNOIO.	Fleet Naval Ordnance Inspecting Officer
FO.	Field Order (Military)
	Finance Officer
	Flag Officer (Navy)
	Flight Officer (OB – Air Force)
	Flight Order (Navy)
	Forward Observer (Military)
FOA.	Football Officials Association
	Foreign Operations Agency
	Foresters of America
FOB	Forward Observer Bombardment (Military)
	Free on Board
FOE	Fraternal Order of Eagles
FOF	Fukouka Occupation Force
FOFA	Foresters of America
FOGA	Fashion Originators Guild of America
FOL	Friends of the Land
FOLNOAVAL. . .	Following items Not Available (Air Force)
FOM	Fishers of Men
FONECON	Telephone Conversation (Military)
FOO	Forward Observation Officer (Military)
	Fraternal Order Orioles
FORESDAT.	Formerly Restricted Data (Military)
FORTRAN	Formula Translator
FOSDIC	Filmed Optical Scanning Device for Input to Computers
FOURATAF	Fourth Allied Tactical Air Force, Central Europe
FOWSAB.	Federation of Women Shareholders in American Business
FP	Flight Pay (Military)
	Freight and Passenger Vessels (Army)
FPA	Flexible Packaging Association
	Flying Physicians Association
	Food Production Administration (OB)
	Foreign Policy Association
	Foreign Press Association
FPAD	Fund for Peaceful Atomic Development
FPANY.	Film Producers Association of New York
FPBAA	Folding Paper Box Association of America
FPC	Federal Power Commission
FPCH	Foreign Policy Clearing House
FPG	Federated Pecan Growers of the US
FPGL	Flight Plan Gas Load (Air Force)
FPHA	Federal Public Housing Authority
FPI.	Federal Prison Industries
FPIS	Forward Propagation Ionospheric Scatter
FPL	Family Protection League of USA
	Final Protective Line (Military)
FPO	Fleet Post Office
FPPI	Frozen Potato Products Institute
FPR	Field Personnel Record (Military)
FPRA	Financial Public Relations Association
FPRS.	Forest Products Research Society

FPT	Full Power Trial (Military)
FPVPC	Federation of Paint and Varnish Production Clubs
FR	Federal Register
	Fighter Reconnaissance (Military)
	Flash Ranging (Military)
	Fleet Reserve
FRA	Fleet Reserve Association
FRAA	Fleet Reserve Association Auxiliary
FRASCO	Foundation for Religious Action in the Social and Civil Order
FRB	Federal Reserve Bank
	Federal Reserve Board
FRC	Facility Review Committee
FRD	Federal Reserve District
FRE	Field Representative, Europe (Air Force)
FRFE	Field Representative, Far East (Air Force)
FRO	Fleet Records Office
FROC	Federated Russian Orthodox Clubs
FRRU	Freight Receiving and Redistribution Unit (Navy)
FRS	Federal Reserve System
FRU	Fleet Requirements Units (Naval aircraft)
FRUPAC	Fleet Radio Unit, Pacific
F/S	Feet per Second
FS	Field Services (Military)
	Film Strip
F/S	Final Statement (Military)
FS	Flying Status (Military)
	Forest Service
FSA	Farm Security Administration
	Federal Security Agency
	Fire Support Area (Military)
FSAA	Family Service Association of America
FSAF	Future Scientists of America Foundation
FSB	Federal Specifications Board
FSC	Family Services Center (Military
	Foreign Service Credits (Military)
FSCC	Fire Support Coordination Center (Military)
	Food Surplus Commodities Corporation
FSD	Foreign Sea Duty (Navy)
	Fuel Supply Depot (Military)
FSE	Field Support Equipment (Military)
FSEC	Federal Specifications Executive Committee (OB)
FSES	Friendly Society of Engravers and Sketchmakers
FSF	Flight Safety Foundation
FSIWA	Federation of Sewage and Industrial Wastes Association
FSLIC	Federal Savings and Loan Insurance Corp. (government agency)
FSMBUS	Federation of State Medical Boards of United States
FSN	Federal Stock Number
FSO	Fleet Supply Officer
	Fuel Supply Office (Military)
FSP	Family Services Program (Military)
	Foreign Service Pay (Military)
FSR	Field Service Regulations (Army)
	Fin Stabilized Rockets
FSRA	Federal Sewage Research Association
FSS	Federal Supply Schedule

ACRONYMS

FSS	Field Service Section (Military)
	Fleet Service School
	Foreign Shore Service (Marine Corps)
FSSD	Foreign Service Selection Date (Military)
FSTI	Formed Steel Tube Institute
FSU	Ferry Service Unit (Navy)
FSUC	Federal Statistics Users Conference
FT	Federal Triangle (Washington, D.C.)
	Firing Tables (Military)
F&T	Fuel and Transportation (Navy)
FTA	Federation of Tax Administrators
	Food Tray Association
	Future Teachers of America
FTAF	Flying Training Air Force (OB)
FTAS	Federation of Turkish-American Societies
FTC	Federal Trade Commission
	Flying Training Command (OB - Air Force)
FTCSC	Flue-Cured Tobacco Cooperative Stabilization Corp.
FTDA	Florists' Telegraph Delivery Association
FTI	Facing Tile Institute
FTP	Fleet Training Publication (Navy)
FTS	Funeral Telegraph Service "Telechapel"
FTT	Free Territory Trieste
FTU	Field Torpedo Unit (Military)
FUA	Farm Underwriters Association
FUBAR	Fouled Up Beyond All Recognition
FUBB	Fouled Up Beyond Belief
FUMTU	Fouled Up More Than Usual
FUSA	First United States Army
FUT	Fleet Utility
FWA	Federal Works Agency (OB)
FWAA	Football Writers Association of America
FWB	Freewill Baptist
FWDA	Federal Wholesale Druggists Association
FWOP	Furloughed Without Pay (Military)
F&WS	Fish & Wildlife Service
FWT	Fair Wear and Tear
FY	Fiscal Year
FYI	For Your Information
FYIG	For Your Information and Guidance
FYSA	Foundation for Youth and Student Affairs

G

G (suit)	Antigravity Suit (Air Force clothing for supersonic flight)
G	Unit of Acceleration (Military)
GA	General Assembly (United Nations)
GAA	General Account of Advances (Navy)
	Grenfell Association of America
GADR	Guided Air Defense Rocket
GAES	Gas Appliance Engineers Society
GAF	German Air Force
	Government Affairs Foundation
GAI	General Accounting Instructions (Navy)
	Governmental Affairs Institute

GALCIT	Guggenheim Aeronautical Laboratory (at California Institute of Technology)
GAM	Guided Aircraft Missile
GAMA	Gas Appliance Manufacturers Association
GAMC	General Agents and Managers Conference of NALU
GAO	General Accounting Office
	General Administrative Order (Navy)
GAPA	Greek American Progressive Association
	Ground-to-Air Pilotless Aircraft
GAR	Grand Army of the Republic (DF - last member, died in 1956)
	Guided-Air-Rocket
GARD	Gamma Atomic Radiation Detector
GARF	Graphic Arts Research Foundation
GARIOA	Government and Relief in Occupied Areas
GLASLA	Great Lakes-St. Lawrence Association
GAT	Greenwich Apparent Time
GATAE	Graphic Arts Trade Association Executives
GATT	General Agreement on Tariffs and Trade (United Nations)
GAW	Guaranteed Annual Wage
GB	General Board (Navy)
	Glide Bomb (OB - Air Force)
	Great Britain
GBBA	Glass Bottle Blowers Association
GBC	Greenland Base Command (Military)
GBF	Great Books Foundation
GBL	Government Bill of Lading
GBR	Gun, Bomb and Rocket
GBSM	Guild of Better Shoe Manufacturers
GBW	Guild of Book Workers
GC	General Counsel
	Government Contribution
	Governors' Conference
	Grolier Club
	Gun Captain (Navy)
GCA	Garden Club of America
	Girls Clubs of America
	Greeting Card Association
	Ground Control Approach (radar)
GCC	Government Contract Committee (government agency)
	Ground Control Center (flying)
GCCA	Greater Clothing Contractors Association
GCFI	Gulf and Caribbean Fisheries Institute
GCI	Ground Control Intercept (radar)
GCIAA	Granite Cutters' International Association of America
GCIS	Ground Control Intercept Squadron (Air Force)
GCL	Ground-Controlled Landing
GCM	General Court-Martial (Military)
GCMC	Good Conduct Medal Clasp (Military)
GCMED	Good Conduct Medal (Military)
GCMI	Glass Container Manufacturers Institute
GCMO	General Court-Martial Order (Military)
GCMP	General Court Martial Prisoner (Military)
GCR	Ground Controlled Radar
GCSA	Golf Course Superintendents Association of America
GCT	General Classification Test (Military)
	Greenwich Civil Time

ACRONYMS

GD .... General Discharge (Military)
GDA .... Gun Defended Area (Military)
GDAA .... Gift and Decorative Accessories Association of America
GDP .... Gun Director Pointer (Navy)
GDPCL ...... Gun Director Pointer Cross Leveler (Navy)
GDPL .... Gun Director Pointer Leveler (Navy)
GDPP .... Gun Director Pointer Pointer (Navy)
GDPSS ...... Gun Director Pointer Sight Setter (Navy)
GDPT .... Gun Director Pointer Trainer (Navy)
GE .... General Electric
GEAPS ...... Grain Elevator and Processing Superintendents
GEC .... Government Employees' Council
GED .... General Educational Development tests (Military)
GEEK .... Geomagnetic Electrokinetograph (equipment for exploring ocean depths)
GENDET ..... General Detail (Coast Guard)
GENESCO .... General Shoe Corp. (now official name of firm)
GEOREF ..... World Geographic Reference system
GERA .... Guard's Expense in Returning Absentee (Military)
GESCO ...... General Electric Supply Corporation
GESTAPO .... Nazi Secret Police (German - Geheime Staatspolizei)
GETLO ...... Obtain by Local Purchase (Military)
GETMA ...... Obtain by Local Manufacture (Military)
GF .... General Fireproofing Corp.
GFAE .... Government Furnished Aircraft Equipment
GFDNA ...... Grain and Feed Dealers National Association
GFE .... Government Furnished Equipment
GFM .... Government Furnished Material
GFP .... Government Furnished Property
GFSA .... Girls' Friendly Society of the USA
GFWC .... General Federation of Women's Clubs
GGMA .... Glassine and Greaseproof Manufacturers Association
GGR .... Ground Gunnery Range (Military)
GH .... General Hospital (Military)
GHA .... Greenwich Hour Angle
GHFA .... Group Health Federation of America
GHQ .... General Headquarters (Army)
GHQAF ...... General Headquarters Air Force (OB)
GI .... Enlisted Man (Military)
            Gastro-Intestinal
            General Issue (Military)
            Government Issue (Military)
GI (Bill) ...... Veterans Benefits Act, PL345, 1944
GIA .... Gemological Institute of America
            Goodwill Industries of America
GIFS .... Gray Iron Founders' Society
GIRO .... General Instructions for Routing and Reporting Officers (Navy)
GIU .... General Intelligence Unit (OB)
GL .... Gun Laying (Military)
GLC .... Great Lakes Commission
GLCA .... Gallery of Living Catholic Authors
GLIBAD ..... Glider Badge (Air Force)
GLIPAR ..... Guide Line Identification Program (for anti-missile research) (Military)
GLO .... Ground Liaison Officer (Military)
            Gunnery Liaison Officer (Navy)
GLOMB ...... Glide Bomb (OB - Air Force)

ACRONYMS

GM	General Motors Corporation
	Guard Mail (Navy)
	Guided Missile
GMA	Grocery Manufacturers of America (Food)
GMAA	Gold Mining Association of America
GMAC	General Motors Acceptance Corporation
GMCM	Guided Missile Countermeasures (Military)
GMD	Guided Missiles Division (Navy)
GMST	General Military Subjects Test
GMT	Greenwich Mean Time
GNI	Gross National Income
GNP	Gross National Product
GO	General Order(s) (Military)
GOB	General Officers Branch (Air Force)
GOC	General Officer Commanding (Army)
	Ground Observer Corps (OB - see Air Reserve Volunteer Support Group)
GOCO	Government-owned Contractor-Operated
GOH	German Order of Harugari
GOM	Government-Owned Material
GOMALCO	Gobel O'Malley Company (George Gobel's firm; O'Malley is business mgr.
GOP	General Operational Plot (Navy)
	Grand Old Party (Republican)
GOYA	Greek Orthodox Youth of America
GP	General Practitioner (medicine)
	General Purpose (Military)
	Geographic Position
	Gun Pointer (Navy)
GPA	Glycerine Producers Association
GPCZ	Governor of Panama Canal Zone
GPF	Gasproof
GP FL	Group Flashing (Navy)
GP (Gas)	Persistent chemical agent gas
GPH	Gallons per Hour
GPI	Ground Position Indicator
GPLD	Government Property Lost or Damaged
GPM	Gallons per Minute
GPMA	Gasoline Pump Manufacturers Association
GPMMA	Grain Processing Machinery Manufacturers Association
GPO	General Post Office
	Government Printing Office
GPOA	Guild of Prescription Opticians of America
GP OCC	Group Occulting (Navy)
GPS	Gallons per Second /Upravlenie) (Russian secret state police)
GPU	Government Political Organization (Gasudarstvennoe Politicheskoe
GQ	General Quarters (Navy)
GR	General Reconnaissance (Marine Corps)
	General Reserve (Military)
	Graves Registration (Military)
	Gunnery Range (Military)
GRA	Governmental Research Association
GRB	Government Reservation Bureau (Navy)
GRC	Gale Research Company
GREPAT	Greenland Patrol (Navy)
GRF	Golden Rule Foundation
GRFO	Gun Range Finder Operator (Military)

ACRONYMS

```
GRI . . . . . . . . . Government of the Ryukyu Islands
GROPAC . . . . . . Group Pacific (Navy)
GRS . . . . . . . . . Graves Registration Service (Military)
GRUCOM . . . . . Group Commander (Navy)
GS . . . . . . . . . . General Schedule (federal employee job classification GS-1 to GS-18
                      General Staff (Army)
G/S . . . . . . . . . General Support (Army)
GS . . . . . . . . . . Geochemical Society
                      Geological Survey (Interior Department)
                      Gerontological Society
GSA . . . . . . . . . Garden Seed Association
                      General Services Administration
                      Genetics Society of America
                      Geological Society of America
                      Girl Scouts of the USA
GSC . . . . . . . . . General Staff Corps (Army)
GSD . . . . . . . . . General Supply Depot (Military)
GSDN . . . . . . . Garden Supply Dealers National
GSF . . . . . . . . . Gulf Sea Frontier (Navy)
GSFC . . . . . . . . Goddard Space Flight Center (NASA)
GSM . . . . . . . . Gold Star Mothers
GSO . . . . . . . . Ground Safety Office(r) (Air Force)
GSR . . . . . . . . . General Service Recruit (Military)
GSS . . . . . . . . . General Service School (Military)
                      General Supply Schedule (Military)
GST . . . . . . . . . Greenwich Sidereal Time
GSU . . . . . . . . . General Service Unit (Marine Corps)
GSUSA . . . . . . . General Staff, US Army
GSWA . . . . . . . Gold Star Wives of America
GTA . . . . . . . . . Graphic Training Aid
                      Gravure Technical Association
GTTC . . . . . . . . Gulf Transportation Terminal Command (Army)
GULFCOBASESERVUNIT . . Gulf Coast Base Service Unit (Navy)
GULFCON . . . . Gulf Control (Navy)
GULFSEAFRON . Gulf Sea Frontier (Navy)
GW . . . . . . . . . General Warning (Military)
GWAA . . . . . . . Garden Writers Association of America
GWI . . . . . . . . . Grinding Wheel Institute
GWMC . . . . . . Galvanized Ware Manufacturers Council
GWSF . . . . . . . . Georgia Warm Springs Foundation
GZ . . . . . . . . . . Ground Zero (Military)

H

HA . . . . . . . . . . Headquarters Administration division (Coast Guard)
                      Home Address (Military)
HAA . . . . . . . . . Heavy Antiaircraft Artillery (Military)
HAB . . . . . . . . . High-Altitude Bombing (Air Force)
HAFMED . . . . . . Headquarters Allied Forces, Mediterranean
HAIC . . . . . . . . Hearing Aid Industry Conference
HAM . . . . . . . . (Am)ateur Radio Operator
                      Heavy Automotive Maintenance (Army)
HAR . . . . . . . . . Honorary Air Reserve (OB - Air Force)
HASC . . . . . . . . Headquarters Air Service Command (OB - Air Force)
HASP . . . . . . . . High-Altitude Sounding Project (Navy)
```

HAU	Hebrew Actors Union
HAWK	Homing All the Way Killer (Air Force)
HAWSEAFRON	Hawaiian Sea Frontier (Navy)
HB	Heavy Bombardment (Air Force)
HBAA	Human Betterment Association of America
HBDC	Home Base Development Committee (Navy)
HBS	Harbor Boat Service (Army)
HBSS	Hospital Bureau of Standards and Supplies
HC	High Capacity
	Historical Commission
	House of Commons (British Commonwealth)
HCA	Absent by reason of being Held by Civil Authorities (Military)
	Hobby Clubs of America
HCBI	Health Conference for Business and Industry
HCCG	Discharge under Honorable Conditions, Convenience of Govt. (Military)
HCCM	Discharge under Honorable Conditions, Convenience of Man (Navy)
HCDP	Discharge under HC, Dependency existing Prior to enlistment (Navy)
HCEE	Discharge under HC, Expiration of Enlistment (Navy)
HCL	High Cost of Living
HCLE	Humanities Center for Liberal Education
HCMS	Discharge under Honorable Conditions, Medical Survey (Navy)
HCMU	Discharge under HC, (Minor) Under age of authorized enlistment (Navy)
HCMW	Discharge under HC, Minors enlisted Without consent, under 18 (Navy)
HCO	Hanger Control Officer (Navy)
HCP	Hanger Control Position (Navy)
HD	Harbor Defense (Army)
	Historical Division (Air Force)
	Honorable Discharge (Military)
HDC	Harbor Defense Command (Army)
HDCG	Honorable Discharge, Convenience of Government (Military)
HDCM	Honorable Discharge, Convenience of Man (Military)
HDDP	Honorable Discharge, Dependency existing Prior to Enlistment (Military)
HDDS	Honorable Discharge, Dependency arising Since enlistment (Military)
HDEE	Honorable Discharge, Expiration of Enlistment (Military)
HDI	House Dress Institute
HDMA	Hardwood Dimension Manufacturers Association
HDMU	Honorable Discharge, (Minor) Under age of authorized enlistment (Navy)
HDMW	Honorable Discharge, Minors enlisted w/o consent, under 18 at discharge
HDR	Home Dockyard Regulations (Navy)
HE	High Explosive (Military)
HEAP	High Explosive Armor-Piercing (Military)
HEAT	High-Explosive Antitank (Military)
HECP	Harbor Entrance Control Post (Army)
HECVES	Harbor Entrance Control Vessel (Army)
HEDCOM	Headquarters Command (Air Force)
HEDRONFAIRWING	Headquarters Squadron Fleet Air Wing
HEI	Heat Exchange Institute
	High Explosive Incendiary (Military)
HEIT	High Explosive Incendiary Traced (Military)
HELIOS	Heteropowered Earth-Launched Interorbital Spacecraft
HELP	Helicopter Electronic Landing Path (Army)
HELREC	Health Record (Military)
HERALDS	Harbor Echo Ranging and Listening Devices
HERDET	Hereby Detached from duty assigned (Military)
HESO	Hospital Educational Services Officer (Navy)

ACRONYMS   HET - HPT

HET	High Explosive Traced (Military)
HEW	Health, Education and Welfare (Department)
HF	Handwriting Foundation
	High Frequency
HFA	Hard Fibres Association
HFAA	Holstein-Friesian Association of America
HFCAUS	Hatters Fur Cutters Association of the US
HF/DF	High Frequency Direction Finder
HFIC	Home Furnishings Industry Committee
HFORL	Human Factors Operation Research Laboratory (OB - Air Force)
HFPS	Hay Fever Prevention Society
HGA	Hobby Guild of America
	Hotel Greeters of America
HHA	Hickory Handle Association
HHE	Household Effects (Military)
HHFA	Housing and Home Finance Agency
HIA	Handkerchief Industry Association
	Hobby Industry Association of America
	Horological Institute of America
	Hospital Industries Association
HIAA	Health Insurance Association of America
HIAS	Hebrew Sheltering and Immigrant Aid Society
HIC	Health Insurance Council
HICOM	High Command (Military)
HICOMRY	High Commissioner of Ryukyu Islands
HIF	Health Information Foundation
HI-FI	High-Fidelity
HII	Health Insurance Institute
HIPA	Home Improvement Products Association
HIRAN	High Precision Shoran (Navigation System)
HISS	High-Intensity Sound Simulator
HIUS	Hispanic Institute in the United States
HL	Herpetologists League
	House of Lords (United Kingdom)
HMA	Hoist Manufacturers Association
	Home Manufacturers Association
HMG	Heavy Machine Gun (Military)
HMI	House Magazine Institute
HMRP	Hurricane Microseismic Research Problem aerology (Navy)
HMSA	Hardware Manufacturers Statistical Association
HNS	Holy Name Society
HO	Hydrographic Office (Navy)
HOI	Headquarters Office Instruction (Military)
HOLUA	Home Office Life Underwriters Association
HOMP	Halifax Ocean Meeting Point (Shipping)
HOPE	Health Opportunity for People Everywhere
HOR	Home of Record (Military)
HP	High Pressure
	Horse-Power
HPF	Harbor Patrol Fleet (Military)
	Highest Possible Frequency
HPI	Hardwood Plywood Institute
	Heifer Project Incorporated
HPS	Health Physics Society
HPT	Horizontal Plot Table (Navy)

HQ	Headquarters (Military)
HQCOM	Headquarters Command (Air Force)
HQMC	Headquarters, Marine Corps
HQUSAF	Headquarters, US Air Force
H&R	Holding and Reconsignment (Military)
HR	House of Representatives
HRAF	Human Relations Area Files
HRAT	Hampton Roads Army Terminal
HRB	Highway Research Board
HREBIU	Hotel and Restaurant Employees and Bartenders International Union
HRET	Hospital Research and Educational Trust
HRI	Height-Range Indicator
H&RP	Holding and Reconsignment Point (Army)
HRRC	Human Resources Research Center (OB - Military)
HRS	Honorary Reserve Section (OB - Military)
H&S	Headquarters and Service (Army)
HSA	Hispanic Society of America
	Hymn Society of America
HSF	Hawaiian Sea Frontier (Navy)
	Hotel Sundry Fund (Air Force)
HSFS	High-Speed Flight Station (National Aeronautics and Space Administration)
HSLWI	Helical Spring Lock Washer Institute
HSMA	Hotel Sales Management Association
HSPA	Hawaiian Sugar Planters' Association
HSR	Hampshire Swine Registry
HSS	History of Science Society
HST	Hawaiian Standard Time
H&STR	Headquarters and Service Troop (Army)
HTA	Heavier-Than-Air (Aircraft)
HTD	Hand Target Designator (Military)
HTRAC	Half-Track (Military vehicle)
HUK	Hunter Killer (of submarines)
HUMRRO	Human Resources Research Office (Military)
HUSAFICPA	Headquarters, US Army Forces in Central Pacific Area (OB)
HV	High Velocity
	High Voltage
HVAP	High Velocity Armor-Piercing
HVAR	High Velocity Aircraft Rocket
HVAT	High Velocity Antitank (Military)
HVWS	Hebrew Veterans of War with Spain
HWNA	Hosiery Wholesalers National Association
HY-COM	Highway Communications

I

IA	Inspection Administration (Navy)
IAA	Independent Airlines Association
	Indian Association of America
	Insurance Accountants Association
	Interment Association of America
	International Acetylene Association
	International Advertising Association
	International Apple Association
IAAAA	Intercollegiate Association of Amateur Athletes of America
IAAHU	International Association of Accident and Health Underwriters

ACRONYMS

IAALD	International Association of Agricultural Librarians and Documentalists
IAAM	International Association of Auditorium Managers
IAATI	International Association of Auto Theft Investigators
IABA	Inter-American Bar Association
IABPAI	International Association of Blue Print and Allied Industries
IABPBD	International Alliance of Bill Posters, Billers and Distributors
IABSOIW	International Association of Bridge, Structural and Ornamental Iron Workers
IAC	Insurance Advertising Conference
IACAC	Inter-American Commercial Arbitration Commission
IACB	International Association of Convention Bureaus
IACD	International Association of Clothing Designers
IACH	Inter-Association Committee on Health
IACP	International Association of Chiefs of Police
IACW	Inter-American Commission of Women
IADA	Independent Aeronautical Dealers Association
IADB	Inter-American Defense Board
	Inter-American Development Bank
IADF	Inter American Association for Democracy and Freedom
IADR	International Association for Dental Research
IAEA	International Atomic Energy Agency (United Nations)
IAEI	International Association of Electrical Inspectors
IAEL	International Association of Electrical Leagues
IAES	International Association of Electrotypers and Stereotypers
IAESC	Inter-American Economic and Social Council
IAF	Industrial Areas Foundation
	International Aeronautics Federation
	International Astronautic Federation
IAFC	International Association of Fire Chiefs
IAFF	International Association of Fire Fighters
IAGFCC	International Association of Game, Fish and Conservation Commissioners
IAGLO	International Association of Governmental Labor Officials
IAHA	Inter-American Hospital Association
	Inter American Hotel Association
	International Arabian Horse Association
IAHFIAW	International Association of Heat and Frost Insulators and Asbestos Workers
IAI	International Association for Identification
IAIABC	International Association of Industrial Accident Boards and Commissions
IAIAS	Inter-American Institute of Agricultural Sciences (OAS)
IAIC	International Association of Insurance Counsel
IAICM	International Association of Ice Cream Manufacturers
IAIU	Insurance Agents International Union
IAL	International Algebraic Language
	International Association of Laryngectomees
IALC	International Association of Lions Clubs
IALSSA	International Air Line Stewards and Stewardesses Association
IAM	Institute of Appliance Manufacturers
	International Association of Machinists
IAMCA	International Association of Milk Control Agencies
IAOD	In Addition to Other Duties (Military)
IAP	International Academy of Pathology
IAPA	Inter American Press Association
IAPES	International Association of Personnel in Employment Security
IAPHC	International Association of Printing House Craftsmen
IAPI	Institute of American Poultry Industries
IAPO	Industrial Accountable Property Officer (Air Force)

Acronym	Expansion
IAPPW	International Association of Pupil Personnel Workers
IAPS	International Association of Pipe Smokers
IAPW	International Association of Personnel Women
IAR	Inactive Air Reserve (OB - Air Force)
IARE	International Association of Railway Employees
IARI	Industrial Advertising Research Institute
IARU	International Amateur Radio Union
IAS	Indicated Air Speed (Flying)
	Institute for Advanced Study
	Institute of Aeronautical Sciences
IASA	Insurance Accounting and Statistical Association
IASAP	Intercollegiate Association for Study of the Alcohol Problem
IASC	Inter-American Safety Council
IASI	Inter American Statistical Institute
IASM	Independent Association of Stocking Manufacturers
IASOR	Ice and Snow on Runway (Flying)
IATA	International Air Transport Association
IATC	International Association of Tool Craftsmen
	International Association of Torch Clubs
IATCB	Interdepartmental Air Traffic Control Board
IATL	International Academy of Trial Lawyers
IATR	Is Amended to Read (Military)
IATSE&MPMO	International Alliance of Theatrical Stage Employees & Motion Picture Machine Operators of US and Canada
IAU	International Astronomical Union
	Italian Actors Union
IAW	In Accordance With (Military)
	International Association of Wholesalers
IAWS	Intercollegiate Association of Women Students
IAZ	Inner Artillery Zone (Military)
IB	Incendiary Bomb (Military)
IBA	Independent Bankers Association
	International Bar Association
	Investing Builders Association
IBAA	Investment Bankers Association of America
IBB	International Brotherhood of Bookbinders
IBBA	International Brangus Breeders Association
IBEC	International Basic Economy Corporation
IBEW	International Brotherhood of Electrical Workers
IBFO	International Brotherhood of Firemen and Oilers
IBH	Initial Beachhead (Army)
IBI	Insulation Board Institute
IBL	International Brotherhood of Longshoremen
IBM	International Brotherhood of Magicians
	International Business Machines Corporation
IBOP	International Brotherhood of Operative Potters
IBR	Institute of Boiler and Radiator Manufacturers
IBRD	International Bank for Reconstruction and Development (United Nations)
IBRL	Initial Bomb Release Line (Military)
IBRM	Institute of Boiler and Radiator Manufacturers
IBS	Intercollegiate Broadcasting System
	International Bible Students
	Island Base Section (Navy)
IC	In Charge (Military)
	Information Center (Military)

ACRONYMS

IC - ID

IC	Interfaith Compassionists
	Interior Communications (Military)
	Internal Combustion
ICA	International Chiropractors Association
	International Claim Association
	International Cooperation Administration
	International Council on Archives
ICAF	Industrial College of the Armed Forces
ICAN	International Commission for Air Navigation
ICAO	International Civil Aviation Organization (United Nations)
ICB	Interior Control Board (Military)
ICBBA	International Cornish Bantam Breeders Association
ICBM	Intercontinental Ballistic Missile
ICBPA	Insurance Company and Bank Purchasing Agents Association
ICC	Indian Claims Commission
	International Chamber of Commerce
	Interstate Commerce Commission
	Institute of Chinese Culture
ICCA	Initial Cash Clothing Allowance (Military)
ICD	Industrial Cooperation Division (Navy)
ICEC	International Council for Exceptional Children
ICEDS	Insurance Company Education Directors Society
ICEI	Internal Combustion Engine Institute
ICEPAT	Iceland Patrol (Navy)
ICESA	Interstate Conference of Employment Security Agencies
ICF	Italian Catholic Federation /(Military)
ICFATCMUTAL . .	Individual is Cleared for Access to Classified Material up to and including
ICFTU	International Confederation of Free Trade Unions
ICG	International Congress of Genetics
	Interviewer's Classification Guide (Navy)
ICIE	International Council of Industrial Editors
ICIR	In Commission, In Reserve (Navy vessel status)
ICITO	Interim Commission for the International Trade Organization (OB - UN)
ICJ	International Court of Justice (World Court)
ICJUB	Intercontinental Jet Unmanned Bomber
ICMA	International City Managers' Association
ICOC	Instructions for Commodores of Convoys (Shipping)
ICOMP	Iceland Ocean Meeting Point (Shipping)
ICPA	International Cooperative Petroleum Association
ICPOA	Intelligence Center, Pacific Ocean Areas (Military)
ICPRB	Interstate Commission on Potomac River Basin
ICR	Institute for Creative Research
ICRDA	Independent Cash Register Dealers Association
IC&RR	Inventory Control and Requirements Review Board (Navy)
ICS	Integrated Communication System (Military in Alaska)
	International College of Surgeons
ICSBC	Interstate Council of State Boards of Cosmetology
ICSS	Inter-University Committee on the Superior Student
ICUS	Inside Continental United States (Military)
ICW	In Compliance with (Military)
	Interrupted Continuous Wave
ICWSG	Infants and Children's Wear Salesmen's Guild
ICWU	International Chemical Workers Union
ID	Identification (Military)
	Inside Diameter

ACRONYMS

```
I of D . . . . . . . Institute of Distribution
ID . . . . . . . . . Intelligence Department (OB - Army)
                     Intelligence Duties (Military)
                     Interior Department
IDA . . . . . . . . Industrial Diamond Association of America
                     Institute for Defense Analysis
                     Intercollegiate Dramatic Association
IDC . . . . . . . . Interdepartmental Committee (also INDEC - Navy)
IDCNA . . . . . . Insulation Distributor-Contractors National Association
IDEA . . . . . . . International Downtown Executives Association
IDFOR . . . . . . Idle waiting convoy Forward (Shipping)
IDG . . . . . . . . Inspector of Degaussing (Navy)
IDI . . . . . . . . Industrial Designers' Institute
IDIOT . . . . . . . Instrumentation Digital On-line Transcriber
IDLOD . . . . . . Idle waiting to Load (Shipping)
IDM . . . . . . . . Interdiction Mission (Air Force)
IDPA . . . . . . . Inland Daily Press Association
IDR . . . . . . . . Infantry Drill Regulations (Military)
IDS . . . . . . . . Instrument Development Section (Navy)
IDSC . . . . . . . International Die-Sinkers' Conference
IDSTO . . . . . . Idle used for Storage (Shipping)
I & E . . . . . . . Information and Education (Military)
IE . . . . . . . . . Initial Equipment (Navy - aircraft)
IEA . . . . . . . . Interment Exchange of America
IEE . . . . . . . . Institute of Environmental Engineers
IEES . . . . . . . International Education Exchange Service (State Department)
IES . . . . . . . . Illuminating Engineering Society
                     Irish Emigrant Society
IESA . . . . . . . Insurance Economics Society of America
IF . . . . . . . . . Ice Fog (Air Force)
                     Intermediate Frequency
IFA . . . . . . . . International Fertility Association
IFB . . . . . . . . Invitation For Bid (Military)
IFC . . . . . . . . International Finance Corporation (United Nations)
IFCA . . . . . . . International Federation of Catholic Alumnae
IFD . . . . . . . . Inter-Fighter Director (Navy)
IFDA . . . . . . . Institutional Food Distributors of America
IFF . . . . . . . . Identification, Friend or Foe (Military)
                     International Film Foundation
IFFJ . . . . . . . International Federation of Free Journalists
IFHOM . . . . . . Idle waiting convoy Homeward (Shipping)
IFI . . . . . . . . Industrial Fasteners Institute
IFIS . . . . . . . Instrument Flight Instructors School (Navy)
IFMA . . . . . . . Institutional Food Manufacturers of America
                     Interdenominational Foreign Mission Association of North America
IFPEC . . . . . . Independent Film Producers Export Corporation
IFR . . . . . . . . Inflight Refueling (Air Force)
                     Instrument Flight Rules
IFRB . . . . . . . International Frequency Registration Board
IFRI . . . . . . . International Fund-Raising Institute
IFRU . . . . . . . Interference Frequency Rejection Unit (Military)
IFT . . . . . . . . Inflight Text (Air Force)
                     Institute of Food Technologists
IFU . . . . . . . . Intelligence Field Unit (Navy)
IG . . . . . . . . . Inspector General (Military)
```

ACRONYMS

IGA – ILT

IGA	Independent Grocers' Alliance Distributing Company
IGAEA	International Graphic Arts Education Association
IGAS	International Graphic Arts Society
	International Grapho Analysis Society
IGD	Inspector General's Department (OB - Army)
IGFA	International Game Fish Association
IGOA	Independent Garage Owners of America
IGT	Institute of Gas Technology
IGTM	Inertial-Guided Tactical Missile
IGWU	International Glove Workers' Union of America
IH	International Harvester
IHA	International Hahnemannian Association
	International House Association
IHCA	In Hands of Civil Authorities (Military)
IHEA	Industrial Heating Equipment Association
IHFA	Industrial Hygiene Foundation of America
IHFM	Institute of High Fidelity Manufacturers
IHOU	Institute of Home Office Underwriters
IHP	Indicated Horsepower
IHPA	Imported Hardwood Plywood Association
IHSA	Italian Historical Society of America
I/I	Inventory and Inspection report (Army)
IIA	Incinerator Institute of America
	Institute of Internal Auditors
	Insurance Institute of America
	Invention Industry Association of America
IIAA	Institute of Inter-American Affairs (United Nations)
IIE	Institute of International Education
IIHSC	Inter-Industry Highway Safety Committee
IIL	Institute of Industrial Launderers
IILI	Institute Internacional de Literatura Iberoamerican
IIO	Institute for International Order
IIRR	Institute of Industrial Race Relations
IIS	Institute for Intercultural Studies
IJA	Institute of Jewish Affairs
IJAJ	Intentional Jitter Antijam (Military)
IJJU	Intentional Jitter Jamming Unit (Military)
IJN	Imperial Japanese Navy
IJS	Institute of Jazz Studies
IJWU	International Jewelry Workers' Union
ILA	Instrument Landing Approach (Flying)
	International Longshoremen's Association
ILAS	Instrument Low Approach System (Flying)
ILGWU	International Ladies' Garment Workers' Union
ILI	Indiana Limestone Institute
	Institute of Life Insurance
ILMA	Incandescent Lamp Manufacturers Association
ILO	In Lieu of (Military)
	International Labor Organization (United Nations)
ILOUE	In Lieu of Until Exhausted (Military)
ILP	Independent Labor Party
ILPA	International Labor Press Association AFL-CIO
ILRM	International League for the Rights of Man
ILS	Instrument Landing System (Flying)
ILT	In Lieu Thereof (Military)

Acronym	Meaning
ILWU	International Longshoremen's and Warehousemen's Union
IM	Impulse Modulation
I&M	Installation and Maintenance (Air Force)
IM	Instrument Man (Air Force)
	Interceptor Missile
	Intermediate Modulation
IMA	Industrial Marketing Associates
	Industrial Medical Association
	International Management Association
IMAC	First (I) Marine Amphibious Corps
IMBA	International Media Buyers Association
IMBT	Iron Masters Board of Trade
IMC	International Mailbag Club
IMCA	International Motor Contest Association
IMCO	Inter-Governmental Maritime Consultative Organization (United Nations)
IME	Institute of Makers of Explosives
IMF	International Monetary Fund (United Nations)
IMFWUNA	International Molders and Foundry Workers Union of North America
IMG	Informational Media Guaranty
IMIB	Inland Marine Insurance Bureau
IMIMI	Industrial Mineral Insulation Manufacturers Institute
IMO	International Meteorological Organization (United Nations)
IMP	Impulse Generator
IMPDAA	Independent Motion Picture Distributors Association of America
IMPPA	Independent Motion Picture Producers' Association
IMR	Individual Medical Record (Military)
IMS	Industrial Management Society
	Industrial Manpower Section (Navy)
	Industrial Mathematics Society
	Institute of Mathematical Statistics
IMSA	International Municipal Signal Association
IMSC	Industry Missile and Space Conference
IMTP	Industrial Mobilization Training Program
IMU	International Mailers Union
IMUA	Inland Marine Underwriters Association
I&N	Immigration and Naturalization Service
INA	Inspector of Naval Aircraft
INACTLANT	Inactive Fleet, Atlantic Fleet
INACTPAC	Inactive Fleet, Pacific Fleet
INA/IC	Inactive-In Commission, In Reserve (Navy - vessel status)
INA/IS	Inactive-In Service, In Reserve (Navy - vessel status)
INA/OC	Inactive-Out of Commission, In Reserve (Navy - vessel status)
INA/OS	Inactive-Out of Service, In Reserve (Navy - vessel status)
INCFO	Institute of Newspaper Controllers and Finance Officers
INCO	International Nickel Company, Inc.
INDAIR	Identification of Aircraft
INDEC	Interdepartmental Committee (also IDC)
INDMAN	Industrial Manager (Navy)
INFO	Information
INFOCEN	Information Center (Military)
INGA	Independent Natural Gas Association of America
INITCCA	Initial Cash Clothing Allowance (Military)
INM	Inspector of Naval Machinery
	Inspector of Naval Material
	Interception Mission (Air Force)

ACRONYMS

INO - IPMANA

INO	Issue Necessary Orders (Military)
INREQ	Information Request (Military)
INS	Immigration and Naturalization Service
	Inspection division (Coast Guard)
	International News Service (MW - United Press International)
INSACS	Interstate Airway Communication Station
INSGEN	Inspector General (Navy)
INSGENPAC	Inspector General, Pacific Fleet and Pacific Ocean Area
INSMACH	Inspector of Naval Machinery
INSMAT	Inspector of Naval Material
INSNAVMAT	Inspector Navigational Material (Navy)
INSORD	Inspector of Ordnance (Navy)
INSPAT	Inshore Patrol (Navy)
INSPETRES	Inspector Petroleum Reserves (Navy)
INSTEP	India Steel Training and Education Program
INSURV	Board of Inspection and Survey (Navy)
INT	Ad Interim Specification (Navy)
	Intelligence and Law Enforcement division (Coast Guard)
INTA	International New Thought Alliance
INTCO	International Code of Signals (Navy)
INTELCEN	Intelligence Center (Military)
INTELCENPAC	Intelligence Center Pacific Ocean Areas
INTERMTRA	Intermediate Training (Naval Air)
INTERPOL	International Criminal Police Organization (United Nations)
INTO	Intelligence Officer (Army)
INTSUM	Intelligence Summary (Military)
IO	Intelligence Officer (Military)
	Intercept Officer (Navy)
	Issuing Office (Navy)
IOC	International Olympic Committee
IOCA	Independent Oil Compounders Association
IOF	Independent Order of Foresters
IOGT	International Order of Good Templars
IOH	Item on Hand (Air Force)
IOL	Initial Outfitting List for advanced base (Navy)
IOMA	Independent Oxygen Manufacturers Association
ION	Institute of Navigation
IOOF	Independent Order Odd Fellows
IORM	Improved Order of Red Men
IOU	I Owe You
IP	Incentive Pay (Military)
	Initial Point (Military)
	Instructor Pilot (Military)
IPA	Institute of Public Administration
	International Publishers Association
IPAA	Independent Petroleum Association of America
	Industrial Photographers Association of America
IPANY	Individual Psychology Association of New York
IPC	Institute of Paper Chemistry
	International Poliomyelitis Congress
IPCEA	Insulated Power Cable Engineers Association
IPEA	Independent Poster Exchanges of America
IPEU	International Photo Engravers Union of North America
IPI	International Press Institute
IPMANA	Interstate Postgraduate Medical Association of North America

Acronym	Meaning
IPPAU	International Printing Pressmen and Assistants' Union
IPRA	International Public Relations Association
IPRB	Inter-Allied Post-War Requirements Bureau (OB)
IPSSG	International Printers Supply Salesmen's Guild
IPTA	International Piano Teachers Association
IPW	Interrogate Prisoner of War (Military)
IQ	Intelligence Quotient
IR	Infra-Red equipment (Military)
	Instrument Reading (Military)
I&R	Intelligence and Reconnaissance (Military)
IR	Interrogator-Responder (Military)
IRA	Indian Rights Association
	International Reading Association
	International Recreation Association
IRAA&A	Increase and Replacement of Armor, Armament and Ammunition (Navy)
IRAC	Interdepartment Radio Advisory Committee (Navy)
IRAN	Inspection and Repair As Necessary (Navy)
IRB	Industrial Readjustment Branch (Navy)
	Industrial Relations Board (Navy)
IRBM	Intermediate Range Ballistic Missile
IRC	Industrial Relations Counselors
	International Red Cross
	International Rescue Committee
IRC&M	Increase and Replacement of Construction and Machinery (Navy)
IRCT	International Research on Communist Techniques
IRE	Increase and Replacement of Emergency construction (Navy)
	Institute of Radio Engineers
IREM	Institute of Real Estate Managers
IRF	International Road Federation
IRFAA	International Rescue and First Aid Association
IRI	Industrial Research Institute
IRIC	Inter-Regional Insurance Conference
IRLA	International Religious Liberty Association
IRLDA	Independent Retail Lumber Dealers Association
IRNV	Increase and Replacement of Naval Vessels
IRO	International Refugee Organization (United Nations)
IRS	Inactive Reserve Section (Military)
	Induction and Recruiting Station (Marine Corps)
	Internal Revenue Service
IRT	Interrogator-Responder-Transponder (Military)
I&S	Board of Inspection and Survey (Navy)
IS	Invalided from Service, medical (Navy)
ISA	Independent Shoemen of America
	Inductee Special Assignment (Navy)
	Instrument Society of America
	Insulating Siding Association
	Insurance Service Association of America
	International Silk Association of the USA
ISAGL	International Shipmasters Association of the Great Lakes
ISBIC	Interservice Balkan Intelligence Committee (OB)
ISC	Indoor Sports Club
ISCB	Inter-Allied Staff Communications Board (OB)
ISCBA	Insulating Siding Core Board Association
ISCC	Inter-Society Color Council
	Inter-Society Cytology Council

ACRONYMS

ISCOM . . . . Island Commander (Navy)
ISCYRA . . . . International Star Class Yacht Racing Association
ISD . . . . Institute of Surplus Dealers
ISEA . . . . Industrial Safety Equipment Association
ISEU . . . . International Stereotypers and Electrotypers' Union
ISF . . . . International Science Foundation
ISFA . . . . Intercoastal Steamship Freight Association
ISGS . . . . International Society for General Semantics
ISIC . . . . Immediate Superior-in-Command (Navy)
ISIR . . . . In Service, In Reserve (Navy - vessel status)
ISIS . . . . Institute of Scrap Iron and Steel
ISLRS . . . . Inactive Status List Reserve Section (Military)
ISM . . . . Institute of Sanitation Management
ISMA . . . . Inter-State Manufacturers Association
ISME . . . . International Society for Music Education
ISNP . . . . International Society of Naturopathic Physicians
ISO . . . . Information Services Officer (Air Force)
ISP . . . . Interamerican Society of Psychology
ISS . . . . International Social Service
ISSCT . . . . International Society Sugar Cane Technologists
ISTDA . . . . Institutional and Service Textile Distributors Association
ISUSAIC . . . . . . Intelligence School, US Army Intelligence Center
ISWC . . . . International Society for the Welfare of Cripples
IT . . . . Institute of Technology (Air Force)
ITA . . . . Industrial Truck Association
ITC . . . . International Toastmistress Clubs
ITE . . . . Institute of Traffic Engineers
ITFO . . . . International Trade Fairs Office (Commerce Department)
ITI . . . . International Theatre Institute
ITM . . . . Inspector of Torpedoes and Mines (Navy)
                Institute of Thread Machiners
ITMA . . . . Institute for Training in Municipal Administration
ITO . . . . Inspecting Torpedo Officer (Navy)
                International Trade Organization (United Nations)
ITT . . . . Individual Technical Training (Military)
IT&T . . . . International Telephone and Telegraph Corporation
ITU . . . . International Telecommunication Union (United Nations)
                International Typographical Union
IU . . . . Interference Unit (Military)
IUCN . . . . International Union for Conservation of Nature and Natural Resources
IUD . . . . Industrial Union Department (of AFL-CIO)
IUEC . . . . International Union of Elevator Constructors
IUJHUSC . . . . . . International Union of Journeymen Horseshoers of the US and Canada
IULIA . . . . International Union of Life Insurance Agents
IUMMSW . . . . . . International Union of Mine, Mill and Smelter Workers
IUMSWA . . . . . . Industrial Union of Marine and Shipbuilding Workers of America
IUOE . . . . International Union of Operating Engineers
IUPW . . . . Independent Union of Petroleum Workers
IV . . . . Initial Velocity
IVS . . . . International Voluntary Services
IWA . . . . Institute of World Affairs
                Insurance Workers of America
                International Woodworkers of America
IWCI . . . . Industrial Wire Cloth Institute
IWL . . . . Italian Welfare League

IWLA	Izaak Walton League of America
IWRMA	Independent Wire Rope Manufacturers Association
IWSB	Insect Wire Screening Bureau
IWVA	International War Veterans' Alliance
IWW	Industrial Workers of the World (OB - AKA "Wobblies")

J

JA	Junior Achievement
	Judge Advocate (Military)
JAA	Judge Advocates Association
JAAC	Joint Aircraft Allocations Committee (Military)
JAAF	Japanese Army Air Force (OB)
	Joint Action Armed Forces
	Joint Army-Air Force
JAAFAR	Joint Army-Air Force Adjustment Regulations
JAAFCTB	Joint Army-Air Force Commercial Traffic Bulletin
JAAFPC	Joint Army-Air Force Procurement Circular
JAAOC	Joint Antiaircraft Artillery Operations Center (Military)
JAB	Joint Amphibious Board (Military)
JABO	Jagbomber or Jagdbomber (German)
JAC	Jet Age Conference (OB - see World Congress of Flight)
	Joint Aircraft Committee (Military)
JACCI	Joint Allocation Committee Civil Intelligence (OB)
JACL	Japanese American Citizens League
JACSPAC	Joint Air Communications of the Pacific (Military)
JADF	Japan Air Defense Force
JAG	Judge Advocate General (Military)
JAGC	Judge Advocate General's Corps (Army)
JAGDUSAF	Judge Advocate General's Department, US Air Force
JAGIT	Joint Air-Ground Instruction Team (Military)
JAGN	Judge Advocate General of the Navy
JAMAC	Joint American Military Advisory Group
JAMMAT	Joint American Military Mission for Aid to Turkey
JAMTO	Joint Airlines-Military Traffic Office
JAN	Joint Army-Navy (OB)
JANAP	Joint Army-Navy-Air Force Publication
JANAST	Joint Army-Navy-Air Force Sea Transportation message
JANCOM	Joint Army-Navy Communications (OB)
JANET	Joint Army-Navy Experimental and Testing Board (OB)
JANFU	Joint Army-Navy Foul Up
JANGRID	Joint Army-Navy Grid (OB)
JANIC	Joint Army-Navy Information Center (OB)
JANIS	Joint Army-Navy Intelligence Studies (OB)
JANMAT	Joint Army-Navy Materiel Program (OB)
JANP	Joint Army-Navy Publication (OB)
JANWSA	Joint Army-Navy-War Shipping Administration (OB)
JAPA	Jane Addams Peace Association
	Japan Area (Military)
JAS	Jewish Agricultural Society
JASA	Joint Anti-Submarine Action (Military)
JASASA	Joint Air-Surface Anti-Submarine Action (Military)
JASCO	Joint Assault Signal Company (Military)
JATO	Jet Assisted Take-Off (Flying)
JAYCEES	Junior Chamber of Commerce

ACRONYMS

JB — JITC

JB	Jet Bomb
	Joint Army-Navy Board (OB)
JBC	Joint Blood Council
JBG	Jewish Board of Guardians
JBHCPIU	Journeymen Barbers, Hairdressers, Cosmetologists & Proprietors' Intl. Union
JBIA	Jewish Braille Institute of America
JBMA	John Burroughs Memorial Association
JBT	Jewelers Board of Trade
JBUSDC	Joint Brazil-US Defense Commission
JBUSMC	Joint Brazil-United States Military Commission
JCA	Jewelry Crafts Association
	Joint Commission on Accreditation of Universities (Military)
	Joint Communication Activity (Military)
JCAC	Joint Civil Affairs Committee (Military)
JCAEC	Joint Congressional Atomic Energy Committee
JCB	Joint Communications Board (Military)
JCC	Joint Communications Center (Military)
JC of C	Junior Chamber of Commerce
JCEC	Joint Communications-Electronics Committee (Military)
JCEE	Joint Council on Economic Education
JCET	Joint Council on Educational Television
JCI	Joint Communications Instruction (Military)
	Junior Chamber International
JCL	Junior Classical League
JCLE	Joint Committee on Library Education
JCMIH	Joint Commission on Mental Illness and Health
JCRR	Joint Commission on Rural Reconstruction
JCS	Joint Chiefs of Staff (Military)
JD	Justice Department
JDA	Joint Defense Appeal
JDCS	Joint Deputy Chiefs of Staff (OB)
JDPC	Joint Defense Production Committee (OB)
JDS	John Dewey Society
JEEP	General Purpose 1/4-ton military utility vehicle
JEIA	Joint Electronics Information Agency (Military)
JERRY	(Ger)man (primarily British)
JFS	Jewish Family Service
JG	Junior Grade
JI	Jazz International
	Jersey Institute
JIB	Jewish Information Bureau
JIC	Jewelry Industry Council
	Joint Intelligence Center (Military)
	Joint Intelligence Committee (Military)
JICA	Joint Intelligence Center, Africa (OB - Military)
	Joint Intelligence Collecting Agency (Military)
JICACBI	Joint Intelligence Collecting Agency, China, Burma, India (OB - Military)
JICAME	Joint Intelligence Collecting Agency, Middle East (Military)
JICANA	Joint Intelligence Collecting Agency, North Africa (Military)
JICARC	Joint Intelligence Collecting Agency, Reception Committee (Navy)
JICPOA	Joint Intelligence Center, Pacific Ocean Areas (Military)
JIG	Joint Intelligence Group (Military)
JIS	Joint Intelligence Staff (Military)
JISPB	Joint Intelligence Studies Publishing Board (Military)
JITC	Jewelry Industry Tax Committee

- 111 -

J&L	Jones & Laughlin Steel Corp.
JLC	Jewish Labor Committee
	Joint Logistics Committee (Military)
JLFB	Joint Landing Force Board (Military)
JLPC	Joint Logistics Plans Committee (Military)
JLPG	Joint Logistics Plans Group (Military)
JM	Johns-Manville
JMAC	Joint Munitions Allocation Committee (Military)
JMB	Jewelers Memorandum Bureau
JMC	Joint Meteorological Committee (Military)
JMCA	Judges, Marshals and Constables Association
JMF	Jewish Music Forum
JMS	John Milton Society
JMTC	Joint Military Transportation Committee (Military)
JMUSDC	Joint Mexico-United States Defense Commission
JMVB	Joint Merchant Vessels Board (Military)
JNHAC	Jewish National Home for Asthmatic Children
JNW	Joint Committee on New Weapons and Equipment (Military)
JOC	Jewish Occupational Council
	Joint Operations Center (Military)
JOSCO	Joint Overseas Shipping Control Office (Military)
JOSPRO	Joint Ocean Shipping Procedure (Military)
JP	Jet Pilot
	Jet Propulsion
	Justice of the Peace
JPB	Joint Planning Board (Military)
	Joint Purchasing Board (Military)
JPC	Joint Planning Committee (Military)
JPL	Jet Propulsion Laboratory (National Aeronautics & Space Administration)
JPPL	Joint Personnel Priority List (Military)
JPR	Joint Procurement Regulation (Military)
JPS	Jewish Publication Society of America
	Joint Planning Staff (Military)
JPSC	Joint Production Survey Committee (Military)
JPWC	Joint Post-War Committee (OB - Military)
JRDB	Joint Research and Development Board
JRPM	Joint Registered Publications Memorandum (Military)
JSA	Jesuit Seismological Association
	Jewelers' Security Alliance of the US
	Junior Statesmen Foundation
JSC	Joint Security Control (Military)
	Joint Strategic Committee (Military)
JSIA	Joint Service Induction Area (Military)
JSOC	Joint Ship Operations Committee (Military)
JSP	Joint Staff Planners (OB - see Joint Chiefs of Staff)
JSPC	Joint Strategic Plans Committee (Military)
JSPG	Joint Strategic Plans Group (Military)
JSRC	Joint Ship Repair Committee (Military)
JSSC	Joint Strategic Survey Committee (Military)
JSV	Jewish Socialist Verband of America
JTF	Joint Task Force (Military)
JTML	Junior Town Meeting League
JTR	Joint Termination Regulations (Military)
	Joint Travel Regulations (Military)
JUSMAG	Joint US Military Advisory Group

ACRONYMS

JUSMAG . . . . . . Joint United States Military Aid Group (to Greece)
JUSMAP . . . . . . Joint US Military Advisory and Planning Group
JUSMG . . . . Joint US Military Group
JUSSC . . . . Joint US Strategic Committee (Military)
JVC . . . . Jewelers Vigilance Committee
JWB . . . . (National) Jewish Welfare Board
JWPC . . . . Joint War Plans Committee (Military)
                    Joint War Production Committee (OB - Military)
JWPS . . . . Joint War Production Staff (OB)
JWV . . . . Jewish War Veterans of the USA
JWVA . . . . National Ladies Auxiliary, Jewish War Veterans of the USA
JWYCC . . . . Jamestown-Williamsburg-Yorktown Celebration Committee

K

KAS . . . . Kroeber Anthropological Society
KATY . . . . Missouri-Kansas-Texas Lines (Railroad)
KBART . . . . Kings Bay Army Terminal
KBO . . . . Kite and Balloon Officer (Navy)
K of C . . . . Knights of Columbus
KCI . . . . Key Clubs International   /D-Day(Navy)
K-DAY . . . . Day set for strike or assault by a carrier's aircraft; corresponds to
KDCW . . . . Katolicky Delnik (Catholic Workman)
KEEP . . . . American Committee for KEEP
KF . . . . Kosciuszko Foundation
KG . . . . Kilogram
KI . . . . Kiwanis International
KIA . . . . Killed in Action (Military)
KKK . . . . Ku Klux Klan
K of L . . . . Knight(s) of Labor
KL . . . . Knights of Lithuania
KMAG . . . . United States Military Advisory Group to the Republic of Korea
KMMA . . . . Knitting Machine Manufacturers Association of US
KNA . . . . Killed Not Enemy Action (Military)
KO . . . . Knockout (pugilism)
KOPS . . . . Keep Off Pounds Sensibly
KP . . . . Kitchen Police (Military)
K of P . . . . Knights of Pythias
KPA . . . . Kraft Paper Association
K of PC . . . . . . Knights of Peter Claver
KPO . . . . Keypunch Operator
KS . . . . Kipling Society
KSKJ . . . . Grand Carniolian Slovenian Catholic Union of USA
KSM . . . . Korean Service Medal
KT . . . . Knights Templar
KVA . . . . Kilovolt Ampere
KW . . . . Kilowatt
                    Korean War
KYCH . . . . Knights York Cross of Honour
KYTOON . . . . . Kite Balloon

L

LA . . . . Low Altitude
LAA . . . . Light Antiaircraft (Guns)

LABS	Low Altitude Bombing System (Air Force)
LACC	Los Angeles City College
LAGE	Los Angeles Grain Exchange
LAM	Latin-American Mission (Air Force)
LAMA	Lead Air Materiel Area (Air Force)
LANAC	Laminar Air Navigation and Anti-Collision
LANCRA	Landing Craft (Navy)
LANCRAB	Landing Craft and Bases (Navy)
LANCRABNAW	Landing Craft and Bases, Northwest African Waters (Navy)
LANDCENT	Allied Land Forces, Central Europe
LANFORASCU	Landing Force Air Support Control Unit (Navy)
LANT	Atlantic (Navy)
LANTCOM	Atlantic Command (Military)
LANTFLT	Atlantic Fleet
LANTRESFLT	Atlantic Reserve Fleet
LAW	Local Air Warning
LB	Light Bombardment (Air Force)
LBI	Library Binding Institute
	Licensed Beverage Industries
LC	Landing Craft (Navy)
	Legitimate Child
	Liaison-Cargo (Air Force)
	Library of Congress
L of C	Line of Communication (Military)
LC	Line of Contact (Military)
LCA	Lake Carriers' Association
	Landing Craft, Assault (Navy)
LCATA	Laundry and Cleaners Allied Trades Association
LCAVAT	Landing Craft and Amphibious Vehicle Assignment Table (Military)
LCBA	Ladies' Catholic Benevolent Association
LCC	Landing Craft, Control (Navy)
	London Communications Committee (OB)
LCCR	Leadership Conference on Civil Rights
LCE	Landing Craft, Emergency repair (Navy)
LCEOP	Landing Craft, Engine Overhaul Parties (Navy)
LCF	Landing Craft, Flak (Navy)
LCFF	Landing Craft, Flotilla Flagship (Navy)
LCFLOTSPAC	Landing Craft, Flotilla, Pacific Fleet
LCG	Landing Craft, Gunboat (Navy)
LCGL	Landing Craft, Gun, Large (Navy)
LCGP	Landing Craft, Group (Navy)
LCI	Landing Craft, Infantry (Navy)
	Livestock Conservation Institute
LCIDIV	Landing Craft Infantry Division (Navy)
LCIFLOT	Landing Craft Infantry, Flotilla
LCIG	Landing Craft, Infantry, Gunboat (Navy)
LCIL	Landing Craft, Infantry, Large (Navy)
LCILFLOT	Landing Craft Infantry, Large, Flotilla (Navy)
LCIM	Landing Craft, Infantry, Mortar Ship (Navy)
LCIR	Landing Craft, Infantry, Rocket Ship (Navy)
LCL	Less than Carload Lot
	Lifting Condensation Level (Air Force)
LCM	Landing Craft, Mechanized (Navy)
LCMA	Lutheran Church Men of America
LCMSO	Landing Craft Material Supply Officer (Navy)

ACRONYMS

LCN	Landing Craft, Navigation
LCNC	Local Cartage National Conference
LCNT	Link Celestial Navigation Trainer (Military)
LCOCU	Landing Craft, Obstruction Clearance Unit (Navy)
LCP	Landing Craft, Personnel (Navy)
LCPL	Landing Craft, Personnel, Large (Navy)
LCPM	Landing Craft, Personnel, Medium (Navy)
LCPN	Landing Craft, Personnel, Nested (Navy)
LCPP	Landing Craft, Personnel, Plastic (Navy)
LCPR	Landing Craft Personnel, Ramp (Navy)
LCPSY	Landing Craft, Personnel, Survey (Navy)
LCRL	Landing Craft, Rubber, Large (Navy)
LCRR	Landing Craft, Rubber, Rocket (Navy)
LCRS	Landing Craft, Rubber, Small (Navy)
LCRU	Landing Craft, Recovery Unit (Navy)
LCSL	Landing Craft, Support, Large (Navy)
LCSM	Landing Craft, Support, Medium (Navy)
LCSR	Landing Craft, Support, Rocket (Navy)
LCSS	Landing Craft, Support, Small (Navy)
LCT	Landing Craft Tank (Navy)
	Latest Closing Time
	Local Civil Time
LCTA	Landing Craft, Tank, Armored (Navy)
LCV	Landing Craft, Vehicle (Navy)
LCVP	Landing Craft, Vehicle and Personnel (Navy)
LD	Labor Department
L/D	Length-Diameter
	Lift-Drag ratio (Air Force)
LD	Line of Departure (Military)
	Line of Duty (Military)
LDC	Light Direction Center (Military)
LDCO	Laundry and Dry-Cleaning Operation (Military)
LDD	Letter of Determination of Dependency (Military)
LDF	Local Defense Forces (Military)
LDO	Limited Duty Officer (Military)
LDRC	Lumber Dealers Research Council
LE	Light Equipment (Military)
	Low Explosive (Military)
LEA	Loss Executives Association
LEAA	Lace and Embroidery Association of America
LED	Library Education Division (of ALA)
LEDC	League for Emotionally Disturbed Children
LEF	Life Extension Foundation
LEG	Logistical Expediting Group (Military)
LEP	Lowest Effective Power
LF	Low Frequency
LFM	Landing Force Manual (Navy)
LFMA	Laminated Foil Manufacturers' Association
LF/MF	Low Frequency, Medium Frequency
LFNGFT	Landing Force Naval Gunfire Team
LG	Landing Gear (Airplane)
	Landing Ground (Navy)
LGAR	Ladies of the Grand Army of the Republic
LH	Left Hand
LHA	Local Hour Angle

Acronym	Meaning
LIA	Lead Industries Association
	Leather Industries of America
LIAA	Life Insurance Advertisers Association
	Life Insurance Association of America
LIAMA	Life Insurance Agency Management Association
LIC	Life Insurers Conference
LICAA	Land Improvement Contractors Association of America
LID	League for Industrial Democracy
LIF	Lone Indian Fellowship
LIFESTA	Lifeboat Station (Coast Guard)
LIMDAT	Limiting Date (Air Force)
LIMRF	Life Insurance Medical Research Fund
LINFT	Linear Foot
LINS	Lightweight Inertial Navigation System
LITFUND	Fund for the Relief of Russian Writers and Scientists in Exile
LIU	Long Island University
	Wood, Wire and Metal Lathers International Union
LKRT	Loyal Knights of the Round Table
LL	Light Line (Military)
LLA	Luther League of America
LLB	Little League Baseball
LLGMA	Luggage and Leather Goods Manufacturers of America
LLGSAA	Luggage and Leather Goods Salesmen's Association of America
LLI	Latitude and Longitude Indicator
LLLO	Lend-Lease Liaison Office (OB)
LLPI	Linen and Lace Paper Institute
LM	Land Mine (Military)
	Legion of Merit (Military)
LMA	Last Manufacturers Association
	Lingerie Manufacturers Association
LMF	Last Meal Furnished (Military)
LMG	Light Machine Gun (Military)
LMI	Lawn Mower Institute
LMNA	Label Manufacturers National Association
LMOA	Locomotive Maintenance Officers Association
LMT	Local Mean Time
LNA	Lithographers National Association
LNC	Local Naval Commander
LO	Law Officer
	Letter Order (Military)
	Liaison Office (r) (Navy)
	Lubrication Order (Military)
LOA	Leave of Absence (Military)
LOB	Loyal Order of the Boar
LOBAR	Long Baseline Radar
LOC	Line of Communication (see LC)
LODC	Local Defense District Craft (Navy)
LODOR	Loaded, Waiting Orders or Assignment (Navy)
LOG	Legion of Guardsmen
LOGAIR	Logistics Transport by Air (Military)
LOGLAND	Logistics Transport by Land (Military)
LOGSEA	Logistics Transport by Sea (Military)
LOM	Loyal Order of Moose
LOMA	Life Office Management Association
LOP	Line of Position (Military)

ACRONYMS

LOP	Local Operational Plot (Military)
LOPU	Logistics Organization Planning Unit (Military)
LORAN	Long-Range Radio Aid to Navigation
LOS	Line of Sight (Military)
LOTS	Loran Operational Training School
LOX	Liquid-Oxygen Explosive (Military)
LP	Last Paid (Military)
	Litter Patient (Military)
	Local Procurement (Military)
	Loss of Pay (Military)
	Low Pressure
LPD	Local Procurement Direct (Military)
LPG	Liquified Petroleum Gas
LPGA	Ladies' Professional Golf Association
LPGA	Liquefied Petroleum Gas Association
	Louisiana Pecan Growers Association
LPI	Lightning Protection Institute
LPMA	Lead Pencil Manufacturers Association
LPRC	Library Public Relations Council
LR or L/R	Leave Rations (Military)
	(Expendable) Limited-Recoverable (Air Force)
	Long Range
LRA	Labor Research Association
LRBM	Long Range Ballistic Missile
LRBR	Long-Range Ballistic Rocket
LRC	Langley Research Center (National Aeronautics and Space Administration)
	Lewis Research Center (National Aeronautics and Space Administration)
LRCE	Little Rock Cotton Exchange
LRNA	Laws Relating to the Navy Annotated
LRPGD	Long Range Proving Ground Division (OB - Air Force)
LRTM	Long Range Training Mission (Military)
LRY	Liberal Religious Youth
LS	Landing Ship (Navy)
	Lepidopterists' Society
	Leukemia Society
	Light Ship or vessel
LSA	Linguistic Society of America
LSAA	Linen Supply Association of America
LSB	Landing Ship, Bombardment (Navy)
LSC	Lincoln Sesquicentennial Committee (government agency)
LSD	Landing Ship, Dock (Navy)
LSF	Louisiana Sugar Exchange
LSHL	Landing Ship, Headquarters, Large (Navy)
LSHS	Landing Ship, Headquarters, Small (Navy)
LSIA	Lamp and Shade Institute of America
LSM	Landing Ship, Medium (Navy)
LSMR	Landing Ship, Medium, Rocket (Navy)
LSMSO	Landing Ship Material Supply Officer (Navy)
LSO	Landing Signal Officer (Navy)
LSPAFRO	Lump Sum Payment to Air Force Reserve Officers
LSPC	Louisiana Sweet Potato Commission
LST	Landing Ship, Tank (Navy)
	Local Sidereal Time
	Local Standard Time
LSTH	Landing Ship, Tank, Hospital (Navy)

LSU	Louisiana State University
LSV	Landing Ship, Vehicle (Navy)
LSX	Landing Ship Experimental (Navy)
LT	Landing Team (Military)
L/T	Line Telecommunications (Military)
LT	Link Trainer Instructor (Military)
LTA	Leave Travel Allowance (Military)
	Lighter-Than-Air (Airships)
	Linen Trade Association
LTEA	Leaf Tobacco Exporters Association
LTF	Lithographic Technical Foundation
LTL	Less Than Truckload
LTS	Landfall Technique School, New York (Navy)
LUF	Lowest Useful high Frequency
LVT	Landing Vehicle, Tracked (Navy)
LVTA	Landing Vehicle, Tracked, Armored Turret Type (Navy)
LVTU	Landing Vehicle, Tracked, Unarmored (Navy)
LW	Light Warning
LWASV	Light Weight Aircraft-to-Surface Vessel (Military)
LWL	Load Water Line
LWMEL	Leonard Wood Memorial for the Eradication of Leprosy
LWOP	Leave Without Pay (Military)
LWUI	Longshoremen's and Warehousemen's Union International
LWVUS	League of Women Voters of the United States
LZ	Landing Zone (Military)

M

MA	Machine Accountant
	Magnesium Association
	Maritime Administration
	Marshalling Area (Military)
	Mediterranean Area (Military)
M/A	Mess Attendant (Military)
MA	Military Attache
MAA	Master-at-Arms (Navy)
	Mathematical Association of America
	Mediaeval Academy of America
MAAC	Mutual Assistance Advisory Committee
MAAF	Mediterranean Allied Air Force (OB)
MAAG	Military Assistance Advisory Group
MAAMA	Middletown Air Materiel Area (Air Force)
MAAN	Mutual Advertising Agency Network
MAATC	Mobile Anti-Aircraft Training Center (Navy)
MAB	Magazine Advertising Bureau (of MPA)
	Marine Air Base
	Munitions Assignment Board (Military)
MABDG	Marine Air Base Defense Group
MABDW	Marine Air Base Defense Wing
MABO	Marianas-Bonins Group (Military)
MABRON	Marine Air Base Squadron
MABS	Marine Air Base Squadron
MAC	Major Air Command (Air Force)
	Marine Amphibious Corps
	Mean Aerodynamic Chord (Air Force)

ACRONYMS

MAC ....Mediterranean Air Command (OB - Military)
MACAIR ......Munitions Assignment Committee, Air (Military)
MACAF.......Mediterranean Allied Coastal Air Forces (OB)
MACG ....Marine Air Control Group
MACR.......Missing Aircrew Report (Air Force)
MACRI ......Mercantile Atlantic Coastal Routing Instructions
MACTU.......Mines and Countermeasures Technical Unit (Navy)
MAD ....Magnetic Airborne Detector (Military)
             Maintenance, Assembly and Disassembly shop (Military)
             Marine Air (or Aviation) Detachment
             Mine Assembly Depot (Navy)
MADAEC.....Military Application Division of the Atomic Energy Commission
MADEPSQ.....Marine Air Depot Squadron
MADP........Main Air Display Plot (Navy)
             Master Air Defense Plan (Military)
MADW ....Military Air Defense Warning Net
MAE.........Medical Air Evacuation (Military)
MAEE........Marine Aircraft Experimental Establishment
MAELU.......Mutual Atomic Energy Liability Underwriters
MAERU.......Mobile Ammunition Evaluation and Reconditioning Unit (Navy)
MAF.........Major Academic Field (Military)
             Marine Air Facility
MAFIA ......Morte Alla Francia Italia Anela (Italian - "death to the French is Italy's cry")
MAFOG ......Mediterranean Area Fighter Operations Grid (OB)
MAFS........Mobilization Air Force Specialty
MAFSC.......Mobilization Air Force Specialty Code
MAFSI ......Manufacturers Agents for Food Service Industry
MAG ....Marine Aircraft Group
             Military Advisory Group
MAIRMAR .....Marine Air Depot, Miramar, California
MAIRU ......Mobile Aircraft Instrument Repair Unit (Navy)
MAL.........Material Allowance List (Military)
MAM ....Medium Automotive Maintenance (Army)
MAMB ....Military Advisory Mission, Brazil
MAMIE ......Minimum Automatic Machine for Interpolation and Extrapolation
MAMS ....Modern Army Maintenance System
MANA ....Manufacturers' Agents National Association
MANIAC......Mathematical Analyzer, Numerical Integrator and Computer
MANMEDDEPT..Manual of the Medical Department (Navy)
MANOP ......Manual of Operations (Military)
MAP.........Manifold Absolute Pressure (Air Force)
             Military Aid Program
             Military Assistance Program
MAPAG ......Military Assistance Program Advisory Group
MAPI ....Machinery and Allied Products Institute
MAPONY .....Maritime Association of the Port of NY
MAPRC.......Mediterranean Allied Photographic Reconnaissance Command (OB)
MAQ ....Monetary Allowance for dependents' Quarters (Military)
MARALLWEAFITRARON ..Marine All-Weather Fighter Training Squadron
MARBRIG .....Marine Brigade
MARC........Manpower Authorization Request for Change (Air Force)
MARCOR......Marine Corps
MARDIV .....Marine Division
MAREGSQ.....Marine Air Regulating Squadron
MARFAIR.....Marine Fleet Air

MARFAIRWEST	Marine Fleet Air, West Coast
MARGARFOR	Marine Garrison Force
MARI	Mercantile Atlantic Routing Instructions
MARPAC	Headquarters, Department of the Pacific (Marine Corps)
MARS	Military Affiliate Radio System
	Military Amateur Radio System (OB - see Military Affiliate Radio System)
MARTRA&REPLCOMS	Marine Training and Replacement Commands
MAS	Military Agency for Standardization
	Monetary Allowance in lieu of Subsistence (Military)
MASA	Mail Advertising Service Association International
MASAF	Mediterranean Allied Strategic Air Force (OB)
MASC	Middletown Air Service Command (OB - Air Force)
MASCU	Marine Air Support Control Unit
MASG	Marine Air Support Group
MASS	Modern Army Supply System
MAT	Mechanical Aptitude Test (Military)
MATA	Motorcycle and Allied Trades Association
MATAF	Mediterranean Allied Tactical Air Force (OB)
MATB	Military Air Transport Board
MATCON	Military Air Traffic Control
MATD	Mine and Torpedo Detector (sonar) (Navy)
MATMU	Mobile Aircraft Torpedo Maintenance Unit (Navy)
MATNO	Material requested Not available (Military)
MATS	Mediterranean Air Transport Service (OB)
	Military Air Transport Service (Air Force)
MATSC	Middletown Air Technical Service Command (OB - Air Force)
MATSO	Material requested being Supplied (Military)
MAV	Manpower Authorization Voucher
MAW	Marine Aircraft Wing
MAWC	Marine Air West Coast
MAWP	Marine Air Wing Pacific
MAWS	Marine Air Warning Squadron
MB	Main Battery (Military)
	Marine Barracks
	Missile Bomber
	Munitions Board (Military)
MBA	Monument Builders of America
	Mortgage Bankers Association of America
MBAA	Master Brewers Association of America
MBC	Mediterranean Bombardment Code (OB)
MBCA	Munitions Board Cataloging Agency (OB-Military)
MBCMC	Milk Bottle Crate Manufacturers Council
MBDG	Marine Base Defense Group
MBF	Milk Bottlers Federation
MBI	May Be Issued (Military)
MBIA	Malting Barley Improvement Association
MBMU	Mobile Base Maintenance Unit (Navy)
MBNAD	Marine Barracks Naval Ammunition Depot
MBNAS	Marine Barracks, Naval Air Station
MBNMD	Marine Barracks, Naval Mine Depot
MBNOB	Marine Barracks, Naval Operating Base
MBNS	Marine Barracks, Naval Station
MBNYD	Marine Barracks, Navy Yard
MBRUU	May Be Retained Until Unserviceable (Military)
MBS	Motor Bus Society

ACRONYMS

MBS	Mutual Broadcasting System
MBSA	Modular Building Standards Association
MBSB	Marine Barracks, Submarine Base
MBW	Munitions Assignment Board, Washington (OB)
MBY&D	Maintenance, Bureau of Yards and Docks (Navy)
MC	Marine Corps
	Maritime Commission
	Master of Ceremonies
	Materiel Command (OB – Air Force – now Air Materiel Command)
	Medical Corps (Military)
	Megacycles
	Megacycles
	Member of Congress
	Memorial Commission (Federal Body)
MCA	Manufacturing Chemists' Association
	Maritime Control Area (Navy)
	Material Coordinating Agency (OB – Military)
	Maternity Center Association
	Mechanical Contractors Association of America
	Medical Correctional Association
	Midwest Curling Association
	Movers Conference of America
	Music Critics Association
	Musicians Club of America
MCAAF	Marine Corps Auxiliary Air Facility
MCAAS	Marine Corps Auxiliary Air Station
MCAB	Marine Corps Air Base
MCAD	Marine Corps Air Depot
MCAF	Marine Corps Air Facility
	Mediterranean Coastal Air Force Headquarters (OB)
MCAPI	Mid-Continent Association of the Pet Industry
MCAS	Marine Corps Air Station
MCASS	Marine Corps Air Station
MCB	Marine Corps Base
	Millwork Cost Bureau
	Mobile Construction Battalion (Navy)
MCBA	Master Car Builders' Association
MCC	Military Coordinating Committee
	Munitions Carriers Conference
MCCD	Marine Corps Clothing Depot
MCCM	Mexican Chamber of Commerce of US
MCE	Memphis Cotton Exchange
	Montgomery Cotton Exchange
MCF	Migrant Children's Fund
MCI	Milk Can Institute
MCKA	Metal Cutting Knife Association
MCL	Marine Corps League
MCLA	Marine Corp League Auxiliary
MCM	Manual for Courts-Martial (Military)
	Marine Corps Manual
MCMI	Malleable Chain Manufacturers Institute
MCO	Main Civilian Occupation (Military)
	Marine Corps Order
MCPD	Marine Corps Procurement District
MCQP	Milk Carton Quality Preforming Council

MCR	Marine Corps Reserve
	Master Change Record (Military)
MCROA	Marine Corps Reserve Officers Association
MCS	Marine Corps School
	Megacycles per Second
MCSC	Marine Corps Supply Center
MCT	Mechanical Comprehension Test (Military)
MCTI	Metal Cutting Tool Institute
MCW	Modulated Continuous Wave
MCWR	Marine Corps Women's Reserve
MD	Marine Detachment
	Medical Department (Military)
	Mine Disposal (Navy)
	Movement Directive (Military)
MDA	Marking Device Association
	Mobile Depot Activities (Air Force)
MDAA	Muscular Dystrophy Associations of America
	Mutual Defense Assistance Act
MDAC	Mutual Defense Assistance, General Area of China
MDAGT	Mutual Defense Assistance, Greece and Turkey
MDAIKP	Mutual Defense Assistance, Iran, Republic of Korea and Philippines
MDANAA	Mutual Defense Assistance, North Atlantic Area
MDAP	Mutual Defense Assistance Program (OB - now Military Assistance Program)
MDF	Manual Direction-Finder
MDNA	Machinery Dealers' National Association
	Mobilehome Dealers National Association
MDRS	Mobilization Designation Reserve Section (Military)
MDRT	Million Dollar Round Table of the NALU
MDT	Mountain Daylight Time
	Mutual Defense Treaty
MDU	Mine Disposal Unit (Navy)
MDW	Military District of Washington, Army
ME	Middle East
MEA	Medical Exhibitors Association
	Music Editors Association
MEAL	Master Equipment Allowance List (Air Force)
	Master Equipment Authorization List (Military)
MEBA	Marine Engineers Beneficial Association (AFL-CIO)
MEBD	Medical Examining Board (Navy)
MEC	Methodist Episcopal Church
MECOM	Middle East Command (Military)
MEDICARE	Dependents' Medical Care (Military)
MEDICOS	Mediterranean Instructions to Convoys (Navy)
MEDOFCOM	Medical Officer-in-Command (Military)
MEDSERVC	Medical Service Corps (Military)
MEDSPECC	Medical Specialist Corps (Military)
MEDSUPDEP	Medical Supply Depot (Navy)
MEE	Minimum Essential Equipment (Military)
MEF	Musicians Emergency Fund
MEI	Manual of Engineering Instructions (Navy)
	Middle East Institute
MEIU	Mobile Explosives Investigation Unit (Navy)
MEMA	Motor and Equipment Manufacturers Association
MEMQ	Married Enlisted Men's Quarters (Military)
MENA	Middle East News Agency

ACRONYMS

MENC .... Music Educators National Conference
MEO .... Major Engine Overhaul (Navy)
MEP .... Mean Effective Pressure
MERCO ...... Mercantile Communications (Shipping)
MERCOS ..... Merchant Codes (Shipping)
MERSIGS .... Merchant Signals (Shipping)
MESA .... Mechanics Educational Society of America
MESC .... Middle East Supply Center (Navy)
METO .... Middle East Treaty Organization
MEW .... Microwave Early Warning (Military)
MEWA .... Motor and Equipment Wholesalers Association
MF .... Medal of Freedom (for civilians)
            Medium Frequency
MFAIRWEST .. Marine Fleet Air, West Coast
MFGA .... Master Furriers Guild of America
MFHA .... Medal for Humane Action (Military - Berlin Airlift, 1948-9)
MFMA .... Maple Flooring Manufacturers Association
            Metal Findings Manufacturers Association
MFOA .... Municipal Finance Officers Association of US and Canada
MFS .... Malleable Founders' Society
            Military Flight Service
MFWC .... Marine Fleet Air West Coast
MG .... Machine Gun (Military)
            Military Government
            Morris Garages (British automobile)
MGA .... Military Government Association
MGCA .... Men's Garden Clubs of America
            Mushroom Growers Cooperative Association
MGE .... Milwaukee Grain Exchange
            Minneapolis Grain Exchange
MGF .... Myasthenia Gravis Foundation
MGI .... Metal Grating Institute
MGM .... Metro-Goldwyn-Mayer
MGO .... Military Government Officer
MGU .... Military Government Unit
MH .... Magnetic Heading
            Medal of Honor (often erroneously called Congressional Medal of Honor)
M-H .... Minneapolis-Honeywell Regulator Company
MHA .... Marine Historical Association
            Modified Handling Authorized (Air Force)
MHC .... Morgan Horse Club
MHD .... Medical Holding Detachment (Military)
MHDNA ...... Mobile Home Dealers National Association
MHE .... Materials Handling Equipment (Air Force)
MHEDA ...... Material Handling Equipment Distributors Association
MHF .... Medium High-Frequency
MHI .... Material Handling Institute
MHMA .... Mobile Homes Manufacturers Association
MI .... Medical Illustrator (Military)
            Military Intelligence
MIA .... Marble Institute of America
            Missing In Action (Military)
MIAA .... Mutual Insurance Advisory Association
MIAPD ...... Mid-Central Air Procurement District (Air Force)
MID .... Military Intelligence Division (OB - Army)

MIDPAC	Middle Pacific (Army)
MIDS	Movement Information Distribution Station (Military)
MIF	Milk Industry Foundation
MIG	Russian aircraft named for designers Mikoyan and Gurevich
MIGA	Merchants Ladies Garment Association
MII	Military Intelligence Interpreter
MIIA	Mine Inspectors Institute of America
MILADGRU	Military Advisory Group
MINBATFOR	Minecraft Battle Force, Pacific Fleet
MINECTRMEASSTA	Mine Counter-Measure Station (Navy)
MINRON	Mine Squadron (Navy)
MINSY	Mare Island Naval Shipyard
MINU	Mobile Instrument Investigation Unit (Navy)
MINY	Mare Island Navy Yard
MIO	Mobile Issuing Office (Navy)
MIP	Manufacturers of Illumination Products
MIPR	Military Interdepartmental Procurement Request
	Military Interdepartmental Purchase Request
MIRB	Mutual Insurance Rating Bureau
MIRS	Military Intelligence Research Section
MISHAP	Missiles High-Speed Assembly Program
MISMA	Major Item Supply Management Agency (Army)
MISR	Major Item Status Report (Military)
MIT	Massachusetts Institute of Technology
	Military Intelligence Translator
	Minimum Individual Training (OB - Military)
MJAO	Mediterranean Joint Air Orders (OB - Military)
MJ&SA	Manufacturing Jewelers & Silversmiths of America
MKA	Machine Knife Association
ML	Military Liaison
	Military payroll Money List
	Missile Launcher
	Money List (Military)
MLA	Maine Lobstermen's Association
	Mechanical Lubricator Association
	Medical Library Association
	Modern Language Association of America
	Music Library Association
MLAUS	Maritime Law Association of the US
MLC	Major Landing Craft (Navy)
	Military Landing Craft (Navy)
MLCAEC	Military Liaison Committee to the Atomic Energy Commission
MLCIM	Marquette League for Catholic Indian Missions
MLG	Main Landing Gear (Air Force)
MLMA	Metal Lath Manufacturers Association
MLPFB	Merrill Lynch, Pierce, Fenner & Bean (now Merrill Lynch, Pierce, Fenner & S
MLPFS	Merrill Lynch, Pierce, Fenner & Smith (Stock Brokers)
MLR	Main Line of Resistance (Military)
MLS	Modern Language Association
MM	Medal of Merit (for civilians)
	Millimeter
MMA	Mirror Manufacturers Association
	Monorail Manufacturers Association
MMB	Mixer Manufacturers Bureau
MMD	Manual of the Medical Department (Military)

ACRONYMS

MMF	Meals for Millions Foundation
MMFPA	Man Made Fiber Producers Association
MMG	Medium Machinegun (Military)
MMI	Mechanized Manufacturing Information
MMM	Minnesota Mining & Manufacturing Company
	Modern Music Masters
MMMA	Meat Machinery Manufacturers Association
MMNIC	Main Mediterranean Naval Intelligence Center
MMP	International Organization of Masters, Mates and Pilots
	Merchant Marine Personnel division (Coast Guard)
MMS	Missile Monitor System (Army)
MMSA	Mining and Metallurgical Society of America
MMT	Merchant Marine Technical division (Coast Guard)
MN	Magnetic North
MNA	Missing Not enemy Action (Military)
MNAO	Mobile Naval Airfield Organization
MNAU	Mobile Naval Airfield Unit
MNF	Millers' National Federation
MNL	Medical Nutrition Laboratory (Army)
M&O	Manpower and Organization (Military)
MO	Medical Officer (Military)
	Mobile station (Air Force)
	Monthly Order (Navy)
	Movement Orders (Military)
MOA	Music Operators of America
MOAA	Mail Order Association of America
MOAMA	Mobile Air Materiel Area (Air Force)
MOARS	Mobilization Assignment Reserve Section (Military)
MOBIDIC	Mobile Digital Computer
MOBOT	Mobile remote-controlled Robot
MOC	Military Order of the Carabao
	Military Order of the Cootie of the US
MODD	Military Order of the Devil Dogs
MOG	Metropolitan Opera Guild
MOGA	Mid-Continent Oil and Gas Association
MOGAS	Motor Gasoline (Military)
MOIC	Medical Officer-in-Charge (Military)
	Medical Officer-in-Command (Military)
MOLB	Military Order of Lady Bugs
MOLLUS	Military Order of Loyal Legion of United States
MOMP	Michigan Ordnance Missile Plant
MONAB	Mobile Naval Air Base
MOP	Mustering Out Pay (Military)
MOPH	Military Order of the Purple Heart of the United States of America
MOPR	Manner-of-Performing Rating (Air Force)
MOPTAR	Multi-Object Phase Tracking and Ranging
MOQ	Married Officers' Quarters (Military)
MOREST	Mobile Arresting Gear (Navy)
MORSEAFRON	Moroccan Sea Frontier (Navy)
MOS	Marking of Overseas Shipments (Military)
	Military Occupational Specialty (Army)
MOSC	Military Oil Sub-Committee (OB)
MOSS	Mutually Owned Society for Songwriters
MOT	Month of Travel (Air Force)
MOTARDIV	Mobile Target Division (Navy)

MOTEL	Motor Hotel
MOTG	Marine Operational Training Group
MOUSE	Minimum Orbital Unmanned Satellite of the Earth
MOV	Manned Orbiting Vehicle (National Aeronautics and Space Administration
MOVPER	Mystic Order of Veiled Prophets of the Enchanted Realm
MOWW	Military Order of the World Wars
MP	Member of Parliament (British Commonwealth)
	Motion Picture Production (Military)
MPA	Magazine Publishers Association
	Mechanical Packing Association
	Metal Powder Association
	Modern Poetry Association
	Motion Picture Alliance for the Preservation of American Ideals
	Music Publishers' Association of the US
MPAA	Motion Picture Association of America
MPBA	Machine Printers Beneficial Association
MPC	Manpower Priorities Committee (OB)
	Military Payment Certificate
	Military Police Corps (Army)
MPCI	Military Police Criminal Investigation Detachment (Army)
MPCO	Military Police Company (Marine Corps)
MPCRI	Mercantile Pacific Coastal Routing Instructions (Shipping)
MPD	Military Pay Division, Finance Center, US Army
MPDFA	Master Photo Dealers and Finishers Association
MPEA	Motion Picture Export Association
MPEAA	Motion Picture Export Association of America
MPERR	Master Personnel Record (Air Force)
MPG	Magazine Promotion Group
MPH	Mile per Hour
MPI	Mean Point of Impact (Military)
	Metal Powder Industries Federation
MPIC	Motion Picture Industry Council
MP&MTD	Motion Picture & Medical Television Department (of AMA)
MPO	Military Pay Order
	Military Permit Office
	Motion Picture Operator (Military)
MPP	Most Probable Position (Military)
MPPA	Music Publishers' Protective Association
MPR	Military Pay Record
MPRC	Motion Picture Research Council
MPRF	Motion Picture Relief Fund
MPRI	Merchant Pacific Routing Instructions (Shipping) (Navy)
MPSC	Material Planning Schedule and Control Division of Inspection Offices
MQO	Marksmanship Qualification Order (Marine Corps)
MR	Machine Records (Military)
M&R	Maintenance and Repair (Air Force)
MR	Medium Range
M/R	Memorandum Receipt (Military)
MR	Mobilization Regulation (Military)
M/R	Morning Report (Military)
MR	Motivational Research
MRA	Moral Re-Armament
MRB	Mutual Reinsurance Bureau
MRBM	Medium Range Ballistic Missile
MRC	Market Research Council

ACRONYMS

MRC	Material Redistribution Center (Navy)
	Movement Report Center (Military)
MRCC	Movement Report Control Center (Military)
MR&D	Material Redistribution & Disposal (Navy)
MRF	Music Research Foundation
MRI	Machine Records Installation (Military)
	Malt Research Institute
	Midwest Research Institute
MRIA	Magnetic Recording Industry Association
MRL	Multiple Rocket Launcher (Military)
MRO	Maintenance, Repair and Operating Supplies (Navy)
	Management Review Officer (Navy)
	Movement Report Office (Military)
MRS	Military Railway Service (Army)
	Movement Report Sheet (Military)
MRTA	Marketing Research Trade Association
MRU	Machine Records Unit (Military)
	Material Recovery Unit (Navy)
	Mobile Radio Unit (Air Force)
M&S	Maintenance and Supply (Air Force)
MS	Manuscript
	Medical Survey (Military)
	Metallurgical Society (of AIME)
	Meteoritical Society
	Motorship
	Multiple Sclerosis
MSA	Magazine Shippers Association
	Masonic Service Association of the United States
	Mineralogical Society of America
	Mutual Security Agency
	Mycological Society of America
MSC	Medical Service Corps (Military)
	Medical Specialist Corps (Military)
MSCI	Mediterranean Secret Convoy Instructions (Shipping)
MSCS	Merchant Ship Control Service
MSE	Midwest Stock Exchange
MSEA	Medical Society Executives Association
MSF	Mobile Striking Force (Military)
	Moroccan Sea Frontier (Navy)
MSGO	Mediterranean Secret General Orders (Military)
MSGP	Mobile Support Group (Military)
MSL	Mean Sea Level
MSP	Mutual Security Program
MSR	Main Supply Route (Military)
	Monthly Status Report (Military)
MSRB	Margaret Sanger Research Bureau
MST	Mountain Standard Time
MSTS	Military Sea Transport Service (Navy)
MSTSO	Military Sea Transportation Service Office (Navy)
MSU	Material Salvage Unit (Navy)
MT	Military Transport
	Motor Transport (Military)
MTAF	Mediterranean Tactical Air Force Headquarters (OB)
MTB	Maintenance of True Bearing
	Motor Torpedo Boat (Navy)

MTBA	Machine Tool Builders' Association
MTBRON	Motor Torpedo Boat Squadron (Navy)
MTBSTC	Motor Torpedo Boat Squadrons Training Center (Navy)
MTC	Medical Training Center (Military)
MTCC	MATS (Military Air Transport Service) Transport Control Center
MTD	Maritime Trades Department (AFL-CIO)
	Metal Trades Department (of AFL-CIO)
	Mobile Target Division, Mine Force (Navy)
MTF	Mechanical Time Fuse (Military)
MTI	Metal Treating Institute
	Moving Target Indicator (Air Force)
MTMA	Military Traffic Management Agency
MTNA	Music Teachers National Association
MTO	Medical Transport Officer (Navy)
	Mediterranean Theater of Operations (OB - Military)
	Mission, Task, Objective (Military)
MTOUSA	Mediterranean Theater of Operations, US Army (OB)
MTP	Mobilization Training Program (Military)
MTU	Mobile Training Unit (Military)
MUE	Meritorious Unit Emblem (Military)
MURA	Midwestern Universities Research Association
MUTT	Military Utility Tactical Truck
MVD	Ministerstvo Vnutrennikh Del (Russian – Soviet Ministry of Internal Affairs)
MVI	Merchant Vessel Inspection division (Coast Guard)
MWA	Modern Woodmen of America
	Mystery Writers of America
MWAA	Movers' and Warehousemen's Association of America
MWO	Modification Work Order (Military)
MWV	Mexican War Veteran
MWWII	Mothers of World War II
M/Y	Marshaling Yards (Military)
MYRAA	Model Yacht Racing Association of America

N

NA	Narcotics Anonymous
	National Airlines
	National Archives
	Naval Academy
	Naval Attache
	Naval Aviator
	North America
	Not Appropriated
NAA	National Academy of Arbitrators
	National Aeronautic Association
	National Arborist Association
	National Archery Association of United States
	National Association of Accountants
	National Auctioneers Association
	Naval Attache for Air
	Northern Attack Area
NAAAP	North American Association of Alcoholism Programs
NAAB	National Association of Artificial Breeders
NAABC	National Association American Business Clubs
NAABI	National Association of Alcoholic Beverage Importers

ACRONYMS

NAACC — NACCA

NAACC	National Association for American Composers and Conductors
	National Association of Angling and Castings Clubs
NAACP	National Association for the Advancement of Colored People
NAAF	Naval Auxiliary Air Facility
NAAG	National Association of Attorneys General
NAAMIC	National Association of Automotive Mutual Insurance Companies
NAAMM	National Association of Architectural Metal Manufacturers
NAAN	National Advertising Agency Network
NAAO	National Association of Assessing Officers
NAAP	National Association of Advertising Publishers
NAAPPB	National Association of Amusement Parks, Pools and Beaches
NAAS	National Association of Art Services
	Naval Auxiliary Air Station
NAATS	National Association of Auto Trim Shops
NAB	Naval Air Base
	Naval Amphibious Base
	National Associated Businessmen
	National Association of Broadcasters
	Navigational Aid to Bombing (Air Force)
NABA	Naval Amphibious Base Annex
NABAC	National Association of Bank Auditors and Comptrollers
NABC	National Association of Basketball Coaches of the US
NABCA	National Alcoholic Beverage Control Association
NABDC	National Association of Blueprint and Diazotype Coaters
NABET	National Association of Broadcast Employees and Technicians
NABIM	National Association of Band Instrument Manufacturers
NABISCO	National Biscuit Company
NABM	National Association of Bedding Manufacturers
	National Association of Blouse Manufacturers
NABOM	National Association of Building Owners and Managers
NABP	National Association of Boards of Pharmacy
NABT	National Association of Biology Teachers
NABTE	National Association for Business Teacher Education
NABTTI	National Association of Business Teacher-Training Institutions
NABU	Naval Advanced Base Unit
NABW	National Association of Bank Women
NAC	National Achievement Clubs
	National Agency Check (Government Security Clearance)
	National Agricultural Chemicals Association
	National Arts Club
	National Association of Cemeteries
	National Association of Concessionaires
	Naval Academy
	North Atlantic Council
NACA	National Acoustical Contractors Association
	National Advisory Comm. for Aeronautics (MW-NASA)
	National Armored Car Association
	National Association of Cost Accountants (NC - Natl. Assn. of Accountants)
NACAA	National Association of County Agricultural Agents
NACAF	Northwest African Coastal Air Force (OB)
NACBS	National Association and Council of Business Schools
NACC	National Association of Collegiate Commissioners
	Norwegian American Chamber of Commerce
NACCA	National Association of Claimants' Compensation Attorneys

NACDS	National Association of Chain Drug Stores
NACE	National Association of Corrosion Engineers
	National Association of County Engineers
NACGG	North American Commercial Gladiolus Growers
NACGM	National Association of Chewing Gum Manufacturers
NACIO	Naval Air Combat Information Office (r)
NACIS	Naval Air Combat Information School
NACLS	National Association of Commission Lumber Salesmen
NACM	National Association of Credit Management
NACO	National Association of Consumer Organizations
	National Association of County Officials
NACPA	National Association of County and Prosecuting Attorneys
NACPDCG	National Association of Catholic Publishers and Dealers in Church Goods
NACRCD	National Advisory Council on Rural Civil Defense
NACS	National Association of College Stores
	National Association of Cosmetology Schools
NACSA	National Association of Casualty and Surety Agents
NACSB	Naval Aviation Cadet Selection Board
NACSDA	National Assn. of Commissioners, Secretaries and Directors of Agriculture
NACSE	National Association of Casualty and Surety Executives
NACTU	Night Attack Combat Training Unit (Navy)
NACWC	National Association of Colored Women's Clubs
NAD	National Academy of Design
	National Association of the Deaf
	Naval Air Depot
	Naval Air Detail
	Naval Ammunition Depot
NADA	National Automobile Dealers Association
NADAR	North American Data Airborne Recorder
NADC	National Anti-Dumping Committee
NADEFCOL	NATO Defense College
NADEVCEN	Naval Air Development Center
NADFPM	National Association of Domestic and Farm Pump Manufacturers
NADI	National Association of Display Industries
NADL	National Association of Dental Laboratories
NADO	Navy Accounts Disbursing Office
NADSA	National Association of Dramatic and Speech Arts
NADSC	National Association of Direct Selling Companies
NADU	Naval Aircraft Delivery Unit
NADUSM	National Association of Deputy United States Marshals
NAE	National Association of Evangelicals
NAEA	National Art Education Association
	Newspaper Advertising Executives Association
NAEB	National Association of Educational Broadcasters
	National Association of Educational Buyers
	North African Economic Board (OB)
NAEBM	National Association of Engine and Boat Manufacturers
NAEC	National Association of Electric Companies
	National Association of Engineering Companies
	National Aviation Education Council
NAED	National Association of Electrical Distributors
NAEGA	North American Export Grain Association
NAEM	National Association of Exhibit Managers
NAEPS	National Academy of Economics and Political Science
NAES	National Association of Educational Secretaries

ACRONYMS

NAES	Naval Air Experimental Station
NAF	National Amputation Foundation
	Naval Air Facility
	Naval Aircraft Factory
	Netherland-America Foundation
	Northern Attack Force (Navy)
NAFBRAT	National Association for Better Radio and Television
NAFC	National Association of Food Chains
	Naval Air Ferry Command (MW - Military Air Transport Service)
	Northern Attack Force Commander (Navy)
NAFD	National Association of Flour Distributors
NAFEC	National Aviation Facility Experimental Center
NAFEM	National Association of Food Equipment Manufacturers
NAFFP	National Association of Frozen Food Packers
NAFGDA	National Auto and Flat Glass Dealers Association
NAFI	Naval Air Fighting Instructions
NAFM	National Association of Fan Manufacturers
	National Association of Flag Manufacturers
	National Association of Furniture Manufacturers
NAFS	Naval Air Fighter School
NAFSA	National Association of Foreign Student Advisers
NAFTF	National Association of Finishers of Textile Fabrics
NAFTRAC	National Foreign Trade Council
NAFV	National Association of Federal Veterinarians
NAG	National Association of Gagwriters
	National Association of Gardeners
NAGA	Negro Actors Guild of America
NAGC	Naval Armed Guard Center
	North American Gladiolus Council
NAGCD	National Association of Glass Container Distributors
NAGCM	National Association of Golf Club Manufacturers
NAGCO	Naval Air Ground Center
NAGM	National Association of Glue Manufacturers
NAGS	Naval Air Gunners School
NAGSCT	National Association of Guidance Supervisors and Counselor Trainers
NAGTC	North American Gasoline Tax Conference
NAGVG	National Association of Greenhouse Vegetable Growers
NAHA	North American Highway Association
	Norwegian-American Historical Association
NAHB	National Association of Home Builders
NAHHIC	National Association of House to House Installment Companies
NAHM	National Association of Hosiery Manufacturers
NAHRMP	National Association of Hotel and Restaurant Meat Purveyors
NAHRO	National Association of Housing and Redevelopment Officials
NAHS	National Association of Horological Schools
NAHW	National Association of Hardwood Wholesalers
NAI	National Apple Institute
NAIA	National Association of Insurance Agents
	National Association of Intercollegiate Athletics
NAIB	National Association of Independent Business
	National Association of Insurance Brokers
NAIC	National Association of Insurance Commissioners
	National Association of Investment Clubs
	National Association of Investment Companies
NAIEHS	National Association of Importers and Exporters of Hides and Skins

Acronym	Meaning
NAII	National Association of Ice Industries
NAIIA	National Association of Independent Insurance Adjusters
NAILM	National Association of Institutional Laundry Managers
NAIOP	Navigational Aid Inoperative for Parts (Air Force)
NAIRE	National Association of Internal Revenue Employees
NAIRO	National Association of Intergroup Relations Officials
NAIT	Naval Air Intermediate Training
NAITC	Naval Air Intermediate Training Command
NAIW	National Association of Insurance Women
NAJAFRA	National Jazz Fraternity
NAJCW	National Association of Jewish Center Workers
NAJD	National Association of Journalism Directors
NALA	National Agricultural Limestone Association
NALAM	National Association of Livestock Auction Markets
NALC	National Association of Letter Carriers
	National Association of Life Companies
	National Association of Litho Clubs
NALCM	National Association of Lace Curtain Manufacturers
NALGM	National Association of Leather Glove Manufacturers
NALHI	National Authority for Ladies Handbag Industry
NALI	National Agricultural Limestone Institute
NALLO	National Association of License Law Officials
NALO	Naval Air Liaison Officer
NALS	National Association of Legal Secretaries
	North American Lily Society
NALT	National Association of the Legitimate Theater
NALU	National Association of Life Underwriters
NAM	National Association of Manufacturers
	Naval Aircraft Modification
NAMA	National Association of Margarine Manufacturers
	National Automatic Merchandising Association
NAMAC	National Association of Men's Apparel Clubs
NAMAE	Northern Air Materiel Area, Europe (Air Force)
NAMAP	Northern Air Materiel Area, Pacific (Air Force)
NAMB	National Association of Merchandise Brokers
	Naval Amphibious Base
NAMBO	National Association of Motor Bus Operators
NAMC	Naval Air Materiel Center
	Naval Air Materiel Command
NAMCC	National Association of Mutual Casualty Companies
NAMD	National Association of Marble Dealers
	National Association of Marine Dealers
	National Association of Market Developers
	Naval Ammunition Depot
NAMDB	National Association of Medical-Dental Bureaus
NAMF	National Association of Metal Finishers
NAMH	National Association for Mental Health
NAMHH	National Association of Methodist Hospitals and Homes
NAMIA	National Association of Mutual Insurance Agents
NAMIC	National Association of Mutual Insurance Companies
NAMILCOM	North Atlantic Military Committee
NAMM	National Association of Margarine Manufacturers
	National Association of Music Merchants
NAMMW	National Association of Musical Merchandise Wholesalers
NAMO	National Association of Marketing Officials

ACRONYMS

NAMO - NAPP

NAMO	Naval Aircraft Maintenance Orders
NAMPBG	National Association of Manufacturers of Pressed and Blown Glassware
NAMRU	Navy Medical Research Unit
NAMS	National Associated Marine Suppliers
NAMSB	National Association of Men's Sportswear Buyers
	National Association of Mutual Savings Banks
NAMT	National Association for Music Therapy
	Naval Aircraft Mobile Trainer
NAMTA	National Art Materials Trade Association
NAMTC	Naval Air Missile Test Center
NAMU	Naval Aircraft Material, Utility
NAMW	National Association of Ministers' Wives
NANA	National Advertising Newspaper Association
	North American Newspaper Alliance
NANBPWC	National Association of Negro Business and Professional Women's Clubs
NANCF	North Atlantic Naval Coastal Frontier
NANE	National Association for Nursery Education
NANEWS	Naval Aviation News
NANFAC	Naval Air Navigation Facility Advisory Committee
NANM	National Association of Negro Musicians
NANP	National Association of Naturopathic Physicians
NANS	Naval Air Navigation School
NANTS	National Association of Naval Technical Supervisors
NAOA	National Apartment Owners Association
NAOEJ	National Association of Oil Equipment Jobbers
NAOT	Naval Air Operational Training
NAOTC	Naval Air Operational Training Command
NAOTS	Naval Aviation Ordnance Test Station
NAP	National Association of Parliamentarians
	National Association of Postmasters
	National Association of Publishers
	Naval Air Priorities
	Naval Aviation Pilot
NAPA	National Amateur Press Association
	National Association of Performing Artists
	National Association of Purchasing Agents
	National Automotive Parts Association
NAPBL	National Association of Professional Baseball Leagues
NAPC	National Association of Plumbing Contractors
NAPE	National Alliance of Postal Employees
	National Association of Power Engineers
NAPECW	National Association for Physical Education of College Women
NAPET	National Association of Photo Equipment Technicians
NAPF	National Association of Plastic Fabricators
NAPFM	National Association of Packaged Fuel Manufacturers
NAPG	Naval Aviation Pilot, Glider
NAPI	National Association of the Pet Industry
NAPIA	National Association of Public Insurance Adjusters
NAPIM	National Association of Printing Ink Makers
NAPL	National Association of Photo-Lithographers
NAPM	National Association of Photographic Manufacturers
NAPNE	National Association for Practical Nurse Education
NAPNM	National Association of Pipe Nipple Manufacturers
NAPO	Naval Air Priorities Office (OB)
NAPP	National Association of Play Publishers

NAPP	Naval Aviation Preparatory Program
NAPPA	National Association of Physical Plant Assn. of Universities & Colleges
NAPPO	National Association of Plant Patent Owners
NAPRE	National Association Practical Refrigerating Engineers
NAPRW	Northwest African Photographic Reconaissance Wing (OB - Air Force)
NAPS	National Association of Postal Supervisors
NAPSG	National Association of Principals of Schools for Girls
NAPT	Naval Air Primary Training
NAPTC	Naval Air Primary Training Command
NAPTCRO	Naval Air Primary Training Command Regional Office
NAPUS	National Association of Postmasters of the United States
NARAS	National Academy of Recording Arts and Sciences
NARB	National Association of Referees in Bankruptcy
NARBW	National Association of Railway Business Women
NARC	National Association for Retarded Children
NARCE	National Association of Retired Civil Employees
NARCF	National Association of Retail Clothiers and Furnishers
NARD	National Association of Retail Druggists
	National Association of Rudimental Drummers
NARDA	National Appliance and Radio-TV Dealers Association
NAREB	National Association of Real Estate Boards
NARGUS	National Association of Retail Grocers of United States
NARHC	National Association of River and Harbor Contractors
NARICM	National Association of Retail Ice Cream Manufacturers
NARM	National Association of Relay Manufacturers
NARMFD	National Association of Retail Meat and Food Dealers
NARS	Non-Affiliated Reserve Section (Military)
NARST	National Association for Research in Science Teaching
NARSTC	Naval Air Rescue Training Command
NARTB	National Assn. of Radio & Television Broadcasters
NARTC	National Association of Railroad Trial Counsel
	Naval Air Research Training Command
NARTS	Naval Aeronautics Test Station
	Naval Air Rocket Test Station
NARTU	Naval Air Reserve Training Unit
NARUC	National Association of Railroad and Utilities Commissioners
NARVRE	National Association of Retired and Veteran Railroad Employees
NARW	National Association of Refrigerated Warehouses
NAS	National Academy of Science
	National Aircraft Standards
	National Association of Sanitarians
	National Audubon Society
	Naval Air Station
	Nocturnal Adoration Society
NASA	National Aeronautics and Space Administration
	National Appliance Service Association
	National Association of Securities Administrators
	National Association Synagogue Administrators
	National Automobile Salesman's Association
	North American Swiss Alliance
NASAB	National Association of Shippers Advisory Boards
NASACT	National Association of State Auditors, Comptrollers and Treasurers
NASAF	Northeast African Strategic Air Force (OB)
NASAO	National Association of State Aviation Officials
NASASP	National Association, State Agencies for Surplus Property

ACRONYMS

NASBERM	Naval Air Station Bermuda
NASBO	National Association of State Budget Officers
NASBP	National Association of Surety Bond Producers
NASC	National Aeronautics and Space Council
	National Association of Student Councils
NASCAR	National Association of Stock Car Auto Racing
NASCD	National Association of Soil Conservation Districts
NASCL	North American Student Cooperative League
NASCRIST	Naval Air Station Corpus Christi
NASCS	National Association of Shoe Chain Stores
NASD	National Association of Schools of Design
	National Association of Securities Dealers
	Naval Aviation Supply Depot
NASDA	National Association of State Departments of Agriculture
NASDIEGO	Naval Air Station San Diego
NASDM	National Association of Special Delivery Messengers
NASDTEC	National Association of State Directors of Teacher Education & Certification
NASDVE	National Association of State Directors of Vocational Education
NAS&FCA	National Automatic Sprinkler and Fire Control Association
NASFT	National Association for the Specialty Food Trade
NASGTMO	Naval Air Station Guantanamo
NASJAX	Naval Air Station Jacksonville
NASLAKE	Naval Air Station Lakehurst
NASM	National Association of Schools of Music
NASMBCM	National Association of Sanitary Milk Bottle Closure Manufacturers
NASMD	National Association of Sheet Metal Distributors
	National Association of Sheet Music Dealers
NAS-NRC	National Academy of Sciences-National Research Council
NASPA	National Association of Student Personnel Administrators
NASPENSA	Naval Air Station Pensacola
NASPM	National Association of Slipper and Playshoe Manufacturers
NASPO	National Association of State Purchasing Officials
NASPSM	National Association of Shirt, Pajama and Sportswear Manufacturers
NASQUON	Naval Air Station Quonset Point
NASRC	National Association of State Racing Commissioners
NASS	National Association of Suggestion Systems
	Naval Air Signal School
NASSB	National Association of Supervisors of State Banks
NASSHE	National Association of State Supervisors of Home Economics
NASSP	National Association of Secondary School Principals
NASSTA	National Association of Secretaries of State Teachers Associations
NASU	National Association of State Universities
NASUP	National Association of Service to Unmarried Parents
NASW	National Association of Science Writers
NASWSO	National Association of Soft Water Service Operators
NAT	Naval Air Training
NATA	National Association of Tax Accountants
	National Association of Tax Administrators
	National Association of Teachers Agencies
	National Association of Transportation Advertising
	National Aviation Trades Association
	North Atlantic Treaty Alliance
NATAS	National Academy of Television Arts and Sciences
NATB	National Automobile Theft Bureau
	Naval Air Training Base

ACRONYMS

NATBASES......Naval Air Training Bases
NATC..........National Air Taxi Conference
              Naval Air Testing Center
              Naval Air Testing Center
              Naval Air Training Center
              Naval Air Training Command
NATD..........National Association of Tobacco Distributors
NATDEFSM......National Defense Service Medal
NATEC.........Naval Air Training and Experimental Command
NATECHTRACEN..Naval Air Technical Training Center
NATESA........National Alliance of Television and Electronic Service Associations
NATL..........National Agricultural Transportation League
NATNAVMEDCEN..National Naval Medical Center (Bethesda, Maryland)
NATO..........National Association of Taxicab Owners
              National Association of Travel Organizations
              North Atlantic Treaty Organization
NATOUSA.......North African Theater of Operations United States Army (OB)
NATRFD........National Association of Television and Radio Farm Directors
NATS..........National Association of Teachers of Singing
              Naval Air Transport Service (MW-Military Air Transport Service)
NATSLANT......Naval Air Transport Service, Atlantic Wing (OB)
NATSPAC.......Naval Air Transport Service, Pacific Wing (OB)
NATT..........Naval Air Technical Training
NATTC.........Naval Air Technical Training Center
NATWA.........National Auto and Truck Wreckers Association
NAUA..........National Automobile Underwriters Association
NAUM..........National Association of Uniform Manufacturers
NAV...........Naval or Navy
NAVA..........National Audio-Visual Association
NAVACT........Communication directed to all Navy Activities
NAVAER........Bureau of Aeronautics Publications (Navy)
NAVAGLOBE.....Long Distance Navigation System, Global (Air Force)
NAVAID........Navigation Aid (Air Force)
NAVAIRFAC.....Naval Air Facility
NAVAIRTRACEN..Naval Air Training Center
NAVALOT.......Allotment Division (Navy)
NAVAMDEP......Naval Ammunition Depot
NAVAR.........Radar Air Navigation and Control System
NAVARHO.......Navigation, Aid, Rho Radio Navigation System (Air Force)
NAVASCOPE.....Airborne Radarscope Used in Navar (Air Force)
NAVASCREEN....Ground Screen Used In Navar (Air Force)
NAVAUTH.......Naval Authority
NAVBASE.......Naval Base
NAVBOILAB.....Navy Boiler Laboratory
NAVC..........Naval Aviation Cadet
NAVCG.........Coast Guard Publications
NAVCLODEP.....Naval Clothing Depot
NAVCM.........Navigation Countermeasures and Deception (Air Force)
NAVCOM........Naval Communications
NAVCOMMSTA....Naval Communication Station
NAVCONTRACEN..Naval Construction Training Center
NAVCONVHOSP...Naval Convalescent Hospital
NAVDAC........Navigation Data Assimilation Center
NAVDET........Navy Detachment
NAVDIS........Naval District

ACRONYMS

NAVDISCBAR... Naval Disciplinary Barracks
NAVDISP ..... Naval Dispensary
NAVDOCKS ... Bureau of Yards and Docks Publications (Navy)
NAVEU....... US Naval Forces in European Waters
NAVEXAM .... Naval Examining Board
NAVEXOS..... Executive Office of the Secretary Publications (Navy)
NAVFAC...... Naval Facility
NAVFE....... Naval Forces Far East
NAVFLIGHTPREPSCOL   Naval Flight Preparatory School
NAVFOR...... US Naval Forces
NAVFOREU.... US Naval Forces Europe (OB - see NAVEU)
NAVFORGER ... US Naval Forces Germany
NAVFROF..... Navy Freight Office
NAVFUELDEP... Naval Fuel Depot
NAVGEN ..... Navy General Publications
NAVGUN ..... Naval Gun Factory
NAVHOME .... US Naval Home (Philadelphia)
NAVHOSP..... US Naval Hospital
NAVINSGEN... Naval Inspector General
NAVINTEL .... Naval Intelligence
NAVDIST ..... Naval District
NAVJAG ..... Judge Advocate General's Office Publications (Navy)
NAVJAP...... US Naval Forces, Japan
NAVMAG..... US Naval Magazine
NAVMC...... Marine Corps Publications
NAVMED ..... Bureau of Medicine and Surgery Publications (Navy)
NAVMINDEP... Naval Mine Depot
NAVMIS...... Naval Mission
NAVMUT ..... Navy Mutual Aid Insurance
NAVNAW..... US Naval Forces, Northwest African Waters (OB - see NAVMED)
NAVNETDEP ... Naval Net Depot
NAVNORSOLS.. Naval Forces, Northern Solomons
NAVNZ ...... Naval Forces, New Zealand
NAVOBSY..... Naval Observatory
NAVOPFAC.... Naval Operation Facility
NAVORD ..... Naval Ordnance Publications
NAVPHIL ..... US Naval Forces Philippines
NAVPOWFAC .. Naval Powder Factory
NAVPREFLIGHTSCOL .. Naval PreFlight School
NAVPRIS...... Naval Prison
NAVPROV..... Naval Proving Ground (Dahlgren, Va.)
NAVPUBSCONBD .. Navy Department Publications Control Board
NAVPUR ...... Navy Purchasing Office
NAVRADSTA ... Naval Radio Station
NAVRES ...... Naval Reserve
NAVRESLAB.... Naval Research Laboratory
NAVRESMIDSCOL.. Naval Reserve Midshipmen's School
NAVRETRAINCOM .. Naval Retraining Command
NAVROUTE.... Navy Routing Office
NAVRYUKYUS .. Naval Forces, Ryukyus
NAVS........ National Association of Variety Stores
NAVSANDA ... Bureau of Supplies and Accounts Publications (Navy)
NAVSHIPS..... Bureau of Ships Publications (Navy)
NAVSHIPYD ... Naval Ship Yard
NAVSTA...... Naval Station

Acronym	Definition
NAVTAC	Tactical Navigation System
NAVTECHJAP	Naval Technical Mission to Japan
NAVTECMISEU	Naval Technical Mission in Europe
NAVTECHTRACEN	Naval Air Technical Training Center
NAVTORPSTA	Naval Torpedo Station
NAVTRADISTCEN	Naval Training and Distribution Center
NAVTRANSAIR	For travel by Naval Transport Aircraft class priority is hereby certified
NAVTRASCOL	Naval Training School
NAVTRASTA	Naval Training Station
NAVWARCOL	Naval War College
NAW	National Association of Wholesalers
NAWA	National Association of Women Artists
NAWAF	Navy with Air Force
NAWAR	Navy with Army
NAWCAS	National Association of Women's and Children's Apparel Salesmen
NAWCC	National Association of Watch and Clock Collectors
NAWDC	National Association of Women Deans and Counselors
NAWF	North American Wildlife Foundation
NAWG	National Association of Wheat Growers
NAWGA	National-American Wholesale Grocers Association
NAWL	National Association of Women Lawyers
NAWLA	National-American Wholesale Lumber Association
NAWM	National Association of Wool Manufacturers
NAWMD	National Association of Waste Material Dealers
NAWU	National Agricultural Workers Union
NAWWO	National Association of Woolen and Worsted Overseers
NAYRU	North American Yacht Racing Union
NAZI	National Socialist (German - Nazional-Sozialist)
NB	Naval Base
NBA	National Bankers Association
	National Banking Association
	National Bar Association
	National Boxing Association of America
	National Button Association
NBAA	National Business Aircraft Association
NBAD	Naval Bases Air Defense
NBBB	National Better Business Bureau
NBBDA	National Burlap Bag Dealers Association
NBBMA	National Beauty and Barber Manufacturers Association
NBBPVI	National Board of Boiler and Pressure Vessel Inspectors
NBC	National Baseball Congress
	National Beef Council
	National Book Committee
	National Bowling Council
	National Broadcasting Company
	National Broiler Council
	Navy Beach Commando
NBCA	National Bituminous Concrete Association
NBCSDA	National Broom Corn and Supply Dealers Association
NBCU	National Bureau of Casualty Underwriters
NBDA	National Barrel and Drum Association
NBER	National Bureau of Economic Research
NBFFO	National Board of Fur Farm Organizations
NBFU	National Board of Fire Underwriters
NBGQA	National Building Granite Quarries Association

ACRONYMS

NBHA........ National Builders' Hardware Association
NBL......... Night Bombardment-Long Distance (OB - Air Force)
NBLP........ National Bureau for Lathing and Plastering
NBMAIA...... National Broom Manufacturers and Allied Industries Association
NBME........ National Board of Medical Examiners
NBOA........ National Ballroom Operators Association
NBP......... National Braille Press
            National Business Publications
NBPA........ Navy Board for Production Awards
NBPW........ National Brotherhood of Packinghouse Workers
NBR......... National Board of Review of Motion Pictures
NBS......... National Bookkeepers' Society
            Bureau of Ships Publication (OB - see NAVSHIPS)
            National Bureau of Standards
            Netherland Benevolent Society of New York
            Night Bombardment-Short Distance (OB - Air Force)
NBSA........ National Bakery Suppliers Association
NBSDI....... National Brands Soft Drinks Institute
NBSS........ Naval Beach Signal Section
NBTA........ National Bus Traffic Association
NBWA........ National Beer Wholesalers' Association of America
NC.......... National Cooperatives (Association)
            Naval Correspondence
            Navy Cross
            Nuclear Congress
NCA......... National Canners Association
            National Charcoal Association
            National Cheerleaders Association
            National Chiropractic Association
            National Civic Association
            National Coal Association
            National Coffee Association of the US
            National Confectioners' Association
            National Constructors Association
            National Costumers Association
            National Council on Alcoholism
            National Cranberry Association
            National Creameries Association
            Naval Communications Annex
NCAA........ National Collegiate Athletic Association
NCAB........ National Collegiate Athletic Bureau
NCAC........ National Council Against Conscription
NCAEG....... National Confederation of American Ethnic Groups
NCAF........ National Committee Against Fluoridation
NCAI........ National Congress of American Indians
            National Council of American Importers
NCAP........ Naval Air Combat Patrol
NCATE....... National Council for Accreditation of Teacher Education
NCAWE....... National Council of Administrative Women in Education
NCB......... National Cargo Bureau
            Naval Communications Board
NC&B........ Naval Courts & Boards
NCBA........ National Chinchilla Breeders of America
NCBC........ Naval Construction Battalion Center
NCBE........ National Conference of Bar Examiners

NCBGCW	National Committee on Boys and Girls Club Work
NCBM	National Council on Business Mail
NCBPE	National Conference of Business Paper Editors
NCBVA	National Concrete Burial Vault Association
NCC	National Castings Council
	National Cotton Council of America
	National Council of Churches of Christ
NCCA	National Catholic Camping Association
NCCB	National Council to Combat Blindness
NCCBS	National Citizens Council for Better Schools
NCCC	National Catholic Cemetery Conference
NCC&CWA	National Cotton Compress & Cotton Warehouse Association
NCCF	National Council on Community Foundations
NCCFL	National Catholic Conference on Family Life
NCCHE	National Conference for Cooperation in Health Education
NCCI	National Council on Compensation Insurance
NCCJ	National Conference of Christians and Jews
NCCM	National Council of Catholic Men
NCCN	National Council of Catholic Nurses
NCCPA	National Cinder Concrete Products Association
NCCPT	National Congress of Colored Parents and Teachers
NCCR	National Council of Chiropractic Roentgenologists
NCCS	National Catholic Community Service
NCCUSL	National Conference of Commissioners on Uniform State Laws
NCCW	National Council of Catholic Women
NCCWHO	National Citizens Committee for the World Health Organization
NCCY	National Council of Catholic Youth
NCCYSA	National Conference of Catholics in Youth Serving Agencies
NCD	Notice of Credit Due (Navy)
NCDC	Naval Contract Distribution Center
NCDH	National Committee Against Discrimination in Housing
NCDI	National Circle Daughters of Isabella
NCDO	Navy Central Disbursing Office
NCDT&E	Naval Combat Demolition Training and Experimental Base
NCDU	Naval Combat Demolition Unit
NCEA	National Catholic Educational Association
NCEC	National Committee for an Effective Congress
NCEW	National Conference of Editorial Writers
NCF	National Cancer Foundation
NCFA	National Consumer Finance Association
NCFC	National Council of Farmer Cooperatives
NCFR	National Council on Family Relations
NCFRF	National Cystic Fibrosis Research Foundation
NCG	Coast Guard Publications (OB - see NAVCG)
NCGA	National Committee on Governmental Accounting
	National Cotton Ginners Association
NCGE	National Council for Geographic Education
NCHA	National Capital Housing Authority
NCHS	National Committee on Homemaker Service
NCI	National Cancer Institute
	National Cheese Institute
	Naval Cost Inspector
NCIH	National Conference on Industrial Hydraulics
NCIMC	National Council of Industrial Management Clubs
NCIS	National Council of Independent Schools

ACRONYMS

NCIT — National Committee for Insurance Taxation
NCJC — National Conference of Judicial Councils
NCJCJ — National Council of Juvenile Court Judges
NCJW — National Council of Jewish Women
NCL — National Consumers League
NCLAVPAE — National Council of Local Admins. of Vocational & Practical Arts Education
NCLC — National Child Labor Committee
NCLI — National Committee for Labor Israel
National Crushed Limestone Institute
NCLTA — National Cigar Leaf Tobacco Association
NCMA — National Concrete Masonry Association
National Council of Millinery Associations
NCMEA — National Catholic Music Educators Association
NCMH — National Committee on Maternal Health
NCMLB — National Council of Mailing List Brokers
NCMUE — National Council on Measurements Used in Education
NCNW — National Council of Negro Women
NCO — Noncommission Officer (Air Force)
Noncommissioned Officer (Military)
NCOIC — Noncommissioned Officer-in-Charge (Military)
NCONAC — National Council on Naturalization and Citizenship
NCOWC — Noncommissioned Officers' Wives Club (Military)
NCPA — National Conference of Police Associations
NCPC — National Capital Planning Commission
National Capital Planning Commission
NCPEA — National Conference of Professors of Education Administration
NCPI — Navy Civilian Personnel Instructions
NCPLA — National Council of Patent Law Associations
NCPMI — National Clay Pipe Manufacturers Inc. (Association)
NCPR — National Congress of Petroleum Retailers
NCPT — National Congress of Parents and Teachers
NCPWB — National Certified Pipe Welding Bureau
NCRAC — National Community Relations Advisory Council
NCRD — Marine Corps Recruit Depot
NCRLC — National Catholic Rural Life Conference
NCRSA — National Commercial Refrigerator Sales Association
NCS — Naval Communication Station
Net Control Station (Navy)
NCSA — National Confectionery Salesmen's Association
National Crushed Stone Association
National Crushed Stone Association
NCSAB — National Council of State Agencies for the Blind
NCSBEE — National Council of State Boards of Engineering Examiners
NCSCEE — National Council of State Consultants in Elementary Education
NCSGC — National Council of State Garden Clubs
NCSI — National Council for Stream Improvement
NCSIRB — National Coat and Suit Industry Recovery Board
NCSL — National Civil Service League
Naval Code and Signal Laboratory
NCSLA — National Conference of State Liquor Administrators
NCSO — National Council of Salesmen's Organizations
NCSP — National Conference on State Parks
NCSRA — National Conference of State Retail Associations
NCSS — National Council for Social Studies
NCSW — National Conference on Social Welfare

NCSWDI	National Combination Storm Window and Door Institute
NCTA	National Community Television Association
NCTC	National Catholic Theatre Conference
	Naval Construction Training Center
NCTCA	National Collegiate Track Coaches Association
NCTE	National Council of Teachers of English
NCTEPS	National Commission on Teacher Education and Professional Standards
NCTM	National Council of Teachers of Mathematics
NCTR	National Council on Teacher Retirement
NCTS	National Council of Technical Schools
NCTW	National Conference of Tuberculosis Workers
NCUTLO	National Committee on Uniform Traffic Laws and Ordinances
NCW	National Council of Women
	Not Complied With (Military)
NCWA	National Candy Wholesalers Association
NCWC	National Catholic Welfare Conference
	National Council of Women Chiropractors
NCWM	National Conference on Weights and Measures
NCWTF	Naval Commander Western Task Force
NCWU	National Catholic Women's Union
ND	Naval District
	Navy Department
NDA	National Dental Association
NDAC	National Defense Advisory Commission (OB)
NDB	Naval Disciplinary Barracks
	Navy Department Bulletin
NDBS	Naval Dispatch Boat Service
NDBULCUMED	Navy Department Bulletins, Cumulative Editions
NDC	National Dairy Council
	National Democratic Club
	New Dramatists Committee
NDD&RF	Naval Dry Dock and Repair Facility
NDF	Naval Dairy Farm
NDFA	National Dietary Foods Association
NDGO	Navy Department General Order
NDGW	Native Daughters of the Golden West
NDHA	National District Heating Association
NDMA	National Door Manufacturers Association
	National Dress Manufacturers Association
NDO	Navy Disbursing Office
NDOS	National Defense Operations Section (Federal Communications Commission)
NDPBC	National Duck Pin Bowling Congress
NDR	Normal Daily Requirement (Military)
NDTC	National Drug Trade Conference
NEA	National Editorial Association
	National Education Association
NEAC	Northeast Air Command (OB - Air Force)
NEAPD	Northeastern Air Procurement District (Air Force)
NEARNAVDIST	Commandant of the Nearest Naval District
NEBF	National Farm Bureau Federation
NEC	National Economic Council
	National Electrical Code
	National Exchange Club
	New England Council
NECA	National Electrical Contractors Association

ACRONYMS

NECA	Near East College Association
NEDA	National Electronic Distributors Association
NEF	Naval Emergency Fund
	Near East Foundation
	Near East Foundation
NEFE	New England Fish Exchange
NEI	Netherlands East Indies
NEL	National Epilepsy League
	Naval Electronics Laboratory
	Naval Explosive Laboratory
NELA	National Electric Light Association
NEMA	National Eclectic Medical Association
	National Electrical Manufacturers Association
NEMI	National Elevator Manufacturing Industry
NEOP	New England Order of Protection
NEPIA	Nuclear Energy Property Insurance Association
NES	Naval Experimenting Station
NESA	National Electric Sign Association
NESLA	New England Shoe and Leather Association
NET	Not Earlier Than (Military)
NEWA	National Electrical Wholesalers Association
NEWCC	Northeastern Weed Control Conference
NEWLON	New London, Connecticut (Navy)
NEWS	Navy Electronic Warfare Simulator
NF	National Foundation
	Nose Fuze (Military)
	Nutrition Foundation
NFA	National Food Administration (OB)
	National Foundry Association
	Naval Fuel Annex
	New Farmers of America
NFAA	National Field Archery Association
NFB	National Federation of the Blind
	Naval Frontier Base
NFBA	National Food Brokers Association
NFBC	Newfoundland Base Command (Military)
NFBPW	National Federation of Business and Professional Women's Clubs
NFC	National Film Carriers
	Not Favorably Considered (Air Force)
NFCA	National Fraternal Congress of America
	National Fuel Credit Association
NFCAA	National Fencing Coaches Association of America
NFCCS	National Federation of Catholic College Students
NFCTA	National Fibre Can and Tube Association
NFD	Naval Fuel Depot
NFDA	National Food Distributors' Association
	National Funeral Directors' Association
NFDMA	National Funeral Directors and Morticians Association
NFFDA	National Frozen Food Distributors Association
NFFE	National Federation of Federal Employees
NFFGB	National Federation of Flemish Giant Breeders
NFFS	National Foundation of Funeral Service
	Non-Ferrous Founders' Society
NFGCA	National Federation of Grandmother Clubs of America
NFGMIC	National Federation of Grange Mutual Insurance Companies

NFHC	National Foot Health Council
NFI	National Fisheries Institute
NFIB	National Federation of Independent Business
NFIS	Naval Fighting Instruction School
NFJM	National Foundation for Junior Museums
NFJMC	National Federation of Jewish Men's Clubs
NFL	National Football League
	National Forensic League
	No Fire Line (Military)
NFLPN	National Federation of Licensed Practical Nurses
NFMC	National Federation of Music Clubs
NFMD	National Foundation for Muscular Dystrophy
NFME	National Fund for Medical Education
NFMLTA	National Federation of Modern Language Teachers Associations
NFMR	National Foundation for Metabolic Research
NFPA	National Fire Protection Association
	National Flaxseed Processors Association
	National Flexible Packaging Association
	National Fluid Power Association
NFPOC	National Federation of Post Office Clerks
NFPOMVE	National Federation of Post Office Motor Vehicle Employees
NFPS	Naval Flight Preparatory School
NFR	No Further Requirement (Military)
NFRW	National Federation of Republican Women
NFS	National Federation of Settlements
NFSAIS	National Federation of Science Abstracting and Indexing Services
NFSC	National Federation of Stamp Clubs
NFSD	National Fraternal Society of the Deaf
NFSE	National Federation of Sales Executives
NFSMA	National Fruit and Syrup Manufacturers Association
NFTB	National Federation of Temple Brotherhoods
	Naval Fleet Training Base
NFTS	National Federation of Temple Sisterhoods
	Naval Flight Training School
NFTY	National Federation of Temple Youth
NFU	National Farmers Union
NFWA	National Furniture Warehousemen's Association
NFWE	National Federation of Women's Exchanges
NG	National Guard
	No Good
NGA	National Gallery of Art
	Needlework Guild of America
NGAA	National Gift and Art Association
	Natural Gasoline Association of America
NGAUS	National Guard Association of the United States
NGB	National Guard Bureau
NGC	National Guinea Club
NGF	National Golf Foundation
	Naval Gun Factory
	Naval Gunfire
NGFT	National Guard on Field Training exercises
NGLO	Naval Gunfire Liaison Officer
NGMA	National Gadget Manufacturers Association
NGNF	National Guard Not in Federal service
NGPT	National Guild of Piano Teachers
NGR	National Guard Regulations

ACRONYMS

NGS .... National Geographic Society
             Naval Gunfire Support
NGSM .... National Gold Star Mothers
NGSMA ...... Natural Gasoline Supply Men's Association
NGTC .... National Grain Trade Council
NGUS .... National Guard of the United States
NH .... Naval Home
             Naval Hospital
NHA .... National Hay Association
             National Health Association (Defunct)
             National Hide Association
             National Holiness Association
             National Housing Act
             National Housing Administration (OB)
             New Homemakers of America
NHAW .... National Heating and Airconditioning Wholesalers
NHC .... National Health Council
             National Housing Conference
NHCA .... National Hairdressers and Cosmetologists Association
NHDAA ...... National Home Demonstration Agents' Association
NHDC .... National Home Demonstration Council
NHENMA ..... National Hand Embroidery and Novelty Manufacturers Association
NHF .... National Hemophilia Foundation
NHFL .... National Home Fashions League
NHFRA ...... National Hay Fever Relief Association
NHHRA ...... National Hereford Hog Record Association
NHLA .... National Hardwood Lumber Association
NHLPA ...... National Hockey League Players' Association
NHMA .... National Handle Manufacturers Association
             National Housewares Manufacturers Association
NHO .... Hydrographic Office Publications (Navy)
NHPAA ...... National Horseshoe Pitchers Association of America
NHPC .... National Historical Publications Commission (Govt. Advisory Committee)
NHRA .... National Hot Rod Association
NHRP .... National Hurricane Research Project
NHS .... National Honor Society
NHSA .... National Horse Show Association of America Ltd.
NHSC .... National Home Study Council
NHWRA ...... National Health and Welfare Retirement Association
NI .... Naval Intelligence
NIA .... National Insurance Association
             Navy Industrial Association
NIAA .... National Industrial Advertisers Association
NIADA ...... National Independent Automobile Dealers Association
NIAE .... National Institute for Architectural Education
NIAL .... National Institute of Arts and Letters
NIAM .... National Institute of Advertising Management
NIAR .... National Institute of Atmospheric Research
NIB .... National Industries for the Blind
             National Information Bureau
NIBCA ...... National Intercollegiate Boxing Coaches Association
NIC .... National Industrial Council
             National Interfraternity Conference
NICB .... National Industrial Conference Board
NICE .... National Institute of Ceramic Engineers

- 145 -

NICMA	National Ice Cream Mix Association
NICO	Navy Inventory Control Office
NID	National Institute of Drycleaning
NIDA	National Independent Dairies Association
	National Industrial Distributors Association
NIDS	National Institute of Diaper Services
	Navigation Instrument Development Unit (Military)
NIFA	National Intercollegiate Flying Association
NIFB	National Institute of Farm Brokers
NIG	Naval Inspector General
NIGP	National Institute of Governmental Purchasing
NIH	National Institutes of Health
NILA	National Industrial Leather Association
NILFP	National Institute of Locker and Freezer Provisioners
NIM	Naval Inspector of Machinery
	Night Intruder Mission (Air Force)
NIMC	National Institute of Management Counsellors
	National Institute of Municipal Clerks
NIMGA	Northern Indiana Muck Growers Association
NIMH	National Institute of Mental Health
NIMLO	National Institute of Municipal Law Officers
NIMPA	National Independent Meat Packers Association
NIO	Naval Inspector Ordnance
	Navigational Information Office (Navy)
NIPHLE	National Institute of Packaging, Handling and Logistics Engineers
NIRA	National Inter-Racial Association
	National Industrial Recreation Association
NIRB	National Industrial Recovery Board
NIRC	National Institute of Rug Cleaning
NIREB	National Institute of Real Estate Brokers
NIS	National Intelligence Survey (Military)
	Naval Inspection Service
	Not in Stock (Military)
NISA	National Industrial Sand Association
	National Industrial Service Association
	National Industrial Stores Association
	National Institute of Supply Associations
NISS	National Institute of Social Sciences
NITEDEVRON	Night Development Squadron (Navy)
NITL	National Industrial Traffic League
NITPA	National Institutional Teacher Placement Association
NIU	Naval Intelligence Unit
NIUC	National Independent Union Council
NIWKC	National Institute of Wood Kitchen Cabinets
NIWU	National Industrial Workers Union
NIZC	National Industrial Zoning Committee
NJA	National Jail Association
NJC	Navy Job Classification Manual
NJCAA	National Junior College Athletic Association
NJCF	National Juvenile Court Foundation
NJCS	National Jewish Committee on Scouting
NJHS	National Junior Honor Society
NJPMB	Navy Jet Propelled Missile Board
NJVGA	National Junior Vegetable Growers Association
NKA	National Kindergarten Association

ACRONYMS

NKOA .... National Knitted Outerwear Association
NKPA .... National Kraut Packers Association
NL .... National League of Professional Baseball Clubs
            Navy League of the United States
            Night Letter
NLA .... National Lime Association
            National Locksmiths Association
NLAA .... National Legal Aid Association
NLAPW ...... National League of American Pen Women
NLBA .... National Licensed Beverage Association
NLC .... National Legislative Council
            National Lutheran Council
NLD .... Not in Line of Duty (Military)
NLDA .... National Luggage Dealers Association
NLDF .... Naval Local Defense Forces
NLEA .... National Lumber Exporters Association
NLF .... Nearest Landing Field (Air Force)
NLFED ...... Naval Landing Force Equipment Depot
NLFM .... Noise Level Monitor (sonar)
NLG .... National Lawyers Guild
            Nose Landing Gear (Air Force)
NLGI .... National Lubricating Grease Institute
NLISA ...... National League of Insured Savings Association
NLMA .... National Lumber Manufacturers Association
NLMC .... National League of Masonic Clubs
NLN .... National League for Nursing
NLNA .... National Landscape Nurserymen's Association
NLO .... Naval Liaison Officer
NLP .... National League of Postmasters
NLRB .... National Labor Relations Board
NLSA .... National Liquor Stores Association
NLSC .... Navy Lockheed Service Center
NLSPA ...... National Live Stock Producers Association
NLT .... Night Letter
            Not Later Than
NLTA .... National League of Teachers' Associations
NM .... Nautical Miles
            Naval Magazine
NMA .... National Management Association
            National Medical Association
            National Microfilm Association
            Navy Mutual Aid Association
            Negligee Manufacturers Association
            Northwest Mining Association
NMAA .... National Machine Accountants Association
            National Metal Awning Association
            Navy Mutual Aid Association
NMB .... National Mediation Board
            Naval Minecraft Base
            Naval Model Basin
NMBF .... National Manufacturers of Beverage Flavors
NMC .... National Manpower Council
            National Music Camp
            National Music Council
            Naval Medical Center

NMCA	National Meat Canners Association
	Navy Mothers' Clubs of America
N&MCM	Navy and Marine Corps Medal
NMCJS	Naval Member Canadian Joint Staff
NMD	Naval Mine Depot
NMDA	National Medical and Dental Association
	National Metal Decorators Association
NMDL	Navy Mine Defense Laboratory
NMDS	Naval Mine Disposal School
NME	National Military Establishment (NC - Department of Defense)
NMEBA	National Marine Engineers' Beneficial Association
NMFEC	National Medical Foundation for Eye Care
NMFH	National Master Farm Homemakers' Guild
NMG	Navy Military Government
NMI	National Macaroni Institute
	No Middle Initial
NMIC	National Meat Industry Council
NML	National Municipal League
NMMA	National Macaroni Manufacturers Association
NMONA	National Mail Order Nurserymen's Association
NMP	Naval Management Program
NMPF	National Milk Producers Federation
NMRA	National Model Railroad Association
NMRC	Navy Material Redistribution Center
NMR&DA	Navy Material Redistribution and Disposition Administration
NMR&DO	Naval Material Redistribution and Disposal Office (r)
NMRS	National Mobile Radio System
NMRTC	Navy and Marine Corps Reserve Training Center
NMS	Naval Meteorological Service
NMSA	National Metal Spinners Association
NMSB	Navy Manpower Survey Board
NMSC	National Merit Scholarship Corporation
NMSD	Naval Medical Supply Depot
NMSS	National Multiple Sclerosis Society
NMTA	National Metal Trades Association
NMTBA	National Machine Tool Builders' Association
NMTS	Naval Mine Testing Center
NMU	National Maritime Union of America
NMWA	National Mineral Wool Association
NMWS	Naval Mine Warfare School
NMWTS	Naval Mine Warfare Test Station
NNA	National Notion Association
NNAC	National Noise Abatement Council
NNBL	National Negro Business League
NNC	Navy Nurse Corps
NNCF	National Newman Club Federation
NND	Naval Net Depot
NNF	National Nephrosis Foundation
NNGA	Northern Nut Growers Association
NNMC	National Naval Medical Center (Bethesda, Maryland)
NNPA	National Newspaper Promotion Association
NNYD	Norfolk Navy Yard
NO	Naval Observatory
NOA	National Opera Association
	National Optical Association

ACRONYMS

NOA . . . . National Orchestral Association
　　　　　　　　Not Otherwise Authorized (Military)
NOART . . . . New Orleans Army Terminal
NOB . . . . Naval Operating Base
NOBFRAN . . . . . Naval Operating Base, San Francisco
NOBNEWT . . . . Naval Operating Base, Newport
NOBSOLO . . . . Naval Operating Base, Coco Solo
NOCT . . . . Navy Overseas Cargo Terminals
NODC . . . . Naval Operating Development Center
NOE . . . . Notice of Exception (Military)
NOF . . . . Naval Operating Facility
NOFA . . . . National Office Furniture Association
NOFMA . . . . . . National Oak Flooring Manufacturers Association
NOFORN . . . . . Classified Information Not releasable to Foreign Nationals (Military)
NOFT . . . . Naval Overseas Freight Terminal
NOI . . . . Non-Operational Intelligence (Military)
NOIBN . . . . . . Not Otherwise Indexed by Name (Military)
NOIC . . . . Naval Officer-in-Charge
NOIO . . . . Naval Ordnance Inspecting Officer
NOJC . . . . National Oil Jobbers Council
NOK . . . . Next of Kin (Military)
NOL . . . . Naval Ordnance Laboratory
NOMA . . . . National Office Management Association
　　　　　　　　National Oil Marketers Association
NOMDA . . . . . . National Office Machine Dealers Association
NONCOM . . . . Noncommissioned officer (Military)
NOP . . . . Naval Officer Procurement
　　　　　　　　Naval Ordnance Plant
NOPCL . . . . . . Naval Officer Personnel Circular Letter
NOPE . . . . New Orleans Port of Embarkation (Military)
NORAD . . . . . . North American Air Defense command
NORBS . . . . . . Northern Base Section, Corsica (Navy)
NORC . . . . National Opinion Research Center
　　　　　　　　Naval Ordnance Computer
NORCALSEC . . . Northern California Section, Western Sea Frontier (Navy)
NORD . . . . Bureau of Ordnance Publication (OB - Navy - see NAVORD)
NORPAC . . . . . . North Pacific area or force (Military)
NORSOLS . . . . . Northern Solomons Area (Navy)
NORVA . . . . . . Norfolk, Virginia (Navy)
NORVAGRP . . . . Norfolk, Virginia Group (Navy)
NORWESSEAFRON . . Northwestern Sea Frontier (Navy)
NORWESSEC . . . Northwestern Sector, Western Sea Frontier (Navy)
NOSLA . . . . . . National Oil Scouts and Landmen's Association
NOSMO . . . . . . Norden Optics Setting, Mechanized Operation (Air Force bombsight)
NOTAL . . . . . . Not at All (Military)
NOTAM . . . . . . Notice to Airmen (Air Force)
NOTC . . . . National Ordnance Traffic Committee
NOTS . . . . Naval Ordnance Test Station
NOTU . . . . Naval Operational Training Unit
NOVS . . . . National Office of Vital Statistics
NOW . . . . Neighbors of Woodcraft
NP . . . . Naval Prison
　　　　　　　　Neuropsychiatry
　　　　　　　　Notary Public
NPA . . . . National Paperboard Association

NPA	National Parking Association
	National Parks Association
	National Personnel Associates
	National Petroleum Association
	National Pharmaceutical Association
	National Pigeon Association
	National Pilots Association
	National Planning Association
	National Preservers Association
	National Proctologic Association
	Naval Procurement Account
	Navy Postal Affairs section publication
NPAB	Navy Price Adjustment Board
NPANX	Naval Potomac Annex
NPB	National Plant Board
NPBEA	National Poultry, Butter and Egg Association
NPBI	National Pretzel Bakers Institute
NPBMA	National Paper Box Manufacturers Association
NPBSA	National Paper Box Supplies Association
NPC	National Panhellenic Conference
	National Peach Council
	National Peanut Council
	National Petroleum Council
	National Pharmaceutical Council
	National Potato Council
	National Press Club
	National Publicity Council for Health and Welfare Services
NPCA	National Pest Control Association
NPCI	National Potato Chip Institute
NPDA	National Plywood Distributors Association
NPDI	Non-Performance of Duty because Imprisoned (Navy)
NPEA	National Printing Equipment Association
NPF	National Paraplegia Foundation
	Naval Powder Factory
	Naval Procurement Fund
NPFFG	National Plant, Flower and Fruit Guild
NPFFPA	National Prepared Frozen Food Processors Association
NPFI	National Plant Food Institute
NPF&PP	Naval Prison Farms and Prison Personnel
NPFS	Naval Pre-Flight School
NPG	Naval Proving Ground
NPIP&NTIP	National Poultry & Turkey Improvement Plans
NPIRI	National Printing Ink Research Institute
NPJPA	National Prune Juice Packers Association
NPL	National Puzzlers' League
NPMA	National Piano Manufacturers Association
NPO	Naval Port Officer
	Navy Post Office
NPOPR	Not Paid on Prior Rolls (Air Force)
NPPA	National Pickle Packers Association
	National Probation and Parole Association
NPPF	National Poultry Producers Federation
NPR	Naval Petroleum Reserve
	New Production Reactor (Electronic)
NPRI	National Psychiatric Reform Institute

ACRONYMS

NPRR . . . . National Public Relations Roundtable
NPS . . . . National Park Service
               National Philatelic Society
               No Prior Service (Military)
NPSA . . . . National Paint Salesmen's Association
NPSB . . . . News Print Service Bureau
NPSC . . . . Naval Personnel Separation Center
NPSD . . . . Naval Photographic Services Depot (Hollywood)
NPSE . . . . National Premium Sales Executives
NPS&PA . . . . . . National Pecan Shellers and Processors Association
NPTA . . . . National Paper Trade Association
               National Piano Travelers Association
               National Postal Transport Association
NPTAUS . . . . . . National Paper Trade Association of the US
NPVLA . . . . National Paint, Varnish and Lacquer Association
NR . . . . Naval Reserve
               Navy Regulations
               (Expendable) Nonrecoverable (Air Force)
NRA . . . . National Reclamation Association
               National Recovery Act (or Administration)
               National Recreation Association
               National Reform Association
               National Rehabilitation Association
               National Renderers Association
               National Restaurant Association
               National Rifle Association of America
               Naval Radio Activity
               Naval Reserve Association
               No Repair Action (Air Force)
NRAA . . . . National Railway Appliances Association
NRAB . . . . Naval Reserve Aviation Base
NRAF . . . . Naval Reserve Auxiliary Field
NRB . . . . Naval Repair Base
               Navy Reservation Bureau
NRC . . . . National Research Council
               Natural Resources Council of America
               Naval Retraining Command
NRCA . . . . National Resources Council of America
               National Retail Credit Association
               National Roofing Contractors Association
NRCI . . . . National Red Cherry Institute
NRD . . . . Office of Naval Research and Development (OB - Office of Naval Research)
NRDFS . . . . Naval Radio Direction Finder Service
NRECA . . . . National Rural Electric Cooperative Association
NRES . . . . Naval Receiving Station
NRFA . . . . National Retail Furniture Association
NRFEA . . . . National Retail Farm Equipment Association
NRFI . . . . Not Ready for Issue (Air Force)
NRHA . . . . National Retail Hardware Association
NRHC . . . . National Rivers and Harbors Congress
NRHS . . . . National Railway Historical Society
NRL . . . . Naval Research Laboratory
NRLCA . . . . National Rural Letter Carriers' Association
NRLDA . . . . National Retail Lumber Dealers Association
NRMA . . . . National Retail Merchants Association

ACRONYMS

NRMC	National Records Management Council
NRMCA	National Ready Mixed Concrete Association
NRMS	Naval Reserve Midshipmen's School
NROTC	Naval Reserve Officer Training Corps
NRP	Nonregistered Publication (Military)
NRPA	National Railway Appliances Association
NRPB	National Research Planning Board (OB)
NRPF	National Railroad Pension Forum
NRPIO	Naval Registered Publications Issuing Office
NRPM	Non-Registered Publications Memoranda (Military)
NRPSA	National Retail Pet Supply Association
NRRS	Naval Radio Research Station
NRS	Naval Radio Station
	Naval Receiving Station
	Naval Recruiting Station
	Navy Relief Society
NRT&CMA	National Retail Tea and Coffee Merchants Association
NRWC	National Right to Work Committee
NS	Naval Shipyard
	Nuclear Ship
NSA	National Secretaries Association
	National Security Agency
	National Shellfisheries Association
	National Sheriffs' Association
	National Shipping Authority
	National Showmen's Association
	National Shuffleboard Association
	National Silo Association
	National Slag Association
	National Slate Association
	National Society of Auctioneers
	National Standards Association
	Naval Supply Account
	Navy Stock Account
	Neurosurgical Society of America
NSAA	National Ski Association of America
	National Supply Association of America
NSAD	National Society of Art Directors
NSAM	Naval School of Aviation Medicine
NSB	Naval Submarine Base
	Newsprint Service Bureau
NSBA	National School Boards Association
	National Sugar Brokers Association
NSBB	National Society for Business Budgeting
NSBMA	National Small Business Men's Association
NSBRO	National Service Board for Religious Objectors
NSC	National Safety Council
	National Security Council
	National Space Council
	Naval Supply Center
	Navy Service Center
NSCA	National Shrimp Canners Association
NSCCA	National Society for Crippled Children and Adults
NSCF	Naval Small Craft Facilities
NSCS	Navy Supply Corps School

ACRONYMS

NSD	Naval Supply Depot
NSDA	National Sprayer and Duster Association
	National Surplus Dealers Association
	Naval Supply Depot Annex
NSE	National Sales Executives
NSF	National Science Foundation
	National Sharecroppers Fund
	Naval Stock Fund
NSGA	National Sand and Gravel Association
	National Sporting Goods Association
NSGC	National Swine Growers Council
NSGW	Native Sons of the Golden West
NSHA	National Steeplechase and Hunt Association
NSI	National Shoe Institute
	Nonstandard Item (Military)
NSIA	National Security Industrial Association
NSID	National Society of Interior Designers
NSL	National Story League
NSLI	National Service Life Insurance
NSM	National Selected Morticians (Association)
NSMA	National Scale Men's Association
	National Shoe Manufacturers Association
	National Soup Mix Association
NSMG	Naval School of Military Government
NSMPA	National Screw Machine Products Association
NSMR	National Society for Medical Research
NSOEA	National Stationery and Office Equipment Association
NSPA	National Society of Public Accountants
	National Soybean Processors Association
	National Split Pea Association
	National Standard Parts Association
NSPB	National Society for Prevention of Blindness
NSPC	National Security Planning Commission
NSPD	Naval Shore Patrol Detachment
NSPE	National Society of Professional Engineers
NSPFA	National Spray Painting and Finishing Association
NSPFEA	National Spray Painting and Finishing Equipment Association
NSPI	National Swimming Pool Institute
NSPRA	National School Public Relations Association
NSPS	National Ski Patrol System
NSPWA	National Society Patriotic Women of America
NSR	National Scientific Register
NSRA	National Shoe Retailers Association
	National Shorthand Reporters Association
NSRB	National Security Resources Board
NSRMCA	National Star Route Mail Carriers Association
NSRP	National Search and Rescue Plan
NSRS	Naval Supply Radio Station
NSS	National Sculpture Society
	National Serigraph Society
	National Slovak Society of the USA
	National Speleological Society
NSSA	National Sanitary Supply Association
	National Skeet Shooting Association
	National Skirt and Sportswear Association

NSSA	National Suffolk Sheep Association
	National Sunday School Association
NSSE	National Society for the Study of Education
NSSEA	National School Supply and Equipment Association
NSSFNS	National Scholarship Service and Fund for Negro Students
NSSTC	National Small Shipments Traffic Conference
NSSTE	National Society of Sales Training Executives
NS&T	Naval Science and Tactics
NSTA	National Science Teachers Association
	National Security Trades Association
	National Shoe Travelers Association
NSTC	National Shade Tree Conference
NSU	Naval Scout Unit
NSWA	National Social Welfare Assembly
	National Stripper Well Association
NSWMA	National Soft Wheat Millers Association
NSY	Naval Shipyard
NT	National Trust for Historic Preservation
	Naval Training
NTA	National Tax Association
	National Technical Association
	Northern Textile Association
	National Tuberculosis Association
NTAA	National Travelers Aid Association
NTC	National Theatre Conference
	National Thrift Committee
	Naval Training Center
NTDC	Naval Training Devices Center
NT&DC	Naval Training and Distribution Center
NTDMA	National Tool and Die Manufacturers Association
NTDRA	National Tire Dealers and Retreaders Association
NTE	Navy Teletypewriter Exchange (OB - see NTX)
NTEA	National Tax Equality Association
NTF	National Turkey Federation
NTFC	National Television Film Council
NTI	Naval Travel Instructions
	No Travel Involved (Military)
NTIOC	No Travel Involved for Officer Concerned (Military)
NTL	National Temperance League
	No Time Lost (Military)
NTLS	National Truck Leasing System
NTMA	National Tank Manufacturers Association
	National Terrazzo and Mosaic Association
NTORS	Naval Torpedo Station
NTPC	National Temperance and Prohibition Council
NTPG	National Textile Processors Guild
NTRA	National Trailer Rental Association
NTRS	Nationwide Trailer Rental System
NTS	National Thespian Society
	National Tulip Society
	Naval Target Sub-division (OB - World War II)
	Naval Torpedo Station
	Naval Training School
	Naval Training Station
	Naval Transportation Service

ACRONYMS

NTSCH	Naval Training School
NTTA	National Tobacco Tax Association
NTTC	National Tank Truck Carriers
	Naval Technical Training Center
NTTR	Naval Torpedo Testing Range (Navy)
NTTTTI	National Truck Tank and Trailer Tank Institute
NTU	Naval Training Unit
NTX	Navy Teletypewriter Exchange
NUCS	National Union of Christian Schools
NUEA	National University Extension Association
NUL	National Urban League
NUSL	Naval Underwater Sound Laboratory
NVATA	National Vocational Agricultural Teachers' Association
NVF	National Vitamin Foundation
NVGA	National Vocational Guidance Association
NVPA	National Visual Presentation Association
NWA	National Wine Association (Dormant)
NWAC	National Weather Analysis Center (Air Force - Navy)
NWAHACA	National Warm Air Heating and Air Conditioning Association
NWB	National Wiring Bureau
	New War Department Building (OB)
NWC	National War College (Military)
	National Writers Club
	Naval War College
NWCA	National Water Carriers Association
	Navy Wives Clubs of America
NWDA	National Wholesale Druggists' Association
NWDGA	National Wholesale Dry Goods Association
NWF	National Wildlife Council
	National Woman's Forum
	Naval Working Fund
NWFA	National Wholesale Furniture Association
NWFMA	Northwest Farm Managers Association
NWGA	National Wool Growers Association
NWI	Netherlands West Indies
NWJA	National Wholesale Jewelers Association
NWLB	National War Labor Board (OB)
NWLDYA	National Wholesale Lumber Distributing Yard Association
NWMA	National Woodwork Manufacturers Association
NWMC	National Wool Marketing Corporation
NWNSA	National Women's Neckwear and Scarf Association
NWP	National Woman's Party
NWPMA	National Wooden Pallet Manufacturers Association
NWSA	National Welding Supply Association
	National Winter Sports Association
NWSF	Northwest Sea Frontier (Navy)
NWTA	National Wool Trade Association
NWTI	National Wood Tank Institute
NWWA	National Water Well Association
NY	Navy Yard
NYA	National Youth Administration (OB)
NYAL	National Yugoslav Army of Liberation (OB)
NYC	New York Central Railroad Company
	New York City
NYCE	New York Cocoa Exchange

ACRONYMS

NYCE	New York Cotton Exchange
NYCSE	New York Coffee and Sugar Exchange
NYGJB	New York Guild for Jewish Blind
NYME	New York Mercantile Exchange
NYPE	New York Port of Embarkation (Military)
	New York Produce Exchange
NYPFO	New York Air Force Procurement Field Office
NYR	Not Yet Reported (Air Force)
NYSE	New York Stock Exchange
NYU	New York University
NYWASH	Navy Yard, Washington
NZLO	New Zealand Liaison Officer
NZSEAFRON	New Zealand Sea Frontier (Navy)

O

OAA	Outdoor Advertising Association of America
OAC	Overseas Automotive Club
OAD	Officers' Accounts Division (Navy)
	Officers Assignment Division, The Adj. General's Office (Army)
OAFC	Office of Air Force Chaplains
OAFIE	Office of Armed Forces Information and Education
OALMA	Orthopedic Appliance and Limb Manufacturers Association
OAO	Orbiting Astronautical Observatories
OAPC	Office of Alien Property Custodian
OAR	Organized Air Reserve (Air Force)
OART	Oakland Army Terminal
OAS	Occupied Areas Section (Military Government)
	Organization of American States
OA&S	Other Arms and Services (Military)
OASDI	Old Age, Survivors and Disability Insurance
OASI	Old Age and Survivors Insurance
OASMS	Ordnance Ammunition Surveillance and Maintenance School (Army)
OAT	Outside Air Temperature
OATC	Oceanic Air Traffic Center (Military)
	Overseas Air Traffic Control (Military)
OB	Obstetrics (Medicine)
	Operating Base (Military)
	Operational Base (Navy)
	Order of Battle (Military)
	Ordnance Battalion (Military)
	Ordnance Board (Military)
OBCA	Outboard Boating Club of America
OBE	Office of Business Economics (Commerce Department)
OBI	Omnibearing Indicator (Air Force)
OBM	Oriental Boat Mission
OBMA	Outboard Boat Manufacturers Association
OBMC	Officers Basic Military Corps (Air Force)
OBR	Office of Budget and Reports (Navy)
OBS	Omnibearing Selector (Air Force)
OBSRON	Observation Squadron (Navy)
OC	Object Class (Military)
	Office of Censorship (Navy)
	Officer Candidate (Military)
	Officer Commanding (Marine Corps)

ACRONYMS

O/C	Officer-in-Charge (Military)
OCA	Office, Comptroller of the Army
	Operational Control Authority (Military)
	Osteopathic Cranial Association
	Oxychloride Cement Association
OCAC	Office, Chief of Air Corps (OB)
OCAFF	Office, Chief of Army Field Forces (OB)
OCAS.	Officer-in-Charge of Armament Supply (Navy)
OCAW	Oil, Chemical and Atomic Workers International Union
OCC	Office of the Comptroller of the Currency (Treasury Department)
OCD	Office of Civil Defense (Now Off. of Civil & Defense Mobilization)
OCDM	Office of Civil & Defense Mobilization)
OCE.	Officer Conducting the Exercise (Military)
OC of F	Office of the Chief of Finance (Army)
OCIAA	Office of Co-ordination of Inter-American Affairs
OCL.	Ordnance Circular Letter (Military)
OCLUS	Outside Continental Limits United States (Military)
OCMH	Office of the Chief of Military History (Army)
OCNO	Office, Chief of Naval Operations (see OPNAV)
OCNPR.	Operation and Conservation of Naval Petroleum Reserves
OCO	Office, Chief of Ordnance (Army - used within Ordnance Corps only)
OCOMS	Office of Community Services (Military)
OCONUS	Outside Continental United States (Military)
OC of ORD	Office, Chief of Ordnance (Army)
OCR.	Office of Civilian Requirements (OB - War Production Board)
OC&R.	Operations, Commitments and Requirements (Military)
OCS.	Office of Contract Settlement (Military)
	Officer Candidate School (Military)
OCSIGO.	Office of the Chief Signal Officer (Army)
OCSPWAR	Office of the Chief of Special Warfare (Army)
OCT.	Office of the Chief of Transportation (Army)
OCTI	Ordnance Corps Technical Instruction (Army)
OD	Officer-of-the-Day (Military)
	Olive-Drab (Military)
	Ordinary Seaman
	Ordnance Data (inspection and test data - Army)
	Outside Diameter
ODM	Office of Defense Mobilization (Now - OCDM)
ODP.	Organized Reservists in drill Pay status (Military)
ODT.	Office of Defense Transportation
OE.	Office of Education
OEEC	Organization for European Economic Cooperation
OEG	Operations Evaluation Group (Military)
OEIU	Office Employees' International Union
OEL	Organizational Equipment List (OB - Air Force)
OEM	Office of Emergency Management (OB)
	Original Equipment Manufacturer
OEMI	Office Equipment Manufacturers Institute
OER	Officer Effectiveness Report (Military)
	Officers' Evaluation Report (Military)
OERL	Officer Education Research Laboratory (Air Force)
OES	Order of the Eastern Star
OEW	Office of Economic Warfare (OB)
OEX.	Office of Educational Exchange
OF.	Ophthalmological Foundation

ACRONYMS

OF	Osteopathic Foundation
OFACS	Overseas Foreign Aeronautical Communications Statician
OFEA	Office of Foreign Economic Administration (OB - Lend Lease)
OFFNAVHIST	Office of Naval History
OFHA	Oil Field Haulers Association
OFLC	Office of Foreign Liquidation Commission
OFP	Operating Force Plan (Military)
OFRRO	Office of Foreign Relief and Rehabilitation Operations
OFS	Office of Field Service (Navy)
OFT	Operational Flight Trainer (Navy)
OG	Office of Geography (Interior Department)
	Officer-of-the-Guard (Military)
OGC	Office of the General Counsel (Military)
	Order of the Golden Chain
OGDANA	Oyster Growers and Dealers Association of North America
OGPU	Obyediaionnoye Gosudarstvennoye Politichiskoye Upravlenie (OB- Russian)
OGR	Ordnance, Gunnery and Readiness division (Coast Guard)
OGU	Outgoing Unit (Navy)
O/H	Over-the-Horizon transmission
OHI	Occupational Health Institute
	Oil-Heat Institute of America
	Ordnance Handling Instructions (Military)
OI	Optimist International
OIA	Oil Insurance Association
OIAA	Office of Inter-American Affairs
OIC	Officer-in-Charge (Military)
OICC	Officer in Charge of Construction (Military)
OIL	Ordnance Investigation Laboratory (Navy)
OILA	Office of International Labor Affairs (Labor Department)
OINA	Oyster Institute of North America
OINC	Officer-in-Charge (Military) /Center (Navy)
OINCABCCTC	Officer-in-Charge, Advanced Base Combat Communication Training
OIR	Office of Industrial Relations (Military)
OIS	Office of Industrial Survey (Navy)
	Office of Information Services (Air Force)
OIT	Office of International Trade (Government)
OITF	Office of International Trade Fairs (Commerce Department)
OJT	On-the-Job Training
OK	All Right (from Old Kinderhook or Oll Korrect)
OL	Operating Location (Military)
OLA	Osteopathic Libraries Association
OLC	Oak-Leaf Cluster (Military)
OLF	Outlying Field (Military)
OLLA	Office of Lend-Lease Administration (OB)
OLP	Office of Labor Production (OB)
O&LS	Ocean and Lake Surveys (Military)
OM	Occupation Medal, as used with special reference to Germany or Japan
	Office Manager
	Officer Messenger (Military)
	Order of Merit
OMA	Office of Military Assistance
	Optical Manufacturers Association
OMB	Outer Marker Beacon (Flying)
OMC	Ordnance Missile Command (OB - Now US Army Ordnance Missile /Command)
OME	Office of Management Engineer (Navy)

ACRONYMS

OMETA	Ordnance Management Engineering Training Agency (Army)
OMGUS	Office of Military Government United States
OMI	Ordnance Modifications Instructions (Navy)
OMM	Office of Minerals Mobilization (Interior Department)
	Officer Messenger Mail (Military)
OMMA	Outboard Motor Manufacturers Association
OMMC	Officer Messenger Mail Center (Military)
OMMMSA	Oil Mill Machinery Manufacturers and Supply Association
OMM(S)C	Officer Messenger Mail (Sub) Center (Military)
OMPUS	Official Munitions Production United States
ONH	Office of Naval History
ONI	Office of Naval Intelligence
ONM	Office of Naval Material
ONO	Office of Naval Operations
ONOP	Office of Naval Officer Procurement
	Officer-in-Charge, Branch Office of Naval Officer Procurement
ONR	Office of Naval Research
OOAA	Olive Oil Association of America
OOAMA	Ogden Air Materiel Area
OOD	Officer-of-the-Deck (Navy)
OOG	Office of Oil and Gas (Interior Department)
OOO	Order of Owls
OOR	Office of Ordnance Research (Army)
O&OS	Ordnance and Ordnance Stores (Navy)
OP	Observation Post (Military)
	Operational Priority (Military)
	Ordnance Pamphlets (Navy)
	Ordnance Personnel (Navy)
OPA	Office of Price Administration (OB)
OPATTYGEN	Opinion of the Attorney General
OPBMA	Ocean Pearl Button Manufacturers Association
OPC	Overseas Press Club of America
OPCMIA	Operative Plasterers and Cement Masons International Association
OPCOM	Operations-Communications (Military)
OPCON	Optimizing Control (Military)
OPDEVFOR	Operations Development Forces (Navy)
OPDL	Office of Production and Defense Lending (Treasury Department)
OPEDA	Organization of Professional Employees of Department of Agriculture
OPET	Organization, Personnel Equipment and Training Group (Navy)
OP&I	Office of Patents and Inventions (Navy)
OPINTEL	Operational Intelligence (Military)
OPL	Outpost Line (Military)
OPLAN	Operation Plan (Military)
OPLR	Outpost Line of Resistance (Military)
OPM	Office of Procurement and Material (Navy)
OPMG	Office of Provost Marshal General (Army)
OPNAV	Office of the Chief of Naval Operations
OPORD	Operations Order (Military)
OPR	Office of Public Relations (OB - Navy)
OPS	Operations (Military)
OP(S)ARMYJAG	Opinion(s) of the Army Judge Advocate General
OPTRA	Air Operational Training (Navy)
OPU	Overseas Plexiglas Unit (Navy)
OPW	Operating Weight (Air Force)
OQMG	Office of the Quartermaster General (Army)

Acronym	Expansion
OQR	Officer's Qualification Record (Military)
OR	Operations Room (Military)
O&R	Overhaul and Repair (Military)
OR	Overseas Replacement (Military)
ORA	Organization de Resistance de L'Armee (OB – French – Maquis)
ORC	Officers' Reserve Corps (Military)
ORCB	Order of Railway Conductors and Brakemen
ORD	Office of Rubber Director (OB)
	Overseas Replacement Depot (Military)
ORDALT	Ordnance Alterations (Navy)
ORDC	Ordnance Research and Development Center (Army)
ORDCAN	Orders Cancelled (Air Force)
ORDCONCAN	Orders Considered Cancelled (Air Force)
ORDCOR	Orders are hereby Corrected (Air Force)
ORDCORPS	Ordnance Corps (Army)
ORDDIS	Ordinary Discharge (Military)
ORDENG	Ordnance Engineering (Military)
ORG	Operations Research Group (Navy)
ORI	Office of Research and Inventions (OB – now, Office of Naval Research)
	Operational Readiness Inspection (Military)
ORIA	Oriental Rug Importers Association of America
ORINS	Oak Ridge Institute of Nuclear Studies
ORNL	Oak Ridge National Laboratory
ORSA	Operations Research Society of America
ORT	Operational Readiness Test (Military)
ORTHO	American Orthopsychiatric Association
OS	Ordnance Specifications (Military)
	Oversea (Military)
OSA	Office of the Secretary of the Army
	Optical Society of America
OSAF	Office of the Secretary of the Air Force
OSB	Ordnance Supply Bulletin (Military)
OSC	Own Ship's Course (Naval)
OSD	Office of the Secretary of Defense
	Ordnance Supply Depot (Military)
OS&D or OS/D	Over, Short and Damaged report (Military)
OSG	Office of the Secretary General (United Nations)
OSI	Office of Special Investigation (Air Force)
OSIGO	Office of Chief Signal Officer (Army)
OSL	Order of St. Luke the Physician of America
OSN	Office of the Secretary of the Navy
OSO	Ordnance Supply Office (Military)
OSR	Office of Scientific Research (Air Force)
	Overseas Returnee (Military) /of Science Research)
OSRD	Office of Scientific Research & Develop. (OB-Air Force-see Office
OSS	Office of Strategic Services (OB – Central Intelligence Agency)
OSSN	Other Specialty Serial Numbers (Air Force)
OSTD	Ordnance Standards (Navy)
OSU	Ohio State University
OSW	Office of Saline Water (Interior Department) /of the Army)
	Office of the Secretary of War (OB – see Office of the Secretary
OT	Observer-Target (Military)
	Office of Territories (Interior Department)
OTA	Operation Town Affiliations
OTAC	Ordnance Tank-Automotive Command (Army)

ACRONYMS

OTANY – PACB

OTANY	Oil Trades Association of New York
OTC	Officer-in-Tactical Command (Military)
	Order of Three Crusades, 1096-1192
	Ordnance Training Command (Army)
	Organization for Trade Cooperation
OTCLANT	Fleet Operational Training Command, Atlantic
OTCPAC	Fleet Operational Training Command, Pacific
OTMA	Oilfield Tank Manufacturers Association
OTS	Office of Technical Services (of Department of Commerce)
	Officer Training School (Military)
O/TSC	Other Than Special Consultants (Military)
OTSG	Office of The Surgeon General (Military)
OTT	One Time Tape (Air Force)
OTU	Operational Training Unit (Military)
OTUS	Office of the Treasurer of the United States
OUTC	Ordnance Unit Training Center (Military)
OUSW	Office of the Under Secretary of War (OB)
OVR	Office of Vocational Rehabilitation (Health, Education and Welfare Dept.)
OW	Overseas Writers (Association)
OWAA	Outdoor Writers Association of America
OWC	Officers' Wives Club (Military)
	Ordnance Weapons Command (Army)
OWI	Office of War Information (OB)
OWM	Office of War Mobilization (OB)
OWM&R	Office of War Mobilization and Reconversion (OB)
OWS	Ordnance Weapon Systems (Army)
OWU	Office of War Utilities (OB)

P

PA	Pending Availability (Military)
	Permanent Appointment (Military)
P/A	Pilotless Aircraft (Military)
PA	Point of Aim (Military)
	Port Agency (Army)
P&A	Procurement and Assignment (Navy)
PA	Proprietary Association
	Public Address
	Puppeteers of America
PAA	Pan-American World Airways
	Peruvian-American Association
	Population Association of America
	Potato Association of America
PAAA	Premium Advertising Association of America
PAAO	Pan-American Association of Ophthalmology
PAB	Price Adjustment Board (OB)
	Priorities Allotment Board (OB)
PAC	Political Action Committee (OB - see Committee for Political Educ.)
	Public Affairs Committee
	Pursuant to Authority Contained in (Military)
PACADV	Pacific Fleet Advance Headquarters (Guam)
PACAF	Pacific Air Forces
PACAFBASECOM	Pacific Air Forces Base Command
PICAO	Provisional International Civil Aviation Org. (OB - see Intl. Civil Aviation Org.)
PACB	Pan-American Coffee Bureau

PACCALL	Pacific Fleet Calls (radio call signs)
PACCOM	Pacific Fleet Communications instructions
PACCS	Pan American Cancer Cytology Society
PACD	Pacific Division (Military)
PACE	Producers of Associated Components for Electronics
PACFLT	Pacific Fleet
PACGO	President's Advisory Committee on Government Organization
PACHEDPEARL	Pacific Headquarters, Pearl Harbor (Navy)
PACORNALOG	Pacific Coast Coordinator of Naval Logistics
PACREP	Port Activities Report (Military)
PACRESFLT	Pacific Reserve Fleet
PACT	Pan American Commission
PACUSA	Pacific Air Command, US Army (OB)
PAD	Pilotless Aircraft Division (Navy)
	Pontoon Assembly Detachment (Navy)
	Port of Aerial Debarkation (Air Force)
PADOC	Pay Adjustment Document (Air Force)
PAE	Port of Aerial Embarkation (Air Force)
PAF	Pacific Air Forces
PAFS	Primary Air Force Specialty
PAGTU	Pan-American Ground Training Unit
PAHEL	Pay and Health record (Air Force)
PAI	Processed Apples Institute
PAL	Personnel Augmentation List (Military)
	Police Athletic League (New York)
	Prisoner-at-Large (Military)
PALCRU	Pay and Allowances Accrue form (Air Force)
PAM	Personnel Actions Memorandum (Military)
	Pulse Amplitude Modulation (Electronic)
PAMA	Pan American Medical Association
PAMO	Port Air Materiel Office(r) (Air Force)
PANAGRA	Pan American-Grace Airways
PAN-AM	Pan-American World Airways System
PANHONLIB	Panama-Honduras-Liberia (Also see PANHONLIBCO)
PANLIBHONCO	Panama-Liberia-Honduras-Costa Rica (Also see PANLIBHON)
PANSEAFRON	Panama Sea Frontier (Navy)
PAOA	Pan American Odontological Association
PAP	Pierced Aluminum Plank (Military)
PAR	Precision Approach Radar (Flying)
PARADROP	An airdrop by Parachute
PARAFRAG	Parachute Fragmentation Bomb (Air Force) /(Air Force)
PARAMEDIC	A medical service person qualified to participate in parachute activities
PARARESCUE	Rescue by individuals parachuted to distressed person or persons (Air Force)
PARATROOPS	Parachute Infantry (Military)
PAREC	Pay Record (Military)
PARS	Pilotless Aircraft Research Station (NASA)
PARU	Photographic and Reproduction Unit (Military)
PAS	Professor of Air Science (Air Force)
PASA	Pacific American Steamship Association
PASEP	Passed Separately (Military)
PA/SO	Port Anti-Submarine Officer (Military)
PAST	Professor of Air Science and Tactics (OB - Air Force)
PASU	Patrol Aircraft Service Unit (Navy)
PASUS	Pan American Society of the US
PAT	Personnel Authorization Table (Air Force)

ACRONYMS

PATA .... Pacific Area Travel Association
PATBOMRON ... Patrol Bombing Squadron (Navy)
PATCA .... Panama Air Traffic Control Area
PATFOR ...... Patrol Force (Navy)
PATRON ...... Patrol Squadron (Navy)
PATS .... Preacademic Training Student (Military)
PATSU .... Patrol Aircraft Service Unit (Navy)
PATWING ..... Patrol Wing (OB - see Fleet Air Wing)
PATWINGLANTFLT .. Patrol Wing Atlantic Fleet (OB)
PATWINGSCOFOR .. Patrol Wing Scouting Force (OB)
PAU .... Pan American Union
             Pilotless Aircraft Unit (Military)
PAV .... Pay Adjustment Voucher (Navy)
             Personnel Allotment Voucher (Military)
PAVA .... Polish Army Veterans Association of America
PAW .... Petroleum Administration for War (OB)
PAYMARCORPS . Paymaster, Marine Corps
PB .... Pilotless Bomber (Air Force)
PBCA .... Paperboard Butter Chip Association
PBI .... Paper Bag Institute
             Paving Brick Institute
             Plumbing Brass Institute
PBMA .... Peanut Butter Manufacturers Association
PBR .... Precision Bombing Range (Air Force)
PBS .... Peninsular Base Section (Navy)
             Prefabricated Bituminous Surface
             Protestant Big Sisters
             Public Buildings Service (Government)
PBX .... Private Branch Exchange (telephone switchboard)
PC .... Port Call (Military)
             Producers' Council
PCA .... Parachute Club of America
             Paraffined Carton Association
             Permanent Change of Assignment (Military)
             Personal Cash Allowance (Military)
             Portland Cement Association
PCC .... Panama Canal Company
             Postal Concentration Center (Navy)
PCCA .... Power and Communication Contractors Association
PCCI .... Paper Cup and Container Institute
PCCNL .... Pacific Coast Coordinator of Naval Logistics
PCD .... Panama Canal Department
PCFA .... Pin, Clip and Fastener Association
PCFO .... Position Classification Field Office (Civil Service)
PCGM .... Pacific Coast Garment Manufacturers
PCI .... Pilot Club International
             Prestressed Concrete Institute
PCO .... Prospective Commanding Officer (Navy)
PCPA .... Protestant Church-Owned Publishers Association
PCRC .... Paraffined Carton Research Council
PCS .... Permanent Change of Station (Military)
             Position, Course and Speed
             Post, Camp, or Station (Military)
PCSA .... Power Crane and Shovel Association
PCSE .... Pacific Coast Stock Exchange

PCSE	President's Committee on Scientists and Engineers
PCU	Portuguese Continental Union of the USA
PCUS	Propeller Club of the US
PD	Police Department
	Port of Debarkation (Military)
	Port Director (Military)
	Priority Directive (Military)
PDA	Parenteral Drug Association
PDC	Package Designers Council
PDCA	Painting and Decorating Contractors of America
	Purebred Dairy Cattle Association
PDD	Physical Damage Division (Navy)
PDI	Pilot's Direction Indicator (Air Force)
	Plumbing and Drainage Institute
PDR	Philippine Defense Ribbon (Military)
P&DSEC	Pioneer and Demolition Section (Military)
PDT	Pacific Daylight Time
PE	Personnel, Enlisted or Englisted Personnel division (Coast Guard)
	Pistol Expert (Military)
	Port of Embarkation (Military)
	Post Exchange (Marine Corps)
P&E	Procurement and Expedition (Military)
PEB	Physical Education Board (Military)
PEC	Production Executive Committee
PEDC	Personal Effects Distribution Center (Military)
PEF	Palestine Endowment Funds
PEI	Porcelain Enamel Institute
PEL	Priests' Eucharistic League
P&EML	Personnel and Equipment Modification List (Air Force)
PENB	Poultry and Egg National Board
PENTENG	Pentagon English (pseudotechnical language)
PEO	Prospective Engineer Officer (Navy)
PEP	Promoting Enduring Peace (Association)
PERAM	Personnel Action Memorandum (Military)
PEREF	Personal Effects (Military)
PERG	Production Equipment Redistribution Group (Military)
PERGRA	Permission Granted (Military)
PERI	Production Equipment Redistribution Inventory (Military)
PERMAFROST	Permanent Frost
PERMR	Permanent Residence (Military)
PERNOGRA	Permission Not Granted (Military)
PERSCON	Personnel Control (Air Force)
PERSD	Personnel Department (Marine Corps)
PERSEXP	Personal Expense Money (Air Force)
PERSOF	Personnel Officer (Navy)
PERSSEPCENT	Personnel Separation Center (Navy)
PERS&TRACOMD	Personnel and Training Command (Navy)
PERSTRAN	Personal Transportation (Navy)
PERU	Production Equipment Records Unit (Military)
PESA	Petroleum Equipment Suppliers Association
PETRES	Petroleum Reserves (Navy)
PF	Physicians Forum
	Pneumatic Float (Military)
	Preflight (Military)
	Proximity Fuze (bomb, rocket or shell)

ACRONYMS   PFCO - PI

PFCO	Position Field Classification Officer (Civil Service and Military)
PFD	Present For Duty (Military)
PFF	Pathfinder Force (Military air troop carriers)
PFI	Pacific Forest Industries
	Pet Food Institute
	Pipe Fabrication Institute
PFMA	Pipe Fittings Manufacturers Association
	Plumbing Fixture Manufacturers Association
PFS	Preflight School (Military)
PG	Permanent Grade (Military)
	Post Graduate
P&G	Proctor and Gamble Company
PG	Proving Ground (Military)
PGA	Professional Golfers Association of America
PGAH	Pineapple Growers Association of Hawaii
PGC	Persian Gulf Command (OB - Army)
	Proving Ground Command (OB - Air Force)
PGCOA	Pennsylvania Grade Crude Oil Association
PGDF	Pilot Guide Dog Foundation
PH	Purple Heart (Military)
PHA	Palomino Horse Association
	Public Housing Administration
PHB	Public Health Service Building
PHCAA	Public Health Cancer Association of America
PHCIB	Plumbing-Heating-Cooling Information Bureau
PHIBCORPAC	Amphibious Corps Pacific Fleet
PHIBDET	Amphibious Detachment (Navy)
PHIBDETIND	Amphibious Detachment India (OB)
PHIBEU	Amphibious Forces Europe (Military)
PHIBFOR	Amphibious Force (Navy)
PHIBLANT	Amphibious Forces Atlantic Fleet
PHIBNAW	Amphibious Forces Northwest African Waters (Navy)
PHIBOPS	Amphibious Operations (Military)
PHIBPAC	Amphibious Forces Pacific Fleet
PHIBSFORPAC	Amphibious Forces Pacific Fleet
PHIBSUKAY	Amphibious Bases United Kingdom (Military)
PHIBTRA	Training Command Amphibious Forces (Navy)
PHIBTRABASE	Amphibious Training Base (Navy)
PHIBTRALANT	Training Command Amphibious Forces, Atlantic Fleet
PHIBTRANS	Amphibious Transport (Navy)
PHIBTRAPAC	Training Command Amphibious Forces, Pacific Fleet
PHIBWARTRACEN	Amphibious Warfare Training Center (Navy)
PHILSEAFRON	Philippine Sea Frontier
PHMA	Plastic Houseware Manufacturers Association
PHNY	Pearl Harbor Navy Yard
PHPC	Post Hostilities Planning Committee (OB)
PHS	Prepared Hessian Surfacing (Air Force)
	Public Health Service
PI	Packaging Institute
	Perlite Institute
	Philippine Islands
	Photo Interpreter (Military)
	Pilotless Intercepter (Air Force)
	Popcorn Institute
	Private Investigator

PIA	Perfumery Importers Association
	Printing Industry of America
	Pumice Institute of America
PIB	Publishing Information Bulletin (Military)
PIBAL	Pilot Balloon (Military)
PIBALS	Pilot Balloon Reports (Navy)
PIC	Photo Interpretation Center (Military)
	Pursuant to Instructions Contained in (Military)
PID	Photo Interpretation Department (Military)
	Public Information Division (Military)
PIEA	Petroleum Industry Electrical Association
PIF	Pilots' Information File (Air Force)
PIO	Public Information Office (r) (Military)
PIR	Philippine Independence Ribbon (Military)
PIREP	Pilots' Report (Air Force)
PIS	Postal Inspection Service
PIU	Photographic Interpretation Unit (Military)
PL	Phase Line (Military)
	Pipeline
	Plain Language (Military)
	Plastic Expert (Navy)
	Public Law
PLANAT	North Atlantic Treaty Regional Planning Group
PLAV	Polish Legion of American Veterans
PLC	Platoon Leaders Class (Marine Corps)
PLCA	Pipe Line Contractors Association
PLF	Parachute Landing Fall (Military)
PLI	Practising Law Institute
PLIB	Pacific Lumber Inspection Bureau
PLM	Production-Line Maintenance (Air Force)
PLOP	Pressure Line of Position (Air Force)
PLR	Philippine Liberation Ribbon (Military)
PLU	Platoon Leaders Unit (Marine Corps)
PM	Paymaster (Coast Guard)
	Post Meridiem (Afternoon)
	Postmaster
	Post Mortem (Latin – After death)
	Prime Minister
	Procurement and Material (Navy)
	Provost Marshal (Army)
PMA	Pencil Makers Association
	Pharmaceutical Manufacturers Association
PMAA	Paper Makers Advertising Association
PMANY	Pattern Makers Association of New York
PMDA	Photographic Manufacturers and Distributors Association
PMG	Paymaster General (Navy)
	Postmaster General
	Provost Marshal General (Army)
PMGS	Provost Marshal General's School (Army)
PMI	Pressed Metal Institute
PMLNA	Pattern Makers' League of North America
PMMI	Packaging Machinery Manufacturers Institute
PMOA	Prospectors and Mine Owners Association
PMOS	Primary Military Occupational Specialty
PMP	Protective Mobilization Plan (Military)

ACRONYMS

PMR — PPA

PMR	Pacific Missile Range
PMS&T	Professor of Military Science and Tactics (Army ROTC)
PMW	Prompt Mobilization designation Withdrawn (Air Force)
PN	Pacific Communications Net (Air Force)
PNA	Paper Napkin Association
PNAUS	Polish National Alliance of the US
PNFD	Present Not For Duty (Air Force)
PNLA	Pacific Northwest Loggers Association
PNMO	Provided No Military Objection Exists
PNNCF	Pacific Northern Naval Coastal Frontier
PNR	Preliminary Negotiation Reports
PNS	Professor of Naval Science
PNSA	Peanut and Nut Salters Association
PNS&T	Professor of Naval Science and Tactics (Navy)
PO	Patent Office
	Personnel Officer
	Port Officer (Military)
	Post Office
	Previous Orders (Military)
POA	Pacific Ocean Area(s) (Military)
POAA	Property Owners' Association of America
POAE	Port of Aerial Embarkation (Air Force)
POAHEDPEARL	Pacific Ocean Areas Headquarters Pearl Harbor (Navy)
POAU	Protestants & Other Americans United (for the Separation of Church & State)
POD	Pay on Delivery
	Port of Debarkation (Military)
	Post Office Department
POE	Port of Embarkation (Military)
POI	Program of Instruction (Military)
POL	Petroleum, Oil and Lubricants (Military)
POM	Preparation for Oversea Movement (Military)
POMAR	Position Operational Meteorological Aircraft Report (Air Force)
POOD	Permanent Officer of the Day or Deck (Navy)
POPA	Property Owners' Protection Association
POPAI	Point-of-Purchase Advertising Institute
POR	Pay on Return
	Preparation for Oversea movement of individual Replacements (Air Force)
PORDIR	Port Director (Military)
POREP	Position Report (Air Force)
POS	Pacific Orchid Society of Hawaii
POSH	Port Outward-bound, Starboard Homeward-bound
POSITRON	Positive Electron
POTANN	Potomac Annex (Navy)
POV	Privately Owned Vehicle (Military)
POW	Prisoner of War (Military)
	Progressive Order of the West
PP	Parcel Post
P/P	Partial Pay (Air Force)
PP	Pellagra Preventive factor
	Permanent Party (Military)
	Private Property
	Public Property (Military)
PPA	Paper Pail Association
	Paper Plate Association
	Parcel Post Association

- 167 -

PPA	Periodical Publishers Association
	Popcorn Processors Association
	Poultry Publishers Association
	Produce Packaging Association
PP of A	Professional Photographers of America
	Public Personnel Association
PPC	Partial Pay Card (Navy)
PPCAA	Parole and Probation Compact Administrators' Association
PPDMG	Popular Priced Dress Manufacturers Group
PPF	Parti Populaire Francais (OB)
PPFA	Planned Parenthood Federation of America
PPG	Personnel Processing Group (Military)
PPI	Plan Position Indicator (radar scope)
PPMA	Plastic Products Manufacturers Association
	Printing Paper Manufacturers Association
	Pulp and Paper Machinery Association
PPMI	Printed Paper Mat Institute
PP&NA	Private Plants and Naval Activities
PPO	Publications and Printing Office (Air Force)
PPPA	Pulp and Paper Prepackaging Association
PPPC	Petroleum Pool Pacific Coast (Military)
PPPI	Precision Plan Position Indicator
PPR	Palomino Pony Registry
	Permanent Pay Record (Military)
PPS	Pulses per Second (radar)
PPSA	Pan-Pacific Surgical Association /(Military)
PPSMEC	Procurement, Precedence of Supplies, Material and Equipment Committee
P&PW	Publicity and Psychological Warfare (Military)
PPWA	Ponderosa Pine Woodwork Association
PQM	Post Quartermaster (Marine Corps)
PR	Parachute Rigger (Military)
	Pay Roll (Military)
	Pershing Rifles (honorary military organization)
	Photoreconnaissance (Air Force)
	Position Report (Air Force)
	Priority Regulation (Military)
	Procurement Regulations (Military)
	Public Relations
PRA	Psoriasis Research Association
PRB	Population Reference Bureau
PRC	Production Readjustments Committee (OB - War Production Board)
PRD	Public Relations Division (Military)
PRECOMMDET	Pre-Commissioning Detail (Navy)
PRECOMMSCOL	Pre-Commissioning School (Navy)
PREFAB	Prefabricated
PRESPROC	Presidential Proclamation
PRESSURETROL	Pressure Control
PRF	Public Relations Foundation
	Pulse Recurrence or Repitition Frequency (radar)
PRI	Paleontological Research Institute
	Pineapple Research Institute of Hawaii
PRIMTRA	Air Primary Training (Navy) /(Navy)
PRISIC	Photographic Reconnaissance Interpretation Section Intelligence Center
PRMG	Piston Ring Manufacturers Group
PRNC	Potomac River Naval Command

ACRONYMS

PRO (pay) . . . . Proficiency Pay (Military)
PRO . . . . Public Relations Officer (Military)
PROLT . . . . . . Procurement Lead Time (Air Force)
PROSIG . . . . . . Procedure Signal (Navy)
PRP . . . . Public Relations Personnel (Military)
PRR . . . . Pulse Repetition Rate
PRRI . . . . Puerto Rico Rum Institute
PRS . . . . Pacific Rocket Society
                 Physically Restricted Status (Military)
PRSA . . . . Public Relations Society of America
PRT . . . . Personnel Research Test (Military)
PRU . . . . Photographic Reconnaissance Unit
PS . . . . Paleontological Society
P&S . . . . Pay and Supply (Coast Guard)
PS . . . . Philippine Scouts (OB - Army)
                 Pistol Sharpshooter (Army)
                 Postscript
PSA . . . . Photographic Society of America
                 Phycological Society of America
                 Play Schools Association
                 Poetry Society of America
                 Poultry Science Association
PSAA . . . . Pakistan Students Association of America
                 Polish Singers Alliance of America
PSC . . . . Public Service Commission
PSCLA . . . . . . Petroleum Supply Committee for Latin America
PSD . . . . Promotion Service Date (Military)
PSDS . . . . Permanently Separated from Duty Station (Military)
PSEA . . . . Physical Security Equipment Agency (Military)
                 Pleaters, Stitchers and Embroiderers Association
PSF . . . . Panama Sea Frontier
                 Philippine Sea Frontier
                 Pounds per Square Foot
                 Psychiatric Research Fund
P&SI . . . . Pay and Supply Instructions (Coast Guard)
PSI . . . . Pounds per Square Inch
PSL . . . . Photographic Science Laboratory (Military)
PS&M . . . . Division of Personnel Supervision and Management (OB - Navy)
PSMA . . . . Power Saw Manufacturers Association
P&SNP . . . . . . Pay and Subsistence of Naval Personnel
PSO . . . . Political Survey Officers (Military)
                 Provisions Supply Office (Military)
PSRF . . . . Profit Sharing Research Foundation
PSS . . . . Plant Science Seminar
                 Precancel Stamp Society
PSSMA . . . . . . Paper Shipping Sack Manufacturers Association
PST . . . . Pacific Standard Time
PS&T . . . . Pay, Subsistence and Transportation (Military)
PSTC . . . . Pressure Sensitive Tape Council
PSTMA . . . . . . Paper Stationery and Tablet Manufacturers Association
PSTO . . . . Principal Sea Transport Offices
PT . . . . Patrol Torpedo boat (Navy)
                 Physical Training (Military)
                 Primary Trainer (OB - Air Force)
PTA . . . . Paper and Twine Association

Acronym	Meaning
PTA	Parent-Teachers' Association
PTAD	Productivity and Technical Assistance Division (Mutual Security Agency)
PTC	Pipe and Tobacco Council
	Power Transmission Council
PTCA	Private Truck Council of America
PTCAD	Provisional Troop Carrier Airborne Division (OB - Army)
PTG	Piano Technicians Guild
PTL	Pocket Testament League
PTM	Pulse-Time Modulation (radar)
PTO	Port Transportation Officer (Military)
PTTC	Pacific Transportation Terminal Command (Army)
PUAA	Public Utilities Advertising Association
PUBINFO	Office of Public Information (Navy)
PUBLINX	Public Links (amateur golf)
PUC	Port Utilization Committee (Military)
	Presidential Unit Citation (Military)
	Production Urgency Committee (OB - War Production Board)
	Provided you Concur (Military)
PUG	Partially Underground (Military)
PVA	Paralyzed Veterans of America
PVAC	Polyvinyl Acetate
P&W	Pratt & Whitney (aircraft engine manufacturer)
PW	Prisoner-of-War (Military)
	Public Works (Military)
PWA	Pacific Western Airlines
	Public Works Administration
PWB	Psychological Warfare Branch (OB - Air Force)
PWC	Pacific War Council (OB)
PWCEN	Public Works Center (Military)
PWD	Psychological Warfare Division (Military)
	Public Works Department
PWE	Prisoner-of-War Enclosure (Military)
PWJC	Paine, Webber, Jackson & Curtis (stock brokers)
PWO	Public Works Office(r) (Military)
PX	Post Exchange (Army)
PXO	Prospective Executive Officer (Navy)

Q

Acronym	Meaning
Q (card)	Qualification Card (Military)
QBACI	Quality Bakers of America Cooperative, Inc.
QCI	Quota Club International
QFCI	Quartermaster Food and Container Institute for the Armed Forces (Army)
QM	Quartermaster (Military)
QMA	Quartermasters Association
QMAO	Qualified for Mobilization Ashore Only (Navy)
QMC	Quartermaster Corps (Army)
QMG	Quartermaster General (Army)
QMS	Quartermaster School (Army)
QMSO	Quartermaster Supply Officer (Military)
QRC	Quick Reaction Capability (Military)
QRDC	Quartermaster Research and Development Command (Army)
QRDEA	Quartermaster Research and Development Evaluation Agency (Army)
QT	Quiet or Sub Rosa
QUADRADAR	Four-Way Radar Surveillance

R

R	Reconnaissance
RA	Rabbinical Assembly of America
R/A	Radius of Action (Air Force)
RA	Regular Army
	Rotogravure Association
RAAF	Royal Australian Air Force
RAB	Radio Advertising Bureau
RAC	Rubber Allocation Committee (OB)
RACCA	Refrigeration and Air Conditioning Contractors Association
RACE	Rapid Automatic Checkout Equipment
RACON	Radar Beacon (Military)
RAD	Released from Active Duty (Military)
	Reported for Active Duty (Military)
	Reservists on Active Duty (Navy)
RADA	Radioactive
RADAN	Radar Navigation
RADAR	Radio Detection and Ranging
RADC	Rome Air Development Center (Air Force)
RADCM	Radar Countermeasures and deception (Military)
RADIAC	Radiation Detection Identification and Computation (Military)
RADIQUAD	Radio Quadrangle (Military)
RADNOS	No Radio (Military)
RADNOTE	Radio Note (Military)
RADOME	Radar Dome (Military)
RADOP	Radar/Optical weapons (Military)
	Radio Operator (Military)
RADPLANBD	Radio Planning Board (Navy)
RADPROPCAST	Radio Propagation Forecast (Air Force)
RADSO	Radiological Survey Officer (Military)
RAF	Royal Air Force
RAILS	Remote Area Instrument Landing System (Army)
RAMAC	Random Access or Memory Accounting
RAMARK	Radar Marker (Military)
RAMD	Random Accessory Memory Device
RAMP	Recovered Allied Military Personnel
RAN	Royal Australian Navy
RAND	Research and Development Corporation (non-profit research organization)
RAOB	Radiosonde Observation (Military)
RAPCON	Radar Approach Control Center (Military)
RARC	Revoked Appointment and Returned to Civilian status (Navy)
RAREP	Radar weather Report (Air Force)
RASC	Rome Air Service Command (OB - Air Force)
RASTA	Radio Station (Coast Guard)
RATO	Rocket Assisted Takeoff (Flying)
RATSC	Rome Air Technical Service Command (OB - Air Force)
RATT	Radio Teletypewriter (Military)
RAWIN	Radar Wind Sounding (Military)
RAWIND	Radio Wind (Coast Guard)
RAWINSONDE	Radiosonde and Radar Wind Sounding (Military)
R/B	Radio Beacon
RB	Renegotiation Board
RBEC	Roller Bearing Engineers Committee
RBH	Regimental Beachhead (Military)

RBO	Russian Brotherhood Organization of the USA
RBPCA	Rare Breeds Poultry Club of America
RBS	Radar Bomb Scoring (Military)
RC	Reception Center (Military)
	Red China
	Roman Catholic
RCA	Radio Corporation of America
	Rodeo Cowboys Association
RCAA	Rocket City Astronomical Association
RCAF	Royal Canadian Air Force
RCC	Rescue Control Center (Military)
RCCC	Regular Common Carrier Conference
RCD	Reinforcement Control Depot (Air Force)
RCIA	Retail Clerks International Association
	Retail Credit Institute of America
RCM	Radar Countermeasures (Military)
	Radio-Controlled Mine (Military)
	Radio Countermeasure (Military)
RCMASA	Russian Consolidated Mutual Aid Society of America
RCMP	Royal Canadian Mounted Police
RCN	Royal Canadian Navy
RCO	Radar Control Officer (Military)
	Remote Control Office (Military)
RCP	Rotation Combat Personnel (Air Force)
RCPR	Resident Commissioner of Puerto Rico
RCRC	Revoked Commission, Returned to Civilian status (Navy)
RCS	Reports Control Symbol (Military)
RCSB	Red Cedar Shingle Bureau
RCT	Regimental Combat Team (Army)
RCTSR	Radio Code Test, Speed of Response (Military)
RD	Readiness Date (Military)
	Research and Development (Military)
RDB	Radar Decoy Balloon (Air Force)
	Research and Development Board
RDF	Radio Direction Finder
RDP	Ration Distributing Point (Military)
RDT	Reserve Duty Training (Military)
RDU	Receipt and Dispatch Unit (Navy)
REA	Railway Express Agency
	Religious Education Association
	Rice Export Association (Defunct)
	Rubber Export Association
	Rural Electrification Administration
REAC	Reeves Electronic Analog Computer
READ	Reserve on Extended Active Duty (Military)
REC	Reserve Equalization Committee (Military)
RECAU	Receipt Acknowledged and Understood (Air Force)
RECGA	Research and Engineering Council of Graphic Arts Industry
RECON	Reconnaissance or reconnoiter (Military)
RECONCO	Reconnaissance Company (Marine Corps)
RECSTA	Receiving Station (Military)
RED	Railroad Employees' Department (of AFL-CIO)
REDOX	Reduction and Oxydization
REEFER	Refrigerator, Refrigerated or Cold Storage (airplane, railway car, truck)
REFCD	Research and Education Foundation for Chest Diseases

ACRONYMS

REFRAD........Release From Active Duty (Military)
REGAF........Regular Air Force
REGS.........Regulations (Military)
REINCO.......Report(ing) In Compliance (Air Force)
REINS........Radio-Equipped Inertial Navigation System
RELBY........When Relieved By (Air Force)
REMCO........Rear Echelon Maintenance Combined Operation (Military)
REO..........Ransom E. Olds Co. (Automobile)
REP..........Range Probable Error (Air Force - formerly range error probable)
REPCAT.......Report Corrective Action Taken (Military)
REPCOMDESPAC.Representative of Commander Destroyers, Pacific Fleet
REPDU........Reporting for Duty (Military)
REPFORMAINT..Representative of Maintenance Force (Navy)
REPIN........Reply In Negative (Air Force)
REPO.........Reporting Officer (Navy)
RER..........Rubberized Equipment Repair (Navy)
RES..........Reserve (Military)
RESCAP.......Rescue Combat Air Patrol (Air Force)
RESCU........Rocket-Ejection Seat Catapult Upward (Flying)
RESDAT.......Restricted Data-Atomic Energy Act of 1954
RESDIST......Reserve District (Navy)
RES/IC.......Reserve-In Commission (Navy - vessel status)
RESLAB.......Research Laboratory
RESMA........Railway Electric Supply Manufacturers Association
RESOJET......Resonant pulse Jet
RETMA........Radio-Electronics Television Manufacturers Association
RF...........Radio Frequency
             Range Finder (Military)
             French Republic (Republique Francaise)
RFA..........Radio Frequency Amplifier
RFAD.........Released from Active Duty not result of demobilization (Navy)
RFB..........Recording for the Blind
RFC..........Reconstruction Finance Corporation (DF)
RFCSE........Retirement Federation of Civil Service Employees
RFD..........Rural Free Delivery
RFE..........Radio Free Europe
RFI..........Ready For Issue (Air Force)
RFM..........Refueling Mission (Air Force)
RF&OOA.......Railway Fuel & Operating Officers Association
RFP..........Radio Finger Printing
RFS..........Ready for Sea
RG...........Reserve Grade (Military)
RH...........Relative Humidity
RHCI.........Radiant Heating and Cooling Institute
RHO..........Railhead Officer (Military)
RHQ..........Regimental Headquarters (Military)
RI...........Recovery Inc.
             Recruit Instruction (Military)
             Rescue Inc.
             Rotary International
RIAA.........Record Industry Association of America
RIAL.........Religion in American Life
RIAS.........Radio In American Sector of Berlin (US Information Agency)
RIC..........Rodeo Information Commission
RIF..........Reduction in Force (Military and Civil Service Commission)

ACRONYMS

RIMR	Rockefeller Institute for Medical Research
RINA	Resident Inspector of Naval Aircraft
RINM	Resident Inspector of Naval Material
RIO	Reporting In and Out (Military)
RIP	Requiescat In Pace (Latin - Rest in Peace)
RISA	Railway and Industrial Spring Association
RIT	Radio Information Test (Military)
RIU	Railroad Insurance Underwriters
RJA	Retail Jewelers of America
RKO	Radio-Keith-Orpheum
	Range Keeper Operator (Military)
RL	Rocket Launcher (Military)
RLEA	Railway Labor Executives' Association
RLF	Religion and Labor Foundation
RLO	Repairs Liaison Officer, Landing Craft and Barges (Navy)
RLPL	Railway Labor's Political League
RLT	Regimental Landing Team (Military)
RLTA	Reenlistment Leave Travel Allowance (Military)
R&M	Redistribution & Marketing (Air Force)
RMA	Rice Millers' Association
	Rubber Manufacturers Association
RMI	Radio Magnetic Indicator
	Roll Manufacturers Institute
RMIA	Rattan Manufacturers and Importers Association
RML	Rescue Motor Launch, Air/Sea Rescue (Air Force)
RMMEA	Rolling Mill Machinery and Equipment Association
RMO	Radio or Radar Material Office (Navy)
RMWAA	Roadmasters and Maintenance of Way Association of America
RN	Registered Nurse
	Royal Navy
	Ruritan National
RNA	Religious Newswriters Association
	Royal Neighbors of America
RNIO	Resident Naval Inspector of Ordnance
RNTWPA	Radio-Newsreel-Television Working Press Association of New York
RNZAF	Royal New Zealand Air Force
RNZN	Royal New Zealand Navy
RO	Recruiting Officer (Military)
	Regimental Orders (Army)
	Route Order (Military)
	Routing Office(r) (Navy)
ROA	Radio Operator's Aptitude Test (Air Force)
	Reserve Officers Association of the United States
ROAT	Radio Operator's Aptitude Test (Military)
ROB	Reserve on Board (Navy)
ROBOMB	Robot Bomb (Air Force)
ROCCM	Controlled devices, countermeasures and deception (Military)
ROCP	Radar Out of Commission for Parts (Air Force)
ROIC	Resident Officer-In-Charge (Military)
ROICC	Resident Officer-in-Charge of Construction (Military)
ROK	Republic of Korea
ROKAF	Republic of Korea Air Force
ROKPUCE	Republic of Korea Presidential Unit Citation Emblem (Military)
RONCOM	Ronald Como, Inc. (Perry Como's production firm; Ronnie is his son)
RONS	Reserve Officers of the Naval Service (MW - Reserve Officers Association

ACRONYMS

ROPA	Reserve Officers Personnel Act
ROS	Reduced Operational Status (Air Force)
ROTC	Reserve Officer Training Corps (Army)
ROTOR	Rotator
RP	Raid Plotter (Navy)
	Rally Point (Air Force)
	Release Point, ground traffic (Military)
	Rocket Projectile
RPA	Rust Prevention Association
RPAO	Radium Plaque Adaptometer Operator (Military)
RPD	Radar Planning Device (Military)
RPG	Religious Publishers Group
RPI	Railway Progress Institute
	Rensselaer Polytechnic Institute
RPIO	Registered Publications Issuing Office (Navy)
RPM	Registered Publications Manual (Navy)
	Registered Publication Memorandum (Military)
	Revolutions per Minute
RPMIO	Registered Publication Mobile Issuing Office (r) (Military)
RPO	Railway Post Office
RPPI	Remote Plan Position Indicator (Military)
RPRA	Railroad Public Relations Association
RPS	Registered Publications Section (Military)
RPS-DL	Registered Publications Section-District Library (Navy)
RPSM	Registered Publication Shipment Memorandum (Military)
R&PT	Rifle and Pistol Team (Military)
RPT	Rocket Propulsion Technician (Air Force)
RPU	Radio Phone Unit (Military)
	Registered Publications Unit (Military)
	Retention Pending Use (Air Force)
RPWDA	Retail Paint and Wallpaper Distributors of America
RQS	Ready Qualified for Standby (Military)
RR	Railroad
	Recruit Roll (Navy)
R&R	Refueling and Rearming (Air Force)
	Reporting and Requisitioning (Air Force)
	Rest and Recuperation (Air Force)
RR	Rifle Range (Military)
R&R	Routing and Record sheet (Air Force)
RR	Rural Route
RRB	Railroad Retirement Board
RRC	Requirements Review Committee (Navy)
	Rubber Reserve Committee (Military)
RRF	Refrigeration Research Foundation
RRI	Rocket Research Institute
RRL	Regimental Reserve Line (Army)
	Reserve Retired List (Military)
RRS	Radiation Research Society
	Reaction Research Society
	Retired Reserve Section (Air Force)
RS	Receiving Ship or Station (Navy)
	Reception Station (Air Force)
	Recruiting Station (Military)
	Regular Station (Military)
	Regulation Station (Air Force)

RS or R/S	Report of Survey (Military)
RS	Revised Statutes
	Road Space (Air Force)
R/S	Routing Slip (Air Force)
RSBA	Rail Steel Bar Association
RSC	Reserve Service Control (Navy)
RSCR	Reserve Special Commendation Ribbon (Military)
RSES	Refrigeration Service Engineers Society
RSI	Research Studies Institute (Air Force)
RSMA	Railway Supply Manufacturers Association
RSNA	Radiological Society of North America
RSO	Regimental Supply Officer (Army)
RSPA	Railway Systems and Procedures Association
RSS	Rifle Sharpshooter (Military)
	Rural Sociological Society
R&SSQ	Repair and Salvage Squadron (Navy)
RSVP	Respondez S'il Vous Plait (French - Please Reply)
RT	Radiotelephone (Air Force)
RT or R/T	Radio Telephony (Navy)
RT	Ranger Tab (Army)
	Receive-Transmit (radio)
	Reduction Table (Military)
	Runup and Taxi (Air Force)
RTA	Railway Tie Association
	Refrigeration Trade Association of America
	Rubber Trade Association of New York
RTC	Replacement Training Center (Military)
RTCA	Radio Technical Commission for Aeronautics
RTDA	Retail Tobacco Dealers of America
RTDG	Radio and Television Directors Guild, International
RTL	Regimental Training Line (Army)
RTNDA	Radio Television News Directors Association
RTO	Rail Transportation Office (r) (Military)
RTPA	Rail Travel Promotion Agency
RTST	Radio Technician Selection Test (Military)
RTTAA	Railway Telegraph and Telephone Appliance Association
RTU	Replacement Training Unit (Military)
R&U	Repairs and Utilities (Air Force)
RUA	Retailer's Uniform Agency (Military)
RUQ	Rifle Unqualified (Military)
RUSNO	Resident United States Naval Officer
RUUR	Regrade Unclassified Upon Receipt (Air Force)
RV	Reading and Vocabulary test (Military)
RVSVP	Respondez Vite, S'il Vous Plait (French - Please Reply at Once)
RVT	Reading and Vocabulary Test (Military)
RW	Rail-Water (Shipping)
	Recreation and Welfare (Military)
	Recruiting Warrant (Navy)
RWA	Railway Wheel Association
RWDSU	Retail, Wholesale and Department Store Union
RWMA	Resistance Welders Manufacturers Association
RWR	Rail-Water-Rail (Shipping)
RYA	Railroad Yardmasters of America

ACRONYMS

S

SA	Salvation Army
	Secretary of the Army
	Semiautomatic (Military)
	Small Arms (Military)
	Society of Actuaries
	South Africa
S/A	Special Activities (Air Force)
SA	Special Assignment (Military)
	Sturm Abteilung (OB - German - storm troops)
	Sugar Association
SAA	Senior Army Advisor
	Signal Appliance Association
	Small Arms Ammunition (Military)
	Society for Applied Anthropology
	Society for American Archaeology
	Society of American Archivists
	Speech Association of America
	Surety Association of America
SAAB	Svenska Aeroplan Aktiebolaget (Swedish automobile)
SAAD	San Antonio Air Depot (Air Force)
SAAMA	San Antonio Air Materiel Area (Air Force)
SAAMI	Sporting Arms and Ammunition Manufacturers Institute
SAASC	San Antonio Air Service Command (OB - Air Force)
SAATSC	San Antonio Air Technical Service Command (OB - Air Force)
SAB	Scientific Advisory Board (Air Force)
	Society of American Bacteriologists (Belgian World Airlines)
SABENA	Societe Anonyme Belge d'Exploitation de la Navigation Aerienne
SAC	Science Advisory Committee (Air Force Advisory Body)
	Strategic Air Command (Air Force)
	Supreme Allied Commander (Military)
SACB	Subversive Activities Control Board
SACEUR	Supreme Commander Allied, Europe
SACLANT	Supreme Allied Commander, Atlantic
SACMED	Supreme Allied Command(er), Mediterranean (OB)
SACO	Sino-American Cooperative Organization
SACSEA	Supreme Allied Command(er), Southeast Asia (OB)
SAD	Support Air Direction (Military)
SAE	Society for Advancement of Education
	Society of Automotive Engineers
SAF	Scandinavian American Fraternity
	Secretary of the Air Force
	Society of American Florists
	Society of American Foresters
	Southern Attack Force (Navy)
	Strategic Air Force (Military)
SAFI	Senior Air Force Instructor
SAFPLAN	Submarine Area Frequency Plan (Navy)
SAFS	Secondary Air Force Specialty
SAG	Screen Actors Guild
SAGA	Stage and Arena Guild of America
SAGE	Semi-Automatic Ground Environment (Air Force)
SAH	Society of American Historians
	Society of Architectural Historians

SAIC	Small Arms Interpost Competition (Military)
SAIM	South America Indian Mission
SAJ	Society for the Advancement of Judaism
SALUT	Sea, Air, Land and Underwater Targets (Navy)
SAM	School of Aviation Medicine (Air Force)
	Society for Advancement of Management
	Society of American Magicians
	Special Air Mission (Air Force)
	Surface-to-Air Missile
	Synchronous Amplitude Modulation
SAMA	Scientific Apparatus Makers Association
	Student American Medical Association
SAMAE	Southern Air Materiel Area, Europe (Air Force)
SAMAP	Southern Air Materiel Area, Pacific (Air Force)
SAME	Society of American Military Engineers
SAO	Staff Administrative Office (Military)
	Support Air Observation (Navy)
SAOTA	Shrimp Association of the Americas
SAP	Semi-Armor Piercing (Military)
	Spot Authorization Plan (OB)
SAPC	Shipowners' Association of the Pacific Coast
	Small Arms Post Competition (Military)
SAPFU	Surpassing All Previous Foul Ups (Military slang)
SAPI	Salesmen's Association of the Paper Industry
SAR	Search and Rescue (Military)
	Semi-Automatic Rifle (Military)
	Society of Authors Representatives
	National Society of the Sons of the American Revolution
	Submarine Advanced Reactor
SARAH	Search and Rescue and Homing (Air Force)
SARCC	Search and Rescue Coordination Center (Air Force)
SART	Seattle Army Terminal
SAS	Scandinavian Airlines System
	Society for Applied Spectroscopy
SASI	Southern Association of Science and Industry
SAST	Society for the Advancement of Space Travel
SATCO	Signal Automatic Air Traffic Control system
SAWE	Society of Aeronautical Weight Engineers
SAWV	Sons of Spanish American War Veterans
SB	Secondary Battery (Military)
	Selection Board (Military)
	Submarine Base (Navy)
	Supply Bulletin (Military)
SBA	Small Business Administration
	Smaller Business of America
SBAMA	San Bernardino Air Materiel Area (Air Force)
SBCA	Soybean Council of America
SBGP	Strategic Bomber Group (Military)
SBI	Steel Boiler Institute
SBIC	Small Business Investment Company (s)
SBME	Society of Business Magazine Editors
SBOAI	Specialty Bakery Owners of America, Inc.
SBP	Society of Biological Psychiatry
	Summary Plot Board (Navy)
SBS	Strategic Balkan Services (OB)

ACRONYMS

SBS .... Strategic Bomb Squadron (Military)
SBWG .... Strategic Bomb Wing (Military)
SC .... Sanitary Corps (OB - Army)
S-C .... Secret and Confidential Files (Military)
SC .... Security Council (United Nations)
            Service Club (Military enlisted men's club)
            Signal Corps (Army)
            Specified Command (Military)
S/C .... Statement of Charges (Military)
SC .... Summary Court (Military)
            Supply Corps (Navy)
            Supreme Court
SCA .... Science Clubs of America
            Screen Composers' Association
            Shipbuilders Council of America
            Stock Company Association
            Synagogue Council of America
SCAEF .... Supreme Commander, Allied Expeditionary Force (OB)
SCAJAP ...... Shipping Control Administrator Japan (OB)
SCAN .... Self-Correcting Automatic Navigation
SCAO .... Senior Civil Affairs Officer (Military)
SCAP .... Supreme Commander Allied Powers (Japan (OB)
SCAR .... Subcaliber Aircraft Rocket
            Submarine Celestial Altitude Recorder (Navy)
SCARWAF ..... Special Category Army Units with Air Force
SCAT .... Service Command Air Transportation (Navy)
SCATE .... Stromberg-Carlson Automatic Test Equipment
SCC .... Society of Cosmetic Chemists
            Standard Commodity Classification (Military)
SCCO .... Security Classification Control Officer (Military)
SCCTSD ...... Society of Catholic College Teachers of Sacred Doctrine
SCCUS .... Swedish Chamber of Commerce of the USA
SCEH .... Society for Clinical and Experimental Hypnosis
SCEL .... Signal Corps Engineering Laboratories (Army)
SCF .... Support Carrier Force (Navy)
SCG .... Society of the Classic Guitar
SCI .... Ship Controlled Intercept (radar)
            Shipping Container Institute
            Supervisory Cost Inspector (Navy)
SCL .... Southeastern Composers' League
SCM .... Sender's Composition Message (Military)
            Summary Court-Martial (Military)
SCMA .... Silk Commission Manufacturers Association
SCMO .... Summary Court-Martial Order (Military)
SCNAWAF ..... Special Category Navy with Air Force
SCO .... Staff Communications Office (Military)
            Statistical Control Office (r) (Military)
SCOFA .... Shipping Control Office, Forward Area (Navy)
SCOFOR ...... Scouting Force (Navy)
SCOMA .... Shipping Control Office, Marianas (Navy)
SCOOP .... Scientific Computation of Optimum Procurement (Air Force)
SCOPE .... Sequential Customer Order Processing Electronically
SCORE .... Signal Communications by Orbiting Relay Equipment
SCORON ...... Scouting Squadron (Navy)
SCOROR ...... Secretary's Committee on Research on Reorganization (Navy)

ACRONYMS

SCORU	Statistical Control and Operations Records Unit (Air Force)
SCOTRACEN	Scouting Training Center (Navy)
SCP	Survey Control Point (Military)
SCPA	Southern Coal Producers' Association
SCPCU	Society of Chartered Property and Casualty Underwriters
SCPI	Structural Clay Products Institute
SCPT	Security Control Point (Military)
SCR	Signal Corps Radio (OB - Air Force)
	Summary Control Report (Planning and Production - Navy)
SCRA	Supreme Council of the Royal Arcanum
SCS	Signal Communications System (OB - Air Force)
	Soil Conservation Service (Agriculture Department)
SCSA	Soil Conservation Society of America
SCST	Society Commercial Seed Technologists
SCTA	Southern California Timing Association
SCTC	Submarine Chaser Training Center (Navy)
SCU	Statistical Control Unit (Military)
SCUBA	Self-Contained Underwater Breathing Apparatus
S/D	Secretary of Defense
SD	Special Duty (Military)
	State Department
	Supply Department (Navy)
SDA	Seventh Day Adventist
	Students for Democratic Action
SDAA	Skein Dyers Association of America
SDC	Society of the Divine Compassion
	Southern Defense Command (Army)
SDCE	Society of Die Casting Engineers
SDCP	Supply Demand Control Point (Military)
SDGA	Screen Directors' Guild of America
SDIT	Service de Documentation et d'Information Techniques de Aeronautique
SDO	Special Duty Only (Military)
	Specialist Duty Only (Military)
	Staff Duty Officer (Military)
SDRNG	Sound Ranging (Air Force)
SE	Single Engine (Air Force)
SEA	Southeast Asia Theater (OB - Military)
SEABEE	(CB) Member of a Construction Battalion (Navy)
SEAC	Southeast Asia Command (OB - Military)
SEAFRON	Sea Frontier (Navy)
SEAS	Sea School (Marine Corps.)
SEATIC	Southeast Asia Translation and Interrogation Center (OB - Military)
SEATO	Southeast Asia Treaty Organization
SEB	Secondary Education Board
SEBM	Society for Experimental Biology and Medicine
SEC	Securities and Exchange Commission
	Sulphur Export Corporation /Washington (Military)
SECAN	Standing Group Communication Security and Evaluation Agency,
SECDEF	Secretary of Defense
SECE	Selfhelp of Emigres from Central Europe
SECNAV	Secretary of the Navy
SECTASKFLT	Second Task Fleet (Navy)
SECWAR	Secretary of War (OB - Army)
SED	Shore Establishments Division (Navy)
SEF	Southern Education Foundation

ACRONYMS

SEF — SFPE

SEF	Space Education Foundation
SEFIC	Seventh Fleet Intelligence Center
SEG	Screen Extras Guild
	Society of Economic Geologists
	Society of Exploration Geophysicists
SEKF	Sister Elizabeth Kenny Foundation
SELSYN	Self-Synchronous
SENAVAV	Senior Naval Aviator
SENL	Standard Equipment Nomenclature List (Military)
SEP	Society of Experimental Psychologists
SEPA	Southeastern Power Administration (Interior Department)
SEPACFOR	Southeast Pacific Force (Navy)
SEPCEN	Separation Center (Military)
SEPE	Seattle Port of Embarkation (Military)
SEPGA	Southeastern Pecan Growers Association
SEPM	Society of Economic Paleontologists and Mineralogists
SEPROS	Separation Processing (Air Force)
SERFORSOPACSUBCOM	Service Force South Pacific Subordinate Command (Navy)
SERON	Service Squadron (Navy)
SERTH	Satisfactory Evidence Received This Headquarters (Air Force)
SERVCOMFMFPAC	Service Command, Fleet Marine Force, Pacific
SERVDIV	Service Division (Navy)
SERVFOR	Service Force (Navy)
SERVLANT	Service Force, Atlantic Fleet
SERVLANTSUBORDCOMD	Service Force, Atlantic Fleet, Subordinate Command
SERVNO	Service Number (Navy)
SERVPAC	Service Force, Pacific Fleet
SERVSOWESPAC	Service Force, Southwest Pacific Fleet
SES	Standards Engineers Society
	Strategic Engineering Survey (Military)
SESA	Society for Experimental Stress Analysis
SESE	Secure Echo-Sounding Equipment (sonar)
SETAF	Southern European Task Force
SETP	Society for Experimental Test Pilots
SF	Security Forces (Japanese army)
	Sound and Flash (Military)
	Specified Forces (Military)
	Standard Form (Military)
SFA	Scandinavian Fraternity of America
	Slide Fastener Association
	Southeastern Fisheries Association
SFBA	Steamship Freight Brokers Association
SFCP	Shore Fire Control Party (Navy)
SFE	Society of Fire Engineers
SFERICS	Electronic detector of electrical discharges in the atmo(spherics)
SFF	Spiritual Frontiers Fellowship
SFI	Sport Fishing Institute
SFIC	San Francisco Information Center (Military)
SFMA	Separator Filter Manufacturers Association
	Soda Fountain Manufacturers Association
	Southern Furniture Manufacturers Association
	Subscription Fulfillment Managers Association
SFMI	Soft Fibre Manufacturers Institute
SFNSY	San Francisco Naval Shipyard
SFPE	Society of Fire Protection Engineers

SFPOE	San Francisco Port of Embarkation (Military)
SFRC	Soya Food Research Council
SFSA	Steel Founders' Society of America
S&FSD	Sea and Foreign Service Duty (Navy)
SG	Standing Group (Military)
	Surgeon General (Military)
SGA	Stained Glass Association of America
SGBI	Santa Gertrudis Breeders International
SGES	Society of Grain Elevator Superintendents
SGI	Sun Glass Institute
SGIS	Student Government Information Service
SGJA	Sporting Goods Jobbers Association
SGLO	Standing Group Liaison Officer to the North Atlantic Council (Military)
SGMAA	Sporting Goods Manufacturers Agents Association
SGN	Standing Group North Atlantic Treaty Organization
SGP	Secondary Gun Pointer (Navy)
	Society of General Physiologists
SGS	Secretary of the General Staff (Army)
SGUS	Slovak Gymnastic Union Sokol of the USA
SH	Soldiers' Home (government agency)
SHA	Sidereal Hour Angle
SHAEF	Supreme Headquarters, Allied Expeditionary Force (OB)
SHAPE	Supreme Headquarters Allied Powers Europe
SHEMA	Steam Heating Equipment Manufacturers Association
SHF	Super High Frequency
SHIPDA	Shipping Data (Air Force)
SHIPDTO	Ship on Depot Transfer Order (Air Force)
SHIPIM	Ship Immediately (Air Force)
SHMI	Saddlery Hardware Manufacturers Institute
SHORAN	Short Range Navigation
SHP	Shaft Horsepower
	Southern Hardwood Producers
SI	Sertoma International
	Smithsonian Institution
	Society of Illustrators
SIA	Sanitary Institute of America
	Self-Insurers Association
	Sprinkler Irrigation Association
SIAM	Signal Information and Monitoring (Military)
	Society for Industrial and Applied Mathematics
SIB	Satellite Ionospheric Beacons (Military)
SIC	Survey Information Center (Military)
SID	Security and Intelligence Service (Army)
	Society for Investigative Dermatology
SIGC	Signal Corps (Army)
SIGO	Signal Officer (Army)
SILO	Security Intelligence Liaison Office (Central Mediterranean Forces - Navy)
SIM	Society for Industrial Microbiology
SIMCA	Societa Industrielle de Mecanique et Carrosserie Automobile (French)
SIME	Security Intelligence, Middle East (Military)
SIMPA	Society of Independent Motion Picture Producers
SINS	Shipboard Inertial Navigation System (Navy)
SIO	Ship's Information Officer (Navy)
SIOE	Special Issue of Equipment (Air Force)
SIP	Standard Inspection Procedure (Military)

ACRONYMS

SIR . . . . Society of Industrial Realtors
              Submarine Intermediate Reactor
SIRSA . . . . Special Industrial Radio Service Association
SIS . . . . Shut-In Society
SITREP . . . . . . Situation Report (Air Force)
SIUNA . . . . Seafarers' International Union of North America
SIW . . . . Self-Inflicted Wounds (Military)
SJA . . . . Staff Judge Advocate (Air Force)
SJART . . . . San Jacinto Army Terminal
SJI . . . . Steel Joist Institute
SL . . . . Sea Level
              Sound Locator (Military)
              Submarine Qualification Lapsed (Navy)
              Support Line (Military)
SLA . . . . Showmen's League of America
              Slovak League of America
              Special Libraries Association
SLC . . . . Searchlight Control (Military)
SLCU . . . . Standard Landing Craft Unit (Navy)
SLEMA . . . . . . Schiffli Lace and Embroidery Manufacturers Association
SLGA . . . . Stained and Leaded Glass Association
SLI . . . . Seal and Label Institute
SLIM . . . . Submarine-Launched Inertial Missile
SLIS . . . . Social Legislation Information Service
SLM . . . . School for Latin America (Air Force)
SLOE . . . . Special List of Equipment (Military)
SLP . . . . Socialist Labor Party
SLRA . . . . Suede and Leather Refinishers of America
SLSDC . . . . . . St. Lawrence Seaway Development Corporation
SLSM . . . . Silver Life Saving Medal
SM . . . . Shipment Memorandum (Navy)
              Society of Medalists
              Soldier's Medal (Army)
              Strategic Missile (Air Force)
SMA . . . . Safe Manufacturers' Association
              Scale Manufacturers Association
              Senior Military Attache
              Service Merchandisers of America (Association)
              Ship's Material Account (Navy)
              Spring Manufacturers Association
              Stoker Manufacturers Association
              Stucco Manufacturers Association
SMACCNA . . . . Sheet Metal and Air Conditioning Contractors National Association
SMACRATRACEN . . Small Craft Training Center (Navy)
SMAMA . . . . . . Sacramento Air Materiel Area (Air Force)
SMART . . . . . . Supersonic Military Air Research Track
              Supersonic Missile and Rocket Track
SMAW . . . . . . Second Marine Aircraft Wing
SMC . . . . Scientific Manpower Commission
SMCAF . . . . . . Society of Medical Consultants to the Armed Forces
SMCC . . . . Society of Memorial Cancer Center
SME . . . . Society of Mining Engineers of AIME
              Standard Medical Examination (Military)
SMG . . . . Sub-Machine Gun (Military)
SMGP . . . . Strategic Missile Group (Air Force)

Acronym	Meaning
SMI	Super Market Institute
SMIU	Stove Mounters International Union
SMLO	Senior Military Liaison Officer
SMM	Specially Meritorious Medal (Military)
SMNA	Safe Manufacturers National Association
SMO	Senior Medical Officer (Military)
	So Much of (Military)
SMOG	Smoke and Fog
SMOP	So Much of Paragraph (Air Force)
SMP	Sound Motion Picture Technician (Military)
SMPE	Society of Marine Port Engineers
SMPO	Sound Motion Picture Operator (Military)
S-MPR	Semi-Monthly Progress Reports (Military)
SMPTE	Society of Motion Picture and Television Engineers
SMR	Special Money Requisition (Military)
SMS	Stereophonic Music Society
	Strategic Missile Squadron (Air Force)
	Subject Matter Specialist (Military)
SMSD	Submarine Detector Ship's Magnet (Navy)
SMT	Shop Mechanic's Test (Military)
	Square Mesh Tracking (Air Force)
SMTA	Sewing Machine Trade Association
SMU	Southern Methodist University
SMW	Society of Magazine Writers
SMWG	Strategic Missile Wing (Air Force)
SMWIA	Sheet Metal Workers' International Association
SN	Service Number (Military)
SNA	Student Naval Aviator
SNAFU	Situation Normal, All Fouled Up (Military slang)
SNAME	Society of Naval Architects and Marine Engineers
SNAP	Senior Naval Aviator Present
	Student Naval Aviator Pilot
	Subsystem for Nuclear Auxiliary Power
SNAP (G)	Student Naval Aviation Pilot (Glider)
SNEA	Student National Education Association
SNL	Standard Nomenclature List (Military)
SNM	Senior Naval Member
	Society of Nuclear Medicine
SNOP	Senior Naval Officer Present
SNORT	Supersonic Naval Ordnance Research Track
SNPJ	Slovene National Benefit Society
SNS	Society of Neurological Surgeons
SNT	Society for Nondestructive Testing
SNTFC	Senior Naval Task Force Commander
SO	Secretary's Office (Military)
	Shipment Order (Military)
	Special Orders (Military)
	Supply Officer (Military)
SOA	Speed of Advance (Military)
	Speed of Approach (Military)
SOAP	Symbolic Optimum Assembly Programming
SOAPD	Southern Air Procurement District (Air Force)
SOCALSEC	Southern California Sector, Western Sea Frontier (Navy)
SOCHINAFOR	South China Force (Navy)
SOCMA	Synthetic Organic Chemical Manufacturers Association of US

ACRONYMS

SOCMC — Special Order of the Commandant of the Marine Corps
SOCONY — Standard Oil Company of N.Y.(OB-Socony Mobil is now official name of firm)
SOD — Small Object Detector (Military)
SODAR — Sound-Detecting and Ranging
SOEASTPAC — Southeast-Pacific force or command (Navy)
SOFAR — Sound Fixing and Ranging
SOFT — Status of Forces Treaty
SOG — Special Operations Group (Military)
SOHIO — Standard Oil Company of Ohio
SOI — Signal Operation Instructions (Military)
SOIC — Supply Officer-in-Charge (Military)
SOINC — Supply Officer-in-Charge (OB - Navy)
SOLANT — South Atlantic force or command (Navy)
SOLANTFOR — South Atlantic Force (Navy)
SOLOG — Standardization of certain aspects of Operations and Logistics (Military)
SOME — Secretary's Office, Management Engineer (Navy)
SONAR — Sound Navigation and Ranging
SOND — Secretary's Office, Navy Department
SONOM — Sonar Countermeasures and Deception
SONRD — Secretary's Office, Off. of Research & Develop. (Now Office of Naval Res.)
SOP — Senior Officer Present (Military)
   Standing Operating Procedure (Military)
SOPA — Senior Officer Present Afloat (Navy)
SOP(A) — Senior Officer Present (Ashore - Navy)
SOPAC — South Pacific area force or command (Navy)
SOPACBACOM — South Pacific Base Command (Navy)
SOPACCOMS — South Pacific Communications (Military)
SOPAT — South China Patrol (Navy)
SOPHE — Society of Public Health Educators
SOPUS — Senior (US) Officer Present (Military)
SOQ — Sick Officer's Quarters (Military)
SOR — Society of Rheology
SORA — Secretary's Office, Records Administration (Navy)
SORD — Society of Record Dealers of America
SORG — Submarine Operations Research Group (Navy)
SORR — Submarine Operations Research Report (Navy)
SOS — Radio Distress Call (letters have no real meaning)
   Services of Supply (OB - Army)
SOSED — Secretary's Office, Shore Establishments Division (OB - Navy)
SOSSPA — Service of Supply, South Pacific Area (OB - Army)
SOSU — Scout Observation Service Unit (Navy)
SOTB — Secretary's Office, Transportation Branch (Navy)
SOWESPAC — Southwest Pacific Command (Military)
SOWESSEAFRON — Southwest Sea Frontier (Navy)
SP — Section Patrol (Navy)
   Security Publication (Military)
   Self-Propelled (Military)
   Shore Party (Navy)
   Shore Patrol (Navy)
   Single Phase
   Single Purpose Gun (Military)
   Smokeless Powder (Military)
   Socialist Party
   Society of Protozoologists
   Strategic Planning chart (Air Force)

SP	Submarine Patrol (Navy)
	Sub-Professional (OB - Civil Service employees designation)
	Summary Plotter (radar)
SPA	Salt Producers Association
	Society for Personnel Administration
	Society of Philatelic Americans
	Songwriters Protective Association
	Southern Pine Association
	Systems and Procedures Association of America
SPAB	Supply, Priorities and Allocations Board (Military)
SPACON	Space Control (Military)
SPAD	Societe Pour Aviation et ses Derives (OB - French - World War I airplane
SPAM	Society for the Publication of American Music
SPAR	Coast Guard Women's Reserve (Semper Paratus - Always Ready, USCG Motto
SPAST	Special Assistant (Navy)
SPATE	Student Personnel Association for Teacher Education
SPATS	South Pacific Air Transportation Service (OB - Military)
SPBA	Specialty Paper and Board Affiliates
SPBOT	Stationers and Publishers Board of Trade
SPC	Standard Products Committee (Military)
SPCC	Ships Parts Control Center (Navy)
SPCM	Spanish Campaign Medal (Military)
	Special Court-Martial (Military)
SPCMO	Special Court-Martial Order (Military)
SPD	Southern Procurement Division (Navy)
SPDC	Spare Parts Distributing Center (Military)
SPE	Society of Petroleum Engineers (of AIME)
	Society of Plastics Engineers
	Special Purpose Equipment (Air Force)
	Subport of Embarkation (Military)
SPEA	Sales Promotion Executive Association /in America
SPEBSQSA	Soc. for the Preservation & Encouragement of Barbershop Quartet Singing
SPECCOM	Specified Command (Military)
SPECDEVCEN	Special Devices Center (Air Force)
SPENAVO	Special Naval Observer
SPF	Society for the Propagation of the Faith
SPFA	Steel Plate Fabricators Association
SPG	Screen Producers Guild
SPGA	Southeastern Pecan Growers Association
SPI	Society of Plastics Industry
SPIB	Southern Pine Inspection Bureau
SPM	Self-Propelled Mount (Military)
SPMA	Soda Pulp Manufacturers Association
	Sump Pump Manufacturers Association
SPMRL	Sulphite Pulp Manufacturers' Research League
SPN	Sponsor Program Number (Military)
SPO	Shore Patrol Officer (Navy)
SPORTFOR	Support Force (Navy)
SPPA	Screen Process Printing Association
SPQR	The Senate and People of Rome (Latin - Senatus Populusque Romanus)
SPR	Society for Pediatric Research
SPS	Special Services (Military)
SPSE	Society of Photographic Scientists and Engineers
SPSSI	Society for the Psychological Study of Social Issues
SPTC	Specified Period of Time Contract (Military)

ACRONYMS

SPTL	Support Line (Military)
SPWA	Steel Products Warehouse Association
SPWWIII	Society for the Prevention of World War III
SR	Senate Resolution
S/R	Service Record (Military)
SR	Ship Repair Ratings (Navy)
	Shipment Request (Military)
	Sound Rating (Army)
	Special Regulations (Military)
SRA	Simultaneous Range Adcock antenna (Military radar)
	Society of Residential Appraisers
	Spanish Refugee Aid
	Station Representatives Association (Advertising)
SRAVBAD	Senior Army Aviator Badge
SRB	Seaplane Repair Base
	Service Record Book (Military)
SRBM	Short-Range Ballistic Missile
SRC	Sound Ranging Control (Military)
	Southern Regional Council
	Standard Requirements Code (Military)
SRCC	Senior Control Center (Air Force)
SRCD	Society for Research in Child Development
SRE	Society of Reproduction Engineers
SRF	Submarine Repair Facility (Navy)
	Sugar Research Foundation
SRFI	Self-Rising Flour Institute
SRGR	Short-Range Guided Rocket
SRI	Southern Research Institute
	Stanford Research Institute
SRL	Save-the-Redwoods League
SRMA	Silk and Rayon Manufacturers Association
SRNC	Severn River Naval Command
SRPARABAD	Senior Parachutist Badge (Military)
SRP&DAA	Silk and Rayon Printers and Dyers Association of America
SRR	Strategic Ready Reserve (Military)
SRTU	Ship Repair Training Unit (Navy)
SRU	Seaplane Reconnaissance Unit (Navy)
	Ship Repair Unit (Navy)
	Submarine Repair Unit (Navy)
SS	Schutz Staffel (OB - German - elite guard)
	Science Service
	Secretary of State
	Selective Service
	Sharpshooter (Military)
	Silver Star (Military)
	Social Security
	Special Staff (Military)
	Staff Specialist (Military)
	Standard Frequency Station
S/S	Statement of Service (Military)
SS	Steamship
	Submarine Studies (Navy)
	Surveillance Station (Military)
	Sworn Statement
SSA	Seismological Society of America

SSA	Ship's Stores Ashore (Navy)
	Signal Security Agency (Navy)
	Soaring Society of America
	Social Security Administration
	Steuben Society of America
	Studio Suppliers Association
SSB	Selective Service Board
	Single Side Band
	Social Security Board
	Society for Study of Blood
SSC	Submarine Supply Center (Navy)
SSCI	Steel Shipping Container Institute
SS&CS	Ship's Stores and Commissary Stores (Navy)
SSD	Stabilized Ship Detector (Navy)
SSDB	Shore Station Development Board (Navy)
SSDG	Society for Study of Development and Growth
SSDPA	Soft-Serv Dairy Products Association
SSDT	Society of Soft Drink Technologists
SSE	Society for the Study of Evolution
SSF	Ship's Service Force (Navy)
	Special Service Force (Military)
SSHSA	Steamship Historical Society of America
SSI	Standing Signal Instructions (Military)
SSIA	Shoe Service Institute of America
	Specification Serial of Individual Assigned (Military)
SSIC	Southern States Industrial Council
SSLORAN	Sky-wave synchronized Loran
SSM	Silver Star Medal (Military)
	Surface-to-Surface Missile
SSMMA	Staple and Stapling Machine Manufacturers Association
SSN	Specification Serial Number (Military; OB - Air Force)
SSO	Statistical Service Office(r) (Military)
SSP	Ship's Stores Profit (Navy)
SSPC	Steel Structures Painting Council
SSPN	Ship's Stores and Profit, Navy
SSR	Spin Stabilized Rockets
SSRS	Society for Social Responsibility in Science
SSS	Selective Service System
	Strategic Support Squadron (Air Force)
SSSA	Soil Science Society of America
SSSP	Society for the Study of Social Problems
SSU	Special Service Unit (Military)
	Squadron Service Unit (Navy)
	Statistical Service Unit (Military)
	Strategic Services Unit (OB - see Central Intelligence Agency)
SSV	Seraphic Society for Vocations
	Ship to Surface Vessel (designation of radar used to detect surface vessels)
SSZ	Society of Systematic Zoology
S/T	Shipping Ticket (Army)
	Sonic Telegraphy
STA	Southern Textile Association
STAD	Special Temporary Aviation Duty (Marine Corps)
STAG	Special Task Air Group (Navy)
STALAG	Stammlager (German - prisoner of war camp)
STALAGLUFT	Stammlagerluft (German - prisoner of war camp for airmen)

ACRONYMS

STANAG	Military Standardization Agency Agreement
STANINE	Standard Nine Score (Military)
STANLANCRU	Standard Landing Craft Unit (Military)
STANOLIND	Standard Oil Company of Indiana
STANVAC	Standard Vacuum Oil Company
STAR	Specialized Training and Reassignment (Army)
STC	Scandinavian Travel Commission
STEM	Special Technical and Economic Mission
STI	Service Tools Institute
	Steel Tank Institute
STL	Space Technology Laboratories
STOL	Short Take-Off and Landing
STRAC	Strategic Army Command
STRAF	Strategic Army Force
STRAFPOA	Strategic Air Force, Pacific Ocean Area (OB)
STRAIRPOA	Strategic Air Force, Pacific Ocean Area (OB)
STRATCOM	Worldwide Strategic Communications System (Air Force)
STU	Service Trials Unit (Military)
STUKA	Sturzkampfflugzeug (German - dive bomber)
STWE	Society of Technical Writers and Editors
SU	Area Service Unit (Army)
SUA	Silver Users Association
	State Universities Association
SUB	Subordinate
	Substitute
	Supplemental Unemployment Benefit(s)
SUBAD	Submarine Force, Pacific Fleet Administration
SUBADMI	Submarine Force, Pacific Fleet Administration, Mare Island
SUBBASE	Submarine Base (Navy)
SUBCOM	Subordinate Command, Service Force, Pacific Fleet
SUBDIV	Submarine Division (Navy)
SUBLANT	Submarine Force, Atlantic Fleet
SUBORCOM	Subordinate Command (Navy)
SUBORCOMDSERVLANT	Subordinate Command, Service Force, Atlantic Fleet
SUBPAC	Submarine Force, Pacific Fleet
SUBPACAD	Submarine Force, Pacific Fleet, Administrative Command
SUBPACSUBORDCOM	Submarine Force, Pacific Fleet, Subordinate Command
SUBRON	Submarine Squadron (Navy)
SUBRU	Submarine Repair Unit (Navy)
SUBSCOFOR	Submarines Scouting Force (Pacific Fleet)
SUBSLANT	Submarines, Atlantic Fleet
SUBSPAC	Submarines, Pacific Fleet
SUBSSOWESPAC	Submarines, Southwest Pacific Force (Navy)
SUDAM	Sunk or Damaged (Navy)
SUIAP	Simplified Unit Invoice Accounting Plan
SUM	Surface-to-Underwater Missile
SUMC	Summary Court (Military)
SUMCM	Summary Court-Martial (Military)
SUNA	Switchmen's Union of North America
SUNFED	Special UN Fund for Economic Development
SUNOCO	Sun Oil Company
SUPIER	Naval Supply Pier
SUPINSMAT	Supervising Inspector of Naval Material
SUPSHIP	Supervisor of Shipbuilding (Navy)
SUS	Society of University Surgeons

ACRONYMS

SUSMOP	Senior US Military Observer Palestine
SUSNO	Senior US Naval Officer
SUVCW	Sons of Union Veterans of the Civil War
SV	Selective Volunteer (Navy)
S/V	Surface Vessel
SVA	Seabee Veterans of America
SVC	Service Command (OB - Army)
SVM	Student Volunteer Movement for Christian Missions
SVP	Society of Vertebrate Paleontology
SW	Secretary of War (OB)
	Special Weapon (Military)
SWA	Southern Woodwork Association
SWC	Special Weapons Command (OB - Air Force)
SWCP	Saline Water Conversion Program (Interior Department)
SWDL	Safe Winter Driving League
SWE	Society of Women Engineers
SWEFCO	Special Weapons Ferry Control Office (Military)
SWEL	Special Weapons Equipment List (Military)
SWETTU	Special Weapons Experimental Tactical Test Units (Military)
SWG	Society of Women Geographers
SWI	Steel Window Institute
SWMA	Southwestern Monuments Association
SWNCC	State, War, Navy Coordinating Committee (OB)
SWOD	Special Weapons Ordnance Devices (Military)
SWP	Sherwin-Williams Paint Co.
	Socialist Workers Party
	Southwest Pacific (Military)
SWPA	Southwest Pacific Area (Military)
	Southwestern Power Administration (Interior Department)
SWPC	Smaller War Plants Corporation (OB)
SWPF	Southwest Pacific Force (Military)
SWR	Standing Wave Ratio (Military)
SWS	Space Weapon Systems (Air Force)
	Special Weapon Systems (Military)
SWSD	Special Weapons Supply Depot (Military)
SWTA	Special Weapons Training Allowance (Military)
SWTTEU	Special Weapons Test and Tactical Evaluation Unit (Military)
SWV	Scottish War Veterans of America
SWVB	Social Work Vocational Bureau

T

T	Trainer (Military)
TA	Table of Allowance (Military)
	Target Area (Military)
	Travel Allowance (Military)
TAA	Technical Assistance Administration (United Nations)
	Transportation Association of America
TAB	Technical Assistance Board (United Nations)
TAC	Tactical Air Command (Air Force)
	Tactical Air Coordinator (Air Force)
	Technical Assistance Committee (United Nations)
	Theater Air Commander (Air Force)
TACA	Tactical Air Coordinator, Airborne (Military)
TACAN	Tactical Air Navigation

ACRONYMS

TACC	Tactical Air Control Center (Air Force)
TACGRU	Tactical Air Control Group (Air Force)
TACNAV	Tactical Air Navigation System
TACP	Tactical Air Control Party (OB - Military)
TACRON	Tactical Air Control Squadron (Air Force)
TAD	Tactical Air Division (Air Force)
	Target Area Designator (Air Force)
	Temporary Additional Duty (Military)
	Training Aids Division (Military)
TADC	Tactical Air Direction Center (OB - Air Force)
	Tactical Air Direction Center (Military)
	Training and Distribution Center (Navy)
TADP	Tactical Air Direction Post (Military)
TAF	Tactical Air Force
TAFCSD	Total Active Federal Commissioned Service Date (Military)
TAFMSD	Total Active Federal Military Service Date
TAG	The Adjutant General (Army)
	Training Aids Guide (Navy)
	Transport Air Group (Ob - Joint Army, Navy and Marine Corp)
TAGA	Technical Association of the Graphic Arts
TAGO	The Adjutant General's Office (Army)
TAGSUSA	The Adjutant General's School, US Army
TAIU	Technical Aircraft Instrument Unit (Navy)
TAL	Training Aids Library (Military)
TALA	Textile Association of Los Angeles
TALO	Tactical Air Liaison Officer (Air Force)
TANKSEC	Petroleum and Tanker Division, Assistant Chief of Naval Operations
TAP	Technical Assistance Program
TAPE	Tactical Air Power Evaluation (OB - Air Force)
TAPPI	Technical Association Pulp and Paper Industry
TARC	Theater Army Replacement Command
TARFU	Things Are Really Fouled Up (Military slang)
TARMAC	Tar Macadam
TARS	Tactical Air Reconnaissance School (Air Force)
	Tactical Air Research and Survey Office (Air Force)
TAS	Technical Assistance Service (United Nations)
	(The) Army Staff
	Training Aids Section (Military)
	True Airspeed (Flying)
TASA	The Aircraft Service Association
TASKFLOT	Task Flotilla (Navy)
TASO	Television Allocations Study Organization
TASS	Telegrafnoe Agenstvo Soyusa Sovetskih Socialisticheskih Respublik (Russian)
TASSA	The Army Signal Supply Agency
TASSO	Transatlantic Air Safety Service Organization (OB)
TAT	To Accompany Troops (Military)
	Torpedo Attack Teacher (Navy)
TATB	Theater Air Transportation Board (Military)
TAUS	Tobacco Association of the US
TB	Technical Bulletin (Military)
	Tubercle Bacillus
	Tuberculosis
T/BA	Table of Basic Allowance (OB - Air Force)
TBA	Television Bureau of Advertising
	Tires, Batteries & Accessories

ACRONYMS

TBA . . . . To Be Activated (Military)
TBD . . . . Target Bearing Designator (Military)
                   To Be Disbanded (Military)
TBEA . . . . Truck Body and Equipment Association
TBGAA . . . . Travel by Government Automobile Authorized (Military)
TBGP . . . . Tactical Bomb Group (Air Force)
TBI . . . . Target Bearing Indicator (Military)
                   To Be Inactivated (Military)
TBMA . . . . Textile Bag Manufacturers Association
TBMAA . . . . Travel by Military Aircraft Authorized
TBS . . . . Tactical Bomb Squadron (Air Force)
                   The Basic School (Air Force)
TBWG . . . . Tactical Bomb Wing (Air Force)
TC . . . . Tariff Commission
                   Training Center (Military)
                   Training Circular (Military)
                   Transaction Code (Military)
                   Transportation Corps
                   Trial Counsel (Military)
                   Troop Carrier (Air Force)
                   True Course
                   Trusteeship Council (United Nations)
                   Turret Captain (Navy)
TCA . . . . Tanners' Council of America
                   Technical Cooperation Administration
                   Theater Commander's Approval
                   Thoroughbred Club of America
                   Tile Council of America
                   Tissue Culture Association
                   Trailer Coach Association
                   Trans-Canada Air Lines
TCC . . . . Tactical Control Center (Military)
                   Transport Control Center (Military)
                   Transportation Control Committee (Military)
                   Troop Carrier Command (OB - Air Force)
TCF . . . . Twentieth Century Fund
TCI . . . . Terrain Clearance Indicator (Military)
TCO . . . . Test Control Officer (Military)
TCP . . . . Traffic Control Post (Military)
TCR . . . . Transportation Corps Release (Army)
TCS . . . . Temporary Change of Station (Military)
                   Traffic Control Station (Army)
TCTW . . . . Tin Can Tourists of the World
TCU . . . . Texas Christian University
TCUS . . . . Tax Court of the United States
TCV . . . . Troop Carrying Vehicle (Military)
TD . . . . Table of Distribution (Army)
                   Tank Destroyer (OB - Army)
                   Testing and Development Division (Coast Guard)
                   Transmitter Distributor
                   Treasury Department
                   Typographic Draftsman (Navy)
TDA . . . . Table of Distribution Augmentation (Army)
TDC . . . . Tank Destroyer Center (OB - Army)
                   Top Dead Center

ACRONYMS

T&DC – TFI

T&DC	Training and Distribution Center (Navy)
TDCO	Torpedo Data Computer Operator (Navy)
TDD	Technical Data Digest (Air Force)
TDI	Textile Distributors Institute
	Tool and Die Institute
TDM	Torpedo Detection Modification (sonar) (Navy)
TDN	Travel as Directed is Necessary in military service
TDP	Target Director Post (Air Force)
TDPFO	Temporary Duty Pending Further Orders (Military)
TDRL	Temporary Disability Retired List (Military)
TDS	Target Designation System (Military)
TDT	Target Designation Transmitter (Military)
TDY	Temporary Duty (Military)
T/E	Tables of Equipment (Army)
TE	Task Element (Military)
	Thermal Efficiency
	Twin Engine (Air Force)
TEA	Technical Engineers Association
TEAM	(The) Evangelical Alliance Mission
TEB	Textile Economics Bureau
TECHREP	Technical Representative (Military)
TECHTAF	Technical Training Air Force (OB)
TECHTRA	Air Technical Training (Navy)
TEDA	Theatre Equipment Dealers Association
TEF	Temperance Education Foundation
	Tennis Educational Foundation
TEFLON	Du Pont Tetrafluoroethylene resin
TEGMA	Terminal Elevator Grain Merchants Association
TEI	Tax Executives Institute
TELCON	Telephone Conversation (Military)
TELECOM	Telecommunications (Military)
TELECON	Teletypwriter Conference (Military)
TELEFLORA	Telegraph Florists Delivery Service
TELEPAK	Telemetering Package
TELERAN	Television, Radar and Air Navigation
TELETYPE	Teletypewriter
TEMA	Tubular Exchanger Manufacturers Association
TEMPO	Technical Military Planning Operation
TERPACIS	Trust Territory of the Pacific Islands
TESMA	Theatre Equipment and Supply Manufacturers Association
TEW	Tactical Early Warning
TEXACO	Texas Company
TF	Task Force (Military)
	Tax Foundation
	Test Flight (Air Force)
	Tolstoy Foundation
	Training Film (Military)
TFA	Textile Fabrics Association
	Tie Fabrics Association
	US Trout Farmers Association
TFC	Time of First Call (Military)
	Trustees for Conservation
TFCSD	Total Federal Commissioned Service Date (Military)
TFGP	Tactical Fighter Group (Air Force)
TFI	Tax Foundation, Inc.

TFS	Tactical Fighter Squadron (Air Force)
TFWG	Tactical Fighter Wing (Air Force)
TG	Task Group (Military)
	Traffic Guidance Ioran (Air Force)
TGA	Toilet Goods Association
TG-ATS	Theatre Guild-American Theatre Society
TGC	Theater Ground Commander (Military)
	Toy Guidance Council
TGCA	Texas Gun Collectors Association
TGF	Treasury Guard Force
TH	True Heading
THART	Theodore Army Terminal
THI	Temperature Humidity Index
	Time Handed In (Military)
THP	Thrust Horsepower (jet engines)
THQ	Theater Headquarters (Military)
TI	Tax Institute
	Thread Institute
	Toastmasters International
	Training Instructor (Navy)
TIAA	Teachers Insurance and Annuity Association of America
TIC	Technical Intelligence Center (Military)
TICER	Temporary Int. Cncl. for Educational Reconstruction (of UNESCO-OB)
TID	Troop Information Division (Military)
TIG	The Inspector General (Military)
TIIC	Technical Industrial Intelligence Committee (Military)
TIMIG	Time In Grade (Military)
TIMS	The Institute of Management Sciences
TINSY	Treasure Island Naval Shipyard
TIO	Target Indication Officer (Navy)
TIP	Troop Information Program (Military)
TIPRO	Texas Independent Producers and Royalty Owners Association
TIR	Target Indication Room (Navy)
TIRB	Transportation Insurance Rating Bureau
TIS	Target Information Sheet (Air Force)
	Technical Information Section (Navy)
	Theater Intelligence Section (Military)
TIU	Target Indication Unit (Navy)
TJA	Trial Judge Advocate (Military)
TJAG	The Judge Advocate General (Military)
TJAGC	The Judge Advocate General's Corps (Army)
TJPOI	Twisted Jute Packing and Oakum Institute
TKA	Toy Knights of America
TKO	technical knockout
TL	Time Lengths
T/L	Training Literature (Navy)
TL	Truckload
TLA	Temperance League of America
	Theatre Library Association
TLCPC	Trunk Line-Central Passenger Committee
TLP	Total Loss of Pay (Military)
TLR	Traingulation-Listening-Ranging (sonar)
TM	Tactical Missile (Air Force)
	Technical Manual (Army)
TMA	Tile Manufacturers Association

- 194 -

ACRONYMS

TMA	Tobacco Merchants Association of the US
	Toiletry Merchandisers Association
TMEA	Typewriter Manufacturers Export Association
TMG	Track Made Good (Flying)
TMS	Tactical Missile Squadron (Air Force)
	Type, Model and Series (Military)
TMSD	Total Military Service Date
TMUS	Toy Manufacturers of the United States
TNA	The National Archives
TNC	Theater Naval Commander
TNT	Trinitrotoluene (explosive)
T/O	Tables of Organization (Army)
TO	Take Off (Flying)
	Technical Order (Air Force)
	Theater of Operations (Military)
TOA	Theatre Owners of America
TOC	Technical Order Compliance (Air Force)
	Theater of Operations Command (Military)
TOD	Time of Delivery (Military)
TOE	Table of Organization and Equipment (Military)
TOF	Time of Filing (Military)
TOFC	Trailer-on-Flat Car (Piggy Back)
TOG	Target-Observer-Gun method (Army)
TOO	Time of Origin (Military)
TOP	Torque Oil Pressure (Air Force)
TOPS	Take Off Pounds Sensibly (Association)
TOPSEC	Top Secret (Military)
TOR	Time of Receipt (Military)
TORPRON	Torpedo Squadron (Navy)
TOS	Term of Service (Military)
TOT	Table of Organization Tentative (Air Force)
	Time on Tape (Military)
	Time on Target or time over target (Air Force)
	Time of Transmission (communications)
TPA	Telephone Pioneers of America
	Transfer of Pay Account (Military)
	Travel by Privately owned conveyance Authorized (Military)
TPI	Target Position Indicator (Military)
TPMG	The Provost Marshal General (Army)
TPNEG	Travel will be Performed at No Expense to the Government (Military)
TPR	Trained Personnel Requirements (Air Force)
TPS	Technical Publishing Society
TPSI	Torque Pressure in pounds per Square Inch (Air Force)
TPSN	Troop Program Sequence Number (Military)
TQMG	The Quartermaster General (Army)
TR	Technical Regulations (Army)
TR or T/R	Transportation Request (Military)
TRA	Thoroughbred Racing Association of the US
	Tire and Rim Association
	Travel Research Association
TRAC	Tracer (Air Force)
	Tractor (Military)
TRACALS	Traffic Control and Landing System (Flying)
TRACDR	Tractor-Drawn (Military)
TRACOMD	Training Command (Navy)

Acronym	Meaning
TRACOMDLANT	Training Command, Atlantic Fleet
TRACOMDPAC	Training Command, Pacific Fleet
TRACOMDSUBPAC	Training Command, Submarines, Pacific Fleet
TRACOMDWESTCOAST	Training Command, West Coast (Navy)
TRADET	Training Detachment (Navy)
TRADIC	Transistor Digital Computer
TRAINBASEFOR	Train Base Force, Pacific Fleet
TRAINLANT	Train Atlantic Fleet
TRAINRON	Train Squadron (OB - Navy - see SERRON)
TRANC	Transient Center (Marine Corps)
TRANSDIV	Transport Division (Navy)
TRANSGRPPHIBFOR	Transportation Group Amphibious Forces (Navy)
TRANSGRPSOPAC	Transport Group, South Pacific Force (Navy)
TRANSLANT	Transports, Atlantic Fleet
TRANSPAC	Trans-Pacific
TRANSPHIBLANT	Transports, Amphibious Force, Atlantic Fleet
TRANSPHIBPAC	Transports, Amphibious Force, Pacific Fleet
TRANSPONDER	Transmission Responder (Communications)
TRANSRON	Transport Squadron (Navy)
TRASTA	Training Station (Navy)
TRCC	Theodore Roosevelt Centennial Commission (government agency)
TR&DL	Tung Research and Development League
TREAT	Transient Reactor Test facilities
TR/FLRES	Transferred to Fleet Reserve
TRGP	Tactical Reconnaissance Group (Air Force)
TRI	Textile Research Institute
	Tin Research Institute
	Tire Retreading Institute
TRICC	Tariff Rules of the Interstate Commerce Commission
TRML	Tropical Research Medical Laboratory (Army)
T&RNP	Transportation and Recruiting Naval Personnel
TRO	Transportation Officer (Air Force)
TRP	Traffic Regulation Point (Military)
TRS	Tactical Reconnaissance Squadron (Air Force)
	Test Research Service
TRU	Transportable Radio Unit (Military)
TRUST	Headquarters Trieste, US Troops
TRWG	Tactical Reconnaissance Wing (Air Force)
TS	Time Shack (Naval Air Station Operations)
	Top Secret (Military)
	Transit Storage (Military)
	Transmittal Sheet (Military)
T/S	Turn-in-Slip (Military)
TSA	Tamworth Swine Association
	Textile Salesmen's Association
	Track Supply Association
TSCC	Top Secret Control Channels (Navy)
TSCO	Top Secret Control Officers (Navy)
TSCP	Top Secret Control Proceeding (Navy)
TSCS	Top Secret Control Section (Navy)
TSD	Theater Shipping Document (Military)
TSG	The Surgeon General (Military)
TSIA	Trading Stamp Institute of America
TSIT	Technical Service Intelligence Team (Military)
TSRC	Tubular and Split Rivet Council

ACRONYMS

TSU	Technical Service Unit (Military)
TT	Target Towing Aircraft (Military)
	Technical Test (Military)
	Teletypewriter
TTA	Travel Time Authorized (Military)
TTAF	Technical Training Air Force (OB)
TTC	Technical Training Command (OB - Air Force)
TTE	Tentative Table of Equipment (Air Force)
TTF	Training Task Force (Navy)
TTG	Time to Go (Air Force)
	Travel with Troops Going (Air Force)
TTMA	Truck-Trailer Manufacturers Association
	Tufted Textile Manufacturers Association
TTP	Total Taxable Pay (Military)
TTPE	Total Taxable Pay Earned (Navy)
TTR	Travel with Troops Returning (Military)
TTSA	Transitional Training Squadron, Atlantic (Navy)
TTSFP	Training Transition School or Squadron, Pacific Fleet
TTSP	Transition Training Squadron, Pacific (Navy)
TU	Task Unit (Military)
	Technical Service Unit (Military)
	Training Unit (Military)
	Russian aircraft named for designer Tupolev
TUCR	Troop Unit Change Request (Military)
TUIFU	The Ultimate In Foul Ups (Military slang)
TURCO	Turn Around Control (Navy)
TUSAFG	The United States Air Force Group (American Mission for Aid to Turkey)
TV	Television
	Terminal Velocity
	Test Vehicle (Military)
TVA	Tennessee Valley Authority
TVOR	Terminal Very High Frequency Omnirange (Air Force)
TWA	Toy Wholesalers Association of America
	Trans-World Airlines
TWE	Textile Waste Exchange
TWHBA	Tennessee Walking Horse Breeders' Association of America
TWHO	The White House Office
TWIU	Tobacco Workers International Union
TWOATAF	Second Allied Tactical Air Force, Central Europe
TWOT	Travel Without Troops (Military)
TWPL	Teletypewriter, Private Line
TWS	Track-While-Scan (Military)
TWT	Travel With Troops (Military)
TWU	Transport Workers Union of America
TWX	Teletypewriter Exchange
TYCOM	Type Commander (Military)
TYSD	Total Years Service Date (Military)

U

UA	Uniform Allowance (Military)
	United Association (of Journeymen & Apprentices of the Plumbing)
UAA	University Aviation Association
UAFSC	Utilization Air Force Specialty Code
UAHC	Union of American Hebrew Congregations

UAL	Unit Authorization List (Air Force)
	United Air Lines
UAM	Underwater-to-Air Missile
	United American Mechanics
UAPA	United Amateur Press Association
UAR	United Arab Republic (Egypt and Syria)
UAW	United Automobile Workers
	United Automobile, Aircraft & Agricultural Implement Workers of America
UBBA	United Boys Brigades of America
UBBR	University Bureaus of Business Research
UBCJ	United Brotherhood of Carpenters and Joiners
UBCW	United Brick and Clay Workers
UBDMA	United Better Dress Manufacturers Association
UBEA	United Business Education Association
U-BOAT-S	Unterseeboot (German-submarine)
UBPVLS	Uniform Boiler and Pressure Vessel Laws Society
UC	Under Construction (Military)
	Unemployment Compensation
UCAR	University Corporation for Atmospheric Research
UCCA	Ukrainian Congress Committee of America
UCEC	Utility Commission Engineers Conference
UCFC	United Community Funds and Councils of America
UCLA	University of California at Los Angeles
UCMJ	Uniform Code of Military Justice
UCPA	United Cerebral Palsy Association
UCR	Uniform Crime Reports (Federal Bureau of Investigation)
UCT	United Commercial Travelers of America
UCW	United Church Women
UCWR	Upon Completion thereof Will Return to (Air Force)
UD	Undesirable Discharge (Military)
UDC	United Daughters of Confederacy
UDCA	Undesirable Discharge, trial by Civil Authorities (Military)
UDDE	Undesirable Discharge, Desertion without trial (Military)
UDFE	Undesirable Discharge, Fraudulent Enlistment (Military)
UDFMA	Upholstery & Drapery Fabric Manufacturers Association
UDT	Underwater Demolition Team (Military)
UDU	Underwater Demolition Unit (Military)
UDUF	Undesirable Discharge, Unfitness (Military)
UE	Unit Equipment (Air Force)
	United Electrical, Radio and Machine Workers of America
	Until Exhausted (Military)
UEA	United Epilepsy Association
UEAC	Unit Equipment Aircraft (Air Force)
UEE	Unit Essential Equipment (Air Force)
UET	United Engineering Trustees
UF	Unified Forces (Military)
	Unit of Fire (Air Force)
	United Foundation
UFDC	United Federation of Doll Clubs
UFFVA	United Fresh Fruit and Vegetable Association
UFMA	United Fur Manufacturers Association
	Upholstered Furniture Manufacturers' Association
UFO	Unidentified Flying Object ("flying saucers")
UFPA	University Film Producers Association
UFSJ	Unitarian Fellowship for Social Justice

ACRONYMS

UFWA........United Furniture Workers of America
UG..........Underground (Military)
UGW.........United Garment Workers of America
UHAA........United Horological Association of America
UHC.........Under Honorable Conditions (Military)
UHCMWIU.....United Hatters, Cap and Millinery Workers International Union
UHF.........Ultra-High Frequency
UHJA........United Hungarian Jews of America
UHRA........United Hunts Racing Association
UHS.........United Hias Service
UI..........Underwear Institute
UIA.........United Israel Appeal
UICWA.......United Infants' and Children's Wear Association
UISA........United Inventors and Scientists of America
UIU.........Upholsterers International Union
UIWU........United Israel World Union
UJA.........United Jewish Appeal
UK..........United Kingdom (Great Britain)
UKML........United Knitwear Manufacturers League
UL..........Underwriters' Laboratories
ULBM........Underwater-Launched Ballistic Missile
ULF.........Ultra Low Frequency
ULL.........Unitarian Laymen's League
ULPA........United Lightning Protection Association
UMA.........Union de Mujeres Americanas (United Women of the Americas)
UMC.........United Motor Courts
UMD.........Unit Manning Document (Air Force)
UMT.........Universal Military Training
UMTS........Universal Military Training Service (or System)
UMWA........United Mine Workers of America, International Union
UN..........United Nations
UNA.........Ukrainian National Association
UNAPOC......United National Association of Post Office Craftsmen
UNCF........United Negro College Fund
UNCMAC......United Nations Command Military Armistice Commission
UNCR........United Nations Command Rear
UNDERSECNAV.Under Secretary of the Navy
UNEF........United Nations Emergency Force
UNESCO......United Nations Educational, Scientific and Cultural Organization
UNGA........United Nations General Assembly
UNICEF......United Nations Intl.Children's Fund ("Intl." no longer used, but acronym /unchanged)
UNICOM......Unified Command (Military)
UNIFOR......Unified Forces (Military)
UNIPRO......Universal Processor (Data Processing)
UNIVAC......Universal Automatic Computer
UNMAC.......United Nations Mixed Armistice Commission
UNODIR......Unless Otherwise Directed (Air Force)
UNRRA.......United Nations Relief and Rehabilitation Administration
UNSC........United Nations Security Council
            United Nations Social Commission
UNSCOB......United Nations Special Committee on the Balkans (Greece)
UNSVM.......United Nations Service Medal
UOGC........United Order of the Golden Cross
UOHC........Under Other than Honorable Conditions (Military)
UP..........Under Provisions of (Air Force)

UP	United Press (MW - United Press International)
UPDMA	United Popular Dress Manufacturers Association
UPGWA	United Plant Guard Workers of America
UPI	United Press International
UPIN	United Press International Newspictures
UPNCA	United Pants and Novelties Contractors Association
UPO	Unit Personnel Office (r) (Military)
UPP	United Papermakers and Paperworkers
UPREAL	Unit Property Record and Equipment Authorization List (Air Force)
UPREC	Upon Receipt (Air Force)
UPREL	Unit Property Record and Equipment List (Air Force)
UPS	Under Provisions of Section (Air Force)
UP&T	Unit Personnel and Tonnage table (Air Force)
UPTT	Unit Personnel and Tonnage Table (Military)
UPU	Universal Postal Union (United Nations)
UPWA	United Packinghouse Workers of America
UR	Unsatisfactory Report (Military)
URA	Urban Renewal Administration
URI	Unpublished Research Information (Conducted by Natl. Science Foundation)
URO	United Rink Operators
URS	UNESCO Relations Staff
URSI	Union Radio Scientifique Internationale (French-Intl. Scientific Radio Union
URW	United Rubber, Cork, Linoleum and Plastic Workers of America
US	Under Secretary
	United States
U/S	Unserviceable (Military)
US of A	Under Secretary of the Army
USA	United Shareholders of America
	United States of America
	United States Army
USAA	United States Armor Association
USAADB	US Army Air Defense Board
USAAMS	US Army Artillery and Missile School
USAARMS	US Army Armor School
USAAVNS	US Army Aviation School
USABF	United States Amateur Baseball Federation
USAC	United States Automobile Club
USACAMGSCH	US Army Civil Affairs and Military Government School
USACDEC	US Army Combat Development Experimentation Center
USACGSC	US Army Command and General Staff College
USACHS	US Army Chaplain School
USACMLCSCH	US Army Chemical Corps School
USACMS	US Army Command Management School
USAEPG	US Army Electronic Proving Ground
USAERDL	US Army Engineer Research and Development Laboratory
USAES	US Army Engineer School
US of AF	Under Secretary of the Air Force
USAF	United States Air Force
USAFA	United States Air Force Academy
USAFACS	United States Air Force Aircrew School
USAFAPS	United States Air Force Air Police School
USAFBMS	United States Air Force Basic Military School
USAFBS	United States Air Force Bombardment School
USAFE	US Air Forces in Europe
USAFECI	US Air Force Extension Course Institute

ACRONYMS

USAFFGS	United States Air Force Flexible Gunnery School
USAFHD	US Air Force Historical Division
USAFI	United States Armed Forces Institute
USAFIT	US Air Force Institute of Technology (OB - now Institute of Technology)
USAFMTC	US Air Force Markmanship Training Center
USAFNS	United States Air Force Navigation School
USAFOCS	United States Air Force Officer Candidate School
USAFPAC	US Air Forces, Pacific
USAFPS	United States Air Force Pilot School
USAFR	United States Air Force Reserve
USAFRS	US Air Force Recruiting Service
USAFSAM	United States Air Force School of Aviation Medicine (OB)
USAFSRA	US Air Force Special Reporting Agency
USAFSS	US Air Force Security Service
USAFTS	United States Air Force Technical School
USAIC	US Army Infantry Center
USAINTB	US Army Intelligence Board
USAINTC	US Army Intelligence Center
USAINTS	US Army Intelligence School
USAIPSG	US Army Industrial and Personnel Security Group
USAIRA	United States Air Attache
USAIRMILCOMUN	US Air Force Representative, United Nations Military Staff Committee
USAIS	US Army Infantry School
USALMC	US Army Logistics Management Center
USALS	US Army Language School
USAM	United States Army Mothers (Association)
USAMOAMA	US Army Medical Optical and Maintenance Activity
USAMP	United States Army Mine Planter
USAMSMADHS	US Army Medical Service Meat and Dairy Hygiene School
USANAFBA	US Army, Navy and Air Force Bandsmen's Association
USAOMC	US Army Ordnance Missile Command
USAORDCORPS	US Army Ordnance Corps
USAOSWAC	US Army Ordnance Special Weapons-Ammunition Command
USAPC	US Army Pictorial Center
USAPWA	United Stone and Allied Products Workers of America
USAR	United States Army Reserve
USARADCOM	US Army Air Defense Command
USARADSCH	US Army Air Defense School
USARAL	United States Army, Alaska
USARCARIB	United States Army Caribbean
USARCEN	US Army Records Center, The Adjutant General's Office
USAREPG	US Army Electronic Proving Ground
USAREUR	United States Army in Europe
USAREURORDCOM	US Army European Ordnance Command
USARFANT	United States Army Forces Antilles
USARIS	US Army Information School
USARJ	US Army Japan
USARMA	United States Army Attache
USARPAC	United States Army, Pacific
USASCS	US Army Signal Corps School
USASESCS	US Army Southeastern Signal Corps School
USASIS	US Army Strategic Intelligence School
USASMSA	US Army Signal Missile Support Agency
USASOS	US Army Services of Supply (OB)
USASTAF	US Army Southern European Task Force

USASTAF	United States Army Strategic Air Forces in the Pacific (OB)
USASWS	US Army Special Warfare School
USAT	US Army Transport
USATSCH	US Army Transportation School
USAW	Underwater Security Advance Warnings (Navy)
USBE	United States Book Exchange
USBF	United States Brewers Foundation
USBG	US Botanic Garden
USBM	United States Bureau of Mines
USBP	US Border Patrol
USC	Under Separate Cover (Military)
	United States Code
	United States Congress
	US Customs
USC	University of Southern California
USCA	US Code Annotated
	United States Copper Association
USCAR	US Civil Administration Ryukyu Islands
USCC	United States Circuit Court
	United States Court of Claims
	United Student Christian Council in United States
USCCA	United States Circuit Court of Appeals
USCCPA	United States Court of Customs and Patent Appeals
USCDC	United States Civil Defense Council
USCG	US Coast Guard
	US Consul General
	United States Civil Service Commission
USCGA	US Coast Guard Academy
	US Coast Guard Auxiliary
USCGAS	US Coast Guard Air Station
USCGASB	US Coast Guard Aircraft and Supply Base
USCGB	US Coast Guard Base
USCGC	US Coast Guard Cutter
USCGD	US Coast Guard Depot
USC&GS	US Coast and Geodetic Survey
USCGR	US Coast Guard Reserve
USCGRC	US Coast Guard Receiving Center
USCGSCF	United States Coast Guard Shore Communication Facilities
USCGTS	US Coast Guard Training Station
USCINCEUR	United States Commander-in-Chief, Europe
USCOLD	US Committee on Large Dams of the International Commission on /Large Dams
USCONARC	United States Continental Army Command
USCS	Universal Ship Cancellation Society
USCSC	United States Cuban Sugar Council
USCSRA	US Cane Sugar Refiners Association
USCSSB	United States Cap Screw Service Bureau
USCUN	United States Committee for the United Nations
USDA	United States Department of Agriculture
USDB	United States Disciplinary Barracks
USDC	United States District Court
USE	Unit Support Equipment (Air Force)
	US Embassy
USES	US Employment Service
USFA	United States Forces in Austria (OB)
USFADTC	US Fleet Air Defense Training Center

ACRONYMS

USFORAZ	United States Forces in Azores
USFSA	United States Figure Skating Association
USFSS	US Fleet Sonar School
USG	United States Standard Gauge
USGA	United States Golf Association
USGLI	US Government Life Insurance
USHA	United States Handball Association
USHGA	United States Hop Growers Association
USIA	US Information Agency /and Drainage
USICID	US National Committee, International Commission on Irrigation
USIS	US Information Service (OB - see USIA)
USITA	United States Independent Telephone Association
USK	US Forces Korea
USKBA	United Strictly Koshed Butchers Association
USL	Underwater Sound Laboratory (Navy)
	United States Legation
USLANT	United States Atlantic Subarea (Air Force)
USLO	US Liaison Officer
USLSA	US Livestock Sanitary Association
USLTA	United States Lawn Tennis Association
USM	Underwater-to-Surface Missile
	United States Mail
	United State Mint
USMA	US Military Academy
USMAPU	US Military Academy Preparatory Unit
USMB	US Marine Barracks
USMC	US Marine Corps
	US Maritime Commission
USMCAS	US Marine Corps Air Station
USMCR	United States Marine Corps Reserve
USMCR (F)	US Fleet Marine Corps Reserve
USMCR (O)	US Organized Marine Corps Reserve
USMCR (V)	US Volunteer Marine Corps Reserve
USMCW	United States Marine Corps, Women
USMCWR	US Marine Corps Women's Reserve
USMH	United States Marine Hospital
USMHS	United States Marine Hospital Service
USMEMILCOMUN	United States Members, UN Military Staff Command
USMILATTACHE	United States Military Attache
USMILCOMUN	United States delegation, UN Military Staff Committee
USMILLIAS	United States Military Liaison Office
USMM	United States Merchant Marine
USMMA	United States Merchant Marine Academy
USMS	US Maritime Service
USMSOS	US Maritime Service Officers School
USMSSB	United States Machine Screw Service Bureau
USMSTS	US Maritime Service Training School
USMTMSA	US Military Training Mission to Saudi Arabia
USN	US Navy (also indicates Regular Navy)
USNA	US Naval Academy
USNAC	US Naval Administrative Command
USNCEREL	US Naval Civil Engineering Research and Evaluation Laboratory
USNDD	US Naval Drydocks
USNH	US Naval Hospital
USNI	United States Naval Institute

Acronym	Meaning
USNM	United States National Museum (Smithsonian Institution)
USNMR	United States National Military Representative
USNPS	US Naval Postgraduate School
USNR	US Naval Reserve
USNS	United States Naval Ship (civilian manned)
USNSA	United States National Student Association
USNSAET	United States National Student Association Educational Travel
USO	United Service Organizations
USOA	United States Olympic Association
USP	United States Pharmacopoeia
USPA	United States Polo Association
	United States Potters Association
USPDO	United States Property and Disbursing Officer
USPEC	United States Paper Exporters Council
USPFO	United States Property and Fiscal Officer
USPHS	United States Public Health Service
USPLTA	United States Professional Lawn Tennis Association
USPO	US Patent Office (Commerce Department)
	United States Post Office
USPPA	United States Pulp Producers Association
USPS	United States Power Squadrons
USPTA	US Paddle Tennis Association
USR	United States (Supreme Court) Reports
USRA	United States Revolver Association
USREPMILCOMUN	United States Representative, UN Military Staff Committee
USRS	United States Reclamation Service
	United States Revised Statutes
	United States Rocket Society
USS	United Seamen's Service
	United States Senate
	United States Ship
	United States Steel Corporation
	United Swedish Societies
USSA	United Saw Service Association
	United States Salvage Association
USSAF	United States Strategic Air Force (OB - now Strategic Air Command)
USSAFE	United States Strategic Air Force in Europe (OB)
USSBD	US Savings Bond Division (Treasury Department)
USSBS	United States Strategic Bombing Survey (OB)
USSC	United States Supreme Court
USSEA	United States Scientific Export Association
USSECMILCOMUN	The Secretary, US Delegation UN Staff Committee
USSF	US Steel Foundation
USSFA	United States Soccer Football Association
USSG	United States Standard Gage
USSIA	United States Shellac Importers Association
USSLL	United States Savings and Loan League
USSR	Union of Soviet Socialist Republics
USSS	US Secret Service
USSTAF	United States Strategic Air Force (OB)
USTA	United States Trademark Association
	United Trotting Association
USTC	US Tariff Commission
USTDA	United States Truck Drivers Association
USTTA	United States Table Tennis Association

ACRONYMS

USVBA	United States Volleyball Association
USW	United Steelworkers of America
USWA	United Shoe Workers of America
USWACS	US Women's Army Corps School
USWB	US Weather Bureau
USWGA	United States Wholesale Grocers' Association
USWSSB	United States Wood Screw Service Bureau
USWV	United Spanish War Veterans
UTM	Universal Transverse Mercator map
UTOA	United Truck Owners of America
UTOCO	Utah Oil Company
UTSE	United Transport Service Employees
UTSEA	United Transport Service Employees of America
UTWA	United Textile Workers of America
UW	Unconventional Warfare
UWATU	Underway Training Unit (Air Force)
UWF	United World Federalists
UWUA	Utility Workers Union of America
UXB	Unexploded Bomb (Air Force)

V

V (bomb)	Vergeltungswaffe Bomb (German – "vengeance weapon")
VA	Veterans Administration
	Voice of America
VAQ	Visiting Airmen's Quarters (Air Force)
VAR	Visual-Aural-Range (communications)
	Volunteer Air Reserve (Air Force)
VART	Volunteer Air Reserve Training (Air Force)
VARTU	Volunteer Air Reserve Training Unit (Air Force)
VB	Vertical Bomb (Air Force)
VC	Veterinary Corps
	Vice Chairman
	Vice Chancellor
	Vice Consul
VCA	Vitrified China Association
VCCUS	Venezuelan Chamber of Commerce of the US
VCI	Variety Clubs International
VCMA	Vacuum Cleaner Manufacturers Association
VCNO	Vice Chief of Naval Operations
VCP	Vehicle Collecting Point (Army)
VCS	Vice Chief of Staff (Military)
VCSA	Vice Chief of Staff, Army
VC/SAF	Vice Chief of Staff, Air Force
VD	Venereal Disease
VDI	Vat Dye Institute
VDP	Vehicle Deadlined for Parts (Military)
V-E	Victory-Europe (9 May 1945)
VEB	Variable Elevation Beam (radar)
VEEP	Jeep Equipped with Very High Frequency Radio (OB)
	Vice President
VERTIJET	Vertical Take-Off and Landing Jet (aircraft)
VES	Veterans' Employment Service (Labor Department)
VF	Video-Frequency
	Vision-Frequency

ACRONYMS

```
VFI . . . . . . . . . Vinyl Fabrics Institute
VFR . . . . . . . . . Visual Flight Rules (Flying)
VFW . . . . . . . . . Veterans of Foreign Wars of the United States
VG . . . . . . . . . Velocity Gravity
VGAA . . . . . . . Vegetable Growers Association of America
VH . . . . . . . . . Very High
VHB . . . . . . . . Very Heavy Bombardment (Air Force)
VHF . . . . . . . . Very High-Frequency
VHF/DF . . . . . . Very High Frequency Direction-Finding
VI . . . . . . . . . Vermiculite Institute
                     Vinegar Institute
VIC . . . . . . . . Virgin Islands Corporation (government agency)
VIL . . . . . . . . Vivisection Investigation League
VIO . . . . . . . . Visual Intercept Officer (Navy)
VIP . . . . . . . . Very Important Passenger (Air Force)
                     Very Important Person (Military)
VIPI . . . . . . . . Very Important Person Indeed (Air Force)
V-J . . . . . . . . Victory-Japan (14 August 1945)
VLA . . . . . . . . Very Low Altitude
VLF . . . . . . . . Very Low Frequency
VLR . . . . . . . . Very Long Range
                     Very Low Range
VMA . . . . . . . . Valve Manufacturers Association
VMI . . . . . . . . Virginia Military Institute
VMWW I . . . . . . Victory Medal, World War I
VMWW II . . . . . . Victory Medal, World War II
VO . . . . . . . . . Verbal Order (Military)
VOA . . . . . . . . Vasa Order of America
                     Volunteers of America
VOC . . . . . . . . Verbal Order of the Commander (Military)
VOCG . . . . . . . Verbal Order of Commanding General (Military)
VOCM . . . . . . . Vehicle Out of Commission for Maintenance (Military)
VOCO . . . . . . . Verbal Orders of Commanding Officer (Military)
VOCP . . . . . . . Vehicle Out of Commission for Parts (Military)
VOCS . . . . . . . Verbal Orders of the Chief of Staff (Military)
VOPNAV . . . . . . Vice Chief of Naval Operations (see VCNO)
VOQ . . . . . . . . Visiting Officer's Quarters (Military)
VOR . . . . . . . . Very high frequency Omnidirectional Range         /with Tacan
VOR/DMET . . . . . Very High Frequency Omni-Range/Distance Measuring Equip. compatible
VORTAC . . . . . . Very High Frequency Omni-Range Tacan
VOSAF . . . . . . . Verbal Orders Secretary of the Air Force
VP . . . . . . . . . Variable Pitch propeller
                     Vice President
                     Vulnerable Point (Military)
VPI . . . . . . . . Virginia Polytechnic Institute
VPLA . . . . . . . Volunteer Prison League of America
VPM . . . . . . . . Vehicles per Mile (Military)
VPMA . . . . . . . Vegetable Parchment Manufacturers Association (Paper)
VRS . . . . . . . . Volunteer Reserve Section (Air Force)
VSD . . . . . . . . Vendor's Shipping Document (Military)
VSR . . . . . . . . Very Short Range
VSTOL or V/STOL . . Vertical or Short Take-Off and Landing (aircraft)
VSTP . . . . . . . Visual Satellite Tracking Program
VT . . . . . . . . . Variable-Time
VTO . . . . . . . . Vertical Take-Off (Air Force)
```

ACRONYMS

VTO	Visual Training Officer (Navy)
	Vocational Training Officer (Navy)
VTOL	Vertical Take-Off and Landing (aircraft)
VTPA	Vertical Turbine Pump Association
VTU	Volunteer Training Unit (Air Force)
VVBAA	Venetian and Vertical Blind Association of America
VW	Volkswagon
VWPI	Vacuum Wood Preservers Institute

W

WA	Wire Association
WAA	War Assets Administration (OB - World War II)
	Wardens' Association of America
	Western Amateur Astronomers
WAABI	Women's Association of Allied Beverage Industries
WAAC	Women's Army Auxiliary Corps (OB - now Women's Army Corps)
WAAF	Women's Auxiliary Air Force (British)
WAB	Western Actuarial Bureau
	When Authorized By (Military)
WAC	Women's Army Corps
	World Aeronautical Chart
	World Affairs Center for the United States
WACA	Women's Apparel Chains Association
WACRES	Women's Army Corps Reserve
WACSM	Women's Army Corps Service Medal
WADC	Wright Air Development Center (Air Force)
WADF	Western Air Defense Force (Air Force)
WAE	When Actually Employed (Air Force)
WAF	Women in the Air Force
WAFS	Women's Auxiliary Ferrying Service (OB)
WAML	Wright Aero Medical Laboratory (Air Force)
WANAP	Washington National Airport
WASP	Westinghouse Advanced Systems Planning group
	Women's Air Force Service Pilots (OB)
WAVES	Women Accepted for Volunteer Emergency Service (USN Women's Reserve)
WB	Wage Board (wage-earning federal workers' classification)
	Way Bill
	Weather Bureau
	Women's Bureau (Labor Department)
WBA	Woman's Benefit Association
WBAN	Weather Bureau, Air Force - Navy
WBF	Workmen's Benefit Fund of the USA
WBFA	Western Bohemian Fraternal Association
WBI	Will Be Issued (Military)
	Wooden Box Institute
WBMA	Wirebound Box Manufacturers Association
WB-S	Wage Board, Supervisor (Civil Service classification)
WC	War College (Air Force)
	Workmen's Compensation
WCBSU	West Coast Base Service Unit (Navy)
WCC	US Conference for the World Council of Churches
WCCA	West Coast Crossarm Association
WCD	Workshop for Cultural Democracy
WCDFMA	Water Cooler and Drinking Fountain Manufacturers Association (OB)

WCEMA	West Coast Electronic Manufacturers' Association
WCEU	World's Christian Endeavor Union
WCF	Water Conditioning Foundation
	World Congress of Flight
WCFA	Wholesale Commission Florists of America
WCLA	West Coast Lumbermen's Association
WCLIB	West Coast Lumber Inspection Bureau
WCMA	West Coast Mineral Association
WCOF	Women's Catholic Order of Foresters
WCOTP	World Confederation of Organizations of Teaching Profession
WCPAB	War Control Price Adjustment Board (OB - World War II)
WCTU	Woman's Christian Temperance Union
WCU	Western Catholic Union
WD	War Department (OB - now Department of the Army)
	When Directed (Air Force)
	Wind Direction (Air Force)
WDA	Wildlife Disease Association
WDC	Washington Document Center
	Western Defense Command (Army)
WDD	Western Development Division (Air Force)
WDGI	Wholesale Dry Goods Institute
WE	World Education (Association)
WEAPD	Western Air Procurement District (Air Force)
WEC	Worldwide Evangelization Crusade
WEFT	Wings, Engines, Fuselage, Tail (system for identifying aircraft)
WEM	Welfare of Enlisted Men (Air Force)
WESCARSUBAREA	Western Carolines Sub-Area (OB - Navy)
WESSEAFRON	Western Sea Frontier (Navy)
WESTAF	Western Transport Air Force
WESTLANT	Western Atlantic area (Military)
WESTOMP	West-Ocean Meeting Point (Shipping)
WESTPACBACOM	Western Pacific Base Command (Military)
WEU	Western European Union
WFCMV	Wheeled Fuel-Consuming Motor Vehicle (Military)
WFEA	World Federation of Educational Associations
WFI	Wheat Flour Institute
WFIA	Western Forest Industries Association
WFPS	Wild Flower Preservation Society
WGA	Western Growers Association
WGCL	Window Glass Cutters League of America
WGDA	Watermelon Growers and Distributors Association
WGMA	Wet Ground Mica Association
WGS	World Government Sponsors
W/H	Withholding
WHAP	When or Where Applicable (Military)
WHCA	White House Correspondents Association
WHI	Western Highway Institute
WHIA	Woolen Hosiery Institute of America
WHMAA	Wool Hat Manufacturers Association of America
WHNPA	White House News Photographers Association
WHO	World Health Organization (United Nations)
WHP	White House Police force
WHPCD	Wage and Hour and Public Contracts Division (Labor Department)
WI	Wine Institute
	Within

WIA	Wounded in Action (Military)
WIBC	Woman's International Bowling Congress
WIF	West Indies Federation
WILCO	Will Comply (Military)
WILPF	Women's International League for Peace and Freedom
WIMS	War Instructions for Merchant Ships (OB)
WISA	West Indian Students Association
WL	Water Line
WLD	West Longitude Date
WLI	Women's League for Israel
WM	Women Marines
WMBA	Wire Machinery Builders Association
WMMA	Woodworking Machinery Manufacturers Association
WMO	World Meteorological Organization (United Nations)
WMS	Woman Medical Specialist (OB)
	Women in the Medical Service (OB - Army)
WMSC	Women's Medical Specialist Corps (OB)
WNAAUS	Women's National Aeronautical Association of the US
WNB	Will Not Be (Military)
WNFGA	Women's National Farm and Garden Association
WNI	Women's National Institute
WNPC	Women's National Press Club
WNSEA	Wood Naval Stores Export Association
WNU	Western Newspaper Union
WO	Warning Order (Military)
WOC	(Government Official Serving) Without Compensation
WOQ	Wave Officers' Quarters (Navy)
WOQT	Warrant Officer Qualification Test (Military)
WP	White Phosphorus
	Will Proceed (Military)
WPA	Western Pine Association
WPB	War Production Board (OB - World War II)
WPBC	Western Pacific Base Command (Navy)
WPF	World Peace Foundation
WPI	Wall Paper Institute
	Waxed Paper Institute
WPM	Words per Minute
WPMA	Waterproof Paper Manufacturers Association
	Writing Paper Manufacturers Association
WPMC	Waxed Paper Merchandising Council
WPRI	Wartime Pacific Routing Instructions (OB - World War II)
WPS	With Prior Service (Military)
WPSA	Welsh Pony Society of America
WPSC	War Plan Shipping Control (OB - World War II)
WPTA	Wooden Pail and Tub Association
WPUC	Waste Paper Utilization Council
WPWOD	Will Proceed Without Delay (Military)
WR	Water-Rail (Transportation)
W&R	Welfare & Recreation (Military)
WR	Wildlife Restoration (Association)
	Women's Reserve (Navy)
WRA	War Relocation Authority (OB - World War II)
WRAIR	Walter Reed Army Institute of Research
WRAMA	Warner-Robins Air Materiel Area (Air Force)
WRAMC	Walter Reed Army Medical Center

WRC	Water Resources Council
WRCLA	Western Red Cedar Lumber Association
WREN	Member of British Women's Reserve Naval Service
WRF	World Rehabilitation Fund
WRI	Weatherstrip Research Institute
WRI	Wire Reinforcement Institute
	Wire Rope Institute
WRMA	Welded Ring Manufacturers Association
WRNS	Women's Reserve Naval Service (Great Britain)
WRSFA	Western Reinforcing Steel Fabricators Association
WS	Water Supply (Military)
	Wilderness Society
	Wildlife Society
WSA	Weed Society of America
	Wholesale Stationers' Association
WSBP	Western Society of Business Publications
WSEG	Weapon Systems Evaluation Group (Military)
WSF	Western Sea Frontier (Navy)
WSMPA	Western States Meat Packers Association
WSMR	White Sands Missile Range (Military)
WSNSCA	Washable Suits, Novelties and Sportswear Contractors Association
WSP	Water Supply Point (Military)
WSPG	Weapon System Phasing Group (Military)
WSPO	Weapon System Project Office (Military)
WSWA	Wine and Spirits Wholesalers of America
WSWMA	Water and Sewage Works Manufacturers Association
WTF	Western Task Force (Navy)
WTN	Western Technical Net (Air Force)
WTP	World Tape Pals
WTSB	Wood Turners Service Bureau
WTWA	World Trade Writers Association
WU	Western Union
WUA	Western Underwriters Association
WUS	World University Service
WUTELCO	Western Union Telegraph Company (Military Designation)
WV	World Vision
WVF	World Veterans Fund
WWA	Wallpaper Wholesalers Association
	Western Writers of America
	Woolens and Worsteds of America (Association)
WWI	World War I
WWII	World War II
WWIII	World War III
WWIS	World Wide Information Service
WWPA	Woven Wire Products Association
WWWV	Women World War Veterans (Association)

X

X	Experimental (Military)
XM	Experimental Missile
XO	Executive Officer

Y

YAK . . . . Russian aircraft named for designer Yakovlev
YANGPAT . . . . . Yangtze Patrol (OB - Navy)
YCS . . . . Young Christian Students
YCW . . . . Young Christian Workers
YDCA . . . . Young Democratic Clubs of America
YMA . . . . Yarn Merchants Association
YMCA . . . . Young Men's Christian Association
YMHA . . . . Young Men's Hebrew Association
YMI . . . . Young Men's Institute
YOAN . . . . Youth of All Nations (Association)
YOB . . . . Year of Birth
YPO . . . . Young President's Organization
YRNF . . . . Young Republican National Federation
YWCA . . . . Young Women's Christian Association
YWHA . . . . Young Women's Hebrew Association

Z

Z . . . . Zone (Military)
ZEL . . . . Zero-Length Launcher (Air Force)
ZF . . . . Zone of Fire (Military)
ZI . . . . Zone of Interior (Military - same as Continental United States)
                    Zonta International
ZMRI . . . . Zinc Metals Research Institute
ZOA . . . . Zionist Organization of America
ZTO . . . . Zone Transportation Office (Military)